AMERICAN HISTORY
VOLUME I

Pre-Colonial Through Reconstruction

Twelfth Edition

Editor

Robert James Maddox
Pennsylvania State University
University Park

Robert James Maddox, distinguished historian and professor of American history at Pennsylvania State University, received a B.S. from Fairleigh Dickinson University in 1957, an M.S. from the University of Wisconsin in 1958, and a Ph.D. from Rutgers in 1964. He has written, reviewed, and lectured extensively, and is widely respected for his interpretations of presidential character and policy.

Annual Editions
A Library of Information from the Public Press

Cover illustration by Mike Eagle

The Dushkin Publishing Group, Inc.
Sluice Dock, Guilford, Connecticut 06437

The Annual Editions Series

Annual Editions is a series of over 55 volumes designed to provide the reader with convenient, low-cost access to a wide range of current, carefully selected articles from some of the most important magazines, newspapers, and journals published today. Annual Editions are updated on an annual basis through a continuous monitoring of over 300 periodical sources. All Annual Editions have a number of features designed to make them particularly useful, including topic guides, annotated tables of contents, unit overviews, and indexes. For the teacher using Annual Editions in the classroom, an Instructor's Resource Guide with test questions is available for each volume.

VOLUMES AVAILABLE

Africa
Aging
American Government
American History, Pre-Civil War
American History, Post-Civil War
Anthropology
Biology
Business Ethics
Canadian Politics
China
Commonwealth of Independent States
Comparative Politics
Computers in Education
Computers in Business
Computers in Society
Criminal Justice
Drugs, Society, and Behavior
Dying, Death, and Bereavement
Early Childhood Education
Economics
Educating Exceptional Children
Education
Educational Psychology
Environment
Geography
Global Issues
Health
Human Development
Human Resources
Human Sexuality
India and South Asia

International Business
Japan and the Pacific Rim
Latin America
Life Management
Macroeconomics
Management
Marketing
Marriage and Family
Microeconomics
Middle East and the Islamic World
Money and Banking
Nutrition
Personal Growth and Behavior
Physical Anthropology
Psychology
Public Administration
Race and Ethnic Relations
Social Problems
Sociology
State and Local Government
Third World
Urban Society
Violence and Terrorism
Western Civilization, Pre-Reformation
Western Civilization, Post-Reformation
Western Europe
World History, Pre-Modern
World History, Modern
World Politics

Library of Congress Cataloging in Publication Data
Main entry under title: Annual editions: American history, volume one.
 1. United States—History—Periodicals. 2. United States—Historiography—Periodicals. 3. United States—Civilization—Periodicals. I. Title: American history, volume one.
E171.A75   973′.05   74–187540
ISBN 1–56134–187–8

Twelfth Edition

Manufactured by The Banta Company, Harrisonburg, Virginia 22801

Printed on Recycled Paper

Editors/ Advisory Board

To the Reader

In publishing ANNUAL EDITIONS we recognize the enormous role played by the magazines, newspapers, and journals of the *public press* in providing current, first-rate educational information in a broad spectrum of interest areas. Within the articles, the best scientists, practitioners, researchers, and commentators draw issues into new perspective as accepted theories and viewpoints are called into account by new events, recent discoveries change old facts, and fresh debate breaks out over important controversies.

Many of the articles resulting from this enormous editorial effort are appropriate for students, researchers, and professionals seeking accurate, current material to help bridge the gap between principles and theories and the real world. These articles, however, become more useful for study when those of lasting value are carefully *collected, organized, indexed,* and *reproduced* in a *low-cost format,* which provides easy and permanent access when the material is needed. That is the role played by *Annual Editions.* Under the direction of each volume's *Editor,* who is an expert in the subject area, and with the guidance of an *Advisory Board,* we seek each year to provide in each ANNUAL EDITION a current, well-balanced, carefully selected collection of the best of the public press for your study and enjoyment. We think you'll find this volume useful, and we hope you'll take a moment to let us know what you think.

Recent trends in historical writing have been to emphasize the lives of ordinary people, and to recognize the diversity of our society by calling attention to the contributions and problems of ethnic and racial minority groups. This development supplements and enriches our understanding of the past, but does not render obsolete the need to understand significant events and leaders. That the Constitution was written one way and not another profoundly affected the course of American history, and individuals such as Franklin D. Roosevelt and Martin Luther King, Jr., *did* make a difference.

American History offers a selection of essays on both traditional and nontraditional subjects. Articles on various aspects of both social and cultural history are included along with those dealing with politics, diplomacy, and military conflicts. Some present analyses of large events, some offer insights on everyday life, and still others convey the "feel" of things through eyewitness accounts. We hope this combination of writings will provide a useful supplement to textbooks, which of necessity have to provide broad coverage at the expense of treating particular topics at length.

This volume contains a number of features designed to be helpful to students, researchers, and professionals. These include a *topic guide* for locating articles on specific subjects; the *table of contents abstracts* that summarize each essay, with key concepts in bold italics; and a comprehensive *index.* Articles are organized into four units. Each unit is preceded by an overview that provides a background for informed reading of the articles, emphasizes critical issues, and presents *challenge questions.*

Every succeeding edition of *American History* includes new articles to replace some old ones. We are eager to continue to improve the quality of the selections, and to consider possible alternatives that might have been missed. If you come across an article that you think merits inclusion in the next edition, please send it along. We welcome your comments about the readings in this volume, and a post-paid reader response card is included in the back of the book for your convenience. Your suggestions will be carefully considered and greatly appreciated.

Robert James Maddox
Editor

Contents

Unit 1

The New Land

Seven selections discuss the beginnings of America, the new land—from the early English explorers, early life of the colonists, and religious intolerance, to the stirrings of liberty and independence.

Unit 2

Revolutionary America

Eight articles examine the start of the American Revolution. The new land offered opportunities for new ideas that led to the creation of an independent nation.

The concepts in bold italics are developed in the article. For further expansion please refer to the Topic Guide and the Index.

Unit 3

National Consolidation and Expansion

Sixteen selections examine the developing United States, the westward movement of people seeking a new life, and the realities of living in early nineteenth-century America.

The concepts in bold italics are developed in the article. For further expansion please refer to the Topic Guide and the Index.

The concepts in bold italics are developed in the article. For further expansion please refer to the Topic Guide and the Index.

Unit 4

The Civil War and Reconstruction

Eleven articles discuss the tremendous effects of the Civil War on America. With the abolishment of slavery, the United States had to reconstruct society.

The concepts in bold italics are developed in the article. For further expansion please refer to the Topic Guide and the Index.

The concepts in bold italics are developed in the article. For further expansion please refer to the Topic Guide and the Index.

Topic Guide

This topic guide suggests how the selections in this book relate to topics of traditional concern to American history students and professionals. It is useful for locating articles that relate to each other for reading and research. The guide is arranged alphabetically according to topic. Articles may, of course, treat topics that do not appear in the topic guide. In turn, entries in the topic guide do not necessarily constitute a comprehensive listing of all the contents of each selection.

TOPIC AREA	TREATED IN:	TOPIC AREA	TREATED IN:
Adams, John Quincy	21. Odd Couple	**Culture**	1. America Before Columbus 6. "Under an Evil Hand" 7. Remapping American Culture 14. Philadelphia 1787 20. Indians in the Land 23. Secret Life of a Developing Country 26. Not Really Greek 27. Legacy of Violence 31. War Against Demon Rum 39. War Inside the Churches 41. What Did Freedom Mean?
African Americans	15. Founding Fathers and Slavery 18. Lives of Slave Women 32. Dred Scott in History 34. Black, Blue, and Gray 36. Lincoln and Douglass: Dismantling the Peculiar Institution 39. War Inside the Church 41. What Did Freedom Mean? 42. New View of Reconstruction		
		Diplomacy	21. Odd Couple
American Revolution	8. Shot Heard Round the World 9. Declaration of Independence 10. Winter at Valley Forge	**Douglass, Frederick**	36. Lincoln and Douglass: Dismantling the Peculiar Institution
Architecture	26. Not Really Greek	**Environment**	20. Indians in the Land 28. Eden Ravished
Articles of Confederation	11. Troubled League	**Exploration**	2. Was America a Mistake? 3. California's Spanish Missions 17. River of the West
Civil War	33. First Blood to the South 34. Black, Blue, and Gray 36. Lincoln and Douglass: Dismantling the Peculiar Institution 37. "Few Appropriate Remarks" 38. Why the Confederacy Lost 39. War Inside the Church 40. War That Never Goes Away	**Government**	11. Troubled League 13. Philadelphia Story 15. Founding Fathers and Slavery 16. 'Nauseous Project' 19. Great Chief Justice 32. Dred Scott in History 42. New View of Reconstruction
Constitution	13. Philadelphia Story 15. Founding Fathers and Slavery 16. 'Nauseous Project'	**Hispanics**	2. Was America a Mistake? 3. California's Spanish Missions

TOPIC AREA	TREATED IN:	TOPIC AREA	TREATED IN:
Immigration	7. Remapping American Culture	Religion	3. California's Spanish Missions 6. "Under an Evil Hand" 39. War Inside the Church
Indentured Servants	4. Colonists in Bondage	Slavery	15. Founding Fathers and Slavery 18. Lives of Slave Women 32. Dred Scott in History 36. Lincoln and Douglass: Dismantling the Peculiar Institution 41. What Did Freedom Mean?
Jackson, Andrew	21. Odd Couple		
Labor	4. Colonists in Bondage 18. Lives of Slave Women 22. From Utopia to Mill Town 30. Forgotten Forty-Niners	Supreme Court	19. Great Chief Justice 32. Dred Scott in History
Lincoln, Abraham	36. Lincoln and Douglass: Dismantling the Peculiar Institution 37. "Few Appropriate Remarks"	Temperance	31. War Against Demon Rum
		Western Expansion	17. River of the West 20. Indians in the Land 21. Odd Couple 28. Eden Ravished 30. Forgotten Forty-Niners
Marshall, John	19. Great Chief Justice		
Native Americans	1. America Before Columbus 2. Was America a Mistake? 3. California's Spanish Missions 20. Indians in the Land	Women	18. Lives of Slave Women 22. From Utopia to Mill Town 29. Act One 30. Forgotten Forty-Niners 31. War Against Demon Rum
Reconstruction	41. What Did Freedom Mean? 42. New View of Reconstruction		

The New Land

The year 1992 marked the 500th anniversary of what used to be called Christopher Columbus's "discovery" of the New World. Although he did discover the Western Hemisphere *for Europeans,* it had been inhabited for at least 12,000 years. The first reading, "America Before Columbus," describes the amazing diversity of cultures that existed at the time Columbus arrived. Some civilizations, such as those created by the Aztecs and Incas, shocked the Europeans with their wealth and sophistication, and north of the Rio Grande there were about 1,000 tribes, which together numbered more than 2 million people.

Columbus Day in the United States traditionally was celebrated in honor of a man regarded as a visionary explorer who changed the course of world history for the better. Although the cruelties inflicted by his and subsequent expeditions were duly noted in the history books—including the diseases they brought with them that devastated indigenous populations—"the age of exploration" usually was presented in positive terms. More recently, individuals and groups have turned this version of history on its head, emphasizing instead the destruction of native peoples and the environment. They see the "invasion of paradise" as an unalloyed disaster. The article "Was America a Mistake?" attempts to present a balanced view. The following reading, "California's Spanish Missions," describes the failure of a well-intentioned Spanish effort to Christianize native peoples begun during the eighteenth century.

The English came to the New World relatively late. Some, like the Spaniards, sought jewels and precious metals. Others came to settle. Land was plentiful in the New World, but there were few to work it. Importing black slaves from Africa was one means of obtaining labor, employing indentured servants was another. These indentured servants were people who contracted for stipulated periods of labor in return for the costs of passage from England, food, clothing, and housing. They became free people after completion of their contract. "Colonists in Bondage: Indentured Servants in America" describes this form of labor.

Religion played an important role in the colonies, as shown in the article "Anne Hutchinson: 'A Verye Dangerous Woman.' " Claiming to have revelations from God, her unorthodox sermons got her into trouble and challenged the religious intolerance of the day.

Witches and wizards were as real to many new Englanders in the seventeenth century as trees and streams. Ordinary people feared that witches might damage their crops or harm their livestock, and some clergy saw a greater threat: a conspiracy to undermind Christianity. "Under an Evil Hand" tells the story of the Salem witch hunts that began in 1692 and led to the execution of 19 people before the hysteria subsided.

The last reading in this unit, "Remapping American Culture," attributes many regional differences in the United States to successive waves of immigration from England, Northern Ireland, and Scotland during colonial days. Despite the impact of immigration from other countries, according to this view, the original folkways still exert strong influence on customs and manners.

Looking Ahead: Challenge Questions

Although the accomplishments of groups such as the Aztecs and Incas have long been recognized, if not fully appreciated, a common assumption about most tribes in North America is that they never learned more than the simplest means of farming and homebuilding. What evidence is there that this assumption is mistaken?

Evaluate the impact of European exploration and settlement on native peoples and on world history.

The practice of indenture seems alien and cruel in modern times. What purpose did it serve and why might it have seemed necessary to those who devised it?

Belief in witchcraft is scoffed at by most people today. Can the spread of hysteria in Salem in 1692 provide any lessons for us?

Using examples, what evidence is there that early immigration from various parts of England has exerted lasting political and cultural patterns?

AMERICA
BEFORE COLUMBUS

They lived in temples as well as teepees, dined on succotash and 9-inch oysters, and developed customs, including daily baths, that Europeans abhorred. They were America's first settlers, and the world they inhabited was anything but new.

Most vacationers on Interstate 70 speed right by ancient Cahokia and its 15-acre ceremonial mound, the one that's 2 acres bigger than the Great Pyramid of Egypt. Only a curious few pull off to learn how a feather-crowned dictator known as the Great Sun used to knell atop the earthen temple every morning and howl when the real sun came up. At its peak, the town across the Mississippi from present-day St. Louis boasted a trade network that stretched from the Gulf of Mexico to the Dakotas and probably had as many residents as did London at that time. But modern textbooks barely take notice. Cahokia's problem is that American history, in the minds of many, started just 500 years ago, back when Columbus discovered the New World. By 1492, Cahokia was an Illinois Babylon, a city that had thrived and vanished.

Like many 20th-century metropolises, 13th-century Cahokia could not handle growth, even though its developers were sharp enough to grasp geometry and astronomy. Besides building more than 100 neatly proportioned mounds, they constructed a circle of tall polls—archaeologists call its "Woodhenge"—that aligned with the sun at equinox and solstice. Despite this evidence of advanced thinking, however, no Cahokian appears to have anticipated the consequences of ecological change and environmental degradation. Cornfields that fed 20,000 to 40,000 urbanites gradually lost their fertility. Forests were stripped of trees not only to fuel thousands of daily household fires but also to form a 2 1/2-mile stockade wall. As hard times set in, Cahokians moved or perished. Centuries later, the French arrived and found only grown-over mounds. The Europeans who peopled America in Columbus's wake believed the land had never been settled, much less civilized. "North America

was inhabited only by wandering tribes who had no thought of profiting by the natural riches of the soil," wrote Alex de Tocqueville in 1835. It was, the French observer concluded, "an empty continent, a desert land awaiting its inhabitants." Tocqueville's "empty continent" phrase endures today in Fourth of July speeches that hail the building of the nation, but in fact the New World was anything but empty in Columbus's day. Give or take several million, the Western Hemisphere in 1492 had as many people as Europe. It was the teeming and majestic civilization of Mexico's Aztecs and Peru's Incas that awed the Spanish conquistadors initially—some gawked like country bumpkins at Montezuma's capital, with its several hundred thousand people—but ancient societies had also been rising and falling for centuries above the Rio Grande. More than 1,000 tribes—with upward of 2 million people—still inhabited the northern forests, prairies and mesas when whites arrived.

Newcomers from Europe, though accustomed to people being burned or beheaded, were shocked at what went on in America. Columbus claimed he had to take hundreds of Carib Indians to Spain for their own good and that of their Arawak neighbors, whom they were eating. (He had a harder time explaining why he also enslaved the gentle Arawaks.) While cannibalism and human sacrifice were rare among Indians north of Mexico, people in some tribes killed unwanted infants, had multiple wives and, in the case of the Hurons, wiped their hands on dogs that ambled by. Other traits seemed alien as well: an awed reverence of nature, a desire to share and, for many, societies free of oppression and class stratification. In addition, most took a daily bath, a practice

the Europeans abhorred. America was not new, but it was different.

As whites moved westward across what is now the United States, they encountered a familiar question among tribesmen in their path: "Why do you call us Indians?" The answer, of course, was that Columbus was mistaken. He thought he was in the distant Indies, somewhere between Japan and India, and labeled his hosts *los Indios.* The Indians had no word for their race. They called their own tribes "people" or "real people," and other tribes names like "friend," "enemy" or "poisonous snake."

The diversity that Americans relish today actually existed long before Columbus arrived. Most of the hundreds of languages the Indians spoke were as different from one another as Farsi is from French. Some Indians loved war. Others hated it. After every reluctant fight, Arizona's Pimas subjected their warriors to a 16-day cure for insanity. Some tribes banned women from their councils. Others were ruled by female chiefs, like Georgia's "Lady of Cofitachequi," who greeted Hernando DeSoto with pearls from the Savannah River. (He ungraciously kidnapped her.) Puppies were a gourmet's delight in some huts. Elsewhere, Indians would rather die than eat dog meat. Premarital sex was unthinkable among the Cheyenne. But Mississippi's Natchez tribe encouraged teenagers to have flings while they could. Once a Natchez girl wed, an extramarital affair could cost her her hair or even an ear.

Every American Indian, from the Abenakis of Maine to the Zunis of New Mexico, descended from immigrant stock. Asian-Americans were the first Americans, and they came over 12,000

 From *U.S. News & World Report,* July 8, 1991, pp. 22-26, 35-37. Copyright © 1991 by U.S. News & World Report.

to 20,000 years ago, probably crossing a glacial land bridge between Siberia and Alaska. For some time, they hunted the mastodon and the long-horned bison, perhaps speeding their extinction. As long ago as 5,000 years, people in Mexico may have cultivated maize, better known as corn, and early residents of Arizona were growing it in A.D. 1. Many people in what is now the United States existed the next 10 or 15 centuries as nomads, moving about in search of game, fish and wild plants for food, but some accomplished much more.

Pioneers who found thousands of abandoned mounds in the Ohio and Mississippi valleys refused to believe they had been built by Indians. "The natural indolence of the Indian and his averseness to any kind of manual labor are well known," wrote author William Pidgeon in 1858. Other 19th-century writers speculated that the mound builders were stray Vikings, Phoenicians or a lost tribe of Israel—obviously an intelligent people who were annihilated by Indian savages. Settlers liked that theory, because it seemed to justify the treatment they inflicted on the Indians on the frontier. Not until the 1890s did educated people agree that the mounds in fact were built by the Indians' ancestors.

The genius of the mound builders has become even more evident in recent years. Just west of the Mississippi in northeast Louisiana lies Poverty Point, a 3,500-year-old collection of concentric semicircles of earth, the biggest nearly three quarters of a mile long. Visitors can stand atop a mound just west of Poverty Point's rings during the spring and fall equinox and see the sun rise over what was the town's central plaza—a view like that at England's Stonehenge during similar conjunctions of earth and sun. On Moundbuilders Golf Course in Newark, Ohio, stands an earthen ring that is 15 centuries old. Its diameter is the same, 1,050 feet, as those of two more circles within 50 miles of Newark. Other precisely measured mounds in central Ohio include three 1,200-foot circles and five 27-acre squares. "Such nice equivalences of shapes and sizes are not the work of savages," says Roger Kennedy, director of the Smithsonian's Museum of American History, who is writing a book entitled "Medieval America." "I doubt that the Harvard freshman class would be capable of similar intellectual achievement."

Every explorer and early settler seemed to notice the aroma of America. Robert Beverley was awed by "the pleasantest Smell" of Virginia's giant magnolias. DeSoto's men admired Georgia's "very savoury, palatable and fragrant" strawberries. Henry Hudson paused in New York's harbor to enjoy the "very sweet smells" of grass and flowers on the New Jersey shore. But the visitors also smelled smoke. Many soon concluded that Indian women did all the work, while the men idled away their time hunting, fishing and setting the woods on fire.

The native men, it turned out, were practicing a form of forest management that put food in their wigwams and longhouses. With torches and stone hatchets, the Nootkas and Haidas of the Pacific Northwest toppled giant redwoods and turned them into whaling canoes. In the eastern forests, Indians slashed and burned to clear the way for cornfields fertilized by the ashes and to create meadows for grazing deer and elk. Every autumn, Indians burned huge chunks of woodland to clear away underbrush. The sprouts that poked each spring through the charred ground boosted populations of game animals, which the Indians could easily spot in the open forests. The trees that survived flourished, too. Sycamores in Ohio grew seven feet in diameter, and the white pines of New England towered 200 to 250 feet. Governor's Island, now in the shadow of Manhattan's skyscrapers, had so many big hickory and walnut trees that the Dutch settlers called it Nut Island.

Colonists enjoyed describing the country they settled as a "howling wilderness"—a phrase from the Book of Jeremiah—and in many places it was. Bamboo canebrakes, 20 to 30 feet high and impenetrable, stretched in parts of the Southeast for 100 miles or more, and tangles of brier and grapevines crowded the cottonwoods of the river bottoms. The forests were so boundless, the settlers like to say, that a squirrel could travel from Maine to the Mississippi and never touch the ground. But wherever Indians hunted, the forest floor was usually clear, reminding one observer of "our parks in England."

Early English settlers, accustomed to woods with only a few doves, were startled by the spectacle in America's skies. The colonists especially admired the green-and gold Carolina parakeet, "a fowle most swift of wing [and] very beautiful." Passenger pigeons passed in flocks "for three or foure houres . . . so thicke they have shaddowed the skie from us." Out west, Meriwether Lewis and William Clark would see huge flocks of pelicans and sandhill cranes along the Missouri and dense clouds of geese over the Columbia River.

Animals were bigger then. Pennsylvania trout, nearly 2 feet long, were easy targets for Algonquian arrows. Virginia sturgeon stretched 6 to 9 feet, and Mississippi catfish topped 120 pounds. Off Cape Cod, a few indians could catch 30 lobsters in a half hour, some weighing 20 pounds, and many Massachusetts oysters had to be sliced into thirds to be swallowed.

Bison roamed not only the Great Plains but also the meadows and open forests of Ohio, Pennsylvania and Virginia. The western bison were infinitely more numerous, thundering along in heards 25 miles long, but the woods buffalo was bigger and blacker with shorter hair and no hump. A few still remained in George Washington's time; he considered crossing them with domestic cattle.

THE WHITE MAN'S BIBLE TAUGHT THAT it is better to give than to receive, and the Indians couldn't agree more. Long after the Arawaks showered Columbus with birds, cloth and "trifles too tedious to describe," natives were offering Europeans virtually anything they had, from fish and turkeys to persimmon bread and the companionship of a chief's daughter. Colonists interpreted the Indians' generosity as evidence they were childlike. That they had no desire to accumulate wealth was seen as a symptom of laziness. The Indians, concluded one New Englander, must develop a love of property. "Wherever this can be established, Indians may be civilized; wherever it cannot, they will still remain Indians."

The Indians felt quite civilized with what they did own, often things a Puritan wouldn't appreciate. Colorado's Pueblos kept parrots that came from Mexico. The Cayuse of Eastern Oregon swapped buffalo robes for the shells of coastal Indians. The Ottawas, whose name meant "to trade," traveled the Great Lakes exchanging cornmeal, herbs, furs and tobacco. The Chinooks of the Northwest even developed their own trade jargon. Their word *hootchenoo*, for homemade liquor, eventually became the slang word "hootch."

1. THE NEW LAND

Above all else, Indians were religious. They saw order in nature and obeyed elaborate sets of rules for fear of disturbing it. Land was to be shared, not owned, because it was sacred and belonged to everyone, like the air and sea. Animals also were precious. A hunter risked stirring the spirits if he killed two deer when one was all his tribe needed. Europe's view of nature, though rooted in religion, was much different. Man should subdue the Earth, Genesis dictated, "and have dominion . . . over every living thing."

Rituals surrounded each important Indian event. To prove their courage, the Arikara of North Dakota danced barefoot on hot coals and, with bare hands, retrieved and devoured hunks of meat from pots of boiling water. Timucuan leaders started council meetings in Florida with a round of emetics brewed from holly leaves. The Hurons of the Great Lakes carried smoldering coals in their mouths to invoke a spirit to cure the sick. But often the rituals were painless. From New York to New Mexico, tradition allowed a woman to end her marriage by putting her husband's belongings outside their door—a sign for him to live with his mother.

Three centuries before the U.S. Constitution took shape, the Iroquois League ran a Congress-like council, exercised the veto, protected freedom of speech and let women choose officeholders. The New Yorkers ran a classless society, as did many tribes across America. But ancient caste systems also endured. The Great Sun of the Natchez, a mound dweller like Cahokia's Great Sun, used his feet to push his leftovers to his noble subordinates. The nobles were not about to complain; below them was a class known as "Stinkards." Besides, the chief's feet were clean. He was carried everywhere, a French guest reported, and his toes never touched ground.

COLUMBUS'S SECOND VOYAGE—THE ONE in which Europeans came to stay—began the process that changed nearly everything. Instead of 90 sailors on the Nina, the Pinta and the Santa Maria as in 1492, Columbus set out in '93 with 1,200 men in 17 ships. In addition to starting the world's most significant movement of people, he delivered a Noah's Ark of animals unknown to the New World— sheep, pigs, chickens, horses and cows— plus a host of Old World diseases. What the Admiral of the Ocean Sea created was the Columbian Exchange, a global swap of animals, plants, people, ailments and ideas that historian Alfred Crosby calls "the most important event in human history since the end of the Ice Age."

For the Old World as well as the New, the event was both salubrious and calamitous. Twenty years after Columbus colonized Hispaniola—the island now shared by Haiti and the Dominican Republic— diseases and taskmasters reduced its Arawaks from a quarter million down to 14,000. Within two centuries, Old World diseases killed probably two thirds of the New World's natives, and America did indeed seem empty. Africans also were dying by the thousands. They were brought to the New World to grow sugar, another import from the Old World.

Yet, thanks to Columbus, Africa's population boomed. Corn, an American staple for thousands of years, augmented African diets, boosting the continent's birth rates and life spans. The same thing happened in Europe with the potato, also from America. The Columbian Exchange thickened Italy's sauces with tomatoes, seeded Kentucky with European bluegrass and covered the gullies of Georgia with Chinese kudzu. China, in return, became the globe's No. 1 consumer of the American-born sweet potato. "The Columbus story is not an Old World, New World story," explains Smithsonian historian Herman Viola, who heads the Museum of Natural History's Columbus Quincentenary programs. "It is two old worlds that linked up, making one new world."

It is also a story of winning and losing, with many of the losers gone before the winners ever showed up. When whites first penetrated the fertile Ohio Valley, they found many mounds but few Indians. The Southeast also seemed vacant when the French came to stay around 1700. As they moved into lands that abounded in natural food resources, the settlers kept wondering where the Indians had gone. Some scholars believe they were wiped out or chased away by epidemics of European diseases that moved north along Indian trade routes in the century after Columbus. Two years before DeSoto visited Cofitachequi's female chief in the 1540s, pestilence swept her province, decimating her town and emptying others nearby. In one village, the Spaniards found nothing but large houses full of bodies. It was the same medical disaster the conquistadors at that time were discovering in Mexico and Peru and the Pilgrims would notice much later in Massachusetts. Four years before the Mayflower landed, disease killed tens of thousands of Indians on the New England coast, including the inhabitants of a village where Plymouth would stand. John Winthrop, admiring the abandoned cornfields, saw the epidemic as divine providence. "God," he said, "hath hereby cleared out title to this place."

Indians in the forests shuddered every time they found honeybees in a hollow tree. The "English flies" moved 100 miles ahead of the frontier—a sign that the white man was on his way. The smart tribes moved west, pushing whatever band was in their way. The Chippewas pushed the Sioux out of the woods of Minnesota into the Dakotas. The Sioux pushed the Cheyenne into Nebraska. The Cheyenne pushed the Kiowas into Oklahoma. Yet not every Indian fled. The Comanches, with horses descended from Columbus's stock, thwarted Spain's colonial designs on Texas with frequent raids on Spanish outposts. Apaches did the same thing in Arizona and New Mexico. Parts of Pennsylvania and New York today might be part of Quebec had the Iroquois rolled over for the French.

Many who didn't move perished. A generation after their gifts of corn saved England's toehold settlement at Jamestown, the Powhatan Indians were systematically wiped out, their crops and villages torched by settlers who wanted more land to grow tobacco. Florida's Timucuas—of whom it was said "it would be good if among Christians there was as little greed to torment men's minds and hearts"—vanished in the early 19th century, victims of epidemics and conflicts with the Spanish, English and Creeks. Natchez's Great Sun wound up with his feet on the ground, enslaved in the West Indies by the French, who eradicated his tribe. California's Chumash shrank from 70,000 to 15,000 toiling for the friars. Soon after the Gold Rush, the tribe, like most in California, ceased to exist. The four-century clash of cultures made 2 of every 3 tribes as extinct as the Carolina parakeet.

The land they left is different now. The white pines that towered over New England became masts for the Royal Navy's sailing ships. The redwoods that stretched from the Rockies to the Pacific, like the cypresses that crowded the Mississippi Valley, exist in pockets smaller than the In-

The Indian Homeland

The first Americans arrived from Asia perhaps 20,000 years ago. No one knows for sure whether they came by boat or, more likely, across a land bridge between Siberia and Alaska. But this is clear: Long before Columbus set sail, America was a land of many different peoples.

1. Folsom

9000 B.C. Excavations in New Mexico in 1927 revealed the stone point of a spear beside a skeleton of the extinct long-horned bison—evidence that American hunters existed 11,000 years ago.

2. Poverty Point

2000 B.C.–700 B.C. The biggest town above the Rio Grande 3,000 years ago was a Louisiana community with six giant earthen semicircles, evident now in infra-red photographs from the air. Poverty Point's trade network extended 1,000 miles along the Mississippi and its tributaries.

3. Two Medicine River

1000 B.C.–A.D. 1800. Western tribes hunted buffaloes by frightening herds into stampedes over cliffs. The practice ended only when Indians acquired horses and guns.

4. Santa Rosa Island

600 B.C.–A.D. 1817. The Chumash moved along California's coast in boats made of brightly painted cedar planks. They ate fish and acorns, lived in domed houses and used sea-lion bristles as needles. An 1812 earthquake drove most of Santa Rosa's Chumash into Catholic missions on the mainland.

5. Serpent Mound

500 B.C.–A.D. 300. In seven giant coils, the Great Serpent Mound stretches a quarter mile from tail to jaw along a creek bluff near Cincinnati. Its builders were members of either the Adena or the Hopewell Culture.

6. Bedford Mound 100 B.C.–A.D. 200.

Buried near a man who smoked tobacco in Illinois 2,000 years ago was a stone pipe shaped like a beaver, with freshwater pearls for eyes and bone for teeth.

7. Mound City

100 B.C.–A.D. 300. Ohio was the home of the mound-building Hopewell people, hunters and fishers who traded with people from Montana to Florida. Many corpses buried in the mounds were bedecked from head to toe in pearls and surrounded with sculptures and pottery.

8. Cahokia

700–1500. In its 13th-century heyday, 30,000 people of the Mississippian Culture resided in this 6-square-mile city across the Mississippi from present-day St. Louis. Monk's Mound, the biggest of Cahokia's 120 mounds, stands 10 stories high with a base larger than that of the Great Pyramid of Egypt. Atop Monk's Mound lived the Great Sun, Cahokia's godlike leader.

9. Mesa Verde

700–1300. The Anasazis, or "ancient ones," lived for centuries on mesa tops. Later they moved into cliff dwellings with protective overhangs, like Colorado's Cliff Palace.

10. Chaco Canyon

950–1200. Apartments were popular in the Southwest. Pueblo Bonito, Chaco Canyon's most impressive ruin, had 800 rooms.

11. Spiro Mounds

950–1400. The first Mississippian artisans in Oklahoma's Spiro community created images of animals. Humanlike figures, carved from stone, wood and copper, were popular later.

12. Moundville

1000–1500. On a bluff overlooking Alabama's Black Warrior River stood the South's largest town and 20 pyramidal mounds. Moundville was the center of a chiefdom with perhaps 10,000 members of the Mississippian Culture.

13. Natchez

1000–1729. The Natchez, the last Indians to use temple mounds, were described by the French as "the most civilized of the native tribes." Yet the 1725 death of the chief's brother, Tattooed Serpent, touched off a sacrificial orgy. To keep him company, several aides and servants plus his two wives joyously agreed to be strangled.

14. Acoma

1100–present. Atop a 375-foot-high mesa stands one of the two oldest continuously inhabited towns in the United States. The other, Oraibi, is nearby. Acoma's residents gave Francisco Coronado's men corn, turkeys and deerskins in the 1540s.

15. Ozette

1200–1400. The Makahs of the Olympic Peninsula used dugout canoes and 18-foot-long harpoons to hunt whales in the Pacific. A mudslide from a steep cliff buried the Makah settlement at Ozette more than 500 years ago, dooming the villagers but preserving their tools, baskets and sculptures.

16. Key Marco

1400–1750. The Calusas . . . traveled widely. With their dugout canoes, some even visited the Arawaks, the first Indians Columbus met in the Caribbean. The tribe disintegrated in the 18th century when the British took many members to the Carolinas as slaves.

17. Plymouth

1616. The Pilgrims, landing in Massachusetts in 1620, chose a cleared site that had been planted in corn. Only four years earlier, a Wampanoag village existed there. The community, like many on the New England coast, was wiped out by a European disease probably spread by visiting fishermen. Some of the surviving Wampanoags helped the Pilgrims get through their first year in America.

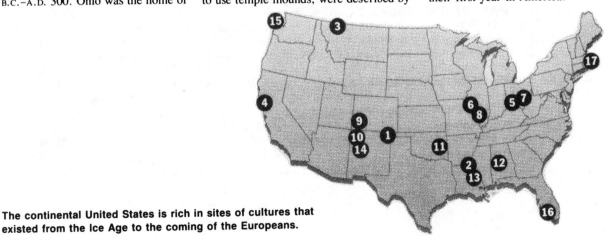

The continental United States is rich in sites of cultures that existed from the Ice Age to the coming of the Europeans.

The Spain that Columbus Left Behind

When Christopher Columbus set sail on the Atlantic, he imagined himself embarked on the final crusade. He would find a route to Asia and enough gold to mount an assault on holy Jerusalem from the east. With the conquest, the man who called himself "bearer of Christ" would usher in the Second Coming and the end of the world.

For all his grandiosity, Columbus was not dismissed by his contemporaries as some wild-eyed fool. He was, in fact, a perfect product of his times. At the close of the 15th century, Spain itself was consumed by a great religious fever, burning heretics, conquering the Moors and expelling or converting tens of thousands of Jews. A country on the cusp of modernity, it had transformed itself into a nation state, made great strides in military technology, mapping and navigation and joined the rest of Europe in the study of classical antiquity. Yet it was still medieval country, too, obsessed with apocalyptic prophecies and nostalgic for chivalry's imaginary past.

Under the canny leadership of Ferdinand and Isabella, Spain amassed in the name of Christianity the largest empire the world had ever seen. "Under the pretext of religion," wrote an admiring Nicolo Machiavelli, "Ferdinand has had recourse to a pious cruelty, and been transformed from a small and weak king into the greatest monarch in Christendom."

Christian soldiers. Just a decade before Ferdinand and Isabella were married in 1469, the Christian world had been thrown into panic with the Muslim conquest of Constantinople. When in 1492 the Spanish rulers defeated the infidel at Granada, they emerged as Europe's supreme defenders of the faith. The Pope rewarded them with the title *Los Reyes Católicos,* "the Catholic monarchs." Three months later, still glowing from the victory, they acceded to Columbus's petition for their patronage of his crusade.

As Spain battled the enemy without, it also waged war within. "Spain had a mission to redeem the world," writes Oxford historian John Elliott, "but had first to cleanse the temple of the Lord of its impurities." Pogroms had begun in the late 1300s, and in 1449 the first "purity of blood" decree excluded all persons of Jewish ancestry—even baptized converts—from certain positions in the government and church. In 1492, Isabella signed the Edict of Expulsion, which banished Spain's 150,000 Jews. The Inquisition, begun in 1481, tossed into prison wayward Catholics accused of blasphemy, homosexuality and bestiality. It burned at the stake the "genuine heretics," converted Jews and Muslims accused of practicing their original faiths in secret and leading authentic Christians astray.

The colonization of the new world was the final step in this purification. The powerful Franciscan religious order saw in the agrarian Amerindians ideal material for a more innocent Christian community, and under its influence Isabella urged conversion of the natives. She could not, in fact, do otherwise, since the papal grant of the new territories was contingent on the promise to redeem the noble savage.

But if there were ulterior motives, Isabella was skillful at masking them with her faith. She was a genius of political spin. At the funeral of her brother, whose death laid open the succession to the throne, Isabella changed hurriedly from mourning into bejeweled finery and marched through the streets with an unsheathed sword, making clear she would brook no opposition. Wisely, she tempered her grandeur with ostentatious humility. Isabella was so chaste, it was said, that when Ferdinand was away she slept surrounded by chambermaids to protect her virtue.

With their combined talents, Ferdinand and Isabella soon achieved unprecedented political control over their empire.

They made Castilian the national language and resurrected the Santa Hermandad, a police force and tribunal that savagely enforced the king's law. In constant need of gold, they became increasingly dependent on colonial plunder—taking a practice standard for the times to new heights.

Like Columbus, the conquistadors were extravagant dreamers. Most were young noblemen, the disinherited second sons of poor families, generally uneducated, but entranced by fancies of armored knights and heroic deeds. These impoverished aristocrats amused themselves with already archaic courtly rituals: elaborate dances, jousting and bearbaiting. They were mocked by Cervantes a century later in his account of the grand delusions of Don Quixote. But like America's cowboy myth, Spain's image of the conquistador gripped the national psyche for centuries.

Beyond Spain's borders, a different and darker myth about the Spanish character prevailed. Enemy nations propagated the belief that the Catholic nation was uniquely barbaric, resulting in what many view as an anti-Spanish, anti-Catholic bias in the writing of American colonial history. The propaganda obscured the fact that Spain, while guilty of atrocities, was alone among European powers in seriously questioning the morality of its practices. Indeed, Isabella in 1500 prohibited expropriation of Indian lands, forced labor and enslavement—in contrast to the English and French. The bias among historians softened only after Franco's death, and today there is renewed debate about medieval Spanish culture and the true nature of the colonists' relations with American natives. Ironically, while most historians are busy beatifying the Indians and vilifying the imperialists, Spain is seeking its own historical redemption.

—By Miriam Horn
with Dana Hawkins

dians' shrunken reservations. The hours-long thunder of bison hooves no longer shakes Kansas or Nebraska, where only a few stretches of grassland remain like the prairie John Muir described a century ago—"one sheet of plant gold, hazy and vanishing in the distance." The prairie now feeds the nation with Old World food like wheat and pork.

Yet at least one ancient American community endures. Shunning electricity, 3,000 Pueblo Indians live today in Acoma atop a mesa in the high New Mexico desert. The town's adobe apartments have been inhabited since the 12th century, through droughts, Apache raids and a brutal occupation in which the enslaving Spaniards chopped off one foot of each adult male. Acomans are reluctant to promote the fact that their settlement is nearly twice as old as St. Augustine, Fla., the Spanish-settled city that is generally considered the nation's oldest community. The people of Acoma figure they have had enough visitors.

By Lewis Lord with Sarah Burke

Was America a Mistake?

*Reflections on the long history of efforts to debunk Columbus
and his discovery*

Arthur Schlesinger, Jr.

Arthur Schlesinger, Jr., received the Pulitzer Prize for history in 1946 and the Pulitzer Prize for biography in 1966. Schlesinger's numerous books include the first three volumes of The Age of Roosevelt *(1957–1960),* A Thousand Days *(1965),* The Imperial Presidency *(1973), and* The Cycles of American History *(1986). He is currently at work on a fourth volume of* The Age of Roosevelt.

October 12, 1992, marks the five-hundredth anniversary of the most crucial of all encounters between Europe and the Americas. In the contemporary global mood, however, the quincentennial of Christopher Columbus's landing in the New World—new, anyway, to the European intruders; old and familiar to its inhabitants—seems an occasion less for celebration than for meditation. Indeed, in some quarters the call is for penitence and remorse.

Christopher Columbus has always been as much a myth as a man, a myth incorporating a succession of triumphs and guilts over what is now five long centuries. The myth has found particular lodgment in the mightiest of the nations to arise in the Western Hemisphere—a nation that may not speak Columbus's language (any of them) but has diligently revered his memory.

Though both the continent and the country bear another's name, Columbus has been surpassed in nomenclatural popularity in the United States only by the great George Washington—and Washington is itself located in the District of Columbia. I make this observation as a native of Columbus, Ohio, the largest of many municipalities called after the great explorer. The preeminent university in the city in which I now live is Columbia—not to mention such other North American institutions as the Columbia Broadcasting System, the *Columbia Encyclopedia,* Columbia Pictures, and a variety of enterprises from banks to space shuttles.

The biography that fixed the nineteenth-century image of Columbus was published in 1828 and written by Washington Irving, Manhattan's first international man of letters, a lover of Spain, the aficionado of Granada and the Alhambra, and in later life the U.S. minister to Madrid. Half a century after, Irish-Americans named a newly founded Roman Catholic fraternal organization the Knights of Columbus. A movement to honor the day of landfall culminated in 1934, when President Franklin D. Roosevelt proclaimed October 12 a national holiday. The holiday is observed in most Latin American countries as well.

The United States also staged the most memorable celebration of the quadricentennial of what it was then widely acceptable to call the "discovery" of America. The World's Columbian Exposition took place in bustling, thrusting, midwestern Chicago, the very heart of the republic. Reconfiguring the great explorer in images of technology and modernity, the Chicago World's Fair saluted the man then regarded, in the words of President Benjamin Harrison, as "the pioneer of progress and enlightenment." In a book especially produced for the fair, the historian Meyer Kayserling summed up the prevailing assessment of Columbus: "In the just appreciation of his great services to mankind, all political, religious and social differences have vanished."

How things have changed in a century! Political, religious, and social differences, far from vanishing, place Columbus today in the center of a worldwide cultural civil war. The great hero of the nineteenth century seems well on the way to becoming the great villain of the twenty-first. Columbus, it is now charged, far from being the pioneer of progress and enlightenment, was in fact the pioneer of oppression, racism, slavery, rape, theft, vandalism, extermination, and ecological desolation.

The revisionist reaction, it must be said, has been under way for a while. As far back as the quadricentennial Justin Winsor, a historian and bibliographer of early America, published a soberly critical biography, arguing that Columbus had left the New World "a legacy of devastation and crime." George Santayana soon wrote of Columbus, in one of his *Odes,*

He gave the world another world, and ruin
Brought upon blameless, river-loving
   nations,
Cursed Spain with barren gold, and made
   the Andes
          Fiefs of Saint Peter.

Today revisionism is in full flood. Much of it is useful and necessary. "The one duty we owe to history," as Oscar Wilde said, "is to rewrite it." The very phrase "discovery of America" is under a ban. It is pointed out, not unreasonably, that America had been discovered centuries earlier by people trickling across the Bering Strait land bridge from East Asia. To call Columbus's landfall a "discovery" therefore convicts one of Eurocentrism. Certainly it is hard to object to the proposal that the arrival of Columbus be seen from the viewpoint of those who met him as well as from the viewpoint of those who sent him.

It is also well that we begin to see the man Columbus not in the nineteenth-century mode, as Benjamin Harrison's "pioneer of progress and enlightenment," but as he saw himself—as, that is, a God-intoxicated man who, for all his superb practical skills as a navigator, believed himself engaged in a spiritual rather than a geographical quest, the messenger not of rationalism and science but of the Almighty, warning that the world would end in another century and a half, prophesying, as he wrote to an intimate of Queen Isabella's, "the new heaven and the new earth which the Lord made, and of which St. John writes in the Apocalypse." We are right, I think, in beginning to read his messianic *Libro de las profecías* not as a cynical attempt to con the Queen nor as the paranoid outburst of an aging and despairing has-been but as the center of the Columbian dream.

REVISIONISM REDRESSES THE BALANCE up to a point; but, driven by Western guilt, it may verge on masochism. Let me cite the resolution on the quincentennial adopted by the National Council of Churches: "What some historians have termed a 'discovery' in reality was an invasion and colonization with legalized occupation, genocide, economic exploitation and a deep level of institutional racism and moral decadence." The Council of Churches' three-page statement is a stern indictment of the criminal history of the European conquest. The quincentennial, the resolution concludes, should be an occasion not for celebration but for "repentance."

The government of Canada has decided not to celebrate the quincentennial at all, on the ground that the arrival of Columbus led to the destruction of the existing American cultures. Russell Means, a leader of the American Indian Movement, opines that Columbus "makes Hitler look like a juvenile delinquent." The novelist Hans Koning finds him "worse than Attila the Hun." Last year on Columbus Day protesters in Washington poured fake blood on the Union Station statue of Columbus. Marlon Brando recently demanded that his name be removed from the credits of a new movie, *Christopher Columbus: The Discovery,* on the ground that the film failed to portray Columbus as "the true villain he was," the man "directly responsible for the first wave of genocidal obliteration of the native peoples of North America." (Brando's role in the film, by the way, was Torquemada.)

In the university town of Berkeley, California, a leaflet charged Columbus with "grand theft; genocide; racism; initiating the destruction of culture; rape,

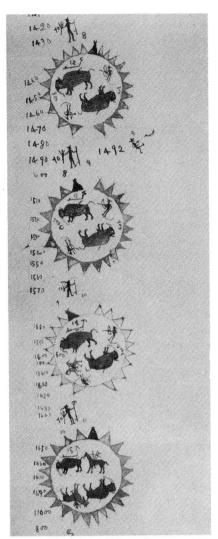

Before and after: a Plains Indian History
LIBRARY OF CONGRESS

torture and maiming of indigenous people; and [being the] instigator of the Big Lie"; city officials thereafter changed October 12 to Indigenous Peoples Day. When Cristobal Colon, a descendant of the explorer's, was appointed grand marshal of Pasadena's annual New Year's Day parade, the Tournament of Roses, the vice-mayor denounced Colon as "a symbol of greed, slavery; rape, and genocide" and his appointment as an insult to American Indians. The protest was stilled only by the naming of Ben Nighthorse Campbell, a congressman and Cheyenne chief, as co-grand marshal.

Recently, in Havana, I asked Fidel Castro how he looks on the impending quincentennial. He replied, "We are critical. Columbus brought many bad things." I said, "If it weren't for Columbus, you wouldn't be here." Castro said, "Well, Columbus brought good things as well as bad." This slightly schizophrenic reaction is not untypical. North and south of

the border Americans of Spanish descent are torn between pride in their Hispanic heritage and romantic identification with indigenous Indian traditions. In the United States some Latinos join the campaign against the Spanish conquest; others take it as an attack on themselves. "My mother sees it as something that brought us religion and civilization," one told Patricia Duarte, of *Newsday.* "Younger people see it as an atrocity."

Still, the "politically correct" image of Columbus as executioner dominates the current discussion. As the art critic Hilton Kramer sums it up,

Columbus is now vilified as a Eurocentric genocidal maniac who, in addition to decimating the native population of the Americas, was also responsible for destroying their ecology and bringing to this part of the world the most atrocious of all economic systems, namely, capitalism.

Had Columbus foreseen even a portion of all the sins he would be held accountable for five centuries later, he might never have bothered to discover America.

WHY THIS SEA CHANGE IN ATTITUDES? Obviously the global mood has shifted since the exaltation of Columbus's heroic aspects at the quadricentennial. This change reflects the end of European domination of the planet. It reflects the revolt of the Third World against economic exploitation, against political control, against cultural despoliation, against personal and national humiliation, even, at times, against modernity itself. It reflects the (belated) bad conscience of the West and the consequent re-examination of the Western impact on the rest of humanity.

No one can doubt the arrogance and brutality of the European invaders, their callous and destructive ways, the human and ecological devastation they left in their trail. Genocide—the calculated and purposeful murder of a race—may be too harsh a term, at least for Spanish America; it applies more to British America, which widely believed that the only good Indian was a dead Indian. Many Spaniards wanted to keep natives alive, if only as slave labor; some, like Father Bartolomé de Las Casas, denounced inhuman treatment in brave and searing language. In both South and North America many more Amerindians died by accident from European diseases—smallpox, cholera, measles—than by design from European swords, harquebuses, and lashes. (And in the transatlantic exchange of diseases, the Europeans apparently received syphilis.)

Revisionists tend to portray pre-Columbian America as an Arcadia. The most readable statement of the case is by Kirkpatrick Sale, in his graceful and passionate book *The Conquest of Paradise* (1990). Sale envisages a continent where people lived in "balanced and fruitful harmony" with nature and with one another, "an untouched world, a prelapsarian Eden of astonishing plenitude . . . functioning to all intents and purposes in its original primal state," green and pure, until European violence smashed the human and ecological utopia.

The myth of innocence is an old one. "In the beginning," John Locke wrote three centuries ago, "all the world was *America,* and more so than that is now; for no such thing as *Money* was any where known." Yet the vision of an uncorrupted pre-Columbian America is in acute conflict with another part of the anti-Columbus campaign: the contention that pre-Columbian America contained elaborate and advanced civilizations that were ruthlessly obliterated by the European invasion.

One has only to recall the soaring temples, exact astronomical calculations, accurate calendars, and complex hieroglyphics of the Maya in Central America; or the wild surmise with which in 1519 stout Cortes and his tiny Spanish band confronted not the Pacific from Keats's peak in Darien but, shimmering in the distance, the Aztec city of Tenochtitlán, a metropolis as impressive as any in sixteenth-century Europe; or the contrast between the brutal Spanish thug Pizarro and the courteous and civilized Inca Emperor Atahualpa; or the wonderful grace, symmetry, and imaginative power of pre-Columbian art.

Yet these empires were also theocratic military collectivisms, quite as arrogant, cruel, and ethnocentric as the Europeans who demolished them. Far from living in harmony with nature, the Maya evidently brought about their own collapse by deforestation and other destructive agricultural practices that upset the rainforest ecosystem of Central America. Far from living in harmony with one another, the Mayan city-states appear to have been engaged in constant warfare, with prisoners ritually tortured and decapitated.

The anthropologist Louis Faron describes the Mundurucú societies of the Amazon basin, whose approach to prisoners of war "ranged from the exotic mutilation of shrinking heads to eating parts of the corpse." After removing the brain and teeth and closing the eyes with beeswax, the Mundurucús parboiled the head and strung cords through the mouth and out the nostrils. The Tupinambas, along the Atlantic coast, "like the Caribs and Cubeos, considered the eating of human flesh a ritual act, part of their belief in consubstantiation."

These were primitive tribes, but the more developed Aztecs brought the processes of ritual torture and human sacrifice to exalted heights. Thousands of captives won in war or exacted in tribute would line up before the 114 steps of the great pyramid waiting for priests to plunge in the obsidian knife and tear out their bleeding hearts—a ceremony no doubt laudably designed to propitiate the sun god, but not easy to reconcile with the revisionist myth of prelapsarian harmony and innocence. Cortes conquered Mexico with such ease because Indian tribes subjugated and persecuted by the Aztecs embraced him as their liberator from unbearable tyranny. As Carlos Fuentes writes, "It was the victory of the *other Indians* over the Aztec overlord."

Given Aztec customs and methods, what, one wonders, would have become of the hapless inhabitants of Spain and Portugal if the Atlantic crossing had been reversed and the Aztecs had conquered Iberia? And those who insist that Aztecs and Incas, Mundurucús and Tupinambas, should be judged by their own values, not by ours, owe the same indulgence to the *conquistadores.*

The melancholy conclusion is that despite the dramatic clash of cultures, one finds in certain respects, as the historian Hugh Thomas argues, little difference between the Europe and the Mexico of 1492: little difference in the uses of power, in prescriptive inequalities, in coercion and torture, in imperialism and violence and destruction, in (to leap centuries forward to contemporary standards) the suppression of individual freedom and of human rights. The record illustrates less the pitiless annihilation of an idyllic culture by a wrecking crew of aliens than it does the criminality of all cultures and the universality of original sin. Cruelty and destruction are not the monopoly of any single continent or race or culture. As William James reminds us, "The trail of the human serpent is thus over everything."

Christopher Columbus, Mario Vargas Llosa observed at a quincentennial conference in Seville last spring, has become a historical counter in a contemporary political game, and British America and Spanish America use him for different purposes. In North America, Columbus is just one more pretext for the already thriving assault mounted against the establishment by apostles of political correctness. The Latin American reaction, Vargas Llosa continues, is far more primary and organic. There Columbus serves not as scapegoat but as alibi. Blaming everything on the conquest provides a perpetual excuse for the failure of Latin American countries to achieve humane, stable, and progressive democracies. Latin America, Vargas Llosa says, must begin to accept responsibility for its own fate. So, too, says Carlos Fuentes: Latin Americans, confronting the questions raised by their "balkanized, fractured politics, failed economic systems, and vast social inequalities," must finally recognize that "we could only answer the questions from within ourselves."

THE GREAT QUINCENTENNIAL DEBATE OVER Columbus and his work awakens echoes in the minds of historians. This is not the first era to advance the proposition that the discovery of the Americas was a mistake. Shortly before the tricentennial of Columbus's landing a spirited debate erupted over precisely this subject. The chief difference is that in the eighteenth century it was Europeans who lamented the opening of the Americas; today Europe seems generally acquiescent, apart from French critics of Euro Disney, and the proposition attracts and agitates the Americas.

For a time Europeans had invented an America peopled by noble savages, men uncorrupted by civilization; as Montaigne wrote, quoting Seneca, they were "fresh from the gods." But Europe has never stopped reinventing the New World. The eighteenth-century debate took off when the Comte de Buffon, the famous French naturalist, proposed a thesis of American biological inferiority, producing an array of quasi-scientific reasons to explain "why the reptiles and insects are so large, the quadrupeds so small, and the men so cold, in the New World." The idea quickly spread. In Britain, Oliver Goldsmith's *The Deserted Village* portrayed a dank and gloomy land where no birds sang and no dogs barked.

Soon the *philosophe* the Abbé Corneille de Pauw described America as "so ill-favored by nature that all it contains is either degenerate or monstrous" and Americans as "a degenerate species of the human race, cowardly, impotent, without physical strength, without vitality, without elevation of mind." As for the conquest of the New World, this, De Pauw concluded, "has been the greatest of all misfortunes to befall mankind."

The Abbé Guillaume Raynal enthusiastically agreed. "How many calamities, which cannot be compensated," he asked, "have not attended the conquest of these regions?" No doubt Europe is in the New World's debt for a few conveniences and a few luxuries. "But before these enjoyments were obtained, were we less healthy, less robust, less intelligent, or less happy? Are these frivolous advantages, so cruelly obtained, so unequally distributed, and so obstinately disputed, worth one drop of that blood which has been spilt, and which will still be spilt for them?"

Raynal elaborated his indictment. "Let us stop here," he finally said,

and consider ourselves as existing at the time when America and India were unknown. Let me suppose that I address myself to the most cruel of Europeans in the following terms. There exist regions which will furnish thee with rich metals, agreeable clothing, and delicious food. But read this history, and behold at what price the discovery is promised to thee. Dost thou wish or not that it should be made? Is it to be imagined that there exists a being infernal enough to answer this question in the affirmative! Let it be remembered, that there will not be a single instant in futurity, when my question will not have the same force.

Raynal did not stop there. After the Declaration of Independence he established a prize of 1,200 francs to be awarded by the Academy of Lyons for the best essay on this piquant topic: "Was the discovery of America a blessing or a curse to mankind? If it was a blessing, by what means are we to conserve and enhance its benefits? If it was a curse, by what means are we to repair the damage?" Contemplating the great debate of 1992, one can only suppose that the Academy of Lyons, if it chose to revive the Raynal prize, would be flooded with entries.

Americans, of course, looked on Raynal with considerable irritation. Benjamin Franklin once had to endure at his own Paris dinner table a monologue by the diminutive abbé on the way everything shrank in the New World. "Let us try this question by the fact before us," Franklin suggested in his practical way, and called on his guests, French and American, to stand up and measure themselves back to back. "There was not one American present," recalled Thomas Jefferson, who was among them, "who could not have tost out of the Windows any one or perhaps two of the rest of the Company."

In one of the earliest Federalist papers, Alexander Hamilton responded with vigor to what he called "these arrogant pretensions of the European." European writers "admired as profound philosophers," Hamilton said, " . . . have gravely asserted that all animals, and with them the human species, degenerate in America—that even dogs cease to bark after having breathed awhile in our atmosphere." Europe, Hamilton continued, had succumbed to the temptation "to plume herself as the Mistress of the World, and to consider the rest of mankind as created for her benefit. . . . Let Americans disdain to be the instruments of European greatness!"

The invention and reinvention of America continue to our day, and so does the argument that opening up America was a bad idea. No less a sage than Sigmund Freud remarked earlier in this century, "America is a mistake; a gigantic mistake, it is true, but none the less a mistake." Whether the discovery was a curse or a blessing was a favorite topic for debate at the Oxford Union between the wars. The Columbus quincentennial charges the old argument with new intensity.

But the terms of the debate, whether in the 1770s or in the 1990s, are inherently defective. Abbé Raynal's question implies what few debaters us could actually believe: that there was some alternative to Europe's discovery of America.

Still, let us for a moment suppose that the Americas could have been indefinitely sealed off from Europe. Would the world be better off? Mario Vargas Llosa has asked, "What would America be like in the 1990s if the dominant cultures were those of the Aztecs and Incas?" The anthropologist Jorge Klor De Alva once speculated that it might be something like contemporary India—a mixture of religions, languages, and castes, somehow extracting coherence out of incoherence. But India had a century and

a half of British imperialism, and therefore a legacy of parliamentary democracy. What would the destiny of the Americas have been without any European infusion?

One must hope that by the twentieth century the Aztecs and the Incas would have learned to read and write and would have abandoned their commitment to torture, obsidian knives, and blood-stained pyramids. But they would most likely have preserved their collectivist cultures and their conviction that the individual had no legitimacy outside the theocratic state, and the result would have been a repressive fundamentalism comparable perhaps to that of the Ayatollah Khomeini in Iran. Aztec and Inca traditions offer little hope for the status of women, for equality before the law, for religious tolerance, for civil liberties, for human rights, and for other purposes deriving uniquely from European culture.

BUT LET US BE REALISTIC. THE IDEA that the Americas could have survived in invincible isolation is fantasy. As a practical matter, America by the fifteenth century was fated to be found by a Europe bursting at the seams with its own dynamism, greed, and evangelical zeal. Columbus happened to make the decisive voyage, but he was not indispensable to that voyage's eventually being made. Europe's westward impulse had already embraced Madeira and the Canaries and the Azores. It would not, could not, halt there. If the "discoverer" was not to be Christopher Columbus, then it would have been Amerigo Vespucci or John Cabot or some mute, inglorious mariner now lost to history. Had Columbus, like his brother Giovanni Pellegrino, died young, the quincentennial might have been delayed a few years, but would still be on its way.

Once the Europeans arrived, could they have pursued more benign policies? Obviously one wishes that in the treatment of natives the Spanish had followed Las Casas rather than Columbus. Perhaps more did so than we know; at least historians generally agree today that the Black Legend of Spanish Catholic villainy was an envenomed Protestant exaggeration. Las Casas, alas, had all too few equivalents in the British and French colonies. In general, the European record in dealing with the indigenous peoples of the Americas was miserable—and indefensible. But it is not clear that Europeans in those war-wracked and religiously fanatical centuries were any more humane in dealing with their enemies at home.

Obviously one also wishes that the Europeans had understood as much about preserving the balance of nature as the Amerindians did, or as our ecologists do today. In their ignorance and arrogance the intruders did indeed bring about extreme ecological disruption. But the migration of peoples has gone on since the beginning of time and cannot be halted; and migrants inevitably bring with them their own habits, technologies, diets, animals, plants, diseases. Even the Amerindians were once migrants. Still, some anti-Columbus revisionists see "ecohubris" as Europe's peculiar sin and, in Kirkpatrick Sale's words, *"warring against species* as Europe's preoccupation as a culture."

Deeper questions are suggested: Does humanity have an obligation to preserve every manifestation of life on the planet? Is every culture equally sacred, no matter how sadistic and horrible? And, assuming the answer is yes, is it possible to freeze history in place and immunize the world against what has heretofore seemed history's one constant—change?

The fact that we cannot stop change complicates one's response to the idea that every culture and species is sacred. And to deny the right to change is to amputate the human spirit. What animated Columbus more than anything else, more than God or glory or gold, must surely have been those primal passions of curiosity and wonder, the response to the challenge of the unknown, the need to go where none had gone before. That everlasting quest for new frontiers continues today as earthlings burst terrestrial bonds and begin the endless voyage beyond planet and galaxy into the illimitable dark.

The fact that Heraclitus was right and nothing stands still does not of course justify all the costs of change, especially unnecessary costs in human suffering and destruction. If we are compelled to give this anniversary a balance sheet, those costs weigh heavily against Columbus and even more against those who followed him.

But there are benefits, too, and these require to be factored into the historical equation. The opening of the Americas ushered in a new era of human history. Not only did the gold and silver and furs of the New World stimulate economic growth, commercial integration, and intellectual analysis in the Old; even more, the age of exploration began to draw the world together into new potentialities of unity, and a new recognition of the varieties of human existence challenged the human intellect and the human imagination.

The era Columbus initiated has seen horror and sadism perhaps worse than the tortures and human sacrifices of the Aztecs. But out of anguish (out, too, of self-criticism and bad conscience) have evolved the great liberating ideas of individual dignity, political democracy, equality before the law, religious tolerance, cultural pluralism, artistic freedom—ideas that emerged uniquely from Europe but that empower people of every continent, color, and creed; ideas to which most of the world today aspires; ideas that offer a new and generous vision of our common life on this interdependent planet. The clash of cultures may yield in the end—not, certainly, to a single global culture (heaven forbid) but to a world in which many differentiated national cultures live side by side in reciprocal enrichment. This, too, is part of the legacy of Columbus.

A century and a quarter ago Walt Whitman brooded on the fate of Columbus at the end of his life, "a batter'd, wreck'd old man . . . stiff with many toils, sicken'd and nigh to death . . . full of woe." The poet perceived what the scholars of his day missed: that Columbus was driven by devotion to the Almighty.

I cannot rest O God, I cannot eat or drink
   or sleep,

Till I put forth myself, my prayer, once
   more to Thee,
Breathe, bathe myself once more in Thee,
   commune with Thee,
Report myself once more to Thee.

Whitman's Columbus had "not once lost nor faith nor ecstasy in Thee," knew that "the urge, the ardor, the unconquerable will, the potent, felt, interior command" were a message from heaven. And how could he measure the result?

By me earth's elder cloy'd and stifled
   lands uncloy'd, unloos'd,
By me the hemispheres rounded and tied,
   the unknown to the known.
The end I know not, it is all in Thee,
Or small or great I know not—haply what
   broad fields, what lands,
Haply the brutish measureless human undergrowth I know,
Transplanted there may rise to stature,
   knowledge worthy Thee.
Haply the swords I know may there indeed
   be turn'd to reaping-tools. . . .

Is it the prophet's thought I speak, or am I
   raving?
What do I know of life? what of myself?
I know not even my own work past or
   present,
Dim ever-shifting guesses of it spread
   before me,
Of newer, better worlds, their mighty
   parturition,
Mocking, perplexing me.

And these things I see suddenly, what
   mean they?
As if some miracles, some hand divine
   unseal'd my eyes,
Shadowy vast shapes smile through the air
   and sky,
And on the distant waves sail countless
   ships,
And anthems in new tongues I hear salut-
   ing me.

With the quincentennial, the dream of newer, better worlds still mocks and perplexes us. But those shadowy vast shapes are there too, giving hope that a happier future lies perhaps more than ever within humanity's grasp. With luck, that may be the work of the next five centuries.

California's Spanish Missions

Louis Kleber tells the story of how a small group of Spanish friars dotted the West Coast of America with outposts of Christianity in the eighteenth century, and of their impact on the native populations they co-opted into their settlement.

Louis Kleber

Louis Charles Kleber is an American writer, presently resident in England.

When one stands in the grounds of the beautiful Spanish missions that climb the California coast, it is easy to imagine a scene of romantic tranquility in the early 1800s—the warmth of the sun, padres strolling through flowered gardens in a courtyard, a few soldiers leisurely talking near a fountain and Indians in an adjoining orchard, gathering fruit. It is all so peaceful and appears so permanent. Not quite.

The beauty is indeed there, but the story of California's twenty-one missions has a dark side, a reflection of colonial aspirations that never lost sight of the search for power, riches and conquest. The biggest losers were the native peoples. Under Spanish, and later Mexican and American rule, their numbers rapidly diminished. In some cases they simply died out.

It was fortunate for Spain that California was off the beaten track of colonial conflict. Her power was in sharp decline at the time the missions were being founded in the late eighteenth century. But that was not so in 1535 when Hernan Cortés led an expedition up the California coast, spurred by a highly romanticised fiction concocted by Garcia Ordónez twenty-five years earlier. In it, he described an island paradise near the Indies, called California, populated solely by warrior women whose only metal was gold. Cortés named the land California, but the only humans he encountered were hunter-gatherer Indians living the simplest existence in a mild land that required little effort to survive. As for gold, that would have to wait another three centuries.

The pace of colonial expansion in California was slow, and it might have been slower had not Sir Francis Drake led an expedition there in 1579, claiming *Nova Albion* for the English crown after landing in the vicinity of San Francisco Bay. The Indians, as usual, were friendly. Although thoroughly disturbed by the presence of their bitter enemy in the Spanish sphere, it took another twenty-three years before Spain sent a well organised and equipped expedition of three ships to California. One of the explorers was a Padre Ascensión. He reported the events in detail and gave his opinion: 'If it should seem lost to His Majesty he can command that his Spaniards go by land to settle . . . (California)'. He suggested settlements at San Diego and Monterey which would eventually become the capital of Spanish, and later Mexican, California. It was the first step toward the establishment of missions; conquest and conversion would go hand-in-hand.

Another century would pass before a Jesuit father, Eusebio Kino, began the actual construction of missions to the south and east of California. Finally, ever more fearful that the English might follow-up on Drake's tenuous claims or that the Russians might come down from the north, Spain acted energetically to secure California. Within four years of his appointment as *Visitador General* of New Spain in 1765, José de Galvez had sea and land expeditions on their way. With them was Father Junipero Serra, a man destined for fame as the father of the California missions.

This Franciscan, whose order had replaced the Jesuits, had extraordinary zeal and vision. His dream was of a string of missions, each within a day's walk of the next, stretching north from the first mission, San Diego de Alcala, established in 1769. By the time of his death in 1784, Father Serra must have been pleased to see the mission system firmly in place. He would have been less pleased had he been able to see ahead. In his *California Pastoral* (1888), Hubert Howe Bancroft portrayed the fatuous promise of mission life for the Indians:

'What benefit should flow from this serene and heavenly life (as a Christian)?' And the Mission Priest Responds:
'Besides religion, your beasts and reptiles and birds of prey will be exterminated, the wilderness will be turned into a garden, famines will cease, pestilence will be controlled, physical forces now antagonistic to your well-being will be subjugated, and you will be less dependent on fitful nature.'

The fate of the Indians, particularly the Chumash, who inhabited the region around present-day Santa Barbara and to the north, is a sad one. Had they been as warlike as the Sioux, Commanche or Apaches, it is doubtful if their numbers would have diminished any faster than they did. But they were peaceful and took to mission life in the early years. The complex and mystical religious ceremonies of the Franciscan padres appealed to them. And they liked music, readily taking to the instruments provided by the Spanish. An innovative padre, Narciso Duran, devised a method for teaching Indians how to harmonise by writing notes in different colours. They sang with great enthusiasm. Santa Barbara Mission still has Padre Duran's *Misa Cataluna*.

Daily life for the mission Indians began at dawn, as it did for the padres. An hour-long religious service was followed by breakfast which commonly consisted of a roasted grain like barley, perhaps supplemented by fruit from the orchards which were planted and tended by the

From *History Today*, September 1992, pp. 42-47. Reproduced by kind permission of History Today, Ltd., 83-84 Berwick Street, London W1V 3PJ England.

1. THE NEW LAND

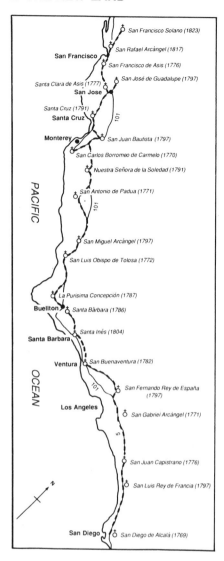

The network of Californian missions established between 1769 and 1823.

Indians. The mild California climate was ideal for agriculture. Peaches, oranges, apples, apricots, figs, grapes and many more varieties of food could be grown with relative ease. Indians who did not work in the fields and orchards were taught skills by the Spaniards; as many as fifty crafts so the missions could be truly self-sustaining. Spinning and weaving, carpentry, shoe-making and other leather-work, candles and soap-making were particularly important.

It was not all work. In the early years, mission Indians had considerable freedom. They could leave to visit their native villages, fish, play games and enjoy leisure time. But it was not to last. Nearly everything worked against the Indians. If they had a friend, it was the Spanish padre, who found himself increasingly shoved aside by officials and soldiers. As time went on, long hours of

work rarely provided rewards for the Indian. His freedom was increasingly restricted, and the original tolerance for continuation of many traditional ways was replaced by the harshest treatment. A.L. Kroeber, an anthropologist, reflected that:

It must have caused many of the Fathers a severe pang to realise, as they could not but do daily, that they were saving souls only at the inevitable cost of lives . . . missionisation, in spite of its kindly flavour and humanitarian root, was only one thing, death.

Conversion, not death, was the keystone of the missionisation concept in California and all of the Americas. It also involved a fundamental question about the moral right of conquest. This was measurably solved by Pope Alexander VI when he endorsed Spain's right to conquer the Americas (except for Brazil, which was Portugal's province), provided the king made certain his soldiers marched under the Christian banner of conversion. Thus, there was both religious and royal assent for men like Junipero Serra to take the cross where their countrymen took the sword. In doing so, they used the mission as an ideal instrument to achieve their goals. They needed to keep the Indians close at hand to deliver the Christian message and lifestyle. And they most certainly needed the Indians for all the work to build missions and keep them as self-sustaining centres.

Undeniably, the missions were part of the Spanish apparatus of conquest. But the religious orders generally did what they could to mollify its harsher evils, and they often exhibited great courage in doing so. A Dominican friar, Antonio de Montesinos, lashed out at the settlers on the island of Hispaniola in 1511: 'You are in mortal sin. You live and die in it, because of the cruelty and tyranny you practise in dealing with these innocent people'. Even the Spanish crown took heed of the need for compassion in conquest. As early as 1549, more than 200 years before the colonisation of California, a royal decree forbad the subjugation of Indians to personal service and labour under threat. They were to be treated as free subjects and reasonably paid for their work. Sadly, proclamations and practice did not go hand-in-hand.

California never experienced the vast scale of excesses that characterised so much of Spain's empire to the south, whether commercial exploitation or blood-letting. The Jesuits in Paraguay,

for example, were successful traders as well as missionaries. Their settlement at Asuncion had over thirty *reducciones* (mission villages), giving them a monopoly on the Indian trade until jealous merchants and landowners engineered their ejection. But actions like this paled next to the ferocity and mercilessness of so many Spanish conflicts with the Indians.

European diseases took an alarming toll. Like other Indians across the American continent, those in California had little resistance to smallpox. Even the lesser illnesses that Europeans could normally withstand, decimated the Indians. At Mission La Purisima Conception de Maria Santisima (Mission of the Immaculate Conception of the Most Holy Mary), there were 1,520 Indians in 1804. Eight years later the number had declined to 999, and by 1824 the number, according to mission records, had dropped to 662. In another twenty years it was down to less than 200.

The cold and damp huts that formed permanent living quarters around the missions, particularly those in the more northern parts of California, contributed to the death rate. The sick and the well were cramped together in a way the Indians had not known before. They had thrived in the outdoor life; if a hut became infested, they would simply burn it or abandon it and build another in just a few hours.

Men and women alike were punished for 'sins' which did not even exist, in many instances, prior to the arrival of the Spaniards. Severe whippings were the order for Indians who ran away from the mission. Women would usually be lashed within a room so their cries would not be heard by the men. The latter would be openly punished in front of everyone. There were, however, limits to what even the peaceful California Indians could take. When one of them was flogged by soldiers at Mission Santa Inez, it released all the pent-up anger. On February 21st, 1824, the Indians burned several buildings. When news of the revolt reached La Purisima, they besieged a handful of soldiers who held out until the following morning when their gunpowder was exhausted. The soldiers were then seized and held as hostages. The triumph was a short one. Three weeks later a relief force of 109 soldiers from the Monterey *presidio* (fort) arrived at La Purisima. Their leader, Lieutenant Estrada, ordered an immediate attack. The Indians were beaten in just two hours.

By this time it was clear that a stand-up fight on their part could only end in defeat. An even more significant defeat had been suffered by both the missions and the Indians two years before. When Mexico won her independence from Spain, the missions lost their unique relationship with the Spanish crown and state. They were no longer part of the imperial spearhead of Spanish expansion and their role as a humanitarian and moderating force on officialdom's excesses rapidly eroded. The collapse of Spanish support to the military and local government, as well as to the missions, had begun in earnest in 1810 when Miguel Hidalgo y Costilla, curate of Dolores, led a revolt against Spain. Although he came from an upper-class background, Hidalgo had felt a growing sense of empathy with the poor. They came to his support and he eventually had an army of 80,000. But, as so often happens in such instances, their numbers were no match for the trained and disciplined Spanish troops who were backed by the existing power structure of officials and wealthy families. He was captured within six months. Three years later a Hidalgo lieutenant, Father José Maria Morelos, led another revolt and proclaimed the independence of Mexico. He and his supporters fared no better than Hidalgo. They were crushed, and Morelos executed, in 1815. Understandably, Spanish government support for California waned in this period of violent political and economic upheaval.

The revolution finally succeeded in 1822-24 when Augustín Iturbide, who had been appointed by the Spanish viceroy to crush insurgents, switched sides and had himself proclaimed emperor. Widespread discontent forced his resignation and Mexico became a federal republic in 1824. It was the end for mission hopes that they would be able to cash letters of credit given by the Spanish government in exchange for supplies provided during the period 1810-22. Additionally, the individual padres lost their annual *memorias* of $1,000 to help with missionary work. The future was indeed growing darker for the missions. To make matters worse, local officials and the military began to turn to the missions for support at the very moment when they could least afford to help.

The secularisation of the missions by the Mexican government in 1834 dealt a near death blow to the missions. The civil administrators, who replaced the padres, were more akin to scavengers than responsible officials. The missions fell into disuse as the Indians were left to supposedly amalgamate with the general society around them. With missions reduced to the level of parish churches, padres at one mission might occasionally visit another to conduct services, but even this token effort waned. Many missions were gradually abandoned and left to fall into ruin. Helen Hunt Jackson's book, *Glimpses of California and the Missions* (1883), gives a poignantly graphic description of La Purisima Mission at the time:

. . . Nothing is left there but one long, low adobe building, with a few arches of the corridor; the doors stand open, the roof is falling in; it has been so often used as a stable and sheepfold, that even the grasses are killed around it. The painted pulpit hangs half falling on the wall, its stairs are gone, and its sounding board is slanting awry. Inside the broken altar rail is a pile of stones, earth, and rubbish thrown up by seekers after buried treasures; in the farther corner another pile and hole, the home of a badger; mud swallows' nests are thick on the cornice, and cobwebbed rags of the old canvas ceiling hang fluttering overhead . . .

The mission system would have come to an end even sooner had foreign powers made California a prime target for expansion. It was quite incredible that Spain held this part of her empire with little more than a skeleton force of soldiers. In 1786 a French exploration party under the Comte de la Pérouse visited some of the missions. His report noted that the Spanish governor in Monterey had:

. . . 282 cavalrymen who must form the garrison of five little forts and furnish squads of four or five men at each of the twenty-five missions or parishes established in Old (lower) and New California.

The foreign danger was there, but it was manifested in trading adventures prior to the Mexican-American War of 1846. As early as 1803, Russian fur hunters and traders were known to be in California. A decade later they established a permanent settlement at Fort Ross, north of San Francisco, to promote the seal and sea otter trade. From here they ranged to such places as the Channel Islands just off the Santa Barbara coast. Sea otters abounded on the islands; their rich fur such an attraction that even Aleutian Islanders were brought in to operate from Russian and American mother ships. The Chumash Indians, who had inhabited the islands, fled to the mainland.

In an ironic twist, the Russians had to turn to the Mexicans for help before their California venture collapsed. The weather in the San Francisco region and to the north can be damp and misty a good part of the year. The Russian harvest failed. In 1839 they bought 1,751 *fanegas* (a Spanish measure equal to 100 lbs) of wheat from the sprawling, 44,000 acre Rancho Petaluma. This enormous rancho had been founded by an extraordinarily resourceful and intelligent entrepreneur, General Marian Guadalupe Vallejo. The secularisation of the missions had proven to be a springboard for Vallejo as huge areas, previously held by the missions, were granted and sold to private citizens and officials. Indeed, the young Vallejo was ordered to secularise Mission San Francisco Solano de Sonoma in 1834 while he was commander of the Presidio of San Francisco. With further crop failures and a vanishing fur trade as the number of seals and otter declined, the Russian presence became increasingly tenuous. Finally, with a hostile Mexican government and an equally hostile General Vallejo facing them, the Russians sold out in 1841 and left.

The early 1840s were tumultuous years of strain between Mexico and the United States. One empire was receding and the other expanding. The fate of the missions was not even a footnote in the broad struggle for land and power. The war that began in 1846 ended in 1848 when the Treaty of Guadalupe Hidalgo was signed and California ceded to the United States. A year later gold was discovered; exciting times for pioneer families, gold miners, outlaws and all the others who made up the American West of fact and fiction. Amidst all this, a group of dedicated padres and the church kept some of the missions alive. It led to a happy ending, in many respects, as California's government, civic-minded groups and individuals eventually realised that the missions were a rich part of history. The story of Mission La Purisima and Mission Santa Barbara illustrates a contrasting example of abandonment, ruin and revival for one (La Purisima) while the other (Santa Barbara) never ceased to function in its evolvement.

Today, La Purisima is the most completely restored of all the California missions. Located a few miles from the present-day town of Lompoc, it was connected to the other missions by *El Cam-

ino Real, the 'Royal Highway'. La Purisima's early years were quite trouble free; from the founding in 1787 until disease began its frightening reduction of the Indian population in 1804. Then, another enemy of the mission struck—earthquake. Just before Christmas, 1812, a violent quake brought down most of the mission buildings, including the church. The damage was so severe that Padre Mariano Payeras decided to rebuild the mission about four miles away. He wrote in his report: 'We shall go to work constructing of poles and grass what is indispensable until the earth becomes quiet'. The mission was rebuilt, but further work ceased around 1818 as the Mexican revolution approached and financial difficulties hounded the padres. Most of the problems were beyond their control; they tended to the needs of the mission as best they could and kept meticulous records. In 1832, La Purisima had 9,200 cattle, 3,500 sheep, 1,000 horses and a small assortment of other animals. It would be lost in the process of secularisation just two years later. In another two years the two resident fathers had left and the ruin of neglect and abandonment began.

Around the turn of the century, some abortive attempts were made to save what was left of La Purisima and do some restoration. Finally, in 1934, real restoration work began by the Civilian Conservation Corps, an agency of the Federal Government. It took seven years of careful work to bring the mission back to its original state. La Purisima is now protected by the State of California.

Events were much kinder to Mission Santa Barbara, 'The Queen of the Missions'. It is a blending of compatible Greek, Roman, Spanish and Moorish styles, coupled with a Chumash Indian influence. The lovely fountain, just outside the front of the mission, is Moorish. The twin-towered church was built of native sandstone by the Chumash between 1815 and 1820. Many items are original; the statue of St Barbara, directly behind the altar, was brought to the mission in 1793, seven years after its founding. The Mission survived secularisation, and in 1842 the first Bishop of California took up residency there. In 1856 it became an Apostolic College to train Franciscans, and in 1896 a seminary was opened to candidates for the priesthood.

The Santa Barbara setting could not be more beautiful, with the mission nestled in the foothills overlooking the Pacific Ocean. It still belongs to the Franciscan Order. There are about thirty friars, dressed in the traditional brown robes and sandals who may be seen strolling through the mission's flowered gardens and in the streets of Santa Barbara. Its appearance today would no doubt please the first padres. Only one thing is missing—the Indians are gone.

FOR FURTHER READING:

Andrew Rolle, *California: A History* (New York, 1969); Sherburne Cook, *The Conflict Between the California Indian and White Civilization* (University of California Press, 1976); John Hawgood, *The American West* (The Chaucer Press, 1967); Wallace Smith, *Garden in the Sun* (Fresno, 1960); John Caughey, *California* (Prentice-Hall, 1963); Owen Francis Da Silva, *Mission Music of California* (Santa Barbara, 1941); Campbell Grant, *The Rock Paintings of the Chumash* (University of California Press, 1965); John Hemming, *The Conquest of the Incas* (Macmillan, 1970).

Colonists in Bondage: Indentured Servants in America

Barbara Bigham

A ship docked at a Virginia harbor in 1635, and from its decks emerged nearly two-hundred newcomers from England, among them twenty-five-year-old Thomas Carter. For some the voyage had cost over £5 sterling. For others, the price was higher still: several years of their lives. Carter, like thousands of other penniless Europeans, had sold himself into bondage as an indentured servant to pay his passage to the colonies. Once there, he lived the life of a virtual slave— the property of his master. But when his indenture was over, he became a free man, and with his "freedom dues" of some clothes and tools, he worked to rise above his humble beginnings and serve as a respected member of the community. Eventually, he had four servants indentured under him at his estate in Isle of Wight County, Virginia. His descendants took an active part in colonial affairs and went on to fight in the Revolution. Some were involved in noble pursuits, others in scandalous incidents, and one—a ninth-generation grandson—became the thirty-ninth president of the United States.

Land was plentiful in the New World, and fertile, but without a large number of laborers to fell trees and work the soil, it was as useless as a desert. Few new settlers could afford to hire a work force of free men, nor could they afford to buy slaves. Of the several schemes employed to entice workers to the colonies, none worked so well as the system of indentured servitude, which established itself almost as soon as the first colonists landed.

The earliest surviving indenture contract is dated 1619, when four owners of a Virginia plantation signed an agreement with Robert Coopy, of Gloucestershire, England. Coopy promised "faythfully to serve . . . for three years from the daye of his landing in the land of Virginia" in return for his benefactors' promise to "transport him (with gods assistance) with all convenient speed into the said land of Virginia at their costs and charges in all things, and there to maintayne him with convenient diet and apparell meet for such a servant, And in the end of the said terme to make him a free man of the said Cuntry . . . And to grant to the said Robert thirty acres of land within their Territory . . ."

The system caught on immediately, and by 1625 there were 487 indentured servants out of a population of 1,227 in the Virginia Company. During the next decade the wording of indenture contracts became fairly uniform, and by 1636, printed forms were available with blank spaces for the names of the servant and master and the details of the contract.

Indentured servitude grew as thousands of men and women in England crammed into cities competing for the few low-paying jobs open to them and for a precariously short food supply. Religious and political pressures, aggravated by famine and disease, made people restless and receptive to the prospect

Few Germans arriving in America under indenture knew the English language. This indenture, written in German, is dated 1736. Courtesy of the Pennsylvania Historical and Museum Commission, Harrisburg, Pennsylvania.

of a better existence elsewhere. Hand-bills and broadsides written by promoters (many of whom had never been to America) to stimulate migration painted the rosiest possible picture of the American colonies, promising abundant land for all and high wages for craftsmen. They neglected to mention the hardships of living in the still-wild country. As the colonies grew, those who had already made the transition sent tantalizing letters home. Robert Parke wrote to his sister in 1725, "There is not one of the family but what likes the country very well and would if we were in Ireland again come here directly; it being the best country for working folk and tradesmen in the world." With such encouragement, "emigration fever" swept through Europe, keeping ships filled with would-be settlers. Those who could afford to do so paid their own passages, arriving in the colonies as free men. Thousands more, with a yearning for the colonies, but no gold in their pockets to pay for the trip, were satisfied by enterprising colonists willing to invest in their passage and maintenance in return for several years of labor.

These early capitalists usually hired an agent (a ship captain was a frequent choice, as were merchants who traveled between the two continents) to contact discouraged workers in England and sign them on as indentured servants. An agreement written in duplicate on a large sheet of paper was signed by both master and servant, then "indented" or cut, in two—one copy for each party. The terms of the contract seldom varied; besides transporting the servant, the master agreed to feed, clothe, and house him for a certain number of years, usually between four and fourteen. At the end of the stipulated time, he was to pay the servant with a small stake and his freedom. Details of the treatment the servant could expect, the rules governing his life, and the freedom dues were rarely set down in writing. They were, instead, to be "according to the custom of the country," which could change with the prosperity, or the personality, of the master.

It was soon evident that great profits were to be made, and many a "middle man" turned professional agent and combed the cities and farm regions in England for men and women willing to become bound servants. He signed their indentures as master and transported them, a shipload at a time, to the colonies. The total cost, including transporta-tion and a few pieces of clothing per person, was seldom more than £10 per head. In the colonies the agent could count on getting £15 to £30 for each servant "set over." (The word sell was consciously avoided when it referred to white men, yet the new owner bought a servant in much the same way he bought a slave.)

Substantial profits to be made in the servant trade led to notoriously deceitful, as well as illegal, methods of recruit-ment. Agents came to be known as "spirits," with reputations for having no qualms about lying to a man or getting him so drunk that he would put his mark on any piece of paper shoved in front of him. If lies and gin didn't work, a whack on the head usually would. Many men and women were forced to the ship and shoved into the hold not to see daylight again until the shores of England were out of sight.

JUST ARRIVED, *in the* Ship JOHN, *Capt.* ROACH, *from* DUBLIN,
A NUMBER of HEALTHY, INDENTED MEN and WOMEN SERVANTS
AMONG THE FORMER ARE,
A Variety of TRADESMEN, with some good FARMERS, and stout LABOURERS: Their Indentures will be disposed of, on reasonable Terms, for CASH, by
GEORGE SALMON.

Many Europeans could afford to come to America only by offering themselves as indentured servants or redemptioners. Newspaper advertisements like the one above regularly announced the arrival of indentured servants.

Public outrage over such forced mi-gration, particularly when it involved children, spurred Parliament to enact laws that protected the citizen from the spirits and, at the same time, protected the honest agent from false accusations of kidnapping by a servant with second thoughts about honoring his indenture. Agents and servants were required to sign the contract before a magistrate, a registry of servants being transported to the colonies was kept, and in some cases, outbound ships were searched so that any passengers with a change of mind could return home. Although these measures were not entirely successful, they helped ensure that most men and women who bound themselves as servants and sailed for America did so because they wanted to.

The English Parliament used inden-tured servitude to rid the country of vagrants roaming England in that time of social upheaval. Frequently these root-less vagabonds were farmers who had been dispossessed of their lands; and unable to find work, they turned in des-peration or bitterness to lives of petty crime and theft. Convicted criminals, many from Newgate Prison, were sent by the state to the colonies as bound servants. Most had a choice of sorts: hanging or America. America was the favored alternative. Prior to 1717, forced exile did not exist in England, but con-victs who would ordinarily be sentenced to die (and a large number of minor crimes were punishable by that harsh sentence) could be pardoned on condi-tion that they leave the country. After 1717, most offenders could be legally transported to America or the West In-dies as indentured servants for not less than seven years.

Besides clearing out overcrowded En-glish jails, bondage supplied much needed labor for the colonies. Of the prisoners convicted at Old Bailey from 1729 to the American Revolution, at least 70 percent were sent to America. Such deportation of criminals did not win favor with colo-nists who likened it to having England "emptying their jakes (privies) on our tables." Maryland and Virginia, destina-tions for most criminal-immigrants, pas-sed restrictive laws forbidding convict ships to land, but such laws were quas-hed by the British crown. Although they complained bitterly, colonists desperate for cheap labor could not afford to be too particular about the past indiscretions of available servants: convict indentures never lacked buyers. About 30,000 con-victs (in reality a small part of those who arrived under indenture) were trans-ported to the colonies, many for petty crimes.

Whether the ships crossing the Atlan-tic were filled with convicts or willing bondsmen, they were filled to overflow-ing. As many as 800 persons might be crowded aboard a single vessel, and even the smaller ships often carried 200 or 300 people. One ship, measured for a safe load of 223, made the crossing with 322 on board; when criticized, the ship owner claimed his craft was far less crowded than many others.

Except for the convict ships, servants rarely had to endure the horrors common on slavers. Still, the voyage was unpleasant at best. Food supplies were as limited as space, and although ships were usually provisioned for a twelve-week voyage, many crossings delayed by bad weather or poor navigation ended as the last rations of wormy food and rancid water were being handed out. Less fortunate voyagers came to the end of provisions before they sighted land.

RUN away the 27th of *August* last, from *James Anderson* Minister of the Gospel in *Donigal*, in the County of *Lancaster* in *Pensilvania*, a Servant Man named *Hugh Wier*, aged about 30 Years of a middle Stature and fresh Complexion, sandy Beard, and short dark brown Hair, he went off very bear in Cloathing, and is supposed to have got himself dress'd in Indian Habit, (He having been used among *Indians*, when he run away from other Masters before) He is by Trade a Flax-dresser, Spinster and Woolcomber, and it is supposed he can Weave; He also does most sort of Women Work, such as washing of Cloaths or Dishes, milking of Cows, and other Kitchen Work, and usually changes his Name, Whoever takes up said Servant and secures him either in this or any of the neighbouring Provinces and let his Master know of it, by Post or otherways, so as his said Master may have him again, shall have *Three Pounds* as a Reward, and all reasonable Charges paid by me, *James Anderson*

Advertisement for a runaway indentured servant in the "American Weekly Mercury" of Philadelphia, December 14, 1733.

Ship captains were notoriously neglectful of cleanliness. Even when they did periodically wash out the ship with vinegar, the vessels were normally steeped in filth. Jammed into cargo holds with few sanitary facilities, the mass of passengers suffered from diseases and sickness made worse by the lack of ventilation. Although they were free to go above deck for fresh air during fair weather, when rough seas or stormy skies threatened, all were sent below the battened-down hatches. One German immigrant cataloged the suffering of fellow passengers during a 1751 crossing as "terrible misery, stench, fumes, horror, vomiting, many kinds of seasickness, fever, dysentery, headache, heat, constipation, boils, scurvy, cancer, mouth-rot, and the like." Another voyager reported that "we had enough in the day to behold the miserable sight of blotches, pox, others devoured with lice til they almost at death's door. In the night fearful cries and groaning of sick and distracted persons. . . ."

By the time the servants reached the colonies they were dirty, sick, and weak. Those with prearranged indentures were taken off the ship by their new masters, while those indentured to agents were readied for sale. Fresh clothing, clean water, and good food were enough to erase most of the visible ill effects of the voyage, and within a few days the cargo was ready for sale. Newspaper advertisements or broadsides announced the arrival of "a number of healthy indented men and women servants . . . a variety of tradesmen, good farmers, stout laborers . . . whose indentures will be disposed of, on reasonable terms, for cash."

The buyers arrived on the day of the sale, and the servants were brought out for inspection. Strong young men, skilled workers, and comely women sold quickly, but the sick or old were harder to dispose of, and at times were given away as a bonus with more desirable servants. In later years, it was not uncommon for one buyer to purchase the indentures of all, or a large part, of the human cargo. These "soul-drivers" loaded their merchandise on wagons and drove through the countryside selling it door-to-door the way the drummer sold sewing needles.

A Pennsylvania soul-driver named McCullough got more than he bargained for when he bought a group of servants in Philadelphia and began a circular swing through the farmlands and towns of the backcountry. He sold all but one of the servants, an Irishman whose rowdy behavior frightened away any potential buyers. The two men stayed one night at an inn but the Irishman woke early and, passing himself off as the master, sold McCullough—still asleep upstairs—to the innkeeper. Before he left the inn he warned the innkeeper that his newly acquired servant was a clever rascal, fond of telling lies and even of persuading gullible people that he was the master.

There were other passengers on those ships who found their way into servitude, although they had not begun their voyages with that in mind. Whole families of German and Swiss immigrants left home to build new lives in the American colonies, making their way down the Rhine to book passage in Rotterdam. But overly-enthusiastic recruitment pamphlets didn't mention the opportunists who overcharged for provisions along the route, or the long waits at the docks until space could be found on some America-bound vessel. Many found that their

money would not stretch far enough to pay their passage. An agent, merchant, or ship captain would step forward to advance the money needed for the voyage, granting the prospective colonist a period of time, usually two weeks, to raise the balance due when he arrived in the colonies. Some managed to find friends or relatives to redeem them, or had the good fortune to fall into the hands of one of the relief societies set up by their countrymen for the unwary victims. Many did not and so, to repay the agent, were sold into servitude. The redemptioner was in no position to quibble over the terms of his indenture, and often had to accept a situation no willing servant would have agreed to before leaving home.

Willing servant, transported convict, or disappointed redemptioner—once bound to a master he was his property, like his house, or horse, or slave. Yet his status was a curious mixture of slave and free man. His services could be bought or sold, rented or even inherited, but the terms of his contract remained the same under each master. He could own property but could not engage in trade. Marriage without his master's consent was strictly forbidden, and fornication and illegitimate pregnancy were serious offenses. Runaway servants were tracked down like runaway slaves and punished just as severely, although a white complexion made eluding capture much more possible. Posters and advertisements offered rewards for their return and warned of the consequences of harboring fugitives. Corporal punishment, including whipping, was accepted practice, often accompanied by a punishment even more hated: the addition of months or even years to the indenture period. A thwarted runaway could expect one month to be added to his term for every week he was gone. Sometimes the extension was confirmed with a whipping or the gift of a heavy iron collar engraved with the master's initials.

But indentured servants were not black slaves—they were white and Christian and as such had an edge over their African counterparts. The most important difference was the right to petition the courts against abuse, a right that was exercised freely and frequently.

At first, the rules regulating the lives of the servants and their treatment were governed by local custom. As the number of servants soared, many of these customs were incorporated into law. Any servant who felt his master was defying a 'custom of the country' or breaking a law could visit the local magistrate and file a petition of grievance.

In 1700, Catherine Douglas of Lancaster County, Virginia, learned that the courts would listen to and judge a case impartially, without bias against a penniless bonded servant. She filed a petition claiming that in England she had signed a four-year indenture with John Gilchrist in exchange for her passage, Gilchrist in turn sold her to Mottron Wright for a seven-year term. Although her own copy of the indenture had been destroyed, Catherine was able to produce three witnesses who testified that they had seen the original and that it had indeed specified four years. Wright argued that his seven-year contract had to be upheld, but the court decided in Catherine's favor; she was set free after serving her four years.

Until the middle of the 17th century, when laws governing black slavery began to be passed, Africans were also imported into the colonies under indenture. Until then, and occasionally after, redress was afforded blacks through the courts. In 1691, a Stafford County, Virginia, court heard an unusual case when black servant Benjamin Lewis petitioned for his freedom, claiming that before leaving England he had been indentured for four years. His term was over but his master refused to set him free, saying that as a Negro, Lewis was not a servant but a slave. The master produced another indenture signed by Lewis for a fourteen year term, but admitted it had been written while the first contract was still in effect. The jury ruled that the original contract was valid and proclaimed Lewis a free man.

Most cases brought before the courts by servants dealt with poor treatment and physical abuse. As with black slaves, the treatment of bonded servants was as varied as the personalities of their masters. Most were dealt with fairly and well, for humanitarian as well as practical reasons, but for some servants, life became a nightmare. Elizabeth Sprigs, indentured in Maryland, wrote of "toiling day and night, and then [being] tied up and whipped to that degree you would not beat an animal, scarce anything but Indian corn and salt to eat and that even begrudged." Some observers reported that when white servants worked side by side with black slaves, the slaves were often fed better and treated with more care since they represented a life-time investment.

The relatively minor charge of providing insufficient clothing was brought against William Miller by his servant William Hust. Court officials in Spotsylvania, Virginia, heard the case in 1758 and issued detailed orders to Miller. "The said Miller [shall] give him one cotton and kersey jacket and britches, 3 Ozanb shirts and sufficient diet and 1 pair of shoes and stockings, 1 hat. . . ." Usually the court found it adequate to reprimand the master and instruct him to properly provide for his servant.

A more serious charge was filed against plantation owners Francis Leaven and Samuel Hodgkins. Their servant, John Thomas, had committed some minor offense, and for punishment, the two hung him up by his hands and placed lighted sticks between his fingers, permanently injuring his hands. The court awarded Thomas not only his freedom, but 5,000 pounds of cotton from each of the masters, who were jailed for the assault.

Most indentured servants lived out their indenture periods without having need to petition the courts, and without the inclination to abscond. They worked hard, as did the free settlers, often learning a trade and gaining valuable experience. When their indenture period ended, freedom dues helped them begin life as free men. The dues varied with locale, but its intent was to give the servant a stake to start out on his own. In 1640, Maryland law required a freedom dues of "one good cloth suit of kersey or broadcloth, a shift of white linen, one new pair of stockings and shoes, two hoes, one axe, 3 barrells of corn and fifty acres of land. . . ." Land as part of the freedom dues was an important incentive for immigration, but as the more desirable tracts were taken up in populated areas, the promise of acreage virtually ended except for wilderness or scrub land. In 1683, the Maryland law dropped the land requirement. In Virginia, a 1748 law gave freed servants a freedom dues of three pounds, ten shillings. The tendency toward cash increased as the colonies prospered.

With his freedom dues, the former servant could make his way in the colonies as a hired laborer or even as a landowner. No stigma attached to his past bondage; with diligent hard work he could become as prosperous and respected as any settler who had paid his own way from Europe with cash. Those who had been lazy and dishonest in Europe before they were bound out probably continued to be so after they were free. Former convicts often ended up on American rather than English gallows, but many others became distinguished citizens and property holders. Seven burgesses in the Virginia assembly of 1629 had been indentured servants, as had fifteen members of the 1637 Maryland Assembly. Charles Thomas, later to serve as Secretary of the Continental Congress, started his American life in bondage, as did Matthew Thornton, a signer of the Declaration of Independence for the colony of New Hampshire. Like many other Americans who could trace their roots to humble beginnings, they had bought their dreams with the most precious commodity they owned: themselves.

Anne Hutchinson

"A Verye Dangerous Woman"

Stephanie Ocko

Even before the *Griffin* docked in Boston harbor in September, 1634, Anne Hutchinson had preached and "vented her opinions" to other passengers aboard. "The fear of man is a snare," she said, as the ship sailed into port, "but they that trust upon the Lord shall be safe." Later, a fellow passenger claimed she uttered these words when she saw the "meanness" of Boston. This she dismissed as absurd, because she had been prepared for Boston. She had said it because "having seen him which is invisible, I fear not what man can do unto me." Anne Hutchinson had had a revelation of the days she would spend in Massachusetts Bay Colony.

The "masterpiece of woman's wit" arrived from Alford, Lincolnshire, with her husband and eleven of her children, of whom the oldest was twenty-one, and the youngest an infant. No stranger to religion, Anne had grown up during the persecution of the Catholics and Separatists under Elizabeth and James I. Her father, Reverend Francis Marbury, had been imprisoned for preaching against the incompetence of English ministers. Now forty-three years old, Anne had undergone her own religious conversion and had followed her beloved minister Reverend John Cotton, whose removal to New England a year earlier had been "a great trouble to me. . . . I could not be at rest but I must come thither."

Merchant William Hutchinson, "a man of very mild temper and weak parts, and wholly guided by his wife," as Governor John Winthrop was later to describe him, settled his family in a spacious house in the center of Boston, a community of about five hundred. Anne, well-bred and wealthy, turned her attention to helping the women of Boston as a midwife.

The religious climate in the six-year-old colony was oppressive. In the rough first days of settlement, religion had served to turn people from asking how they could go back to England to how they could go to heaven. As the colony took hold, ministers emphasized everyone's pious duty to pray, fast, and discipline oneself. Reminded that hypocrites could appear to be "saved," colonists were urged to examine their hearts daily as their only means to salvation.

Under the anxiety of never being sure they were saved, women in particular suffered. One Boston woman threw her child into a well because "now she was sure she should be damned."

It was not long before Anne Hutchinson began to hold women's meetings. At first the women discussed the previous Sunday's sermons, but before long, Anne began interpolating her own beliefs which differed from those of the Boston ministers. Those who would be saved, she said, were those in whom the Holy Spirit lived; this was signalled by a personal love of Christ and an inner light. The ministers of Boston, she said, preached too much that people could be saved only by "works," that is, by following the Scriptures and the Ten Commandments.

In what was to become known as the argument between a covenant of grace versus a covenant of works, Anne further exacerbated the local elders by claiming that only two Boston ministers were "elect," or saved, John Cotton and her brother-in-law John Wheelwright.

Anne's Thursday night meetings took on a new importance. As many as eighty people filled her house, including "some of the magistrates, some gentlemen, some scholars and men of learning, some burgesses, . . . some of our captains and soldiers. . . . She had more resort to her for counsell about matters of conscience," Winthrop observed, "than any minister in the country."

Among them was Sir Henry Vane, who became governor of the colony in 1636.

What started as an ecclesiastical point of difference grew into a schism that threatened the political stability of the colony. When Anne, with the support of Governor Vane and John Cotton, attempted to have her brother-in-law installed as minister of the Boston church, most of the congregation supported her. But the pastor of the church, Reverend John Wilson, a man "whom orthodoxy in New England had no champion more cruel and more ungenerous," gave a speech on the "inevitable dangers of separation" caused by the religious dissensions, and joined with John Winthrop. Because they feared that England would hear of their troubles and cut off the colony (Charles I had tried to squelch it in 1635), a meeting was called with Vane, Cotton, Wheelwright, and Hutchinson to try to settle their religious differences. Cotton conceded that their differences were slight, but the others still maintained that a personal union with the Holy Spirit was possible.

"It began to be as common here," Winthrop said early in 1637, "to distinguish between men, by being under a covenant of grace or a covenant of works, as in other countries between

Protestants and Papists." Thomas Weld complained, "Now after our sermons were ended, you might have seen half a dozen pistols discharged at the face of the preacher, (I mean) so many objections were made by the opinionists in the open assembly." When a call to arms went out for men to fight in the Pequot War, a contingent from Boston "came near refusing to march" because the chaplain (Reverend Wilson) was under a covenant of works.

By now Anne Hutchinson's followers were called Antinomians, a term coined originally by Martin Luther to designate those who believed they were above the Mosaic Law, or the Ten Commandments. In fact, the term, intended to be derogatory, was erroneously applied to Hutchinson's followers, who did not believe that the indwelling of the Holy Spirit released them from obligation to moral law.

In May 1637, a general election was called, and Vane lost to John Winthrop, who took command of the divided colony. To prevent new Antinomians from settling Winthrop imposed a restriction on immigrants, among them Anne's brother and several of her friends who were forced to return to England. In August, eighty-two "heresies" committed by the Antinomians were read at a synod, and a ban was placed on all private meetings.

But Wheelwright continued to preach, and Anne now held her meetings twice a week. Therefore, in November, Wheelwright and Anne were charged and called to account at a meeting of the General Court.

Intending to prove that Anne's behavior was immoral, Winthrop described her meetings as "a thing not tolerable nor comely in the sight of God, nor fitting for your sex," and accused her of breaking the Fifth Commandment by not honoring her father and mother (in this case, the magistrates of the colony).

Answering deftly, Anne came close to clearing herself of all charges. But suddenly, she mentioned that she had had several revelations, including one in which she saw that she "should be persecuted and suffer much trouble" in Boston. The Lord revealed himself to her, she said, "upon a Throne of Justice, and all the world appearing before him, and though I must come to New England, yet I must not fear nor be dismaied," she said. "Therefore, take heed. For I know that for this that you goe about to doe

unto me," she threatened, "God will ruin you and your posterity, and this whole State."

Winthrop answered quickly. "I am persuaded that the revelation she brings forth is delusion," he said.

"We all believe it!" the other members cried.

The court voted to banish her.

"I desire to know wherefore I am banished," she demanded.

"Say no more, the court knows wherefore, and is satisfied," Winthrop replied.

Wheelwright was exiled and shortly left for New Hampshire, and Hutchinson was put under house arrest for the winter to await a church trial in the spring. Fearing that the Antinomians would "make some suddaine irruption upon those that differ from them in judgment," the court ordered that all their arms be seized.

The winter was particularly harsh. Snow stood one-and-a-half feet deep from November to March, 1638. In February Winthrop reported that local Indians repeatedly saw the devil, who told them to desert the English. If Winthrop was uneasy about Anne's revelation of disaster to the colony, he did not have far to look to find a sign of the devil connected to her. Sometime during the winter it was revealed that Anne's friend, Mary Dyer, "notoriously infected with Mrs. Hutchinson's errors," had given birth to a monster described by the midwife as a horned, scaly creature with its facial features scattered over its torso. At the first thaw, Winthrop and "above a hundred persons" opened the monster's grave and were satisfied to see "horns, and claws, . . . and some scales, &c."

On March 15, 1638, Anne was brought to trial before the elders of the church of Boston. Charged with sixteen ecclesiastical errors, she acknowledged some misunderstandings. But when her sons and sons-in-law attempted to speak on her behalf, John Cotton cautioned them against "hindering" the work of God in healing her soul. To the women of the congregation, he said to be careful in listening to her "for you see she is but a woman and many unsound and daygerous Principles are held by her."

If Cotton had once been her friend, he now turned full force against her, attacked her meetings as a "promiscuous and filthie coming together of men and women without Distinction or Relation of Marriage," and accused her of believing in free love.

"Your opinions frett like a Gangrene," Cotton mercilessly pursued, "and spread like a Leprosie, and will eate out the very Bowells of Religion."

The elders admonished her and gave her a week in which to repent. She was sent to Cotton's house.

On March 22, the interrogation was resumed. She admitted several errors, but denied that she was not bound to the Law and held to her belief in inherent grace. Several elders expressed doubt that she had fully repented her "fowle and Damnable Herisies." One called her a "Notorious Imposter."

Then Reverend Wilson, whom she had once tried to evict from the Boston church, delivered her excommunication. "I doe cast you out and in the name of Christ I doe deliver you up to Satan, that you may learne no more to blaspheme, to seduce, and to lye."

A crowd was gathered at the church as she left with Mary Dyer. "Who is that young woman?" someone in the crowd asked. "It is the woman who had the monster!" someone replied.

To Anne, a bystander shouted, "The Lord sanctify this unto you."

"The Lord judgeth not as man judgeth," she replied. "Better to be cast out of the church than to deny Christ." Winthrop reported that after the excommunication, "her spirits . . . revived again, and she gloried in her sufferings, saying that it was the greatest happiness, next to Christ, that ever befel her."

Within a week, Anne left Boston and walked with several of her children to the Island of Aquidneck in Rhode Island where she joined her husband and several others. On land purchased from the Indians, the small band of Antinomians set up a colony which they named Portsmouth.

Shortly after arriving, Anne "perceived her body to be greatly distempered, and her spirits failing, and in that regard, doubtful of her life." With Dr. John Clarke as attending physician, she expelled what a modern pathologist has termed a hydatidiform mole, or a uterine growth. Word quickly reached Boston, and John Cotton announced that she had given birth to "twenty-seven lumps of man's seed without any mixture of anything from the woman." Governor Winthrop perceived that she had had not one, but "30 monstrous births."

Now forty-eight years old, cast out by the minister she had followed to America, and in exile, Anne Hutchinson did not retire. Winthrop kept his eye on her and on the "Isle of Errours," as well as on the strange happenings in Boston. A day after his re-election in May, 1638, he fell ill with a fever that "brought him near death" for a month. Corn planted in the spring "rotted in the ground." And on June 1, a great earthquake roared "like a continued thunder or the rattling of coaches in London." At Portsmouth, he noted, it had come while Mrs. Hutchinson and some friends were at prayer. "The house being shaken thereby, they were persuaded (and boasted of it)," he said, "that the Holy Ghost did shake it in coming down upon them, as he did upon the apostles."

Early in 1639 the Boston church sent a delegation to Portsmouth to dissuade Anne from preaching, but she refused to acknowledge the presence of a church in Boston. When they tried to talk to her husband, William, "he told us that he was more nearly tied to his wife than to the church and he thought her a dear saint and servant of God."

In 1642 William died. Always her supporter, he left her at a time when Massachusetts Colony was threatening to gain possession of Rhode Island, because of an ill-defined boundary. In the company of fifteen members of her family, including her three youngest children, all under ten, and her grandchildren, Anne headed for the Dutch colony in New York. Despite the fact that Governor Winthrop claimed she left Aquidneck because she was weary of the island, "or rather, the island being weary of her," Anne sought a friendlier atmosphere near present-day Eastchester Bay, New York.

But a few months later, fifteen Dutchmen were slain in a battle between the Mohegans and the Narragansetts. In August, 1643, having swept across Long Island, the Mohegans raided the Hutchinson house. They killed cattle, set fire to the house, and slaughtered Anne and thirteen members of her family.

The reaction in Boston was predictable. "I never heard that the Indians in those parts did ever before this commit the like outrage upon any one family," Governor Winthrop said, "and therefore God's hand is more apparently seene herein, to pick out this wofull woman, to make her and those belonging to her, an unheard of heavie example of their cruelty above al others. Thus," he concluded, "the Lord heard our groanes to heaven, and freed us from this great and sore affliction."

Neither martyr nor successful reformer, Anne Hutchinson nevertheless identified and challenged the colony's palpable weakness. Her "ready wit and bold spirit" aroused a fear that moved the founding fathers to an inelegant harshness. Confounded, Winthrop saw her eloquence as the work of the devil, her cleverness in answering the ridiculous charges at her trials as "circumlocutions," her religious differences as atheism. To him, she was a "Prophetesse, . . . an American Jesabel." Had she been a man, she might have wrested political power from Governor Winthrop. As it was, she used her considerable influence as a woman to test the colony's religious tolerance, which, ironically, had been the reason for settlement.

"Under an Evil Hand"

Three hundred years ago the largest witch hunt in American history gripped Salem, Massachusetts. Before the hysteria finally subsided, nineteen people were executed and more than a hundred others convicted of or charged with practicing witchcraft.

Larry Gragg

History professor at the University of Missouri-Rolla, Larry Gragg specializes in early American history with a special emphasis on seventeenth-century New England. His book The Salem Witch Crisis *is published by Praeger Publishers, NY.*

Early in 1692, several young girls in Salem Village, Massachusetts were "led away with little sorceries," according to Cotton Mather, Boston's eminent man of God. Their experiments, which involved little more than divining what their future husbands would be like, began in the household of the village minister, the Reverend Samuel Parris. Elizabeth, Parris's nine-year-old daughter, and Abigail Williams, his eleven-year-old niece, under the guidance of Tituba, the family's West Indian slave, fashioned a crude crystal ball by dropping an egg into a bowl of water. To the impressionable girls, the undulating egg white appeared to float in the shape of a coffin.

Confronted with this horrific image, the frightened youngsters began to act in peculiar ways. Neighbors were shocked by their "afflictions," which seemed to worsen each day. One clergyman claimed that the children "were bitten and pinched by invisible agents; their arms, necks, and backs turned this way and that way, and returned back again, so as it was impossible for them to do of themselves, and beyond the power of any epileptic fits, or natural disease to effect."

Unable to determine a physical cause for their "distemper," William Griggs, the village doctor, confided to Parris that the children were "under an Evil Hand"—the blanket seventeenth-century diagnosis for maladies physicians were unable to understand.

Anxious to ease the girls' suffering and to prevent further spread of the afflictions (several teens who lived near the parsonage had begun to exhibit similar symptoms), Parris consulted with neighboring ministers. Upon observing the girls, the clergymen confirmed the physician's diagnosis—"the hand of Satan was in them." The reactions of the Reverend Parris and civil authorities to these assessments led to the largest witch hunt in American history.

To the modern mind, the tragic epic of the Salem witch trials seems virtually incomprehensible. But to the seventeenth-century mind, sorcery and the occult were very real. With few exceptions, everyone—even the most highly educated individuals—believed in witchcraft and feared the evil associated with it.

WHEN PARRIS AND THE OTHER MINISters repeatedly asked the girls who was afflicting them, they finally obliged by naming Tituba and two other village women, Sarah Good and Sarah Osborne—both likely candidates fitting the stereotypical witch "mold." The destitute pipe-smoking Good wandered from house to house begging food, while Osborne was a semi-invalid old woman known for depression and erratic behavior. Salem magistrates Jonathan Corwin and John Hathorne swiftly issued warrants for the arrest of the accused, and on March 1 constables took them into custody for questioning.

The large crowd that filed into the village meetinghouse to witness the "examination" of the suspects brought with them their profound belief in the occult. Well educated and poorly educated alike gleaned from almanacs the astronomical data needed to practice astrology, relied on charms, and heeded the words of fortune tellers. They considered comets, lightning, and thunder as omens of catastrophe and gossiped about prophecies, visions, and disembodied voices.

Cotton Mather claimed many "would often cure hurts with spells, and practice detestable conjurations with sieves, and keys, and peas, and nails, and other implements, to learn the things for which they had a forbidden and impious curiosity." What most worried the Puritan divine was his conviction that this interest inevitably led to a greater fascination with the more insidious practice of witchcraft.

Mather had good reason for his concern. Many seventeenth-century immigrants to New England brought with them their Old World belief that witches or wizards, through curses, charms, or the evil eye, could cause harm in their villages. While ordinary folk worried about witches damaging their crops, harming their livestock, or making someone in their family ill, Mather and some of his clerical colleagues had a much greater fear. They had come to believe that a well-organized witch conspiracy existed in New England, bent upon the overthrow of Christianity.

While the community's members might disagree on the threat posed by witchcraft, most agreed on the means employed by Satan to recruit witches. Preying upon those with financial difficulty, marital problems, or religious ca-

From *American History Illustrated*, March/April 1992, pp. 54-59. Reprinted through the courtesy of Cowles Magazines, publishers of *American History Illustrated*.

res, the devil offered happiness and material success for their allegiance.

Two aspects of this alleged pact became important in the witch prosecutions of 1692. Puritans believed that the devil gave to witches natural and unnatural creatures known as "familiars" to aid them in carrying out their evil deeds. Some also contended that the witch, in turn, granted Satan permission to use her shape or her "specter" to afflict others. Indeed, testimony of someone's specter doing harm became the most crucial form of evidence in the 1692 trials.

For four days during the first week of March, Salem Villagers heard magistrates Corwin and Hathorne interrogate the first three suspects about familiars, specters, and incidents in their past that might shed light on the afflictions of the suffering girls. Sarah Good and Sarah Osborne denied complicity in the affair, but Tituba, impressed by the spectacle and fearful of reprisals, confessed to a number of malicious actions. The devil had forced her to harm the girls on several occasions and to sign a pact, she testified. As she wrote in the devil's book, Tituba claimed she saw numerous names, including Good's and Osborne's. Moreover, she offered detailed descriptions of the two villagers' familiars. Good had a yellow bird, a wolf, and a cat. Osborne had one with "wings and two legs and a head like a woman" and the other "all over hairy."

While the magistrates questioned Good and Osborne in the meetinghouse, the afflicted girls, who listened during their testimony, suffered numerous fits—convincing proof to the judges of the accused witches' frightful powers. Even Sarah Good's husband and daughter offered evidence against her; William Good admitted that he thought his wife was a witch, and six-year-old Dorothy claimed to have seen her mother's familiars—three birds of various colors.

Sarah Good's examination led some villagers to recall past confrontations with her, and a few of them came forward later in the year to offer damning evidence in her trial. Sarah Gadge, for example, remembered an argument that had ended with Good threatening that "she should give [Gadge] something." The following day, one of Gadge's cows had mysteriously died—an occurrence she attributed to Good's evil powers.

On March 7, magistrates Corwin and Hathorne, convinced they had assembled enough evidence to justify an indictment,

ordered the three women held in a Boston jail to await their day in court.

To seventeenth-century eyes, there had been little extraordinary about this particular episode of accusations. The three women fit contemporary ideas on witches and the practice of witchcraft. Almost eighty percent of the roughly one hundred people accused of witchcraft in New England prior to 1692 were women; most of them were poor and more than forty years of age. Several had sullied reputations, being known for supposedly having magical powers, criminal backgrounds, or simply disagreeable dispositions. Robert Calef, in one of the contemporary accounts of the Salem trials, explained that because the accused in this case included a confessing slave, as well as "Sarah Good, who had long been counted a melancholy or distracted woman, and one Osborne, an old bed-rid woman; which two were persons so ill thought of, that the accusation was the more readily believed."

Usually, after suspects in witchcraft trials were jailed, the afflicted recovered. In 1692, however, not only did the girls' symptoms worsen, the number of those suffering afflictions increased. Widespread panic, which would soon escalate into hysteria, set in.

Initially, then, the accusations of early March seemed little different from previous ones. As Salem's John Higginson recalled a decade later, the situation was "looked on at first as an ordinary case which had fallen out before at several times in other places, and would be quickly over."

USUALLY, AFTER SUSPECTS IN WITCHcraft episodes were jailed, the afflicted recovered. In 1692 Salem Village, however, not only did the girls' symptoms worsen, the number of those suffering afflictions increased. When fasts and prayer meetings failed to afford relief, villagers concluded that additional, as-

yet unidentified witches must be in their midst. Widespread panic, which would soon escalate into mass hysteria, set in.

On March 11, the afflicted youths named Martha Corey, and days later they accused Rebecca Nurse of harming them. Because both of these women were members of the Congregational Church, their arrest posed a fundamental crisis of faith for the people of Salem Village.

For three generations, ministers had taught settlers in Massachusetts that even though man was born in sin and deserving of damnation, God had chosen to save a few "elect" souls. In most congregations, membership was based largely upon the applicant's explanation of his or her conversion experience. In churches accepting this evidence of God's gift of grace, few believed that an elect person could fall from grace after having once been saved. But now two of God's apparent elect stood accused of witchcraft. Confused Salem Villagers looked to their spiritual leader for guidance.

On March 27, the Reverend Samuel Parris responded with a sermon entitled "Christ Knows How Many Devils There Are in His Churches and Who They Are." This discourse became the key to the rapid acceleration in accusations that made the Salem episode unique in American history. "Let none then build their hopes of salvation merely upon this," Parris explained, "that they are church members this you and I may be, and yet devils for all that." Church members may have once considered their congregation a sanctuary safely out of the devil's reach, but no more. "Christ knows how many devils among us," said Parris, "whether one or ten or twenty."

When Parris said that the devil had breached the walls of the church and entered into covenants with two of the elect, he was arguing that virtually anyone could be suspect. Parris's dismal prospect that the church no longer offered refuge from evil heightened the atmosphere of distrust enveloping Salem Village. As one minister described the mood during the examination of Rebecca Nurse, "they were afraid that those that sat next to them were under the influence of witchcraft."

There is little question that Parris's sermon changed the pace and character of the accusations. During the following two months more than sixty people stood accused of practicing witchcraft. Increasingly the "specters" of people from across the social spectrum harmed the afflicted. Farmers, merchants, artisans, and clergymen, or more often their wives and daughters, as well as the deviants of the villages surrounding Salem, now faced the prospect of a witchcraft trial. By late May, Thomas Newton, who received a commission to handle the prosecution of the witches, marveled that "the afflicted spare no person of what quality soever."

ON MAY 14, AS THE JAILS BETWEEN Salem and Boston filled with suspects, William Phips, the new royal governor of Massachusetts, arrived from England. He was greeted with frightful stories of the sufferings of the increasing number of afflicted. Their relatives told him of family members "taken with preternatural torments some scalded with brimstone some had pins stuck in their flesh others hurried into the fire and water and some dragged out of their houses and carried over the tops of the trees and hills for many miles together."

Phips faced a legal dilemma. The Massachusetts Bay colony had made the practice of witchcraft a felony under the authority of a charter granted by Charles I in 1629. That document, however, had been revoked in 1686. Two years later, the colony became part of the Dominion of New England. Since the 1689 overthrow of Edmund Andros, the Dominion governor, Massachusetts had existed in a legal limbo while its agents negotiated with William III for a new charter. Technically, then, no law against witchcraft existed. Governor Phips, who had arrived with a new charter, was unable to convene another provincial legislature to confirm the old statute until June 8.

Not wanting to wait that long, Phips appointed a special Court of Oyer and Terminer (a judicial body to hear and determine) on May 27. He selected Deputy Governor William Stoughton and eight leading merchants and landowners to serve on the court. All but one of the nine had some experience with witchcraft cases.

The judges spent the brief time between their appointment and the first trial consulting clergymen, reviewing the transcripts of the preliminary examinations, reading accounts of earlier trials, and studying English guidebooks on proper procedures in witchcraft cases.

Out of their deliberations, the judges agreed to admit three types of evidence.

Accepting the proposition that a witch had to nourish her familiars, the judges ordered a physical search of suspects for a "witch's teat," a peculiar growth or "preternatural excrescence." Acknowledging the tradition that the devil gave witches the power to harm people by thrusting pins into or twisting images of them, the judges also ordered constables to search suspects' homes for puppets or dolls. Beyond this physical evidence, the judges decided to accept testimony from any who recalled confrontations with the accused and then experienced some misfortune.

Most importantly, however, they concluded that "specter evidence" would be the key to convictions. If the afflicted or other villagers came forward with testimony of the accused's shape or specter doing harm, the judges saw that as the best evidence of complicity with Satan on the grounds that the devil could not use humans' shapes without their permission.

In all, twenty-seven individuals in Salem underwent jury trials for witchcraft between June 2 and September 17. Because prosecutors Thomas Newton and Anthony Checkley were able to introduce specter evidence in all of the trials, the juries rendered guilty verdicts in each case.

Among the convicted were George Burroughs, a former Salem Village minister, and church members Martha Corey and Rebecca Nurse. The latter's trial drew particular attention because of the high regard most people held for her. Perhaps no one had been more surprised by the charges against her than Nurse herself. Upon learning of her impending arrest, the pious seventy-one-year-old Nurse asked, "what sin hath God found out in me unrepented of that he should lay such an affliction upon me in my old age?"

For Nurse's June 30 trial, almost forty people signed a petition attesting that "her life and conversation" had always been that of a Christian and they "never had any cause or grounds to suspect her of any such thing as she is now accused of."

When the jury, on the strength of this overwhelming affirmation of Nurse's character, found her innocent, the afflicted "made an hideous outcry." Justice Stoughton then asked the jury to reconsider their verdict. Jury foreman Thomas Fisk agreed to do so on the basis of a puzzling remark Nurse had made upon seeing accused witch Deliverance Hobbs

and her daughter being led into the courtroom. "What, do these persons give in evidence against me now?" Nurse asked, "They used to come among us." The jury wanted to know if Nurse's "us" meant a group of suspects or a group of witches. When Fisk asked the accused to clarify the statement, the nearly deaf, distracted woman made no reply. Taking the suspect's failure to respond as an admission of guilt, the jury reversed its verdict.

By September 22, nineteen of the convicted, including Rebecca Nurse, had been wheeled in carts up Gallows' Hill in Salem and hanged. In addition, the judges had ordered that one suspect, Giles Corey, be "pressed." Corey, in an apparent protest against the trials, had pleaded not guilty but then refused to put himself on trial "by God and my country." This strategy prevented the court from trying him before a jury. Under English law, however, the judges were permitted to impose the sentence of *piene forte et dure* (hard and severe punishment) to coerce a change of mind. Consequently, they ordered Sheriff George Corwin to pile great weights upon Corey. The seventy-two-year-old man refused to relent and died after two days of this torture.

MORE THAN ONE HUNDRED SUSPECTS awaited their trial when Governor Phips returned to Boston in early October from a military campaign against Native Americans on the frontier. Appalled at the scope and spectacle of the trials and upset because even his own wife was named by the afflicted, Phips forbade any more arrests and, at the end of the month, dismissed the Court of Oyer and Terminer. His decision reflected a rapidly developing opposition to the trials.

Ever more people had grown skeptical of the testimony and actions of the afflicted. In his May examination, John Alden had called them "wenches . . . who played their juggling tricks, falling down, crying out, and staring in peoples' faces." During Elizabeth Proctor's June 30 trial, Daniel Elliott testified that he had overheard one of the afflicted claim "she did it for sport they must have some sport." Mary Warren, one of the afflicted who accused more than a dozen people, even admitted to several villagers that "her head was distempered" when she had made those allegations. Moreover, "when she was well again she could not say that she saw any of [the] apparitions at the time aforesaid."

By early October many also came to realize that several of the more than fifty people who had confessed to familiarity with the devil had done so under great duress. They had been intimidated by the afflicted or by the persistent questions of the magistrates and sometimes even family members who thought a confession might spare their lives. (Only those who refused to confess were hanged; confession was one way to avoid death.)

Those who later recanted their confessions had explanations similar to that of Margaret Jacobs, who told the judges, "I was cried out upon by some of the possessed persons, as afflicting them; whereupon I was brought to my examination, which persons at the sight of me fell down which did very much to startle and affright me. The Lord above knows I knew nothing in the least measure how or who afflicted them; they told me, without doubt I did, or else they would not fall down at me; they told me, if I would not confess, I should be put down into the dungeon and would be hanged, but if I would confess I should have my life, the which did so affright me, with my own vile wicked heart, to save my life; made me make the like confession I did, which confession, may it please the honored court, is altogether false and untrue."

As well as harboring doubts about the testimony of the confessors and accusations of the afflicted, many Salem villagers were impressed by the deportment of the condemned. Shortly before her execution, Rebecca Nurse's sister Mary Esty petitioned the court not for her own life but "that no more innocent blood be shed." The five victims executed on August 19 had likewise expressed the hope that "their blood might be the last innocent blood shed." The Reverend George Burroughs left a particularly vivid impression. According to one contemporary, the former Salem Village minister's protestation of innocence and recitation of the Lord's Prayer (that witches were allegedly unable to utter) "drew tears from many" who had attended the public execution.

The people of Salem Village and surrounding communities demonstrated their opposition to the trials most forcefully by coming forward to support the accused. Before Governor Phips halted the trials, almost three hundred family members, neighbors, clergymen, and even jailers either had signed petitions or testified on behalf of the accused. As Cotton Mather reported on October 20, the "humors of this people now run" against a continuation of the trials.

Although important, this shift in public opinion was not as significant to Phips as the opinion of the colony's leading minister, Increase Mather (Cotton's father). Phips had an obvious reason for his high regard for Increase. The minister not only had been instrumental in securing the new charter for Massachusetts but also in persuading the king to select Phips as the new governor.

In late September, several clergymen persuaded Mather to draft a treatise detailing the problems with the evidence used in the trials. In a work he called *Cases of Conscience,* Mather presented a synthesis of what several ministers had been arguing privately since late May. He maintained that specter evidence, the most critical in all convictions, was seriously flawed. Satan could assume any shape. Consequently, testimony of a person's image doing harm did not provide conclusive proof that the individual had made a pact with the devil. Although specter evidence could be used to raise suspicion, it was insufficient for a conviction. If the court accepted his argument, Mather acknowledged that there was little chance it could gain any more convictions, and some witches might escape justice. That was a price, however, that Mather and most of the province's clergy were willing to pay "It were better," he wrote, "that ten suspected witches should escape, than that one innocent person should be condemned."

In 1697 the Massachusetts colony sought to pay penance for the suffering caused by the witchcraft trials, ordering all to observe a day of prayer and fasting, in the hope this would bring a pardon from God for "all the errors of his servants and people."

In explaining to officials in London his decision to suspend the trials, Phips emphasized his reliance upon Mather and other ministers who "did give it as their judgment that the Devil might afflict in the shape of an innocent person and that the look and touch of the suspected persons was not sufficient proof against them." In December, Phips appointed a new court to deal with the remaining cases. Because the judges agreed to use specter evidence only as presumptive evidence, only three individuals were convicted; Phips subsequently pardoned them.

DURING THE NEXT TWO DECADES, Massachusetts colonists struggled with the consequences of the witchcraft crisis. Several people who had been instrumental in the accusations and trials acknowledged that they had committed grievous errors. In 1694, for example, the Reverend Samuel Parris admitted to his congregation that his sermons two years earlier had contributed to the crisis atmosphere in Salem Village. While he maintained that he had sought "to avoid the wronging of any," Parris apologized to the families who had "unduly suffered in these matters." Twelve years later, Ann Putnam, Jr., who had accused twenty-one individuals of witchcraft, sought membership in the Salem Village congregation. She pleaded with the congregation to forgive her 1692 actions "particularly, as I was a chief instrument of accusing Goodwife Nurse and her two sisters."

Samuel Sewall, a judge on the Court of Oyer and Terminer, likewise publicly acknowledged his role. In 1696, as Sewall stood in front of his Boston congregation, he had his pastor read a confession in which the judge accepted "the blame and shame" of agreeing to the executions of nineteen of the convicted. Twelve of the jurors joined Sewall in expressing their sorrow in the "condemning of any person" during the great witch hunt.

Indeed, the entire colony sought to pay penance for the suffering of 1692 when the provincial legislature ordered all to observe a day of prayer and fasting in January 1697. Civil and religious leaders hoped this special day would bring a pardon from God for "all the errors of his servants and people" in the witchcraft episode.

Slowly, civil and religious leaders came to the conclusion that true reconciliation could not be achieved until the government reversed the convictions of

1692 and compensated the victims or their surviving family members. In 1703 and 1710, responding to petitions from these individuals and groups, the provincial government reversed the guilty verdicts of all but seven of those convicted.* In 1710, the legislature also voted to award partial compensation to many of the accused witches or their survivors for jail expenses, court costs, and property confiscated in 1692.

This cumulative effort to make amends for the errors and mass hysteria of 1692 did not eliminate all the bitterness resulting from the year of prosecutions. For

---

*Bridget Bishop, Elizabeth Johnson, Susanna Martin, Alice Parker, Ann Pudeator, Wilmot Redd, and Margaret Scott. Because no advocates came forward on behalf of these individuals, their convictions remain on the record.

Salem Village, a community wracked by factional strife for decades, controversy ultimately focused on the Reverend Parris's role in the witchcraft crisis. After a fierce five-year struggle with a faction led by Rebecca Nurse's relatives, who never could forgive the man they called the "great prosecutor," Parris lost his job.

Nor did the provincials' attempt to heal the wounds caused by the prosecutions prevent contemporary and subsequent generations from heaping infamy upon the trials' supporters, notably Cotton Mather. Because he had written an uncritical account of the trials called *Wonders of the Invisible World,* Mather quickly gained an enduring reputation as the leading apologist of the Court of Oyer and Terminer. Boston merchant Robert Calef made that charge in a 1700

work he sarcastically entitled *More Wonders of the Invisible World,* in which he largely ignored Mather's advice to the judges throughout the summer to use spectral evidence cautiously. Instead, he focused upon the painfully deferential Mather's defense of jurists he respected and found difficult to criticize in print. As New England historian Samuel Eliot Morison put it, Calef "tied a tin can to him after the frenzy was over; and it has rattled and banged through the pages of superficial and popular historians."

Although the year-long struggle against occult forces deterred New Englanders from engaging in massive witch hunts ever again, the majority of these highly religious and superstitious settlers never renounced their belief in witchcraft. Rather, they concluded that no sufficiently just method existed for routing out the evil force.

Remapping American Culture

A New U.S. history traces today's regionalism to colonial days

For nearly a century, historians have searched for the wellspring of American politics and culture. Herbert Baxter Adams found it in the Teutonic forests, where Saxon warriors had gathered in an early version of the New England town meeting. Frederick Jackson Turner looked westward to the American frontier, while Richard Hofstadter and Daniel Boorstin looked to the economic abundance and inventiveness that produced a broad-based middle class. Now, historian David Hackett Fischer is bidding to join their ranks with a provocative new theory of the roots of the American experience.

The Brandeis University historian has uncovered America's political and cultural roots in the countryside of Britain. In his new book, *Albion's Seed* (Oxford University Press, $39.95), Fischer argues that settlers from different sections of England—called Albion by the ancient Greeks—brought divergent values to the new world, where they established distinctive regional cultures that remain central to the nation's fabric even today. Fischer contends that everything from contrasting New England and Southern accents to what makes the South far more politically conservative than the Northeast can be explained by looking at the differences among the early settlers.

This bold thesis, called "a revisionist blockbuster" by one critic, is nothing less than an attempt at a new synthesis of U.S. history. Before the 1960s, American history had been written as a smooth narrative of the achievements of the famous and powerful that left little room for the lives of ordinary citizens. But the '60s turned American history—and the nation itself—on its head, and shattered the old scholarly synthesis. The once neglected masses became the focus of research as "the new social history" moved to the fore and historical scholarship fragmented into numerous sub-

specialties. Many leading historians wondered whether, like Humpty Dumpty, U.S. history could ever be put back together again. Fischer is trying to do just that.

His America, hardly the "melting pot" described in many history texts, is a land that from its very beginning was marked by diversity, not homogeneity. It is a land in which the early settlers all spoke English but otherwise had remarkably little in common. They arrived here at different times and from different regions of England, each fleeing a different form of oppression. Most of the Puritans came from the east of England to Massachusetts between 1629 and 1641. A small Royalist elite and large numbers of indentured servants arrived in the Chesapeake region from the south and west of England between 1642 and 1675. Quakers from England's north midlands and Wales arrived in the Delaware Valley between 1675 and 1725, and immigrants from Northern Ireland, parts of Scotland and the border area of north England settled in Appalachia from 1717 to 1775. "They carried across the Atlantic four different sets of British folkways which became the basis of regional cultures in the New World," says Fischer.

Almost from the beginning, there was little love lost among the colonists. The Anglicans of Virginia and the Puritans of New England agreed on little other than their loathing of Quakers, who were regarded as dangerous radicals. The Puritans and Quakers, in turn, disliked the Virginians. In 1651, one Puritan observed of Virginians: "I think they are the farthest from conscience and moral honesty of any such number together in the world." And Puritans, Virginia cavaliers and Quakers united in the view that the backcountry settlers of Appalachia were—barbarians.

These sometimes feuding groups left 20th-century America a rich and diverse legacy, especially when it came to regional tongues. Fischer traces the unique dialect of Massachusetts and much of New England to a high-pitched nasal accent called the "Norfolk whine" that the Puritans brought to the new world. Even today, the distinctive pronunciation of the letter *r* that characterizes Yankee speech, transforming a word such as *Harvard* into *Haa-v'd*, can be heard in England's East Anglia region. In contrast, the slow drawl of the South comes from the south and west of England, where ancestors of the Virginia cavaliers uttered such words as *chitlins* and *no-count*.

Even what is controversially labeled today as black dialect may have been an English import. The people of Virginia, even those of high rank, preferred "I be," "she ain't," "it don't" and "I hain't" to such phrases as "I am" and "you are," bays Fischer, who found that American travelers to England in the 19th century were startled by the resemblance of the dialect of rural Sussex to Virginia speech. A different and equally persistent language variation was introduced into Appalachia by Scottish and Irish settlers who pronounced *where* as *whar* and *there* as *thar* and used such constructions as *he come in* and *she done finished*, which show up today in everything from country music to comedy routines. The more subtle linguistic peculiarities of the Quakers sowed the seeds of the flat accent of the Midwest.

Not only did the early settlers speak differently, they also held dramatically different attitudes toward education. The Puritans were members of a sturdy middle class steeped in the Bible who transmitted to their descendants the importance they placed on literacy and learning. That is why even today there are excep-

The Puritan legacy

*Centuries later, the imprint of an austere,
sober people remains indelible*

Modern New England may be best known for leafy
autumns and high tech, but the legacy of the Puritans lives
on in the form of boiled dinners, town meetings and Cape
Cod houses. Puritans associated their diet with piety, not
the palate, so they preferred cold baked beans and boiled
vegetables to bountiful seafood. The austerity of the diet
was leavened, however, by the baked pie, which became a
special culinary delight. For housing, the Puritans utilized two styles from East Anglia, the saltbox—boasting
two stories in front and one in back—and the 1½-story
Cape Cod, which remains popular today.

Their fashion statement came in the form of such "sadd
colors" as tawny, russet and purple, which continue as
part of the region's official culture. They show up in
ceremonies at institutions like Brown University, whose
idea of high color is dark brown trimmed with black.

Ordered liberty, the belief that individual liberties belong to all within a framework of an active town-meeting
government, became a Puritan bench mark. John Quincy
Adams and his father, John Adams, before him were
among 16 U.S. Presidents descended from the settlers.

tionally—high levels of college attendance in New England, home to some of
the nation's finest colleges. The Quakers,
ambivalent about education, were slower
to found colleges, but put more emphasis
on schooling than residents of the Southern highlands—West Virginia, Arkansas,
Kentucky, Alabama and Mississippi—
where even now levels of educational
attainment are comparatively low. Fischer
traces this to educational practices brought
from Northern Ireland, the north of England and parts of rural Scotland to—the
backcountry, "where there were no institutions comparable to New England's
town schools or even to Virginia's system of parish education."

In domestic matters—sexual relations
and family violence, especially—the past
was also prologue. Violence was much
greater in the patriarchal cultures of the
backcountry and the Chesapeake than
among the Puritans and Quakers. This
colonial pattern manifests itself today in
regional variations in the homicide rate,
which is much lower in the North than in

the South and Southwest. And from the
beginning, it appears, there was an intimate connection between domestic violence and attitudes toward women. In
Puritan Massachusetts, for instance, the
Christian ideal of spiritual equality between the sexes held sway, and every
woman was entitled by law to physical
protection from both physical and verbal
abuse. Men and women were also punished equally for sexual transgressions.
The Quakers went further. They held the
revolutionary view that the family was a
union of individuals who were equal in
the sight of God, and Quaker law was the
first to routinely use the pronouns "he or
she."

In the backcountry, by contrast, men
were considered warriors and women
workers—an inequitable domestic relationship that led to high levels of household violence. And in the Chesapeake
region, women were held inferior even
by the law. While rape was a hanging
crime in New England, in the Southern
colonies it was sometimes punished less
severely than petty theft.

This history helps explain why support for women's suffrage and for the
equal-rights amendment has been strongest across the Northern tier of the
nation and weakest in the South and
Southwest, Fischer contends. Most
states in the Southern highlands voted
against the ERA, while every state in the
Northern tier supported it. The nation's
politics, he believes, reflect at heart the
philosophical differences spread by Albion's seed.

Even the participation of Americans in
wars of all kinds may be traceable to
unique regional experiences. Fischer offers the controversial argument that
Northeastern liberals joined World War
II because they saw it as a moral crusade
against Fascism and militarism, while
Southern conservatives were drawn by a
kinship with Britain that dated back to
the cavaliers. Backcountry descendants
fought for national honor, while Quakers
nonviolently supported what they saw as
a battle against the warrior spirit.

What is most remarkable is that these
differences have persisted through waves
of subsequent immigration. Although
fewer than 20 percent of Americans now
have British ancestors, says Fischer, the
nation remains a product of Albion's
seed because newer waves of immigrants
"tended to adopt the folkways of the
regions in which they settled." He draws
on his own experience teaching at Bran-

deis, a predominantly Jewish school,
where his Protestant stereotypes about
the culture of Judaism were exploded by
encountering everything from Yankee
Jews to "backslapping Texas Jews in
cowboy boots and 10-gallon hats."

Still, Fischer readily acknowledges
that since the 18th century the original
four cultures of British America have
commingled with others. Today, he finds
at least seven regional cultures in the
U.S., and perhaps more. The Albion
four, which have spread out across the
nation, have been joined by the cultures
of Greater New York—"a very heavy
infusion of Middle European and Jewish
culture—grafted on the old Dutch root"—
the predominantly Mormon Great Basin
and heavily Hispanic Southern California.

Myth of homogeneity. By focusing on
England, Fischer opens himself to the
charge that he is offering nothing more
than a WASP's-eye view of history while
slighting the centuries-old contributions
of other cultures, most notably that of
African Americans. Fischer will deal

Cavaliers and servants

*The rich led an opulent life, while the rest
settled for much slimmer pickings*

The Civil War notwithstanding, the "distressed cavaliers"
and their plantation style remain a cornerstone of Southern culture. Stately mansions with large rooms, high
ceilings and elaborate gardens were built by Virginians
who were accustomed to housing extended patriarchal
families. The homes served as reminders of the manors of
southern England. Not surprisingly, the cavaliers did not
stint on their dining pleasure. Prosperous planter William
Byrd enjoyed fried chicken, often cooked with bacon or
ham, now a staple of the American diet. A favorite of
many Virginians was "fricagy," or fricassee, chicken or
meat simmered with herbs in an open pan.

In the colony, clothes did not make the man, they
showed who he was. While servants and commoners wore
garments of canvas, the elite dressed in bright silks and
satins, often displaying family coats of arms on rings,
silverware and furniture.

Virginians believed in the hierarchical concept of freedom. Liberty belonged to free-born Englishmen, not to
all people. George Washington and Thomas Jefferson are
among the 10 Chief Executives from their ranks.

with African American culture in the second volume of his projected five-volume series. The 53-year-old scholar, who has been working on the project for almost two decades, has finished drafts of two volumes and rough drafts of the others.

The second volume, tentatively titled *American Plantations,* will focus on two strains of black culture, one brought to the Chesapeake region from West Africa and the other to South Carolina from the Congo basin. The book will also examine native-American culture and the Dutch culture that was instrumental in the development of New York. Hispanic culture is several volumes away, since Fischer argues that its impact was not significant until the 19th century.

Critics fault Fischer for sometimes offering fuzzy evidence to back up claims of the continuing strength of Albion's seed in the 20th century. He has also been accused of underplaying differences within a regional culture and of presenting a framework that, all in all, is a little too tidy. But whatever the shortcomings of his encyclopedic, 946-page work, historians who have read it generally agree that the book is a masterpiece of scholarship. Cornell University's Michael Kammen lauds the Brandeis scholar for producing "the finest work of synthesis in early American history in more than 50 years." The University of Florida's Bertram Wyatt-Brown predicts that the book will "raise a firestorm," but he believes that Fischer's overall "thesis and its proof are so sweeping that critics will find it hard to refute."

What Fischer has done is to shatter the myth that America has evolved into one homogeneous mass culture. As his portrait shows, although we share the same films, TV shows and fast-food restaurants, we remain a remarkably diverse people.

DELAWARE VALLEY
Quaker simplicity
They brought a social conscience to their dining table and abhorred excess in all things except moderation

Function, not frills, marked the Quaker way of life. The Quakers opposed excess and refused to touch foods they regarded as tainted by social evil, a harbinger of such modern movements as the grape boycott. Their main culinary contribution was a special form of food preservation that spawned products like cream cheese.

Their homes were built of stone and brick and came primarily in the "Quaker plan" (three rooms on the first floor and a full second story) and the "four-over-four" (four large rooms with central halls on both the top and bottom floors).

Quakers believed that costly costumes created envy and divisiveness. A man's wardrobe often consisted of leather breeches and a wide leather apron, derived from the folk costume of England's North Midlands. Women wore modest dresses and put no powder or color on their faces.

Reciprocal liberty, in which every freedom demanded for oneself should be extended to others, was a credo of the Quakers. They did not approve of politics, and hence the culture sired few Presidents, among them Herbert Hoover.

APPALACHIA
Backcountry folk
Although they were the last of Albion's seed to arrive, they have given the nation 18 Presidents

The settlers of Appalachia were hard-living and hard-working and believed in self-reliance and individual responsibility. Their diet would shock today's cholesterol-sensitive citizenry; it leaned heavily to milk, butter and clabber, a blend of sour milk, curds and whey. They brought with them their beverage of choice: Whisky. But they had to adapt to their new home's native grains, replacing Scotch with bourbon.

Privacy was not a concern, so families lived in stone or log cabins, made into one large room, that were similar in style to homes in England's northern border country. Clothing emphasized the differences between the sexes in a culture that stressed sensuality. Single women often wore a full bodice with deep décolletage, a short full skirt and a hem high above the ankle. The men wore shirts cut full in the chest and shoulders and pants that were loose and flowing. This attire, considered the prototype of frontier dress, was similar to clothing in Britain's borderlands.

The idea of natural liberty flourished in their remote environs. Although back-country residents were the last of the immigrant groups to arrive, they produced 18 Presidents, including Lyndon Johnson.

Revolutionary America

To English officials, the American colonies were but part of a remote empire. Their value, under the prevailing economic theory known as "mercantilism," was to provide foodstuffs and raw materials for the mother country, and markets for English manufactured goods. A major goal for the empire, aside from economic prosperity, was to attain self-sufficiency—especially in time of war. It was unwise, for instance, to rely on another nation for shipbuilding materials that might be cut off in the event of conflict. There was little inclination for London to interfere with the colonies so long as they served their function. Aside from some regulations on commercial matters, often ignored in practice, many colonies gained virtual autonomy over their own affairs.

What Americans called the French and Indian War changed all that. British victory in 1763 resulted in the expulsion of France from North America, thereby eliminating colonial reliance on the British government for protection. At the same time, the war had brought England to the verge of bankruptcy. As the colonists had benefited from the war's outcome, British officials thought it only fair that they bear their fair share of taxes to reduce the deficit. Many colonists thought otherwise. The series of new taxes and regulations imposed by the British government seemed to them a radical departure from long-standing tradition. What began as a protest against purely economic measures soon became entangled with issues of political and religious freedom. A family squabble led to revolution.

News of the American Revolution spread quickly throughout the capitals of Europe. The Declaration of Independence had radical implications for the "enlightened despots" who feared challenges to their legitimacy. Was the American Revolution a product of political repression and constitutional differences as suggested in "The American Revolution: A War of Religion?" "The Shot Heard Round the World" indicates that the American Revolution was not perceived merely as a rebellion, but as a movement of universal appeal. The article "Declaration of Independence" evaluates its domestic impact, then and now. The author sees it as one of the most fundamental American documents, despite its having no standing in law. In "Winter at Valley Forge," how the Continental Army was transformed from a dispirited mob into a disciplined army that helped the revolution succeed is described.

America's first government, the Articles of Confederation, was less a national government than a confederation of states. Important legislation required a two-thirds majority to pass, and amending the Articles required unanimity. Despite important accomplishments, the Articles increasingly came to be perceived as inadequate. "A Troubled League," by Brian McGinty, shows how dissatisfaction led to the demand for a new form of government. Jack Rakove, in "Philadelphia Story," analyzes the deliberations that formed the writing of the Constitution, and "Philadelphia 1787" provides a portrait of that city as it was while the convention met. In "The Founding Fathers and Slavery," the author offers the view that while the Constitution did not end slavery, the Founding Fathers took "positive steps that demonstrated their antislavery instincts" and ultimately undermined that terrible institution.

Looking Ahead: Challenge Questions

What was there about the American Revolution and the Declaration of Independence that aroused both admiration and fear in Europe?

What were the strengths and weaknesses of the Articles of Confederation? What were the major compromises made at the Constitutional Convention? How did the final document remedy the weaknesses of the Articles?

Discuss the attitudes of the Founding Fathers toward slavery. What steps did they take that restricted and weakened that form of bondage?

The Shot Heard Round the World

Henry Fairlie

"Here once the embattled farmers stood
And fired the shot heard round the
   world."
> —Hymn sung at the completion
> of the Battle Monument
> Concord, July 4, 1837

The claim in Emerson's line is expansive. Can it be true that the shot was heard round the world—when there were no satellites, no television, no radio, no telephone? Let us see.

It then took from five to six weeks for news to cross the Atlantic. (The first regular passenger service between England and the colonies was instituted in 1755.) Thus the news of the "battles" of Lexington and Concord, fought on April 19, 1775, appeared on May 29 in the London press, from which the French papers, as usual, took their news of America; and from them the press in the rest of Europe picked up the story. By June 19 it appeared in a newspaper as far away as St. Petersburg. Similarly the news of the Declaration of Independence was first published in a London newspaper on August 17, 1776; a week later it appeared in papers in Hamburg, on August 30 in Sweden, and on September 2 in Denmark. The actions in Lexington and Concord had been no more than skirmishes in two villages whose names Europeans can never have heard before. Yet the news excited editors across Europe, and they knew it would arouse their readers. The saw *at once* the size of the event.

In 1775-76 the French Revolution had not sounded its tocsin to the peoples of Europe. Most of them lived under the rule of a few absolute monarchs: Louis XVI in France; Maria Theresa (as dowager empress) and her son Joseph II in Austria and the Holy Roman Empire;

Frederick the Great in Prussia; Catherine the Great in Russia; and Christian VII in Denmark. It was the age of the "enlightened despots," who genuinely had the welfare of their subjects at heart, but though they proclaimed the right of their peoples to be well governed, they did not acknowledge their right to govern themselves. The only monarch who had (sourly) learned the ABCs of freedom was, paradoxically, the one against whom the colonists were rebelling. The English were far freer than any peoples on the Continent. But the English reaction to the news from America is more interesting if we know how the shot was heard on the other side of the English channel.

Maria Theresa had ascended the throne in 1740 at the age of 23. Even then she realized that the old order could not survive, and set about instituting a series of effective reforms. Her scarcely less remarkable son, who succeeded his father as co-regent in 1765, produced the most thought-out exposition of the duties of an enlightened despot. They received the news of the Declaration at about the same time it reached London, and two weeks before it found its way through the heavy censorship into the daily press in Vienna. Taking a dim view of popular uprisings, Maria Theresa expressed to George III her "hearty desire to see the restoration of obedience and tranquility in every quarter of his dominions," and Joseph told the British ambassador, "The cause in which England is engaged . . . is the cause of all sovereigns who have joint interest in the maintenance of due subordination . . . in all the surrounding monarchies."

The rulers feared that their subjects would see the American action not as a rebellion against a rightful monarch in his own territories—there had been plenty of rebellions against European

sovereigns—but as the proclamation of a revolutionary doctrine of universal application, as the Declaration indeed announced it to be. Thus, although the Declaration was at last allowed through the censorship in Vienna, when the *Wienerisches Diarium* the next year explained the War of Independence as a clash between two political principles— monarchy and popular sovereignty— Maria Theresa was outraged, even though the paper had covered itself by printing an editorial saying that this view of the rebellion was mistaken.

Similarly, when the news of Lexington and Concord got through the censors into the *Sanktpeterburgskie Vedemosti,* the Americans were, in deference to the Empress Catherine, firmly called "rebels." In 1780, when Catherine read the Abbé Raynal's history of Europe's dominions overseas and came to his chapter on the American Revolution, she wrote to a friend: "The American record is filled with declarations in which there is too little that is reasonable and too much that is unbecoming impertinence."

IN BELGIUM, WHICH WAS THEN UNDER the rule of Austria, it was clear that the subjects of the enlightened despots might take the American "impertinence" as an example. From as early as 1766, when the *Gazette des Pays-Bas* in Brussels reported the remonstrations of colonial assemblies in America, the Belgian press followed American affairs intently. In four Belgian newspapers and journals the Maryland Constitution was printed in 1777, the Massachusetts Constitution in 1780, some of a collection of the constitutions of all 13 states in 1783, Virginia's Code of Civil and Criminal Laws in 1786, and in the following year the U.S. Constitution in full. This steady flow of news (including the reports of the war and of American victories) could only stir up the middle class in Belgium. They enjoyed neither national independence nor a constitution guaranteeing any basic political rights, while each day the Americans were remaking their political and civil society before the eye of the world. By 1787 a strong movement for independence and a new constitution was growing in Belgium.

In the debates that were provoked in Europe we can see how the shot was heard. We can follow them (as they were conducted in the press) through the 25 or so out-of-the-way historical monographs, memoirs, and so on, that are the main source of this story. Throughout the debates a constant appeal was made to the example of America. Liberty had been crushed in Poland, was struggling in Holland, said Lambert d'Outrement, a lawyer in Liege, but it had been maintained in England, and triumphed in America: "What will be the lot of the Austrian Low Countries?" There could be only one answer. Belgium would try itself. Toward the end of 1789 the States-General of the Austrian Netherlands deposed Joseph II and proclaimed the *United States* of Belgium. The Belgian Declaration of Independence (and the equivalent declarations of the provinces of Belgium, like the states in America) followed the American Declaration faithfully. In the Manifeste de la Province de Flandre (1790), "the Course of Human Events" became *Un Concours de circonstances . . . extraordinaires,"* and continued: *"En conséquence . . . au juge suprême de l'Univers . . . a droit d'être un Etat libre et indépendant"*—almost word for word the American original.

Thus, although the French Revolution had by then erupted, the inspiration was coming from America. The working people of Europe, it was said in the Belgian debates, must inevitably look to America. They had learned that conditions for the likes of them were better there, and many were emigrating. A telling use was made of America's distance from the mother country, since Belgium, like many of the territories of the Austrian Empire, was remote from the imperial capital and government in Vienna. Moreover when, during the War of Independence, the absolute monarchs of Europe entered into relations (and even alliances) with the Americans, they were in effect endorsing revolution. The

monarchs might say that the American Revolution was intolerable, but by their actions they were telling their peoples that revolution was not a crime, but as d'Outrement said, *"un beau monument élevé à La Liberté."*

THE SIGNIFICANCE EUROPEANS ATTACHED to America was underlined by the deftness and even courage with which editors across the Continent managed to circumvent the censorship. In 1775-76 Denmark was a significant power. It included Norway (and Greenland, a Norwegian possession), Schleswig and Holstein, Iceland, and three West Indian islands, St. Croix, St. Thomas, and St. John (which were later sold to the United States). Given the insanity of Christian VII, it was governed by a court party as an enlightened despotism, and as usual a significant part of the extensive bureaucracy was the ever watchful censorship.

On August 23, 1776, the *Altonaischer Mercurius* (a German-language newspaper published in Altona in Holstein) printed an edited version of the Declaration, which was then translated and printed at the top of the front page of the *Kiobenhavske* [Copenhagen] *Tidender,* the newspaper with the largest circulation in Denmark. In both papers it appeared uncut as far as the sentence "The History of the present King of Great-Britain is a History of repeated Injuries and Usurpations, all having in direct Object the Establishment of absolute Tyranny over these States." The trouble was that the intermittently insane George III was one of the demented Christian's closest allies. So in the above sentence, the words "King of Great-Britain" were replaced by "the present ministry of Great Britain." But the Declaration continued with the long list of grievances against George, and it was all too likely that any Danish reader would have begun ticking off in his mind his own grievances against the Danish monarchy. Ingeniously, the *Mercurius* solved the problem by publishing the Declaration in two halves, the second (with the grievances) appearing on August 26, in which all the references to King George were replaced by the anonymous *"Er"* (he). This appeased the censors; it cannot have fooled the readers.

How different it was in the New World. Over in the West Indies, the only Danish newspaper, the *Royal Danish American Gazette,* published (signifi-

cantly) in English, printed the complete Declaration as early as August 17, even placing it prominently on the front page, which was otherwise reserved for advertising. The Danes in the colonies seemed themselves to have become Americans.

It was not only the editors in Denmark (and elsewhere), nosy for news, who were excited by the events in America. As early as October 22, 1776, A. P. Bernstorff, the great Danish minister for foreign affairs, wrote to a friend: "The public here is extremely occupied with the rebels [in America], not because they know the cause, but because the mania of independence in reality has infected all the spirits, and the poison has spread imperceptibly from the works of the philosophes all the way out to the village schools." Those last eight words, from such a source, tell us something we need to know.

So does a firsthand glimpse of the popular mood in Copenhagen. The *Aftenpost* carried a column—as we would now call it—by one Edmund Balling, describing life in the city; it sounds like a city column by Jimmy Breslin or Mike Royko. Balling dropped into alehouses, which he described as "our political schools of Fencing, those bourgeois Art of War Listening Rooms, where our little Politici, during a Glass of Ale, a Pinch of Snuff and a Pipe of Tobacco," tossed about the issues of the day. At the end of 1776 he found them debating the War of Independence. One said the Americans were rebels, and "ought to be beaten over the Forehead like Bullocks"; another countered that "the English ought to be thrashed"; a third had no doubt that the English had got "something to chew on"; and a sausage-stuffer called it an "accursed War" because the rice from South Carolina had become so dear, and what could he now stuff his sausages with in place of meat? On January 12, 1778, Balling told of a man entering an alehouse (after reading the news, one guesses, of Burgoyne's defeat): "Good evening, Gentlemen! Ha! Ha! Have we the newspapers? Well, what does England say now? . . . Yes, this War will likely make a rather considerable Change in Europe."

As in Belgium, the impact did not lessen even after America achieved its independence. In 1820 a Danish civil servant, C. F. von Schmidt-Phiseldeck, called the Fourth of July "this forever memorable day." And in our own time a Danish historian has said that "the Declaration of Independence had a decisive impact on the course of events leading to the attainment in 1849 of Denmark's first democratic constitution.''

BUT AS WE COME ACROSS THE EDITORS, their newspapers, and their readers, the European response is telling us something very important about the American Revolution itself. It was carried in the colonies and overseas by the assertiveness of the American middle class. One of George III's more apt comments was that his sovereignty was being challenged by a lot of ''grocers.'' Marx was really saying no more when he declared that ''the American Revolution sounded the tocsin for the European bourgeoisie,'' and gave ''the first impulse to the European Revolution.'' Lenin later said the War of Independence was ''one of those great, truly liberating, truly revolutionary wars''—something that cannot be said of the revolution he wrought in Russia.

Two vigorous merchant cities—Hamburg and Dubrovnik—illustrate the response of a newly aggressive merchant class in Europe. Hamburg was a free port, as most of its dock area still is (its official name even now is the Free and Hanseatic City of Hamburg), and since the Reformation had been the proud refuge of Protestants, other dissidents, and refugees. Ports are naturally liberal, being used to strangers, with their different cultures and ideas. When the Declaration was published in the *Staats und Gelehrte Zeitung,* its citizens naturally sympathized with the colonies in their claim to be a free trading nation, with which Hamburg could expand its commercial ties (as it did after the war), greatly reinforcing its prosperity. Completing the story, another cargo would eventually stream through Hamburg: a vast number of immigrants to the New World from Russia and Eastern Europe. Dubrovnik had risen to be a powerful merchant republic in the Middle Ages, and had existed since then (virtually independent) under the protection, in succession, of Venice, Hungary, and Turkey—until Napoleon, with his usual disrespect for history, abolished the republic in 1806, the same year in which he occupied Hamburg. Again, far away on the Adriatic, the citizens of a strong merchant port were stimulated by the news from America, a point made in a book published by the city of Dubrovnik to celebrate the bicentennial of the Declaration.

IT IS THE RESPONSE OF THE MIDDLE class in Europe that throws light on the attitudes in England. To the ruling class in England the Declaration of Independence did not herald the dawn of a new age, or introduce new abstract principles of freedom and equality that had a universal application. In fact, it seemed to them less of a threat than it did to the ruling monarchs on the Continent, since they enjoyed many of the freedoms the Americans were claiming. It was to them a very local document, a list (as indeed it was) of very local grievances. Neither it nor any shot, in their view, was heard round the world. Both had been aimed, after all, at them; and on the whole they took it like gentlemen.

Here was a war in which the First British Empire, as it is known to history, was falling, and it is natural we should wish that the author of *The Decline and Fall of the Roman Empire,* who was a member of Parliament throughout the war, had offered a long historical perspective or a few grand philosophical reflections on so great an event. But Edward Gibbon's attitude was not only devious; it was corrupt, even if in the accepted manner of the day. No one can blame him for wishing to write the great book, or for wishing to receive some patronage as he labored at his task. He looked, of course, to the government for an appointment, and accepted the post of one of the Lords Commissioner of Trade and Plantations. With this sinecure, his voice and vote were bought by George III and his ministers, which makes one appreciate even more the king's dig at him one day, ''Scribble, scribble, scribble, eh, Mr. Gibbon?''

At the end of the difficult parliamentary session in 1775, Gibbon was glad to get away, saying that ''having saved the British I must destroy the Roman Empire.'' But this little jest was capped by an American. Horace Walpole reported with delight in a letter in 1781: ''Dr. [Benjamin] Franklin . . . said he would furnish Mr. Gibbon with materials for writing the History of the Decline of the British Empire.'' A lampoon went the rounds in London during the war. Attributed to Charles James Fox, a dauntless leader of the opposition and staunch friend of the Americans, two verses ran:

King George in a fright
Lest Gibbon should write
The history of England's disgrace
    Thought no way so sure
    His pen so secure

As to give the historian a place.
    His book well describes
    How corruption and bribes
O'erthrew the great empire of Rome;
    And his rantings declare
    A degeneracy there
Which his conduct exhibits at home.

We do not get wit like that from our politicians now.

Whether in Gibbon's own jest, Franklin's quip, or Fox's lampoon, there is nothing to suggest that the governing class in London could work itself into any great passion over the American war—neither the supporters nor the opponents of the American cause. (Though the consummate and by then aged orator William Pitt, for whom Pittsburgh was named, reinforced his impassioned philippic in defense of the American colonists by collapsing unconscious on the floor of the House at the end.)

WE ALSO KNOW HOW THE AMERICAN news was received outside London. In December 1775 the daily journal of the Rev. James Woodforde (a country parson in Weston, Norfolk, of ordinary loyalty to the Crown) gave ''notice of a Fast being kept on Friday next concerning the present war between America and us.'' Note that the colonists are not called subjects or rebels, as on the Continent, but *America,* as if they were already a nation. The war then seems to have aroused little interest until there was another official Day of Prayer in 1780, for it was by then clear that God was not pulling his weight. So the good parson ''read the proper prayers on the Occasion, but there was no sermon preached. My Squire and Lady at the Church. . . . Sister Clarke, Nancy, Sam and myself all took it into our heads to take a good dose of Rhubarb on going to bed.'' Rhubarb is an astringent purgative—a very English way of disposing of the news of fresh disasters, rather like taking a ''nice cup o' tea'' in the Blitz.

In 1781 he recorded the news that ''Cornwallis and his whole army . . . are all taken by the Americans and French in Virginia.'' That is all; not dismay, no commotion, no anger. When it was all over, the news of the Treaty of Versailles was a ''joyful'' event, though England had suffered a great defeat and lost a vast possession. There remained only the aftermath, an entry as late as December 9, 1785: '' . . . to a poor soldier laterly [sic] arrived from America that had been wounded & is now ill gave 1 [shilling] and 6 [pence]"—a neglected veteran of an unpopular, unsuccessful war.

Throughout the war we could have found Horace Walpole at home in London, writing to his friends the letters that now fill 36 volumes in the Yale edition. One of Europe's most intelligent and cultivated men, he chose (happily for us) to be a spectator of great events rather than an actor in them. He returned again and again to the American question, urbane, tart, and outraged. Why are we in America? he asked, as 200 years later he might have asked about Vietnam. "We could even afford to lose America," he wrote as early as March 28, 1774. After Washington's victory at Trenton he wrote: "What politicians are those that have preferred the empty name of *sovereignty* to that of *alliance!* and forced subsidies to the golden age of oceans and commerce." The Americans, he pointed out to a friend, "do not pique themselves upon modern good breeding, but level at the officers, of whom they have slain a vast number." This savage amusement at the fact that the Americans "impertinently" fired on English officers is a wholly accurate reflection of "the amazing heights which pro-Americanism could reach in London," as one researcher found it in even the popular novels of the day. The Boston Tea Party was to him the symbol of English official stupidity: "Mrs. Britannia orders her senate to proclaim America a continent of cowards, and vote it should be starved unless it drink tea with her."

By the end of 1777 Walpole was writing: "We have been horribly the aggressors." A week after the capitulation at Yorktown, but before he had news of it, he proclaimed: "The English in America are as much my countrymen as those born in the parish of St. Martin's in the Field; and when my countrymen quarrel, I think I am free to wish better to the sufferers than to the aggressors; nor can I see how my love of my country obliges me to wish well to what I despise. . . . Were I young and of heroic texture, I would go to America." It is clear from all the evidence that the English people as a whole could not have their hearts in a war against their "countrymen."

BUT THERE WAS ONE EXCEPTION TO THIS generally unexcited and unideological response in England, and it is illuminated by the reaction on the Continent. The merchants of the City of London and of other expanding cities of the new middle class in England identified their own interests closely with those of the colonists. The London press, almost without exception, was the voice of this class. With the introduction of the tax on the colonists' trade in molasses and sugar in 1764, the *London Chronicle* at once reported from the west coast port of Bristol, which depended on the American trade, that "the principal merchants of the city intend to support with all their interest the independent free trade of the American colonies." In the numerous and remarkably free English newspapers we can trace how this argument from interest developed steadily into an ideological assertion. As the Americans, during those extraordinary ten years from 1765 to 1775, worked out the philosophical grounds on which they would claim independence, the English merchant class found itself examining and then adopting the same arguments.

In resisting taxation "without representation" by the English Parliament, the Americans (those "grocers") argued that in *English custom* and "natural law" there was a power above Parliament—in short, the Constitution in revolutionary thinking, in the work of the Founding Fathers, and forever afterward in the mind of America. The idea that Parliament was sovereign was then a fairly new development, and there were many at home who objected to it, but it was the American colonists who clarified the issue by their dogged resistance. Moreover, the English middle class had its own doubts about the justice of the parliamentary system as it then existed. The Industrial Revolution was reaching its flood, and beyond London many of the rising middle-class cities such as Manchester and Sheffield were not represented at all. So the American cry of "no taxation without representation" drew a strong echo from them.

When the news of the Boston Tea Party reached England, the *London Packet* called such resistance lawful and even honorable against "tyrannic" measures. After Lexington and Concord the *London Evening Post* said that "the prevailing toast in every company of true Englishmen is, 'Victory to the Americans, and re-establishment to the British Constitution.' " (No one was arrested or imprisoned in England for supporting the Americans.) Thus in England as in Europe the American cause had been translated into a universal cause—by a rising class. The American Revolution represented the spontaneously international ideology of this class, which was feeling its strength in Europe, growing assertive in England, and already established in America, even able to organize and arm itself for war.

Of all the dramatic assertions in the Declaration of Independence, none is more "impertinent" than the assurance with which the 13 colonies said they had decided to "assume among the Powers of the Earth, the separate and equal Station" to which they were entitled. Yet the presumption was not as great as it seems. As early as 1765 a correspondent in the *London Magazine* said: "Little doubt can be entertained, that this vast country will in time become the most prosperous empire that perhaps the world has ever seen." This was widely appreciated, and both the English and Europeans were aware of the rapid increase in America's population, and of Franklin's estimate that it would double every 25 years. Shortly after Lexington and Concord the *Chester Chronicle* quoted Bishop Berkeley's poem, "Westward the course of Empire takes its way."

ONCE THE NEWS OF THE FATEFUL SHOT reached the courts of Europe, the monarchs were alert to the effect the American rebellion might have on the balance of power in Europe. George III at once dispatched a personal envoy to Catherine the Great, to request fewer than 20,000 Russian troops for help in suppressing the American insurrection. But Catherine did not have a high opinion of George, and refused to supply any soldiers or to make the treaty that Britain wanted. She and her government were extremely well informed about American affairs, and on receiving news of the Declaration, the counselor of the Russian Embassy in London wrote to the Russian foreign minister, N. I. Panin, saying that both it and the prosecution of a formal war against Britain "offer evidence of all the courage of leadership" in America.

King George had no better luck in Vienna. Austria had been allied with France since 1756, but by 1775 it was exhausted by the Seven Years' War, and urgently trying to resist the rise of Prussia in the east under Frederick the Great. Maria Theresa saw that Austria needed to secure its position in the west by friendship with both England and France,

2. REVOLUTIONARY AMERICA

and by 1776 wished to revive her earlier friendship with England. In 1777 she wrote to her daughter Marie Antoinette (who had none of her inquiring intelligence or even savvy, and paid the price at the guillotine) that the "war in America" troubled her, as well it might since it pitted France and England against each other. She therefore skillfully maintained Austria's neutrality throughout the war, and forbade both English and American recruiting in Hapsburg lands.

This response of the European monarchs—Denmark also remained neutral, in spite of its alliance with England and its far-flung shipping and trading interests—was the clearest recognition that America had indeed become a new nation on something like equal terms with the oldest and most imperious in the Old World, at once acting and being accepted on the stage of Europe as one of the "Powers of the Earth."

It must be remembered that the enlightened despots were significant figures of the Enlightenment; Catherine corresponded regularly with Voltaire.

There was therefore nothing particularly remarkable in the fact that the chief assistant to Panin as the Russian foreign minister was D. I. Fonvizin, whose plays boldly satirized the Russian aristocracy and the institution of serfdom. When Fonvizin traveled through Europe in 1777-78, he met Benjamin Franklin at a *rendez-vous des gens de lettres,* calling him in a letter to his sister "the glorious Franklin." (Franklin wrapped the European intellectuals around his little finger.) Another Russian, commenting on this meeting, wrote: "The representative of the young enlightenment of Russia was an interlocutor with the representative of young America." The excitement at such a meeting demonstrates yet another way in which the new United States, a child of the Enlightenment, impressed itself on Europe as already a mature nation.

THE STORY OF HOW THE SHOT WAS heard round the world carries obvious instructions. Any notion that the War of Independence was only a rebellion falls to the ground. Both rulers and their subjects saw it as a revolution of universal appeal. The dynamism of that appeal was derived from the fact that the Americans had already built a great trading nation and created not only a strong middle class in the process, but a society that as a whole was middle-class in its temper and energy. What is more, as a result of the preparation between 1765 and 1775—ten of the most creative years in political thinking in the history of the world—the Americans entered the War of Independence with a profound political philosophy that immediately lit fires round the world. They are not yet extinguished.

The names of two unknown villages, Lexington and Concord, became household words even as far as Dubrovnik and St. Petersburg. And on any Fourth of July one cannot help thinking of the few minutemen who took their stand on a bridge and sent the drilled Redcoats running with their tails between their legs back into Boston.

Declaration of Independence

★ ★ ★ ★

Dennis J. Mahoney

Dennis J. Mahoney is visiting assistant professor of political science at Claremont McKenna College. He received his Ph.D. in government from Claremont Graduate School, and he is assistant editor of the Encyclopedia of the Constitution.

America's most fundamental constitutional document was adopted by the United States in Congress on July 4, 1776. The Declaration of Independence may carry little weight in the courts; it may, for all its being placed at the head of the *Statutes at Large* and described in the United States Code as part of the "organic law," have no legally binding force. Yet it is the Declaration that constitutes the American nation. John Hancock, president of the Continental Congress, transmitting the Declaration to the several states, described it as "the Ground & Foundation of a future Government." James Madison, the Father of the Constitution, calls it "the fundamental Act of Union of these States."

The Declaration of Independence is the definitive statement for the American policy of the ends of government, of the necessary conditions for the legitimate exercise of political power, and of the sovereignty of the people who establish the government and, when circumstances warrant, may alter or abolish it. No mere tract in support of a bygone event, the Declaration was and remains the basic statement of the meaning of the United States as a political entity.

The historical event, the Revolution, provided the occasion for making that statement. Richard Henry Lee, on instructions from the Virginia convention, introduced three resolutions on June 7, 1776: to declare the colonies independent, to establish a confederation, and to seek foreign alliances. Each of the resolutions was referred to a select committee, one of which was charged with preparing "a declaration to the effect of the first resolution." Lee's motion was adopted on July 2, the Declaration two days later.

Although the Congress had appointed for the task a distinguished committee, including John Adams of Massachusetts, Benjamin Franklin of Pennsylvania, Roger Sherman of Connecticut, and Robert Livingston of New York, Thomas Jefferson of Virginia actually penned the Declaration. So well did Jefferson express the sentiments of the Congress that his committee colleagues made only a few changes in his draft.

Jefferson, by his own account, turned to neither book nor pamphlet for ideas. Nor did he seek to expound a novel political theory. His aim was to set forth the common sense of the American people on the subject of political legitimacy. To be sure, there are ideas, and even phrases, that recall John Locke: the Declaration follows Locke in stressing the natural rights of man as the foundation of the political order. But the concept of man's natural autonomy, modifiable only by his consent to the rule of others in a social compact, was long acknowledged in the American colonies; it inhered in congregational church polity, and it was transmitted through such theoretical and legal writers as Emerich de Vattel, Jean-Jacques Burlamaqui, and Samuel Pufendorf, as well as by the authors of *Catos' Letters* and other popular works.

The Declaration of Independence has a structure that emphasizes its content. It begins with a preamble, by which the document is addressed not to the king of Great Britain nor to the English public, but to the world at large, to the "opinion of mankind." Moreover, the purpose of the document is said explicitly to be to "declare the causes" that impelled the Americans to declare their independence from Britain.

There had been other revolutions in British history, but this one was different. From the barons at Runnymede to the Whigs who drove James II from the throne, British insurgents had appealed to the historic rights of Englishmen. The declarations they extracted—from Magna Carta to the Bill of Rights—were the assurances of their kings that the ancient laws obtaining in their island would be respected. The preamble of the Declaration of Independence makes clear that this is not the case with the American Revolution. The case of Britain's rule in America was to be held up to a universal standard and exposed as tyrannical before a "candid world." Against the self-same standard all government everywhere could be measured. Everyone who reads the Declaration with his eyes open must be struck by this fact: the Declaration justifies the independence of the American nation by appeal not to an English or an Anglo-American standard, but to the universal standard of human rights.

There follows next a statement of the ends of government and of the conditions under which obedience to government is proper. "All men are created equal . . . endowed by their Creator with certain unalienable rights . . . among [which] are life, liberty, and the pursuit of happiness." Equality is the condition of men prior to government—logically prior, not chronologically. But that equality is not equality of condition, or even equality of opportunity; certainly it is not equality of intelligence, strength, or skill. The equality that men possess by nature is equality of right. There is, among human beings, none with a right to rule the others; God may claim to rule human beings by right, human beings may rule the brutes by right, but no human being has a claim to rule another by right.

The rights with which men are endowed are said to be "unalienable." That is, human rights may be neither usurped nor surrendered, neither taken away nor given up. The Declaration rejects the false doctrine of Thomas Hobbes (more gently echoed by William Blackstone) that men on entering society and submitting to government yield their natural rights and retain only "civil" rights, dispensed and revoked at the pleasure of the sovereign.

"To secure these rights, governments are instituted among men." The purpose of government is to protect the natural rights that men possess, but which, in the absence of government, they are not secure enough to enjoy. Government in society is not optional, it is a necessary condition for the enjoyment of natural rights. But the institution of government does not create an independent motive or will in society. All just powers of government derive "from the consent of the governed."

The Declaration asserts that the people retain the right of revolution, the right to substitute new constitutions for old. But it also asserts that the exercise of that right is properly governed by prudence—a prudence that the Americans had shown in the face of great provocation.

The next section of the Declaration is a bill of indictment against George III on the charge of attempted tyranny. The specifications are divided almost evenly between procedural and substantive offenses. The fact that the king—by his representatives in America—assembled the provincial legislatures at places far from their capitals or required persons accused of certain crimes to be transported to England for trial, evinced a tyrannical design by disregard of procedural safeguards. But even when the established procedures were followed, as in giving or withholding assent to legislation, the result could be tyrannical; for example, the suppression of trade, the discouragement of population growth, and the keeping of standing armies in peacetime were acts according to the forms of due process that unjustly deprived the Americans of their liberty. Still other acts, such as making the royal assent conditional on surrender of the right of representation and withholding assent from bills to create provincial courts, were tyrannical in both form and substance.

The most critical charge, the thirteenth, was that the king had conspired with others—the British Parliament—to subject the Americans to a jurisdiction foreign to their constitution. The Americans had come to see that a compact existed between the British king and each of his American provinces by which the king exercised executive power in each even as he did in the home island, and that the common executive was the sole governmental connection between America and Britain. The imperial constitution, as the Americans had come to understand it, no more permitted the British legislature to regulate the internal affairs of Massachusetts or Virginia than it did the provincial legislatures to regulate the internal affairs of England or Scotland. But the British legislature could not breach the compact between the king and the provinces because Parliament was not a party to that compact. The king, however, by conniving at that usurpation, did breach the compact.

The final five accusations deal with the fact that Britain and America were at war. One charge that Jefferson included, but Congress struck out, accused the king of waging "cruel war against human nature itself" by tolerating the introduction of slavery into the colonies and sanctioning the slave trade. Only two states, Georgia and South Carolina, objected to the passage, but the others acquiesced to preserve unanimity. In any case, the condemnation of slavery was implicit in the opening paragraphs of the Declaration.

The conclusion of the document asserts that the Americans had tried peaceably to resolve their differences with the mother country while remaining within the empire, and in a final paragraph contains the actual declaration that the erstwhile colonies were now independent states.

Whether the colonies became independent collectively or individually was a matter of debate for at least a hundred years. At the Constitutional Convention of 1787, James Wilson and Alexander Hamilton advanced the former position, while Luther Martin maintained the latter position. At least until the Civil War, different theories of the union arose based on differing interpretations of the act of declaring independence.

Considered as a tract for the times, as a manifesto for the revolutionary cause, the Declaration marks an important step in American constitutional development. The resistance to British misrule in America had, at least since the French and Indian Wars, been based on an appeal to the British constitution. The Americans had charged that the imposition of taxes by a body in which they were not represented and the extension to them of domestic legislation by a Parliament to whose authority they had not consented violated the ancient traditions of British government. The constitution, that is, the arrangement of offices and powers within the government and the privileges of the subjects, had been overridden or altered by the British Parliament. Although the differences between the American provinces and the mother country were great, they were differences about, and capable of resolution within, the British constitutional framework. The liberties that the colonists had claimed were based on prescription.

When independence was declared, the British constitution became irrelevant. The liberties claimed in the Declaration are grounded in natural law; they are justified by reason, not by historical use. The American Revolution was, therefore, the first and most revolutionary of modern revolutions. Not the quantity of carnage but the quality of ideas distinguishes the true revolution. In the declaration was recognized a higher law to which every human law—constitution or statute—is answerable. The British constitution, as it then existed, was tried by the standards of that higher law and found guilty of tyranny. As the British constitution, so every constitution, including the American Constitution, may be tried; and on conviction the sentence is that the bonds of allegiance are dissolved.

Much of American constitutional history has revolved around the attempt to reconcile the nation's political practice with the teachings of the Declaration. The gravest problem in our constitutional history was slavery. Although the Congress struck out Jefferson's condemnation of slavery as "cruel war against human nature," the founders clearly understood that slavery was incompatible with the principles of liberty and equality that they espoused.

Chief Justice Roger B. Taney, in *Dred Scott* v. *Sandford* in 1857, tried to read the black man out of the Declaration. This was a distortion of the history and the plain meaning of the document. Even John C. Calhoun had not stooped to this, choosing rather to denounce the Declaration than to pervert its meaning. The antithesis between the Declaration and the existence of chattel slavery was recognized by the slave power in Congress when, during the gag rule controversy, any petition referring to the Declaration of Independence was automatically treated as a petition against slavery and laid on the table.

The intimate connection between the Declaration of Independence (and therefore of antislavery) and the Constitution became the theme of the political career of Abraham Lincoln. When the slavery question divided the nation, Lincoln, with the voice of an Old Testament prophet, called for rededication to the principles of the Declaration. During Lincoln's presidency, the Civil War, begun as a challenge to the Union, was won as a struggle to vindicate the Declaration of Independence. It was fought to prove that a nation "dedicated to the proposition that all men are created equal" could endure.

The putative antagonism between America's two basic documents, invented by the slave power in the nineteenth century, was revived as a political theme during the Progressive movement. Authors like J. Allen Smith and Charles A. Beard contended that the Constitution's system of federalism, separation of powers, checks and balances, and bicameralism frustrated the unfettered will of the people allegedly set free by the Declaration. Smith and Beard posited a virtually bloodless coup d'e'tat by wealthy conservatives—a "Thermidorian reaction" to the success of the democratic revolution. Thus constitutional forms were attacked as illegitimate, not withstanding that they were intended to preserve the Declaration's regime of limited government.

The Beard-Smith thesis remained popular as long as the Constitution seemed to be a barrier to social reform and redistribution of wealth and income by the government. The later twentieth century witnessed another change in the attitude of intellectuals toward the two documents. President Franklin D. Roosevelt appointed a sufficient number of Supreme Court justices to insure that the Court would ratify his policies as constitutional. Later, the Warren Court devised a host of new "constitutional" rights and remedies for criminal defendants, ethnic minorities, and political dissenters. The Constitution was transformed into a "living" document, that is, one almost infinitely malleable in the hands of enlightened judges. History, understood as progress, rather than nature thereafter dictated the ends of government. The Declaration of Independence, with its references to "the laws of nature and of nature's God," although revered as a symbol of American nationality, ceased to be regarded as the source of authoritative guidance for American politics.

The Constitution of the United States is sometimes pronounced, by scholars or politicians, to be neutral with respect to political principles. But the Constitution was not framed in a vacuum. It was devised as the Constitution of the nation founded by the Declaration of Independence. The Declaration prescribes the ends and limits of government, and proclaims the illegitimacy of any government that fails to serve those ends or observe those limits. The Constitution is thus ruled by the Declaration. The Constitution provides for the government of the regime created by the Declaration: the regime of equality and liberty.

READINGS SUGGESTED BY THE AUTHOR:

Becker, Carl L. *The Declaration of Independence.* Cambridge: Harvard University Press, 1922.

Diamond, Martin. "The Declaration and the Constitution: Liberty, Democracy and the Founders." *The Public Interest* 42 (1975): 39-55.

Hawke, David. *A Transaction of Free Men: The Birth and Course of the Declaration of Independence.* New York: Charles Scribner's Sons, 1964.

Jaffa, Harry V. *The Crisis of the House Divided.* New York: Doubleday, 1959.

White, Morton. *The Philosophy of the American Revolution.* New York: Oxford University Press, 1978.

Winter at Valley Forge

***Although they suffered from privation, hunger, and cold, the soldiers of the
Continental Army emerged from this encampment a revitalized
and trained combat force.***

Joan Marshall-Dutcher

*Joan Marshall-Dutcher is park historian
at Valley Forge.*

Valley Forge, Pennsylvania. December
19, 1777. Under the command of General George Washington, the Continental
Army of the newly formed United States
of America—recently defeated at Brandywine and stalemated at Germantown—
arrived at the frigid site to face a nightmare winter. A light snow fell as twelve
thousand weary men trudged up Gulph
Road to the area designated only days
before as winter quarters.

Cold. Hungry. Diseased. Dirty. Wet.
Cramped. Ragged. These images characterize the Continental soldiers who endured the six-month encampment that
today symbolizes the epitome of suffering and sacrifice during the struggle to
win American independence.

They came from Virginia, North Carolina, Rhode Island, New York, Pennsylvania, New Hampshire, and every other
American colony: Lewis Hurd, age seventeen, a private from Connecticut; Benjamin Blossom, about thirty-one years
old, a soldier from Massachusetts; George
Ewing, twenty-three, an ensign of the
Seventh Company in the Third New Jersey Regiment; Joseph Plumb Martin,

only fifteen when he enlisted in Connecticut's Third Company on July 6, 1776,
sixteen when he arrived at Valley Forge.
Some still boys as young as twelve, and
others in their fifties and sixties, the
soldiers included blacks and native
Americans as well as Caucasians.

The men carried with them what few
possessions they had, including their
muskets (by far the most popular weapon).
If he did not have a cartouche or cartridge box, the infantryman carried a
powder horn, hunting bag, and bullet
pouch. His knapsack or haversack held
any extra clothing he was fortunate
enough to own, along with a blanket, a
plate and spoon, and perhaps a knife,
fork, and tumbler. Canteens were often
shared with others and six to eight men
shared cooking utensils. According to
Joseph Plumb Martin, "We had always,
in the army, to carry our cooking utensils
in our hands by turns. [At] this time, as
we were not overburdened with provisions, our mess had put ours into our
kettle, it not being very heavy, as it was
made of plated iron."

Many a soldier's shoes had been destroyed by the long marches, and clothing
and blankets were tattered almost beyond
serviceability. Hundreds of men were
declared unfit for duty owing to these
shortages.

The first order of business was shelter.
An active field officer was appointed for

each brigade to superintend the business
of hutting. General Orders December 18
specified the size and design for these log
structures: fourteen by sixteen feet, a
door at the front, and a fireplace in the
rear. Twelve men were to occupy each
hut. The officers' huts, located to the
rear, would house fewer men. Each brigade would also build a hospital, fifteen
by twenty-five feet. Many of the brigadier generals used local farmhouses as
their quarters. (Some, including Henry
Knox, later moved into huts to be closer
to their men.)

Despite these specifications, hut size
and location varied. Few of the men
were skilled craftsmen; tools were at a
premium; the troops were exhausted;
and clothing was in short supply. On
Christmas Day, Jonathan Todd, a surgeon's mate from Connecticut, recorded:
"We have but one Dull ax to build a
Logg Hutt When it will be done knows
not." Yet on the nineteenth of January,
Todd wrote to his father: "I will give you
a description of our hutt which is built
Nearly after the same Model of the
Others—it is 18 Feet Long & 16 broad
two rooms and two chimneys at opposite
Corners of the house—the Floor is made
of split Loggs as is the Partition &
Door—the Whole of it was made with
one Poor ax & not another Tool—we
were not more than a fortnight in making
of it although Never more than three men

From *American History Illustrated,* November/December 1990, pp. 36-41. Reprinted through the courtesy of Cowles
Magazines, publishers of *American History Illustrated.*

Work'd at once-the Roof is not the best in Wet weather oak slabs Cover's with Turf & Earth—Our Inards work is not yet Completed."

The primitive cabins provided greater comfort and warmth than the tents used by the men when on campaign. But after months of housing unwashed men and food waste, these cramped quarters fostered discomfort and disease. Albigence Waldo complained, "my Skin & eyes are almost spoil'd with continual smoke."

Thousands of Continental troops suffered from physical afflictions, including putrid fever, itch, diarrhea, dysentery, pneumonia, and rheumatism. Hundreds died. In January the Hospital Department inoculated between two and three thousand men against smallpox. Jedediah Huntington wrote to his brother, "The Troops who have not had the Small Pox are to receive the Infection in Camp in a few Days. Should any Men be coming this Way, on Business to be done in Camp, twill be necessary they should be those who have had that Distemper."

The army was continually plagued with shortages of food, clothing, and equipment. Soldiers relied both on their home states and on the Continental Congress for these necessities. Poor organization, a shortage of wagoners, limited forage for the horses, the devaluation of the Continental currency, spoilage, and capture by the British all contributed to prevent these critical supplies from arriving at camp. An estimated 34,577 pounds of meat and 168 barrels of flour per day were needed to feed the army. Shortages were particularly acute in December and February.

"To see men without clothes to cover their nakedness," Washington wrote admiringly of his soldiers on December 23, "without blankets to lie on, without shoes . . . without a house or hut to cover them until those could be built, and submitting without a murmur, is a proof of patience and obedience which, in my opinion, can scarcely be paralleled."

To alleviate the critical food shortage, Washington sent foraging expeditions into the surrounding countryside to round up cattle. In February three public markets opened. Farmers were encouraged to sell their produce. "Fresh pork, fat turkey, goose, rough skinned potatoes, turnips, Indian meal, sourcrout, leaf tobacco, new milk, cider, and small beer" were included in the list of articles published in the *Pennsylvania Packet* and circulated in handbills.

Throughout the winter and early spring, men were frequently "on command," leaving camp on a variety of assignments. Some were away on the foraging expeditions, others were absent on furlough, and still others returned to their home states to recruit new troops. In January Jeremiah Greenman reported that "all ye spayr officers sent home to recrute a nother regiment & sum on furlow."

ON FEBRUARY 23, FRIEDRICH WILHELM Augustus Heinrich Ferdinand, Baron von Steuben, arrived at Valley Forge to offer his military skills to the patriotic cause. Washington assigned him the duties of acting inspector general and gave him the task of developing and carrying out a practical training program. One hundred men from various states were detailed to augment Washington's all-Virginian guard. Steuben personally trained this nucleus to march, to load and fire muskets, and to charge with bayonets. The life guard became a model company for drilling the entire army.

As no standard American training manuals existed, Steuben drafted his own, which he wrote at night in French. His aides translated this manual to English to be copied and given to the individual regiments and companies. The prescribed drill was then taught the following day. One soldier recalled, "I was kept constantly, when off duty, engaged in learning the Baron de Steuben's new Prussian exercise. It was a continual drill."

Steuben's aide, Pierre Duponceau, with the ability to enjoy his own mistakes, relates the following incident: " . . . the commander in chief ordered a sham fight to be executed by two divisions of our troops, one of which was under the command of Baron Steuben. In the capacity of his aide-de-camp I was sent to reconnoitre with orders to return immediately at full gallop, as soon as the enemy should be in sight. I rode on to the distance of about a quarter of a mile when I was struck with the sight of what I was since informed to be some red petticoats hanging on a fence to dry which I took for a body of British soldiers. I had forgotten, it seems, the contending parties were all Americans, and none of them clothed in scarlet regimentals. Full of my hallucination, I returned in haste to the camp, with the news that the enemy were marching upon us. Our division took the road I had indicated, and behold! the sight of the red petticoats was all the result of their movement. It excited of course a great deal of merriment, to my utter confusion and dismay."

Foreign officers were an essential part of the Continental Army, providing the military skills that the Americans lacked. Some, including Steuben and the Marquis de Lafayette, came as volunteers. Accompanying the young Lafayette as interpreter, Baron Johannes De Kalb quickly proved himself to Washington and won a commission as major general. Others, such as engineer Louis Lebèque de Presle Duportail, who designed the Valley Forge encampment, and his associates de Gouvion, de Laumoy, and de La Radiére had been given leave from the French Army to provide "covert" assistance to the Americans.

LITTLE IS KNOWN ABOUT THE WOMEN present at Valley Forge. Duponceau wrote: "Mrs. Washington had the courage to follow her husband in that dismal abode; other ladies also graced the scene. Among them was the lady of General (Nathanael] Greene, a handsome, elegant, and accomplished woman. Her dwelling was the resort of the foreign officers, because she understood and spoke the French language, and was well versed in French literature. There was also Lady Stirling, the wife of Major General Lord Stirling [William Alexander]; her daughter, Lady Kitty Alexander . . . and her companion Miss Nancy Brown, then a distinguished belle. There was Mrs. Biddle, the wife of Colonel Clement Biddle, who was at the head of the forage department, and some other ladies whose names I do not at present recollect. They often met at each other's quarters, and sometimes at General Washington's, where the evening was spent in conversation, over a dish of tea or coffee. There were no levees or formal soirees; no dancing, card playing, or amusement of any kind, except singing. Every gentleman or lady who could sing, was called upon in turn for a song."

Junior officers' wives probably remained in their husbands' homes and socialized among themselves. The enlisted men's wives lived and labored among the troops, some working as housekeepers for the officers; others as cooks, nurses, or laundresses.

Despite the privation, harsh weather, and long hours of drill, the troops occasionally found time and energy for recreation. The officers liked to play cricket (known also as wicket), and on at least one occasion were joined by His Excellency, the commander in chief. Amateur theatrical companies staged several dramas, including Joseph Addison's *Cato,* which played to a packed audience. Drinking provided a common recreation when spirits were available.

Duponceau relates an entertaining evening: "Once, with the Baron's [Steuben's] permission, his aides invited a number of young officers to dine at our quarters; on condition that none should be admitted that had on a whole pair of breeches. This was, of course, understood as 'pars pro toto'; but torn clothes were an indispensable requisite for admission; and in this, the guests were very sure not to fail. The dinner took place; the guests clubbed their rations, and we feasted sumptuously on tough beefsteaks and potatoes, with hickory nuts for our dessert. In lieu of wine, we had some kind of spirits, with which we made 'Salamanders'; that is to say, after filling our glasses, we set the liquor on fire and drank it up, flame and all. Such a set of ragged, and at the same time merry fellows were never brought together."

SPRING'S ARRIVAL SHIFTED THE BALANCE in favor of the beleaguered Continental soldiers. Under Steuben's direction, the Continentals had become professionals, if not career soldiers. New recruits arrived daily. South Carolina sent a regiment; Maryland provided two; another arrived from New York. Nathanael Greene accepted an appointment as quartermaster general and began to correct the supply problems plaguing the encampment. Morale steadily increased as confidence grew and weather and supplies improved.

Then, on Tuesday, May 5, 1778, an official alliance with France was announced; plans were quickly made "to set apart a day for gratefully acknowledging the divine Goodness" credited for this positive turn of events.

Historian Charles Royster described the celebration and the elevated troop morale: "[On] Wednesday, May 6, the troops assembled by brigades to hear a summary of the treaty. A cannon fired in the Artillery Park signaled the troops to be under arms. A second cannon was fired to signal the beginning of the march to the alarm posts on the lines. The brigades wheeled to the right by platoons and marched in order of battle. Once the brigades were in place, Washington and the general officers made a circuit round the lines to review the whole army at its posts. A person watching the soldiers could see 'the remarkable animation with which they performed the necessary salute as the general passed along.'

"When the review was over, Washington, his aides, and his guard took post on high ground to the rear. A flag on the redoubt was dropped, and the third cannon signaled the beginning of the 'feu de joie.' Washington's guard fired their muskets. Then thirteen cannon—six-pounders on a height in the northwest corner of the camp—were fired one by one. After the thirteenth, a running fire of musketry began on the right of the First Virginia Brigade and continued around the lines through the whole front line of the army. The second line took it up on the left and continued it back around to the starting place. A fourth cannon shot signaled the whole army to huzza, 'Long live the King of France.' The battalions reloaded, and again the thirteen cannon began a second running fire twice around the camp, with the huzza, and 'Long live the friendly European Powers.' Another reloading, another thirteen cannon, another 'feu de joie,' and then came the last huzza, 'To the American States.' "

With the arrival of warmer weather, the soldiers removed the chinking from their hut walls and burned musket cartridges inside "to purify the air." By May 14, the men began returning to tents. On June 10, the men "marcht about a mild [sic] over School kills River & Piched our tents in a field in providance town Ship."

ON JUNE 18, WASHINGTON DECLARED to the president of Congress: "Sir: I have the pleasure to inform Congress, that I was this minute advised by Mr. Roberts, that the Enemy evacuated the City [of Philadelphia] early this morning. . . . I have put Six Brigades in motion, and the rest of the Army are preparing to follow with all possible dispatch."

On June 19, 1778, six months to the day following their arrival, commander in chief George Washington and the Continental Army departed Valley Forge and marched to Monmouth, New Jersey, where, just nine days later, they engaged the British in battle. The army then continued on to eventual victory at Yorktown.

Proud. Spirited. Self-confident. Disciplined. Vigorous. Dignified. Valley Forge, June 19, 1778.

Recommended additional reading: Charles Royster's A Revolutionary People at War: The Continental Army and American Character 1775-1783 *(University of North Carolina, 1979) contains an excellent chapter on Valley Forge.*

A Troubled League

America had gained independence and a degree of unity, but shortcomings
in the Articles of Confederation prompted national leaders to seek
"a more perfect Union."

Brian McGinty

"The Republic is sick," Alexander Hamilton wrote in 1781, "and wants powerful remedies." Looking over the nation that boldly called itself the "United States of North America," Hamilton saw "a number of petty states, with the appearance only of union, jarring, jealous and perverse, without any determined direction, fluctuating and unhappy at home, weak and insignificant by their dissensions in the eyes of other nations." Virginia's Congressman William Grayson thought that, if things did not change, the United States would soon be "one of the most contemptible nations on the face of the Earth."

George Washington, in retirement at his beloved Mount Vernon, watched the nation's deterioration with a sense of grim foreboding. "No morn ever dawned more favourably than ours did," Washington wrote Congressman James Madison in November 1786, "and no day was ever more clouded than the present."

The troubles that alarmed Hamilton, Grayson, Washington, and business and government leaders all over the country were partly social and partly economic. However, most Americans frankly perceived them as political, and when they sought solutions for these troubles, it was *political* solutions they sought. It was entirely natural for the men who defied King George in 1776, boldly declaring their "inalienable" right to establish their own government, to see the nation's problems in political terms. Independence had been seen as a political solution to a whole range of social and economic problems. By altering the form of their government—by revising the terms of their "social contract"—Revolutionary patriots believed they could

shape their destinies, direct their futures, safeguard their lives and liberty.

If the United States in the 1780s was, as Hamilton charged, "sick," its malady must surely be the fault of its government. The "government" under which the country functioned was a weak and hesitant structure, hardly suited to the grand ideals of safeguarding American freedom and independence. It was, in name, a "confederation," although, in practice, it was little better than a diplomatic assembly—an association of autonomous states whose "ambassadors" met from time to time to discuss common problems but rarely, if ever, agreed on solutions to those problems.

The idea of organizing the thirteen former British colonies into a confederation was not exactly new. Benjamin Franklin had suggested it as early as 1754. In that year, the Pennsylvanian had drafted the so-called "Albany Plan of Union," under which the colonies would have joined together in a "permanent union" governed by a "Grand Council" with power to impose taxes, regulate military affairs, nominate executive officers, and regulate affairs with the Indian tribes. But the colonies, jealous of their own prerogatives, had refused to approve the plan. Franklin had renewed his suggestion for a confederation in 1775, although the plan he proposed then was to be a temporary association only, designed to coerce the British Parliament into revising its American policies.

The germ of the idea eventually adopted by the independent American states was set forth in the resolution that Virginia's Richard Henry Lee submitted to the Continental Congress in 1776. On June 7 of that fateful year, in the same resolution in which he proposed that "these United Colonies are, and of right ought to be, free and independent States," Lee pro-

posed that "a plan of confederation be prepared and transmitted to the respective Colonies for their consideration and approbation."

Congress responded to Lee's resolution by appointing Thomas Jefferson to head a committee to draft a Declaration of Independence and by naming John Dickinson of Delaware leader of a committee to write a charter of confederation. Dickinson's draft of a document he titled "Articles of Confederation and Perpetual Union" was submitted to Congress a little over a month later—and promptly tabled.

In 1776, Congress was concerned with more immediate matters than the adoption of a charter of government. There was an army to be raised and sent into the field, a navy to be outfitted, treaties to be negotiated with the foreign powers the patriots hoped would help the colonies throw off the British yoke, and money to be raised to accomplish all these goals. Not until November 15, 1777, was a final draft of the "Articles of Confederation" approved by Congress. And it was July 9, 1778, before an engrossed copy was ready for the members' signatures.

ALTHOUGH SOMETIMES CALLED "THE FIRST constitution of the United States," the Articles of Confederation bore little resemblance to the great document that was adopted in 1787. All power under the Confederation was vested in a single legislative body (called, somewhat awkwardly, "the United States, in Congress assembled") composed of members elected by the state legislatures. Although the states were free to select any number of members between two and seven, each state, regardless of its area or population, had only one vote.

From *American History Illustrated*, Summer 1987, pp. 19-23. Reprinted through the courtesy of Cowles Magazines, publishers of *American History Illustrated*.

2. REVOLUTIONARY AMERICA

The Articles gave Congress the power to make war and peace, to send and receive ambassadors, to enter into treaties and alliances, to establish post offices, to set standards of weights and measures, to coin money, and to regulate affairs with the Indian tribes. But they stated explicitly that each state retained "its sovereignty, freedom and independence" and that "every Power, Jurisdiction and Right" not expressly delegated to Congress was reserved to the states. Sounding a hopeful note, the Articles declared their purpose to the creation of "a firm league of friendship" among the states by providing for "their common defence, the security of their Liberties, and their mutual and general welfare."

But the government established by the Articles was poorly conceived to achieve its goals. Because Congress had no power to levy taxes, it had to rely for its finances on "requisitions" from among the several states. It could request specific sums, but the state legislatures were free to comply or not with the requests. Members of Congress, who served at the whim of their legislatures, could be recalled at any time, and they were forbidden from holding office more than three years out of any six. As a result, men of strong conviction often refused to accept seats in Congress, and those who agreed to serve had little opportunity to speak to national constituencies.

Not surprisingly, many members of Congress under the Articles of Confederation exhibited no more than a perfunctory interest in its activities. Between October 1, 1785, and January 1, 1786, a quorum (nine states) was present in Congress for only ten days. From October 1, 1785, to April 30, 1786, there was a quorum only three days.

Furthermore, the Articles made no provision for a chief executive or for any independent executive officers. The "president" of Congress was its presiding officer, with no power beyond what was given him by the other members. John Adams's daughter Abigail (who preferred to be called Amelia) dined with President Cyrus Griffin and other members of Congress in 1788 (before the Constitution had been ratified and put into effect) and later wrote her mother: "Had you been present you would have trembled for your country, to have seen, heard and observed the men who are its rulers."

No national judiciary existed to resolve disputed questions of law or to settle quarrels between the states, and Congress had no power to enforce its decisions. A glaring deficiency of the charter was its failure to provide any workable method for modifying its provisions. The Articles specifically provided that they could be amended only by the states' unanimous consent. This meant that a majority of the electors of Delaware, which had a population of less than 60,000, could overrule the decisions of the more than three million residents of the twelve other states.

The obvious defects of the Articles help to explain the lethargy with which the states proceeded to ratify them. Pennsylvania approved the Articles in July 1778; New Jersey did not act until November 1778; and Maryland delayed its ratification until February 1781. Maryland, a small state with a clearly defined western border, had insisted that large states like New York, Massachusetts, and Virginia, which claimed vast tracts of land beyond the Appalachians, first be made to surrender those claims to the Confederation.

A notable lapse in the Articles was their total failure to make any provision for the western lands which, following the successful conclusion of the war, assumed an increasingly larger role in the nation's planning. Although Congress had no constitutional power to deal with the western domain, it proceeded, even before the Articles were approved, to make rules for its settlement; and it was only after Maryland approved the Articles in February 1781 that Virginia—following the earlier examples of Massachusetts, Connecticut, and New York—relinquished its claims to all land north and west of the Ohio River. On March 1, nearly five years after they were proposed, the Articles of Confederation went into effect.

The ratification of the charter went almost unnoticed in the country at large. After the event, Congress continued to operate in much the same manner as it had before: maintaining ministers in European capitals; selling large tracts of land in what was now called the "North-West Territories"; negotiating treaties with the Indians; trying without much success to convince the states to send the money it needed to maintain the semblance of an American army and navy.

Despite its obvious handicaps, Congress managed under the Articles of Confederation to achieve some notable accomplishments. It laid the groundwork for eventual statehood in the western lands by passing (in 1787) the Northwest Ordinance, a comprehensive plan for territorial self-government that was to establish a pattern for the later settlement of all American territories. It successfully negotiated an end to the Revolutionary War. (The Treaty of Paris was signed by John Adams, Benjamin Franklin, and John Jay in September 1783 and ratified by Congress in January 1784.) And it managed, though haltingly, to stave off the financial disaster that the economic troubles of the 1780s threatened to bring upon the country.

In other matters, Congress showed itself to be almost helpless. It was unable to set tariffs or deal effectively with foreign challenges to American shipping. When the Spanish, who held the vast Louisiana territory, refused to permit American ships to sail down the Mississippi to New Orleans, Congress could do little more than protest. When the British, taking advantage of the Confederation's military weakness, refused to surrender wilderness forts in the Northwest Territory (which under the Treaty of Paris belonged to the United States), Congress could complain, but it could not take action. When Barbary pirates harassed American merchant ships off the coast of Africa, Congress could neither pay the ransoms the pirates demanded nor muster the naval forces necessary to stop their plundering.

Congress's requests for funds from the states met with humiliating denials. Between November 1, 1781, and January 1, 1786, the Confederation received less than two-and-a-half million dollars from the states, a sum that was barely enough to pay its operating expenses for the period. Twice Congress tried to amend the articles so as to give it a dependable source of revenue, and twice its efforts were rebuffed. In 1781 Congress proposed that it be authorized to levy a five percent duty on imports, but tiny Rhode Island refused to agree to it. Two years later, Congress made a modified version of the same proposal, only to see it fail when New York, which derived most of its income from customs, would not approve it.

There were repeated and often bitter disputes between the states, and Congress was entirely powerless to resolve them. New York and New Hampshire both laid claims to the territory of Vermont, which had been promised statehood during the war; but, because of

Congress's inability to make good on its promise, Vermont had to wait until 1791 to be admitted to the Union. Virginia and Maryland laid conflicting claims to navigation rights on the Potomac, and New York and New Jersey quarreled over the Hudson River.

And when they were not arguing among themselves, the states were haggling with Congress—or going their own ways, oblivious to the needs of the Confederation. Several states borrowed (or tried to borrow) money in foreign markets, thus undercutting similar efforts by Congress. Nine states, ranging from Massachusetts in the north to South Carolina in the south, organized navies of their own, and virtually all regarded their militias as state armies. After the Treaty of Paris had been negotiated, Virginia insisted on ratifying the treaty to signify its belief that Congress had no power to make peace for residents of the Old Dominion.

Starved for money, stripped of all but the most rudimentary authority, Congress found that it commanded little respect among the people. Former Continental Army soldiers demanding back pay chased it out of Philadelphia in June 1783, and thereafter Congress wandered in search of a home. It was in Princeton, New Jersey, at the end of June; in Annapolis, Maryland, in November; in Trenton, New Jersey, in 1784; and in New York City in 1785, where it remained, more out of necessity than choice, for the final years of the Confederation.

Economic troubles were, in large measure, responsible for the problems the nation faced in the 1780s. Burdened by heavy debts incurred during the war, the states, as well as the Confederation, found it nearly impossible to meet their financial obligations. Maritime trade, badly hurt by Britain's decision to seal off West Indian ports from American ships, was slow and halting. And the scarcity of gold and silver coins (British pounds and shillings, Dutch guilders, and Spanish dollars formed the bulk of hard money in the country) forced small merchants and farmers to barter goods for services.

But economic problems did not fully explain the deep discontent that was sweeping through the states. Even before the Articles of Confederation were ratified, influential public leaders were suggesting that the government was inadequate to meet the needs of the nation, that nothing short of a major overhaul of the Confederation could re-establish confidence in public institutions or recapture the enthusiasm of the early years of the Revolution.

Hamilton toyed for a while with the idea of establishing a government on the British model, while Robert Morris (Pennsylvania) argued for the establishment of a central banking system. John Hancock (Massachusetts) was not sure what form the new government should take, but he knew there had to be a change. "How to strengthen and improve the Union so as to render it completely adequate," Hancock said, "demands the immediate attention of these states. Our very existence as a free nation is suspended upon it."

THREE EVENTS WERE SOON TO SUGGEST a national course of action. The first was the outbreak, in the summer and fall of 1786, of the popular uprising known as "Shays' Rebellion." This attack on civil authority in Massachusetts did not seriously threaten the integrity of either the Confederation or the Commonwealth of Massachusetts, but it demonstrated the weaknesses of both. When Daniel Shays, a poor farmer and one-time Continental Army captain, set his rag-tag army of "Regulators" against state and federal troops at Springfield, Massachusetts, on January 25, 1787, it seemed for a while as if the very fabric of freedom was threatened. "We are fast verging to anarchy and confusion," an excited George Washington wrote to James Madison.

The second two events were less dramatic than "Shays' Rebellion," but no less important for the nation's future. Delegates from Maryland and Virginia were commissioned by their state legislatures to meet in Alexandria in March 1785 to discuss navigation rights on the Potomac, an issue that had long divided the two states. When the meeting was delayed by the tardiness of the Virginia commissioners, George Washington invited the delegates to reconvene at Mount Vernon. The conference concluded three days later with an agreement that declared the Potomac "a common High Way," provided for common fishing rights in Chesapeake Bay, and recommended that the paper money and customs duties of the two states be made uniform. Steering the compact to approval in the Virginia Legislature, James Madison proposed a meeting of Virginia delegates with commissioners from other states to discuss "such commercial regulations [as] may be necessary to their common interest and personal harmony." Five states—New York, New Jersey, Pennsylvania, Delaware, and Virginia—responded to Madison's proposal and sent delegates to a convention that met in Annapolis, Maryland, on September 11, 1786.

The twelve delegates who met there quickly realized they could accomplish very little. No New England delegates attended, and that region was vital to any truly national consensus. Alexander Hamilton, who attended as a delegate from New York, seized upon the opportunity to set the stage for a later and, he hoped, more momentous convention of all the states. Hamilton suggested that the state legislatures appoint representatives to meet at Philadelphia on the second Monday of the following May "to devise such further provisions as shall appear to them necessary to render the constitution of the Federal Government adequate to the exigencies of the Union." The resolution quickly passed.

Congress was now faced with a ticklish question: should it oppose or approve the proposed Philadelphia convention? A convention to devise "further provisions" for the country's government seemed to many members a usurpation of authority. If it was not exactly illegal, it was certainly extralegal, for the Articles made no allowance for such a convention. But Congress had neither the means nor, at this late stage in the life of the Articles of Confederation, the *will* to express its opposition. And so, on February 21, 1787, after several months of delay, Congress passed a cautious resolution approving the proposed convention for "the sole and express purpose of revising the Articles of Confederation."

But Congress's actions were irrelevant to the events that were now pressing forward. Even before the Congress had expressed its tentative approval of the new convention, delegates had been chosen in several states, and the selection process was accelerating. The stage was now set for the next act in a great national drama, and the actors were already gathering in the wings.

The American Revolution
A War of Religion?

Jonathan Clark probes the anti-Catholic actions and millenarian rhetoric of eighteenth-century America, challenging the assumption that 1776 was solely a product of secular and constitutional impulses.

Jonathan Clark is a Fellow of All Souls College, Oxford and author of Revolution and Rebellion: State and Society in England in the Seventeenth and Eighteenth Centuries *(Cambridge University Press, 1986).*

Thanks to our ruling picture of the American Revolution, a major premise of British and American history remains unrevised: the belief that both societies have pursued the uninterrupted evolution of a secular, libertarian, constitutional ideal, and that its progressive implementation has progressively freed them from internal revolutionary threat. A longer perspective is a crucial corrective: through all the vicissitudes of English politics from the 1530s to the 1820s and beyond, the most consistent theme both of popular sentiment and of ideological exegesis was anti-Catholicism. From the sixteenth century, Englishmen pictured the Roman Church not merely as a system of cruelty and intolerance, but as an international conspiracy operating through secret agents and with the covert sympathy of fellow travellers. Deliverances were attributed to direct divine intervention in favour of Protestant England. An apocalyptic or millenarian perspective on England's and America's history was generated principally in the context of Protestantism's conflict with Rome.

By the late seventeenth century, anti-Catholic paranoia was even stronger in America than in England, despite the presence in the colonies of an even smaller Catholic minority. This heightened sensibility reacted strongly against the exercise of executive power by James II and produced a situation of extreme tension: in 1689 news of events in England triggered violent rebellions in three colonies—Massachusetts, New York and Maryland—and peaceful changes of government where the authorities did not resist the proclamation of William and Mary. The Massachusetts rebellion was aimed at restoring Puritan hegemony and local autonomy, enjoyed from Charles I's charter of 1629 until its cancellation when the colony was unwillingly incorporated in the Dominion of New England in 1684. This swift and violent reaction was in part a response to a

'An attempt to land a bishop in America'; a cartoon reflecting resistance to attempts at transplanting an Anglican state church into New England.

theory of popish conspiracy, manifest in recent English history:

We have seen more than a decade of Years rolled away since the English World had the Discovery of an horrid Popish Plot; wherein the bloody Devotees of Rome had in their Design and Prospect no less than the Extinction of the Protestant Religion . . . And we were of all Men the most insensible, if we should apprehend a Countrey so remarkable for the true Profession and pure Exercise of the Protestant Religion as New-England is, wholly unconcerned in the Infamous Plot.

In New York the rebellion, headed by Jacob Leisler, was in part an ethnic Dutch backlash against English encroachment since the conquest of the colony in 1664, in part an attempt by one set of magnates to dispossess another set of the spoils of office. Nevertheless, the popish phobia created a political idiom in New York and could be exploited.

All shortcomings in the administration of proprietary Maryland could be similarly attributed to the religion of its administrators, and political parties were already polarised on sectarian lines. By 1689, this division had generated paranoid complaints of 'Not only private but publick outrages, & murthers committed and done by papists upon Protestants without redress, but rather connived at and tolerated by the chief in authority'. In March 1689 the colony was gripped by a rumour that the Catholic ruling group was conspiring with the Indians to massacre the Protestants. According to the Council's report to London, people had 'gathered themselves together in great parties to defend themselves, as they were persuaded, against a groundless and imaginary plott and designe contrived against them as was rumoured and suspected by the Roman Catholicks inviting the Indians to joyne with them in that detestable and wicked Conspiracy'.

The American colonies rehearsed certain libertarian issues in 1689, but they had not obtained all or even most of what they had sought. The issues therefore remained; but their significance was transformed by the change of dynasty. No longer could antipopery sentiments transform practical objections to English rule: William III's Calvinism aligned him squarely with New England Puritanism, and the Lutheranism of George I and George II similarly established their credentials. The enemy was henceforth an external one. If the practical threat of popery receded, it did not disappear: in

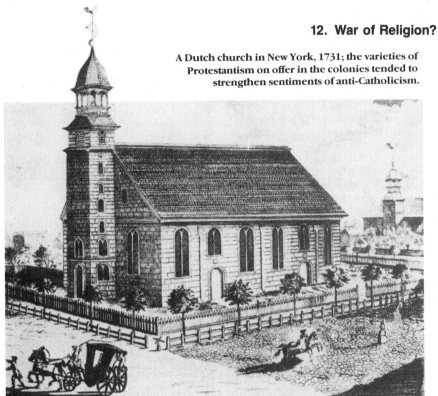

A Dutch church in New York, 1731; the varieties of Protestantism on offer in the colonies tended to strengthen sentiments of anti-Catholicism.

Europe the Protestant interest often seemed on the defensive until the Seven Years' War; French Canada and Spanish Florida similarly served as reminders to Americans. An added peril now began to prey on the psyche of the southern colonist: the fear that he would be murdered by the negro, either in an isolated incident or as part of a mass insurrection which would necessarily result (as with anti-Catholic phobias) in a general massacre of white Protestants. Isolated incidents certainly occurred. Would they run together to constitute a revolution?

The early Hanoverian era saw a series of plots or uprisings by negro slaves in America, equally savage in their impact and in the punishments with which they were repressed. Conspiracies were discovered and rebellion prevented in Virginia in 1687 and 1709, South Carolina in 1720, New Jersey in 1734, Maryland in the late 1730s, South Carolina in 1740 and elsewhere. Violent rebellions occurred in New York City in 1712 and 1741, in South Carolina (the Stono Rebellion) in 1739 and on other occasions. In the 1730s and 40s slave disorder has been linked to the evangelical movement known as the Great Awakening: the first movement to sweep large numbers of negroes into sectarian participation, it acted to challenge hierarchical distinctions of white and black even more forcibly than those of white and white.

Despite the special circumstances of slave revolts, religion could appear both

in their motivation and in the white response. In 1741 New York was convulsed by fears of a negro insurrection: outbreaks of arson and robbery seemed to be its preliminaries; informers fuelled the panic, and trials rehearsed the issues in the public eye. Paranoia now inflated public disorder into a full-scale conspiracy. Much of the blame was attributed to revivalist religion, ignited by the recent visit of the Calvinist George Whitefield, and directed to the subversive end of the conversion of blacks as well as whites. Wartime conflict between Spanish Florida and the colony of Georgia soon introduced another ancient preoccupation into the mounting New York frenzy: the Catholic plot. Suspicion of the enthusiasm or superstition which was seen as common to both Methodism and Catholicism now joined with the ancient horror of a Catholic massacre. These events were seen as part of the divine scenario: 'so bloody and Destructive a Conspiracy was this, that had not the mercifull hand of providence interposed and Confounded their [the negroes'] Divices, in one and the Same night the Inhabitants would have been butcher'd in their houses, by their own Slaves, and the City laid in ashes'. Within such a context, New York's response to this fictional conspiracy is explicable as motive rather than mere rhetoric: four whites were hanged as conspirators; so were eighteen blacks; and thirteen more negroes were burnt at the stake. Similar conspiracies continued to be uncovered up to and long after the Revolution. Such was the emotional background against which the lofty issues of 1776 were rehearsed.

In England, millennial expectations receded after the 1650s; in the colonies, especially Puritan New England, they evolved into the eighteenth century as an orthodoxy, though without the revolutionary threat implicit in English sectarianism. New England society had earlier come close to being a theocracy; the sense of America as a religious experiment, as the new Israel, still gave stability and practical content to millenarian hopes. In the southern colonies, these traditions may have been refreshed by the Calvinism of Scots and Scots-Irish immigrants. The Great Awakening, in turn, was explicitly millenarian; when it lost its first impetus, England's wars of the 1740s and 50s against France and Spain renewed the identification of Antichrist with Catholicism and revitalised the old images of Catholic persecution. As a preacher warned, 'our inveterate and popish Enemies both without and within the Kingdom, are restless to enslave and ruin us'. If France won, 'Cruel *Papists* would quickly fill the *British Colonies,* and seize our Estates, abuse our Wives and Daughters, and barbarously murder us; as they have done the like in *France* and *Ireland*'.

In the 1740s and 50s, Britain overcame the major threats to her internal stability—threats to the religious and dynastic order. In the American colonies they survived; indeed they were exacerbated. Apart from the conflict of loyalist and republican, in the period following the Peace of Paris, a common thread ran through the conflicts which saw colonial Americans in armed conflict with each other: the clash of material interests between the pioneers, the settlers of the western backcountry, and the long-established settlers of the eastern seaboard with their control first of colonial, then of republican government. This applied to the march of the Paxton Boys against Philadelphia (1764); the Regulator movement in North and South Carolina (1768–71); the clashes in the Wyoming Valley of Pennsylvania between Pennamite and Yankee (1770–1); the disorders of the Green Mountain Boys in Vermont (early 1770s); Shays' Rebellion in Massachusetts (1786–7); the Whiskey Rebellion in Pennsylvania (1794); and Fries' Rebellion (1799). Such conflicts were once held to owe everything to the

material grievances of the back-country and equally little either to the pursuit of secular constitutional ideals or to formal sectarian allegiance. Yet these instances of civil disobedience can now be seen to share important features with other colonial insurrections since 1676, especially the religious catalyst; their ethnic composition brings their sectarian nature into sharp relief.

The wide availability of millennial thought meant that British legislation on the American colonies in the 1760s could at once be seen in an 'apocalyptical perspective'. The Stamp Act therefore quickly reversed a whole nexus of ideas which had grown up in a fervent identification of civil and religious liberty with British rule. George Grenville's stamps were described in the language of the Book of Revelation as 'the mark of the beast'; In cartoons, British policy was often personified as the devil. This paranoia had been expressed again in the New England controversy of 1763–5 over the threatened appointment of an Anglican bishop. In 1774 it received an immense boost: the Quebec Act, granting toleration to Canadian Catholics, was taken as proof of an imperial plot to promote popery. From the 1740s, American imagery had steadily strengthened the identity between tyranny and sin, civil liberty and grace. This was partly a consequence of a religious revivalist movement sufficiently dramatic and distinct to acquire a capitalised name: the Great Awakening.

Several decades before British political authority was systematically challenged in the colonies, a similar challenge had been launched against conventional ecclesiastical authorities of several denominations by the 'New Light' preachers of the religious revival. The significance of their appeal to personal revelation, a right of private judgement and a duty of secession from sinful congregations was interpreted by the established powers in the same terms as that of the rebels of 1776. The New Light clergy were 'Innovators, disturbers of the peace of the church, sowers of heresies and seditions'; they were 'foremost in propagating the Principles of Sedition, and Disobedience to Authority'. George Whitefield recorded in 1739 the unpopularity of the New Light ministers who graduated from William Tennent's famous Log College: 'Carnal ministers oppose them strongly; and, because people, when awakened by Mr. Tennent or

his brethren, see through them, and therefore leave their ministry, the poor gentlemen are loaded with contempt, and looked upon as persons who turn the world upside-down'.

Few of the implications of New Light theology were brought to bear against British rule before the early 1760s: until the conclusion of the Seven Years War, the threat to liberty, property and Protestantism clearly emanated from French Canada. In New England especially, Britain was depicted as the main bulwark of freedom against the antichrist of Rome. From the mid-1760s, however, colonists were free to redirect their rhetoric of Protestant virtue. In this they were encouraged by the perspective of still more recent immigrants from Scotland and Ireland, including the clergymen John Witherspoon and Alexander Craighead, who re-emphasised the Covenanter roots of political contractarianism. Witherspoon exercised his influence as President of Princeton from 1768 to 1794, Craighead in more humble surroundings as a minister in Mecklenburg County, North Carolina, from 1755 to his death in 1766. Craighead had already been expelled from ministering in two presbyteries for imposing the Solemn League and Covenant and the National Covenant: his affinities with the Cameronians made him a difficult neighbour. Among the Scots-Irish of the backcountry, however, he found a receptive audience. To them he appealed both by his preaching and his published works. Among the latter has been claimed the anonymous pamphlet *Renewal of the Covenants* (Philadelphia, 1743, 1748) which reviewed their history in Scotland and their violation under the persecution of Stuart and Hanoverian monarchs.

Like the Covenanters, Craighead preached 'a defensive War against all Usurpers of the Royal Prerogative of the glorious Lamb of God'. After his death, this message was sustained by other New Light clergy in the neighbourhood, like the influential David Caldwell: their teaching flowed directly into the Regulator movement. Although other denominations including New England Congregationalism shared this religious impetus to political engagement, the popular movement which bore that name had a special place in the tradition of disorder. The history of colonial British America was punctuated with a series of backcountry rebellions against east coast authorities. The last and greatest of these

'The Mitred Minuet' - an attack on the ill-timed Quebec Act of 1774, where the British government's provision to allow the Catholic church to keep its privileges there inflamed anti-Popish sentiment and suspicion in the colonies. The devil hovers over George III's ministers, Lords Bute and North, onlookers at the episcopal dance.

occurred only shortly before the larger Revolution of 1776, for from 1768 until their military destruction at the battle of Alamance in May 1771 the piedmont of North and South Carolina was increasingly under the control of the self-styled Regulators, local activists usurping by force the authority of colonial magistrates and tax officials.

What prompted certain Americans to rebel? The old constitutional scenario of a sinister and concerted attempt by George III to resurrect monarchical absolutism is now untenable; so is the related notion that the ministry of Lord North rested on a revived Tory party. Nevertheless, the historiographical tradition which made a neo-Harringtonian libertarianism into the almost universal American idiom even before 1776 required that the trigger of revolution should be external to the colonies, a reassertion of authoritarian ideology in 1760s Britain. A fuller picture of the monarchical, Anglican nature of the early-Hanoverian regime removes the significant elements in this contrast between the years before and after 1760, and reopens the question of internal colonial triggers to the rebellion of 1776.

Before the 1760s, the main idioms of political discourse in mainland colonies had echoed English norms: they were determined by the dynastic and religious questions fought over by Englishmen since 1679. But why was it thought appropriate by some people to use Whig rhetoric against a Whig regime? After 1760, the pattern in the New World again corresponded closely to that in the Old. The external threats disappeared, together with the internal polarity they had induced. The confluence of former Whigs and Tories in support of George III simultaneously reawakened old fears and provided new targets for existing opposition rhetoric.

In both 1688 and 1766, the constitutional problems raised by questions of taxation, executive prerogative and parliamentary jurisdiction were turned from grievances into issues which evoked the passionate commitment of great numbers of ordinary men by their engagement with a much wider nexus of ideas and feelings. Contemporaries recognised the part played by religious enthusiasm in the American cause. 'Enthusiasm' now came to take on a wider secular meaning: John Adams echoed Shaftesbury's eulogy of 'noble enthusiasm' as a quality which 'raised the imagination to an opinion or conceit of something majestic and divine'. But its secular sense had most

importance only to the small circle of men who formed part of the Jeffersonian Enlightenment. The political commitments of most men were still an aspect of their religion; and this was already taking forms which were both new and distinctively American.

Richard Price rightly sensed that the American colonies in 1776 were 'animated by piety'. They were, indeed, in the grip of one of the more momentous of religious revivalist movements. The evangelical phenomenon known in the colonies as the Great Awakening began slowly in the 1740s, under the inspiration of the New Light Presbyterians, a highly politicized élite associated in the foundation of Princeton. From the 1740s it grew to become a mass movement, turning into a 'landslide' in the decade following 1765. By 1776, the Great Awakening had inspired in many colonists a vision of an imminent millennium. The expectation of a future moral transformation was matched by a condemnation of the sinfulness, luxury and corruption of past life, and, especially, of English modes. It was the millenarian impulse which gave immediacy to the academic neo-Harringtonian critique of 'corruption', and the social constituency of the evangelical movement which gave these religious insights their populist focus as an attack on privilege and hierarchy, an assertion of divinely-sanctioned popular sovereignty against the divine right of the English monarchy.

In the decade before 1776, the rhetoric of American clergy subtly changed. 'The familiar jeremiad about the sins of God's chosen people and the need for a collective act of atonement was increasingly combined with an implication that that repentance had already been demonstrated by the resistance to tyranny, so that Providence was now enlisted in the rebel cause. The doctrine that God stood in a contractual relation with his chosen people—a doctrine especially emphasised in New England Congregationalism and by Presbyterians—became more generally available to all Americans, and the burden of guilt for the breach of this eternal contract was by implication transferred to the mother country.

Indeed, argued Perry Miller, it was not the 'genial Anglicanism' of the established clergy nor the 'urbane rationalism' of the Washingtons, Jeffersons and Franklins that

brought the rank and file of American Protestants into the war. What aroused a Christian patriotism that needed staying power was a realization of the vengeance God denounced against the wicked; what fed their hopes was not what God promised as a recompense to virtue, but what dreary fortunes would overwhelm those who persisted in sloth; what kept them going was an assurance that by exerting themselves they were fighting for a victory thus providentially predestined.

It has been suggested that colonial Americans were able to mobilise so quickly between 1773 and 1776 because a millennial tradition of thought was available for instant activation, overriding the tradition of a remedy for present corruption in the return to former virtue. Mobilisation on the scale of 1776 is evidence against religious imagery being mere rhetoric. A break in the tie with Britain, a renunciation of existing rationales for American society, demanded and was easily given an alternative rationale, a biblically-supported vision of a new future.

Within the millenarian vision, one component in particular still acted as an emotional catalyst and a political trigger: the fear of Popery. Its role was already an ancient one. The New England colonies were founded at a time of frenzied anti-Catholicism in England, and carried this

Burning the Stamp Act in Boston, 1765 – several of its colonial opponents had described the actual stamps in apocalyptic terms as 'the mark of the beast'.

inheritance as a lasting and vivid theme in their moral and political discourse. Laudian persecution of Puritans added the element of paranoia. Consequently, the imperial challenges of the 1670s and 80s produced an even more hysterical reaction in the colonies than in England. By the mid-Eighteenth century the vocabulary of tyranny, slavery and arbitrary power was still grounded on the meanings of the key term 'popery'; but, under the impact of such early eighteenth century English texts as *Cato's Letters,* these meanings had been stretched to cover the exercise of power by any established, episcopal church. Whatever its origin, this heightened emotional temperature acted to sweep up and distort patterns of argument which might otherwise have provided grounds for caution rather than insurrection.

American rhetoric in the 1760s and 1770s combined the same inconsistent elements as did that of England: beside

contract theory and natural rights theory went the doctrine of the ancient constitution. As important as the specific form of the ancient constitution was the long record of sacrifice in its defence: colonists revered the 'ancestors [who] have liberally shed their blood to secure to us the rights we now contend for'; but such a rhetoric carried the implication that the constitution could only be maintained 'at the hazard of our lives and fortunes'. A theory of past achievement became itself an incitement to present excess: in the frenzy of an evangelical religious movement, the theory of the ancient constitution demanded sacrifice and atonement rather than negotiation, compromise or humility.

From soon after the accession of George III, English Dissenters cooperated with their colonial co-religionists to confirm and strengthen the Americans in their belief that a transatlantic conspiracy was being hatched against both civil and religious liberty. These issues were revitalised, for English Dissenters also, by the Anglican church's intermittent moves to appoint a bishop for the colonies. Only when viewed against the background of the history of English, Irish and Scots sectarian emigration to the colonies did this modest proposal assume the sinister shape of a bid to reimpose those claims which the Americans had fled their homelands to escape. The Wilkes affair and Anglican resistance to the Feathers Tavern petition against subscription to the Thirty-Nine Articles fell into place as episodes in the royal conspiracy.

It required the Dissenting perspective to arrange these unconnected incidents into a scenario of impending tyranny. Anglicans explained the innocence of a scheme for a bishop in America: as a memorandum of Shelburne re-emphasised in 1764, it was proposed to 'model every thing upon the most extensive Principles of the *Toleration* . . . No Coersive Powers are desired over the Laity'. But the ancient intolerance of New England Congregationalism was given a new object by the loyal behaviour of Anglican clergy during the Stamp Act crisis; by 1771 the clergy of New York and New Jersey, petitioning once more for a bishop, could warn that 'Independency in Religion will naturally produce Republicanism in the State'. Anglicanism had changed greatly from the persecutory creed it had been as recently as Anne's reign; colonial Dissenters still largely lived with their ancient shibboleths, nursing atavistic hatreds.

Yet the perspective of the Jeffersonian Enlightenment blocked any deeper understanding of the causes of rebellion. At the same time, a right of rebellion, once asserted so successfully, had become part of American culture. It could not be

removed by Britain's recognition of the independence of thirteen of her colonies in 1783. Rebellions therefore continued, adding to fears that the new republic would break into its component parts, either between northern and southern or between eastern and western states. In Shays' Rebellion (1786), the Whiskey Rebellion (1794), and Fries' Rebellion (1799), Americans fought Americans in a continuing conflict over the issues that had been at stake in 1776; but now it was a US Federal government which asserted its authority with the whiskey excise of 1791, and the stamp and land taxes of 1798. This continuing conflict sets 1776 in the perspective of a civil war rather than a war of national liberation, a war to emancipate a pre-existing nation; and it reopens the question of its religious origins.

Evidence does survive of these later rebels identifying the cause of their east coast opponents with Antichrist. Many were active Presbyterians, and although their church officially disavowed rebellion, the religious element continued to do more than strengthen their group identity. Even Fries' Rebellion contained an echo of dynastic, anti-Anglican fears. The Presbyterianism of the Whiskey rebels, too, bound them closely into a transatlantic tradition. Opposition to internal taxes in England in the 1730s, as in the colonies in the 1760s and 1790s, was articulated by the élite in the familiar terms of arbitrary power. Popular perceptions showed why such language was activated: according to Lord Hervey, during the Excise Crisis of 1733 'the universal cry of the kingdom was "No slavery, no excise, no wooden shoes"'. The *London Journal* claimed that the opposition had spread the effective

rumour 'that a great many Pair of *Wooden Shoes* were lately *imported,* on purpose to be carried about the City on Poles or Sticks, as *Emblems* or *Signs* to the People, of what a dismal State they are coming to'. Popery and poverty (wooden shoes) were as much a popular identity as a literary trope, as the Gordon Riots of 1780 once more emphasised.

Social stability combined with political instability was the norm in early modern societies of western Europe. This is particularly apparent in England's Atlantic empire during the seventeenth and eighteenth centuries. Conflict, massacre, schism and sometimes successful rebellion were set against steady but irregular structural change and commercial development, always threatened by the stresses and outcomes of war or insurrection. Why was the intellectual tradition of Common Law and parliamentary representation activated, turned from a defensive to an offensive creed? Why were great numbers of men periodically seized by revolutionary frenzy? From Venner's rising in 1661 through 1688 and 1776 to the Irish rebellion of 1798, we find not a monocausal explanation but a common thread on both sides of the Atlantic in religion.

FOR FURTHER READING:

Ruth M. Bloch, *Visionary Republic: Millennial Themes in American Thought, 1756–1800* (Cambridge, 1985); Patricia U. Bonomi, *Under the Cope of Heaven: Religion, Society and Politics in Colonial America* (Oxford, 1986); Nathan O. Hatch, *The Sacred Cause of Liberty: Republican Thought and the Millennium in Revolutionary New England* (New Haven, 1977); Winthrop D. Jordan, *White over Black: American Attitudes towards the Negro, 1550–1812* (Chapel Hill, NC, 1968); Cushing Strout, *The New Heavens and New Earth* (New York, 1974).

Philadelphia Story

Jack N. Rakove

Jack N. Rakove, 39, is associate professor of history at Stanford University. Born in Chicago, he received a B.A. from Haverford College (1968), and a Ph.D. from Harvard (1975). He is the author of The Beginnings of National Politics: An Interpretive History of the Continental Congress *(1979).*

"There never was an assembly of men, charged with a great and arduous trust, who were more pure in their motives, or more exclusively or anxiously devoted to the object committed to them."

It probably was shortly before his death, in 1836, that Virginia's James Madison, the sole surviving Framer of the Constitution, dictated those closing words of the preface to his notes of the debates at the Constitutional Convention. This was how Madison wanted his countrymen to imagine the Convention. In many ways we have followed his wishes—and will be asked to do so again during the bicentennial celebrations.

Yet, for most of this century, this popular image of the Founding has coexisted with another, less heroic portrait etched by scholars since Charles A. Beard published *An Economic Interpretation of the Constitution* (1913).

Rather than treat the Constitution as the product of a highly principled debate conducted by an extraordinary group of men who resolved *all* of the great questions before them, these historians have emphasized everything that was practical and tough-minded about the task of creating a national government: the threats and bargains that dominated the politics of the Convention, and the determination of the delegates to protect the interests of their states and, for that matter, of their own propertied class.

To strike an accurate balance between these two contrasting images is the great challenge that confronts anyone who studies the making of the Constitution.

That task is more important now than it has been at any point in our recent history. Today's controversy over constitutional jurisprudence, sparked by U.S. attorney general Edwin Meese III, requires that Americans ask again how much weight the "original intent" of the Framers should carry in interpreting the Constitution.

One thing is clear: The 55 delegates to the Philadelphia Convention were not all cut from the same cloth. Six had signed the Declaration of Independence, 14 were land speculators, 21 were military veterans of the Revolution, at least 15 owned slaves, and 24 served in Congress. Thirty-four were lawyers.

Present were many of the most outstanding men that the new Republic could muster. Among them were Benjamin Franklin, the president of Pennsylvania's Supreme Executive Council and the leading American scientist of the century, so disabled by gout and other ailments at the age of 81 that he was carried from his lodgings to the Convention in a sedan chair borne by four convicts; Virginia's George Washington, then 55, who came to Philadelphia very reluctantly after three years of retirement from public life at Mount Vernon; New York's Alexander Hamilton, 30, Washington's wartime aide; George Mason, a 60-year-old Virginia plantation owner and (said Thomas Jefferson) "the wisest man of his generation."

Also in attendance were men of somewhat less distinction. One of the more interesting examples was Luther Martin, "the rollicking, witty, audacious Attorney General of Maryland," as Henry Adams later described him, "drunken, generous, slovenly, grand . . . the notorious reprobate genius."

Missing from the Convention were Thomas Jefferson, 44, author of the Declaration of Independence 11 years earlier, who was overseas serving as the American minister to France, and former congressman John Adams, 51, likewise engaged in England. The great firebrands of the Revolution—Samuel Adams, Thomas Paine, Patrick Henry—were also absent.

A HUMID SUMMER

No delegates came from Rhode Island. "Rogue Island," as a Boston newspaper called it, was in the hands of politicians bent on inflating the currency to relieve farm debtors; they would have nothing to do with a strong national government and the monetary discipline it would impose. For lack of lunds, New Hampshire's delegates arrived more than two months late, bringing the number of states represented to 12. Indeed, during the Convention's debates, the cost and difficulties of travel would occasionally be cited as looming obstacles to effective national government. Nearly a year, Madison predicted, would be "consumed in preparing for and travelling to and from the seat of national business."

The delegates were supposed to gather in Philadelphia on May 14, 1787, but it was the rare public assembly in 18th-century America that met on time. Only on Friday the 25th did delegates from seven states—a quorum—assemble in the spacious east room of the Pennsylvania State House, the same chamber where the Declaration of Independence had been signed. The delegates sat two or three to a desk. George Washington was immediately elected president of the Convention. Serious discussion began on the 29th. Thereafter, the delegates met six days a week until they finally adjourned on September 17, taking only one recess. It was, by contemporary standards, an arduous schedule. The delegates met for four, six, sometimes even eight hours a day.

In the afternoons, when the Convention adjourned, the delegates often repaired to local taverns—the Indian Queen, the George, the Black Horse—or turned to other amusements. These included visiting Mrs. Peale's Museum, with its fossils, stuffed animals, and portraits of the Revolution's heroes (by her husband, Charles), browsing through libraries and book and stationery shops, reading the city's eight newspapers, and watching the occasional horse race through the city streets, paved with bricks and cobblestones. Down by the busy docks and brick warehouses along the Delaware River, spectators could watch as inventor John Fitch demonstrated a novel contraption: a steam-powered boat.

Although there was a large and growing German population, the Quakers, in their broadbrim hats, still set the tone in Philadelphia, and the tone was sober but cosmopolitan. George Mason, from rural Virginia, complained after his arrival that he was growing "heartily tired of the etiquette and nonsense so fashionable in this city."

It was hot and humid that summer. "A veritable torture," moaned one French visitor. But the delegates had to keep their windows closed as they slept: Obnoxious stinging flies filled the air. The dyspeptic Elbridge Gerry of Massachusetts sent his family to the healthier clime of New York City, where the U.S. Congress was sitting. A few of his colleagues, such as Charles Pinckney, the young delegate from South Carolina, rented houses and brought their families to Philadelphia; others lived alone in rented rooms above the taverns or boarded in Mrs. Mary House's place at the corner of Fifth and Market streets near the State House. Most brought servants. George Washington was the guest of Pennsylvania delegate Robert Morris, Philadelphia's great merchant prince, who owned a large mansion a block from the State House.

A typical session of the Convention would find perhaps 35 or 40 delegates from 10 or 11 states in attendance. Some delegates came and went, others sat silently the entire time—and a few would have been better advised to say less. Washington did not so much as venture an opinion until the last day of debate. But his stern presence in the chair did much to preserve the decorum of the meeting.

MADISON'S FEARS

The debates were held in secrecy. Otherwise, candor would have been impossible, since the delegates knew that their opinions and votes, if made public, would become live ammunition in the hands of political foes back home. Moreover, the threat of deadlock would have quickly arisen had the dissidents within the Convention been allowed to stir up a hue and cry among their constituents. "Their deliberations are kept inviolably secret, so that they set without censure or remark," observed Francis Hopkinson, a Philadelphia musician and signer of the Declaration, "but no sooner will the chicken be hatch'd but every one will be for plucking a feather."

Nevertheless, we know a great deal about what was said at the Convention, thanks chiefly to the copious daily note-taking of Virginia's James Madison, then just turned 36, who is now generally regarded as the "father of the Constitution."

Were he alive today, the slight, soft-spoken Madison would probably be happily teaching history or political theory at his alma mater, Princeton University (or the College of New Jersey, as it was then known). He took a distinctively intellectual approach to politics, reinforced by a decade of experience in the Virginia legislature and the U.S. Congress. He had read deeply in the history of ancient and modern confederacies and pondered the shortcomings of the Articles of Confederation and the state constitutions. (It was Madison's frustration with the scanty archives left by earlier confederacies that prompted him to take meticulous notes at the Convention.) He arrived in Philadelphia 11 days early to begin drafting, with his fellow Virginians, the Virginia Plan. After the state's 34-year-old governor, Edmund Randolph, presented the plan on May 29, it became, in effect, the agenda of the Convention.

The starting point for all of Madison's proposals was his belief, based on the nation's unhappy experiences under the Articles and under the state constitutions, that the state legislatures could not be counted on to respect the national interest, the concerns of other states, or even the "private rights" of individuals and minorities.

Like most other Federalists, Madison thought that the legislatures were dominated by demagogues who sought office for reasons of "ambition" and "personal interest" rather than "public good." Such men—e.g., Patrick Henry, his great rival in Virginia—could always "dupe" more "honest but unenlightened representative[s]" by "veiling [their] selfish views under the professions of public good, and varnishing [their] sophistical arguments with the glowing colors of popular eloquence."

From this condemnation of state politics, Madison drew a number of conclusions that appeared in the Virginia Plan. First, unlike the existing Congress, which relied upon the good will of the states to see its resolutions carried out, the new government would have to be empowered to impose laws and levy taxes directly upon the population, and to enforce its acts through its own executive and judiciary. Second, he hoped that membership in the new Congress would result from "such a process of elections as will most certainly extract from the mass of the society the purest and noblest characters it contains."

ONE STATE, ONE VOTE?

Yet, because Madison also doubted whether popularly chosen representatives could ever be entirely trusted, he hoped to make an indirectly elected Senate (with members nominated by the legislatures but elected by the people) the true linchpin of government. Not only would this Senate thwart the passage of ill-conceived laws by the lower house, it would manage the nation's foreign relations and appoint all major federal officials. But since even the Senate could not always be counted upon to legislate wisely, Madison sought an additional check in the form of a joint executive-judicial Council of Revision that would possess a limited veto over all acts of Congress.

Most important of all, Madison wanted to arm the national government with a "negative in all cases whatsoever" over the acts of the states. This radical veto power would be shared jointly by Congress (or the Senate) and the Council of Revision.

In Madison's mind, the whole edifice of the Virginia Plan rested on the adoption of some form of proportional representation in Congress. If the Confederation's "one state, one vote" scheme were retained, for example, each citizen of tiny Delaware (population in 1790: 59,000) would, in effect, carry the same weight in the powerful new government as 12 Virginians. Delegates from Massachusetts and Pennsylvania, the Confederation's other two largest states, reached the same conclusion.

The Pennsylvanians, in fact, wanted to deny the small states an equal vote even within the Convention. But in a private caucus held before the Convention, the Virginians persuaded Pennsylvania's leading delegates—James Wilson (the Convention's finest legal mind), Gouverneur Morris (its wiliest advocate and its most talkative delegate, with 173 speeches), and Robert Morris (the former superintendent of finance for the Confederation)—that they could prevail over the small states by force of reason. And sooner rather than later. For the large states' delegates also agreed that the problem of representation had to be solved first.

Two of the small states' leaders tried to avoid the clash: Roger Sherman, a 66-year-old Connecticut farmer and store-keeper turned politician, and John Dickinson of Delaware, who had gained fame as the "penman of the Revolution" during the late 1760s for his antitax *Letters from a Farmer in Pennsylvania.* Sherman was among the signers of the Declaration of Independence; Dickinson had refused to put his name to it, still hoping for reconciliation with Great Britain. Both men had taken leading roles in drafting the Articles of Confederation a decade before the Convention. Now, during the early days of debate in Philadelphia, they tried to head off full discussion of the dangerous issue of representation.

Let the Convention first determine what it wanted the national government to do, they suggested. Perhaps it might vest Congress with only a few additional powers; then there would be no need to propose any changes in the system of representation.

TOWARD THE GREAT COMPROMISE

Their opponents would not waver. "Whatever reason might have existed for the equality of suffrage when the union was a federal one among sovereign states," Madison flatly declared, "must cease when a national government should be put into the place."

Although interrupted by discussion of other issues, such as fixing the qualifications for legislative office, the struggle over representation would go on for seven grueling weeks. It lasted until July 16, when the Great Compromise, as scholars now call it, allowed the Convention to move forward.

The fight went through three phases. During the first (May 29–June 13), the large states exploited the initiative they had seized with the Virginia Plan to gain an early endorsement of the principle of proportional representation in both houses. The small-state men rallied after June 14, when William Paterson, 42, a diminutive country lawyer and New Jersey attorney general—"of great modesty," noted Georgia's William Pierce, "whose powers break in upon you and create wonder and astonishment"—presented the New Jersey Plan.* This second round of debate came to a dramatic end on July 2, when the convention deadlocked (five states to five, with Georgia divided, and thus losing its vote) over a motion by Oliver Ellsworth of Connecticut to give each state an equal vote in the Senate.

Round Three began immediately, with the appointment of a committee made up of one member from each delegation and explicitly charged with finding a compromise. The Convention received its report on July 5, debated it until the 14th, and finally approved it by a narrow margin two days later.

These seven weeks were the Convention's true testing time. The tension is apparent to anyone who reads Madison's daily notes. The character of debate covered a wide spectrum, from highly principled appeals to heavy-handed threats and pokerfaced bluffs.

In the speeches of the large states' leading advocates—Madison, Wilson, and Rufus King, the 32-year-old lawyer from Massachusetts—one finds powerful and profound briefs for the theory of majority rule. Indeed, the spokesmen for the other side rarely met the arguments on their own terms. Delaware's hot-tem-

---

*The New Jersey Plan would have amended the Articles of Confederation, leaving the unicameral Congress intact, but empowering it to elect a plural executive and granting the national government the power to impose taxes directly on the citizens of states that failed to meet the contributions quotas assigned them by Congress. The government would also have the power to compel the states to abide by its laws by force of arms. This was a crucial concession, for it acknowledged the fundamental weakness of confederation.

pered Gunning Bedford, Jr., claimed, for example, that the large states would "crush the small ones whenever they stand in the way of their ambitious or interested views." But when Madison and his allies demanded to know what common interest could ever unite societies as diverse as those of Massachusetts, Pennsylvania, and Virginia, the small-state men could not come up with an answer.

What was finally at issue was a question not so much of reason as of will. John Dickinson had made sure that Madison got the point immediately after the New Jersey Plan was introduced on June 15. "You see the consequences of pushing things too far," he warned, as the delegates filed out of the chamber at the end of the day. "Some of the members from the small states wish for two branches in the general legislature, and are friends to a good national government: but we would sooner submit to a foreign power, than submit to be deprived of an equality of suffrage in both branches of the legislature, and thereby be thrown under the domination of the large states."

SKEPTICISM ABROAD

When the large states hinted that perhaps they might confederate separately, or that the Union might dissolve if their demands were not met, Bedford retorted that the small states would "find some foreign ally of more honor and good faith, who will take them by the hand and do them justice."

In the end, it was the bluff of the large states that was called. Once the deadlock of July 2 demonstrated that the small states would not buckle, the necessity for compromise became obvious. And the committee, called the Grand Committee, that the Convention elected to that end was stacked in favor of the small states. The three members chosen for the most populous states—Elbridge Gerry of Massachusetts, Benjamin Franklin of Pennsylvania, and George Mason of Virginia—were less militant than others in their delegations.

While the Grand Committee labored, the other delegates observed the 11th anniversary of American Independence. Philadelphia marked the occasion in fine fashion. A fife-and-drum corps paraded about the city; the militia fired three cannonades. In the local taverns, revelers toasted the day.

The 'Nefarious Institution'

James Madison was somewhat surprised by the intensity of the debates between the large and small states at Philadelphia. After all, he told the delegates on June 30, the states were really not divided so much by size as by "the effects of their having, or not having, slaves."

Yet slavery did not become a major issue at the Constitutional Convention. In August, Gouverneur Morris passionately denounced it as "a nefarious institution." But, as John Rutledge of South Carolina quickly reminded the delegates, "the true question at present is whether the Southern states shall or shall not be parties to the union."

As they would time and again during the Convention, the delegates turned away from divisive social issues to focus on what historian James MacGregor Burns has called the "mundane carpentry" of making a constitution.

Abolitionist sentiment was widespread but not deep in 1787. Traffic in imported African slaves was outlawed everywhere except in Georgia and the Carolinas, yet only Massachusets had banned slave ownership. Many delegates, Northerners and Southerners alike, disliked slavery; some also believed, as Connecticut's Oliver Ellsworth said, that the arrival of cheap labor from Europe would ultimately "render slaves useless."

Such hopes, combined with the delegates' sense of the political realities, led them to reduce the slavery issue to a series of complicated tradeoffs.

Early in June, the large states accepted the famous "three-fifths" compromise: Slaves (carefully referred to as "all other Persons") would each count as three-fifths of a free white "person" in any scheme of representation by population. In return, the Georgians and Carolinians tacitly agreed to support the large states' ideas for a strong national government.

But on August 6, a report by the Committee of Detail upset the agreement. The Committee recommended several measures that would weaken the new national government, including a ban on national taxes on exports. More important, it proposed a ban on any federal regulation of the slave trade.

The debate was heated. Rufus King of Massachusetts reminded the Southerners of the earlier bargain and added that he could not agree to let slaves be "imported without limitation and then be represented in the National Legislature." A slave influx could give undue legislative power to the South.

Another committee—the Committee of Eleven—was named to mediate the dispute. After more haggling, the ban on export taxes was retained. The government would be empowered to halt the slave trade in 1808. But the new Constitution also mandated the return to their owners of escaped slaves.

Congress did abolish the slave trade in 1808, but the "peculiar institution" did not die. Inevitably, the North-South division that Madison saw in 1787 widened, while the heated conflict between the large and small states faded almost as soon as the delegates left Philadelphia. The Framers' artful compromises, later denounced by abolitionists as "A Covenant with Death and an Agreement with Hell," could not contain the nation's passions over slavery.

The delegates kept their worries to themselves. "We were on the verge of dissolution," wrote Luther Martin, "scarce held together by the strength of an hair, though the public papers were announcing our extreme unanimity." Indeed, up and down the Atlantic seaboard, editors were speculating about the proceedings in Philadelphia. "With zeal and confidence, we expect from the Federal Convention a system of government adequate to the security and preservation of those rights which were promulgated by the ever memorable Declaration of Independency," proclaimed the *Pennsylvania Herald*. "The world at large expect something from us," said Gerry. "If we do nothing, it appears to me we must have war and confusion."

In Britain, France, and Spain, royal advisers awaited news from America with detached curiosity. The Spaniards were particularly interested in the proceedings at Philadelphia, for if an effective government were not formed, American settlers in the lands west of the Appalachians might fall into their orbit. Even after the adoption the Constitution, wrote historians Samuel Eliot Morison and Henry Steele Commager, "most European observers believed that the history of the American Union would be short and stormy."

On July 5, the committee presented its report to a glum Convention. The compromise it proposed was one in name only. In return for accepting an equal state representation in the Senate, the large states would gain the privilege of having all tax and appropriations bills originate in the House of Representatives, whose members were apportioned on the basis of population, with no changes by the upper chamber allowed. (Later, the Convention decided to allow the Senate to alter tax and spending laws.) Madison and his allies dismissed the proposed tradeoff as worthless, neither desirable in theory nor useful in practice; the Senate, they said, could simply reject a bill it disliked.

AVERTING A COLLAPSE

But, by this time, argument no longer mattered.

The key vote of July 16 found five states for the compromise, four against, and Massachusetts divided by Gerry and Caleb Strong, who insisted that "an accommodation must take place." The compromise won, but not by much.

Emotions were still running high. New York's two remaining delegates, Robert Yates and John Lansing, Jr., had departed on July 10, declaring that the Convention was exceeding its authority. This point was raised several times during the proceedings, and brushed aside. As James Wilson had put it, the Convention was "authorized to *conclude nothing,* but . . . at liberty to *propose anything.*"

Next on the Convention's agenda for the afternoon of July 16th was the difficult task of beginning to define the extent of the legislative authority of Congress.

But the large states' delegates were unprepared to go on. The broad powers the Virginia Plan had proposed for Congress had rested on the expectation that both houses would be selected by proportional voting. "The vote of this morning had embarrassed the business extremely," Edmund Randolph declared during the afternoon of the 16th. He suggested that the Convention adjourn to give both sides a chance to rethink their positions. Mistakenly believing that Randolph was calling for an adjournment *sine die* (indefinitely), William Paterson of New Jersey immediately jumped to his feet and enthusiastically agreed that "it was high time for the Convention to adjourn, that the rule of secrecy ought to be rescinded, and that our constituents should be consulted."

But that, Randolph apologized, was not what he had meant. All he sought was an overnight adjournment. Tempers cooled, a few members hastened to remind their colleagues that even if "we could not do what was best, in itself, we ought to do something," and the Convention broke up for the day.

A SINGLE EXECUTIVE?

The next morning, the large states' delegates caucused to decide whether to pull out and confederate separately. "The time was wasted in vague conversation on the subject," Madison noted, "without any specific proposition or agreement." The Convention, despite the large states' unhappiness, would continue.

The critical vote of July 16, then, was not a compromise as we ordinarily use the term. One side had won its point, the other had lost. But the outcome of this struggle did cause a series of other changes and "accommodations" that profoundly affected both the structure of the future U.S. government and its powers.

In its preoccupation with representation in Congress, the Convention had barely discussed the other two branches of government. Most of the delegates agreed with Madison that the central problem was to find a way to enable the executive and the judiciary to withstand the "encroachments" of the legislature. But how was that to be accomplished?

At an early point, the Convention had rejected Madison's scheme for a joint executive-judicial Council of Revision. The judiciary could simply overturn unconstitutional laws by itself, the members felt, and it would be most effective if "free from the bias of having participated" in writing the laws.

It is remarkable how little time the Framers spent discussing the role of the judiciary. Harvard's Raoul Berger noted some years ago that "the very casualness with which the [Convention's] leadership assumed that judicial review was available . . . suggests that the leaders considered they were dealing with a widely accepted doctrine." In their focus on the powers of the other branches of gov-

ernment, however, the Framers never sought to prescribe either the scope of the courts' power to declare laws unconstitutional or the basis on which this power could be exercised.

Far more of the Convention's time was devoted to the subject of executive power. But here, too, it is difficult to fathom exactly what the Framers intended.

Something of the uncertainty the convention had to overcome was illustrated when the subject of the executive was first raised on June 1. After James Wilson moved that "the executive consist of a single person," the delegates sat speechless in their chairs, reluctant to begin discussing so great an issue. "A considerable pause ensuing," noted Madison, "and the chairman asking if he should put the question, Dr. Franklin observed that it was a point of great importance and wished that the gentlemen would deliver their sentiments on it before the question was put." A lively debate began, and it immediately revealed two things.

The delegates agreed that a republican executive could not be modeled on the British monarchy. Second, most members thought that considerations of efficiency and responsibility alike required an executive headed by a single person—though a few dissenting members joined Randolph in fearing that such an office would prove "the foetus of monarchy." The dissenters variously favored either a plural executive, a kind of government by committee, or some form of ministerial government, akin to the British cabinet.

The great puzzle was how the executive was to be elected.

Today, Americans regard the strange device that the Framers finally invented, the electoral college, as evidence of how far they were prepared to go to prevent a popular majority from choosing a potential tyrant. What the Framers actually feared, however, was that a scattered population could never "be sufficiently informed of characters," as Roger Sherman put it, to choose wisely among what the Framers assumed would be a large field of candidates.*

Believing that popular election was impractical, then, many delegates saw no alternative to having Congress choose the executive. But this only raised other objections. An election by Congress would be "the work of intrigue, cabal, and of faction," Gouverneur Morris asserted. "Real merit" would be passed over.

Moreover, the executive could not be expected to discharge his duties consci-

entiously, free from improper legislative influence, unless he were made ineligible for reelection. But that, Morris noted, would "destroy the great motive to good behavior, the hope of being rewarded by a reappointment." Such an executive, he continued, would be tempted to "make hay while the sun shines."

The desire for reelection would be an incentive to good behavior. But would that not leave open the possibility that a leader's fondness for the powers and perquisites of office—or a public that had grown too used to a leader—might lead to the creation of a monarchy in everything but name?

FISHING FOR TROUT

Just before it recessed on July 26, the Convention agreed (six states to three, with Virginia divided) to have Congress appoint a single executive, to serve for a single seven-year term. It then turned the task of recasting all the resolutions approved thus far over to a Committee of Detail composed of Randolph, Wilson, Ellsworth, John Rutledge of South Carolina, and Nathaniel Gorham of Massachusetts.

The muggy weather continued. "At each inhaling of air," wrote one visitor to Philadelphia, "one worries about the next one. The slightest movement is painful." Many of the delegates from nearby states took the opportunity to return home. Others fled to the countryside. General Washington, in his usual terse style, recorded in his journal: "In company with Mr. Govr. Morris and in his Phaeton with my horses, went up to one Jane Moore's (in whose house we lodged) in the vicinity of Valley Forge to get Trout."

When they reconvened on August 6, the delegates were eager to move the business toward a conclusion. During the remaining six weeks, the debates became more rushed—and more focused. They centered on specific clauses and provi-

*Article II, Section 1 of the Constitution grants each state "a Number of Electors, equal to the whole Number of Senators and Representatives to which the State may be entitled in the Congress." The small states thus enjoyed more influence than they would have under a strictly proportional system. It was hoped that the electors would be the wisest and ablest men of their states. The Constitution does not require electors to bind themselves to particular candidates: In 1968, a North Carolina elector designated as a Republican cast his vote for George Wallace.

sions; decisions that would figure prominently in later controversies over the Constitution were reached with surprisingly little discussion, revealing far less about the Framers' intentions than modern commentators would like to know.

Far and away the most momentous changes that took place were those involving the powers of the executive.

In the report of the Committee of Detail, the major duties of the president (as the committee now named the executive) were confined to seeing that the laws were "duly and faithfully executed" and to serving as commander-in-chief of the armed forces. He would also enjoy a limited veto over acts of Congress. Two of the powers that provide the foundation for much of the political authority of the modern presidency remained in the Senate: the power to make treaties and the power to appoint ambassadors and justices of the Supreme Court (and perhaps even the heads of major executive departments, though this was left unclear).

In Britain, these powers were critical elements of the royal prerogative, and the Framers were reluctant to grant them to the president. Yet, with the report of the Committee of Detail in their hands, many began to reconsider. Madison, Wilson, Gouverneur Morris, and other delegates from the large states now opposed giving sole power over foreign affairs to the Senate, a body in which the small states would enjoy disproportionate influence, and whose members would be elected by the presumably reckless state legislatures.

SHAPING THE PRESIDENCY

From this unhappiness with the Great Compromise over representation in Congress, a new concept of the presidency began to emerge. Though many of the Framers worried about the potential abuse of executive power, some now described the president, in Gouverneur Morris's words, as "the general guardian of the national interests." He would not only carry out the national will as it was expressed by the legislature, but also act independently to define a national interest larger than the sum of the legislators' concerns.

The best evidence for this enlarged conception of executive power is circumstantial, resting less on anything the delegates said than on the final changes that led to the adoption of the electoral col-

lege. Unfortunately, the key discussions took place within the Committee on Postponed Parts, appointed on August 31 to consider a potpourri of unresolved issues. Very little is known about what was said during its debates.

In the Committee's major report, read September 4, the president suddenly enjoyed significant responsibility for foreign affairs and the power to appoint ambassadors, judges, and other officials, with the "advice and consent" of the Senate. At the same time, his election by an electoral college promised to make the president politically independent of Congress. The report also specified a four-year term and eligibility for reelection.

The Committee had clearly sought to preserve the Great Compromise. The large states, it was assumed, would enjoy the advantage in promoting candidates for the presidency. (None of the Framers anticipated the formation of powerful political parties.) But if an election failed to produce a majority—as many delegates thought it usually would—the election would fall to the Senate. There, the small states would have greater influence.

SAVING THE DAY

James Wilson rose to object. If the Senate controlled the ultimate power of election, he warned, "the President will not be the man of the people as he ought to be, but the Minion of the Senate." Many members agreed, but nobody could find a solution that would not erode the Great Compromise.

It was only after the report had been adopted that Roger Sherman and North Carolina's Hugh Williamson had the idea of sending deadlocked elections into the House of Representatives, with the members voting by states. This had the ingenious effect of preserving both the president's independence from the Senate and the Great Compromise. The amendment was adopted almost without debate.*

---

*The House of Representatives has been called upon to decide an election only twice: In 1800, it selected Thomas Jefferson over Aaron Burr; in 1824, John Quincy Adams over Andrew Jackson, Henry Clay, and William H. Crawford. The possibility that a candidate might prevail in the electoral college without winning a majority of the popular vote—which has occurred only once, when Benjamin Harrison defeated Grover Cleveland in 1888—has sparked many proposals for reform over the years.

On September 12, George Mason broached the subject of a Bill of Rights. "It would give great quiet to the people," he argued, if trial by jury and other rights were guaranteed in the new Constitution. Roger Sherman replied that a Bill of Rights was unnecessary. The states, he said, could protect these rights: Eight of them had already incorporated such provisions into their constitutions. The discussion was brief. The Convention voted against including a Bill of Rights, 10 states to none. Only later, after several state ratifying conventions demanded it, were the guarantees that Americans now associate with the Constitution introduced in Congress and ratified by the states as the first 10 amendments.

Despite this progress, Madison was gloomy. As he informed Jefferson seven weeks later, he was discouraged because the Convention had rejected the Virginia Plan's scheme for an unlimited national veto of all state laws, instead vesting the courts with narrower powers of review. Madison was convinced that an independent judiciary, as framed by the Convention, would lack the political strength to override the improper acts of the legislatures, which could always claim to express the will of the people.

Madison had entered the Convention with higher hopes and more ambitious goals than any of the other delegates. What they saw as compromises and accommodations he regarded as defeats. He privately thought that the worst "vices of the political system" would go unchecked even if the new national government worked as planned. He did not cheer the end result.

So it fell to Benjamin Franklin to claim the privileges of age and reputation to urge the 41 delegates still present as the Convention drew to a close to make their final approval of the Constitution unanimous. That would speed its ratification by Congress and the states.

A HOPEFUL EXPERIMENT

"When you assemble a number of men to have the advantage of their joint wisdom," Franklin reminded them, "you inevitably assemble with those men, all their prejudices, their passions, their errors of opinion, their local interests, and their selfish views. From such an assembly," he asked, "can a perfect production be expected? It therefore astonishes me,

Sir, to find this system approaching so near to perfection as it does; and I think it will astonish our enemies, who are waiting with confidence to hear that our councils are confounded like those of the Builders of Babel. . . . Thus I consent, Sir, to this Constitution, because I expect no better, and because I am not sure that it is not the best."

On September 15, 1787, the delegates, voting by states, did endorse the Constitution. But Franklin's appeal failed to sway three of the delegates. Mason, Randolph, and Gerry refused, for various reasons, to sign the Constitution. Mason worried, among other things, about the extent of the president's powers and the absence of a Bill of Rights.

For what Franklin invoked was not simply the cumulative wisdom of what the Framers had wrought, but also the character of the deliberations themselves. No one could better gauge the range of intentions, honorable and otherwise, that had entered into the making of the Constitution than Franklin, who was perhaps the most worldly and calculating of all the Framers. No one could better grasp both the limits as well as the possibilities of human reason than the leading American experimental scientist of his century.

Franklin was bold enough to observe how "near to perfection" the completed Constitution came, yet he was just as prepared to concede that the objections against it might have merit. (Franklin himself favored a unicameral national legislature and a plural executive.) With his usual cleverness, he asked only that "every member of the Convention who may still have objections to it, would with me, on this occasion doubt a little of his own infallibility."

It took Madison a while to appreciate Franklin's wisdom. But when he dictated the final paragraphs of his preface to the Philadelphia debates, he took the same philosophical view. "Of the ability and intelligence of those who composed the Convention," he wrote, "the debates and proceedings may be a test." But, he went on, "the character of the work which was the offspring of their deliberations must be tested by the experience of the future, added to that of the nearly half century which has passed."

To see the Constitution as Franklin asked its very first critics to see it, or as Madison later learned to view it, does not require later generations to invest the Framers with perfect knowledge, to conclude that they had closely considered and conclusively resolved every issue and problem that they faced.

The Framers were patriotic men of varied capacities who rose above their passions and self-interest to forge a grand document. But they left Philadelphia viewing the Constitution as a hopeful experiment whose results and meanings would be made known only through time.

Nothing would have struck the Framers as more unrealistic than the notion that their original intentions must be the sole guide by which the meaning of the Constitution would ever after be determined. They did not bar future generations from trying to improve upon their work, or from using the lessons of experience to judge the "fallibility" of their reason. They asked only that we try to understand the difficulties that they had encountered and the broad array of concerns, variously noble and self-serving, that they had labored to accommodate during nearly four months of debate in the City of Brotherly Love.

Philadelphia 1787

The host city for the Constitutional Convention was the largest, most cosmopolitan, and progressive in America—but not without its share of urban problems.

Harold Holzer

Harold Holzer, who works for New York Governor Mario Cuomo, is also a free lance writer specializing in political history.

Philadelphia could not have been the most agreeable place to live and work in the summer of 1787.

A torrid heat wave had made America's largest city almost unbearable that year. Older Philadelphians could recall no hotter summer in nearly forty years. "At each inhaling of air," a tormented visitor recorded, "one worries about the next one. The slightest movement is painful." But the heat was not the city's only discomfort. Mud choked the unpaved streets. Polluted by latrines, drinking water from private wells grew more bitter. Swarms of flies and other insects plagued people night and day. And to make matters worse, sewers in the center of the city were being dug up and reconstructed. Acrid odors from the sewers, stables, breweries, tan-yards, and gutters pervaded the city.

But it was in this sweltering, teeming metropolis, rife with discomfort and pollution, that fifty-five men from twelve* of the United States lived and worked for four months, trying to craft what one of them, James Madison, prayed would be a "firm, wise, manly system of federal government."

Even before the Constitutional Convention, Philadelphia had earned its position as the cradle of national liberty. It was here that America had declared itself free in 1776 under "the laws of Nature and Nature's God." Here, too, the first sessions of Congress had met—at least until its members fled the city in the summer of 1783 in the wake of Continen-

---

*Rhode Island refused to send representatives to the Constitutional Convention.

tal Army veterans who marched into town to demand back pay.

Although the summer heat of Philadelphia in 1787 was anything but conducive to industriousness, the delegates met at the revered old State House—the monument now known as Independence Hall—from five to seven hours a day, five or six days a week, beginning May 25.

There they had to decide whether to open or close the windows. If they kept them closed, they would inevitably sweat and suffer profusely, even if they shed their coats in the privacy of their deliberations. New England delegates to the Convention, such as John Langdon Jr. and Nicholas Gilman from New Hampshire and most likely Elbridge Gerry from Massachusetts, had brought and wore only their heavy woolen suits and tight wigs. Some of the southerners had known enough to bring light clothes, such as they were two hundred years ago, but at best they suffered only slightly less than their fellow countrymen from the North. If the delegates, clothed so warmly, chose to let in some air, they would hear the incessant pounding of hooves and wooden wheels over the cobblestones on Walnut Street. And more flies—a "veritable torture," according to one visitor to the city—would invade the premises.

It is not known what the delegates decided about the windows because the president of the convention, George Washington, steadfastly barred the press and public from the proceedings, "lest our transactions get into the newspapers and disturb the public repose." But what is known is that the city tried to accommodate the states's representatives. On June 22, local street commissioners directed that gravel from the sewer site be carted over to the vicinity of the State House and spread along the pavement to muffle the noise.

No matter how appalling its sanitation and amenities seem retrospectively, however, Philadelphia was not unlike other large American cities of the age: busy, dirty, noisy—but exhilarating. Not a single delegate left a record of complaint or regret about the city.

OF COURSE SOME DELEGATES, IN FACT all those from Pennsylvania, lived in Philadelphia year-round. Benjamin Franklin, the city's first citizen and a delegate to the convention, lived across the street from "The Market," an immaculately clean but boisterously busy three-block-long enclosed produce fair that, three days a week, attracted a veritable riot of shoppers, representing "some of every nation under heaven."

The original renaissance American, Franklin had only recently returned from his years of diplomatic triumph in France. Now a "short, fat, trunched old man" with a "bald pate and white locks," as one visitor described him, and all but immobilized from gout and kidney stones, the eighty-one-year-old Franklin nonetheless attended sessions as a delegate, held court at his house, welcomed guests to a dining room that seated twenty-four, and simultaneously oversaw some new additions to his property, including a print shop for his grandson.

Some say that as Franklin more and more emerged as a man of the world he was less and less trusted as a man of his city. Whether Philadelphians liked it or not, each working day they were presented with the unforgettable sight of this living monument commuting grandly to and from the State House. Because ordinary carriages jostled his aching body, Franklin imported from Paris a glass-windowed sedan chair, which he rode daily like some potentate, carried by local jail prisoners.

From *American History Illustrated*, May 1987, pp. 20-25. Reprinted through the courtesy of Cowles Magazines, publishers of *American History Illustrated*.

At night, Franklin's exhausted bearers would return to their cells in the Walnut Street Gaol, that, to the mortification of some local officials, stood directly across from State House yard. Delegates were frequently confronted with the sight of convicts thrusting makeshift sacks on poles through their cell bars, shouting "foul and horrid" profanities at the passersby. The day before Washington arrived in town, men were executed there. And yet the twelve-year-old fortress was considered a model prison of its day.

SURELY THE MOST WONDROUS PLACE IN Philadelphia was Charles Willson Peale's museum, opened in his home in 1786. Peale was a portrait painter and an incurable collector. His museum was the Smithsonian of its day, an eclectic attic full of artworks, natural wonders, and scientific curiosities.

Here, Peale's advertisements claimed, visitors would be "gratified in the sight of many of the Wonderful Works of Nature which are now closeted and but seldom seen." Such claims were not overstated. Peale's manmade beach boasted a wide assortment of mummified "turtles, frogs, toads, lizards, water snakes," and "a collection of fish with their skins stuffed, water fowls . . . all having the appearance of life." It was a taxidermist's dream: "birds . . . partridge, quail, heath-hen . . . geese, ducks, cranes, herons," and animals as well: "bear, deer, leopard, tiger, wildcat, fox." Even the branches of the trees were "loaded with birds." Everything was "real, either their substance or their skins finely preserved."

Peale personally greeted guests when he could, admonishing them not to touch the stuffed birds, which they invariably did anyway, ignoring the large sign that read: "THEY ARE TREATED WITH ARSNIC [sic] POISONING." The museum was a "school of education for children," a treasure-trove of wonders for adults—irresistible to both.

There was nothing else quite like Peale's unusual house in all of Philadelphia, although there were many great homes. There was William Shippen's on Prune Street, for example, which in addition to hosting several delegates had the distinction of housing a camel in its back yard. William Bingham's mansion on the south side of town boasted a greenhouse and exotic fruit trees, as well as a rare circular driveway off Third Street.

Just up the block was the Willing plot, with a lovely home occupied by the owner, a leading merchant, and an even larger one he rented to Benjamin Chew, former Chief Justice of Pennsylvania. Judge Chew's daughter would be married there during the convention, with George Washington in attendance as a special guest.

Nearby, William Lewis lived in "Fort Wilson," so named because during the Revolution, its owner, James Wilson, had been besieged there by a mob of Patriots protesting his acting as attorney for local Loyalists. Friends, among them several who would later become Convention delegates, rushed off to nearby Carpenters' Hall, the guild headquarters off Chestnut Street, to gather muskets to hold off the attack.

During the Convention, Carpenters' Hall was occupied by the Library Company of Philadelphia. Many delegates went there during the summer to borrow books. (Two failed to return them.) Built in 1773, the little hall still stands, once again run by the Carpenters' Company.

Intermingled with the stately and imposing homes were the inns and boarding houses, bursting with Convention activity. Right next door to the Franklin residence were the stables of the Indian Queen, the city's largest and most popular tavern. A visitor from New York once described the place as "a large pile of buildings with many spacious halls and numerous small apartments appropriated for lodging rooms, and kept in an elegant style." Washington dined here at least twice that summer, and many of his colleagues did so more often, although the inn directly fronted the block-long excavation of the Fourth Street sewer.

At City Tavern on Second Street, a highly popular gathering spot, Rufus King of Massachusetts rented a room, and fellow delegates met there often for informal meetings and receptions. For inspiration, just across the street was the Slate Roof House, where William Penn had resided at the dawn of the century. At the time of the Convention, however, it housed clothes-cleaning and tailor shops.

Among the larger of the local inns was Mary House's "genteel" establishment only minutes from Independence Hall. Although it was only two blocks from the aromatic Potts Brewery, it became the favorite of the Virginia delegates. Here Edmund Randolph and James Madison stayed, and Washington would have, too, had he not accepted a last-minute invitation from Robert Morris to room at his fine, four-story brick mansion.

The Morris house became extremely crowded. Robert and Mary Morris had seven children and two servants, and Washington brought along servants of his own from Mount Vernon. The Morrises entertained lavishly and frequently during the summer, serving lemonade from silver urns and providing harpsichord music during meals. Mrs. Morris recalled she had never had a less demanding guest than Washington. The president of the convention would "come in and be about the house for hours, without any one of the family being aware of it." He spent much time reading, writing, and meditating. And his tranquil stay was disturbed but once, when, to the family's horror, Washington witnessed what he recorded in his diary as "a little malapropos" at the front door, some business associate come to harangue Mr. Morris, known as the richest man in Philadelphia, about paying his London bills. Washington could not have imagined it, but only eleven years later, Morris, the man who had helped finance the Revolution, would spend more than three years in the debtors's prison on Prune Street.

That summer in Philadelphia the Presbyterians were also holding a convention, as was, more importantly, the Society of the Cincinnati, composed of Revolutionary War officers. Philadelphia was alive with hospitality, an ambience that successfully combined business with pleasure.

Philadelphia had another side as well. It was very much a Quaker city, with deep religious roots and a host of churches to show for it. There were the Friends Meeting House and the Old Buttonwood Presbyterian Church in the northeast corner of town, right near Claypoole and Dunlap's shop, where the first copies of the finished constitution were printed. There was Christ Church on Second Street, where delegate James Wilson would be buried in 1798. Washington worshipped "with impartial zeal" during the Convention, visiting a number of churches, including St. Mary's Roman Catholic on May 27.

With such a schedule Washington must have been much in demand in Philadelphia that year—at table, at services, at the portrait painter's. An observer noted that he "lived the life of a national hero" throughout his four months in Philadelphia—eclipsing even Franklin as an object of curiosity and adulation. He had been welcomed into the city by throngs of well-wishers when he arrived at Gray's Landing on the Schuylkill River on Sunday, May 13. Church bells rang, artillery salutes were fired, and crowds followed the General to his first stop—Franklin's home. He would subsequently be wined and dined in "all the leading homes of the city."

As THE CAPITAL CITY OF THE YOUNG nation, and thanks to Washington and the conclave over which he was presiding that summer, Philadelphia became the center of American society. But foreigners remained unimpressed, many still finding the city hopelessly provincial, its men "grave," its women "serious." French visitors complained about everything from the lack of "casement windows" and "coffee-houses" to the absence of "libertine wives."

Another tourist admitted the local girls were attractive, but predicted they'd be "faded at twenty-three, old at thirty-five, decrepit at forty or forty-five." To others the city seemed horribly crowded. "How busy the city by day," complained one, "and how noisy." And yet, "there is no city in the world, perhaps, so quiet" at night. At 11 P.M., "you may walk over half the town without seeing the face of a human being except the watchman" (the town crier who called out the time and weather conditions hourly until daybreak, and would even rouse residents who needed to wake up early). "What a gloomy Sunday reigns," a visitor lamented about the typical Philadelphia Sabbath. "One can imagine that some violent epidemic or plague had obliged everyone to shut himself up at home."

And yet the city had much to offer: miles of beautiful riverfront; the Market, "neat and clean as a dining hall;" the endless but magnificent chiming of bells from churches and street peddlers alike; street lighting, libraries, and a fire company—all proposed or created by Franklin; and shops of every description, selling every convenience a visitor could imagine—even the new fad from Europe, the toothbrush. Without doubt, Philadelphia was the most prosperous, enterprising, and progressive of American cities. It even boasted a municipal clinic that dispensed medical care and drugs to the poor, although many local residents continued to rely on such home remedies

as their favored cure for jaundice: a dose of white wine laced with goose dung and earthworms.

Foreign visitors may have poked fun at Philadelphia's Quaker plainness and pre-Victorian inhibitions, but having watched the delegates to this historic convention walk freely about town, open their own doors, and shop for themselves, even the most jaded observers knew they were witnessing something magnificent in its simplicity. After witnessing this, the Marquis de Berbe-Marbois admitted: "I am not sure that people who have porters, stewards, butlers, and covered carriages with springs would have offered the same resistance to despotism."

Of course the enduring monument to this spirit—the shrine to the emerging nation, was the State House, where the delegates met. It did not look exactly as it now does; in fact the building appeared rather run-down that summer. Its famous steeple had decayed so much that it had been removed after the war, leaving a "naked tower" that would not be crowned again until 1828. One of the streets surrounding the State House square was unpaved. There was excavation for a new Congress Hall on the west side of the square, and another gaping hole on the east side where the new American Philosophical Society would be built.

Yet, despite its deteriorated condition, there was something undeniably compelling about the State House. Built more than fifty years earlier at a cost of six thousand pounds Pennsylvania currency, its graceful federal architecture, gentle piazzas, and spacious interiors made it uniquely attractive for its time. But far more important than what it looked like was what had happened there and what was happening now. For here, as a local paper pointed out that year, a "revolution in favor of liberty" had been forged in 1776. And here a "revolution in government" was taking place in 1787.

In this shrine the Constitution of the United States was formally adopted by the convention in September. As it was being signed by the delegates, James Madison glanced at Benjamin Franklin and observed the old doctor staring intently at Washington's elevated chair, the back of which bore a carved and painted sunburst. Madison then heard Franklin tell the delegates nearby "that Painters had found it difficult to distinguish in their art a rising from a setting sun. I have," said he, "often and often in the

course of the Session, and the vicissitudes of my hopes and fears as to its issue, looked at that behind the President without being able to tell whether it was rising or setting: But now at length I have the happiness to know that it is a rising and not a setting sun."

AND SO IT ENDED—FOR THE DELEGATES, that is, not for Philadelphia. Yet to come was the state convention called to consider ratification, and the official vote of approval on December 12. Not until June of the next year, however, did New Hampshire become the ninth state to ratify, making the Philadelphia-born constitution the official law of the land.

And then, on July 4, 1788, Philadelphia exploded in a "hilarious and picturesque" celebration, a three-mile-long "grand Federal procession" of 17,000 marchers, and floats, such as the huge eagle drawn by six horses, displaying a large, framed copy of the Constitution fixed on a staff crowned by a liberty cap ornament, and accompanied by ten men, each representing a state that had ratified, walking arm-in-arm to symbolize the Union.

Then came the "New Roof" float, a huge dome, with thirteen Corinthian columns and a cupola with the figure of "Plenty" at the pedestal, drawn by ten white horses. The "New Roof" was a symbol based on an allegorical poem composed the previous December by Francis Hopkinson in which he criticized the Anti-Federalists for preferring an old roof to a new one. A banner on the float read: "In Union the fabric stands strong."

Finally, to demonstrate that the people of Philadelphia stood squarely behind the Constitution created in their city, came the ordinary people: the City Troop, of course, the company that had escorted Washington into town to begin the convention, but also a parade of gilders, glovers, tallow chandlers, saddlers, stay makers, coopers, engravers, brass-founders, druggists, bricklayers, gunsmiths, and printers—representatives of every trade, craft, and walk of life from the city where America had sent its best and brightest that torrid summer of 1787.

Suggested additional reading: Miracle at Philadelphia: The Story of the Constitutional Convention, May to September 1787 *by Catherine Drinker Bowen (Little, Brown, 1966).*

The Founding Fathers and Slavery

William W. Freehling

Only a few years ago in a historical age now grown as arcadian as Thomas Jefferson himself no man needed to defend the Founding Fathers on slavery. However serious were their sins and however greedy seemed their pursuits, the men who made the American Revolution were deemed to have placed black slavery at bay. Patriots such as George Washington, historians used to point out, freed their slaves. If Jefferson emancipated few of his, the condemnation of Jeffersonian ideology and the curse of a declining economy were fast driving Virginia's slavery to smash. Only the fabulous profits made possible by Whitney's invention of the cotton gin and the reactionary abstractions perpetuated by Calhoun's repudiation of Jefferson breathed life into the system and waylaid the Fathers' thrust toward peaceful abolition.

This happy tale, once so important and so widely believed, now lies withered by a decade of attack. Scholars such as Robert McColley, Staughton Lynd, William Cohen, and Winthrop Jordan have assaulted every aspect of the old interpretation.[1] Some revisionists write to correct excesses in the former view. Others are driven by a New Leftist contempt for reformers who repudiate radicalism and a modern-day repugnance for liberals contaminated by racism. Whatever their separate reasons and however qualified their individual positions, these scholars, taken together, have hammered out a new image of the Founding Fathers. The image is not attractive. In an era of racial turmoil the racist taints portrayed by Jordan seem even more grotesque than the grasping materialism described by Beard.

The Declaration of Independence, it is now argued, was a white man's document that its author rarely applied to his or to any slaves. The Constitution created aristocratic privilege while consolidating black bondage. Virginia shrank from abolition, for slave prices were too high and race fears too great. Jefferson himself suspected blacks were innately inferior. He bought and sold slaves; he advertised for fugitives; he ordered lashes well laid on. He lived in the grand manner, burying prayers for freedom under an avalanche of debt. In all these evasions and missed opportunities Jefferson spoke for his age. For whatever the virtues of the Founding Fathers, concludes the new view, they hardly put slavery on the road to ultimate extinction. It seems fitting, then, that when Southerners turned their backs on the Declaration and swung toward reaction in the wake of the Missouri crisis, the sage of Monticello himself helped point the way.

Many admirers of Jefferson, aware of a brighter side, scorn this judgment and yearn for a reassessment. The following essay, while in sympathy with their position, is not written for their reasons. More is at stake than Thomas Jefferson: indeed Jefferson's agonized positions on slavery are chiefly important as the supreme embodiment of a generation's travail. Moreover, the historian's task is not to judge but to explain; and the trouble with the new condemnatory view is not so much that it is a one-sided judgment of the Founding Fathers as that it distorts the process by which American slavery was abolished. The new charge that the Founding Fathers did next to nothing about bondage is as misleading as the older notion that they almost did everything. The abolitionist process proceeded slowly but inexorably from 1776 to 1860: slowly in part because of what Jefferson and his contemporaries did not do, inexorably in part because of what they did. The impact of the Founding Fathers on slavery, like the extent to which the American Revolution was revolutionary, must be seen in the long run not in terms of what changed in the late eighteenth century but in terms of how the Revolutionary experience changed the whole of American antebellum history. Any such view must place Thomas Jefferson and his contemporaries, for all their ironies and missed opportunities, back into the creeping American antislavery process.

If men were evaluated in terms of dreams rather than deeds everyone would concede the antislavery credentials of the Founding Fathers. No American Revolutionary could square the principles of the Declaration with the perpetuation of human bondage. Only a few men of 1776 considered the evil of slavery permanently necessary. None dared proclaim the evil a good. Most looked forward to the day when the curse could be forever erased from the land. "The love of justice and the love of country," Jefferson wrote Edward Coles in 1814, "plead equally the cause of these people, and it is a moral reproach to us that they should have pleaded it so long in vain."[2]

If the Founding Fathers unquestionably dreamed of universal American freedom, their ideological posture was weighed down equally unquestionably with conceptions of priorities, profits, and prejudices that would long make the dream utopian. The master passion of the age was not with extending liberty to blacks but with erecting republics for whites. Creative energies poured into designing a political City on the Hill; and the blueprints for utopia came to be the federal Constitution and American union. When the slavery issue threatened the Philadelphia Constitutional Convention the Deep South's ultimatums were quickly met. When the Missouri crisis threatened the Union Jefferson and fellow spirits beat a retreat. This pattern of valuing the Union more than abolition—of marrying the meaning of America to the continuation of a particular government—would persist, producing endless

From *The American Historical Review*, February 1972. Reprinted through the courtesy of Cowles Magazine, publishers of *American Historical Review*.

compromises and finally inspiring Lincoln's war.

The realization of the Founding Fathers' antislavery dream was blocked also by the concern for property rights articulated in their Declaration. Jefferson's document at once denounced slave chains as immoral and sanctioned slave property as legitimate. It made the slave's right to freedom no more "natural" than the master's right to property. Liberty for blacks became irrevocably tied to compensation for whites; and if some proposed paying masters for slaves, no one conceived of compensating South Carolina planters for the fabulous swamp estates emancipation would wreck.

The financial cost of abolition, heavy enough by itself, was made too staggering to bear by the Founding Fathers' racism, an ideological hindrance to antislavery no less important than their sense of priorities and their commitment to property. Here again Jefferson typified the age. As Winthrop Jordan has shown, Jefferson suspected that blacks had greater sexual appetites and lower intellectual faculties than did whites. This racism was never as hidebound as its twentieth-century varieties. Jefferson kept an open mind on the subject and always described innate differences as but his suspicion. Still it is significant, as Merrill Peterson points out, that Jefferson suspected blacks were inferior rather than suspecting blacks were equal.[3] These suspicions, together with Jefferson's painfully accurate prophecy that free blacks and free whites could not live harmoniously in America for centuries, made him and others tie American emancipation to African colonization. The alternative appeared to be race riot and sexual chaos. The consequence, heaping the cost of colonization on the cost of abolition, made the hurdles to emancipation seem unsurmountable.

Jefferson and the men of the Revolution, however, continually dreamed of leaping ahead when the time was ripe. In 1814, while lamenting his own failure, Jefferson urged others to take up the crusade. "I had always hoped," he wrote Edward Coles, "that the younger generation receiving their early impressions after the flame of liberty had been kindled in every breast . . . would have sympathized with oppression wherever found, and proved their love of liberty beyond their own share of it." As late as 1824, five years after his retreat in the Missouri crisis, Jefferson suggested a federally financed postnati abolition scheme that would have ended slavery faster than the plan proposed by his grandson, Thomas Jefferson Randolph, in the famed Virginia slavery debate of 1832.[4]

The ideological stance of Jefferson and other Founding Fathers on slavery, then, was profoundly ambivalent. On the one hand they were restrained by their overriding interest in creating the Union, by their concern for property rights, and by their visions of race war and miscegenation; on the other hand they embraced a revolutionary ideology that made emancipation inescapable. The question is, how was this theoretical ambivalence resolved in practical action?

The answer, not surprisingly, is also ambivalent. Whenever dangers to Union, property, or racial order seemed to them acute, the Founding Fathers did little. In the short run, especially in those Deep Southern states where the going was stickiest, they did almost nothing. But whenever abolition dangers seemed to them manageable Jefferson and his contemporaries moved effectively, circumscribing and crippling the institution and thereby gutting its long-range capacity to endure.

The revisionist view of the Founding Fathers is at its best in emphasizing slavery's short-run strength in Jefferson's South. In Virginia both secure slave prices and frenzied race fears made emancipation a distant goal. Jefferson as legislator did no more than draft abolitionist resolutions, and his revisions of the Virginia slave code did little to ease the lot of slaves and something to intensify the plight of free blacks. Jefferson's proposed clause, requiring a white woman who had a black child to leave the state within a year or be placed "out of the protection of the laws," speaks volumes on why abolition came hard in Virginia. South of Virginia, where percentages of slaves and profits from staple crops ran higher, abolition was more remote. Planters who worked huge gangs of slaves in pestilential Georgia and South Carolina's lowlands never proposed peacefully accepting the end of their world.

The federal Constitution of 1787 also reflected slavery's short-run strength. Garrison's instinct to consign that document to the flames was exactly right, for the Constitution perpetually protected an institution the Fathers liked to call temporary. Safeguards included the three-fifths clause, destined to help make the minority South political masters of the nation for years, and the fugitive slave clause, destined to help return to thralldom men who had risked everything for freedom. Moreover, to lure Georgia and South Carolina into the Union, the Fathers agreed to allow any state to reopen the African slave trade for twenty years. When South Carolina seized the option from 1803 to 1807, the forty thousand imported blacks and their hundreds of thousands of slave descendants paid an awesome price for the creation of the white man's republic.

After the Constitution was ratified, slavery again showed its strength by expanding over the West. "The years of slavery's supposed decline," Robert McColley points out, "were in fact the years of its greatest expansion."[5] In the age of Jefferson black bondage spread across Kentucky and engulfed Alabama and Mississippi. Furthermore, Jefferson as president acquired slave Louisiana, and Jefferson as elder statesman gave his blessings to the resulting diffusion of the system. If in the 1780s Jefferson had believed, as he did in 1819, that diffusing slavery made it more humane, the antislavery clause in the Northwest Ordinance might have been scotched and this essay could not have been written.

Slavery showed its strength not only in Jefferson's Virginia legislature, Philadelphia's Constitutional Convention, and Louisiana's black deltas but also at Monticello itself. By freeing their slaves George Washington and John Randolph lived up to Revolutionary ideals. These men, however, were exceptions. Thomas Jefferson, who freed nine while blithely piling up debts that precluded freeing the rest, was the rule. The plantation life style, with its elegant manner and extravagant tastes, lessened the chance of reducing debts and allowing quick manumission on a massive scale. That life style, in Virginia and throughout the South, was as integral a part of slavery as was South Carolina's hunger for Africans and the Southwest's commitment to cotton.

The master of Monticello, finally, revealed the towering practical strength of slavery in the notorious case of Sally Hemings, his mulatto house servant. Those who enjoy guessing whether Jefferson sired Sally's many offspring can safely be left to their own speculations. The evidence is wildly circumstantial and the issue of dubious importance.

Of greater significance is the way Jefferson and his contemporaries handled the ugly controversy. Alexander Hamilton could cheerfully confess to illicit relations with a white woman and continue with his career. Jefferson's supporters had to ward off all talk of the embarrassing Sally, for interracial sex would ruin anyone's reputation. Nor could Jefferson handle the problem resolutely in the privacy of his own mansion. Firm action would, as Dumas Malone points out, "have looked like a confession that something was wrong on the mountain."[6] Better to look the other way as Sally's light-skinned children multiplied. Better to keep blacks enchained for a time than risk a nation polluted by allegedly lascivious Sallys. Better, in short, to live uneasily in a corrupted City on the Hill than blurt out the full horror of America's nightmare.[7]

The old view, then, that slavery was dying in Jefferson's South cannot withstand the revisionist onslaught. The system was strong and, in places, growing stronger; and the combination of economic interest, concern for the Union, life style, and race prejudice made emancipationists rare in Virginia and almost nonexistent in South Carolina. Jefferson, no immediate emancipationist, refused as president to endorse an antislavery poem that had been sent to him for his approval. He could not, he said, "interpose with decisive effect" to produce emancipation. To interpose at all was to toss away other reforms.[8] Here as always Jefferson reveals himself as the pragmatic statesman, practicing government as the art of the possible. An idealist might fault him for refusing to commit political suicide by practicing utopian politics. But all the evidence of Robert McColley shows that as a practical politician Jefferson accurately gauged impassable obstacles. The point is crucial: long before Garrison, when Jefferson ruled, peaceful abolition was not possible.

What could be done—what Jefferson and his contemporaries did—was to attack slavery where it was weakest, thereby driving the institution south and vitiating its capacity to survive. In a variety of ways the Founding Fathers took positive steps that demonstrated their antislavery instincts and that, taken together, drastically reduced the slavocracy's potential area, population, and capacity to endure.

The first key reform took place in the North. When the American Revolution began slavery was a national institution, thriving both north and south of the Mason-Dixon line. Slaves comprised 14 percent of the New York population, with other figures ranging from 8 percent in New Jersey to 6 percent in Rhode Island and 3 percent in Connecticut and Pennsylvania. In these states, unlike Virginia, percentages of slaves were low enough to permit an unconvulsive variety of reform.

Still, prior to 1776, abolitionists such as John Woolman found the North barren soil for antislavery ideas. As John Jay recalled, "the great majority" of Northerners accepted slavery as a matter of course, and "very few among them even doubted the propriety and rectitude of it."[9] The movement of 1776 changed all this. The humanitarian zeal of the Revolutionary era, together with nonslaveholder hatred of slave competition and universal acknowledgment that the economy did not need slavery, doomed Northern slavery to extinction. In some states the doom was long delayed as Northern slaveholders fought to keep their bondsmen. Slavery was not altogether ended in New York until 1827 and in New Jersey until well into the 1840s. By 1830, however, less than one per cent of the 125,000 Northern blacks were slaves. Bondage had been made a *peculiar* institution, retained alone in the Southern states.[10]

No less important than abolition in old Northern states was the long and bitter fight to keep bondage from expanding. In 1784 Jefferson drafted a congressional ordinance declaring slavery illegal in all Western territories after 1800. The proposed law, keeping bondage out of Alabama and Mississippi no less than Illinois and Indiana, lost by a single vote, that of a New Jerseyite ill in his dwelling. Seldom has a lone legislator lost so good a chance to turn around the history of a nation. "The fate of millions unborn," Jefferson later cried, was "hanging on the tongue of one man, and heaven was silent in that awful moment."[11]

Three years later, in the famed Northwest Ordinance of 1787, Congress decreed slavery illegal immediately in the upper Western territories. The new law left bondage free to invade the Southwest. But without the Northwest Ordinance slavery might have crept into Illinois and Indiana as well, for even with

it bondage found much support in the Midwest.

In the years before 1809 Indiana settlers, led by William Henry Harrison and the so-called Virginia aristocrats, petitioned Congress again and again to allow Midwestern slavery. Indiana's pro-Harrison and anti-Harrison parties were both proslavery; they disagreed only on the tactical question of how to force Congress to budge. When Congress refused to repeal the ordinance, the Indiana legislature in 1805 passed a black indentured servitude act, in effect legalizing slavery. Indiana census takers, more honest than the legislature, counted 237 slaves in the territory in 1810 and 190 in 1820.

In 1809, when the part of Indiana that was most in favor of slavery split off as the new territory of Illinois, the battleground but not the issue shifted. The climax to the territorial phase of the Midwestern quest for slavery came in the Illinois Constitutional Convention of 1818, when proslavery forces, after winning a bitterly contested election to the convention, settled for a renewal of the territorial indentured servitude law because they feared that an explicit slavery law might jeopardize statehood.

With statehood secured, the battle over slavery in Illinois continued in the 1820s. The hero of the antislavery forces was Edward Coles, an enlightened Virginian deeply influenced by Madison and Jefferson. Coles, who came to Illinois to free his slaves and stayed to protect the Northwest Ordinance, narrowly defeated his proslavery rival for governor in 1822. In 1824 he helped secure, by the close vote of 6,640-4,973, final victory in a referendum on a proslavery constitutional convention. With Coles's triumph slavery had again been restricted to the South.[12]

The crusade for slavery in Illinois and Indiana, lasting over a quarter of a century and so often coming so close to victory, forms a dramatic example of the institution's expansive potential in the age of the Founding Fathers. The proslavery drive was turned back in part because of race phobias and economic desires that obsessed nonslaveholding Midwestern farmers. But in an area where victory came so hard no one can deny the importance of the Northwest Ordinance and Edward Coles's crusade in keeping slavery away.

A third antislavery victory of the Founding Fathers, more important than

Northern abolition and the Northwest Ordinance, was the abolition of the African slave trade. This accomplishment, too often dismissed as a non-accomplishment, shows more clearly than anything else the impact on antislavery of the Revolutionary generation. Furthermore, nowhere else does one see so clearly that Thomas Jefferson helped cripple the Southern slave establishment.

The drive to abolish the African slave trade began with the drafting of the Declaration of Independence. Jefferson, with the concurrence of Virginia and the upper South, sought to condemn King George for foisting Africans on his colonies. South Carolina and Georgia, less sure they had enough slaves, demanded the clause be killed. Jefferson acquiesced. Thus was prefigured, at the first moment of national history, the split between upper and lower South that less than a century later would contribute mightily to the disruption of the republic.

At the Constitutional Convention, as we have seen, lower South delegates again postponed a national decision on slave importations. This time a compromise was secured, allowing but not requiring Congress to abolish the trade after twenty years. A year before the deadline Jefferson, now presiding at the White House, urged Congress to seize its opportunity. "I congratulate you, fellow citizens," he wrote in his annual message of December 2, 1806, "on the approach of the period when you may interpose your authority constitutionally" to stop Americans "from all further participation in those violations of human rights which have been so long continued on the unoffending inhabitants of Africa, and which the morality, the reputation, and the best interests of our country have long been eager to proscribe." Although the law could not take effect until January 1, 1808, noted Jefferson, the reform, if passed in 1807, could make certain that no extra African was dragged legally across the seas.[13] In 1807 Congress enacted Jefferson's proposal.

The new law, although one of the most important acts an American Congress ever passed, did not altogether end African importations. Americans illegally imported approximately one thousand blacks annually until 1860. This is, however, a tiny fraction of the number that could have been imported if the trade had been legal and considered legitimate. Brazil imported over a million and a half slaves from 1807 to 1860, and the Deep

South's potential to absorb bondsmen was greater. South Carolina alone imported ten thousand blacks a year in the early nineteenth century, before the law of 1808 went into effect. Louisiana creole planters sought unsuccessfully to make Jefferson's administration grant them the same privilege.[14] The desire of Virginia slaveholders to keep slave prices high no doubt helped feed the abolition of the trade, just as the desire of Illinois nonslaveholders to keep out blacks helped give Edward Coles his triumph. In both cases, however, the Revolutionary generation's conception of slavery as a moral disaster was of undeniable significance.

The law that closed the trade and saved millions of Africans from servitude on new Southwestern plantations also aided slaves already on those plantations. The great Southwestern boom came after the close of the African trade. Slaves could not be "used up," no matter how fantastic yearly profits were, for the restricted supply kept slave prices high. By mid-nineteenth century, moreover, almost all blacks were assimilated to the Southern way, making possible a paternal relationship between master and slave that could ease exploitation. One does not have to romanticize slave life or exaggerate planter paternalism to recognize that bondage would have been crueler if millions of Africans had been available in Mississippi and Louisiana to escalate profits. The contrast with nineteenth-century South America, where the trade remained open, makes the point with precision. Wherever Latin Americans imported so-called raw Africans by the boatload to open up virgin territories, work conditions reached a level of exploitation unparalleled in the New World. Easy access to fresh recruits led to using up laborers; and the fact that slaves were unassimilated foreigners precluded the development of the kind of ameliorating relationship that was possible between master and bondsman in North America.[15]

The law profoundly affected North American whites as well as blacks. Most notably, it shut off the South's importation of labor during the period when immigrants were pouring into the North and the two societies were locked in mortal combat. If the trade had remained open, the operation of the three-fifths clause would have given the South greater congressional representation, and a massive supply of Africans might well have helped Southerners to compete

more successfully in the race to Kansas and the campaign to industrialize. As it was, with the trade closed, fresh immigration fed the Northern colossus by the hour while Southerners fell ever more desperately behind.

Perhaps the most important long-run impact of closing the trade was to help push bondage deeper into the South, thereby continuing the work the Fathers had begun with Northern abolition and the Northwest Ordinance. Now that African markets were closed the new Southwest had to procure its slaves from Northern slave states. By 1860 the resulting slave drain had significantly reduced percentages of slaves and commitments to slavery throughout the border area stretching from Delaware through Maryland and Kentucky into Missouri. Whereas in 1790, almost 20 percent of American slaves lived in this most northern tier of border slave states, the figure was down to 10 percent and falling by 1860. On the other hand, in 1790, the area that became the seven Deep South states had 20 percent of American slaves and by 1860 the figure was up to 54 percent and rising. During the cotton boom the shift was especially dramatic. From 1830 to 1860 the percentage of slaves in Delaware declined from 4 to 1 percent; in Maryland from 23 to 13 percent; in Kentucky from 24 to 19 percent; in Missouri from 18 to 10 percent; and in the counties to become West Virginia from 10 to 5 percent.[16]

By both reducing the economic reliance on slavery and the psychic fear of blacks this great migration had political consequences. Antislavery politicians, echoing Hinton R. Helper's appeals to white racism, garnered thousands of votes and several elections, especially in Missouri, during the 1850s.[17] It was only a beginning, but it was similar to the early stages of the demise of slavery in New York.

While the end of the slave trade indirectly drained slaves from the border South, another Revolutionary legacy, the tradition of individual manumissions, further weakened the institution in the Northern slave states. Although Jefferson did not live up to his dictum that antislavery planters should free their slaves many upper South masters followed precept rather than example in the antebellum years. The Virginia law of 1806, forcing freed slaves to leave the state in a year, did not halt the process as absolutely as some have supposed. Virginia laws passed in 1819 and 1837 allowed county courts to grant exceptions. The ensuing trickle of manumissions was a festering sore to the Virginia slave establishment.[18]

Meanwhile, in two border states, manumission sabotaged the institution more insistently. Delaware, which had 9,000 slaves and 4,000 free blacks in 1790, had 1,800 slaves and 20,000 free blacks in 1860. Maryland, with 103,000 slaves and 8,000 free blacks in 1790, had 87,000 slaves and 84,000 free blacks in 1860. These two so-called slave states came close to being free Negro states on the eve of Lincoln's election. Indeed, the Maryland manumission rate compares favorably with those of Brazil and Cuba, countries that supposedly had a monopoly on Western Hemispheric voluntary emancipation.[19]

The manumission tradition was slowly but relentlessly changing the character of states such as Maryland in large part because of a final Jeffersonian legacy: the belief that slavery was an evil that must some day be ended. Particularly in the upper South, this argument remained alive. It informed the works of so-called proslavery propagandists such as Albert T. Bledsoe; it inspired Missouri antislavery activists such as Congressman Frank Blair and the mayor of St. Louis, John M. Wimer; and it gnawed at the consciences of thousands of slaveholders as they made up their wills.[20] Jefferson's condemnation of slavery had thrown the South forever on the defensive, and all the efforts of the George Fitzhughs could never produce a unanimously proslavery society.

In summary, then, the Revolutionary generation found slavery a national institution, with the slave trade open and Northern abolitionists almost unheard. When Jefferson and his contemporaries left the national stage they willed to posterity a crippled, restricted, peculiar institution. Attacking slavery successfully where it was weakest they swept it out of the North and kept it away from the Northwest. They left the antebellum South unable to secure more slaves when immigrants rushed to the North. Most important of all, their law closing the slave trade and their tradition concerning individual manumissions constituted a doubly sharp weapon superbly calculated to continue pushing slavery south. By 1860 Delaware, Maryland, Missouri, and the area to become West Virginia all had fewer slaves than New York possessed at the time of the Revolution, and Kentucky did not have many more. The goal of abolition had become almost as practicable in these border states as it had been in the North in 1776. As the Civil War began, slavery remained secure in only eleven of the fifteen slave states while black migration toward the tropics showed every capacity to continue eroding the institution in Virginia and driving slavery down to the Gulf.

If the Founding Fathers had done none of this—if slavery had continued in the North and expanded into the Northwest; if millions of Africans had been imported to strengthen slavery in the Deep South, to consolidate it in New York and Illinois, to spread it to Kansas, and to keep it in the border South; if no free black population had developed in Delaware and Maryland; if no apology for slavery had left Southerners on shaky moral grounds; if, in short, Jefferson and his contemporaries had lifted nary a finger—everything would have been different. Because all of this was done slavery was more and more confined in the Deep South as the nineteenth century progressed.

No one spied these trends better than the men who made the Southern revolution of 1860-61. Secessionist newspaper editorials in the 1850s can almost be summed up as one long diatribe against Jeffersonian ideology and the policy to which it led. Committed lower South slaveholders knew the world was closing in on them at the very time the more Northern slave states could not be relied on. Seeing the need not only to fight off Republicans from without but also to halt erosion from within, radical Southerners applauded the movement to re-enslave free blacks in Maryland; many of them proposed reopening the slave trade so that the Gulf states' hunger for slavery could be fed by imported Africans instead of black Virginians; and they strove to gain Kansas in large part to keep Missouri.

When this and much else failed and Lincoln triumphed, lower South disunionists believed they had reached the moment of truth. They could remain in the Union and allow the noose to tighten inexorably around their necks. They would then watch slavery slowly ooze out of the border South and permit their own domain to shrink to a handful of Gulf and lower Atlantic states. Or they could strike for independence while the upper South retained some loyalty to bondage, thereby creating a confrontation and forcing wavering slave states to make their choice. This view of the options helped to inspire the lower South's secession, in part a final convulsive effort to halt the insidious process the Founding Fathers helped begin.[21]

When war came the lower South's confrontation strategy was half successful. Four of the eight upper South states seceded in the wake of Sumter. But four others remained loyal to the North. In the most Northern slave states, Delaware, Maryland, Kentucky, Missouri, and the area to become West Virginia, the slave drain and manumission processes had progressed too far. When the crunch came, loyalty to the Union outweighed loyalty to slavery. Abraham Lincoln is said to have remarked that while he hoped to have God on his side he had to have Kentucky. The remark, however apocryphal, clothes an important truth. In such a long and bitter war border slave states were crucial. If they too had seceded, the Confederacy might have survived. The long-run impact of the Founding Fathers' reforms, then, not only helped lead lower South slavocrats to risk everything in war but also helped doom their desperate gamble to failure.

Any judgment of the founding fathers' record on slavery must rest on whether the long or the short run is emphasized. In their own day the Fathers left intact a strong Southern slave tradition. The American Revolution, however, did not end in 1790. Over several generations, antislavery reforms inspired by the Revolution helped lead to Southern division, desperation, and defeat in war. That was not the most desirable way to abolish slavery, but that was the way abolition came. And given the Deep South's aversion to committing suicide, both in Jefferson's day and in Lincoln's, perhaps abolition could not have come any other way.

This conclusion would have brought tears to the eyes of Thomas Jefferson. Jefferson wrote St. George Tucker in 1797 that "if something is not done, and soon done" about slavery, "we shall be the murderers of our own children."[22] In 1820 he saw with a prophet's eye how that murder would take place. The Missouri crisis, coming upon him like "a Firebell in the Night," almost caused him to shrink from even his own antislavery actions. The "momentous question," he knew, was the "knell of the Union," if not in his own time inevitably soon enough. "I regret that I am now to die in the belief," he wrote John Holmes, "that the useless sacrifice of themselves by the generation of 1776, to acquire self-government and happiness in their country, is to be thrown away by the unwise and unworthy passions of their sons, and that my only consolation is to be, that I live not to weep over it."[23]

No sadder note survives in American literature than this scream of failure from one of the most successful of the Founding Fathers. The irony is that the ambiguous antislavery posture of Jefferson and his contemporaries helped place the nation, unintentionally but perhaps irrevocably, in lockstep toward the blowup. In the late eighteenth century a statesman had two ways to lessen the chance of civil war over slavery. He could ease the racial, sexual, and materialistic fears that made the lower South consider emancipation anathema. Or he could scotch the antislavery idealism the slavocracy found disquieting. Jefferson, mirroring his generation and generations yet unborn, could do neither. Both his antislavery beliefs and his fear of the consequences of those beliefs went too deep. He was caught up too completely in America's most anguishing dilemma. The famed wolf he complained of holding by the ears was his own revolutionary tradition no less than blacks chained in violation of that tradition.

Like reluctant revolutionaries before and since, Jefferson sought to have it both ways. He succeeded, as such men will, in starting something destined to get out of hand. He helped protect slavery where it was explosive and helped demolish it where it was manageable. Meanwhile, he helped give informal sanction to the lower South's worst racial fears at the same time that he helped intensify those fears by unintentionally driving more blacks toward the tropics. Over a seventy-five year period the Founding Fathers' reforms added claustrophobia to a lower South psyche in-

flamed enough in 1787. When that happened the day of the soldier was at hand.

If in 1820 Jefferson pulled back shuddering from the horror he saw ahead, his imperfect accomplishments had taken on a life of their own. And less than a half century later, though hundreds of thousands lay slain by bullets and slaves were but half free, mournful bells in the night would herald the realization of his most radical dream.

NOTES

1. Robert McColley, *Slavery and Jeffersonian Virginia* (Urbana, 1964); Staughton Lynd, *Class Conflict, Slavery and the United States Constitution* (Indianapolis, 1968); William Cohen, "Thomas Jefferson and the Problem of Slavery," *Journal of American History*, 56 (1969): 503–26; Winthrop D. Jordan, *White Over Black: American Attitudes Towards the Negro, 1550–1812* (Williamsburg, 1968). For the fullest summation of the position, see Donald L. Robinson, *Slavery in the Structure of American Politics* (New York, 1971).

2. Thomas Jefferson to Edward Coles, Aug. 25, 1814, in Paul Leicester Ford, ed., *The Works of Thomas Jefferson* (New York, 1904–05), 11: 416.

3. Jordan, *White Over Black*, 429–81; Merrill D. Peterson, *Thomas Jefferson and the New Nation: A Biography* (New York, 1970), 263.

4. Jefferson to Coles, Aug. 25, 1814. Jefferson to Jared Sparks, Feb. 4, 1824, in Ford, *Works of Jefferson*, 11: 416, 12: 335–36.

5. McColley, *Slavery in Jeffersonian Virginia*, 3.

6. Dumas Malone, *Jefferson the President: First Term, 1801–1805* (Boston, 1970), 498.

7. See the stimulating comments on the matter in Jordan, *White Over Black*, 468, and Eric McKitrick, "The View from Jefferson's Camp," *New York Review of Books*, Dec. 17, 1970, p. 37.

8. Jefferson to George Logan, May 11, 1805, in Ford, *Works of Jefferson*, 10:141–42.

9. Jay to Granville Sharp [1788], in Henry P. Jackson, ed., *The Correspondence and Public Papers of John Jay* (New York, 1890–93), 3: 342.

10. Arthur Zilversmit, *The First Emancipation: The Abolition of Slavery in the North* (Chicago 1967).

11. Quoted in Peterson, *Jefferson*, 283.

12. The Indiana-Illinois story can best be followed in Jacob P. Dunn, Jr., *Indiana: A Re-*demption from Slavery* (Boston, 1888); theodore Calvin Pease, *The Story of Illinois* (Chicago, 1949), 72–78; and Adrienne Koch, *Madison's "Advice to My Country"* (Princeton, 1966), 144–51.

13. James D. Richardson, ed., *A Compilation of the Messages and Papers of the Presidents* (Washington, 1910), 1: 396.

14. Philip D. Curtin, *The Atlantic Slave Trade: A Census* (Madison, 1969).

15. See the judicious remarks in C. Vann Woodward, *American Counterpoint: Slavery and Racism in the North-South Dialogue* (Boston, 1971), 97–106.

16. U.S. Census Bureau, *The Statistics of the Population of the United States: Ninth Census—Volume 1* (Washington, 1872), 3–8.

17. Helper is too often treated as a lone voice crying in the wilderness when in fact he was the man who summed up in book form an argument heard constantly in the upper South. See, for example, the files of the St. Louis *Democrat*, Baltimore *Patriot*, and Wheeling *Intelligencer* during the 1850s.

18. See, for example, John C. Rutherfoord, *Speech of John C. Rutherfoord of Goochland, in the House of Delegates of Virginia, on the Removal from the Commonwealth of the Free Colored Population* (Richmond, 1853).

19. James M. Wright, *The Free Negro in Maryland, 1634–1860* (New York, 1921).

20. The Wimer-Blair position is best laid out in the St. Louis *Democrat*. See also Albert T. Bledsoe, *An Essay on Liberty and Slavery* (Philadelphia, 1856), and the ambiguities omnipresent in such upper South newspapers as the Baltimore *American* and Louisville *Courier* throughout the fifties.

21. I hope to demonstrate at length the positions outlined in the last two paragraphs in my forthcoming *History of the South, 1850–61*, to be published by Harper and Row. The best sources on fire-eater positions in the 1850s are the Charleston *Mercury*, New Orleans *Delta*, and *DeBow's Review*. The clearest statements of the connection between lower South secession and upper South wavering are in John Townsend, *The South Alone Should Govern the South* (Charleston, 1860), and Henry L. Benning, *Speech . . . November 6, 1860* (Milledgeville, Ga., 1860). For a preliminary estimate of how the same thinking affected the Virginia Secession Convention, see William W. Freehling, "The Editorial Revolution, Virginia, and the Coming of the Civil War: A Review Essay," *Civil War History*, 16 (1970): 64–72.

22. Jefferson to St. George Tucker, Aug. 28, 1797, in Ford, *Works of Jefferson*, 8: 335.

23. Jefferson to John Holmes, Apr. 22, 1820, in *ibid.*, 12: 158–60.

National Consolidation and Expansion

"From the beginning," two scholars have recently written, "the language of America has been the language of rights." Practically all the complaints that colonists had against England involved violation of one or another of what they perceived as their rights. Critics of the Constitution complained that it included no bill of rights as had many of the state constitutions. In "A Nauseous Project," James Hutson traces the background and the writing of the Bill of Rights and how it came to be adopted by Congress in 1789.

The Constitution also failed to make entirely clear the role of the Supreme Court. During its first decade of existence, the Court was subordinate to the executive and legislative branches. "The Great Chief Justice" shows how John Marshall redefined the Court's powers and established the principle of judicial review.

Exploration and expansion were constant themes throughout the period. Despite numerous expeditions by Europeans, some areas on the western coast of North America remained uncharted. "River of the West" describes how Captain Robert Gray in 1792 located and navigated what he named the Columbia River, thereby establishing American claims to the Oregon territory. "The Odd Couple Who Won Florida and Half the West" is an account of the way John Quincy Adams exploited Andrew Jackson's questionable behavior to acquire territory. Two essays deal with use of these areas. In "Indians in the Land," environmental historians discuss differences between the way Native Americans and whites viewed nature, and "Eden Ravished" tells how the latter plundered natural resources.

Although slavery gradually became extinct in the North, it continued to flourish in the South until the Civil War.

"The Lives of Slave Women" explains what they shared in common with slave men and what set them apart. Their experiences tended to produce more cooperation than among males, but disputes and violences sometimes occurred. Three more articles deal primarily with women. "From Utopia to Mill Town" provides an account of an experimental effort to employ young women in factory work while providing them with a healthy environment in which to live. "Act One" analyzes the early women's rights movement, and "Forgotten Forty-Niners" reveals that women who joined the gold rush were by no means limited to being dance hall girls and prostitutes.

Four essays deal with manners, morals, and life-styles during the period. "The Secret Life of a Developing Country (Ours)" explores a variety of customs and habits that varied regionally and changed over time. "Not Really Greek" provides a sampling of architectural styles favored by the wealthy. "Legacy of Violence" offers a provocative interpretation of modern urban violence, tracing one cause to pre–Civil War Southern concepts of "honor." The early history of the temperance movement is the subject of "The War Against Demon Rum."

Looking Ahead: Challenge Questions

Why did critics of the Constitution insist that a Bill of Rights be added? What kinds of rights were enumerated in the Bill? How did John Marshall help shape constitutional precedents?

How did expansion influence the American people? How did it influence those who were its targets?

Discuss the conditions under which slave women had to live. What rights did white women seek to achieve through political action? How well did they succeed?

THE SEPARATION OF THE MOTHER AND CHILD.

'A Nauseous Project'

James H. Hutson

James H. Hutson is Chief of the Manuscript Division at the Library of Congress. Born in Bridgeport, West Virginia, he received a B.A. (1959) and Ph.D. (1964) from Yale University. He is the author of several books, including John Adams and the Diplomacy of the American Revolution *(1981). This essay is taken from* A Culture of Rights: The Bill of Rights in Philosophy, Politics, and Law—1791 and 1991, *edited by Michael J. Lacey and Knud Haakonssen, published in the Woodrow Wilson Center Series by Cambridge University Press, 1991.*

"From the beginning," write Philip Kurland and Ralph Lerner in a recent book on the framing of the Constitution, "the language of America has been the language of rights." Although this statement might not apply to 17th-century America, few scholars would deny that it accurately describes the situation during the 18th century, especially the period after the passage of the Stamp Act in 1765.

The eagerness of 18th-century Americans to claim rights exasperated those trying to govern them. As early as 1704, James Logan, an agent of William Penn, the founder of the Pennsylvania colony, ridiculed the colonists' obsession with the "Rattle of Rights and Privileges." Three years later this same functionary assailed "the infatuated people of this province" for their "ridiculous contending for rights unknown to others of the Queen's subjects." That the colonists had inflated ideas of their rights was, in fact, a stock complaint of royal officials for as long as the King's writ ran in America. Reverence for rights was not grounded, however, in widespread intellectual mastery of the subject; there were frequent assertions and admissions that Americans did not fully understand the object of their devotion. But they perceived that they could not afford to wait for perfect enlightenment before claiming rights in opposition to the pretensions of an intrusive British government. Thus, the 18th century was a period (not, perhaps, unlike our own) in which the public's penchant for asserting its rights outran its ability to analyze them and to reach a consensus about their scope and meaning.

I

Congress shall make no law respecting an establishment of religion, or prohibiting the free exercise thereof; or abridging the freedom of speech, or of the press; or the right of the people peaceably to assemble, and to petition the government for a redress of grievances.

As the century progressed, and especially after independence set off searching debates in the states about the formation of new governments, Americans reached a common understanding about some aspects of the rights question, and this rough consensus informed the drafting of the Bill of Rights in 1789. To understand what the drafters of that document meant requires, therefore, an explanation of the context from which the Bill of Rights emerged, an investigation that must begin in the reign of King George III and pick its way through a complicated clutter of ideas emanating from moral philosophy, jurisprudence, political theory, and theology.

On whose authority can it be said that Americans did not comprehend the rights they claimed? On Thomas Hutchinson's, for one. "I am sensible," the royal governor lectured the Massachusetts legislature on March 6, 1773, "that nice Distinctions of Civil Rights and Legal Constitutions are far above the reach of the Bulk of Mankind to comprehend." Since Hutchinson was a Loyalist who soon retired to London, his statement might be dismissed as so much Tory superciliousness. Modern scholars have agreed with him, however. Assessing the events in 1773 upon which Hutchinson was commenting, one concluded that "the people at large . . . were too little informed in political theory to have possessed any clear ideas [about rights], and so they voted in ignorance for opinions presented to them by a handful of local leaders."

Just how much difficulty the "people at large" had in dealing with the rights question is revealed by a plaintive letter to a Baptist minister from a back-country delegate to the Massachusetts Constitutional Convention of 1780. "I am sensible," wrote Noah Allen to the Reverend Isaac Backus, that "the work is grate and my gifts Small and I am inexperienced in work of this sort. Dear brother I pray you to favor me with your mind on the subject Expesualy what are the Rights of the people and how that Bill of Rights ought to be drawn." That Allen's perplexity was widespread is attested to by pleas from various Massachusetts towns to the draftsmen of the state constitution to describe rights in language "so explicitly as the lowest capacity may fully understand," to use words "leveled as much as may be to the Capacities of the Subjects in common."

Even the well-informed were vexed by the "numerous and various" opinions on rights. "I consider that there are very few who understand the whole of these rights," Philadelphia lawyer James Wilson complained in 1787. "All the political writers, from Grotius and Puffendorf down to Vattel, have treated on this subject, but in no one of these works, nor in the aggregate of them all, can you find a complete enumeration of rights appertaining to the people as men and citizens."

Formidable though the subject of rights was, John Adams contended in 1765 that many Americans were having trouble coming to grips with it not because they were unable to understand it but because they were unwilling to try to do so. "We have been afraid to think," claimed Adams. "We have felt a reluctance to examine into the grounds of our privileges and the extent to which we have an indisputable right to demand them." Scholars have agreed with Adams, arguing, as one put it, that in the years before 1763 Americans were "noticeably hesitant about spelling out the rights and liberties they claimed." Why was this so? Adams cited "certain prudent reasons" for his countrymen's diffidence. Some Americans, he believed, were opportunists, seekers after political loaves and fishes, who did not want to antagonize potential patrons in the British colonial administration by raising the rights issue. Others, Adams implied, recoiled from a searching investigation of rights when they saw where it might lead. Consequently, when Britain brought on the crisis of 1764–65 by taxing the colonies, Americans were caught intellectually unprepared. They knew they had rights, but they had no coherent, authoritative statement, nothing resembling an intercolonial position paper, on the origin, sum, and scope of those rights. To forge a common understanding on rights became one of the principal challenges confronting American thinkers during the next quarter century.

II

A well regulated Militia, being necessary to the security of a free State, the right of the people to keep and bear Arms, shall not be infringed.

The Stamp Act, announced in Parliament in 1764 and passed in 1765, taxed legal instruments, business documents, and newspapers in the colonies and subjected violators of the act to trial in the vice-admiralty courts, where judges, applying Roman law, sat without juries. This statute started the rights controversy on the most elementary level because everyone in America believed that Magna Carta and other basic documents of the British Constitution forbade the taking of an Englishman's property without his consent. Since the colonists were Englishmen and since they were not represented in Parliament, the Stamp Act violated their constitutional rights. So plain was this proposition that people in Britain, including the officials who drafted the Stamp Act, agreed with it, although they countered with the specious argument that American rights had not been violated after all because the

colonists were "virtually" represented in Parliament. (The doctrine of virtual representation held that members of Parliament represented the citizenry at large, not just the citizens of the particular districts that happened to elect them.)

As the dispute with America intensified, George III's ministers tried to tighten their controls in the colonies. Refractory Massachusetts required special attention. The colony's legislature paid the salaries of the judges of its Superior Court. To deprive the locals of this lever of financial control over the administration of justice, London proposed in 1772 to pay the judges itself. Massachusetts Whigs believed that royal payment of judges serving during royal pleasure might subvert the rule of law by creating an irresponsible and tyrannical judiciary. The proposal was, in their view, politically and morally wrong. But did it violate their rights? The British Constitution was no help here, for it certainly permitted the king to pay his servants. Massachusetts Whigs, therefore, used another voice in the repertoire of rights. Speaking through the Boston Committee of Correspondence, they issued on November 20, 1772 a statement listing the "Natural Rights of the Colonists as Men" and protesting that the payment of the judges violated those rights.

In issuing statements in the language of natural rights, Americans, according to legal scholar John Philip Reid of New York University, "went off the constitutional deep end." What Reid apparently means is that since natural rights (and the law of nature from which they were derived) were unwritten and hence undefined, they could be issued to dignify any desire, to package any prejudice. Indeed, the citizens of Andover, Massachusetts, announced in 1780 that it was "one of the natural and civil rights of a free People" to limit public office to Protestants, and a writer in the *Boston Gazette* claimed in the same year that Congregational ministers had "a natural and unalienable right" to be paid salaries by the state legislature.

Reid also accuses historians of overemphasizing the "nonsense" of natural rights during the revolutionary controversy. In his opinion the primary authority for rights between 1763 and 1776 was the British Constitution; it followed, therefore, that "the revolutionary controversy was concerned with positive constitutional rights, not abstract natural

rights." Not so, argues the political scientist Harry Jaffa: "Natural law always took precedence in the order of importance. The primacy of rights and right, understood in the light of the law of nature, was the argument of the American Revolution from the beginning."

The dispute among contemporary scholars echoes a debate in the First Continental Congress between natural law advocates and proponents of the British Constitution. The First Congress split the difference by agreeing to found American claims on both the "immutable law of nature" and the "principles of the English Constitution." The British paid little attention to these nice distinctions, however, and as they moved toward a military solution to the colonial problem, Americans moved toward a reliance on natural law as the chief source of their rights. Typical of this trend was Alexander Hamilton's assertion in 1775 that "the sacred rights of mankind are not to be rummaged for, among old parchments, or musty records. They are written, as with a sunbeam, in the whole volume of nature, by the hand of divinity itself."

III

No Soldier shall, in time of peace be quartered in any house, without the consent of the Owner, nor in time of war, but in a manner to be prescribed by law.

Independence cemented the preference for natural law. "How in the world," Jaffa asks, could Americans be expected "to appeal to their rights under the laws of England at the precise moment that they were telling the world they were no longer Englishmen?" The situation was, in fact, more complicated than this statement suggests, for Americans claimed all through the revolutionary controversy that their quarrel was not with the British Constitution, but with the unprincipled politicians who were defiling it. The mother country's constitution was extolled at the Constitutional Convention in 1787 and for decades thereafter. These tributes, however, were almost always paid to the institutional contrivances of the British Constitution that were designed to control the excesses of democracy. Admiration for the stabilizing properties of Britain's

Constitution, mostly voiced by political conservatives, did not translate into a willingness of the citizens of the new republic to concede that they were beholden to the British for their rights. Rather, they considered, with James Wilson, that "by the Revolution [they] have attained all their natural rights," that, as a Pennsylvania newspaper claimed, they had "nobly resumed those rights which God and nature bestowed on man."

If "the natural rights philosophy seized the minds . . . of the rebellious patriots of 1776," as Leonard Levy of the Claremont Graduate School has recently argued, a contributing factor was the use Americans made of the theory of the state of nature to explain the events of 1776. Thomas Hobbes employed the state of nature as a major presumption in *Leviathan* (1651), but most Americans absorbed the more benign version of the concept used by John Locke in his *Two Treatises of Government* (1690).

IV

The right of the people to be secure in their persons, houses, papers, and effects, against unreasonable searches and seizures, shall not be violated, and no Warrants shall issue, but upon probable cause, supported by Oath or affirmation, and particularly describing the place to be searched, and the persons or things to be seized.

The state of nature began appearing in American writing less than 30 years after the publication of Locke's work. By the middle of the 18th century, writes Yale's Edmund S. Morgan, "Locke's political doctrines were assimilated by American clergymen and dispensed in their sermons along with older ideas." In 1764 it was reported that New Englanders believed themselves entitled "to form a new government as full to all intents and purposes as if they had been in a state of nature and were making their first entrance into civil society."

Not every American believed that a state of nature literally existed at some point in the past. James Otis, a leading Boston rebel, labelled the doctrine "a piece of metaphysical jargon and systematic nonsense." Yet Otis conceded that the state of nature was an indispensable fiction. Even if imaginary, it "hinders not but that the natural and original rights of each individual may be illustrated and explained in this way better than in any other."

Many Americans regarded the British Parliament's passage of the Intolerable Acts in 1774 as an act of aggression which converted the fictional state of nature into fact. This was Patrick Henry's view. At the First Continental Congress in September 1774, he declared: "Government is dissolved. Fleets and Armies and the present State of Things show that Government is dissolved. . . . We are in a State of Nature." The state of nature was a popular topic among Henry's Virginia constituents, for a writer in Virginia's leading newspaper warned in the same month that "if the king violated his sacred faith" with the American colonies, "he dismembers them from the empire and reduces them to a state of nature." From the eye of the storm, Massachusetts Whig leader James Warren wrote John Adams in 1774 that "It can be no longer a question whether any People ever subsisted in a State of Nature. We have been and still remain in that Situation."

The source of the new nation's rights was simple, James Madison said in 1785; they were "the gift of nature." Since Americans believed that the law of nature embodied the will of God, was "dictated by God himself," as Sir William Blackstone described it, many identified God—the more secular-minded substituted the "Creator" of the Declaration of Independence—as the source of American rights. For the Founding generation, rights were grounded in religion.

The constitutions which the new states began adopting in 1776 signaled the states' emergence from the state of nature (whether real or theoretical) to which British oppression had reduced them. Bills of rights were added to most of the new constitutions and they contained all the contradictory and incoherent thinking about rights that existed before 1776. Historian Gordon Wood observes that the new documents combined a "jarring but exciting combination of ringing declarations of universal principles with a motley collection of common law procedures." If they contained too much for Wood's taste, they included too little to suit Leonard Levy. Reproving the drafters of the documents for proceeding "in an haphazard fashion that verged on ineptness," Levy deplored their omissions: "Two states passed over a free press guarantee; four neglected to ban excessive fines, excessive bail, compulsory self-incrimination, and general search warrants. Five ignored protections for the rights of assembly, petition, counsel, and trial by jury in civil cases. Seven omitted a prohibition of *ex post facto* laws. Nine failed to . . . condemn bills of attainder. Ten said nothing about freedom of speech, while 11 were silent on double jeopardy."

People at the time were not satisfied with the first bills of rights either. The citizens of Albemarle County, Virginia, for example, in the fall of 1776 sent instructions to their delegates in the state assembly, complaining that, although the recently adopted Virginia Declaration of Rights "will be an honorable Memorial to the memory of its Compilers . . . we find, that the true sense of it is not understood; for which reason a good many still remain ignorant of their rights."

What were the people of Albemarle unable to comprehend? Perhaps they could not tell how secure their rights were, for by using the verb "ought" to state certain rights—trial by jury "ought to be held sacred," excessive bail "ought not to be required"—the drafters of the Declaration seemed to make the enjoyment of rights optional. There were also doubts in the Old Dominion about the relationship of the bill of rights to the state constitution. "Virginia," said Governor Edmund Randolph, "has a bill of rights, but it is no part of the Constitution. By not saying whether it is paramount to the Constitution or not, it has left us in confusion."

V

No person shall be held to answer for a capital, or otherwise infamous crime, unless on a presentment or indictment of a Grand Jury, except in cases arising in the land or naval forces, or in the Militia, when in actual service in time of War or public danger; nor shall any person be subject for the same offence to be twice put in jeopardy of life or limb, nor shall be compelled in any criminal case to be a witness against himself, nor be deprived of life, liberty, or property, without due process of law; nor shall private property be taken for public use, without just compensation.

Another confusing aspect of the first state bills of rights was what appeared to be their strong British flavor. Sections from the English Bill of Rights, the Habeas Corpus Act of 1679, and even Magna Carta seemed to have been imported wholesale into the first bills, raising the question of whether the British Constitution was not, after all, the source of rights in independent America.

The eminent continental jurist, Georg Jellinek, dismissed such a conclusion as "superficial," because there was a fundamental difference in spirit between the English and American bills of rights. The American instruments recognized the individual's "inalienable and indefeasible rights. The English laws know nothing of this. They do not wish to recognize an eternal, natural right, but one inherited from their fathers."

VI

In all criminal prosecutions, the accused shall enjoy the right to a speedy and public trial, by an impartial jury of the State and district wherein the crime shall have been committed, which district shall have been previously ascertained by law, and to be informed of the nature and cause of the accusation; to be confronted with the witnesses against him; to have compulsory process for obtaining Witnesses in his favor, and to have the Assistance of Counsel for his defence.

Americans of the revolutionary generation tended to interpret the British Constitution as being, no less than their own fundamental charters, grounded in nature. Most of them did not subscribe to our modern view that rights can be created; rather they believed that in formulating rights, individuals merely declared the presence of what Madison called "pre-existent rights." (Hence the preference of many states for the phrase "declaration" of rights in describing their earliest bills of rights.) Since rights were not considered to be created or invented, the British were thought to have appropriated to their use natural, pre-existent rights. Therefore, in the American view, the British Constitution was itself a natural rights document. As the Massachusetts Assembly asserted in 1765, Americans "have a just value for those inestimable rights which are derived to

all men from nature, and are happily interwoven in the British Constitution."

The idea that all rights and liberties were natural or naturally derived had by 1787 become the analytical tool Americans used to make sense of the bills of rights they had reflexively written in 1776. Bills of rights, it was widely held by 1787, were in theory repositories of reserved natural rights. How this notion evolved from the confused and conflicting ideas about rights abroad in 1776 is worth noting.

The starting point was the pervasive concept of the state of nature. As noted above, Locke postulated that individuals who left the state of nature surrendered some of their rights to society but retained others. Americans subscribed to this idea. George Mason, author of the Virginia Declaration of Rights, America's first bill of rights, believed that individuals who formed societies "entered into compacts to give up some of their natural rights, that by union and mutual assistance they might secure the rest." Civis, as one writer in the *Virginia Gazette* called himself in 1776, asserted that "the use of speech is a natural right, which must have been reserved when men gave up their natural rights for the benefit of society." When the Observer wrote in a Boston paper two years later that "every natural right, not expressly given up, remains," he was merely repeating what had been claimed for years in the state of Massachusetts.

What were the natural rights retained by individuals who had entered society? In theory, there were two kinds: alienable and inalienable. Alienable natural rights were those that individuals could have ceded to society, if they wished; inalienable natural rights were so fundamental to human welfare that they were not considered to be in the power of individuals to surrender. George Mason named three of them in the Virginia Declaration of Rights: life, liberty, and "the means of acquiring and possessing property." He appears to have borrowed this trio from the three "absolute" rights in Sir William Blackstone's famous *Commentaries on the Laws of England* (1765–69). They also appeared in five of the seven remaining state bills of rights, suggesting that from the beginning Americans recognized that, at a minimum, declarations of rights must contain these inalienable natural rights.

Quite soon it became apparent to some Americans that around natural rights

they could construct a theory about what the state bills of rights were. Writing as Ludlow in the *Pennsylvania Journal* in 1777, Benjamin Rush complained that his state's "Bill of Rights has confounded the *natural* and *civil* rights in such a manner as to produce endless confusion in society." Presuming to speak as an expert on the subject, the future author of the *Rights of Man* (1791), Thomas Paine, replied over his familiar signature Common Sense that "a Bill of Rights . . . should retain such natural rights as are either consistent with or absolutely necessary toward our happiness in a state of society."

As a result of such writing, something approaching a national consensus emerged by 1787. Whatever else a bill of rights might include, its distinguishing characteristic was that it contained reserved natural rights.

VII

In Suits at common law, where the value in controversy shall exceed twenty dollars, the right of trial by jury shall be preserved, and no fact tried by a jury, shall be otherwise re-examined in any Court of the United States, than according to the rules of the common law.

The consensus was evident in the debates over the ratification of the federal Constitution in 1787–88. "A bill of rights may be summed up in a few words," Patrick Henry declared in the Virginia Ratifying Convention. "What do they tell us? That our rights are reserved." Pennsylvania Antifederalist leader Robert Whitehill agreed, describing a bill of rights as "an explicit reservation of those rights with which the people ought not, and mean not to part."

What happened to those rights that *were* surrendered to society? By 1787 a consensus had also emerged about their status.

"The Legislature," asserted Noah Webster in 1787, "has all the power, of all the people," the reason being, Alexander Contee Hanson explained, that "when people entered into a compact of government" they "thereby parted with the whole legislative power." "When general legislative powers are given," James Wilson told the Pennsylvania Ratifying Convention, "the people part with their authority, and . . . retain nothing." Nothing, Wilson should have added, except the natural rights they reserved in their bills of rights.

The Federalists and Antifederalists agreed, then, on the theory of the bills of rights adopted by the American states, a theory that was a marriage of Blackstone and Locke. Both groups held that the American bills of rights reserved certain natural rights; those rights not expressly reserved were considered to be transferred to an omnicompetent legislature.

If Federalists and Antifederalists agreed about the nature of American bills of rights, how can historians claim that the issue divided them during the ratification campaign? Antifederalists, it is true, assailed the new constitution because of the absence of a bill of rights and Federalists aggressively refuted their charges. But what was at issue was not contrasting understandings of the nature of bills of rights, but a disagreement over who the parties to the new constitution were. The Antifederalists claimed that in writing the Constitution the Federalists had flouted their instructions, which called for a mere revision of the Articles of Confederation, and had taken the unprecedented step of dissolving the social compact and throwing the country into a state of nature. Individuals were thus obliged to come together and reconstitute the social and political order. The creation of the Constitution was, in Antifederalist eyes, nothing more than a replay on a continental scale of the creation of the state governments.

If the federal Constitution was, in theory, the state constitutions writ large, if it was a compact of individuals leaving a state of nature, then the other lessons of the state constitutions followed. If the individuals forming the constitution reserved no rights by adapting a bill of rights, all rights and powers were ceded to the new federal government. But Federalists scorned the Antifederalist premises. "The absurd idea of the federal constitution being a government of individuals," complained a Maryland Federalist, "seems too nugatory to merit a serious reflection."

But if individuals did not create the Constitution, who did? The people did, the Federalists answered, albeit the people in a corporate capacity. As James Madison explained in *Federalist* 39, assent was given to the Constitution "by the people, not as individuals composing one entire nation, but as composing the distinct and independent states to which they respectively belong. It is to be the assent and ratification of the several States, derived from the supreme authority in each state—the authority of the people themselves." The Constitution, therefore, as the product of a collective people, could not, in theory, be a vehicle of individual rights, a fact obvious to common scribblers in the newspapers. "In the proposed Compact among the same thirteen individual sovereignties no Bill of Rights of Individuals has been or could be introduced," asserted a Federalist writer in a Baltimore newspaper. But this commentator recognized that a state government was a different matter, for "in Articles of Agreement among a Number of People forming a Civil Society, a Bill of Rights of Individuals comes in of course, and it is indispensably necessary."

VIII

Excessive bail shall not be required, nor excessive fines imposed, nor cruel and unusual punishments inflicted.

The Federalists' support for state bills of rights gave the lie to Antifederalist accusations that they were enemies to rights in general. The Federalists were, as scholars have recognized, "civil libertarians," who could genuinely claim, as John Marshall did at the Virginia Ratifying Convention, "the title of being firm friends of liberty and the rights of mankind." They accepted with equanimity the possibility that rights might vary from state to state—as former Supreme Court Justice William Brennan, Jr., did when he observed recently that "our federalism permits diversity" in rights from state to state.

Believing that rights were a state responsibility, the Framers said little about them in Philadelphia. According to one authority, the Framers' "immediate business gave them little occasion" to discuss rights. What was their "immediate business"? Power, they would have responded. "Every member who attended the Convention," said Charles Cotesworth Pinckney at the South Caro-

lina Ratifying Convention, "was from the beginning sensible of the necessity of giving greater powers to the federal government." To some Federalists the Constitution was nothing more than a "great power of attorney." In 1789 Madison described it as a "Bill of Powers [that] needs no bill of R[ig]hts."

The Federalist argument was adumbrated during the final days of the Philadelphia Convention by Roger Sherman of Connecticut, who parried a demand that a written guarantee for the freedom of the press be included in the Constitution with the reply that "it is unnecessary. The power of Congress does not extend to the Press."

The Federalist attitude was summed up in a phrase: "There cannot be a more positive and unequivocal declaration of the principle of the adoption," said Madison in the Virginia Ratifying Convention, than that "everything not granted is reserved." This aphorism became the Federalists' principal political weapon to "prove" that a bill of rights was unnecessary. Believing that a bill of rights was unnecessary, Federalists also concluded that it would be dangerous, reasoning that the principle of the state bills of rights—everything not reserved was granted—posed the danger that rights omitted from a bill of rights might be considered to have been surrendered to the government. The case against a bill of rights seemed so clear to the Federalists that they did not conceal their contempt for the counter-arguments in its favor. Bills of rights, Federalists jeered, were "absurd and dangerous," "idle and superfluous," "preposterous and dangerous," not to mention full of "inutility and folly."

But ridicule could not assuage the public's anxiety, and the Federalists were obliged, beginning in the Massachusetts Constitution Convention in February 1788, to promise their opponents that they would consider adding rights amendments after the Constitution was ratified. More than 200 amendments (many duplicating one another) had been suggested in various state conventions, and these were used by James Madison as he guided the Bill of Rights through the First Congress, which convened in New York City in April 1789.

Acclaimed as the "Father of the Bill of Rights," Madison in fact was a reluctant parent. In the Virginia Convention he joined in denouncing proposals for a bill of rights as "unnecessary and dangerous'' and he suffered politically at the hands of supporters of bills of rights in Virginia. Patrick Henry prevented the Virginia legislature from electing him to the U.S. Senate and forced him to run for a House seat in a district gerrymandered in favor of the Antifederalists. To win election, Madison was forced to promise the local voters that he would support a bill of rights. This he dutifully did, by introducing rights amendments in the House of Representatives on June 8, 1789.

Madison rejected out of hand the model of the state bills of rights, which were placed as discrete entities at the head of state constitutions. Like a modern Procrustes, he compressed the rights amendments into the frame of the Constitution to make them as indistinguishable as possible, structurally and theoretically, from that document. Madison tucked what became the Bill of Rights' first eight amendments ''into article 1st, section 9, between clauses 3 and 4.'' Article I, section 9, is, of course, the part of the Constitution that limits the powers of Congress, forbidding it to prohibit the slave trade for 20 years, to pass bills of attainder, to tax exports from the states, etc. During the ratification debates, these ''express restrictions'' on the powers of Congress were considered by some as a truncated bill of rights. What better place, then, Madison appears to have reasoned, to insert rights amendments?

This strategy gave the Bill of Rights the curious shape it finally assumed. To make the amendments consistent with the language already there, Madison was obliged to express rights, not positively and affirmatively, as they were phrased in the state bills of rights, but in language that seemed to link them to restraints on power, that seemed to make them in some sense dependent on the forbearance of government. For example, Madison wrote, ''nor shall the full and equal rights of conscience be in any manner, or on any pretext infringed.''

As Madison's rights amendments made their way through Congress in the summer of 1789, they were placed at the end of the Constitution. In the case of religion, the press, and speech, Congress also deleted Madison's assertions that these were rights, but retained his language stating that Congress had no power to infringe them. This is the reason freedom of religion, press, and speech are not explicitly claimed as rights in the First Amendment. That they

are rights must be inferred from Congress's obligation to refrain from exercising power.

Madison's June 8 amendments also contained the precursor of what became the Ninth Amendment. Refined by the First Congress, Madison's words became: ''The enumeration in the Constitution of certain rights shall not be construed to deny or disparage others retained by the people.''

Both the embryonic language of June 8 and the Ninth Amendment repudiated the philosophy of the state bills of rights, that what is not reserved is granted. Both documents stated that, in addition to rights reserved (i.e. enumerated), other undefined rights were retained by the people. Some modern scholars contend that these undefined rights must be natural rights or some other species of unwritten rights, but this argument collapses in the face of Madison's resolve, which is reflected in his careful interweaving of rights amendments into Arti-

---

IX

The enumeration in the Constitution, of certain rights, shall not be construed to deny or disparage others retained by the people.

---

cle I, Section 9, to preserve the integrity of the Constitution by crafting amendments to be consistent with it.

As we have seen, a fundamental conviction of Madison and the Federalists was that the Constitution was created not by individuals leaving a state of nature but by the people acting collectively through their state governments and that, therefore, the natural rights of individuals had no place in the Constitution. During the deliberations of the Committee of Detail at the Philadelphia Convention, Edmund Randolph stated the Federalist position precisely: ''We are not working on the natural rights of men not yet gathered into society, but upon those rights modified by society.'' Leonard Levy has recently shown how Convention delegates scrupulously observed this distinction by proposing only measures to protect rights incident to civil society, such as freedom of the press and the inviolability of the writ of habeas corpus.

''No natural rights were constitutionally protected,'' Levy asserted, nor were any proposed to be protected in the meetings at Philadelphia.

In 1789, American society was further removed from the state of nature than it had been in 1787, because the adoption of the Constitution had overlaid the existing state governments with a powerful new national government. To conceive, therefore, of a bill of rights or of any other law passed by the federal Congress in 1789 as protecting the rights of individuals emerging from a state of nature was ludicrous.

That Madison deliberately omitted natural rights can be seen from the use he made of the Virginia Ratifying Convention's proposed amendments. Madison had them at his elbow when he prepared his June 8 amendments, and he incorporated parts of them word for word. What he did not incorporate from the Virginia document was its assertion of ''certain natural rights'' shared by all men, the familiar trio of life, liberty, and property. In a word, Madison stripped rights of their natural status when drafting the Bill of Rights.

If the ''others'' mentioned in the Ninth Amendment, those other rights ''retained by the people,'' are not natural rights or collateral unwritten rights, what are they?

One clue is the linkage between rights and power in the embryonic ninth amendment language of Madison's June 8 proposals. Another is the Virginia Convention's amendment from which Madison copied some of his ninth amendment language of June 8: It used the word ''power,'' where we should have expected the term ''right.'' The rights retained in the Ninth Amendment seem, therefore, to have been intimately related, in Madison's mind, to power, although we have been assured by scholars that power and right are utterly incompatible. The two concepts, historian Bernard Bailyn insists, occupied ''innately antagonistic spheres . . . the one [power] must be resisted, the other [right] defended, and the two must never be confused.'' In fact, revolutionary Americans fused the two concepts, and they did so not because they were confused but because they had on their side the authority of the foremost students of rights in the Western intellectual tradition.

For example, Jean Jacques Burlamaqui, whose impact on Jefferson, James

Wilson, and others was substantial, wrote simply: "We must define Right a power." Blackstone asserted that the rights of man consist "properly in a power of acting as one thinks fit, without any restraint or control, unless by the law of nature." Confining rights and power within the bounds of the law of nature (dictated, Blackstone believed, by God) gave rights a moral dimension which every writer back to William of Ockham proclaimed and to which Americans of the revolutionary generation were committed. Emmerich de Vattel spoke their mind when he said that right was "nothing more than the power of doing what is morally possible."

The founding generation's equation of rights and power clarifies the meaning of the Ninth Amendment. It was, as I have said, a disclaimer of the philosophy of the state bills of rights, that everything not reserved was granted to the government.

Had there been no Ninth Amendment, Madison and his colleagues feared that it could be assumed that the people retained only the rights contained in the first eight amendments. As soon as people outside Congress saw the Ninth Amendment, they perceived that this was its purpose. It was, said Edmund Randolph in the Virginia General Assembly, a "reservation against constructive power." No one considered it a repository of natural or unwritten rights, as indeed it was not.

What was the extent of those rights/powers declared by the Ninth Amendment to be retained by the people? The answer was supplied by the Tenth Amendment. The curious aspect of the Tenth Amendment was that it was a kind of anti-bill of rights. It repeated the stock Federalist charge used during the ratification campaign to deny that a bill of rights was needed: Powers not granted to the government were reserved to the people. This being so, it was absurd to list rights to be protected against the abuse of power that did not exist. During the ratification contest partisans on both sides recognized that language similar to the Tenth Amendment would obviate the necessity of a bill of rights. The Articles of Confederation, said Samuel Spencer of North Carolina, stated "that all was not given up to the United States was retained by the respective states. If such a clause had been inserted in the Constitution, it would have superseded the necessity of a bill of rights." Yet the Tenth

Amendment was needed as a gloss on the Ninth. Scholars have recognized that the two amendments are complementary, but they have not appreciated that the Tenth Amendment was designed to explain the Ninth. To the question posed by the Ninth Amendment—what other rights/powers are retained by the people—the Tenth Amendment answers: All powers not delegated to the United States.

The Bill of Rights is a strange document indeed. The first eight amendments are a list of rights. The Ninth Amendment is a disclaimer, denying that the federal bill of rights is similar to any of the other American bills of rights adopted since independence. The Tenth Amendment is an anti-bill of rights, a repetition of the argument used by the Federalists to repudiate a bill of rights during the ratification controversy. No wonder that

---

X

The powers not delegated to the United States by the Constitution, nor prohibited by it to the States, are reserved to the States respectively, or to the people.

Roger Sherman, in a House debate that August, criticized the document as a potpourri of "heterogeneous articles." It was a document that could not stand in the esteem of either its sponsors or opponents.

The approval of the Bill of Rights by Congress on September 25, 1789 was a defeat for the Antifederalists, who had criticized the Constitution's alleged failure to protect civil liberties in hopes of forcing a revision of the document to enhance state power.* Once it became apparent that Congress would pass a bill of rights that protected individual rather than states' rights, Antifederalist leaders began depreciating its importance. Speak-

---

*Two amendments approved by Congress were not ratified by the states. One would have changed the basis of representation in the House of Representatives, the other would have required the approval of two Congresses for congressional pay increases. Because the state legislatures left few records of their deliberations, historians do not know why these amendments failed.

---

ing for many of his colleagues, Antifederalist Senator William Grayson of Virginia dismissed the amendments sent to the states as "good for nothing and, I believe, as many others do, that they will do more harm than benefit."

Nor did the Federalists consider the passage of the Bill of Rights a famous victory. Madison's colleagues were exasperated with him for pushing it through Congress. They accused him of headline hunting and denounced his proposals as "watergruel amendments," "milk and water amendments," and placebos prescribed for "imaginary ailments." They persisted in considering a bill of rights absurd and dangerous and justified passing it as a means of placating the misguided Antifederalist rank and file, an exercise they cynically described as "tossing a tub to a whale." (When sailing ships of the era ran afoul of whales at sea, crews often diverted them by tossing empty tubs or barrels into the water.) Weary of rowing against the tide of friend and foe, Madison confided to a correspondent that August that the Bill of Rights business was a "nauseous project."

Federalists in Congress were not inclined to take much credit for a measure they passed with so little enthusiasm, and their Antifederalist adversaries wrote the Bill of Rights campaign off as a bad investment of their time. Taking their cue from Congress, the state parties received and ratified the Bill of Rights so unceremoniously that, except in Virginia, which became the 11th and last state to ratify on December 15, 1791, they left scarcely any record of what they had done. The Bill of Rights forthwith fell into a kind of national oblivion, as Cornell's Michael Kammen reminded us in 1987, not to be "discovered" until the beginning of World War II (when the two remaining states ratified). A 1941 census of the 13 copies of the Bill of Rights sent to the states in October 1789 revealed that the document had been literally forgotten. Only four copies could be found, although a diligent search, propelled by patriotic ardor, later uncovered additional copies in Rhode Island, New Jersey, and South Carolina, the latter "crumpled, and torn" and caked with "much dust."

Of course, as a result of momentous Supreme Court decisions since World War II, the Bill of Rights has enjoyed a remarkable resurgence in our national consciousness. What of natural law, considered by Americans in the years after 1776 to be the bedrock of rights in the new nation? One scholar recently has found natural law prospering in American jurisprudence from 1789 to 1820, and another has described it as a principle of considerable, though declining jurisprudential importance up to the Civil War.

Today, natural law and natural rights are said to be rejected by spokesmen of every ideological stripe.

The result is that natural law, considered indispensable by the Founders' generation, is now dismissed as unnecessary, while the Bill of Rights, considered unnecessary in 1787, is held to be indispensable. Such reversals are not uncommon in the history of ideas, nor are they unknown in the history of law. What they indicate is that the most strongly held convictions often change and that the current reverence for the Bill of Rights cannot be taken for granted in the future.

River of the West

Separated from European influence by Asia and the trackless Pacific in one direction and by the vast Atlantic and an imposing continental barrier in the other, America's Northwest Coast long remained one of earth's most isolated regions. Finally, during the late eighteenth century, far-ranging mariners seeking furs, new territories to exploit, and the legendary Northwest Passage penned in most of the gaps along the long-uncharted shores. This era of accelerated activity reached a zenith in May 1792 when American merchant captain Robert Gray confirmed the existence of one of the region's most elusive prize—the great waterway that he named "Columbia's River."

Thomas Vaughan

An international scholar of Russian expansion and of trade in the North Pacific, Thomas Vaughan was for thirty-five years executive director of the Oregon Historical Society. In recognition of his work with British museums and collections of Captain James Cook, Queen Elizabeth II in 1975 decorated Vaughan with the Most Excellent Order of the British Empire. In 1989 the Oregon state legislature unanimously voted him the life designation of Oregon Historian Laureate.

During this quincentennial year the epic 1492 voyage of Christopher Columbus casts a giant shadow that virtually eclipses the exploits of previous and subsequent adventurers. Nevertheless, the achievements of another pathfinder—American merchant captain Robert Gray—also richly deserve anniversary remembrance during 1992. Two hundred years ago this May, Gray, commanding the trading ship *Columbia Rediviva* ("Columbia Reborn"), became the first nonnative mariner to enter the Columbia River—the elusive "River of the West." In confirming the existence of this fabled waterway (which, like the legendary Strait of Anian, long had intrigued mapmakers and tantalized explorers), Gray laid the foundation for subsequent American claims to and eventual possession of the Oregon country*

The coincidental juxtaposition of these two discoverers from different centuries offers interesting parallels. History reveals that Gray, like Columbus, always placed more importance on opening trade routes than on exploration for its own sake. The basic drive for both men, it seems, was "goods" rather than "glory"; the principle of the flag following trade is well-supported.

To carry the association one step further, it was aboard a ship obviously named in the spirit of the Columbian tradition that Gray and his superior, a somewhat capricious John Kendrick, eventually reached the harbors of China and the shores of Japan—the very ports the Genoese Colon had sought so aggressively three centuries earlier.

Finally, just as Columbus's 1492 voyage opened an era of great maritime

*Providing ease of communication between the coast and interior, the Columbia River became an artery for Pacific Northwest exploration, trade, and settlement during the nineteenth century. Transcontinental explorers Lewis and Clark wintered at Fort Clatsop near the river's mouth (1805-06); American and British fur interests established important posts on the Columbia at Astoria (1811) and Vancouver (1825); and American settlers concentrated along its southern tributary in the fertile Willamette Valley.

discoveries in the Americas, so did Gray's 1792 voyage virtually close that epoch. In locating the largest watercourse on the Pacific slope of the two continents, Gray filled in the last major void on mariners' charts of the New World.**

THE THREE-HUNDRED-YEAR ODYSSEY leading from Columbus's first landfall in the "Indies" to Gray's arrival off the "River of the West" was circuitous, with many fits and starts as mariners from a host of rival nations gradually scribed in the margins of the Pacific in their quest for knowledge, territory, and riches. To retrace the chain of events leading up to the great river's initial sighting (and eventual rediscovery) we must follow in the wakes of a host of Pacific navigators.

In 1520, a short generation after Columbus, another great sailing master, Ferdinand Magellan—with five ships and great courage—pushed around South America toward the great "South Sea" that the conquistador Vasco Nuñez de

**The Columbia River drains more than one hundred and fifty lesser rivers and one quarter of a million square miles, including portions of present-day Washington, Oregon, Idaho, Montana, Wyoming, and British Columbia. In North America its flow is surpassed only by the Mississippi, MacKenzie, and St. Lawrence rivers.

 From *American History Illustrated*, May/June 1992, pp. 29-43. Reprinted through the courtesy of Cowles Magazines, publishers of *American History Illustrated*.

Balboa first had viewed from the Isthmus of Panama in 1513.

Magellan, who had renounced his Portuguese career for Spanish service, sought to reach the wealth-giving Spice Islands (Moluccas) by sailing west instead of east. After a tortuous passage through the South American strait that later would bear his name, the much-vexed explorer embarked upon the "Pacific" sea on a voyage whose privations and difficulties we can scarcely comprehend today—a thirteen-thousand-mile, ninety-nine-day passage devoid of landfalls, fresh provisions, or potable water.

The intrepid Portuguese eventually crossed the line of the Moluccas, as he had said he would, and entered the archipelagic maze of the Philippines. Although the great navigator and others of his command were killed by inflamed natives on some Philippine shore, his name is first linked, and rightfully so, with a circumnavigation of the globe. Late in the summer of 1522, the expedition's lone remaining ship, the *Victoria*, manned by the durable Basque captain Juan Sebastian del Cano and seventeen other emaciated and scurvy-ridden survivors, returned to Seville. The conclusion of that epic voyage firmly established, by European reasoning, Spain's claim to the world's greatest ocean. For the next two centuries the Spaniards regarded the Pacific as their private "lake."

ONE MIGHT SAY THAT THE PACIFIC WAS almost "holy" water, because by papal decree Spain in 1494 had signed a treaty with Portugal whereby the rival monarchs reached agreement on colonizing new territories. Portugal obtained exclusive rights to trade with and possess new lands in a hemisphere extending eastward from a meridian near the Cape Verde Islands in the Atlantic, while Spain secured precedence to the regions to the west—including most of the Americas and their bordering seas.

Immense vision, fortitude, and bottomless greed soon gave Spain a giant stance astride much of the New World, including the southern flank of North America and all of South America (barring Brazil). But with its eyes on the newly established Manila trade and with the papal division firmly in mind, sixteenth-century New Spain felt no great urgency concerning any northward advance along the Pacific Coast. Most secrets of that remote sector remained unplumbed despite the hardiest efforts of such mariners as Juan Rodriguez Cabrillo and Bartolomé Ferrelo. While searching for the fabled Strait of Anian* in September 1542, Cabrillo made probably the first landing by a European in California, at the bay he called San Miguel. The following year Ferrelo, assuming command of Cabrillo's expedition after the leader's death, may have sailed as far north as California's Humboldt Bay or even Oregon's Rogue River.

ONE AMONG AN EMERGING GROUP WHO refused to recognize papal treaties or any Spanish rights was the audacious English marauder Francis Drake of Devon. In 1578 the "sunnes' fellow traveller," who had for several years terrorized the Spanish Main, now found a new way around Cape Horn and sailed his *Pelican* into virgin Spanish waters. Cruising up the west coast of South America, "Francisco Draque" pillaged lightly defended treasure towns from Chile to Peru and captured several ships filled with silks, porcelains, and silver and gold from the American mines.

Laden with treasure and accompanied by a captured Spanish pilot boat, Drake's ship, now renamed the *Golden Hind,* continued north past California and into unknown seas. Perhaps seeking the elusive shortcut home that later would attract other great English mariners to these same waters, Drake instead encountered freezing weather and "the most vile, thicke and stinking fogges." In early June 1579 the two ships sought shelter somewhere along the Oregon coast, anchoring for several days "in a bad bay, the best roade we could for the present meet with." From that exposed roadstead they moved south once again. On June 17 a "convenient and fit harborough was found" on the California coast north of as-yet-undiscovered San Francisco Bay. There Drake claimed "New Albion" for Queen Elizabeth, and his crews careened and repaired the legendary *Hind* in anticipation of the long voyage home across the Pacific and around Africa. Thus ended England's first foray into the North Pacific.

WITH ITS COLONIAL ADMINISTRATION PREoccupied with the transpacific trade and Old World concerns, New Spain's northward advance along the Pacific Coast continued at a torpid pace at best. We thus can appreciate the frustrations experienced at the beginning of the seventeenth century by Frey Antonio de la Asenscion and mariner Sebastian Vizcaino.

Asenscion stated to all who would listen or read that political, religious, and lesser reasons dictated that New Spain, regardless of all obstacles, must continue to push north from Mexico. His essential concern—subsequently validated—was the gradual awakening of other European sea powers and his geopolitical sense of their naturally greedy intentions.

The friar's ambitions at least were temporarily realized in 1599 when Vizcaino—a professional soldier and adventurer by trade—was appointed to lead an expedition into northern waters. Finally sailing from Acapulco in May 1602 (with Asenscion as a member of the enterprise), Vizcaino reached the California coast in November, where he renamed Cabrillo's previously discovered bay after his own flagship *San Diego*. Farther north the mariner took note of another bay that he named for his superior, the Conde de Monterey, Viceroy of Mexico. Then, in January 1603, a grand storm carried Vizcaino's flagship sufficiently far north for him to note Cape Blanco, the westernmost promontory in Oregon. His second ship, the *Tres Reyes* under the command of Martín Aguilar, was blown perhaps as far north as Oregon's Coos Bay.

After returning to Mexico, Vizcaino urged a second northern voyage, but he was turned down by the Marques de Montesclaros, the new viceroy, who held the remarkable view that the northern coasts at best should left unexplored, unsettled by Europeans, and in essence unmentioned.**

Spanish interest in the North Pacific thereafter languished for the next 150 years, not to be revived until the hidalgos belatedly realized that Russian mariners were making serious incursions into the northern reaches of Spain's exclusive preserve.

---

*For nearly three hundred years New World geographers sought a Strait of Anian and/or Northwest Passage. This dreamed-of strait, they hoped, would provide European mariners with a shortcut to the Pacific and its riches.

**The viceroy's head-in-the-sand approach perhaps could be attributed to Spain's recent decline as a world sea power. If Spanish mariners probing the frontier were to find the Strait of Anian, colonial leaders reasoned, such a discovery would only enable other, ascending powers to trespass into the Spanish preserve.

3. NATIONAL CONSOLIDATION AND EXPANSION

BY THE EIGHTEENTH CENTURY, THE RUSsians, whose trappers and traders occupied northern Asia's Kamchatka peninsula after a headlong continental trek across the boundless tangle of Siberia, were engaged full-bore in a quest for knowledge of the regions bordering their recently acquired territory. The great Russian march east had been a staggering, costly achievement that had quadrupled the imperial land holdings.

Jogged by the accomplishments of Western European questers and by sharp questions from his newly founded Russian Academy of Sciences, Peter the Great sent a series of expeditions onto the broad Pacific to determine whether the Asian and North American continents were joined in the frigid Arctic waters.* Even as he lay wracked by bouts of delirium on his death-bed in 1725, Peter dispatched another expedition. His admiral selected as leader a half-pay Dane, Vitus Bering, promoting the twenty-year Russian naval veteran to senior captain and handing him one of the last regal statements from Peter's hand. He should go to Kamchatka, build two ships, and "sail near the land which goes to the north, which (since no one knows where it ends) it seems is part of America."

More than four hundred men were involved. It took three years simply to transport the expedition and its equipment 4,800 miles from the Neva to Kamchatka and the primitive *ostrog* of Petropavlovsk. En route the stoic plodders were reduced to eating their requisitioned horses, then their saddles and saddle bags, and finally even their leather clothing and boots.

Finally sailing north along the Asian coast and through today's Bering Strait, the explorers crossed the Arctic Circle— but failed to sight the American coast. In the absence of contrary evidence, Bering logically concluded that the two continents were not connected.

Despite some skepticism and opposition, another attempt to locate the Amer-

---

*Cossack voyager Semen Dezhnev in fact had resolved this question in 1648 when his ninety-man expedition navigated a vessel with reindeer-hide sails from the Arctic Kolyma River down around the huge Chukotsk Peninsula, and through today's Bering Strait. Unfortunately, the report of Dezhnev's brilliant geographical accomplishment was lost in the files in Iakutsk, along with a request for back pay for the surviving crew members—not to be rediscovered until the 1740s.

ican continent was approved in 1732. Bering's second Kamchatka expedition, more than six hundred strong, consumed eight years simply in crossing Siberia once again and refitting the Baltic-type packets *St. Peter* and *St. Paul.*

Eventually, despite grueling physical hardships and costs in lives and treasure, Bering and the commander of his second ship, Alexei Chirikov, sailed east into the foggy Pacific and independently sighted portions of the Alaskan coast. Bering himself was not fated to enjoy his triumph for long; marooned on a barren island while attempting to return to Petropavlovsk, he and many of his men died miserably. But the geographical puzzle finally had been unraveled, and in the Russian sense, America was "rediscovered" in 1741.

Unwittingly, Bering's sailors found not only land but also treasure. The Alaskan waters teemed with the same "soft gold" that had opened up Siberia so speedily. Soon legions of Russian fur entrepreneurs — *promyshleniki* — fanned out across the North Pacific archipelagos, ruthlessly subduing native tribes (notably the Aleuts) and gathering immense quantities of sea otter pelts. Within a few years this rich North Pacific bounty would attract not only Russians, but also English and American traders.

IN 1761, THROUGH THEIR AGENTS IN ST. Petersburg, the Spanish finally become aware of the Russian encroachments into Alaskan waters. These theoretically secret undertakings impelled the Madrid court and then its viceroy in Mexico to place renewed interest in the long-fallow "northern enterprise." Commencing an aggressive defense of her "lake," Spain established out-posts at San Diego and Monterey, plus other missions in Alta California.

The Spanish also resumed probing the waters along the Northwest Coast, achieving significant new discoveries. In 1774 naval officer Juan Pérez sailed the frigate *Santiago* from San Blas and Monterey all the way to the Queen Charlotte Islands, near the present British Columbia-Alaska border. During his homeward-bound passage the explorer skirted Vancouver Island and sighted Nootka Sound, later to become a favorite rendezvous for fur trading ships in these northern waters.

A two-ship expedition with Pérez as pilot and Bruno Heceta y Dudogoitia as

commander returned to the Northwest the following year. One of these vessels, the thirty-eight-foot tender *Sonora,* commanded by naval lieutenant Juan Francisco de La Bodega y Quadra, made an extraordinary passage as far north as Mount Edgecumbe (present-day Sitka). The flagship *Santiago,* under Heceta, a thirty-year-old naval officer who had journeyed to Mexico from Spain the preceding year, reached the vicinity of Vancouver Island after making the first recorded landing on the coast of today's Washington State.

Early in August, with his crew seriously weakened by malnutrition and scurvy, Heceta turned back toward Monterey. In the predawn hours of August 16, after a run that had carried him due south off the coast of Washington, Heceta veered east-southeast "looking toward the coast." Hours later the mariner made a notable observation; one that hitherto had eluded European voyagers and that would continue to frustrate them for another seventeen years. "In the afternoon of this day I discovered a large bay that I named Bahia de Asunción [Assumption Bay], the shape of which is shown on the map" [a chart that survives today in the Archives of the Indies in Seville].

Continuing to peer through the haze, Heceta further recorded in his journal that "I sounded in 24 brazas [144 feet]. The swirling currents were so swift that despite having a full press of sail it was difficult to get clear or separate myself from the cape to the extreme north. . . . These currents and the seething waters had led me to believe that it may be the mouth of some great river, or the passage to another sea."

There is now no doubt from Heceta's log and the fine chart he drew that he had found the great river known today as the Columbia. Astronomical calculations for that day suggest that tidal conditions might have been ideal for crossing the treacherous bar, but after consultation with Captain Pilot Don Juan Pérez and pilot Don Cristobal Revilla, Heceta reluctantly decided to move on. His crew was so weakened by sickness that "they insisted that I should not attempt it, for in letting go the anchor we did not have men with which to get it up, nor to attend to the work that would thereby result."

In retrospect, it is probably best that caution prevailed. Bad weather blew in the next day.

As he resumed his course toward California and Mexico, Heceta very possibly realized that he had been on the verge of a momentous discovery. The tenacious Basque had another thirty-one years to reflect on what might have been—but one doubts that was his disposition.*

AT THE SAME TIME THAT SPANISH MARIners were countering Russian encroachments into the North Pacific, another dynamic imperial power began to focus on that region. The English long had maintained their thin but wiry connection to the western shore of North America through the timeless exploits of Francis Drake. Now, two centuries later, the new British Empire produced perhaps the most skilled of all sea surveyors, Captain James Cook, R.N.

During two extraordinary voyages between 1768 and 1775, Cook explored vast portions of the South Pacific, discovering numerous islands, charting the coasts of Australia and New Zealand, and disproving the existence of a great Southern Continent.

In July 1776, aboard the HMS *Resolution* and accompanied by the HMS *Discovery,* Cook embarked on yet another great voyage, this time focusing his quest on the long-dreamed-of Northwest Passage. The search offered tantalizing monetary as well as scientific rewards; Parliament had pledged a £20,000 prize to the discoverer of the rumored shortcut between the seas.

Sailing at a leisurely pace, Cook rounded the Cape of Good Hope and consumed a year revisiting the South Seas. Then, sailing north from Tahiti, he added to his list of impressive discoveries the Sandwich [Hawaiian] Islands, which he encountered in January 1778.

After briefly exploring this mid-Pacific paradise, the British navigator resumed his voyage to the Northwest Coast, arriving off Oregon in early March. Moving slowly northward through spring storms and fog, Cook had the misfortune of completely missing the large "bay" noted by Heceta two years earlier. One can only speculate what the region's subsequent history—and nationality—might have been had conditions allowed this meticulous explorer to examine the coast more closely.

Also failing to note the broad entrance to Puget Sound, Cook arrived off the huge island later named for a midshipman in his command (George Vancouver) and anchored in a roadstead already identified by Spanish sailors as San Lorenzo—today's Nootka. There the explorers made extensive repairs to their sea-worn ships, and the shivering crews engaged in a lively trade with the natives for sea otter pelts.** This seemingly incidental commerce would later lead to perhaps the most far-reaching consequence of the expedition.

As they continued north, Cook and his colleagues made countless contacts and perceptive observations during visits to Prince William Sound, Kodiak, Unalaska, and other windswept islands. Cruising through the Bering Strait, the Yorkshireman rounded the northern capes of Siberia. Despite every scrutiny of hazardous passages to the east, he found no way home, thus failing to secure the £20,000 prize. Then, turning south to winter over in the Sandwich Islands, Cook sailed on to death and glory—slain in a February 1779 encounter with Hawaiians over a stolen ship's boat.

Cook's second-in-command, Charles Clerke, returned to the Arctic in an attempt to continue the search but soon died of tuberculosis near Petropavlovsk, where he was buried. Under the command of John Gore, a Virginian, the homeward-bound ships later stopped at Macao and Canton. To the sailors' astonishment and pleasure, the sea otter pelts they had obtained for next to nothing commanded high prices from Russian traders and even more handsome remuneration from the Chinese.

Within eight years at least five British traders were working the islands and inlets of the Northwest, eager to exchange nails, saw blades, tobacco, hatchets, or whatever else it took to obtain pelts worth $50 to $70 each in Canton harbor. Three of these captains, George Dixon, James Colnett, and Nathaniel Portlock, had sailed with "the great navigator."

AMERICANS, ANXIOUS TO REBUILD THEIR commerce after the Revolution, soon heard about the remarkable opportunities the Northwest Coast offered. Perhaps most telling was the report of Captain James King in Volume 3 of Cook's report, published in London in 1784. King stated that sea otter pelts obtained by the expedition's sailors had subsequently brought as much as $120 in Canton—each. The impatience of the sailors to return to the Northwest had been "not far short of mutiny."

The American merchants were also aware of the scheme proposed by John Ledyard, a tenacious Connecticut visionary who had served as a young corporal of Marines aboard Cook's ship. In 1784 Ledyard managed to interest Thomas Jefferson (then U.S. minister to France) and naval hero John Paul Jones in a French-financed fur trading venture to the North Pacific. The undertaking collapsed, but the concept clearly had been sound.

Responding to these glowing reports, Boston entrepreneur Joseph Barrell gathered together a group of his moneyed friends to formulate a merchant venture to China via the North Pacific. His associates were Samuel Brown and Charles Bulfinch of Boston, a Cambridge sea captain named Crowell Hatch, John Derby of Salem, and John M. Pintard, a New York merchant.

American commerce with Asia had heretofore seemed impractical, because U.S. merchants had only limited gold with which to buy foreign products, and virtually no goods of interest to the Chinese. But now, taking their cue from Ledyard's aborted scheme, the Boston businessmen envisioned a triangular trade route between their city, the North Pacific coast, and Canton. After obtaining furs from Northwest natives in exchange for cheap goods, traders employed by the merchants would sell the pelts in Asia and there secure other cargos for return to the United States.

The combine purchased and outfitted two American-built ships at a cost of $50,000. The three-masted, Rhode Island-built *Columbia* measured eighty-eight feet in length and was of about 212 tons burden. Her consort, the elegant *Lady Washington,* was a beautifully laid out sloop of somewhat different design. Carrying a single mast with an unusually long boom, she was at ninety tons judged small for sailing around the Horn—but ideal for trading excursions into shallow bays and harbors.

The expedition's planners placed forty-seven-year-old John Kendrick, an experienced merchant sailor of imposing stature, in overall charge of the enterprise and

---

*Following his service in New Spain, Heceta moved on to fight Horatio Nelson at Trafalgar and scale the long ladder of Spanish advancement to the Admiralty.

**To obtain trade items at Nootka the English sailors pilfered their own ships' metal fittings, "so that before we left the place, hardly a bit of brass was left . . . except what was in the necessary instruments."

named him captain of the *Columbia Rediviva.* Kendrick had commanded several privateers during the Revolution. As captain of the *Lady Washington,* the sponsors named taciturn thirty-two-year-old Robert Gray, also a veteran of maritime service during the late war.

Departing from Boston on September 30, 1787, the *Columbia* and *Lady Washington* sailed first to the Cape Verde Islands, where their crews took on water and provisions, then continued on to the Falklands off South America. Kendrick, who had been chosen for his supposedly decisive qualities, now proved otherwise, dawdling for weeks and losing the confidence of his crews.

Finally resuming their voyage in February 1788, the two ships headed west around stormy Cape Horn—the first American vessels of record to attempt this difficult passage. Blown far south into Antarctic waters, they nearly foundered in the gale-swept seas. On April 1 they became separated, not to rejoin for more than five months.

On August 2, Gray, who had left the more cautious Kendrick far behind, sailed within view of the California coast. By the fourteenth the *Lady Washington* reached northern Oregon, where Gray sighted a "tolerably commodious" harbor. His crew, now suffering from scurvy, had not stepped ashore since leaving the Falklands six months earlier. The trader, who would prove time and again to be an audacious inshore sailor, successfully threaded his way in through the treacherous entrance of Tillamook Bay. Gray and his men were the first known non-natives to set foot in Oregon.

With fresh provisions and prime sea otter skins in mind, "trafic on a very friendly footing" was immediately established with the Tillamook natives. But two days later relations took a disastrous turn. Gray's black cabin boy Marcus Lopius became involved in a fracas over a stolen sword and was dispatched by the local villagers. The other members of the landing party barely escaped with their lives. This was a hard lesson the Yankees never forgot, to the point of ruthless reprisals in later encounters. Resuming his northward course, Gray bitterly named his first port of call "Murderers Harbour."

A FEW HOURS BEFORE ENTERING TILLA-mook Bay, Gray had noted a strong, south-moving current. Unbeknownst to the trader at the time, he had encountered the same "seething waters" (which during flood periods extend as far as fifty miles offshore) that Heceta experienced off the Columbia's mouth thirteen years earlier.

Although foggy weather denied Gray a sighting of the great estuary as he continued north, barely a month earlier another trader had ventured right up to the "River of the West." Early in July, English captain John Meares* sailed south along the Washington coast on a fur trading reconnaissance. At noon on the sixth he sighted a prominent headland "and we pleased ourselves with the expectation of its being Cape St. Roc of the Spaniards, near which they are said to have found a good port."

"After we had rounded the promontory," recorded Meares, "a large bay, as we had imagined, opened to our view, that bore a very promising appearance, and into which we steered with every encouraging expectation.... As we steered in, the water shoaled to nine, eight, and seven fathoms, when breakers were seen from the deck, right ahead, and, from the mast head, they were observed to extend across the bay."

Thwarted by the unbroken shoals that seemed to bar entrance to the "bay," Meares turned away in defeat, renaming Heceta's Cape St. Roc "Cape Disappointment" and his Bahia de Asunción "Deception Bay." "We can now with safety assert," concluded the trader, "that there is no such river as that of St. Roc exists, as laid down in the Spanish charts." Meares was the first (but not quite the last) English mariner who nearly held the region's greatest prize in his grasp—only to let it go.

CONTINUING HIS PASSAGE NORTH TO VAN-couver Island's Nootka Sound, Gray there awaited Kendrick, whose *Columbia Rediviva* finally caught up with the *Lady Washington* in late September.

The two ships lay at anchor in Nootka Sound until March 1789, when Gray set out on an exploring and fur-gathering expedition. Scouring the coast for pelts, he sailed south to the Strait of Juan de Fuca, entering that passage to a depth of fifty miles. Turning back north again, he sailed as far as Bucareli Bay in Alaska,

---

*In 1789 Meares found himself the central figure in the "Nootka Controversy," a diplomatic conflict between Spain and England over claims, rights, and sovereignty in Northwest waters.

where the *Lady Washington* was blown ashore on a rocky coast and nearly sunk.

One wonders what Gray's reaction must have been upon returning to the Nootka roadstead on June 16. He had pushed the *Lady Washington* into every kind of hair-raising situation, winning a reputation for reckless behavior among his crew. Kendrick, an exasperating puzzle for his subordinate, had never left the anchorage.

As a result of various deliberations, Gray's furs were now transferred to the *Columbia* and the remaining trade goods shifted to the *Lady Washington.* Kendrick, fifteen years Gray's senior and now at age fifty perhaps simply worn out, moved to the smaller *Washington* and ordered Gray to take the other ship and her cargo to China.

Gray, now in command of the *Columbia Rediviva,* left Clayoquat Sound on July 30, 1789, bound for the Hawaiian Islands. After a three-week stop (the first visit there by an American ship), he continued on to Macao and Canton, where he sold the furs in exchange for six hundred cases of choice tea. The intrepid mariner then sailed toward home via the Cape of Good Hope, arriving back in Boston on August 9, 1790. During a voyage lasting nearly three years he had logged 48,889 sea miles and accomplished the first circumnavigation of the globe by an American captain.**

DESPITE UNIMPRESSIVE FINANCIAL RE-sults (seawater had damaged part of Gray's cargo of tea), the *Columbia's* backers immediately readied her for a return voyage. Derby of Salem and Pintard of New York dropped out of the enterprise, but Gray and two others took their places.

With Gray still in command, the *Columbia Rediviva* left Boston for her second Northwest voyage on September 28, 1790. By early June of the following year, having accomplished the outward-

---

**Kendrick followed Gray to China, arriving in January 1790. But neither he nor the *Lady Washington* ever returned to the United States. Forsaking allegiance to the merchants who had financed the expedition, he appropriated the *Lady Washington* and became a rogue trader. Kendrick met a bizarre end in the Hawaiian islands in December 1794 when, exchanging salutes with the English trader *Jaekal,* he was struck by shot inadvertently fired from the other vessel's cannon. The *Lady Washington,* under another captain, disappeared with all hands in Asian waters in about 1800.

bound passage in eight months, Gray again was actively trading among the northern islands.

Late in November 1791, Gray established winter quarters on Clayoquat Sound. There, in an inlet he named Adventure Cove, the ship's crew erected a crude fort and spent the next several months building a small sloop whose keel and frames had been carried from Boston in the hold of the *Columbia.*

On April 2, 1792, after a tense winter beleaguered with sickness, dissembling, and in Gray's mind native treachery (the Americans apparently thwarted a plot by local natives to massacre them), the trader resumed active operations. Placing the newly-completed *Adventure* under command of his youthful second officer Robert Haswell, Gray sent it north in search of furs. Gray himself, aboard the *Columbia Rediviva,* turned south for a reconnaissance of the Washington and Oregon coasts, apparently hoping to find new sources for trade.

By April 11, Gray reached the vicinity of the present Oregon-California border. There he reversed course and headed north again. Throughout this passage, chief mate Owen Smith took the jolly boat in through the rough coastal waters, marking hidden bays and estuaries. By mid-April the *Columbia Rediviva* was back in the vicinity of the Columbia River.

UNKNOWN TO GRAY, A BRITISH NAVAL expedition was following in his wake, conducting a detailed reconnaissance of the American coast. On April 17 the sloop of war *Discovery* and armed tender *Chatham* arrived off northern California, en route from Hawaii. Captain George Vancouver, who as a midshipman had visited the Northwest Coast with Cook's third expedition, was now returning to that same region with a twofold mission: to finally prove or disprove the myth of a navigable Northwest Passage; and to conclude negotiations with the Spanish commander at Nootka regarding national sovereignty in the roiled Northwest waters. Vancouver was particularly interested in exploring the Strait of Juan de Fuca—there being some hope this might be the western entrance to the supposed passage.

Slowly sailing north, Vancouver (aboard the *Discovery,* accompanied by Lieutenant William Broughton, commanding the *Chatham)* made a careful examination of

the shoreline, lying-to at night and resuming the survey each morning. On April 27 the British captain reached latitude 46° 19' North, where at noon he sighted the prominent headland that four years earlier Meares had renamed "Cape Disappointment." Just to its south lay the broad opening that Meares had called "Deception Bay."

In his journal the ever-observant Vancouver wrote, "the sea had now changed from its natural, to river-coloured water; the probable consequence of some streams falling into the bay, or into the opening north of it, through the lowland."

Vancouver's botanist, Archibald Menzies, noted a strong offshore current and debris "like the overflowings of a considerable river." Thomas Manby, master of the *Chatham,* recorded that the ships approached the opening "as near as safety would permit, [and] as a continued roll of breakers lay right across its entrance, it may [be] from a River, and perhaps admisible at certain periods."

Vancouver now was poised at the edge of what could have been a glorious moment in the explorers life—and (like Meares before him) he let it slip away. "Not considering this opening worthy of more attention," he recorded, "I continued our pursuit to the north-west, being desirous to embrace the advantages of the prevailing breeze and pleasant weather, so favourable to our examination of the coasts."

Two days later, near the entrance to the Strait of Juan de Fuca, the British explorers sighted and hailed the first ship they had seen in eight months—Gray's *Columbia Rediviva.*

TWO OF VANCOUVER'S OFFICERS, MENzies and Peter Puget, boarded the *Columbia* to visit with Gray. The American shared information on the Strait of Juan de Fuca and, according to Vancouver's journal, told of "having been off the mouth of a river in the latitude of 46° 10', where the outset, or reflux, was so strong as to prevent his entering for nine days."

Gray sailed into the Strait of Juan de Fuca as far as Neah Bay with the British explorers, then returned to the open sea and pressed south. On May 7 the *Columbia* followed her longboat into a hitherto unknown harbor on Washington's central coast.

Here the traders had a murderous night clash with a group of Native Americans they had bartered with through the

daylight hours on May 8. "After it was bright moon light," recorded fifth mate John Boit, "we see the canoes approaching to the Ship. We fier'd several cannon over them but still [they] persist'd to advance with their war Hoop." When a large canoe with twenty men pressed to within half a pistol shot, the gunners lowered their aim and "dash'd her all to pieces & no doubt kill'd every soul in her." Alas, this doleful act was several times repeated by apprehensive or rapacious traders through the years.

Again Gray pushed south, on May 11 leaving the harbor his crew named in his honor. It would appear the trader was now moving directly for the site that, according to what he told Vancouver, had frustrated him for several days the preceding month.

It was Boit, a solid product of the Boston Latin School, who entered the laconic description that would have had Gray's approbation. "Just so! May [11], 1792. This day saw an appearance of a spacious harbour abrest th Ship, haul'd our wind for itt, observ'd two sand bars making off, with a passage between them to a fine river. Out pinnance and sent her in ahead and followed with the Ship under short sail. . . . The River extended to the NE as far as eye cou'd reach . . . we directed our course up this noble river in search of a Village. The beach was lin'd with Natives, who ran along shore following the Ship. Soon after above 20 Canoes came off, and brought a good lot of Furs and Salmon, which last they sold two for a board Nail. The furs we likewise bought cheap, for Copper and Cloth. They appear'd to view the Ship with greatest astonishment and no doubt we was the first civilized people they ever saw."

Gray remained in the broad estuary until May 20, maneuvering the *Columbia* freely about in the high spring runoff. He drew the first chart of the interior waters, with soundings marking his progress near the northern shore to a point some thirty miles from the river's entrance. The plentitude of everything was favorably noted, including good food and pure water drawn from the river.

Many canoes visited the several anchorages, and Boit stated that more than fifty villages were reported along the estuary. This observation alone would demand further exploration, but here Gray, still the bold and consummate trader, revealed a basic character trait:

though in possession of long-sought knowledge of international import, he made little use of it. His primary drive was ever the pursuit of cargo.

LATER THAT SUMMER, BEFORE HE LEFT the Northwest Coast for China and home, Gray presented to the Spanish commander at Nootka—Bodega y Quadra of *Sonora* fame—the chart that he had drawn of the lower Columbia. It showed beyond all doubt that the American had entered the long-sought river. When Quadra subsequently gave the chart to Vancouver, the British commander had no recourse but to acknowledge Gray's accomplishment, though his mistrustful officers regarded the trader as a purveyor of "impudent humbug" and "egregious falsehoods."

Following on Gray's information, the British surveyors wanted to see for themselves. Early in October the two warships arrived off Cape Disappointment, and Lieutenant Broughton navigated the *Chatham* over the breaker-swept bar and into the estuary. Captain Vancouver, out of concern for the *Discovery's* deeper keel, was obliged to remain at sea; with the winter rains not yet begun, the great river was now at low ebb.

For three weeks Broughton explored the Columbia, ascending the majestic waterway with the *Chatham's* cutter for a distance of nearly a hundred miles and charting and naming a profusion of islands, points, hillocks, rivers, creeks, and mountains. On October 30 he stepped ashore near present-day Vancouver and formally claimed the river for Great Britain. But nothing Broughton could do or impugn could erase the fact that Gray, the quiet but audacious American mariner, had entered and named "Columbia's River" before him. When the tea-laden *Columbia Rediviva* returned to Boston in July 1793, successful and renowned, "Empire followed in its wake."

Recommended additional reading: Two new books focus on the Northwest voyages of Robert Gray and John Kendrick. Already in print is *Columbia's River: The Voyages of Robert Gray, 1787-1793* by J. Richard Nokes (Washington Historical Society, 352 pages, illustrated, $39.95 hardcover, $24.95 softcover). Soon to be released is *Hail, Columbia!* by John Scofield, a descendant of Kendrick (Oregon Historical Society, about $20.00). Also available is a new edition of *Voyages* of *the Columbia to the Northwest Coast,* containing the logs from that ship, edited by Frederic W. Howay (Oregon Historical Society, 576 pages, $40.00). Also of interest is *Northwest Explorations* by Gordon Speck (Binfords & Mort, 1954).

The Lives of Slave Women

Deborah Gray White

Deborah Gray White is associate professor of history and Africana studies at Rutgers University, New Brunswick, New Jersey. This chapter is adapted from her book, Ar'nt I a Woman? Female Slaves in the Plantation South, *published in 1985 by W. W. Norton.*

Slave women have often been characterized as self-reliant and self-sufficient, yet not every black woman was a Sojourner Truth or a Harriet Tubman. Strength had to be cultivated. It came no more naturally to them than to anyone else, slave or free, male or female, black or white. If slave women seemed exceptionally strong it was partly because they often functioned in groups and derived strength from their numbers.

Much of the work slaves did and the regimen they followed served to stratify slave society along sex lines. Consequently slave women had ample opportunity to develop a consciousness grounded in their identity as females. While close contact sometimes gave rise to strife, adult female cooperation and dependence of women on each other was a fact of female slave life. The self-reliance and self-sufficiency of slave women, therefore, must be viewed in the context not only of what the individual slave woman did for herself, but what slave women as a group were able to do for each other.

It is easy to overlook the separate world of female slaves because from colonial times through the Civil War black women often worked with black men at tasks considered by Europeans to be either too difficult or inappropriate for females. All women worked hard, but when white women consistently performed field labor it was considered temporary, irregular, or extraordinary, putting them on a par with slaves. Actress Fredericka Bremer, visiting the ante-bellum South, noted that usually only men and black women did field work; commenting on what another woman traveler sarcastically claimed to be a noble admission of female equality, Bremer observed that "black [women] are not considered to belong to the weaker sex."[1]

Bremer's comment reflects what former slaves and fugitive male slaves regarded as the defeminization of black women. Bonded women cut down trees to clear lands for cultivation. They hauled logs in leather straps attached to their shoulders. They plowed using mule and ox teams, and hoed, sometimes with the heaviest implements available. They dug ditches, spread manure fertilizer, and piled coarse fodder with their bare hands. They built and cleaned Southern roads, helped construct Southern railroads, and, of course, they picked cotton. In short, what fugitive slave Williamson Pease said regretfully of slave women was borne out in fact: "Women who do outdoor work are used as bad as men."[2] Almost a century later Green Wilbanks spoke less remorsefully than Pease in his remembrances of his Grandma Rose, where he implied that the work had a kind of neutering effect. Grandma Rose, he said, was a woman who could do any kind of job a man could do, a woman who "was some worker, a regular man-woman."[3]

It is hardly likely, though, that slave women, especially those on large plantations with sizable female populations, lost their female identity. Harvesting season on staple crop plantations may have found men and women gathering the crop in sex-integrated gangs, but at other times women often worked in exclusively or predominantly female gangs.[4] Thus women stayed in each other's company for most of the day. This meant that those they ate meals with, sang work songs with, and commiserated with during the work day were people who by virtue of their sex had the same kind of responsibilities and problems. As a result, slave women appeared to have developed their own female culture, a way of doing things and a way of assigning value that flowed from their perspective as slave women on Southern plantations. Rather than being squelched, their sense of womanhood was probably enhanced and their bonds to each other strengthened.

Since slaveowners and managers seemingly took little note of the slave woman's lesser physical strength, one wonders why they separated men and women at all. One answer appears to be that gender provided a natural and easy way to divide the labor force. Also probable is that despite their limited sensitivity regarding female slave labor, and the double standard they used when evaluating the uses of white and black female labor, slaveowners did, using standards only they could explain, reluctantly acquiesce to female physiology. For instance, depending on their stage of pregnancy, pregnant women were considered half or quarter hands. Healthy nonpregnant women were considered three-quarter hands. Three-quarter hands were not necessarily exempt from some of the herculean tasks performed by men who were full hands, but usually, when labor was being parceled out and barring a shortage of male hands to do the very heavy work or a rush to get that work completed, men did the more physically demanding work. A case in point was the most common differentiation where men plowed and women hoed.[5]

Like much of the field labor, nonfield labor was structured to promote cooperation among women. In the Sea Islands, slave women sorted cotton lint according to color and fineness and removed cotton seeds crushed by the gin into the cotton and lint. Fence building often found men splitting rails in one area and women doing the actual construction in another. Men usually shelled corn, threshed peas, cut potatoes for planting, and platted shucks. Grinding corn into meal or hominy was women's work. So too were spinning, weaving, sewing, and washing.[6] On Captain Kinsler's South Carolina plantation, as on countless others, "old women and women bearin' chillun not yet born, did cardin' wid handcards." Some would spin, others would weave, but all would eventually learn from some skilled woman "how to make clothes for the family . . . knit coarse socks and stockins."[7]

"When the work in the fields was finished women were required to come home and spin one cut a night," reported a Georgian. "Those who were not successful in completing this work were punished the next morning."[8] Women had to work in the evenings partly because slaveowners bought them few ready-made clothes. On one South Carolina plantation each male slave received annually two cotton shirts, three pairs of pants, and one jacket. Slave women, on the other hand, received six yards of woolen cloth, six yards of cotton drilling, and six yards of cotton shirting a year, along with two needles and a dozen buttons.[9]

A great deal of both field labor and nonfield labor was structured to promote cooperation among slave women.

Perhaps a saving grace to this "double duty" was that women got a chance to interact with each other. On a Sedalia County, Missouri plantation, women looked forward to Saturday afternoon washing because, as Mary Frances Webb explained, they "would get to talk and spend the day together."[10] Quiltings, referred to by former slaves as female "frolics" and "parties," were especially convivial. Anna Peek recalled that when slaves were allowed to relax, they gathered around a pine wood fire in Aunt Anna's cabin to tell stories. At that time "the old women with pipes in their mouths would sit and gossip for hours."[11] Missourian Alice Sewell noted that sometimes women would slip away and hold their own prayer meetings. They cemented their bonds to each other at the end of every meeting when they walked around shaking hands and singing, "fare you well my sisters, I am going home."[12]

The organization of female slave work and social activities tended not only to separate women and men, but also to generate female cooperation and interdependence. Slave women and their children could depend on midwives and "doctor women" to treat a variety of ailments. Menstrual cramps, for example, were sometimes treated with a tea made from the bark of the gum tree. Midwives and "doctor women" administered various other herb teas to ease the pains of many ailing slaves. Any number of broths—made from the leaves and barks of trees, from the branches and twigs of bushes, from turpentine, catnip, or tobacco—were used to treat whooping cough, diarrhea, toothaches, colds, fevers, headaches, and backaches.[13] According to a Georgia ex-slave, "One had to be mighty sick to have the services of a doctor." On his master's plantation "old women were . . . responsible for the care of the sick."[14] This was also the case on Rebecca Hooks's former Florida residence. "The doctor," she noted, "was not nearly as popular as the 'granny' or midwife, who brewed medicines for every ailment."[15]

Female cooperation in the realm of medical care helped foster bonding that led to collaboration in the area of resistance to abuses by slaveholders. Frances Kemble could attest to the concerted efforts of the black women on her husband's Sea Island plantations. More than once she was visited by groups of women imploring her to persuade her husband to extend the lying-in period for childbearing women. On one occasion the women had apparently prepared beforehand the approach they would take with the foreign-born and sympathetic Kemble, for their chosen spokeswoman took care to play on Kemble's own maternal sentiments, and pointedly argued that slave women deserved at least some of the care and tenderness that Kemble's own pregnancy had elicited.[16]

Usually, however, slave women could not be so outspoken about their needs, and covert cooperative resistance prevailed. Slaveowners suspected that midwives conspired with their female patients to bring about abortions and infanticides, and on Charles Colcock Jones's Georgia plantation, for example, this seems in fact to have been the case. A woman named Lucy gave birth in secret and then denied that she had ever been pregnant. Although the midwife attended her, she too claimed not to have delivered a child,

as did Lucy's mother. Jones had a physician examine Lucy, and the doctor confirmed what Jones had suspected, that Lucy had indeed given birth. Twelve days later the decomposing body of a full-term infant was found, and Lucy, her mother, and the midwife were all hauled off to court. Another woman, a nurse, managed to avoid prosecution but not suspicion. Whether Lucy was guilty of murder, and whether the others were accessories, will never be known because the court could not shatter their collective defense that the child had been stillborn.[17]

The inability to penetrate the private world of female slaves is probably what kept many abortions and infanticides from becoming known to slaveowners. The secrets kept by a midwife named Mollie became too much for her to bear. When she accepted Christianity these were the first things for which she asked forgiveness. She recalled, "I was carried to the gates of hell and the devil pulled out a book showing me the things which I had committed and that they were all true. My life as a midwife was shown to me and I have certainly felt sorry for all the things I did, after I was converted."[18]

Health care is not the only example of how the organization of slave work and slave responsibilities led to female cooperation and bonding; slave women also depended on each other for child-care. Sometimes, especially on small farms or new plantations where there was no extra woman to superintend children, bondswomen took their offspring to the field with them and attended to them during pre-scheduled breaks. Usually, however, infants and older children were left in the charge of an elderly female or females. Josephine Bristow, for example, spent more time with Mary Novlin, the nursery keeper on Ferdinand Gibson's South Carolina plantation, than she spent with her mother and father, who came in from the fields after she was asleep: "De old lady, she looked after every blessed thing for us all day long en cooked for us right along wid de mindin'."[19] In their complementary role as nurses, they ministered to the hurts and illnesses of infants and children.[20] It was not at all uncommon for the children's weekly rations to be given to the "grannies" as opposed to the children's parents.[21] Neither the slaveowner nor slave society expected the biological mother of a child to fulfill all of her child's needs. Given the circumstances, the responsibilities of motherhood had to be shared, and this required close female cooperation.

Cooperation in this sphere helped slave women overcome one of the most difficult of predicaments—who would provide maternal care for a child whose mother had died or been sold away? Fathers sometimes served as both mother and father, but when slaves, as opposed to the master, determined maternal care, it was usually a woman who became a child's surrogate mother. Usually that woman was an aunt or a sister, but in the absence of female relatives, a non-kin woman assumed the responsibility.[22] In the case of Georgian Mollie Malone, for example, the nursery superintendent became the child's substitute mother.[23] When Julia Malone's mother was killed by another Texas slave, little Julia was raised by the woman with whom her mother had shared a cabin.[24] On Southern plantations the female community made sure that no child was truly motherless.

Because black women on a plantation spent so much time together, they inevitably developed some appreciation of each other's skills and talents. This intimacy enabled them to establish the criteria by which to rank and order themselves. The existence of certain ''female jobs'' that carried prestige created a yardstick by which bondswomen could measure each other's achievements. Some of these jobs allowed for growth and self-satisfaction, fringe benefits that were usually out of reach for the field laborer. A seamstress, for example, had unusual opportunities for self-expression and creativity. On very large plantations the seamstress usually did no field work, and a particularly good seamstress, or ''mantua-maker,'' might be hired out to others and even allowed to keep a portion of the money she earned.[25] For obvious reasons cooks, midwives, and female folk doctors also commanded the respect of their peers. Midwives in particular often were able to travel to other plantations to practice their art. This gave them an enviable mobility and also enabled them to carry messages from one plantation to the next.

Apart from the seamstresses, cooks, and midwives, a few women were distinguished as work gang-leaders. On most farms and plantations where there were overseers, managers, foremen, and drivers, these positions were held by men, either black or white. Occasionally, however, a woman was given a measure of authority over slave work, or a particular aspect of it. For instance Louis Hughes noted that each plantation he saw had a ''forewoman who . . . had charge of the female slaves and also the boys and girls from twelve to sixteen years of age, and all the old people that were feeble.''[26] Similarly, a Mississippi slave remembered that on his master's Osceola plantation there was a ''colored woman as foreman.''[27]

Clearly, a pecking order existed among bondswomen—one which they themselves helped to create. Because of age, occupation, association with the master class, or personal achievements, certain women were recognized by other women—and also by men—as important people, even as leaders. Laura Towne met an aged woman who commanded such a degree of respect that other slaves bowed to her and lowered their voices in her presence. The old woman, Maum Katie, was according to Towne a ''spiritual mother'' and a woman of ''tremendous influence over her spiritual children.''[28]

A slaveowner lamented that Big Lucy, one of his oldest slaves, had more control over his female workers than he did.

Sometimes two or three factors combined to distinguish a particular woman. Aunt Charlotte was the aged cook in John M. Booth's Georgia household. When Aunt Charlotte spoke, said Booth, ''other colored people hastened to obey her.''[29] Frederick Douglass's grandmother wielded influence because of her age and the skills she possessed. She made the best fishnets in Tuckahoe, Maryland, and she knew better than anyone else how to preserve sweet potato seedlings and how to plant them successfully. She enjoyed what Douglass called ''high reputation,'' and accordingly ''she was remembered by others.''[30] In another example, when Elizabeth Botume went to the Sea Islands after the Civil War, she employed as a house servant a young woman named Amy who performed her tasks slowly and sullenly, until an older woman named Aunt Mary arrived from Beaufort. During slavery Amy and Aunt Mary had both worked in the house but Amy had learned to listen and obey Aunt Mary. After Aunt Mary arrived the once obstreperous Amy became ''quiet, orderly, helpful and painstaking.''[31]

The leadership of some women had a disruptive effect on plantation operations. Bennet H. Barrow repeatedly lamented the fact that Big Lucy, one of his oldest slaves, had more control over his female workers than he did: ''Anica, Center, Cook Jane, the better you treat them the worse they are. Big Lucy the Leader corrupts every young negro in her power.''[32] A self-proclaimed prophetess named Sinda was responsible for a cessation of all slave work for a considerable period on Butler Island in Georgia. According to a notation made by Frances Kemble in 1839, Sinda's prediction that the world would come to an end on a certain day caused the slaves to lay down their hoes and plows in the belief that their final emancipation was imminent. So sure were Sinda's fellow slaves of her prediction that even the lash failed to get them into the fields. When the appointed day of judgment passed uneventfully Sinda was whipped mercilessly. Yet, for a time, she had commanded more authority than either master or overseer.[33]

Bonded women did not have to go to such lengths in order to make a difference in each other's lives. The supportive atmosphere of the female community was considerable buffer against the depersonalizing regimen of plantation work and the general dehumanizing nature of slavery. When we consider that women were much more strictly confined to the plantation than men, that many women had husbands who visited only once or twice a week, and that slave women outlived slave men by an average of two years, we realize just how important the female community was to its members.

If we define a stable relationship as one of long duration, then it was probably easier for slave women to sustain stable emotional relationships with other bondswomen than with bondsmen. This is not to say that male-female relationships were unfulfilling or of no consequence. But they were generally fraught with more uncertainty about the future than female-to-female relationships, especially those existing between female blood kin. In her study of ex-slave interviews, Martha Goodson found that of all the relationships slaveowners disrupted, through either sale or dispersal, they were least likely to separate mothers and daughters.[34] Cody found that when South Carolina cotton planter Peter Gaillard divided his estate among his eight children, slave women in their twenties and thirties were twice as likely to have a sister with them, and women over 40 were four times more likely to have sisters with them than brothers. Similarly, daughters were less likely than sons to be separated from their mother. Over 60 percent of women aged 20 to 24 remained with their mothers when the estate was divided, as did 90 percent of those aged 25 to 29.[35] A slave song reflected the bonds between female siblings by indicating who took responsibility for the motherless female slave child. Interestingly enough, the one designated was neither the father nor the brother:

A motherless chile see a hard time.
  Oh Lord, help her on de road.
Er sister will do de bes' she kin,
  Dis is a hard world, Lord, fer a motherless chile.[36]

If female blood ties did indeed promote the most enduring relationships among slaves, then we should probably assume that like occupation, age, and personal achievement these relationships helped structure the female slave community. This assumption should not, however, obscure the fact that in friendships and dependency relationships women often treated non-relatives as if a consanguineous tie existed. This is why older women were called Aunt and Granny, and why unrelated women sometimes called each other Sister.[37]

While the focus here has been on those aspects of the bondswoman's life that fostered female bonding, female-to-female conflict was not uncommon. It was impossible for harmony always to prevail among women who saw so much of each other and who knew so much about one another. Lifelong friendships were founded in the hoe gangs and sewing groups, but the constant jockeying for occupational and social status created an atmosphere in which jealousies and antipathies smoldered. From Jesse Belflowers, the overseer of the Allston rice plantation in South Carolina, Adele Petigru Allston heard that "mostly mongst the Women" there was a "goodeal of quarling and disputing and telling lies."[38] The terms of a widely circulated overseer's contract advised rigorous

punishment for "fighting, particularly amongst the women."[39] Some overseers followed this advice. According to Georgian Isaac Green, "Sometimes de women uster git whuppin's for fightin'."[40]

Occasionally, violence between women could and did get very ugly. Molly, the cook in James Chesnut's household, once took a red hot poker and attacked the woman to whom her husband had given one of her calico dresses.[41] Similarly, when she was a young woman in Arkansas, Lucretia Alexander came to blows with another woman over a pair of stockings that the master had given Lucretia.[42] In another incident on a Louisiana cotton plantation, the day's cotton chopping was interrupted when a feisty field worker named Betty lost her temper in the midst of a dispute with a fellow slave named Molly and struck her in the face with a hoe.[43]

The presence of conflict within interpersonal relationships between female slaves should not detract from the more important cooperation and dependence that prevailed among them. Conflict occurred *because* women were in close daily contact with each other and because the penalties for venting anger on other women were not as severe as those for striking out at men, either black or white. It is not difficult to understand how dependency relationships could become parasitical, how sewing and washing sessions could become "hanging courts," how one party could use knowledge gained in an intimate conversation against another.

Just how sisterhood could co-exist with discord is illustrated by the experience of some black women of the South Carolina and Georgia Sea Islands between 1862 and 1865. On November 7, 1861, Commodore S. F. DuPont sailed into Port Royal Sound, quickly defeated the Confederates, and put Union troops ashore to occupy the islands. Almost before DuPont's guns ceased firing, the entire white population left the islands for the mainland. A few house servants were taken with the fleeing whites but most of the slaves remained on the islands. The following year they and the occupying army were joined by a host of government agents and Northern missionaries. Several interest groups were gathered in the islands and each had priorities. As Treasury agents concerned themselves with the cotton, and army officers recruited and drafted black soldiers, and missionaries went about "pre-

paring" slaves for freedom, the black Sea Islanders' world was turned upside down. This was true for young and middle-aged men who served in the Union army, but also for the women who had to manage their families and do most of the planting and harvesting in the absence of the men.[44]

During the three years of upheaval, black female life conformed in many ways to that outlined here. Missionaries' comments indicate that certain women were perceived as leaders by their peers. Harriet Ware, for instance, identified a woman from Fripp Point on St. Helena Island named Old Peggy as "the leader." This woman was important because she, along with another woman named Binah, oversaw church membership. Ware's housekeeper Flora told her, "Old Peggy and Binah were the two whom all that came into the Church had to come through, and the Church supports them."[45]

On the Coffin's Point Plantation on St. Helena Island, a woman named Grace served her fellow women at least twice by acting as spokeswoman in disputes over wages paid for cotton production. On one occasion the women of the plantation complained to Mr. Philbrick, one of the plantation superintendents, that their wages were not high enough to permit them to purchase cloth at the local store. They were also upset because the molasses they bought from one of the other plantation superintendents was watered down. As Grace spoke in their behalf, the women shouted words of approval. At least part of the reason for Grace's ascendancy stemmed from the fact that she was among the older women of the island. She was also a strong and diligent worker who was able despite her advanced age to plant, hoe, and harvest cotton along with the younger women.[46]

Ample evidence exists of dependency relationships and cooperation among Sea Island women throughout the war years. In slavery sick and "lying-in" women relied on their peers to help them, and the missionaries found this to be the case on the islands during the Union occupation as well. For instance, Philbrick observed that it was quite common for the blacks to hire each other to hoe their tasks when sickness or other inconveniences kept an individual from it. In 1862 some of the Coffin's Point men were recruited by government agents to pick cotton elsewhere in the Sea Islands. This left many of the women at Coffin's Point completely responsible for hoeing the land allotted to each. Women who were sick or pregnant stood to lose their family's allotment since neglected land was reassigned to others. However, the women saw to it, according to Philbrick, that "the tasks of the lying-in women [were] taken care of by sisters or other friends in the absence of their husbands." No doubt these "other friends" were women, since in the same letter Philbrick noted that the only men left on the plantation were those too old to work in the cotton.[47]

Another missionary, Elizabeth Hyde Botume, related similar episodes of female cooperation. Regardless of the circumstances surrounding a pregnancy, it was common for the women of Port Royal to care for, and keep company with, expectant and convalescing mothers. Several times Botume was approached by a spokeswoman seeking provisions for these mothers. Sometimes she gave them reluctantly because many of the women were not married. Usually, however, she was so impressed by the support that the pregnant women received from their peers that she suspended judgment and sent clothes and groceries for the mothers and infants. On one occasion she was approached by several women who sought aid for a woman named Cumber. The women were so willing to assist one of their own that Botume remarked abashedly: " . . . their readiness to help the poor erring girl made me ashamed."[48] These were not the only instances of cooperation among the black women. Some moved in with each other and shared domestic duties; others looked after the sick together.[49] With so many of the men away, women found ways of surviving together and cooperating. Predictably, however, along with the "togetherness" went conflict.

Many situations held possibilities for discord. Charles P. Ware, a missionary from Boston, wrote that the work in the crops would go more smoothly if only he could get the women to stop fighting. At least some of the fights were caused by disputes over the distribution of the former mistress's wardrobe. According to Ware, when a woman said, "I free, I as much right to ole missus' things as you," a fight was sure to erupt.[50] Harriet Ware witnessed a fight in which the women "fired shells and tore each other's clothes in a most disgraceful way." The cause of the fight was unknown to her but she was sure it was the "tongues of the women." Jealousy, she noted, ran

rampant among the women, and to her mind there was "much foundation for it."[51]

The experiences of the Sea Islands women in the early 1860s comprised a special episode in American history, but their behavior conformed to patterns that had been set previously by bonded women on large plantations. Historians have shown that the community of the quarters, the slave family, and slave religion shielded the slave from absolute dependence on the master and that parents, siblings, friends, and relatives served in different capacities as buffers against the internalization of degrading and dependent roles. The female slave network served as a similar buffer for black women, but it also had a larger significance. Treated by Southern whites as if they were anything but self-respecting women, many bonded females helped one another to forge their own independent definitions of womanhood, their own notions about what women should be and how they should act.

NOTES

1. Fredericka Bremer, *Homes of the New World*, 2 vols. (New York, 1853), 2: 519; Frances Anne Kemble, *Journal of a Residence on a Georgian Plantation*, ed. John A. Scott (New York, 1961 [1863]), p. 66. See also: Harriet Martineau, *Society in America*, 3 vols. (London, 1837), 2: 243, 311-12.

2. Benjamin Drew, *The Refugees: A North Side View of Slavery*, in *Four Fugitive Slave Narratives* (Boston, 1969), p. 92.

3. George Rawick, ed., *The American Slave, A complete Autobiography*, 19 vols. (Westport, CT, 1972), Ga., vol. 13, pt. 4: 139.

4. Frederick Olmsted, *A Journey in the Seaboard Slave States* (New York, 1856), pp. 430-32; Olmsted, *The Cotton Kingdom*, ed. David Freeman Hawke (New York, 1971), p. 176; William Howard Russell, *My Diary North and South (Canada, Its Defenses, Condition and Resources)*, 3 vols. (London, 1865), 1: 379-80; Solomon Northup, *Twelve Years a Slave, Narrative of Solomon Northup* in Gilbert Osofsky, ed., *Puttin' on Ole Massa* (New York, 1969), pp. 308-09; Rawick, *American Slave*, Ark., vol. 10, pt. 5: 54; Ala., vol. 6: 46, 336; Newstead Plantation Diary 1856-58, entry Wednesday, May 6, 1857, Southern Historical Collection (SHC), University Of North Carolina at Chapel Hill; Adwon Adams Davis, *Plantation Life in the Florida Parishes of Louisiana 1836-1846 as Reflected in the Diary of Bennet H. Barrow* (New York, 1943), p. 127; Frederick Olmsted, *A Journey in the Back Country* (New York, 1907), p. 152; *Plantation Manual*, SHC, p. 4; Eugene Genovese, *The Political Economy of Slavery: Studies in the Economy and Society of the Slave South* (New York, 1961), p. 133; Stuart Bruchey, ed., *Cotton and the Growth of the American Economy: 1790-1860* (New York, 1967), pp. 176-80.

5. See note 4.

6. J. A. Turner, ed., *The Cotton Planters Manual* (New York, 1865), pp. 97-98; Guion B. Johnson, *A Social History of the Sea Islands* (Chapel Hill, NC, 1930), pp. 28-30; Jenkins Mikell, *Rumbling of the Chariot Wheels* (Columbia, SC, 1923), pp. 19-20; Bruchey, *Cotton and the Growth of the American Economy*, pp. 176-80.

7. Rawick, *American Slave*, S.C., vol. 2, pt. 2: 114.

8. Ibid., Ga., vol. 13, p. 3: 186.

9. *Plantation Manual*, SHC, p. 1.

10. Rawick, *American Slave*, Ok., vol. 7: 315.

11. George P. Rawick, Jan Hillegas, and Ken Lawrence, ed., *The American Slave: A Composite Autobiography, Supplement, Series 1*, 12 vols. (Westport, CT, 1978), Ga., Supp. 1, vol. 4: 479.

12. Rawick, *American Slave*, Mo., vol. 11: 307.

13. For examples of cures see: Ibid., Ark., vol. 10, pt. 5: 21, 125; Ala., vol. 6: 256, 318; Ga., vol. 13, pt. 3: 106.

14. Ibid., Ga., vol. 12, pt. 1: 303.

15. Ibid., Fla, vol. 17: 175; see also: Rawick et al., *American Slave, Supplement*, Miss. Supp. 1, vol. 6: 317; Ga. Supp. 1, vol. 4: 444; John Spencer Bassett, *The Southern Plantation Overseer, as Revealed in His Letters* (Northampton, MA, 1923), pp. 28, 31.

16. Kemble, *Journal of a Residence on a Georgian Plantation*, p. 222.

17. Robert Manson Myers, ed., *The Children of Pride: A True Story of Georgia and the Civil War* (New Haven, CT, 1972), pp. 528, 532, 542, 544, 546.

18. Charles S. Johnson, ed., *God Struck Me Dead: Religious Conversion Experiences and Autobiographies of Negro Ex-Slaves* in Rawick, *American Slave*, vol. 19: 74.

19. Rawick, *American Slave*, S.C., vol. 2, pt. 1: 99.

20. Ibid., Ga., vol. 12, pt. 2: 112; S.C., vol. 2, pt. 2: 55; Fla., vol. 17: 174; see also Olmsted, *Back Country*, p. 76.

21. See, for instance, *Plantation Manual*, SHC, p. 1.

22. Rawick, *American Slave*, Ala., vol. 6: 73.

23. Rawick et al., *American Slave, Supplement*, Ga. Supp. 1, vol. 4, pt. 3: 103.

24. Rawick, *American Slave*, Tex., vol. 5, pt. 3: 103.

25. Hughes, *Thirty Years a Slave*, p. 39; Rawick, *American Slave*, Fla., vol. 17: 158; S.C., vol. 2, pt. 1: 114; White Hill Plantation Books, SHC, p. 13.

26. Hughes, *Thirty Years a Slave*, p. 22.

27. Ophelia Settle Egypt, J. Masuoha, and Charles S. Johnson, eds., *Unwritten History of Slavery: Autobiographical Accounts of Negro Ex-Slaves* (Washington, 1968 [1945]), p. 41.

28. Laura M. Towne, *Letters and Diary of Laura M. Towne Written from the Sea Islands of South Carolina 1862-1884*, ed. Rupert Sargent Holland (New York, 1969 [1912]), pp. 144-45. See also: Kemble, *Journal of a Residence on a Georgian Plantation*, p. 55.

29. Rawick, *American Slave*, Ga. vol. 13, pt. 3: 190.

30. Frederick Douglass, *My Bondage and My Freedom* (New York, 1968 [1855]), p. 36.

31. Elizabeth Hyde Botume, *First Days Amongst the Contrabands* (Boston, 1893), p. 132.

32. Davis, *Plantation Life in the Florida Parishes*, p. 191. See also pp. 168, 173.

33. Kemble, *Journal of a Residence on a Georgian Plantation*, pp. 118–19.

34. Martha Graham Goodson, ''An Introductory Essay and Subject Index to Selected Interviews from the Slave Narrative Collection,'' (Ph.D. diss., Union Graduate School, 1977), p. 33.

35. Cheryll Ann Cody, ''Naming, Kinship, and Estate Dispersal: Notes on Slave Family Life on a South Carolina Plantation, 1786 to 1833,'' *William and Mary Quarterly* 39 (1982): 207–09.

36. Rawick, *American Slave*, Ala., vol. 7:73.

37. Herbert G. Gutman, *The Black Family in Slavery and Freedom, 1750–1925* (New York, 1976), pp. 216–22.

38. J. H. Easterby, ed., *The South Carolina Rice Plantations as Revealed in the Papers of Robert W. Allston* (Chicago, 1945), p. 291.

39. Bassett, *The Southern Plantation Overseer*, pp. 19–20, 32.

40. Rawick, *American Slave*, Ga., vol. 12, pt. 2: 57.

41. C. Vann Woodward, ed., *Mary Chesnut's Civil War* (New Haven, CT, 1981), pp. 33–34.

42. Norman Yetman, *Voices from Slavery* (New York, 1970), p. 13.

43. J. Mason Brewer, *American Negro Folklore* (New York, 1968), p. 233.

44. Willie Lee Rose, *Rehearsal for Reconstruction: The Port Royal Experiment* (New York, 1964), p. 11.

45. Elizabeth Ware Pearson, ed., *Letters from Port Royal: Written at the Time of the Civil War* (New York, 1969 [1906]), p. 44.

46. Ibid., pp. 250, 303–04.

47. Ibid., p. 56.

48. Botume, *First Days Amongst the Contrabands*, p. 125.

49. See for instance: Ibid., pp. 55–56, 58, 80, 212.

50. Pearson, *Letters from Port Royal*, p. 1133.

51. Botume, *First Days Amongst the Contrabands*, pp. 210–11.

The Great Chief Justice

Under the leadership of John Marshall, the nation's highest tribunal became a court supreme in fact as well as in name.

Brian McGinty

Brian McGinty is a California attorney and writer.

He was a tall man with long legs, gangling arms, and a round, friendly face. He had a thick head of dark hair and strong, black eyes—"penetrating eyes," a friend called them, "beaming with intelligence and good nature." He was born in a log cabin in western Virginia and never wholly lost his rough frontier manners. Yet John Marshall became a lawyer, a member of Congress, a diplomat, an advisor to presidents, and the most influential and respected judge in the history of the United States. "If American law were to be represented by a single figure," Supreme Court Justice Oliver Wendell Holmes, Jr., once said, "sceptic and worshipper alike would agree without dispute that the figure could be but one alone, and that one John Marshall."

To understand Marshall's preeminence in American legal history it is necessary to understand the marvelous rebirth the United States Supreme Court experienced after he became its chief justice in 1801. During all of the previous eleven years of its existence, the highest judicial court in the federal system had been weak and ineffectual—ignored by most of the nation's lawyers and judges and scorned by its principal politicians. Under Marshall's leadership, the court became a strong and vital participant in national affairs. During his more than thirty-four years as Chief Justice of the United States, Marshall welded the Supreme Court into an effective and cohesive whole. With the support of his colleagues on the high bench, he declared acts of Congress and of the president unconstitutional, struck down laws that infringed on federal prerogatives, and gave force and dignity to basic guar-

antees of life and liberty and property. Without John Marshall, the Supreme Court might never have been anything but an inconsequential junior partner of the executive and legislative branches of the national government. Under his guidance and inspiration, it became what the Constitution intended it to be—a court system in fact as well as in name.

Born on September 4, 1755, in Fauquier County, Virginia, John Marshall was the oldest of fifteen children born to Thomas Marshall and Mary Randolph Keith. On his mother's side, the young Virginian was distantly related to Thomas Jefferson, the gentlemanly squire of Monticello and author of the Declaration of Independence. Aside from this kinship, there was little similarity between Marshall and Jefferson. A son of the frontier, Marshall was a backwoodsman at heart, more comfortable in the company of farmers than intellectuals or scholars. Jefferson was a polished aristocrat who liked to relax in the library of his mansion near Charlottesville and meditate on the subtleties of philosophy and political theory.

The contrast between the two men was most clearly drawn in their opposing political beliefs. An advocate of limiting the powers of central government, Thomas Jefferson thought of himself first and foremost as a Virginian (his epitaph did not even mention the fact that he had once been president of the United States). Marshall, in contrast, had, even as a young man, come to transcend his state roots, to look to Congress rather than the Virginia legislature as his government, to think of himself first, last, and always as an American. Throughout their careers, their contrasting philosophies would place the two men at odds.

Marshall's national outlook was furthered by his father's close association with George Washington and his own

unflinching admiration for the nation's first president. Thomas Marshall had been a schoolmate of Washington and, as a young man, helped him survey the Fairfax estates in northern Virginia. John Marshall served under Washington during the bitter winter at Valley Forge and later became one of the planter-turned-statesman's most loyal supporters.

Years after the Revolution was over, Marshall attributed his political views to his experiences as a foot soldier in the great conflict, recalling that he grew up "at a time when a love of union and resistance to the claims of Great Britain were the inseparable inmates of the same bosom;—when patriotism and a strong fellow feeling with our suffering fellow citizens of Boston were identical;—when the maxim 'united we stand, divided we fall' was the maxim of every orthodox American . . ." "I had imbibed these sentiments so thoughroughly [sic] that they constituted a part of my being," wrote Marshall. "I carried them with me into the army where I found myself associated with brave men from different states who were risking life and everything valuable in a common cause believed by all to be most precious; and where I was confirmed in the habit of considering America as my country, and Congress as my government."

After Washington's death, Marshall became the great man's biographer, penning a long and admiring account of Washington's life as a farmer, soldier, and statesman, expounding the Federalist philosophy represented by Washington and attacking those who stood in opposition to it. Jefferson, who detested Federalism as much as he disliked Marshall, was incensed by the biography, which he branded a "five-volume libel."

Frontiersman though he was, Marshall was no bumpkin. His father had person-

From *American History Illustrated*, September 1986, pp. 8-14, 46-47. Reprinted through the courtesy of Cowles Magazines, publishers of *American History Illustrated*.

Jefferson and Marshall: Two Great Minds in Conflict

PROFILE PORTRAITS
BY M. FEVRET DE SAINT MEMIN
AMERICAN HISTORY ILLUSTRATED COLLECTION

Fellow Virginians Thomas Jefferson and John Marshall (next page) had contrasting philosophies regarding the roles of government. Jefferson believed in state sovereignty and in a limited role for national government.

ally attended to his earliest schooling, teaching him to read and write and giving him a taste for history and poetry (by the age of twelve he had already transcribed the whole of Alexander Pope's *Essay on Man).* When he was fourteen, Marshall was sent to a school a hundred miles from home, where future president James Monroe was one of his classmates. After a year, he returned home to be tutored by a Scottish pastor who had come to live in the Marshall house. The future lawyer read Horace and Livy, pored through the English dictionary, and scraped at least a passing acquaintance with the "Bible of the Common Law," William Blackstone's celebrated *Commentaries on the Laws of England.*

In 1779, during a lull in the Revolution, young Marshall attended lectures at the College of William and Mary in Williamsburg. He remained at the college only a few weeks, but the impression made on him by his professor there, George Wythe, was lasting. A lawyer, judge, and signer of the Declaration of Independence, Wythe is best remembered today as the first professor of law at any institution of higher learning in the United States. As a teacher, he was a seminal influence in the development of American law, counting among his many distinguished students Thomas Jefferson, John Breckinridge, and Henry Clay.

Marshall did not remain long at William and Mary. It was the nearly universal custom then for budding lawyers to "read law" in the office of an older lawyer or judge or, failing that, to appeal to the greatest teacher of all—experience—for instruction. In August 1780, a few weeks before his twenty-fifth birthday, Marshall appeared at the Fauquier County Courthouse where, armed with a license signed by Governor Thomas Jefferson of Virginia, he was promptly admitted to the bar.

His first cases were not important, but he handled them well and made a favorable impression on his neighbors; so favorable that they sent him to Richmond in 1782 as a member of the Virginia House of Delegates. Though he retained a farm in Fauquier County all his life, Richmond became Marshall's home after his election to the legislature. The general courts of Virginia held their sessions in the new capital, and the commonwealth's most distinguished lawyers crowded its bar. When Marshall's fortunes improved, he built a comfortable brick house on the outskirts of the city, in which he and his beloved wife Polly raised five sons and one daughter (four other offspring died during childhood).

Marshall's skill as a lawyer earned him an enthusiastic coterie of admirers and his honest country manners an even warmer circle of friends. He liked to frequent the city's taverns and grog shops, more for conviviality than for refreshment, and he was an enthusiastic member of the Barbecue Club, which met each Saturday to eat, drink, "josh," and play quoits.

Marshall liked to do his own shopping for groceries. Each morning he marched through the streets with a basket under his arm, collecting fresh fruits, vegetables, and poultry for the Marshall family larder. Years after his death, Richmonders were fond of recalling the day when a stranger came into the city in search of a lawyer and found Marshall in front of the Eagle Hotel, holding a hat filled with cherries and speaking casually with the hotel proprietor. After Marshall went on his way, the stranger approached the proprietor and asked if he could direct him to the best lawyer in Richmond. The proprietor replied quite readily that the best lawyer was John Marshall, the tall man with the hat full of cherries who had just walked down the street.

Marshall believed in a strong central government, in the Constitution as the key to the laws of the land, and in courts as the supreme custodians of those laws—views that would influence his shaping of the Supreme Court.

COURTESY OF THE CORCORAN GALLERY OF ART, WASHINGTON, D.C.

But the stranger could not believe that a man who walked through town so casually could be a really "proper barrister" and chose instead to hire a lawyer who wore a black suit and powdered wig. On the day set for the stranger's trial, several cases were scheduled to be argued. In the first that was called, the visitor was surprised to see that John Marshall and his own lawyer were to speak on opposite sides. As he listened to the arguments, he quickly realized that he had made a serious mistake. At the first recess, he approached Marshall and confessed that he had come to Richmond with a hundred dollars to hire the best lawyer in the city, but he had chosen the wrong one and now had only five dollars left. Would Marshall agree to represent him for such a small fee? Smiling good-naturedly, Marshall accepted the five dollars, then proceeded to make a brilliant legal argument that quickly won the stranger's case.

Marshall was not an eloquent man; not eloquent, that is, in the sense that his great contemporary, Patrick Henry, a spellbinding courtroom orator, was eloquent. Marshall was an effective enough speaker; but, more importantly, he was a rigorously logical thinker. He had the ability to reduce complex issues to bare essentials and easily and effortlessly apply abstract principles to resolve them.

Thomas Jefferson (himself a brilliant lawyer) was awed, even intimidated, by Marshall's powers of persuasion. "When conversing with Marshall," Jefferson once said, "I never admit anything. So sure as you admit any position to be good, no matter how remote from the

> *"If American law were to be represented by a single figure . . . the figure could be but one alone, and that one John Marshall."*

conclusion he seeks to establish, you are gone. . . . Why, if he were to ask me if it were daylight or not, I'd reply, 'Sir, I don't know, I can't tell.' "

THOUGH MARSHALL'S LEGAL PROWESS and genial manner won him many friends in Richmond, his political views did little to endear him to the Old Dominion's political establishment. While Jefferson and his followers preached the virtues of agrarian democracy, viewing with alarm every step by which the fledgling national government extended its powers through the young nation, Marshall clearly allied himself with Washington, Alexander Hamilton, and John Adams and the Federalist policies they espoused.

Marshall was not a delegate to the convention that met in Philadelphia in 1787 to draft a constitution for the United States, but he took a prominent part in efforts to secure ratification of the Constitution, thereby winning the special admiration of George Washington. After taking office as president, Washington offered Marshall the post of attorney general. Marshall declined the appointment, as he did a later offer of the prestigious post of American minister to France, explaining that he preferred to stay in Richmond with his family and law practice.

He did agree, however, to go to Paris in 1798 as one of three envoys from President John Adams to the government of revolutionary France. He did this, in part, because he was assured that his duties in Paris would be temporary only, in part because he believed he could perform a real service for his country, helping to preserve peaceful relations between it and France during a time of unusual diplomatic tension.

After Marshall joined his colleagues Elbridge Gerry and Charles Pinckney in Paris, he was outraged to learn that the French government expected to be paid before it would receive the American emissaries. Marshall recognized the French request as a solicitation for a bribe (the recipients of the payments were mysteriously identified as "X," "Y," and "Z"), and he refused to consider it.

Thomas Jefferson, who was smitten with the ardor and ideals of the French Revolution, suspected that Marshall and his Federalist "cronies" were planning war with France to promote the interests of their friends in England. But the American people believed otherwise. When they received news of the "XYZ Affair," they were outraged. "Millions for defense," the newspapers thundered, "but not one cent for tribute!" When Marshall returned home in the summer of 1798, he was welcomed as a hero. In the elections of the following fall, he was sent to Congress as a Federalist representative from Richmond.

Jefferson was not pleased. He declined to attend a dinner honoring Marshall in Philadelphia and wrote worried letters to his friends. Though he deprecated his fellow Virginian's popularity, alternatively attributing it to his "lax, lounging manners" and his "profound hypocrisy," Jefferson knew that Marshall was a potentially dangerous adversary. A half-dozen years before the Richmonder's triumphal return from Paris, Jefferson had written James Madison a cutting letter about Marshall that included words he would one day rue: "I think nothing better could be done than to make him a judge."

In Congress, Marshall vigorously supported the Federalist policies of President John Adams. Adams took note of the Virginian's ability in 1800 when he appointed him to the important post of secretary of state, a position that not only charged him with conduct of the country's foreign affairs but also left him in effective charge of the government during Adams's frequent absences in Massachusetts.

John Marshall's future in government seemed rosy and secure in 1800. But the elections in November of that year changed all that, sweeping Adams and the Federalists from power and replacing them with Jefferson and the Democratic Republicans.

After the election, but before Adams's term as president expired, ailing Supreme Court Chief Justice Oliver Ellsworth submitted his resignation. Casting about for a successor to Ellsworth, Adams sent John Jay's name to the Senate, only to have Jay demand that it be withdrawn. The thought of leaving the appointment of a new chief justice to Jefferson was abhorrent to Adams, and the president was growing anxious. He summoned Marshall to his office to confer about the problem.

"Who shall I nominate now?" Adams asked dejectedly. Marshall answered that he did not know. He had previously suggested that Associate Justice William Paterson be elevated to the chief justiceship, but Adams had opposed Paterson then and Marshall supposed that he still did. The president pondered for a moment, then turned to Marshall and announced: "I believe I shall nominate you!"

Adams's statement astounded Marshall. Only two years before, Marshall had declined the president's offer of an associate justiceship, explaining that he still hoped to return to his law practice in Richmond. "I had never before heard myself named for the office," Marshall recalled later, "and had not even thought of it. I was pleased as well as surprised [sic], and bowed my head in silence."

Marshall's nomination was sent to the Senate and promptly confirmed, and on February 4, 1801, he took his seat as the nation's fourth chief justice. As subse-

John Marshall's Richmond home, completed in 1790, still survives and is open to the public. Completely restored and furnished following extensive archaeological and historical research, the elegant Federal-style two-story residence—the only eighteenth-century brick house still standing in Richmond—retains its original woodwork, floors, and paneling. Ninety percent of the home's furnishings, silver, and china are original to the Marshall family, and John Marshall's judicial robes and his wife Polly's wedding dress are also on display. Located at 818 Marshall Street, the John Marshall House is administered by the Association for the Preservation of Virginia Antiquities and is open Tuesday through Saturday, 11:00 AM to 4:00 PM. For further information, call (804) 648-7998.

quent events would prove, it was one of the most important dates in American history.

WITH THOMAS JEFFERSON IN THE EXEC-utive Mansion and John Marshall in the chief justice's chair, it was inevitable that the Supreme Court and the executive branch of the government should come into conflict. Marshall believed firmly in a strong national government and was willing to do all he could to strengthen federal institutions. Jefferson believed as firmly in state sovereignty and the necessity for maintaining constant vigilance against federal "usurpations." In legal matters, Jefferson believed that the Constitution should be interpreted strictly, so as to reduce rather than expand federal power.

Marshall, in contrast, believed that the Constitution should be construed fairly so as to carry out the intentions of its framers. Any law or executive act that violated the terms of the Constitution was, in Marshall's view, a nullity, of no force or effect; and it was the peculiar prerogative of the courts, as custodians of the laws of the land, to strike down any law that offended the Supreme Law of the Land.

Jefferson did not question the authority of the courts to decide whether a law or executive act violated the Constitution, but he believed that the other branches of the government also had a duty and a right to decide constitutional questions. In a controversy between the Supreme Court and the president, for example, the Supreme Court could order the president to do whatever the Court thought the Constitution required him to do; but the president could decide for himself whether the Supreme Court's order was proper and whether or not it should be obeyed.

As he took up the duties of the chief justiceship, Marshall contemplated his role with uncertainty. The Supreme Court in 1801 was certainly not the kind of strong, vital institution that might have been expected to provide direction in national affairs. There were six justices when Marshall joined the Court, but none (save the chief justice himself) was particularly distinguished. One or two men of national prominence had accepted appointment to the Court in the first eleven years of its existence, but none had remained there long. John Jay, the first chief justice, had resigned his seat in 1795 to become governor of New York. During the two years that John

Rutledge was an associate justice, he had regarded the Court's business as so trifling that he did not bother to attend a single session, and he finally resigned to become chief justice of South Carolina. The Court itself had counted for so little when the new capitol at Washington was being planned that the architects had made no provision for either a courtroom or judges' chambers, and the justices (to everyone's embarrassment) found that they had to meet in a dingy basement room originally designed for the clerk of the Senate.

How could Chief Justice Marshall use his new office to further the legal principles in which he believed so strongly? How could he strengthen the weak and undeveloped federal judiciary when most of the nation's lawyers and judges regarded that judiciary as superfluous and unnecessary? How could he implement his view of the Supreme Court as the final arbiter of constitutional questions when the President of the United States—his old nemesis, Thomas Jefferson—disagreed with that view so sharply? It was not an easy task, but John Marshall was a resourceful man, and he found a way to accomplish it.

His opportunity came in 1803 in the case of *Marbury v. Madison*. William Marbury was one of several minor federal judges who had been appointed during the closing days of John Adams's administration. When Jefferson's secretary of state, James Madison, refused to deliver the commissions of their offices, the judges sued Madison to compel delivery. In 1789, Congress had passed a law granting the Supreme Court authority to issue writs of mandamus, that is, legally enforceable orders compelling public officials to do their legal duties. Following the mandate of Congress, Marbury and the other appointees filed a petition for writ of mandamus in the Supreme Court.

Marshall pondered the possibilities of the case. He was sure that Marbury and his colleagues were entitled to their commissions, and he was just as sure that Jefferson and Madison had no intention of letting them have them. He could order Madison to deliver the commissions, but the secretary of state would certainly defy the order; and, as a practical matter, the Court could not compel obedience to any order that the president refused to acknowledge. Such an impasse would weaken, not strengthen, the federal union, and it would engender un-

precedented controversy. No, there must be a better way. . . .

All eyes and ears in the capitol were trained on the lanky chief justice as he took his seat at the head of the high bench on February 24, 1803, and began to read the Supreme Court's opinion in *Marbury* v. *Madison*.

The evidence, Marshall said, clearly showed that Marbury and the other judges were entitled to their commissions. The commissions had been signed and sealed before John Adams left office and were, for all legal purposes, complete and effective. To withhold them, as Jefferson and Madison insisted on doing, was an illegal act. But the Supreme Court would not order the secretary of state to deliver the commissions because the law authorizing it to issue writs of mandamus was unconstitutional: the Constitution does not authorize the Supreme Court to issue writs of mandamus; in fact, it prohibits it from doing so. And any law that violates the Constitution is void. Since the law purporting to authorize the Supreme Court to act was unconstitutional, the Court would not—indeed, it could not—order Madison to do his legal duty.

If historians and constitutional lawyers were asked to name the single most important case ever decided in the United States Supreme Court, there is little doubt that the case would be *Marbury v. Madison*. Though the dispute that gave rise to the decision was in itself insignificant, John Marshall used it as a springboard to a great constitutional pronouncement. The rule of the case—that the courts of the United States have the right to declare laws unconstitutional—was immediately recognized as the cornerstone of American constitutional law, and it has remained so ever since.

MORE THAN A HALF-CENTURY WOULD pass before the Supreme Court would again declare an act of Congress unconstitutional, but its authority to do so would never again be seriously doubted. Marshall had made a bold stroke, and he had done so in such a way that neither Congress, nor the president, nor any other public official had any power to resist it. By denying relief to Marbury, he had made the Supreme Court's order marvelously self-enforcing!

Predictably, Thomas Jefferson was angry. If the Supreme Court could not issue writs of mandamus, Jefferson asked, why did Marshall spend so much time

discussing Marbury's entitlement to a commission? And why did the chief justice lecture Madison that withholding the commission was an illegal act?

The president thought for a time that he might have the chief justice and his allies on the bench impeached. After a mentally unstable federal judge in New Hampshire was removed from office, Jefferson's supporters in the House of Representatives brought a bill of impeachment against Marshall's colleague on the Supreme Court, Associate Justice Samuel Chase. Chase was a Federalist who had occasionally badgered witnesses and made intemperate speeches, but no one seriously contended that he had committed an impeachable offense (which the Constitution defines as "treason, bribery, or other high crimes and misdemeanors"). So the Senate, three-quarters of whose members were Jeffersonians, refused to remove Chase from office. Marshall breathed a deep sigh of relief. Had the associate justice been impeached, the chief had no doubt that he himself would have been Jefferson's next target.

Though he never again had occasion to strike down an act of Congress, Marshall delivered opinions in many cases of national significance; and, in his capacity as circuit judge (all Supreme Court justices "rode circuit" in the early years of the nineteenth century), he presided over important, sometimes controversial, trials. He was the presiding judge when Jefferson's political arch rival, Aaron Burr, was charged with treason in 1807. Interpreting the constitutional provision defining treason against the United States, Marshall helped to acquit Burr, though he did so with obvious distaste. The Burr prosecution, Marshall said, was "the most unpleasant case which has been brought before a judge in this or perhaps any other country which affected to be governed by law."

On the high bench, Marshall presided over scores of precedent-setting cases. In *Fletcher v. Peck* (1810) and *Dartmouth College v. Woodward* (1819), he construed the contracts clause of the Constitution so as to afford important protection for the country's growing business community. In *McCulloch v. Maryland* (1819), he upheld the constitutionality of the first Bank of the United States and struck down the Maryland law that purported to tax it. In *Gibbons v. Ogden* (1824), he upheld federal jurisdiction over interstate commerce and lectured those (mainly Jeffersonians) who persistently sought to enlarge state powers at the expense of legitimate federal authority.

Though Marshall's opinions always commanded respect, they were frequently unpopular. When, in *Worcester v. Georgia* (1832), he upheld the treaty rights of the Cherokee Indians against encroachments by the State of Georgia, he incurred the wrath of President Andrew Jackson. "John Marshall has made his decision," "Old Hickory" snapped contemptuously "Now let him enforce it!" Marshall knew, of course, that he could not enforce the decision; that he could not enforce any decision that did not have the moral respect and acquiescence of the public and the officials they elected. And so he bowed his head in sadness and hoped that officials other than Andrew Jackson would one day show greater respect for the nation's legal principles and institutions.

Despite the controversy that some of his decisions inspired, the chief justice remained personally popular; and, during the whole of his more than thirty-four years as head of the federal judiciary, the Court grew steadily in authority and respect.

WELL INTO HIS SEVENTIES, MARSHALL continued to ride circuit in Virginia and North Carolina, to travel each year to his farm in Fauquier County, to attend to his shopping duties in Richmond, and to preside over the high court each winter and spring in Washington. On one of his visits to a neighborhood market in Richmond, the chief justice happened on a young man who had been sent to fetch a turkey for his mother. The youth wanted to comply with his mother's request, but thought it was undignified to carry a turkey in the streets "like a servant." Marshall offered to carry it for him. When the jurist got as far as his own home, he turned to the young man and said, "This is where I live. Your house is not far off; can't you carry the turkey the balance of the way?" The young man's face turned crimson as he suddenly realized that his benefactor was none other, than the chief justice of the United States.

Joseph Story, who served as an associate justice of the Supreme Court for more than twenty years of Marshall's term as chief justice, spent many hours with the Virginian in and out of Washington. Wherever Story observed Marshall,

he was impressed by his modesty and geniality. "Meet him in a stagecoach, as a stranger, and travel with him a whole day," Story said, "and you would only be struck with his readiness to administer to the accommodations of others, and his anxiety to appropriate the least to himself. Be with him, the unknown guest at an inn, and he seemed adjusted to the very scene, partaking of the warm welcome of its comforts, wherever found; and if not found, resigning himself without complaint to its meanest arrangements. You would never suspect, in either case, that he was a great man; far less that he was the Chief Justice of the United States."

In his youth, Marshall had been fond of corn whiskey. As he grew older, he lost his appetite for spirits but not for wine. He formulated a "rule" under which the Supreme Court judges abstained from wine except in wet weather, but Story said he was liberal in allowing "exceptions." "It does sometime happen," Story once said, "the the Chief Justice will say to me, when the cloth is removed, 'Brother Story, step to the window and see if it does not look like rain.' And if I tell him that the sun is shining brightly, Judge Marshall will sometimes reply, 'All the better; for our jurisdiction extends over so large a territory that it must be raining somewhere.' "You know," Story added, "that the Chief was brought up upon Federalism and Madeira, and he is not the man to outgrow his early prejudices."

In Richmond, Marshall held regular dinners for local lawyers, swapped stories with old friends, and tossed quoits with his neighbors in the Barbecue Club. An artist named Chester Harding remembered seeing the chief justice at a session of the Barbecue Club in 1829. Harding said Marshall was "the best pitcher of the party, and could throw heavier quoits than any other member of the club." "There were several ties," he added, "and, before long, I saw the great Chief Justice of the United States, down on his knees, measuring the contested distance with a straw, with as much earnestness as if it had been a point of law; and if he proved to be in the right, the woods would ring with his triumphant shout."

In 1830, a young Pennsylvania congressman and future president of the United States commented on Marshall's enduring popularity among his neighbors. "His decisions upon constitutional

questions have ever been hostile to the opinions of a vast majority of the people in his own State," James Buchanan said, "and yet with what respect and veneration has he been viewed by Virginia? Is there a Virginian whose heart does not beat with honest pride when the just fame of the Chief Justice is the subject of conversation? They consider him, as he truly is, one of the great and best men which this country has ever produced."

MARSHALL WAS NEARLY EIGHTY YEARS old when he died in Philadelphia on July 6, 1835. His body was brought back to Virginia for burial, where it was met by the longest procession the city of Richmond had ever seen.

In the contest between proponents of strong and weak national government, Marshall had been one of the foremost and clearest advocates of strength. The struggle—between union and disunion, between federation and confederation, between the belief that the Constitution created a nation and the theory that it aligned the states in a loose league—was not finally resolved until 1865. But the struggle *was* resolved. "Time has been on Marshall's side," Oliver Wendell Holmes, Jr., said in 1901. "The theory for which Hamilton argued, and he decided, and Webster spoke, and Grant fought, is now our cornerstone.

Justice Story thought that Marshall's appointment to the Supreme Court contributed more "to the preservation of the true principles of the Constitution than any other circumstances in our domestic history." "He was a great man," Story said. "I go farther; and insist, that he would have been deemed a great man in any age, and of all ages. He was one of those, to whom centuries alone give birth."

John Adams and Thomas Jefferson both lived long and distinguished lives, but neither ever gave an inch in their differences of opinion over Marshall. Jefferson went to his grave bemoaning the "cunning and sophistry" of his fellow Virginian. Adams died secure in the belief that his decision to make Marshall chief justice had been both wise and provident. Years later, Adams called Marshall's appointment "the pride of my life." Time has accorded Thomas Jefferson a great place in the affections of the American people; but, in the controversy over John Marshall, the judgment of history has come down with quiet strength on the side of John Adams.

Indians in the Land

Did the Indians have a special, almost noble, affinity with the American environment—or were they despoilers of it? Two historians of the environment explain the profound clash of cultures between Indians and whites that has made each group almost incomprehensible to the other.

A conversation between William Cronon and Richard White

When the historian Richard White wrote his first scholarly article about Indian environmental history in the mid–1970s, he knew he was taking a new approach to an old field, but he did not realize just how new it was. "I sent it to a historical journal," he reports, "and I never realized the U.S. mail could move so fast. It was back in three days. The editor told me it wasn't history."

Times have changed. The history of how American Indians have lived in, used, and altered the environment of North America has emerged as one of the most exciting new fields in historical scholarship. It has changed our understanding not only of American Indians but of the American landscape itself. To learn more about what historians in the field have been discovering, *American Heritage* asked two of its leading practitioners, Richard White and William Cronon, to meet and talk about their subject.

White, who is thirty-nine, teaches at the University of Utah. While earning his B.A. from the University of California at Santa Cruz in the late 1960s, he became involved in Indian politics. He wrote his doctoral dissertation at the University of Washington on the environmental history of Island County, Washington. That work, which became his first book—*Land Use, Environment, and Social Change*—earned him the Forest History Society's prize for the best book published in 1979–1980. This was followed by *The Roots of Dependency*, an environmental history of three Indian tribes: the Choctaws of the Southeast, the Pawnees of the Great Plains, and the Navajos of the Southwest. In it he

showed how each had gradually been forced into economic dependency on the now-dominant white society.

William Cronon, thirty-two, teaches history at Yale University. His first book, *Changes in the Land: Indians, Colonists, and the Ecology of New England,* examined the different ways Indians and colonists had used the New England landscape. It won the Francis Parkman Prize in 1984. Cronon recently became a MacArthur Fellow, and is working on several projects in environmental history and the history of the American West.

This conversation, which was arranged and edited by William Cronon, took place late last year at Richard White's home in Salt lake City.

William Cronon If historians thought about the environment at all up until a few years ago, they thought of it in terms of an older school of American historians who are often called "environmental determinists." People like Frederick Jackson Turner argued that Europeans came to North America, settled on the frontier, and began to be changed by the environment.

Richard White In a delayed reaction to Turner, historians in the late 1960s and early 1970s reversed this. They began to emphasize a series of horror stories when they wrote about the environment. The standard metaphor of the time was "the rape of the earth," but what they were really describing was the way Americans moving west cut down the forests, ploughed the land, destroyed the grasslands, harnessed the rivers—how

they in effect transformed the whole appearance of the North American landscape.

WC Since then, I think, we've realized that both positions are true, but incomplete. The real problem is that human beings reshape the earth as they live upon it, but as they reshape it, the new form of the earth has an influence on the way those people can live. The two reshape each other. This is as true of Indians as it is of European settlers.

RW My first connections with Indians in the environment was very immediate. I became interested because of fishing-rights controversies in the Northwest, in which the Indians' leading opponents included several major environmental organizations. They argued that Indians were destroying the fisheries. What made this odd was that these same groups also held up Indians as sort of primal ecologists. I remember reading a Sierra Club book which claimed that Indians had moved over the face of the land and when they left you couldn't tell they'd ever been there. Actually, this idea demeans Indians. It makes them seem simply like an animal species, and thus deprives them of culture. It also demeans the environment by so simplifying it that all changes come to seem negative—as if somehow the ideal is never to have been here at all. It's a crude view of the environment, and it's a crude view of Indians.

WC Fundamentally, it's an historical view. It says not only that the land never changed—"wilderness" was always in this condition—but that the people who lived upon it had no history, and existed outside of time. They were "natural."

RW That word *natural* is the key. Many of these concepts of Indians are quite old, and they all picture Indians as people without culture. Depending on your view of human nature, there are two versions. If human beings are inherently evil in a Calvinistic sense, then you see Indians as inherently violent and cruel. They're identified with nature, but it's the nature of the howling wilderness, which is full of Indians. But if you believe in a beneficent nature, and a basically good human nature, then you see Indians as noble savages, people at one with their environment.

WC To understand how Indians really did view and use their environment, we have to move beyond these notions of "noble savages" and "Indians as the original ecologists." We have to look instead at how they actually lived.

RW Well, take the case of fire. Fire transformed environments all over the continent. It was a basic tool used by Indians to reshape landscape, enabling them to clear forests to create grasslands for hunting and fields for planting. Hoe agriculture—as opposed to the plow agriculture of the Europeans—is another.

WC There's also the Indians' use of "wild" animals—animals that were not domesticated, not owned in ways Europeans recognized. Virtually all North American Indians were intimately linked to the animals around them, but they had no cattle or pigs or horses.

RW What's hardest for us to understand, I think, is the Indians' different way of making sense of species and the natural world in general. I'm currently writing about the Indians of the Great Lakes region. Most of them thought of animals as a species of *persons*. Until you grasp that fact, you can't really understand the way they treated animals. This is easy to romanticize—it's easy to turn it into a "my brother the buffalo" sort of thing. But it wasn't. The Indians *killed* animals. They often overhunted animals. But when they overhunted, they did so within the context of a moral universe that both they and the animals inhabited. They conceived of animals as having, not rights—that's the wrong word—but *powers*. To kill an animal was to be involved in a social relationship with the animal. One thing that has impressed me about Indians I've known is their realization that this is a harsh planet, that they survive by the deaths of

other creatures. There's no attempt to gloss over that or romanticize it.

WC There's a kind of debt implied by killing animals.

RW Yes. You incur an obligation. And even more than the obligation is your sense that those animals have somehow surrendered themselves to you.

WC There's a gift relationship implied . . .

RW . . . which is also a *social* relationship. This is where it becomes almost impossible to compare Indian environmentalism and modern white environmentalism. You cannot take an American forester or an American wildlife manager and expect him to think that he has a special social relationship with the species he's working on.

WC Or that he owes the forest some kind of gift in return for the gift of wood he's taking from it.

RW Exactly. And it seems to me hopeless to try to impose that attitude onto Western culture. We distort Indian reality when we say Indians were conservationists—that's not what conservation means. We don't give them full credit for their view, and so we falsify history.

Another thing that made Indians different from modern Euro-Americans was their commitment to producing for *security* rather than for maximum yield. Indians didn't try to maximize the production of any single commodity. Most tried to attain security by diversifying their diet, by following the seasonal cycles: they ate what was most abundant. What always confused Europeans was why Indians didn't simply concentrate on the most productive part of the cycle: agriculture, say. They could have grown more crops and neglected something else. But once you've done that, you lose a certain amount of security.

WC I like to think of Indian communities having a whole series of ecological nets under them. When one net failed, there was always another underneath it. If the corn died, they could always hunt deer or gather wild roots. In hard times—during an extended drought, for instance—those nets became crucial.

All of this was linked to seasonal cycles. For me, one of the best ways of understanding the great diversity of environmental practices among Indian peoples is to think about the different ways they moved across the seasons of the year. Because the seasons of North America differ markedly between, say, the Eastern forests and the Great Plains

and the Southwestern deserts, Indian groups devised quite different ways of life to match different natural cycles.

New England is the region I know best. For Indians there, spring started with hunting groups drawing together to plant their crops after having been relatively dispersed for the winter. While women planted beans, squash, and corn, men hunted the migrating fish and birds. They dispersed for summer hunting and gathering while the crops matured, and then reassembled in the fall. The corn was harvested and great celebrations took place. Then, once the harvest was done and the corn stored in the ground, people broke up their villages and fanned out in small bands for the fall hunt, when deer and other animals were at their fattest. The hunt went on until winter faded and the season of agriculture began again. What they had was agriculture during one part of the year, gathering going on continuously, and hunting concentrated in special seasons. That was typical not just of the Indians of New England but of eastern Indians in general.

To regard Indians as primal ecologists is a crude view.

RW For me the most dramatic example of seasonal changes among Indian peoples would be the horticulturists of the eastern Great Plains. The Pawnees are the example I know best. Depending on when you saw the Pawnees, you might not recognize them as the same people. If you came upon them in the spring or early fall, when they were planting or harvesting crops, you would have found a people living in large, semi-subterranean earth lodges and surrounded by scattered fields of corn and beans and squash. They looked like horticultural people. If you encountered the Pawnees in early summer or late fall, you would have thought you were seeing Plains nomads—because then they followed the buffalo, and their whole economy revolved around the buffalo. They lived in tepees and were very similar, at least in outward appearance, to the Plains nomads who surrounded them.

For the Pawnees, these cycles of hunting and farming were intimately connected. One of my favorite examples is a conversation in the 1870s between the

Pawnee Petalesharo and a Quaker Indian agent who was trying to explain to him why he should no longer hunt buffalo. Suddenly a cultural chasm opens between them, because Petalesharo is trying to explain that the corn will not grow without the buffalo hunt. Without buffalo to sacrifice at the ceremonies, corn will not come up and the Pawnee world will cease. You see them talking, but there's no communication.

WC It's difficult for a modern American hearing this to see Petalesharo's point of view as anything other than alien and wrong. This notion of sacrificing buffalo so corn will grow is fundamental to his view of nature, even though it's utterly different from what *we* mean when we call him a conservationist.

RW And yet, if you want to understand people's actions historically, you have to take Petalesharo seriously.

WC Environmental historians have not only been reconstructing the ways Indians used and thought about the land, they've also been analyzing how those things changed when the Europeans invaded. A key discovery of the last couple of decades had been our radically changed sense of how important European disease was in changing Indian lives.

RW It was appalling. Two worlds that had been largely isolated suddenly came into contact. The Europeans brought with them diseases the Indians had never experienced. The resulting death rates are almost impossible to imagine: 90 to 95 percent in some places.

WC The ancestors of the Indians came to North America from ten to forty thousand years ago. They traveled through an Arctic environment in which many of the diseases common to temperate and tropical climates simply couldn't survive. They came in groups that were biologically too small to sustain those diseases. And they came without the domesticated animals with which we share several of our important illnesses. Those three circumstances meant that Indians shed many of the most common diseases of Europe and Asia. Measles, chicken pox, smallpox, and many of the venereal diseases vanished during migration. For over twenty thousand years, Indians lived without encountering these illnesses, and so lost the antibodies that would ordinarily have protected them.

RW Most historians would now agree that when the Europeans arrived, the Indian population of North America was between ten and twelve million (the old estimate was about one million). By the early twentieth century it had fallen to less than five hundred thousand. At the same time, Indian populations were also under stress from warfare. Their seasonal cycles were being broken up, and they were inadequately nourished as a result. All these things contributed to the tremendous mortality they suffered.

WC Part of the problem was biological; part of it was cultural. If a disease arrived in mid-summer, it had quite different effects from one that arrived in the middle of the winter, when people's nutrition levels were low and they were more susceptible to disease. A disease that arrived in spring, when crops had to be planted, could disrupt the food supply for the entire year. Nutrition levels would be down for the whole subsequent year, and new diseases would find readier victims as a result.

RW The effects extended well beyond the original epidemic—a whole series of changes occurred. If Indian peoples in fact shaped the North American landscape, this enormous drop in their population changed the way the land looked. For example, as the Indians of the Southeast died in what had once been a densely populated region with a lot of farmland, cleared areas reverted to grassy woodland. Deer and other animal populations increased in response. When whites arrived, they saw the abundance of animals as somehow natural, but it was nothing of the sort.

Disease also dramatically altered relationships among Indian peoples. In the 1780s and 1790s the most powerful and prosperous peoples on the Great Plains margins were the Mandans, the Arikaras, the Hidatsas, the Pawnees, all of whom raised corn as part of their subsistence cycles. Nomadic, nonagricultural groups like the Sioux were small and poor. Smallpox changed all that. Those peoples living in large, populous farming villages were precisely those who suffered the greatest death rates. So the group that had once controlled the region went into decline, while another fairly marginal group rose to historical prominence.

WC That's a perfect example of biological and cultural interaction, of how complex it is. A dense population is more susceptible to disease than a less dense one: that's a biological observation true of any animal species. But which Indian communities are dense and which are not, which ones are living in clustered settlements and which ones are scattered thinly on the ground—these aren't biological phenomena but *cultural* ones.

RW Perhaps the best example of this is the way different Plains Indians responded to the horse, which, along with disease, actually preceded the arrival of significant numbers of Europeans in the region. The older conception of what happened is that when the horse arrived, it transformed the world. That may have been true for the Sioux, but not for the Pawnees. The Sioux became horse nomads; the Pawnees didn't. They were not willing to give up the security of raising crops. For them, the horse provided an ability to hunt buffalo more efficiently, but they were not about to rely solely on buffalo. If the buffalo hunt failed, and they had neglected their crops, they would be in great trouble. As far as I know, there is no agricultural group, with the exception of the Crows and perhaps the Cheyennes, that *willingly* gave up agriculture to rely solely on the buffalo. The people like the Sioux who became Plains nomads had always been hunters and gatherers, and for them horses represented a *more* secure subsistence, not a less secure one.

WC It's the ecological safety net again. People who practiced agriculture were reluctant to abandon it, because it was one of their strongest nets.

RW And they didn't. When given a choice, even under harsh circumstances, people tried to integrate the horse into their existing economy, not transform themselves.

The horse came to the Sioux at a time when they were in trouble. Their subsistence base had grown precarious: the buffalo and beavers they'd hunted farther east were declining, and the decline of the farming villages from disease meant the Sioux could no longer raid or trade with them for food. The horse was a godsend: buffalo hunting became more efficient, and the buffalo began to replace other food sources. Having adopted the horse, the Sioux moved farther out onto the Plains. By the time they had their famous conflicts with the United States in the 1860s and 1870s, they were the dominant people of the Great Plains. Their way of life was unimaginable without the horse and buffalo.

WC The result was that the Sioux reduced the number of ecological nets that sustained their economy and way of life. And although the bison were present in enormous numbers when the Sioux began to adopt the horse, by the 1860s the bison were disappearing from the Plains; by the early eighties they were virtually gone. That meant the Sioux's main ecological net was gone, and there wasn't much left to replace it.

RW To destroy the buffalo was to destroy the Sioux. Of course, given time, they might have been able to replace the buffalo with cattle and become a pastoral people. That seems well within the realm of historical possibility. But they were never allowed that option.

WC Disease and the horse are obviously important factors in Indian history. But there's a deeper theme underlying these things. All North American Indian peoples eventually found themselves in a relationship of dependency with the dominant Euro-American culture. At some point, in various ways, they ceased to be entirely autonomous peoples, controlling their own resources and their own political and cultural life. Is environmental history fundamental to explaining how this happened?

RW I think it's absolutely crucial. Compare the history of European settlement in North America with what happened in Asia and Africa. Colonialism in Asia and Africa was very important, but it was a passing phase. It has left a strong legacy, but Africa is nonetheless a continent inhabited by Africans, Asia a continent inhabited by Asians. American Indian peoples, on the other hand, are a small minority in North America. Part of what happened was simply the decline in population, but as we've said, that decline was not simple at all. To understand it, we have to understand environmental history.

Many Indians were never militarily conquered.

Many Indians were never militarily conquered. They nonetheless became dependent on whites, partly because their subsistence economy was systematically undercut. Virtually every American Indian community eventually had to face the fact that it could no longer feed or shelter itself without outside aid. A key aspect of this was the arrival of a market economy in which certain resources came to be overexploited. The fur trade is the clearest example of this.

WC No question. The traditional picture of the fur trade is that Europeans arrive, wave a few guns and kettles and blankets in the air, and Indians come rushing forward to trade. What do they have to trade? They have beaver pelts, deerskins, bison robes. As soon as the incentive is present, as soon as those European goods are there to be had, the Indians sweep across the continent, wipe out the furbearing animals, and destroy their own subsistence. That's the classic myth of the fur trade.

RW It simply didn't happen that way. European goods often penetrated Indian communities slowly; Indian technologies held on for a long time. Indians wanted European goods, but for reasons that could be very different from why *we* think they wanted them.

WC One of my favorite examples is the kettle trade. Indians wanted kettles partly because you can put them on a fire and boil water and they won't break. That's nice. But many of those kettles didn't stay kettles for long. They got cut up and turned into arrowheads that were then used in the hunt. Or they got turned into high-status jewelry. Indians valued kettles because they were such an extraordinarily flexible resource.

RW The numbers of kettles that have turned up in Indian graves proves that their value was not simply utilitarian.

WC The basic facts of the fur trade are uncontestable. Europeans sought to acquire Indian furs, food, and land; Indians sought to acquire European textiles, alcohol, guns, and other metal goods. Indians began to hunt greater numbers of furbearing animals, until finally several species, especially the beaver, were eliminated. Those are the two end points of the fur-trade story. But understanding how to get from one to the other is very complicated. Why did Indians engage in the fur trade in the first place? That's the question.

RW We tend to assume that exchange is straightforward, that it's simply giving one thing in return for another. That is not how it appeared to Indian peoples.

WC Think of the different ways goods are exchanged. One is how we usually perceive exchange today: we go into the local supermarket, lay down a dollar, and get a candy bar in return. Many Europeans in the fur trade thought that was what they were doing—giving a gun, or a blanket, or a kettle and receiving a number of furs in return. But for the

Indians the exchange looked very different.

RW To see how Indians perceived this, consider two things we all know, but which we don't ordinarily label as "trade." One is gifts. There's no need to romanticize the giving of gifts. Contemporary Americans exchange gifts at Christmas or at weddings, and when those gifts are exchanged, as anybody who has received one knows, you incur an obligation. You often have relatives who never let you forget the gift they've given you, and what you owe in return. There's no *price* set on the exchange, it's a gift, but the obligation is very real. That's one way Indians saw exchange. To exchange goods that way, the two parties at least had to pretend to be friends.

At the other extreme, if friendship hadn't been established, goods could still change hands, but here the basis of exchange was often simple theft. If you had enemies, you could rob them. So if traders failed to establish some friendship, kinship, or alliance, Indians felt perfectly justified in attacking them and taking their goods. In the fur trade there was a fine line between people who sometimes traded with each other and sometimes stole from each other.

WC To make that more concrete, when the Indian handed a beaver skin to the trader, who gave a gun in return, it wasn't simply two goods that were moving back and forth. There were *symbols* passing between them as well. The trader might not have been aware of all those symbols, but for the Indian the exchange represented a statement about their friendship. The Indian might expect to rely on the trader for military support, and to support him in return. Even promises about marriage, about linking two communities together, might be expressed as goods passed from hand to hand. It was almost as if a language was being spoken when goods were exchanged. It took a long time for the two sides to realize they weren't speaking the same language.

RW Right. But for Indians the basic meanings of exchange were clear. You gave generously to friends; you stole from enemies. Indians also recognized that not everybody could be classified simply as a friend or an enemy, and this middle ground is where trade took place.

But even in that middle ground, trade always began with an exchange of gifts. And to fail to be generous in your gifts, to push too hard on the price—Indians read that as hostility. When Europeans tried to explain the concept of a "market" to Indians, it bewildered them. The notion that demand for furs in London could affect how many blankets they would receive for a beaver skin in Canada was quite alien to them. How on earth could events taking place an ocean away have anything to do with the relationship between two people standing right here who were supposed to act as friends and brothers toward each other?

WC So one thing Indian peoples had trouble comprehending at certain stages in this dialogue was the concept of *price:* the price of a good fluctuating because of its abundance in the market. Indian notions were much closer to the medieval "just price." This much gunpowder is always worth this many beaver skins. If somebody tells me they want twice as many skins for the same gunpowder I bought last year at half the price, suddenly they're being treacherous. They're beginning to act as an enemy.

RW Or in the words Algonquians often used, "This must mean my father doesn't love me any more." To Europeans that kind of language seems ludicrous. What in the world does love have to do with giving a beaver skin for gunpowder? But for Indians it's absolutely critical.

The concepts of price and market bewildered Indians.

Of course, exchange became more commercial with time. Early in the fur trade, Indians had received European goods as gifts, because they were allies against other Indians or other Europeans. But increasingly they found that the only way to receive those goods was through direct economic exchange. Gift giving became less important, and trading goods for set prices became more important. As part of these commercial dealings, traders often advanced loans to Indians before they actually had furs to trade. By that mechanism, gifts were transformed into debts. Debts could in turn be used to coerce greater and greater hunting from Indians.

WC As exchange became more commercial, the Indians' relationship to animals became more commercial as well. Hunting increased with the rise in trade, and animal populations declined in re-

sponse. First the beaver, then the deer, then the bison disappeared from large stretches of North America. As that happened, Indians found themselves in the peculiar position of relying more and more on European goods but no longer having the furs they needed to acquire them. Worse, they could no longer even *make* those same goods as they once had, in the form of skin garments, wild meat, and so on. That's the trap they fell into.

RW And that becomes dependency. That's what Thomas Jefferson correctly and cynically realized when he argued that the best way for the United States to acquire Indian lands was to encourage trade and have government storehouses assume Indian debts. Indians would have no choice but to cede their lands to pay their debts, and they couldn't even renounce those debts because they now needed the resources the United States offered them in order to survive. Not all tribes became involved in this, but most who relied on the fur trade eventually did.

Of course, the effects go both ways. As whites eliminated Indians and Indian control, they were also, without realizing it, eliminating the forces that had shaped the landscape itself. The things they took as natural—why there were trees, why there weren't trees, the species of plants that grew there—were really the results of Indian practices. As whites changed the practices, those things vanished. Trees began to reinvade the grassland, and forests that had once been open became closed.

WC Once the wild animals that had been part of the Indians' spiritual and ecological universe began to disappear, Europeans acquired the land and began to transform it to match their assumptions about what a "civilized" landscape should look like. With native animals disappearing, other animals could be brought in to use the same food supply that the deer, the moose, and the bison had previously used. And so the cow, the horse, the pig—the animals so central to European notions of what an animal universe looks like—began to move across the continent like a kind of animal frontier. In many instances the Indians turned to these domesticated European species to replace their own decreasing food supply and so adopted a more pastoral way of life. As they lost their lands, they were then stuck with the problem of feeding their animals as well as themselves.

RW The Navajos are a good example of this. We tend to forget that Indians don't simply vanish when we enter the twentieth century. The Navajos are perhaps the group who maintained control over their own lands for the longest time, but their control was increasingly subject to outside pressures. They very early adopted European sheep, which became more and more important to their economy, both because wild foods were eliminated and because the government strongly encouraged the Navajos to raise more sheep. They built up prosperous herds but were gradually forced to confine them to the reservation instead of the wider regions they had grazed before.

The result was a crisis on the Navajo reservation. The land began to erode. By the 1920s and 1930s the Navajos had far more sheep than could be sustained during dry years. And here's where one of the more interesting confrontations between Indians and conservationists took place. The government sought to reduce Navajo stock, but its own motives were mixed. There was a genuine fear for the Navajos, but the main concern had to do with Boulder Dam. Conservationists feared Lake Mead was going to silt up, and that the economic development of the Southwest would be badly inhibited.

What they didn't understand were the causes of erosion. They blamed it all on Navajo sheep, but it now appears that there was a natural gullying cycle going on in the Southwest. Anybody familiar with the Southwest knows that its terrain is shaped by more than sheep and horses, no matter how badly it is overgrazed. So the result of government conservation policy for the Navajos was deeply ironic. Having adjusted to the European presence, having prospered with their sheep, they found their herds being undercut by the government for the good of the larger economy. It's a classic case of Indians—as the poorest and least powerful people in a region—forced to bear the brunt of economic-development costs. So the Navajo economy was again transformed. As the Navajos became poorer and poorer, they grew more willing to lease out oil and allow strip mining on the reservation. They found themselves in the familiar situation of being forced to agree to practices that were harmful, even in their view, to the land. They had to do it in order to survive, but they were then attacked by white conservationists for abandoning their own values.

3. NATIONAL CONSOLIDATION AND EXPANSION

WC A real no-win situation.

RW There are lessons in all this. We can't copy Indian ways of understanding nature, we're too different. But studying them throws our own assumptions into starker relief and suggests shortcomings in our relationships with nature that could cost us dearly in the long run.

WC I think environmental history may be capable of transforming our perspective, not just on Indian history, but on all human history. The great arrogance of Western civilization in the industrial and postindustrial eras has been to imagine human beings existing somehow apart from the earth. Often the history of the industrial era has been written as if technology has liberated human beings so that the earth has become increasingly irrelevant to modern civilization—when in fact all history is a long-standing dialogue between human beings and the earth. It's as if people are constantly speaking to the earth, and the earth is speaking to them. That's a way of putting it that Indians would be far more capable of understanding than most modern Americans. But this dialogue, this conversation between earth and the inhabitants of earth, is fundamental to environmental history. With it we can try to draw together all these pieces—human population changes, cultural changes, economic changes, environmental changes—into a complicated but unified history of humanity upon the earth. That, in rather ambitious terms, is what environmental historians are seeking to do.

The Odd Couple Who Won Florida and Half the West

The General's invasion outraged Congress and the King of Spain, but the Secretary of State turned the scandal into a diplomatic coup

**James Chace
and Caleb Carr**

The Congress knew nothing of the operation. The President later denied that he had ever given it a green light. But the brash American officer who did the deed in the name of American national security claimed he had the full backing of the executive branch of his government. The escapade caused an international furor, indeed an international crisis, and outraged members of both the Senate and the House of Representatives called for investigations. Many congressmen demanded public disavowal by the President and punishment of the officer in question. Just at the moment when such consequences seemed unavoidable, the Secretary of State stepped boldly forward to salvage the officer's name, silencing criticism at home and abroad.

It was the troubled winter of 1817–18. The United States had still not recovered from the War of 1812 with Great Britain, which had bitterly divided the nation and seen the near-secession of the New England states, whose livelihood depended on shipping. Because the British had burned the White House, the Capitol and many public buildings (Smithsonian, September 1987), James Monroe, a forthright if sometimes indecisive Virginian, became the first American President to take the oath of office out-of-doors. The wrangling Congress, meanwhile, was obliged to carry on its often-raucous proceedings in the Patent Office. New England's leaders had been prevented from shattering the American Union during the war only by the eleventh-hour negotiation of the Treaty of Ghent in December 1814, and by the astonishing American victory won at New Orleans under the command of Andrew Jackson a month later.

President Monroe was eager to put his energy and talent to the task of avoiding any new international crises, hoping to mend not only the American capital but also the divided national spirit. Soon after his Inauguration, he embarked on a personal tour of New England prompting at least one observer to predict the start of an "era of good feelings."

Nonetheless, in 1817 two powerful Americans did not share Monroe's desire for a pacific posture at home and abroad. One was Andrew Jackson, an ambitious general and bellicose frontier nationalist whose driving obsession was the security of the United States. The other was the country's new Secretary of State, John Quincy Adams of Massachusetts, son of a President, America's foremost diplomat and a man whose ascetic, intellectual lifestyle stood in sharp contrast to that of the whip-wielding slaveholder, Jackson.

Adams had headed the American negotiating team at Ghent, barely winning a stalemate. As the architect of the victory at New Orleans, Jackson was well aware that he had simply smashed one badly led British army, doing little to change Britain's global reach and strident grasp. The border and trade disputes that had originally helped force James Madison into declaring war against Great Britain were still unresolved. So it was that in the early months of the Monroe Administration, Jackson and Adams shared an overriding concern for the nation's security. As they saw it, despite the war, the United States of 1817 was every bit as vulnerable as the United States of 1812.

As depicted in the fairly rough maps of North America of the time, the area that preoccupied both men was that sizable tract of land south of the border, whose outline resembled a massive, threatening pistol—the Spanish provinces of East and West Florida (see map). The butt of this pistol was the peninsula of East Florida, a largely swampy region with a long and strategic coastline. The pistol's trigger guard, the valley of the Apalachicola River, then the boundary between East and West Florida, was made up of some of the best farmland in the Southeast. And its barrel, a long strip of fertile land slicing under Alabama and Mississippi, pointed menacingly at the Mississippi River, the most coveted commercial artery in North America.

Adams and Jackson held that without control of these provinces, then filled with hostile Indians, runaway slaves, foreign adventurers and duplicitous Spanish officials, there could be no real territorial security for the United States, and no safe process of westward expansion, let alone a secure export route through New Orleans. Spain, though officially bound by the Pinckney Treaty of 1795 to restrain Indian tribes and British adventurers from raiding American settlers over the border, had neither the will nor the troops to do so. For decades, Spanish governors of Florida had allowed runaway American slaves to live just inside its borders as free farmers or members of the friendly Creek and Seminole tribes. To an unapologetic slave owner like Jackson, this was an outrage. Adams was personally repelled by slavery. But as Secretary of State, he was alive to foreign threats and plottings, and could not allow American laws to be ignored with impunity by a neighboring power.

In their determination to do something about the Spanish Floridas, the two men made a formidable, if mismatched, pair. As a boy, Jackson had seen most of his family die at the hands of the British during the American Revolution. He had enjoyed a wild young manhood as a gambler and duelist. After being admitted to the North Carolina bar at 20, he moved to Tennessee where he created a thriving law practice in Nashville, using his profits to acquire land and slaves. Despite the lack of a formal, classical education, the young Jackson was already a fervent nationalist and an articulate, outspoken supporter of the landed class. By 1798, at the age of 31, he had become a strict justice of the Superior Court of Tennessee. "I have an opinion of my own on all subjects," he later said, "and when that opinion is formed I pursue it *publickly,* regardless of who goes with me."

In short, Jackson in politics was a bit like Jackson in war. By 1817 his celebrity (and his nickname, Old Hickory) had taken on many of the heroic public and private attributes that we still recognize, among them a passionate devotion to his wife, Rachel, who had not been officially divorced when they were first married and whose good name Jackson was ever ready to defend—to the death, if need be. His gaunt body was wracked by the pain of chronic ailments that could only be eased by periods of respite at his famed home, the Hermitage. And his drawn, determined face had become the image we see in portraits today, with its remarkably piercing eyes surmounted by a bold shock of silvery hair. Largely because of New Orleans, Jackson's place among American heroes was assured before he turned to the problem of the Floridas.

Not so with John Quincy Adams. He had served his country with equal zeal, but was hardly the type to capture the imagination of the American people. The new Secretary of State had first become a public servant in 1781, at the age of 14, when he served as secretary to the American Minister in St. Petersburg. Since that time, in addition to negotiating the Treaty of Ghent, he had been Minister to The Hague and later to Prussia, then Senator from Massachusetts, then abroad again as Minister—first to Russia and then to Great Britain. Many years spent wrangling with grasping and some-

times-patronizing foreign governments had shaped in Adams a sharply nationalistic political credo. Advocating a strong Union and a firmly nonaligned stance abroad, he had become a force to be reckoned with at home and in every European capital. Now he was preparing to make the United States, as he once wrote, a "nation, coextensive with the North American continent, destined by God and nature to be the most populous and powerful people ever combined under one social compact."

Adams was a linguist and a compulsive reader who nevertheless took time out for rigorous physical exercise. As the nation's scrupulous but not very successful sixth President, from 1825–29, he would become famous for swimming in the muddy Potomac, clad in nothing but a bathing cap and goggles. Adams managed to fit two or three days' work into every 24 hours, yet his intricate personality was marked by paradox. America's greatest diplomat, he was also capable of extraordinarily offensive bluntness, sarcasm and open intolerance. He adored the theater but distrusted theatrical folk; loved his children but was a harsh taskmaster to them.

When choosing the renowned diplomat from Quincy to run the State Department in 1817, equable James Monroe did not concern himself with Adams' personal quirks. The President knew that Adams possessed a mind whose mastery of international relations knew no equal, a mind as refined as Andrew Jackson's was rough-hewn. As a New Englander, moreover, Adams' appointment helped balance Monroe's Southern and Western political ties.

Like many events in those troubled Spanish provinces, the Florida crisis of 1817–19 was set in motion by murder. In the spring of 1817, the War Department received a message from one of its agents on the Georgia-Florida border saying that the Red Stick Creeks (so called because of their large, red war clubs) had killed a white woman, one Mrs. Garrett, and her two children, and had "commenced their Red Stick dancings, again." In response to the widely reported killings, Gen. Edmund Gaines, the American military commander in Georgia, called a conference of the local Seminole Indian chiefs to berate them. The Indians kept a running account of how many of their people had been killed by whites, and they viewed retaliatory attacks as a fair way of settling the score.

The deaths, they explained, were retribution for the recent killing of several of their own.

Gaines accused the chiefs of harboring runaway slaves; indeed of themselves making slaves of the runaways. The Indians told him that this was true; but slavery in a Seminole tribe merely meant the paying of tribute to a chief. Slaves were allowed to farm their own fields and live fairly independently. It was only natural that captive, hard-driven blacks from over the border in Georgia would be drawn to Florida. The longtime friendship and intermarriage of former slaves and Seminoles, the chiefs maintained, was not the business of the white general; controlling murderous American settlers was.

But by fall the Georgia settlers were demanding revenge for the deaths of Mrs. Garrett and her children. And American troops dispatched to the Seminole village of Fowltown discovered something that was far more explosive than murdered whites: British uniforms, as well as other circumstantial evidence indicating that British military agents were at work in the area.

Nothing could have been worse for the Seminoles and the Creeks. Incitement of Indian tribes on American borders had been a British method of harassing the United States ever since the Revolution. For months before the Fowltown discoveries, rumors had been flying that Indians in the Floridas were under the sway of British agents, foremost among them Alexander Arbuthnot, a burly, white-bearded Scot who traded not only in blankets and rum but in guns and powder, and Lt. Robert Christie Armbrister, a professional adventurer thought to be training runaway slaves to fight their former masters. The finding of British uniforms in a Seminole village inside the Georgia border so exasperated General Gaines that on November 12, 1817, he had Fowltown burned to the ground. In executing this order, American soldiers killed five Indians. The tally of deaths was again unbalanced.

On November 30, an American lieutenant, R. W. Scott, was taking a party of American women, children and soldiers—most of them ill—by boat up the Apalachicola for treatment at an American fort, when the boat was ambushed. Thirty-four soldiers, along with six women and four children, were killed. Scott himself, or so angry rumor soon had it, was tortured to death. Several days later, another group of boats taking supplies to Fort Scott, 75 miles upriver in Georgia, was attacked and got away only after fierce fighting. These raids were in evident retaliation for the events at Fowltown.

FACED WITH INFLAMMATORY RHETORIC and the outrage of its Southern citizens, President Monroe's Administration began to realize that, right or wrong, some forceful response might be necessary. Sentiment, in fact, was growing for a large-scale move against the Indians in Spanish Florida. General Gaines had written Secretary of War John Calhoun, the "poisonous cup of barbarism cannot be taken from the lips of savages with the mild voice of reason alone." On December 16, Calhoun sent a dispatch to Gaines saying that "should the Seminole Indians still refuse to make reparations for the outrages and depredations on the citizens of the United States, it is the wish of the President that you consider yourself at liberty to march across the Florida line and attack them . . . unless they should shelter themselves under a Spanish post. In the last event, you will immediately notify this department."

TWO WEEKS LATER, THE PRESIDENT transferred the job to Jackson, still commander of the U.S. Army's Division of the South and a man who had earlier led expeditions against both Creeks and Seminoles. He began to collect volunteers for a long march to the Florida border. The news that Jackson was to lead the American assault prompted the Florida Indians to prepare for a campaign with no quarter asked and none given. Events would prove their assessments chillingly accurate.

Meanwhile in Washington, John Quincy Adams had just opened a series of negotiations with the Spanish Minister, Don Luis de Onís, on the dual questions of the Floridas and the western boundary of the United States. Spain had consistently refused to recognize America's purchase of the Louisiana Territory from France in 1803 and denied all American claims to land west of the Mississippi River. Adams hoped to resolve both issues with de Onís, and to do so quickly, for he realized that the killings in Florida were steadily edging President Monroe toward significant military action—in January 1818, Adams bluntly informed de

Onís "that if we should not come to an early conclusion of the Florida negotiation, Spain would not have the possession of Florida to give us."

Late in that month, de Onís offered a plan under which, in return for Spain's formally ceding the Floridas to the United States, the Monroe government would agree to limit its western claims to a borderline just beyond the Mississippi. It was an unrealistic offer, given Spain's weakness and America's wholehearted belief in her title to the Louisiana Purchase, which, as negotiated with Napoleon, extended west of the Mississippi into Spanish claims on what is now Texas, New Mexico and Colorado. The negotiations eventually deadlocked. What Adams could not yet have known was that on March 10, 1818, General Jackson ordered all available livestock at the Georgia border of the Apalachicola to be slaughtered, and had issued to each of his men a three-day ration of meat, and one of corn—and then marched into Florida.

Jackson, who inherited Gaines' original orders, almost immediately questioned the limitations they put upon him. In a secret note to President Monroe on January 6, 1818, the general asserted that the "whole of East Florida [ought to be] seized and held as an indemnity for the outrages of Spain upon the property of our citizens; This done, it puts all opposition down, secures for our citizens a complete indemnity, and saves us from a war with Great Britain, or some Continental Powers combined with Spain; this can be done without implicating the Government; let it be signified to me through any channel . . . that the possession of the Floridas is desirable to the United States, and in sixty days it will be accomplished."

In the months to come, this remarkable missive would stir hot debate within the Monroe Administration and in Congress. The question was not what did Monroe know and when did he know it, but did Jackson have Presidential approval when he invaded Florida? Monroe, who was ill at the time the note reached Washington, said that he offered no comment on it at all, but simply passed it along to Secretary of War Calhoun and Treasury Secretary William Crawford. Jackson always stoutly maintained he had received—through channels he did not precisely identify—an unofficial but definite green light. Time has shown both Monroe's and Jackson's

claims difficult to prove. But, as anyone who has listened to the recent Iran-Contra hearings can well imagine, in the spring of 1818 among aroused political parties, such considerations were fairly academic.

On March 25, General Jackson wrote Calhoun that the Seminoles to his east had taken refuge in the Spanish fort of St. Mark's. Despite Monroe's instructions, the general decided on his own authority that this was grounds for taking possession of a Spanish military post. On April 6, he took the fort. He then pressed farther east to subdue a force of Indians and runaway slaves operating in the Suwanee River region. The Seminoles there were led by a chief of great distinction, called Bolecks or Bolicks or, more commonly, Bowlegs. But military leadership was left to Bowlegs' head slave, a runaway black named Nero, and to the Englishman Armbrister. The trader Arbuthnot gave a warning to the Indians and Armbrister of Jackson's approach, and when the Americans, now several thousand strong, reached the Suwanee they were faced only by a small force of runaway slaves who were quickly dispersed.

Still, Jackson's men captured Arbuthnot and two Seminole chiefs, whom they lured in by flying a British flag on one of their boats, as well as Armbrister. From him, the general learned of Arbuthnot's warning to the Seminoles, and on the basis of this a special military court was convened in St. Mark's to try the two Englishmen and two chiefs.

The result of the trial was preordained. Despite the fact that the board of 12 officers reduced its initial death sentence to 50 lashes and a year's confinement for Armbrister, it was clear that the Tennessee judge intended to execute his own brand of law. As a "necessary warning" to future Indian agitators, Jackson had all four men summarily put to death.

On May 24, he moved on to occupy the fort of St. Michael's, overlooking Pensacola in West Florida. Well aware of whom he was dealing with, the governor of the province, Don José Masot, retreated to a nearby fort and after firing off his cannon in a gesture of defense, quickly surrendered. Along with all his officers, Masot was allowed passage to Havana, and Jackson appointed one of his own colonels governor of West Florida.

Jackson, for once, seemed to have exhausted even his capacity for creating a furor. By attacking St. Mark's and Pensacola—not to mention appointing an American officer governor of a Spanish province—the general had deeply offended the integrity of Spain and insulted the person (or so it would later be said) of King Ferdinand VII. By executing Arbuthnot and Armbrister, he had given good cause to those in Great Britain who favored yet another war with the United States. Through his brutal treatment of the Florida Indians and their chiefs, he had fanned the already strong anti-American sentiments among those peoples. At the end of the month, weary, sick and longing for the company of his wife, he returned to Tennessee.

Much of official Washington was shocked by Jackson's behavior. But Minister de Onís was outraged. The details of the invasion reached the capital in early June, and Don Luis swiftly fired off a stinging rebuke to the Monroe Administration for a perfidious attack made in the midst of negotiations, adding, "General Jackson has omitted nothing that characterizes a haughty conqueror.

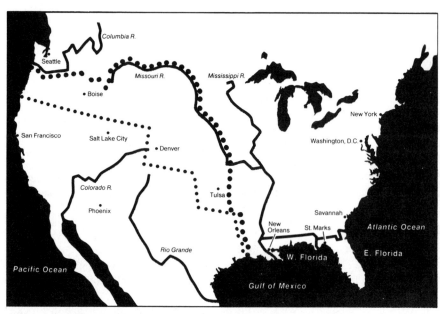

Map shows Floridas and disputed westward boundaries. In 1819 Spain claimed all land below the large dots, finally settled for the small dots, ceding a way to the Pacific and an area that would become most of seven states. Modern cities are for reference.

WHILE DE ONÍS' INDIGNATION WAS overstated considering Spanish toleration of violence by Indians in the Floridas and the presence there of British agents who trained them, his remarks about Jackson's methods went straight to the heart of the matter. Before the invasion, to be sure, most Americans would have agreed that acquiring Florida was necessary. Yet to acquire this area through an invasion unauthorized by Congress, resulting in the execution of British subjects by a military court, was high-handed and warlike behavior. The action troubled many Americans, including most of the Cabinet and the President.

Monroe saw the reasons for Jackson's invasion but worried about the political uproar it was leading to. Even in his own Cabinet the only support for Jackson came from John Quincy Adams. On July 15, the day the Cabinet first took up the issue, the Secretary of State noted in his diary that the question was "embarrassing and complicated," involving as it did "actual war with Spain" and "the Executive power to authorize hostilities" without a declaration from Congress. "The President and all the members of the cabinet, except myself," he wrote "are of [the] opinion that Jackson acted not only without, but against, his instructions;

that he has committed war upon Spain, which cannot be justified, and in which, if not disavowed by the Administration, they will be abandoned by the country." But in Adams' view, Jackson's headstrong "proceedings were justified by the necessity of the case."

The Secretary of State was aware of one issue above all: if the government disavowed Jackson, of whom the Spanish were clearly frightened, the United States' position in the negotiations for a boundary treaty with Spain would be so weakened that Adams' hope of getting a northwestern border stretching all the way to the Pacific would be impossible to obtain. And unfortunately there was no diplomatic middle ground in the issue; Jackson and his invasion either had to be abandoned or supported.

Sensing American disunity and the public pressure on Monroe, the Spanish put forward a set of dramatic demands: the return of Pensacola, the payment of indemnities and, above all, the "lawful punishment" of General Jackson. Despite the Spanish threat to break off treaty negotiations, Adams replied to these demands by making a counterproposal for a western boundary that included a line to the Pacific along the 42d parallel. De Onís was shocked.

Meanwhile, to the President and the Cabinet, Adams insisted that disavowal would not only be a dangerous display of

weakness on the part of the nation and of the Administration, it would also be "unjust" because "in principle" Jackson's actions were "strictly justifiable." If Adams' arguments did not prompt Cabinet approval, they at least succeeded in delaying disavowal.

But political pressure for disavowal kept growing. By autumn there was talk of a full-scale Congressional investigation into Jackson's invasion, prompting de Onís to make another boundary offer, strongly restating the previous Spanish claims to much of the Louisiana Purchase west of the Mississippi. President Monroe, a reasonable man by nature, found himself at a loss as to what course to pursue. Never fully in favor of disavowing Jackson, Monroe was more and more impressed by Adams' continued insistence that disavowal would mean an end to the prospect of gaining Florida and would cripple the American position in the western boundary negotiations. As President, however, Monroe could not simply ignore the pressures being applied by the Congress and his Cabinet. The confusion and impatience brought on by these conflicting considerations eventually caused the President to turn to the simplest solution: force. He instructed Adams to let it be known to Congress, when it reconvened, and to the Spanish Minister that he had not ruled out the possibility of annexing the

Floridas through a formal invasion. A war with Spain at least, and perhaps Great Britain as well, seemed a real possibility.

IT WAS THEN THAT, IN A SINGLE STROKE, John Quincy Adams suddenly and dramatically turned the tables on his foreign and domestic opponents. The Spanish government's demand that Jackson be punished had been addressed to the American Minister in Madrid, George Erving, who forwarded it to Washington. Adams' reply, therefore, was also addressed to Erving, who was instructed to deliver a copy of the lengthy note to the court of Ferdinand VII. In addition, copies were sent to other American ministers in European capitals, especially including Richard Rush in London.

Dated November 28, 1818, the celebrated "Instructions to Erving" were the fruit of weeks of work on the part of the Secretary of State. Adams' aim seemed almost impossible. It was nothing less than to deal a mortal blow to the idea of disavowing Jackson's invasion; to show that it was Madrid's and not Washington's position in Florida that was indefensible; and to make it clear to Great Britain that America would actively respond to any British meddling in the affairs of North America. The extent of Adams' success was remarkable.

He began by stating, in a tone of moral indignation, that Jackson's invasion was wholly justifiable on grounds of self-defense against the marauding Indians and their British sponsors, and that punishment of the general was therefore out of the question. As for King Ferdinand's "profound indignation" at having his territory invaded, Adams pointed out that the British had used Florida as a base of operations for years, and asked, "Where was His Majesty's profound indignation at that?"

THE SECRETARY OF STATE SAVED HIS strongest language for Great Britain, a nation that "yet engages the alliance and cooperation of savages in war. . . . From the period of our established independence to this day, *all* the Indian wars with which we have been afflicted have been distinctly traceable to the instigation of English traders or agents. Always dis-

avowed, yet always felt; more than once detected, but never before punished; two of them, offenders of the deepest dye . . . have fallen, *flagrante delicto,* into the hands of an American general; and the punishment inflicted upon them has fixed them on high, as an example awful in its exhibition, but, we trust, auspicious in its results."

The document leveled all opposition to the Monroe Administration in the Congress. Richard Rush soon wrote from London to say that the British Foreign Secretary, Lord Castlereagh, was now determined to avoid war with America at any cost. John Adams Smith, John Quincy's nephew and a member of the London legation, reported that "there has scarcely been a pistol flashed since the great gun from Washington to Madrid."

In a bold, and some would have said, outrageously independent style, using closely reasoned argument, Adams had preempted the interference of Great Britain and Europe generally in the affairs of North America. At home, the vindication of Andrew Jackson was complete. Largely as a result of Adams' "Instructions to Erving," both the House and Senate investigations into the invasion of Florida were aborted. The general even embarked on a triumphant tour of the Northeast.

In Madrid, where the Spanish empire suddenly found itself politically isolated, the note sounded the death knell of Spanish procrastination on the issues of Florida and the western boundary of the United States. On February 22, 1819, Secretary Adams and Don Luis de Onís signed the Transcontinental Treaty. In exchange for a sum of $5 million, King Ferdinand transferred possession of all his territories in the Floridas to the United States. The newly defined western border established unchallenged American control over the vaguely named regions that had been bought from France, and included a line to the Pacific along the 42d parallel—now the northern boundary of Utah, Nevada and California. It was the most significant treaty that had yet—or perhaps has ever—been signed by the United States.

JUST FOUR YEARS LATER, JOHN QUINCY Adams once more called upon the argu-

ments and eloquent powers that had been fine-tuned during the Florida crisis. It was he who drafted for James Monroe the foreign policy declaration that became known as the Monroe Doctrine—extending American warnings against any European meddling in the Western Hemisphere.

The political alliance between Jackson and Adams forged during the Florida crisis was short-lived, though. In 1824 Adams was elected President, and in 1828 Jackson ran against him in one of the most below-the-belt election campaigns in American history. Jackson's supporters leveled totally unsubstantiated charges of corruption at the Adams Administration, and personal invective abounded. Some of Adams' sympathizers made scurrilous charges about Jackson's wife and even his mother. The President had bought a billiard table and a chess set for the White House; Jackson's people called these "gambling furniture" and some of his supporters even accused Adams of pimping for the czar during his residency in Moscow. Adams refused to answer such charges, claiming that to do so would degrade the office of the President. This stance may well have cost him reelection. When Jackson—whose good reputation owed so much to the efforts of the then Secretary of State ten years earlier—arrived for the most riotous Inauguration ever, to begin a term that dramatically extended the power of the Presidency, he found that his spiteful predecessor had slipped out of the White House the night before.

There would be no traditional transfer of power, and rarely another word exchanged, between Andrew Jackson and John Quincy Adams.

REFERENCES

John Quincy Adams and the Foundations of American Foreign Policy by Samuel Flagg Bemis, Knopf, 1949

Andrew Jackson and the Course of American Empire, 1767–1821 by Robert V. Remini, Harper & Row, 1977

" 'A perpetual harrow upon my feelings': John Quincy Adams and the American Indian" by Lynn Page Parsons, *New England Quarterly,* September 1983

Diplomacy and the Borderlands: The Adams-Onís Treaty of 1819 by Philip Coolidge Brooks, University of California Press (Berkeley), 1939

The Era of Good Feelings by George Dangerfield, Harcourt, Brace, 1952

The Florida Wars by Virginia Bergman Peters, Archon Books (Hamden, Connecticut), 1979

From Utopia to Mill Town

The Boston Associates wanted to build the perfect industrial community. But could they become more than Lords of the Loom?

Maury Klein

Tennessee native Maury Klein is presently a professor of history at the University of Rhode Island. A 1965 Ph.D. recipient from Emory University in Georgia, he has written a total of four books and several dozen articles and reviews. For further reading on Lowell, he suggests Steven Dunwell's The Run of The Mill *(1978) and* The Golden Threads *(1949), by Hannah Josephson.*

They flocked to the village of Lowell, these visitors from abroad, as if it were a compulsory stop on the grand tour, eager to verify rumors of a utopian system of manufacturers. Their skepticism was natural, based as it was on the European experience where industry had degraded workers and blighted the landscape. In English manufacturing centers such as Manchester, observers had stared into the pits of hell and shrank in horror from the sight. Charles Dickens used this gloomy, putrid cesspool of misery as a model in *Hard Times*, while Alexis de Tocqueville wrinkled his nose at the "heaps of dung, rubble from buildings, putrid, stagnant pools" amid the "huge palaces of industry" that kept "air and light out of the human habitations which they dominate. . . . A sort of black smoke covers the city. . . . Under this half daylight 300,000 human beings are ceaselessly at work. A thousand noises disturb this damp, dark labyrinth, but they are not at all the ordinary sounds one hears in great cities."

Was it possible that America could produce an alternative to this hideous scene? It seemed so to the visitors who gaped in wonderment at the village above the confluence of the Concord and Merrimack rivers. What they saw was a planned community with mills five to seven stories high flanked by dormitories for the workers, not jammed together but surrounded by open space filled with trees and flower gardens set against a backdrop of the river and hills beyond. Dwelling houses, shops, hotels, churches, banks, even a library lined the streets in orderly, uncrowded rows. Taken whole, the scene bore a flavor of meticulous composition, as if a painting had sprung to life.

The contrast between so pristine a vision and the nightmare of Manchester startled the most jaded of foreigners. "It was new and fresh, like a setting at the opera," proclaimed Michel Chevalier, a Frenchman who visited Lowell in 1834. The Reverend William Scoresby, an Englishman, marveled at how the buildings seemed "as fresh-looking as if built within a year." The indefatigable Harriet Martineau agreed, as did J.S. Buckingham, who pronounced Lowell to be "one of the most remarkable places under the sun." Even Dickens, whose tour of America rendered him immune to most of its charms, was moved to lavish praise on the town. "One would swear," he added "that every 'Bakery,' 'Grocery' and 'Bookbindery' and every other kind of store, took its shutters down for the first time, and started in business yesterday."

If Lowell and its social engineering impressed visitors, the mill workers dazzled them. Here was nothing resembling Europe's *Untermenschen*, that doomed proletariat whose brief, wretched lives were squeezed between child labor and a pauper's grave. These were not men or children or even families as found in the Rhode Island mills. Instead Lowell employed young women, most of them fresh off New England farms, paid them higher wages than females earned anywhere else (but still only half of what men earned), and installed them in dormitories under strict supervision. They were young and industrious, intelligent, and entirely respectable. Like model citizens of a burgeoning republic they saved their money, went to church, and spent their leisure hours in self-improvement.

More than one visitor hurried home to announce the arrival of a new industrial order, one capable of producing goods in abundance without breaking its working class on the rack of poverty. Time proved them wrong, or at best premature. The Lowell experiment lasted barely a generation before sliding back into the grinding bleakness of a conventional mill town. It had survived long enough to tantalize admirers with its unfulfilled promise and to reveal some harsh truths about the incompatibility of certain democratic ideals and the profit motive.

The founding fathers of Lowell were a group known as the Boston Associates, all of whom belonged to that tight knit elite whose dominance of Boston society was exceeded only by their stranglehold on its financial institutions. The seed had been planted by Francis Cabot Lowell, a shrewd, far-sighted merchant who took up the manufacture of cotton cloth late in life. A trip abroad in 1810 introduced him to the cotton mills of Lancashire and to a fellow Boston merchant named Nathan Appleton. Blessed with a superb memory and trained in mathematics, Lowell packed his mind with details about the machinery shown him by unsuspecting mill owners. The Manchester owners jealously hoarded their secrets and patents, but none regarded the wealthy American living abroad for his health as a rival.

From *American History Illustrated*, October 1981, pp. 34-40, 48. Reprinted through the courtesy of Cowles Magazines, publisher of *American History Illustrated*.

Once back in America, Lowell recruited a mechanical genius named Paul Moody to help replicate the machines he had seen in Manchester. After much tinkering they designed a power loom, cottonspinning frame, and some other machines that in fact improved upon the English versions. As a hedge against inexperience Lowell decided to produce only cheap, unbleached cotton sheeting. The choice also enabled him to use unskilled labor, but where was he to find even that? Manchester drew its workers from the poorhouses, a source lacking in America. Both the family system and use of apprentices had been tried in Rhode Island with little success. Most men preferred farming their own land to working in a factory for someone else.

But what about women? They were familiar with spinning and weaving, and would make obedient workers. Rural New England had a surplus of daughters who were considered little more than drains on the family larder. To obtain their services Lowell need only pay decent wages and overcome parental reservations about permitting girls to live away from home. This could be done by providing boarding houses where the girls would be subject to the strict supervision of older women acting as chaperones. There would be religious and moral instruction enough to satisfy the most scrupulous of parents. It was an ingenious concept, one that cloaked economic necessity in the appealing garb of republican ideals.

Lowell added yet another wrinkle. Instead of forming a partnership like most larger businesses, he obtained a charter for a corporation named the Boston Manufacturing Company. Capitalized at $300,000, the firm started with $100,000 subscribed by Lowell and a circle of his caste and kin: Patrick Tracy Jackson and his two brothers, Nathan Appleton, Israel Thorndike and his son, two brothers-in-law, and two other merchants. Jackson agreed to manage the new company, which chose a site at the falls on the Charles River at Waltham. By late 1814 the first large integrated cotton factory in America stood complete, along with its machine shop where Lowell and Moody reinvented the power loom and spinner.

Production began in 1815, just as the war with England drew to a close. The mill not only survived the return of British competition but prospered in spectacular fashion: during the years 1817–1824 dividends averaged more than nineteen percent. Moody's fertile mind devised one new invention after another, including a warp-yarn dresser and double speeder. His innovations made the firm's production methods so unique that they soon became known as the "Waltham system." As Gilman Ostrander observed, "The Waltham method was characterized by an overriding emphasis upon standardization, integration, and mechanization." The shop began to build machinery for sale to other mills. Even more, the company's management techniques became the prototype on which virtually the entire textile industry of New England would later model itself.

Lowell did not live to witness this triumph. He died in 1817 at the age of forty-two, having provided his associates with the ingredients of success. During the next three years they showed their gratitude by constructing two more mills and a bleachery, which exhausted the available water power at Waltham. Eager to expand, the Associates scoured the rivers of New England for new sites. In 1821 Moody found a spot on the Merrimack River at East Chelmsford that seemed ideal. The river fell thirty-two feet in a series of rapids and there were two canals, one belonging to the Pawtucket Canal Company and another connecting to Boston. For about $70,000 the Associates purchased control of the Canal Company and much of the farmland along the banks.

From that transaction arose the largest and most unique mill town in the nation. In this novel enterprise the Associates seemed to depart from all precedent, but in reality they borrowed much from Waltham. A new corporation, the Merrimack Manufacturing Company, was formed with Nathan Appleton and Jackson as its largest stockholders. The circle of investors was widened to include other members of the Boston elite such as Daniel Webster and the Boott brothers, Kirk and John. Moody took some shares but his ambitions went no further; he was content to remain a mechanic for the rest of his life. The memory of Francis Cabot Lowell was honored by giving the new village his name.

The task of planning and overseeing construction was entrusted to Kirk Boott. The son of a wealthy Boston Anglophile, Boott's disposition and education straddled the Atlantic. He obtained a commission in the British army and fought under Wellington until the War of 1812 forced his resignation. For several years he studied engineering before returning home in 1817 to take up his father's business. A brilliant, energetic, imperious martinet, Boott leaped at the opportunity to take charge of the new enterprise. As Hannah Josephson observed, he became "its town planner, its architect, its engineer, its agent in charge of production, and the leading citizen of the new community."

The immensity of the challenge appealed to Boott's Ordered mind. He recruited an army of 500 Irish laborers, installed them in a tent city, and began transforming a pastoral landscape into a mill town. A dam was put across the river, the old canal was widened, new locks were added, and two more canals were started. The mills bordered the river but not with the monotony of a wall. Three buildings stood parallel to the water and three at right angles in a grouping that reminded some of Harvard College. Trees and shrubs filled the space between them. The boarding houses, semi-detached dwellings two-and-a-half stories high separated by strips of lawn, were set on nearby streets along with the superintendents' houses and long brick tenements for male mechanics and their families. It was a standard of housing unknown to working people anywhere in the country or in Europe. For himself Boott designed a Georgian mansion ornamented with a formidable Ionic portico.

Lowell emerged as the nation's first planned industrial community largely because of Boott's care in realizing the overall concept. At Waltham the boarding houses had evolved piecemeal rather than as an integral part of the design. The Associates took care to avoid competition between the sites by confining Lowell's production to printed calicoes for the higher priced market. While Waltham remained profitable, it quickly took a back seat to the new works. The machine shop provided a true barometer of change. It not only produced machinery and water wheels for Lowell but also oversaw the construction of mills and housing. Shortly before Lowell began production in 1823, the Associates, in Nathan Appleton's words, "arranged to equalize the interest of all the stockholders in both companies" by formally purchasing Waltham's patterns and pat-

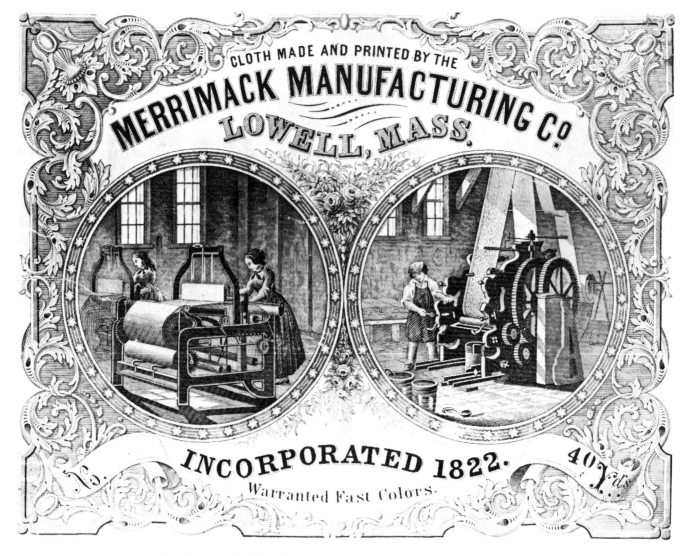

Merrimack trade label. Courtesy of the American Antiquarian Society.

ent rights and securing Moody's transfer to Lowell. A year later the entire machine shop was moved to Lowell, leaving Waltham with only a maintenance facility.

The success of the Lowell plant prompted the Associates to unfold ambitious new plans. East Chelmsford offered abundant water power for an expanding industry; the sites were themselves a priceless asset. To use them profitably the Associates revived the old Canal Company under a new name, the Locks and Canals Company, and transferred to it all the land and water rights owned by the Merrimack Company. The latter then bought back its own mill sites and leased the water power it required. Thereafter the Locks and Canals Company sold land to other mill companies, leased water power to them at fixed rates per

spindle, and built machinery, mills, and housing for them.

This organizational arrangement was as far advanced for the times as the rest of the Lowell concept. It brought the Associates handsome returns from the mills and enormous profits from the Locks and Canals Company, which averaged twenty-four percent in dividends between 1825 and 1845. As new companies like the Hamilton, Appleton, and Lowell corporations were formed, the Associates dispersed part of their stock among a widening network of fellow Brahmins. New partners entered their exclusive circle, including the Lawrence brothers, Abbott and Amos. Directories of the companies were so interlocked as to avoid any competition between them. In effect the Associates had created industrial harmony of the sort J.P. Morgan

would later promote under the rubric "community of interest."

By 1836 the Associates had invested $6.2 million in eight major firms controlling twenty five-story mills with more than 6,000 employees. Lowell had grown into a town of 18,000 and acquired a city charter. It boasted ten churches, several banks to accommodate the virtue of thrift on the part of the workers, long rows of shops, a brewery, taverns, schools, and other appurtenances of progress. Worldwide attention had transformed it into a showcase. Apart from the influx of foreigners and other dignitaries, it had already been visited by a president the Associates despised (Andrew Jackson), and by a man who would try three times to become president (Henry Clay).

The Associates basked in this attention because they viewed themselves as benevolent, far-seeing men whose sense of duty extended far beyond wealth. To be sure the life blood of the New England economy flowed through their counting houses from their domination of banks, insurance companies, railroads, shipping, and mills elsewhere in New England. Yet such were the rigors of their stern Puritan consciences that for them acquisition was all consuming without being all fulfilling. Duty taught that no fortune was so ample that more was not required. Economist Thorstein Veblen later marveled at the "steadfast cupidity" that drove these men "under pain of moral turpitude, to acquire a 'competence,' and then unremittingly to augment any competence acquired."

Not content with being an economic and social aristocracy, the Associates extended their influence to politics, religion, education, and morality. Lowell fit their *raison d'etre* so ideally because it filled their coffers while at the same time reflecting their notion of an orderly, paternal community imbued with the proper values. The operatives knew their place, deferred to the leadership of the Associates, shared their values.

Or so they thought. In reality the homogeneity of Lowell had always been, like a painting, somewhere between an illusion and a contrivance. The planned community stopped just beyond the border of the mills and boarding houses. No provision had been made for the Irish who built the mills; they huddled together in a squalid settlement, the pioneer settlers of what became the town. Shopkeepers overwhelmed the space provided by the Associates until their stores and homes sprawled in the same indiscriminate manner of other towns. Gradually the growth of Lowell threw the Associates into the familiar role of dominant taxpayer demanding economy and reluctant to approve services that cost money.

While the town mushroomed in chaotic manner, the mills also underwent profound changes. Between 1836 and 1850 they doubled in number, reflecting the enormous growth of the industry as a whole. The press for space filled the breathing room around the original buildings with solid five-story walls that blotted out all view of the river. The rising tide of operatives overwhelmed the boarding houses and flooded into tenement neighborhoods, leading one observer to complain that "few cities are so crowded as Lowell."

During those same years the Associates had to contend with falling prices, a major depression, and by 1840, reduced dividends. Once docile stockholders grumbled about inefficiency and demanded changes. The Associates realized that to restore dividends to their accustomed levels, falling prices had to be offset by increased volume. This could be done by reducing wages on piecework and assigning each worker more looms or spindles to tend, practices known as speedup and stretch-out. The workday grew both harder and longer, about twelve-and-a-half hours, and working conditions harsher. As a final inspiration the Associates introduced the premium system whereby overseers and second hands received bonuses for getting more work than usual out of the operatives.

By 1860 the industrial utopia had given way to a grim mill town, and its operatives were fast sliding down into that abyss of misery and despair once reserved for the English working class. The Associates had lost their bloom as models of propriety and benevolence. Some called them "lords of the loom" and consigned them to the same terrace of Inferno as the South's "lords of the lash." How ironic it was for Nathan Appleton, the most beloved of souls with an unmatched reputation for philanthropy and civic virtue, that his mills were the first to be called "soulless corporations."

Robert Owen, that ardent utopian capitalist, had once declared, "I can make manufacturing pay without reducing those whom I employ to misery and moral degradation." The Associates had thought to do as much, but the lesson of buying cheap and selling dear was too deeply etched in their characters. The harsh truth was that benevolence cost money, and when the cost grew so dear as to compel a choice between ideals and dividends, idealism went the way of all utopias. Gradually their paternalism shriveled into the narrow, impersonal wage relationship typical of other factories. As for the workers, by 1845 they were, in Hannah Josephson's words, "putting in more time under less agreeable working conditions, turning out more cloth and receiving less pay than when the industry was first established."

After that date they ceased even to be the same workers. The pride and joy of Lowell had always been its girls, those sturdy daughters of New England farms, but they were fast departing the mills. In their place came hordes of Irish immigrants fleeing the famine and desperate for work. Those who remained in the mills struggled helplessly against their declining position. Like Lowell itself the bloom had fled their cheeks, left them older and wiser about the ways of the world and its unfilled promises.

The Secret Life of a Developing Country

(Ours)

Forget your conventional picture of America in 1810. In the first half of the nineteenth century, we were not at all the placid, straitlaced, white-picket-fence nation we imagine ourselves to have been. By looking at the patterns of everyday life as recorded by contemporary foreign and native observers of the young republic and by asking the question that historians often didn't think to ask of another time—what were people really like? how did they greet one another on the street? how did they occupy their leisure time? what did they eat?—Jack Larkin brings us a detailed portrait of another America, an America that was so different from both our conception of its past life and its present-day reality as to seem a foreign country.

Jack Larkin

Jack Larkin is Chief Historian at Old Sturbridge Village. This article is adapted from his book The Reshaping of Everyday Life in the United States, 1790-1840, *published by Harper & Row.*

WE LOOKED DIFFERENT

Contemporary observers of early-nineteenth-century America left a fragmentary but nonetheless fascinating and revealing picture of the manner in which rich and poor, Southerner and Northerner, farmer and city dweller, freeman and slave presented themselves to the world. To begin with, a wide variety of characteristic facial expressions, gestures, and ways of carrying the body reflected the extraordinary regional and social diversity of the young republic.

When two farmers met in early-nineteenth-century New England, wrote Francis Underwood, of Enfield, Massachusetts, the author of a pioneering 1893 study of small-town life, "their greeting might seem to a stranger gruff or surly, since the facial muscles were so inexpressive, while, in fact, they were on excellent terms." In courtship and marriage, countrymen and women were equally constrained, with couples "wearing all unconsciously the masks which custom had prescribed; and the onlookers who did not know the secret would think them cold and indifferent."

Underwood noted a pervasive physical as well as emotional constraint among the people of Enfield; it was rooted, he thought, not only in the self-denying ethic of their Calvinist tradition but in the nature of their work. The great physical demands of unmechanized agri-

culture gave New England men, like other rural Americans, a distinctively ponderous gait and posture. Despite their strength and endurance, farmers were "heavy, awkward and slouching in movement" and walked with a "slow inclination from side to side."

Yankee visages were captured by itinerant New England portraitists during the early nineteenth century, as rural storekeepers, physicians, and master craftsmen became the first more or less ordinary Americans to have their portraits done. The portraits caught their caution and immobility of expression as well as recording their angular, long-jawed features, thus creating good collective likenesses of whole communities.

The Yankees, however, were not the stiffest Americans. Even by their own impassive standards, New Englanders found New York Dutchmen and Pennsyl-

A dour face of the early 1800s.

vania German farmers "clumsy and chill" or "dull and stolid." But the "wild Irish" stood out in America for precisely the opposite reason. They were not "chill" or "stolid" enough, but loud and expansive. Their expressiveness made Anglo-Americans uncomfortable.

The seemingly uncontrolled physical energy of American blacks left many whites ill at ease. Of the slaves celebrating at a plantation ball, it was "impossible to describe the things these people did with their bodies," Frances Kemble Butler, an English-born actress who married a Georgia slave owner, observed, "and above all with their faces. . . ." Blacks' expressions and gestures, their preference for rhythmic rather than rigid bodily motion, their alternations of energy and rest made no cultural sense to observers who saw only "antics and frolics," "laziness," or "savagery." Sometimes perceived as obsequious, childlike, and dependent, or sullen and inexpressive, slaves also wore masks—not "all unconsciously" as Northern farm folk did, but as part of their self-protective strategies for controlling what masters, mistresses, and other whites could know about their feelings and motivations.

American city dwellers, whose daily routines were driven by the quicker pace of commerce, were easy to distinguish from "heavy and slouching" farmers attuned to slow seasonal rhythms. New Yorkers, in particular, had already acquired their own characteristic body language. The clerks and commercial men

who crowded Broadway, intent on their business, had a universal "contraction of the brow, knitting of the eyebrows, and compression of the lips . . . and a hurried walk." It was a popular American saying in the 1830s, reported Frederick Marryat, an Englishman who traveled extensively in the period, that "a New York merchant always walks as if he had a good dinner before him, and a bailiff behind him."

Northern and Southern farmers and city merchants alike, to say nothing of Irishmen and blacks, fell well short of the standard of genteel "bodily carriage" enshrined in both English and American etiquette books and the instructions of dancing masters: "flexibility in the arms . . . erectness in the spinal column . . . easy carriage of the head." It was the ideal of the British aristocracy, and Southern planters came closest to it, expressing the power of their class in the way they stood and moved. Slave owners accustomed to command, imbued with an ethic of honor and pride, at ease in the saddle, carried themselves more gracefully than men hardened by toil or preoccupied with commerce. Visiting Washington in 1835, the Englishwoman Harriet Martineau contrasted not the politics but the postures of Northern and Southern congressmen. She marked the confident bearing, the "ease and frank courtesy . . . with an occasional touch of arrogance" of the slaveholders alongside the "cautious . . . and too deferential air of the members of the North." She could recognize a New Englander "in the open air," she claimed, "by his deprecatory walk."

Local inhabitants' faces became more open, travelers observed, as one went west. Nathaniel Hawthorne found a dramatic contrast in public appearances only a few days' travel west of Boston. "The people out here," in New York State just west of the Berkshires, he confided to his notebook in 1839, "show out their character much more strongly than they do with us," in his native eastern Massachusetts. He compared the "quiet, silent, dull decency . . . in our public assemblages" with Westerners' wider gamut of expressiveness, "mirth, anger, eccentricity, all showing themselves freely." Westerners in general, the clergyman and publicist Henry Ward Beecher observed, had "far more freedom of manners, and more frankness and spontaneous geniality" than did the city or country people of the New England and Middle

In marriage, couples wore "all unconsciously the masks which custom had prescribed."

Atlantic states, as did the "odd mortals that wander in from the western border," that Martineau observed in Washington's political population.

WE WERE DIRTY AND SMELLY

Early-nineteenth-century Americans lived in a world of dirt, insects, and pungent smells. Farmyards were strewn with animal wastes, and farmers wore manure-spattered boots and trousers everywhere. Men's and women's working clothes alike were often stiff with dirt and dried sweat, and men's shirts were often stained with "yellow rivulets" of tobacco juice. The locations of privies were all too obvious on warm or windy days. Unemptied chamber pots advertised their presence. Wet baby "napkins," today's diapers, were not immediately washed but simply put by the fire to dry. Vats of "chamber lye"—highly concentrated urine used for cleaning type or degreasing wool—perfumed all printing offices and many households. "The breath of that fiery bar-room," as Underwood described a country tavern, "was overpowering. The odors of the hostlers' boots, redolent of fish-oil and tallow, and of buffalo-robes and horse-blankets, the latter reminiscent of equine ammonia, almost got the better of the all-pervading fumes of spirits and tobacco."

Densely populated, but poorly cleaned and drained, America's cities were often far more noisome than its farmyards. Horse manure thickly covered city streets, and few neighborhoods were free from the spreading stench of tanneries and slaughterhouses. New York City accumulated so much refuse that it was generally believed the actual surfaces of the streets had not been seen for decades. During her stay in Cincinnati, the English writer Frances Trollope followed the practice of the vast majority of American city housewives when she threw her household "slops"—refuse food and dirty dishwater—out into the street. An irate neighbor soon informed her that

Freely moving pigs fed on the city's trash.

municipal ordinances forbade "throwing such things at the sides of the streets" as she had done; "they must just all be cast right into the middle and the pigs soon takes them off." In most cities hundreds, sometimes thousands, of free-roaming pigs scavenged the garbage; one exception was Charleston, South Carolina, where buzzards patrolled the streets. By converting garbage into pork, pigs kept city streets cleaner than they would otherwise have been, but the pigs themselves befouled the streets and those who ate their meat—primarily poor families—ran greater than usual risks of infection.

PRIVY MATTERS

The most visible symbols of early American sanitation were privies or "necessary houses." But Americans did not always use them; many rural householders simply took to the closest available patch of woods or brush. However, in more densely settled communities and in regions with cold winters, privies were in widespread use. They were not usually put in out-of-the-way locations. The fashion of some Northern farm families, according to Robert B. Thomas's *Farmer's Almanack* in 1826, had long been to have their "necessary planted in a garden or other conspicuous place." Other countryfolk went even further in turning human wastes to agricultural account and built their out-houses "within the territory of a hog yard, that the swine may root and ruminate and devour the nastiness thereof." Thomas was a long-standing critic of primitive manners in the countryside and roundly condemned these traditional sanitary arrangements as demonstrating a "want of taste, decency, and propriety." The better arranged necessaries of the prosperous

emptied into vaults that could be opened and cleaned out. The dripping horse-drawn carts of the "nocturnal gold-finders," who emptied the vaults and took their loads out for burial or water disposal—"night soil" was almost never used as manure—were a familiar part of nighttime traffic on city streets.

The humblest pieces of American household furniture were the chamber pots that allowed people to avoid dark and often cold nighttime journeys outdoors. Kept under beds or in corners of rooms, "chambers" were used primarily upon retiring and arising. Collecting, emptying, and cleaning them remained an unspoken, daily part of every housewife's routine.

Nineteenth-century inventory takers became considerably more reticent about naming chamber pots than their predecessors, usually lumping them with miscellaneous "crockery," but most households

Chamber pots were dumped in the streets.

probably had a couple of chamber pots; genteel families reached the optimum of one for each bedchamber. English-made ceramic pots had become cheap enough by 1820 that few American families within the reach of commerce needed to go without one. "Without a pot to piss in" was a vulgar tag of long standing for extreme poverty; those poorest households without one, perhaps more common in the warm South, used the outdoors at all times and seasons.

The most decorous way for householders to deal with chamber-pot wastes accumulated during the night was to throw them down the privy hole. But more casual and unsavory methods of disposal were still in wide use. Farm families often dumped their chamber pots out the most convenient door or window. In densely settled communities like York, Pennsylvania, the results could be more serious. In 1801, the York

diarist Lewis Miller drew and then described an event in North George Street when "Mr. Day an English man [as the German-American Miller was quick to point out] had a bad practice by pouring out of the upper window his filthiness . . . one day came the discharge . . . on a man and wife going to a wedding, her silk dress was fouled."

LETTING THE BEDBUGS BITE

Sleeping accommodations in American country taverns were often dirty and insect-ridden. The eighteenth-century observer of American life Isaac Weld saw "filthy beds swarming with bugs" in 1794; in 1840 Charles Dickens noted "a sort of game not on the bill of fare." Complaints increased in intensity as travelers went south or west. Tavern beds were uniquely vulnerable to infestation by whatever insect guests travelers brought with them. The bedding of most American households was surely less foul. Yet it was dirty enough. New England farmers were still too often "tormented all night by bed bugs," complained *The Farmer's Almanack* in 1837, and books of domestic advice contained extensive instructions on removing them from feather beds and straw ticks.

Journeying between Washington and New Orleans in 1828, Margaret Hall, a well-to-do and cultivated Scottish woman, became far more familiar with intimate insect life than she had ever been in the genteel houses of London or Edinburgh. Her letters home, never intended for publication, gave a graphic and unsparing account of American sanitary conditions. After sleeping in a succession of beds with the "usual complement of fleas and bugs," she and her party had themselves become infested: "We bring them

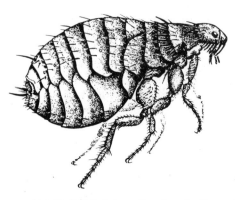

Insects infested many American beds.

along with us in our clothes and when I undress I find them crawling on my skin, nasty wretches." New and distasteful to her, such discoveries were commonplace among the ordinary folk with whom she lodged. The American children she saw on her Southern journey were "kept in such a state of filth," with clothes "dirty and slovenly to a degree," but this was "nothing in comparison with their heads . . . [which] are absolutely crawling!" In New Orleans she observed women picking through children's heads for lice, "catching them according to the method depicted in an engraving of a similar proceeding in the streets of Naples."

Davy Crockett, like many Americans, preferred to wash himself in the great outdoors.

BIRTH OF THE BATH

Americans were not "clean and decent" by today's standards, and it was virtually impossible that they should be. The furnishings and use of rooms in most American houses made more than the most elementary washing difficult. In a New England farmer's household, wrote Underwood, each household member would "go down to the 'sink' in the lean-to, next to the kitchen, fortunate if he had not to break ice in order to wash his face and hands, or more fortunate if a little warm water was poured into his basin from the kettle swung over the kitchen fire." Even in the comfortable household of the prominent minister Lyman Beecher in Litchfield, Connecticut, around 1815 all family members washed in the kitchen, using a stone sink and "a couple of basins."

Southerners washed in their detached kitchens or, like Westerners in warm weather, washed outside, "at the doors . . . or at the wells" of their houses. Using basins and sinks outdoors or in full view of others, most Americans found anything more than "washing the face and hands once a-day," usually in cold water, difficult, even unthinkable. Most men and women also washed without soap, reserving it for laundering clothes; instead they used a brisk rubbing with a coarse towel to scrub the dirt off their skins.

Gradually the practice of complete bathing spread beyond the topmost levels of American society and into smaller towns and villages. This became possible as families moved washing equipment out of kitchens and into bedchambers, from shared space to space that could

be made private. As more prosperous households furnished one or two of their chambers with washing equipment—a washstand, a basin, and a ewer, or large-mouthed pitcher—family members could shut the chamber door, undress, and wash themselves completely. The daughters of the Larcom family, living in Lowell, Massachusetts, in the late 1830s, began to bathe in a bedchamber in this way; Lucy Larcom described how her

We were not "clean and decent" by today's standards; washing was difficult.

oldest sister started to take "a full cold bath every morning before she went to her work . . . in a room without a fire," and the other young Larcoms "did the same whenever we could be resolute enough." By the 1830s better city hotels and even some country taverns were providing individual basins and pitchers in their rooms.

At a far remove from "primitive manners" and "bad practices" was the genteel ideal of domestic sanitation embodied in the "chamber sets"—matching basin and ewer for private bathing, a cup for brushing the teeth, and a chamber pot with cover to minimize odor and spillage—that American stores were beginning to stock. By 1840 a significant minority of American households owned chamber

sets and wash-stands to hold them in their bedchambers. For a handful there was the very faint dawning of an entirely new age of sanitary arrangements. In 1829 the new Tremont House hotel in Boston offered its patrons indoor plumbing: eight chambers with bathtubs and eight "water closets." In New York City and Philadelphia, which had developed rudimentary public water systems, a few wealthy households had water taps and, more rarely, water closets by the 1830s. For all others flush toilets and bathtubs remained far in the future.

The American people moved very slowly toward cleanliness. In "the back-country at the present day," commented the fastidious author of the *Lady's Book* in 1836, custom still "requires that everyone should wash at the pump in the yard, or at the sink in the kitchen." Writing in 1846, the physician and health reformer William Alcott rejoiced that to "wash the surface of the whole body in water daily" had now been accepted as a genteel standard of personal cleanliness. But, he added, there were "multitudes who pass for models of neatness and cleanliness, who do not perform this work for themselves half a dozen times— nay once—a year." As the better-off became cleaner than ever before, the poor stayed dirty.

WE DRANK AND FOUGHT WHENEVER WE COULD

In the early part of the century America was a bawdy, hard-edged, and violent land. We drank more than we ever had

Backwoodsmen have a "knock down" in this 1841 woodcut from *Crockett's Almanack.*

before or ever would again. We smoked and chewed tobacco like addicts and fought and quarreled on the flimsiest pretexts. The tavern was the most important gateway to the primarily male world of drink and disorder: in sight of the village church in most American communities, observed Daniel Drake, a Cincinnati physician who wrote a reminiscence of his Kentucky boyhood, stood the village tavern, and the two structures "did in fact represent two great opposing principles."

The great majority of American men in every region were taverngoers. The printed street directories of American cities listed tavernkeepers in staggering numbers, and even the best-churched parts of New England could show more "licensed houses" than meetinghouses. In 1827 the fast-growing city of Rochester, New York, with a population of approximately eight thousand, had nearly one hundred establishments licensed to sell liquor, or one for every eighty inhabitants.

America's most important centers of male sociability, taverns were often the scene of excited gaming and vicious fights and always of hard drinking, heavy smoking, and an enormous amount of alcohol-stimulated talk. City men came to their neighborhood taverns daily, and "tavern haunting, tippling, and gaming," as Samuel Goodrich, a New England historian and publisher, remembered, "were the chief resources of men in the dead and dreary winter months" in the countryside.

City taverns catered to clienteles of different classes: sordid sailors' grog-

shops near the waterfront were rife with brawling and prostitution; neighborhood taverns and liquor-selling groceries were visited by craftsmen and clerks; well-appointed and relatively decorous places were favored by substantial merchants. Taverns on busy highways often specialized in teamsters or stage passengers, while country inns took their patrons as they came.

In the 1820s America was a bawdy and violent land. We drank more than we ever would again.

Taverns accommodated women as travelers, but their barroom clienteles were almost exclusively male. Apart from the dockside dives frequented by prostitutes, or the liquor-selling groceries of poor city neighborhoods, women rarely drank in public.

Gambling was a substantial preoccupation for many male citizens of the early republic. Men played billiards at tavern tables for money stakes. They threw dice in "hazard," slamming the dice boxes down so hard and so often that tavern tables wore the characteristic scars of their play. Even more often Americans sat down to cards, playing brag, similar to modern-day poker, or an elaborate table game called faro. Outdoors they wagered with each other on horse

races or bet on cockfights and wrestling matches.

Drink permeated and propelled the social world of early-nineteenth-century America—first as an unquestioned presence and later as a serious and divisive problem. "Liquor at that time," recalled the builder and architect Elbridge Boyden, "was used as commonly as the food we ate." Before 1820 the vast majority of Americans considered alcohol an essential stimulant to exertion as well as a symbol of hospitality and fellowship. Like the Kentuckians with whom Daniel Drake grew up, they "regarded it as a duty to their families and visitors . . . to keep the bottle well replenished." Weddings, funerals, frolics, even a casual "gathering of two or three neighbors for an evening's social chat" required the obligatory "spirituous liquor"—rum, whiskey, or gin—"at all seasons and on all occasions."

Northern householders drank hard cider as their common table beverage, and all ages drank it freely. Dramming—taking a fortifying glass in the forenoon and again in the afternoon—was part of the daily regimen of many men. Clergymen took sustaining libations between services, lawyers before going to court, and physicians at their patients' bedsides. To raise a barn or get through a long day's haying without fortifying drink seemed a virtual impossibility. Slaves enjoyed hard drinking at festival times and at Saturday-night barbecues as much as any of their countrymen. But of all Americans they probably drank the least on a daily basis because their masters could usually control their access to liquor.

In Parma, Ohio, in the mid-1820s, Lyndon Freeman, a farmer, and his brothers were used to seeing men "in their cups" and passed them by without comment. But one dark and rainy night

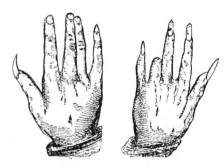

The hands of a celebrated gouger.

they discovered something far more shocking, "nothing less than a *woman beastly drunk* . . . with a flask of whiskey by her side." American women drank as well as men, but usually much less heavily. They were more likely to make themselves "tipsy" with hard cider and alcohol-containing patent medicines than to become inebriated with rum or whiskey. Temperance advocates in the late 1820s estimated that men consumed fifteen times the volume of distilled spirits that women did; this may have been a considerable exaggeration, but there was a great difference in drinking habits between the sexes. Americans traditionally found drunkenness tolerable and forgivable in men but deeply shameful in women.

By almost any standard, Americans drank not only nearly universally but in large quantities. Their yearly consumption at the time of the Revolution has been estimated at the equivalent of three and one-half gallons of pure two-hundred-proof alcohol for each person. After 1790 American men began to drink even more. By the late 1820s their imbibing had risen to an all-time high of almost four gallons per capita.

Along with drinking went fighting. Americans fought often and with great relish. York, Pennsylvania, for example, was a peaceable place as American communities went, but the Miller and Weaver families had a long-running quarrel. It had begun in 1800 when the Millers found young George Weaver stealing apples in their yard and punished him by "throwing him over the fence," injuring

---

To get through a long day's haying without drink seemed an impossibility.

---

him painfully. Over the years hostilities broke out periodically. Lewis Miller remembered walking down the street as a teenaged boy and meeting Mrs. Weaver, who drenched him with the bucket of water she was carrying. He retaliated by "turning about and giving her a kick, laughing at her, this is for your politeness." Other York households had their quarrels too; in "a general fight on Beaver Street," Mistress Hess and Mistress Forsch tore each other's caps from their

---

In isolated areas it was not uncommon to meet men who had lost an eye in a fight.

---

heads. Their husbands and then the neighbors interfered, and "all of them had a knock down."

When Peter Lung's wife, Abigail, refused "to get up and dig some potatoes" for supper from the yard of their small house, the Hartford, Connecticut, laborer recalled in his confession, he "kicked her on the side . . . then gave her a violent push" and went out to dig the potatoes himself. He returned and "again kicked her against the shoulder and neck." Both had been drinking, and loud arguments and blows within the Lung household, as in many others, were routine. But this time the outcome was not. Alice Lung was dead the next day, and Peter Lung was arrested, tried, and hanged for murder in 1815.

In the most isolated, least literate and commercialized parts of the United States, it was "by no means uncommon, wrote Isaac Weld, "to meet with those who have lost an eye in a combat, and there are men who pride themselves upon the dexterity with which they can scoop one out. This is called *gouging.*"

THE SLAVE'S LOT

Slaves wrestled among themselves, sometimes fought one another bitterly over quarrels in the quarters, and even at times stood up to the vastly superior force of masters and overseers. They rarely, if ever, reduced themselves to the ferocity of eye gouging. White Southerners lived with a pervasive fear of the violent potential of their slaves, and the Nat Turner uprising in Virginia in 1831, when a party of slaves rebelled and killed whites before being overcome, gave rise to tighter and harsher controls. But in daily reality slaves had far more to fear from their masters.

Margaret Hall was no proponent of abolition and had little sympathy for black Americans. Yet in her travels south she confronted incidents of what she ironically called the "good treatment of slaves" that were impossible to ignore. At a country tavern in Georgia, she summoned the slave chamber-maid, but "she could not come" because the mis-

tress had been whipping her and she was not fit to be seen. Next morning she made her appearance with her face marked in several places by the cuts of the cowskin and her neck handkerchief covered with spots of blood."

Southern stores were very much like Northern ones, Francis Kemble Butler observed, except that they stocked "negro-whips" and "mantraps" on their shelves. A few slaves were never beaten at all, and for most, whippings were not a daily or weekly occurrence. But they were, of all Americans, by far the most vulnerable to violence. All slaves had, as

A white master takes a baby from its mother.

William Wells Brown, an ex-slave himself, said, often "heard the crack of the whip, and the screams of the slave" and knew that they were never more than a white man's or woman's whim away from a beating. With masters' unchecked power came worse than whipping: the mutilating punishments of the old penal law including branding, ear cropping, and even occasionally castration and burning alive as penalties for severe offenses. In public places or along the road blacks were also subject to casual kicks, shoves, and cuffs, for which they could retaliate only at great peril. "Six or seven feet in length, made of cow-hide, with a platted wire on the end of it," as Brown recalled it, the negro-whip, for sale in most stores and brandished by masters and overseers in the fields, stood for a pervasive climate of force and intimidation.

PUBLIC PUNISHMENT

The penal codes of the American states were far less blood-thirsty than those of England. Capital punishment was not often imposed on whites for crimes other than murder. Yet at the beginning of the nineteenth century many criminal offenses were punished by the public infliction of pain and suffering. "The whipping post and stocks stood on the green near the meetinghouse" in most of the towns of New England and near courthouses everywhere. In Massachusetts before 1805 a counterfeiter was liable to have an ear cut off, and a forger to have one cropped or partially amputated, after spending an hour in the pillory. A criminal convicted of manslaughter was set up on the gallows to have his forehead branded with a letter M. In most jurisdictions town officials flogged petty thieves as punishment for their crime. In New Haven, Connecticut, around 1810, Charles Fowler, a local historian, recalled seeing the "admiring students of [Yale] college" gathered around to watch petty criminals receive "five or ten lashes . . . with a rawhide whip."

A man in the stocks awaits a flogging.

Throughout the United States public hangings brought enormous crowds to the seats of justice and sometimes seemed like brutal festivals. Thousands of spectators arrived to pack the streets of courthouse towns. On the day of a hanging near Mount Holly, New Jersey, in the 1820s, the scene was that of a holiday: "around the place in every direction were the assembled multitudes—some in tents, and by-wagons, engaged in gambling and other vices of the sort, in open day." In order to accommodate the throngs, hangings were usually held not in the public square but on the outskirts of town. The gallows erected on a hill or set up at the bottom of a natural amphitheater allowed onlookers an unobstructed view. A reprieve or stay of execution might disappoint a crowd intent on witnessing the deadly drama and

provoke a riot, as it did in Pembroke, New Hampshire, in 1834.

RISE OF RESPECTABILITY

At a drunkard's funeral in Enfield, Massachusetts, in the 1830s—the man had strayed out of the road while walking home and fallen over a cliff, "his stiffened fingers still grasping the handle of the jug"—Rev. Sumner G. Clapp, the Congregationalist minister of Enfield, mounted a log by the woodpile and preached the town's first temperance sermon before a crowd full of hardened drinkers. In this way Clapp began a campaign to "civilize" the manners of his parishioners, and "before many years there was a great change in the town; the incorrigible were removed by death, and others took warning." Drinking declined sharply, and along with it went "a general reform in conduct."

Although it remained a powerful force in many parts of the United States, the American way of drunkenness began to lose ground as early as the mid-1820s. The powerful upsurge in liquor consumption had provoked a powerful reaction, an unprecedented attack on all forms of drink that gathered momentum in the Northeast. Some New England clergymen had been campaigning in their own communities as early as 1810, but their concerns took on organized impetus with the founding of the American Temperance Society in 1826. Energized in part by a concern for social order, in part by evangelical piety, temperance reformers popularized a radically new way of looking at alcohol. The "good creature" became "demon rum"; prominent physicians and writers on physiology, like Benjamin Rush, told Americans that alcohol, traditionally considered healthy and fortifying, was actually a physical and moral poison. National and state societies distributed anti-liquor tracts, at first calling for moderation in drink but increasingly demanding total abstinence from alcohol.

To a surprising degree these aggressive temperance campaigns worked. By 1840 the consumption of alcohol had declined by more than two-thirds, from close to four gallons per person each year to less than one and one-half. Country storekeepers gave up the sale of spirits, local authorities limited the number of tavern licenses, and farmers even abandoned hard cider and cut down their

apple orchards. The shift to temperance was a striking transformation in the everyday habits of an enormous number of Americans. "A great, though silent change," in Horace Greeley's words, had been "wrought in public sentiment."

But although the "great change" affected some Americans everywhere, it had a very uneven impact. Organized temperance reform was sharply delimited by geography. Temperance societies were enormously powerful in New England and western New York and numerous in eastern New York, New Jersey, and Pennsylvania. More than three-fourths of all recorded temperance pledges came from these states. In the South and West, and in the laborers' and artisans' neighborhoods of the cities, the campaign against drink was much weaker. In many places drinking ways survived and even flourished, but as individuals and families came under the influence of militant evangelical piety, their "men of business

---

Liquor consumption provoked a powerful reaction: an unprecedented attack on drinking.

---

and sobriety" increased gradually in number. As liquor grew "unfashionable in the country," Greeley noted, Americans who wanted to drink and carouse turned increasingly to the cities, "where no one's deeds or ways are observed or much regarded."

Closely linked as they were to drink, such diversions as gambling, racing, and blood sports also fell to the same forces of change. In the central Massachusetts region that George Davis, a lawyer in Sturbridge, knew well, until 1820 or so gaming had "continued to prevail, more and more extensively." After that "a blessed change had succeeded," overturning the scenes of high-stakes dice and card games that he knew in his young manhood. Impelled by a new perception of its "pernicious effects," local leaders gave it up and placed "men of respectable standing" firmly in opposition. Racecourses were abandoned and "planted to corn." Likewise, "bear-baiting, cock-fighting, and other cruel amusements" began to dwindle in the Northern countryside. Elsewhere the rude life of

AMERICAN ANTIQUARIAN SOCIETY

A popular temperance print of 1826 shows a drunkard's progress from a morning dram to loss of his home.

the tavern and "cruel amusements" remained widespread, but some of their excesses of "sin and shame" did diminish gradually.

Over the first four decades of the nineteenth century the American people increasingly made churchgoing an obligatory ritual. The proportion of families affiliated with a local church or Methodist circuit rose dramatically, particularly after 1820, and there were fewer stretches of the wholly pagan, unchurched territory that travelers had noted around 1800. "Since 1830," maintained Emerson Davis in his retrospect of America, *The Half Century,* " . . . the friends of the Sabbath have been gaining ground. . . . In 1800, good men slumbered over the desecration of the Sabbath. They have since awoke. . . ." The number of Sunday mails declined, and the campaign to eliminate the delivery of mail on the Sabbath entirely grew stronger. "In the smaller cities and towns," wrote Mrs. Trollope in 1832, worship and "prayer meetings" had come to "take the place of almost all other amusements." There were still communities near the edge of settlement where a traveler would "rarely find either churches or chapels, prayer or preacher," but it was the working-class neighborhoods of America's larger cities that were increasingly the chief strongholds of "Sunday dissipation" and "Sabbath-breaking."

Whipping and the pillory, with their attentive audiences, began to disappear from the statute book, to be replaced by terms of imprisonment in another new American institution, the state penitentiary. Beginning with Pennsylvania's abolition of flogging in 1790 and Massachusetts's elimination of mutilating pun-

ishments in 1805, several American states gradually accepted John Hancock's view of 1796 that "mutilating or lacerating the body" was less an effective punishment than "an indignity to human nature." Connecticut's town constables whipped petty criminals for the last time in 1828.

Slaveholding states were far slower to change their provisions for public punishment. The whipping and mutilation of blacks may have become a little less ferocious over the decades, but the whip remained the essential instrument of punishment and discipline. "The secret of our success," thought a slave owner, looking back after emancipation, had been "the great motive power contained in that little instrument." Delaware achieved notoriety by keeping flogging on the books for whites and blacks alike through most of the twentieth century.

Although there were important stirrings of sentiment against capital punishment, all American states continued to execute convicted murders before the mid-1840s. Public hangings never lost their drawing power. But a number of American public officials began to abandon the long-standing view of executions as instructive communal rituals. They saw the crowd's holiday mood and eager participation as sharing too much in the condemned killer's own brutality. Starting with Pennsylvania, New York, and Massachusetts in the mid-1830s, several state legislatures voted to take executions away from the crowd, out of the public realm. Sheriffs began to carry out death sentences behind the walls of the jailyard, before a small assembly of representative onlookers. Other states clung much longer to tradition and continued

public executions into the twentieth century.

SEX LIFE OF THE NATIVES

Early-nineteenth-century Americans were more licentious than we ordinarily imagine them to be.

"On the 20th day of July" in 1830, Harriet Winter, a young woman working as a domestic in Joseph Dunham's household in Brimfield, Massachusetts, "was gathering raspberries" in a field west of the house. "Near the close of day," Charles Phelps, a farm laborer then living in the town, "came to the field where she was," and in the gathering dusk they made love—and, Justice of the Peace Asa Lincoln added in his account, "it was the Sabbath." American communities did not usually document their inhabitants' amorous rendezvous, and Harriet's tryst with Charles was a commonplace event in early-nineteenth-century America. It escaped historical oblivion because she was unlucky, less in

Early-nineteenth-century Americans were more licentious than we imagine them to be.

becoming pregnant than in Charles's refusal to marry her. Asa Lincoln did not approve of Sabbath evening indiscretions, but he was not pursuing Harriet for immorality. He was concerned instead with economic responsibility for the child. Thus he interrogated Harriet about the baby's father—while she was in labor, as was the long-customary practice—in order to force Charles to contribute to the maintenance of the child, who was going to be "born a bastard and chargeable to the town."

Some foreign travelers found that the Americans they met were reluctant to admit that such things happened in the United States. They were remarkably straitlaced about sexual matters in public and eager to insist upon the "purity" of their manners. But to take such protestations at face value, the unusually candid Englishman Frederick Marryat thought, would be "to suppose that human nature is not the same everywhere."

The well-organized birth and marriage records of a number of American communities reveal that in late-eighteenth-century America pregnancy was frequently the prelude to marriage. The proportion of brides who were pregnant at the time of their weddings had been rising since the late seventeenth century and peaked in the turbulent decades during and after the Revolution. In the 1780s and 1790s nearly one-third of rural New England's brides were already with child. The frequency of sexual intercourse before marriage was surely higher, since some couples would have escaped early pregnancy. For many couples sexual relations were part of serious courtship. Premarital pregnancies in late-eighteenth-century Dedham, Massachusetts, observed the local historian Erastus Worthington in 1828, were occasioned by "the custom then prevalent of females admitting young men to their beds, who sought their company in marriage."

Pregnancies usually simply accelerated a marriage that would have taken place in any case, but community and parental pressure worked strongly to assure it. Most rural communities simply accepted the "early" pregnancies that marked so many marriages, although in Hingham, Massachusetts, tax records suggest that the families of well-to-do brides were considerably less generous to couples who had had "early babies" than to those who had avoided pregnancy.

"Bundling very much abounds," wrote the anonymous author of "A New Bundling Song," still circulating in Boston in 1812, "in many parts in country towns." Noah Webster's first *Dictionary* of *the American Language* defined it as

Lovers await Cupid's dart in this woodcut.

the custom that allowed couples "to sleep on the same bed without undressing"—with, a later commentator added, "the shared understanding that innocent endearments should not be exceeded." Folklore and local tradition, from Maine south to New York, had American mothers tucking bundling couples into bed with special chastity-protecting garments for the young woman or a "bundling board" to separate them.

In actuality, if bundling had been intended to allow courting couples privacy and emotional intimacy but not sexual contact, it clearly failed. Couples may have begun with bundling, but as courtship advanced, they clearly pushed beyond its restraints, like the "bundling maid" in "A New Bundling Song" who would "sometimes say when she lies down/She can't be cumbered with a gown."

Young black men and women shared American whites' freedom in courtship and sexuality and sometimes exceeded it. Echoing the cultural traditions of West Africa, and reflecting the fact that their marriages were not given legal status and security, slave communities were somewhat more tolerant and accepting of sex before marriage.

Gradations of color and facial features among the slaves were testimony that "thousands," as the abolitionist and former slave Frederick Douglass wrote, were "ushered into the world annually, who, like myself, owe their existence to white fathers, and those fathers most frequently their own masters." Sex crossed the boundaries of race and servitude more often than slavery's defenders wanted to admit, if less frequently than

the most outspoken abolitionists claimed. Slave women had little protection from whatever sexual demands masters or overseers might make, so that rapes, short liaisons, and long-term "concubinage" all were part of plantation life.

As Nathaniel Hawthorne stood talking with a group of men on the porch of a tavern in Augusta, Maine, in 1836, a young man "in a laborer's dress" came up and asked if anyone knew the whereabouts of Mary Ann Russell. "Do you want to use her?" asked one of the bystanders. Mary Ann was, in fact, the young laborer's wife, but she had left him and their child in Portland to become "one of a knot of whores." A few years earlier the young men of York, Pennsylvania, made up a party for "overturning and pulling to the ground" Eve Geese's "shameful house" of prostitution in Queen Street. The frightened women fled out the back door as the chimney collapsed around them; the apprentices and young journeymen—many of whom had surely been previous customers—were treated by local officials "to wine, for the good work."

From medium-sized towns like Augusta and York to great cities, poor American women were sometimes pulled into a darker, harsher sexual world, one of vulnerability, exploitation, and commerce. Many prostitutes took up their trade out of poverty and domestic disaster. A young widow or a country girl arrived in the city and, thrown on her own resources, often faced desperate economic choices because most women's work paid too poorly to provide decent food, clothing, and shelter, while other women sought excitement and independence from their families.

As cities grew, and changes in transportation involved more men in long-distance travel, prostitution became more visible. Men of all ages, married and unmarried, from city lawyers to visiting country storekeepers to sailors on the docks, turned to brothels for sexual release, but most of the customers were young men, living away from home and unlikely to marry until their late twenties. Sexual commerce in New York City was elaborately graded by price and the economic status of clients, from the "parlor houses" situated not far from the city's best hotels on Broadway to the more numerous and moderately priced houses that drew artisans and clerks, and finally to the broken and dissipated women who haunted dockside grogshops in the Five Points neighborhood.

From New Orleans to Boston, city theaters were important sexual marketplaces. Men often bought tickets less to see the performance than to make assignations with the prostitutes, who sat by custom in the topmost gallery of seats. The women usually received free admission from theater managers, who claimed that they could not stay in business without the male theatergoers drawn by the "guilty third tier."

Most Americans—and the American common law—still did not regard abortion as a crime until the fetus had "quickened" or began to move perceptibly in the womb. Books of medical advice actually contained prescriptions for bringing on delayed menstrual periods, which would also produce an abortion if the woman happened to be pregnant. They suggested heavy doses of purgatives that created violent cramps, powerful douches, or extreme kinds of physical activity, like the "violent exercise, raising great weights . . . strokes on the belly . . . [and] falls" noted in William Buchan's *Domestic Medicine,* a manual read widely through the 1820s. Women's folklore echoed most of these prescriptions and added others, particularly the use of two American herbal preparations—savin, or the extract of juniper berries, and Seneca snake-root—as abortion-producing drugs. They were dangerous procedures but sometimes effective.

REINING IN THE PASSIONS

Starting at the turn of the nineteenth century, the sexual lives of many Americans began to change, shaped by a growing insistence on control: reining in the passions in courtship, limiting family size, and even redefining male and female sexual desire.

Bundling was already on the wane in rural America before 1800; by the 1820s it was written about as a rare and antique custom. It had ceased, thought an elderly man from East Haddam, Connecticut, "as a consequence of education and refinement." Decade by decade the proportion of young women who had conceived a child before marriage declined. In most of the towns of New England the rate had dropped from nearly one pregnant bride in three to one in five or six by 1840; in some places prenuptial pregnancy dropped to 5 per-

Just say no: Quaker lovers hold back.

cent. For many young Americans this marked the acceptance of new limits on sexual behavior, imposed not by their parents or other authorities in their communities but by themselves.

These young men and women were not more closely supervised by their parents than earlier generations had been; in fact, they had more mobility and greater freedom. The couples that courted in the new style put a far greater emphasis on control of the passions. For some of them—young Northern merchants and professional men and their intended brides—revealing love letters have survived for the years after 1820. Their intimate correspondence reveals that they did not give up sexual expression but gave it new boundaries, reserving sexual intercourse for marriage. Many of them were marrying later than their parents, often living through long engagements while the husband-to-be strove to establish his place in the world. They chose not to risk a pregnancy that would precipitate them into an early marriage.

Many American husbands and wives were also breaking with tradition as they began to limit the size of their families. Clearly, married couples were renegotiating the terms of their sexual lives together, but they remained resolutely silent about how they did it. In the first two decades of the nineteenth century, they almost certainly set about avoiding childbirth through abstinence; coitus interruptus, or male withdrawal; and perhaps sometimes abortion. These contraceptive techniques had long been traditional in preindustrial Europe, although previously little used in America.

As they entered the 1830s, Americans had their first opportunity to learn, at least in print, about more effective or

less self-denying forms of birth control. They could read reasonably inexpensive editions of the first works on contraception published in the United States: Robert Dale Owen's *Moral Physiology* of 1831 and Dr. Charles Knowlton's *The Fruits of Philosophy* of 1832. Both authors frankly described the full range of contraceptive techniques, although they solemnly rejected physical intervention in the sexual act and recommended only douching after intercourse and coitus interruptus. Official opinion, legal and religious, was deeply hostile. Knowlton, who had trained as a physician in rural Massachusetts, was prosecuted in three different counties for obscenity, convicted once, and imprisoned for three months.

But both works found substantial numbers of Americans eager to read them. By 1839 each book had gone through nine editions, putting a combined total of twenty to thirty thousand copies in circulation. An American physician could write in 1850 that contraception had "been of late years so much talked of." Greater knowledge about contraception surely played a part in the continuing decline of the American birthrate after 1830.

The sexual lives of Americans began to change, reshaped by a new emphasis on self-control.

New ways of thinking about sexuality emerged that stressed control and channeling of the passions. Into the 1820s almost all Americans would have subscribed to the commonplace notion that sex, within proper social confines, was enjoyable and healthy and that prolonged sexual abstinence could be injurious to health. They also would have assumed that women had powerful sexual drives.

Starting with his "Lecture to Young Men on Chastity" in 1832, Sylvester Graham articulated very different counsels about health and sex. Sexual indulgence, he argued, was not only morally suspect but psychologically and physiologically risky. The sexual overstimulation involved in young men's lives produced anxiety and nervous disorders, "a shocking state of debility and excessive irritability." The remedy was diet, exercise, and a regular routine that pulled the mind away from animal lusts. Medical writings that discussed the evils of masturbation, or "solitary vice," began to appear. Popular books of advice, like William Alcott's *Young Man's Guide,* gave similar warnings. They tried to persuade young men that their health could be ruined, and their prospects for success darkened, by consorting with prostitutes or becoming sexually entangled before marriage.

A new belief about women's sexual nature appeared, one that elevated them above "carnal passion." Many American men and women came to believe during the nineteenth century that in their true and proper nature as mothers and guardians of the home, women were far less interested in sex than men were. Women who defined themselves as passionless were in a strong position to control or deny men's sexual demands either during courtship or in limiting their childbearing within marriage.

Graham went considerably farther than this, advising restraint not only in early life and courtship but in marriage itself. It was far healthier, he maintained, for couples to have sexual relations "very seldom."

Neither contraception nor the new style of courtship had become anything like universal by 1840. Prenuptial pregnancy rates had fallen, but they remained high enough to indicate that many couples simply continued in familiar ways. American husbands and wives in the cities and the Northern countryside were limiting the number of their children, but it was clear that those living on the farms of the West or in the slave quarters had not yet begun to. There is strong evidence that many American women felt far from passionless, although others restrained or renounced their sexuality. For many people in the United States, there had been a profound change. Reining in the passions had become part of everyday life.

SMOKING AND SPITTING

Everyone smokes and some chew in America," wrote Isaac Weld in 1795. Americans turned tobacco, a new and controversial stimulant at the time of colonial settlement, into a crucially important staple crop and made its heavy use a commonplace—and a never-ending source of surprise and indignation to

After 1800, in public and private it became nearly impossible to avoid tobacco chewers.

visitors. Tobacco use spread in the United States because it was comparatively cheap, a homegrown product free from the heavy import duties levied on it by European governments. A number of slave rations described in plantation documents included "one hand of tobacco per month." Through the eighteenth century most American smokers used clay pipes, which are abundant in colonial archeological sites, although some men and women dipped snuff or inhaled powdered tobacco.

Where the smokers of early colonial America "drank" or gulped smoke through the short, thick stems of their seventeenth-century pipes, those of 1800 inhaled it more slowly and gradually; from the early seventeenth to the late eighteenth century, pipe stems became steadily longer and narrower, increasingly distancing smokers from their burning tobacco.

In the 1790s cigars, or "segars," were introduced from the Caribbean. Prosperous men widely took them up; they were the most expensive way to consume tobacco, and it was a sign of financial security to puff away on "long-nines or principe cigars at three cents each" while the poor used clay pipes and much

On the home front: a smoker indulges.

cheaper "cut plug" tobacco. After 1800 in American streets, barrooms, stores, public conveyances, and even private homes it became nearly impossible to avoid tobacco chewers. Chewing extended tobacco use, particularly into workplaces; men who smoked pipes at home or in the tavern barroom could chew while working in barns or workshops where smoking carried the danger of fire.

An expert spitter takes aim.

"In all the public places of America," wrote Charles Dickens, multitudes of men engaged in "the odious practice of chewing and expectorating," a recreation practiced by all ranks of American society. Chewing stimulated salivation and gave rise to a public environment of frequent and copious spitting, where men every few minutes were "squirting a mouthful of saliva through the room."

Spittoons were provided in the more meticulous establishments, but men often ignored them. The floors of American public buildings were not pleasant to contemplate. A courtroom in New York City in 1833 was decorated by a "mass of abomination" contributed to by "judges, counsel, jury, witnesses, officers, and audience." The floor of the Virginia House of Burgesses in 1827 was "actually flooded with their horrible spitting," and even the aisle of a Connecticut meetinghouse was black with the "ejection after ejection, incessant from twenty mouths," of the men singing in the choir. In order to drink, an American man might remove his quid, put it in a pocket or hold it in his hand, take his glassful, and then restore it to his mouth. Women's dresses might even be in danger at fashionable balls. "One night as I was walking upstairs to valse," reported Margaret Hall of a dance in Washington in 1828, "my partner began clearing his throat. This I thought ominous. However, I said to myself, 'surely he will turn his head to the other side.' The gentleman, however, had no such thought but deliberately shot across me. I had not courage enough to examine whether the result landed in the flounce of my dress."

The segar and the quid were almost entirely male appurtenances, but as the nineteenth century began, many rural and lower-class urban women were smoking pipes or dipping snuff. During his boyhood in New Hampshire, Horace Greeley remembered, "it was often my filial duty to fill and light my mother's pipe."

After 1820 or so tobacco use among women in the North began to decline. Northern women remembered or depicted with pipe or snuffbox were almost all elderly. More and more Americans adopted a genteel standard that saw tobacco use and womanliness— delicate and nurturing—as antithetical, and young women avoided it as a pollutant. For them, tobacco use marked off male from female territory with increasing sharpness.

In the households of small Southern and Western farmers, however, smoking and snuff taking remained common. When women visited "among the country people" of North Carolina, Frances Kemble Butler reported in 1837, the "proffer of the snuffbox, and its passing from hand to hand, is the usual civility." By the late 1830s visiting New Englanders were profoundly shocked when they saw the women of Methodist congregations in Illinois, including nursing mothers, taking out their pipes for a smoke between worship services.

FROM DEFERENCE TO EQUALITY

The Americans of 1820 would have been more recognizable to us in the informal and egalitarian way they treated one another. The traditional signs of deference before social superiors—the deep bow, the "courtesy," the doffed cap, lowered head, and averted eyes—had been a part of social relationships in colonial America. in the 1780s, wrote the American

poetess Lydia Huntley Sigourney in 1824, there were still "individuals . . . in every grade of society" who had grown up "when a bow was not an offense to fashion nor . . . a relic of monarchy." But in the early nineteenth century such signals of subordination rapidly fell away. It was a natural consequence of the Revolution, she maintained, which, "in giving us liberty, obliterated almost every vestige of politeness of the 'old school.'" Shaking hands became the accustomed American greeting between men, a gesture whose symmetry and mutuality signified equality. Frederick Marryat found in 1835 that it was "invariably the custom to shake hands" when he was introduced to Americans and that he could not carefully grade the acknowledgment he would give to new acquaintances according to their signs of wealth and breeding. He found instead that he had to "go on shaking hands here, there and everywhere, and with everybody." Americans were not blind to inequalities of economic and social power, but they less and less gave them overt physical expression. Bred in a society where such distinctions were far more clearly spelled out, Marryat was somewhat disoriented in the United States; "it is impossible to know who is who," he claimed, "in this land of equality."

Well-born British travelers encountered not just confusion but conflict when they failed to receive the signs of respect they expected. Margaret Hall's letters home during her Southern travels outlined a true comedy of manners. At every stage stop in the Carolinas, Georgia, and Alabama, she demanded that country tavernkeepers and their households give her deferential service and well-prepared meals; she received instead rancid bacon and "such an absence of all kindness of feeling, such unbending frigid heartlessness." But she and her family had a far greater share than they realized in creating this chilly reception. Squeezed between the pride and poise of the great planters and the social debasement of the slaves, small Southern farmers often displayed a prickly insolence, a considered lack of response, to those who too obviously considered themselves their betters. Greatly to their discomfort and incomprehension, the Halls were experiencing what a British traveler more sympathetic to American ways, Patrick Shirreff, called "the democratic rudeness which assumed or presump-

tuous superiority seldom fails to experience."

LAND OF ABUNDANCE

In the seventeenth century white American colonials were no taller than their European counterparts, but by the time of the Revolution they were close to their late-twentieth-century average height for men of slightly over five feet eight inches. The citizens of the early republic towered over most Europeans. Americans' early achievement of modern stature—by a full century and more—was a striking consequence of American abundance. Americans were taller because they were better nourished than the great majority of the world's peoples.

Yet not all Americans participated equally in the nation's abundance. Differences in stature between whites and blacks, and between city and country dwellers, echoed those between Europeans and Americans. Enslaved blacks were a full inch shorter than whites. But they remained a full inch taller than European peasants and laborers and were taller still than their fellow slaves eating the scanty diets afforded by the more savagely oppressive plantation system of the West Indies. And by 1820 those who lived in the expanding cities of

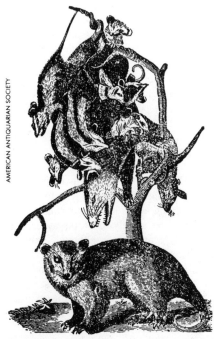

AMERICAN ANTIQUARIAN SOCIETY

Possum and other game were dietary staples.

the United States—even excluding immigrants, whose heights would have reflected European, not American, conditions—were noticeably shorter than the people of the countryside, suggesting an increasing concentration of poverty and poorer diets in urban places.

Across the United States almost all country households ate the two great American staples: corn and "the eternal pork," as one surfeited traveler called it, "which makes its appearance on every American table, high and low, rich and poor." Families in the cattle-raising, dairying country of New England, New York, and northern Ohio ate butter,

---

Americans were better nourished than the great majority of the world's peoples.

---

cheese, and salted beef as well as pork and made their bread from wheat flour or rye and Indian corn. In Pennsylvania, as well as Maryland, Delaware, and Virginia, Americans ate the same breadstuffs as their Northern neighbors, but their consumption of cheese and beef declined every mile southward in favor of pork.

Farther to the south, and in the West, corn and corn-fed pork were truly "eternal"; where reliance on them reached its peak in the Southern uplands, they were still the only crops many small farmers raised. Most Southern and Western families built their diets around smoked and salted bacon, rather than the Northerners' salt pork, and, instead of wheat or rye bread, made cornpone or hoecake, a coarse, strong bread, and hominy, pounded Indian corn boiled together with milk.

Before 1800, game—venison, possum, raccoon, and wild fowl—was for many American households "a substantial portion of the supply of food at certain seasons of the year," although only on the frontier was it a regular part of the diet. In the West and South this continued to be true, but in the Northeast game became increasingly rare as forests gave way to open farmland, where wild animals could not live.

Through the first half of the eighteenth century, Americans had been primarily concerned with obtaining a sufficiency of

Families began to sit down at mealtime.

meat and bread for their families; they paid relatively little attention to foodstuffs other than these two "staffs of life," but since that time the daily fare of many households had grown substantially more diverse.

COMING TO THE TABLE

Remembering his turn-of-the-century Kentucky boyhood, Daniel Drake could still see the mealtime scene at the house of a neighbor, "Old Billy," who "with his sons" would "frequently breakfast in common on mush and milk out of a huge buckeye bowl, each one dipping in a spoon. Old Billy" and his family were less frontier savages than traditionalists; in the same decade Gov. Caleb Strong of Massachusetts stopped for the night with a country family who ate in the same way, where "each had a spoon and dipped from the same dish." These households ate as almost all American families once had, communally partaking of food from the same dish and passing around a single vessel to drink from. Such meals were often surprisingly haphazard affairs, with household members moving in and out, eating quickly and going on to other tasks.

But by 1800 they were already in a small and diminishing minority. Over the eighteenth century dining "in common" had given way to individualized yet social eating; as families acquired chairs and dining utensils, they were able to

make mealtimes more important social occasions. Most Americans expected to eat individual portions of food at a table set with personal knives, forks, glasses, bowls, and plates. Anything that smacked of the old communal ways was increasingly likely to be treated as a sin against domestic decency. The clergyman Peter Cartwright was shocked at the table manners of a "backward" family who ate off a "wooden trencher," improvised forks with "sharp pieces of cane," and used a single knife, which they passed around the table.

"One and all, male and female," the observant Margaret Hall took note, even in New York's best society, ate "invariably and indefatigably with their knives." As a legacy of the fork's late arrival in the colonies, Americans were peculiar in using their "great lumbering, long, two-pronged forks," not to convey food to the mouth, as their English and French contemporaries did, but merely to keep their meat from slipping off the plate while cutting it. "Feeding yourself with your right hand, armed with a steel blade," was the prevalent American custom, acknowledged Eliza Farrar's elaborate *Young Lady's Friend* of 1836. She added that it was perfectly proper, despite English visitors' discomfort at the sight of a "prettily dressed, nice-looking young woman ladling rice pudding into her mouth with the point of a great knife" or a domestic helper "feeding an infant of seventeen months in the same way.

Mrs. Farrar acknowledged that there were stirrings of change among the sophisticated in the 1830s, conceding that some of her readers might now want "to imitate the French or English . . . and put every mouthful into your mouth with your fork." Later in the nineteenth century the American habit of eating with the knife completely lost its claims to gentility, and it became another relic of "primitive manners." Americans gradually learned to use forks more dexterously, although to this day they hold them in the wrong hand and "upside down" from an Englishman's point of view.

The old ways, so startlingly unfamiliar to the modern reader, gradually fell away. Americans changed their assumptions about what was proper, decent, and nor-

---

Primitive manners succumbed to campaigns for temperance and gentility.

---

mal in everyday life in directions that would have greatly surprised most of the men and women of the early republic. Some aspects of their "primitive manners" succumbed to campaigns for temperance and gentility, while others evaporated with the later growth of mass merchandising and mass communications.

Important patterns of regional, class, and ethnic distinctiveness remain in American everyday life. But they are far

less powerful, and less central to understanding American experience, than they once were. Through the rest of the nineteenth century and into the twentieth, the United States became ever more diverse, with new waves of Eastern and Southern European immigrants joining the older Americans of Northern European stock. Yet the new arrivals—and even more, their descendants—have experienced the attractiveness and reshaping power of a national culture formed by department stores, newspapers, radios, movies, and universal public education. America, the developing nation, developed into us. And perhaps our manners and morals, to some future observer, will seem as idiosyncratic and astonishing as this portrait of our earlier self.

The Jacksonian Revolution

Robert V. Remini

Robert V. Remini is professor of history at the University of Illinois Circle Campus in Chicago, and author of a multivolume biography of Andrew Jackson.

"What?" cried the outraged North Carolina lady when she heard the dreadful news. "Jackson up for president? Jackson? Andrew Jackson? The Jackson that used to live in Salisbury? Why, when he was here, he was such a rake that my husband would not bring him into the house! It is true, he might have taken him out to the stable to weigh horses for a race, and might drink a glass of whiskey with him there. Well, if Andrew Jackson can be president, anybody can!"

Indeed. After forty years of constitutional government headed by presidents George Washington, John Adams, Thomas Jefferson, James Madison, James Monroe, and John Quincy Adams, the thought of Gen. Andrew Jackson of Tennessee—"Old Hickory" to his devoted soldiers—succeeding such distinguished statesmen came as a shock to some Americans in 1828. And little did they know at the time that Old Hickory would be followed in succession by the little Magician, Tippecanoe and Tyler, too, Young Hickory, and then Old Rough and Ready.

What had happened to the American political process? How could it come about that the Washingtons, Jeffersons, and Madisons of the world could be replaced by the Van Burens, Harrisons, Tylers, and Taylors? What a mockery of the political system bequeathed by the Founding Fathers!

The years from roughly 1828 to 1848 are known today as the Age of Jackson or the Jacksonian era. To many contemporaries, they initiated a "revolution," a shocking overthrow of the noble republican standards of the founders by the "common people," who in 1828 preferred as president a crude frontiersman like Andrew Jackson to a statesman of proven ability with a record of outstanding public service like John Quincy Adams.

An entirely new generation of politicians appeared at the outbreak of the War of 1812.

Over the forty years following the establishment of the American nation under the Constitution, the United States had experienced many profound changes in virtually all phases of life. Following the War of 1812, the industrial revolution took hold and within thirty years all the essential elements for the creation of an industrial society in America were solidly in place. At the same time, a transportation revolution got underway with the building of canals, bridges, and turnpikes, reaching a climax of sorts in the 1820s with the coming of the railroads. The standard of living was also improved by numerous new inventions. Finally, many of the older eastern states began to imitate newer western states by democratizing their institutions, for example, amending their constitutions to eliminate property qualifications for voting and holding office, thereby establishing universal white manhood suffrage.

The arrival of many thousands of new voters at the polls in the early nineteenth century radically changed American politics. In the past, only the wealthy and better educated were actively involved in government. Moreover, political parties were frowned upon by many of the Founding Fathers. Parties stood for factions or cliques by which greedy and ambitious men, who had no interest in serving the public good, could advance their private and selfish purposes. John Adams spoke for many when he declared that the "division of the republic into two great parties . . . is to be dreaded as the greatest political evil under our Constitution."

But times had changed. An entirely new generation of politicians appeared at the outbreak of the War of 1812, men like Henry Clay, John C. Calhoun, Martin Van Buren, and Daniel Webster, who regarded political parties more favorably. Indeed, the party structure that had emerged before the end of President Washington's administration had been their corridor to power, since none of them could offer to their constituents a

From *The World & I*, January 1988, pp. 549-563. *The World & I*, a publication of The Washington Times Corporation.

public record to match what the founders had achieved.

NONE HAD FOUGHT IN THE REVOLUTION. None had signed the Declaration or participated in the debates leading to the writing and adoption of the Constitution. Some of them—Martin Van Buren is probably the best example—actually considered parties to be beneficial to the body politic, indeed essential to the proper working of a democratic society. Through the party system, Van Buren argued, the American people could more effectively express their will and take measures to ensure that that will was implemented by their representatives. "We must always have party distinctions," he wrote, "and the old ones are the best. . . . Political combinations between the inhabitants of the different states are unavoidable and the most natural and beneficial to the country is that between the planters of the South and the plain Republicans of the North."

In supporting Andrew Jackson for the presidency in 1828 and trying to win support from both planters and plain Republicans, Van Buren affirmed his belief in the American need for a two-party system. Jackson's election, he told Thomas Ritchie, editor of the Richmond *Enquirer*, "as the result of his military services without reference to party, and, as far as he alone is concerned, scarcely to principle, would be one thing. His election as the result of combined and concerted effort of a political party, holding in the main, to certain tenets and opposed to certain prevailing principles, might be another and far different thing."

Van Buren eventually formed an alliance with John C. Calhoun and a number of other southern politicians, and led the way in structuring a political organization around the presidential candidacy of Andrew Jackson. That organization ultimately came to be called the Democratic Party. Its leaders, including Jackson, Van Buren, Calhoun, and Thomas Hart Benton, claimed to follow the republican doctrines of Thomas Jefferson. Thus they opposed both a strong central government and a broad interpretation of the Constitution, and they regarded the states, whose rights must be defended by all who cared about preserving individual liberty, as a wholesome counterweight to the national government. Many of them opposed the idea of the federal government sponsoring public

works, arguing that internal improvements dangerously inflated the power of the central government and jeopardized liberty. As president, Andrew Jackson vetoed the Maysville road bill and contended that the national government should avoid internal improvements as a general practice, except for those essential to the national defense.

The political philosophy these Democrats espoused was fundamentally conservative. It advocated economy in operating the government because a tight budget limited government activity, and Jackson swore that if ever elected president he would liquidate the national debt. True to his word, he labored throughout his administration to cut expenditures by vetoing several appropriations bills he tagged as exorbitant, and he finally succeeded in obliterating the national debt altogether in January 1835—a short-lived accomplishment.

The organization of the Democratic Party in its initial stages included a central committee, state committees, and a national newspaper located in Washington, D.C., the *United States Telegraph*, which could speak authoritatively to the party faithful. In time it was said that the Democratic organization included "a chain of newspaper posts, from the New England States to Louisiana, and branching off through Lexington to the Western States." The supporters of Jackson's election were accused by their opponents of attempting to regulate "the popular election by means of organized clubs in the States, and organized presses everywhere."

Democrats took particular delight in celebrating the candidacy of Andrew Jackson. They found that Old Hickory's personality and military accomplishments made him an attractive and viable candidate for the ordinary voter. Indeed his career and personality stirred the imagination of Democratic leaders around the country and they devised new methods, or improved old ones, to get across the message that Andrew Jackson was a "man of the people." "The Constitution and liberty of the country were in imminent peril, and he has preserved them both!" his supporters boasted. "We can sustain our republican principles . . . by calling to the presidential chair . . . ANDREW JACKSON."

Jackson became a symbol of the best in American life—a self-made man, among other things—and party leaders

adopted the hickory leaf as their symbol. Hickory brooms, hickory canes, hickory sticks shot up everywhere—on steeples, poles, steamboats, and stage coaches, and in the hands of all who could wave them to salute the Old Hero of New Orleans. "In every village, as well as upon the corners of many city streets," hickory poles were erected. "Many of these poles were standing as late as 1845," recorded one contemporary, "rotten momentoes [*sic*] of the delirium of 1828." The opponents of the Democratic Party were outraged by this crude lowering of the political process. "Planting hickory trees!" snorted the Washington *National Journal* on May 24, 1828. "Odds nuts and drumsticks! What have hickory trees to do with republicanism and the great contest?"

The Democrats devised other gimmicks to generate excitement for their ticket. "Jackson meetings" were held in every county where a Democratic organization existed. Such meetings were not new, of course. What was new was their audience. "If we go into one of these meetings," declared one newspaper, "of whom do we find them composed? Do we see there the solid, substantial, moral and reflecting yeomanry of the country? No. . . . They comprise a large portion of the dissolute, the noisy, the discontented, and designing of society." The Democratic press retorted with the claim that these so-called dissolute were actually the "bone and muscle of American society. They are the People. The real People who understand that Gen. Jackson is one of them and will defend their interests and rights."

The Jacksonians were also very fond of parades and barbecues. In Baltimore a grand barbecue was scheduled to commemorate the successful defense of the city when the British attacked during the War of 1812. But the Democrats expropriated the occasion and converted it into a Jackson rally. One parade started with dozens of Democrats marching to the beat of a fife and drum corps and wearing no other insignia save "a twig of the sacred [hickory] tree in their hats." Trailing these faithful Jacksonians came "gigantic hickory poles," still live and crowned with green foliage, being carted in "on eight wheels for the purpose of being planted by the democracy on the eve of the election." These poles were drawn by eight horses, all decorated with "ribbons and mottoes." Perched in the branches of each tree were a dozen Democrats, waving flags and shouting, "Hurrah for Jackson!"

"Van Buren has learned you know that the *Hurra Boys* were for Jackson," commented one critic, "and to my regret they constitute a powerful host." Indeed they did. The number of voters in the election of 1828 rose to 1,155,340, a jump of more than 800,000 over the previous presidential election of 1824.

The Hurra Boys brought out the voters in 1828, but at considerable cost. The election set a low mark for vulgarity, gimmickry, and nonsensical hijinks. Jackson's mother was accused of being a prostitute brought to America to service British soldiers, and his wife was denounced as an "adulteress" and bigamist. "Ought a convicted adulteress and her paramour husband to be placed in the highest offices of this free and Christian land?" asked one editor. But the Democrats were no better, accusing John Quincy Adams of pimping for the czar of Russia.

The tone and style of this election outraged many voters who feared for the future of American politics.

The tone and style of this election outraged many voters who feared for the future of American politics. With so many fresh faces crowding to the polls, the old republican system was yielding to a new democratic style and that evolution seemed fraught with all the dangers warned against by the Founding Fathers. Jackson's subsequent victory at the polls gave some Americans nightmares of worse things to come.

At his inauguration people came from five hundred miles away to see General Jackson, wrote Daniel Webster, "and they really seem to think that the country is rescued from some dreadful danger!" They nearly wrecked the White House in their exuberance. Their behavior shocked Joseph Story, an associate justice of the Supreme Court, and sent him scurrying home. "The region of KING MOB seemed triumphant," he wailed. But a western newspaper disagreed. "It was a proud day for the people," reported the

Argus of Western America. "General Jackson is *their own* President."

Jackson himself was fiercely committed to democracy. And by democracy he meant majoritarian rule.

Jackson himself was fiercely committed to democracy. And by democracy he meant majoritarian rule. "The people are the government," he wrote, "administering it by their agents; they are the Government, the sovereign power." In his first message to Congress as president, written in December 1829, Jackson announced: "The majority is to govern." To the people belonged the right of "electing their Chief Executive." He therefore asked Congress to adopt an amendment that would abolish the College of Electors. He wanted all "intermediary" agencies standing between the people and their government swept away, whether erected by the Founding Fathers or not. "The people are sovereign," he reiterated. "Their will is absolute."

So committed was Jackson to the principle of popular self-rule that he told historian-politician George Bancroft that "every officer should in his turn pass before the people, for their approval or rejection." And he included federal judges in this sweeping generalization, even justices of the Supreme Court. Accordingly, he introduced the principle of rotation, which limited government appointments to four years. Officeholders should be regularly rotated back home and replaced by new men, he said. "The duties of all public officers are . . . so plain and simple that men of intelligence may readily qualify themselves for their performance." Otherwise abuse may occur. Anyone who has held office "a few years, believes he has a life estate in it, a vested right, & if it has been held 20 years or upwards, not only a vested right, but that it ought to descend to his children, & if no children then the next of kin—This is not the principles of our government. It is rotation in office that will perpetuate our liberty." Unfortunately, hack politicians equated rotation with patronage and Jackson's enemies quickly dubbed his principle "the spoils system."

But it was never meant to be a spoils system. Jackson wanted *every* office of government, from the highest to the lowest, within the reach of the electorate, arguing that "where the people are everything . . . there and there only is liberty." Perhaps his position was best articulated by Alexis de Tocqueville, the French visitor in the 1830s whose *Democracy in America* remains one of the most profound observations about American life in print. "The people reign in the American political world," declared Tocqueville, "as the Deity does in the universe. They are the cause and aim of all things; everything comes from them, and everything is absorbed in them." The "constant celebration" of the people, therefore, is what Jackson and the Democratic Party provided the nation during his eight years in office. It is what Jacksonian Democracy was all about.

Jackson wanted every office of government, from the highest to the lowest, within the reach of the electorate.

As president, Jackson inaugurated a number of important changes in the operation of government. For example, he vetoed congressional legislation more times than all his predecessors combined, and for reasons other than a bill's presumed lack of constitutionality. More importantly, by the creative use of his veto power he successfully claimed for the chief executive the right to participate in the legislative process. He put Congress on notice that they must consider his views on all issues *before* enacting them into law or run the risk of a veto. In effect he assumed the right to initiate legislation, and this essentially altered the relationship between the executive and the Congress. Instead of a separate and equal branch of the government, the president, according to Jackson, was the head of state, the first among equals.

Jackson also took a dim view of the claim that the Supreme Court exercised the final and absolute right to determine the meaning of the Constitution. When the court decided in *McCulloch vs. Maryland* that the law establishing a national bank was constitutional, Jackson disagreed. In his veto of a bill to recharter the Second National Bank in 1832, he claimed among other things that the bill lacked authority under the Constitution, despite what the high court had decided. Both the House and the Senate, as well as the president, he continued, must decide for themselves what is and what is not constitutional before taking action on any bill. The representatives of Congress ought not to vote for a bill, and the president ought not to sign it, if they, in their own good judgment, believe it unconstitutional. "It is as much the duty of the House of Representatives, of the Senate, and of the President to decide upon the constitutionality of any bill or resolution which may be presented to them for passage or approval as it is of the supreme judges when it may be brought before them for judicial decision." Jackson did not deny the right of the Supreme

Jackson took a dim view of the claim that the Supreme Court has the final right on the meaning of the Constitution.

Court to judge the constitutionality of a bill. What he denied was the presumption that the Court was the final or exclusive interpreter of the Constitution. All three branches should rule on the question of constitutionality, Jackson argued. In this way the equality and independence of each branch of government is maintained. "The authority of the Supreme Court," he declared, "must not, therefore, be permitted to control the Congress, or the Executive when acting in their legislative capacities, but to have only such influence as the force of their reasoning may deserve." What bothered Jackson was the presumption that four men could dictate what 15 million people may or may not do under their constitutional form. To Jackson's mind that was not democratic but oligarchic. But that was precisely the intention of the Founding Fathers: to provide a balanced mix of democratic, oligarchic, and monarchical forms in the Constitution.

Of course Jackson was merely expressing his own opinion about the right of all three branches to pass on the constitutionality of all legislation, an opinion the American people ultimately rejected. The great fear in a democratic system—one the Founding Fathers knew perfectly well—was the danger of the majority tyrannizing the minority. Jackson would take his chances. He believed the American people were virtuous and would always act appropriately. "I for one do not despair of the republic," he wrote. "I have great confidence in the virtue of a great majority of the people, and I cannot fear the result. The republic is safe, the main pillars [of] virtue, religion and morality will be fostered by a majority of the people." But not everyone shared Jackson's optimism about the goodness of the electorate. And in time—particularly with the passage of the Fourteenth Amendment—it fell to the courts to guard and maintain the rights of the minority.

Jackson summed up his assertion of presidential rights by declaring that he alone—not Congress, as was usually assumed—was the sole representative of the American people and responsible to them. After defeating Henry Clay in the 1832 election, he decided to kill the Second National Bank by removing federal deposits because, as he said, he had received a "mandate" from the people to do so. The Senate objected and formally censured him, but Jackson, in response, merely issued another statement on presidential rights and the democratic system that had evolved over the last few years.

By law, only the secretary of the treasury was authorized to remove the deposits, so Jackson informed his secretary, William Duane, to carry out his order. Duane refused pointblank. And he also refused to resign as he had promised if he and the president could not agree upon a common course of action with respect to the deposits. Thereupon, Jackson sacked him. This was the first time a cabinet officer had been fired, and there was some question whether the president had this authority. After all, the cabinet positions were created by Congress and appointment required the consent of the Senate. Did that not imply that removal also required senatorial consent—particularly the treasury secretary, since he handled public funds that were controlled by Congress? The law creating the Treasury Department never called it an "executive" department, and it required its

secretary to report to the Congress, not the president. None of this made a particle of difference to Andrew Jackson. All department heads were *his* appointees and they would obey *him* or pack their

Jackson declared that he alone—not Congress—was the sole representative of the American people.

bags. The summary dismissal of Duane was seen by Jackson's opponents as a presidential grab for the purse strings of the nation. And in fact presidential control over all executive functions gave the chief executive increased authority over the collection and distribution of public funds.

THE JACKSONIAN REVOLUTION

By the close of 1833 many feared that Andrew Jackson was leading the country to disaster. Henry Clay regularly pilloried the president on the Senate floor. On one occasion he accused Jackson of "open, palpable and daring usurpation" of all the powers of government. "We are in the midst of a revolution," Clay thundered, "hitherto bloodless, but rapidly tending towards a total change of the pure republican character of the Government."

A "revolution"—that was how the opposition Whig Party characterized Jackson's presidency. The nation was moving steadily away from its "pure republican character" into something approaching despotism. What the nation was witnessing, cried Clay, was "the concentration of all power in the hands of one man." Thereafter Whig newspapers reprinted a cartoon showing Jackson as "King Andrew the First." Clad in robes befitting an emperor, he was shown wearing a crown and holding a scepter in one hand and a scroll in the other on which was written the word "veto."

Democrats, naturally, read the "revolution" differently. They saw it as the steady progress of the country from the gentry republic originally established by the Founding Fathers to a more democratic system that mandated broader representation in government and a greater responsiveness to popular will.

Andrew Jackson did not take kindly to Clay's verbal mauling. "Oh, if I live to get these robes of office off me," he snorted at one point, "I will bring the rascal to a dear account." He later likened the senator to "a drunken man in a brothel," reckless, destructive, and "full of fury."

Other senators expressed their opposition to this "imperial" president and seconded Clay's complaints. John C. Calhoun, who by this time had deserted to the enemy camp, adopted the Kentuckian's "leading ideas of revolution" and charged that "a great effort is now making to choke and stifle the voice of American liberty." And he condemned Jackson's insistence on taking refuge in democratic claims. The president "tells us again and again with the greatest emphasis," he continued, "that he is the immediate representative of the American people! What effrontery! What boldness of assertion! Why, he never received a vote from the American people. He was elected by electors . . . who are elected by Legislatures chosen by the people."

Sen. Daniel Webster and other Whigs chimed in. "Again and again we hear it said," rumbled Webster, "that the President is responsible to the American people! . . . And this is thought enough for a limited, restrained, republican government! . . . I hold this, Sir, to be a mere assumption, and dangerous assumption." And connected with this "airy and unreal responsibility to the people," he continued, "is another sentiment . . . and that is, that the President is the direct representative of the American people." The sweep of his language electrified the Senate. And "if he may be allowed to consider himself as the sole representative of all the American people," Webster concluded, "then I say, Sir, that the government . . . has already a master. I deny the sentiment, and therefore protest against the language; neither the sentiment nor the language is to be found in the Constitution of this Country."

Jackson's novel concept that the president served as the people's tribune found immediate acceptance by the electorate, despite the warnings of the Whigs. In effect, he altered the essential character of the presidency. He had become the head of government, the one person who would formulate national policy and direct public affairs. Sighed Senator Benjamin W. Leigh of Virginia: "Until the President developed the faculties of the Executive power, all men thought it infe-

rior to the legislature—he manifestly thinks it superior: and in his hands [it] . . . has proved far stronger than the representatives of the States."

JACKSON INTERPRETED

From Jackson's own time to the present, disagreement and controversy over the significance of his presidency has prevailed. In the twentieth century the disagreements intensified among historians. Confusion over the meaning of Jacksonian Democracy, varying regional support for democratic change, and the social and economic status of the Democrats and Whigs have clouded the efforts of scholars to reach reliable conclusions about the Old Hero and the era that bears his name.

That Andrew Jackson can still generate such intense partisan feeling is evidence of his remarkable personality.

Andrew Jackson himself will always remain a controversial figure among historians. That he can still generate such intense partisan feeling is evidence of his remarkable personality. He was an aggressive, dynamic, charismatic, and intimidating individual. And although modern scholars and students of history either admire or dislike him intensely, his rating as president in polls conducted among historians over the past thirty years varies from great to near great. He carries an enormous burden in winning any popularity contest because of his insistence on removing the eastern Indians west of the Mississippi River and on waging a long and vicious war against the Second National Bank of the United States.

His first biographer, James Parton, wrote a three-volume *Life of Andrew Jackson* (1859, 1860), and came away with mixed feelings about the man and his democracy. At times Parton railed against the mindless mob "who could be wheedled, and flattered, and drilled," but at other times he extolled democracy as the mark of an enlightened society. What troubled Parton particularly was

the spoils system. Rotation, he wrote, is "an evil so great and so difficult to remedy, that if all his other public acts had been perfectly wise and right, this single feature of his administration would suffice to render it deplorable rather than amiable."

William Graham Sumner's *Andrew Jackson* (1882) was relentlessly critical of his subject, deploring in particular Jackson's flawed moral charter and emotional excesses. Sumner and other early historians, such as Herman von Holst and James Schouler, constituted what one student of the Jacksonian age called a "liberal patrician" or "Whig" school of history. These individuals came from European middle- or upper middle-class families with excellent backgrounds of education and public service. Because their class had been ousted from political power, these historians were biased against Jacksonian Democracy, and their books reflect their prejudice.

The interpretation of Old Hickory and his adherents took a sharp about-face with the appearance in 1893 of the vastly influential article by Frederick Jackson Turner, "The Significance of the Frontier in American History." Turner argued that American democracy emerged from the wilderness, noting that universal white manhood suffrage guaranteed by the new western states became something of a model for the older, eastern states. Naturally Jackson and his followers were seen as the personification of this frontier democracy. The thesis was advanced and sometimes amplified by Charles A. Beard, Vernon L. Parrington, and other western and southern historians of the early twentieth century who were caught up in the reform movement of the Progressive era. They dubbed the Jacksonian revolution an age of egalitarianism that produced the rise of the common man. Jackson himself was applauded as a man of the people. Thus the liberal patrician school of historiography gave way to the Progressive school.

This interpretation dovetailed rather well with the views of Tocqueville. During his visit, Tocqueville encountered a widespread belief in egalitarianism but worried that majoritarian rule could endanger minority rights. There are so many sharp and accurate insights into American society and institutions in *Democracy in America* that it ought to be the first book anyone reads in attempting to understand the antebellum period of

American history. Among other things, he catches the American just as he is emerging from his European and colonial past and acquiring many of the characteristics of what are generally regarded as typically American today.

Tocqueville's democratic liberalism, augmented by the works of the Progressive historians—especially Turner, Beard and Parrington—dominated historical thought about the American past for the next fifty years or more. Almost all the Progressive historians stressed the role of geographic sections in the nation, and Turner at one point even denied any class influence in the formation of frontier democracy. The only important negative voice concerning Jackson during this period came from Thomas P. Abernethy, whose *From Frontier to Plantation in Tennessee: A Study in Frontier Democracy* (1932) insisted that Jackson himself was a frontier aristocrat, an opportunist, and a land speculator who strongly opposed the democratic forces in his own state of Tennessee.

The virtual shattering of the Progressive school's interpretation of Jacksonian Democracy came with the publication of one of the most important historical monographs ever written concerning American history: *The Age of Jackson* (1945), by Arthur M. Schlesinger, Jr. This classic work virtually rivals in importance the frontier thesis of Frederick Jackson Turner. It is a landmark study and represents the beginning of modern scholarship on Jackson and his era.

Schlesinger argued that class distinctions rather than sectional differences best explain the phenomenon of Jacksonian Democracy. He interpreted Jackson's actions and those of his followers as an effort of the less fortunate in American society to combat the power and influence of the business community. The working classes in urban centers as well as the yeoman farmers, he argued, were the true wellsprings of the Jacksonian movement. Jacksonian Democracy evolved from the conflict between classes and best expressed its goals and purposes in the problems and needs facing urban laborers. Schlesinger singled out the bank war as the most telling example of the conflict and as the fundamental key to a fuller understanding of the meaning of Jacksonian Democracy. What attracted many historians to this path-breaking study, besides its graceful and majestic style, was Schlesinger's

perceptive definition of Jacksonian Democracy and a precise explanation of its origins.

The reaction to Schlesinger's work was immediate and dramatic. It swept the historical profession like a tornado, eliciting both prodigious praise and, within a relatively short time, fierce denunciations. Bray Hammond, in a series of articles as well as his *Banks and Politics in America from the Revolution to the Civil War* (1957), and Richard Hofstadter, in his *The American Political Tradition and the Men Who Made It* (1948), contended that the Jacksonians were not the champions of urban workers or small farmers but rather ambitious and ruthless entrepreneurs principally concerned with advancing their own economic and political advantage. They were "men on the make" and frequently captains of great wealth. According to Hofstadter, the Jacksonians were not so much hostile to business as they were hostile to being excluded from entering the confined arena of capitalists. Where Schlesinger had emphasized conflict in explaining the Jacksonian era, Hofstadter insisted that consensus best characterized the period. The entrepreneurial thesis, as it was called, found strong support among many young scholars who constituted the Columbia University school of historians. In a series of articles and books produced by these critics, Jackson himself was described as an inconsistent opportunist, a strikebreaker, a shady land speculator, and a political fraud. Marvin Meyers, in his *The Jackson Persuasion* (1957), provides a slight variation on the entrepreneurial thesis by arguing that Jacksonians did indeed keep their eyes on the main chance but yearned for the virtues of a past agrarian republic. They hungered after the rewards of capitalism but looked back reverentially on the blessings of a simpler agrarian society.

A major redirection of Jacksonian scholarship came with the publication of Lee Benson's *The Concept of Jacksonian Democracy: New York as a Test Case* (1961). This work suggested a whole new approach to the investigation of the Jacksonian age by employing the techniques of quantification to uncover solid, factual data upon which to base an analysis. Moreover, Benson emphasized social questions and found that such things as ethnicity and religion were far more important than economics in determining how a person voted or which party won

his allegiance. He dismissed Jacksonian rhetoric about democracy and the rights of the people as "claptrap" and contended that local issues in elections meant more to the voters than national issues. Andrew Jackson himself was dismissed as unimportant in understanding the structure and meaning of politics in this period. In time, some college textbooks virtually eliminated Jackson from any discussion of this period except to mention that he opposed social reforms and that his removal of the Indians was one of the most heinous acts in American history.

An ethnocultural school of historical writing soon emerged that rejected class difference as an important factor in political determinism. German and Irish Catholics, for example, were more likely to vote Democratic because of their ethnicity and religion than anything else. Besides, some argued, Whigs were not materially richer than Democrats. Edward Pessen, in a series of books and articles, took the argument one step further and insisted that Jacksonian America was not particularly egalitarian in terms of wealth, as Tocqueville had stated. He rejected the argument that the common man politically came into his own during the Jacksonian age. In a nice turn of phrase concluding his *Jacksonian America: Society, Personality, and Politics* (1969), Pessen declared that there was only "*seeming* deference to the common man by the uncommon men [the rich and powerful] who actually ran things."

By the end of the 1970s the ethnocultural approach had quieted down and was replaced by newer kinds of social analyses, most particularly by cultural Marxists who reemphasized class conflict in understanding voter preference. Other historians took a different approach and sought to describe what might be called a "political culture" for the period. However, many of the insights of Benson and the other students of the ethnocultural school have been incorporated into the whole to form a more sophisticated analysis. Joel Silbey, Sean Wilentz, Harry L. Watson, and others have shown that the electorate normally develops a wide set of values based on class, religion, nationality, family, residence, and several other factors and then invariably votes to safeguard those values as they perceive them. Watson particularly has demonstrated by his study of North Carolina politics that national issues did in fact matter in general elections. Even Jackson has been somewhat restored to his former importance, if not his former heroic stature. My own three-volume life of Old Hickory, *Andrew Jackson and the Course of American Empire, 1767–1821; Andrew Jackson and the Course of American Freedom, 1822–1832; Andrew Jackson and the Course of American Democracy, 1833–1845* (1977, 1981, 1984) highlights Schlesinger's findings and Jackson's faith and commitment to liberty and democracy. I contend that Jackson was in fact a man of the people,

just as the Progressive historians had argued, and that he actively attempted to advance democracy by insisting that all branches of government, including the courts, reflect the popular will. I also tried to show that, for a number of reasons, the president's policy of Indian removal was initiated to spare the Indian from certain extinction. And Francis Paul Prucha has argued persuasively that Indian removal was probably the only policy possible under the circumstances.

The study of the Jacksonian era is

essential for any serious examination of the evolution of the American presidency. This has been widely recognized since the avalanche of articles and books triggered by the appearance of Schlesinger's monumental work. Jackson himself has never lost his ability to excite the most intense passions and interest among students of American history. No doubt scholars and popular writers will continue to debate his role as a national hero and as an architect of American political institutions.

"Texas Must Be Ours"

On the 150th anniversary of Texan independence, we trace the fierce negotiations that brought the republic into the Union after ten turbulent years

Robert V. Remini

Robert Remini, a professor of history at the University of Illinois at Chicago, won the American Book Award for Andrew Jackson and the Course of American Democracy.

From the moment he entered the White House in March 1829, Andrew Jackson of Tennessee turned a cold and calculating eye on Texas. Sitting in his study on the second floor of the mansion, maps strewn around the room, the white-haired, sharp-featured, cadaverous President breathed a passion for Texas that was soon shared by other Americans.

Old Hickory always believed—or so he said—that Texas had been acquired by the United States as part of the Louisiana Purchase in 1803 and then had been recklessly thrown away when "that old scamp J. Q. Adams" negotiated the Florida treaty with Spain in 1819 and agreed to the Sabine River as the western boundary of the country. The claim was questionable at the very least, but many Southerners, outraged by Northern reaction to the slavery issue during the debates over the admission of Missouri and

chagrined over the institution's prohibition in the Louisiana Territory north of 36° 30′, decided to press it anyway.

The loss of Texas by virtue of the Florida treaty dismayed some Americans. It infuriated Jackson. "How infatuated must have been our councils who gave up the rich country of Texas," he wrote. Such action, in his mind, verged on treason. And why had it happened? "It surely must have been with the view to keep the political ascendance in the North, and east," he fumed, "& cripple the rising greatness of the West." No matter. He would attend to it at the first opportunity. And indeed he did—or tried to. "I have long since been aware of the importance of Texas to the United States," he wrote a friend just a few months after taking office as President, "and of the real necessity of extending our boundary west of the Sabine. . . . I

shall keep my eye on this object & the first propitious moment make the attempt to regain the Territory as far south & west as the great Desert."

All his attempts at acquiring Texas proved feeble, however, mostly because he had assigned a freewheeling, fast-talking, double-dealing incompetent to represent the United States in Mexico. Col. Anthony Butler made numerous "diplomatic" efforts to purchase Texas from Mexico, and when those failed, he turned to bribery. "I have just had a very singular conversation with a Mexican," he wrote Jackson in October of 1833, and this Mexican "has much influence with the Presidt. Genl. St. Anna." The Mexican had bluntly asked Butler, "Have you command of Money?"

"Yes, I have money," Butler responded.

The price would be high, said the Mexican, in excess of half a million dollars. The Mexican himself required two or three hundred thousand, and Butler allowed that "there are others amongst whom it may become necessary to distribute 3 or 4 Hundred thousand more."

"Can you command that Sum?" the Mexican demanded.

"Yes," Butler assured him.

He was wrong. "I have read your confidential letter with care, and astonishment," a furious Jackson replied, " . . . astonishment that you would entrust such a letter, without being in cypher, to the mail." Moreover, wrote Jackson, he was astounded by Butler's presumption that "my instructions authorized you to apply to corruption, when nothing could be farther from my intention than to convey such an idea."

At length Jackson had to recall Butler. The President was discouraged not only by the diplomatic failure and the shady operations of his minister but also by the resistance of the Mexicans to his assurance that a "natural boundary" at the Rio Grande River would work to the mutual benefit of both nations. Such a boundary, Jackson insisted, would eliminate "collisions" that two peoples of "conflicting laws, habits and interests" were bound to have. Moreover, it would provide the Mexicans with needed cash to bolster their economy: the President was willing to go as high as five million dollars to purchase the territory. Failure of the sale was sure to encourage the many Americans who had moved to Texas over the previous ten years to establish an independent republic. And such a turn of events, the President feared, would sever that "crazy old man, John Quincy Adams." In the election, he won 170 electoral votes to Clay's 105. The popular vote was even closer: 1,337,243 to 1,299,062. Polk defeated Clay by a 1.4 percent margin. "A mere *Tom Tit,*" growled John Quincy Adams, had triumphed over the "old Eagle. The partial associations of Native Americans, Irish Catholics, abolition societies, liberty party, the Pope of Rome, the Democracy of the sword, and the dotage of a ruffian [Andrew Jackson] are sealing the fate of this nation, which nothing less than the interposition of Omnipotence can save."

Two months after Texas won her independence, the United States and Mexico were on the brink of war.

ARTS OF THE BOOK COLLECTION (WESTERN AMERICANA), YALE UNIVERSITY LIBRARY, NEW HAVEN, CONN.

YOUNG TEXAS IN REPOSE.

An abolitionist view of the new republic featured a murderous cowboy and his victim.

Between the time of his election and inauguration, Polk met several times with Jackson at the Hermitage. Old Hickory instructed his friend on the necessity of annexing Texas in order to "put to rest the vexing question of abolitionism, the dangerous rock to our Union, and put at defiance all combined Europe, if combined to invade us." But Polk needed no instruction. Upon his arrival in Washington, he was queried by many members of Congress about his plans and goals. "He is for Texas, Texas, Texas," reported Sen. Willie P. Mangum of North Carolina, "& talks of but little else."

The outgoing President, John Tyler, saw his opportunity to capitalize on Polk's victory, and he helped arrange a joint resolution of annexation for both houses of Congress. After considerable

politicking the House and Senate gave their approval, and Tyler signed the resolution on March 1, 1845, just three days before he was to leave office. A messenger was immediately dispatched to Texas with the "glorious" news.

"Texas is ours," trumpeted the newspapers. "The Union is safe." A feeble old man who had only a few months to live added his voice to the general acclaim. Andrew Jackson thanked God that he had lived to see this happy day. "I . . . congratulate my beloved country [that] Texas is reannexed," he wrote, "and the safety, prosperity, and the greatest interest of the whole Union is secured by this . . . great and important national act."

But others expressed more disturbing views. They feared that the admission of Texas would lead inevitably to war with Mexico and possibly civil war. And their direst predictions proved correct. Texas ratified annexation on July 4 and was admitted into the Union as a slave state on December 29, 1845. The following spring—on May 11, 1846—the United States declared war against Mexico. Later the North and South submitted their dispute over slavery to a frightful test of arms. Within twenty years the Union cracked apart, and to weld it back together did indeed take "oceans of blood & hundreds of millions of money." the "bonds of amity and good understanding" between the United States and Mexico.

Since the early 1820s, Americans had been migrating to Texas, particularly from the South and West. Motivated to a large extent by the hard times generated by the Panic of 1819, they sought relief in Texas because the Mexicans encouraged them to settle there. Led by Moses Austin and his son Stephen F., they established an American colony in Texas and accepted Mexican authority. Slave owners from Alabama, Mississippi, and Tennessee were particularly attracted to this haven. By 1830 over twelve thousand Americans had emigrated to Texas, and Mexico, alarmed, eventually prohibited all immigration from the north.

Many Texans desired immediate annexation by the United States, especially after 1829, when slavery was forbidden throughout Mexican territory. The blatant and hostile intentions of these Texans naturally provoked the Mexicans, and Jackson's fumbling efforts to purchase the territory only exacerbated an already worsening situation. Despite his passion for Texas, the President wanted neither war with Mexico nor domestic strife over the wisdom of adding what might become another slave state. Still, he would not abandon his dream of territorial expansion. "The boundary between the U. States and Mexico," he jotted into his private memorandum book, " . . . must be altered."

Jackson's apprehensions deepened when he learned that his old friend and protégé Sam Houston, late governor of Tennessee, had fled to Texas after a disastrous marriage and reportedly "would conquer Mexico or Texas, & be worth two millions in two years." These were the "efusions of a distempered brain," said Jackson; Houston would never place millions before the welfare of his country, but that did not guarantee a peaceful resolution to the problem.

Perhaps, given Mexico's stiff opposition to territorial dismemberment, no one in the United States possessed the diplomatic skill to bring about the peaceful acquisition of this valuable and strategically important landmass. But certainly Jackson botched what little chance he may have had by appointing Butler and then keeping him long after Jackson had reason to believe that his minister was a scoundrel. Gen. Antonio López de Santa Anna was convinced that the United States had acted dishonorably and had violated its neutrality laws by encouraging filibustering expeditions into Texas and by arming Americans to instigate revolution.

The failure of American diplomacy did indeed spur the Texans to take matters into their own hands. A war party was formed at the same time that the Mexican government was moving to centralize control over all parts of the Mexican republic, including Texas. The struggle for independence ignited in October 1835 and roared to its climax when General Santa Anna marched into Texas at the head of a five-thousand-man army. Texas proclaimed its independence on

March 2, 1836, and on April 21 a Texan army commanded by Sam Houston defeated Santa Anna at the Battle of San Jacinto. Santa Anna himself was captured and forced to sign a treaty (later repudiated) recognizing Texan independence.

No American doubted that annexation by the United States would soon follow. Some Texans might have preferred to remain a republic, but probably many more desired eventual statehood.

The Mexican minister to the United States, Manuel Eduardo de Gorostiza, peppered President Jackson with angry protests. He raged against American treachery and ultimately demanded his passports. Relations between Mexico and the United States rapidly deteriorated, and within two months it appeared that war between the two countries would break out momentarily. The secretary of the Navy, Mahlon Dickerson, reported at a cabinet meeting that Com. Alexander J. Dallas had notified him that the American consul and residents at Tampico had suffered innumerable "indignities" at the hands of Mexican authorities. Moreover, American armed vessels in the area had been refused water, and their officers had been denied permission to go ashore. Worse, these authorities had threatened to put to death all Americans in Tampico in retaliation for the capture of Santa Anna.

Dickerson concluded his report. Benjamin Butler, in a letter to his wife, explained what happened next. Jackson "broke out in his most impassioned manner." He jumped to his feet, gesticulated wildly, and shook his fist at invisible enemies. It was one of the most frightening displays of the President's anger that the cabinet had ever witnessed. The members sat frozen, staring; nobody dared interrupt the wild outburst.

Then, wrote Butler, Old Hickory barked, "Write immediately to Commodore Dallas & order him to *blockade* the harbour of Tampico, & to suffer nothing to enter till they allow him to land and obtain his supplies of water & communicate with the Consul, & if they touch the hair of the head of one of our citizens, tell him *to batter down & destroy their town & exterminate the inhabitants from the face of the earth!*"

The cabinet sucked in its collective breath, but said nothing. Could he be serious?

Finally, Jackson addressed his secretary of state, John Forsyth. "Have you recd any information on this subject?"

Forsyth shook his head.

"Then let the Secy of the Navy furnish you the papers," Jackson ordered, "& do you write immediately to Mr. Gorostiza informing him of the orders we have given to Commodore Dallas, & that we shall not permit a jot or tittle of the treaty to be violated, or a citizen of the United States to be injured without taking immediate redress."

FORTUNATELY, COOLER HEADS ON BOTH sides prevented the extermination of the citizens of Tampico, but American-Mexican relations continued to deteriorate: Texans were doing everything possible to force U.S. recognition of their independence and eventual annexation. Commissioners dispatched to lobby in Washington were all warmly received by the President. During one such meeting Jackson turned to Special Commissioner Samuel Carson and said, "Is it true, Mr. Carson, that your Government has sent Santa Anna back to Mexico?" Carson responded that Santa Anna was indeed expected to depart shortly to assist in winning ratification of the treaty recognizing the independence of Texas.

"Then I tell you, Sir," said Jackson, "if ever he sets foot on Mexican ground, your Government may whistle; he, Sir, will give you trouble, if he escapes, which you dream not of."

Then there would be war, Carson said.

"Where is your means, Sir, to carry on an offensive war against Mexico?"

"In the enthusiasms of the American people," said Carson happily, "their devotion to the cause of Liberty are the ways and means, to defray the expenses of the War."

Jackson blanched. It was one thing for the President of the United States to threaten war, quite another for "outsiders" from Texas to presume they could manipulate this country into one. The United States had a treaty with Mexico, and the annexation of Mexican territory would most certainly be viewed around the world as a betrayal. Civilized countries would label it a brutal and aggressive act, a violation of the "law of nations." The "Texians," as Jackson frequently called them, must realize that annexation would take time and careful planning. Thus, when Stephen F. Austin sent him an impassioned letter requesting assistance, Jackson wrote the following endorsement: "[Austin] does not reflect that we have a treaty with Mexico, and our national faith is pledged to support it. The Texians before they took the step to declare themselves Independent, which has aroused and united all Mexico against them ought to have pondered well, it was a rash and premature act. Our neutrality must be faithfully maintained."

And there were other problems. Abolitionists, for one. These troublemakers would exploit any issue to attack slavery, said Jackson, even if it ruptured relations between North and South. They intended to oppose the admission of Texas because it represented the continued expansion of slavery. Texas, therefore, posed a possible threat to the Union, which hobbled Jackson's efforts to negotiate a swift treaty of admission. His passion for Texas could never match his passion for the Union. "Prudence," he later wrote, seemed to dictate that "we should stand aloof" and see how things would develop. No doubt he was also fearful of jeopardizing the election of his hand-picked successor to the Presidency, Martin Van Buren.

At this juncture Sam Houston decided to send Santa Anna to Washington to meet Jackson in the hope that their talks together would help the cause of Texas annexation. Houston released the Mexican, presented him with a handsome horse, and headed him (under armed escort) to the capital. Santa Anna arrived on January 17, 1837.

At the moment, Old Hickory was recovering from a severe "hemorrhage of the lungs" that had almost ended his life. For months he remained in his room, not daring to expose himself to a relapse by needless movement around the White House. In fact, he left his room only four times during the final six months of his administration. Still, on state occasions,

Jackson could muster great presence and exude the appearance of enormous strength. For his part, Santa Anna, despite his long trip, looked refreshed and relaxed. He was amused and rather pleased by the notoriety that his arrival in the capital had provoked. Many assumed he would look malevolent. They

> *Jackson believed passionately that national safety rested on acquiring Texas "peaceably if we can, forcibly if we must."*

were surprised to find him a gracious and cultivated man of impeccable manners and dress.

On Thursday, January 19, 1837, the Mexican general was escorted into the presence of the American general at the White House. The two men greeted one another politely and with a degree of dignified reserve. Always the gentleman, Old Hickory assured his guest that he was most welcome in Washington and expressed pleasure in meeting him at long last. "General Andrew Jackson greeted me warmly," Santa Anna later wrote, "and honored me at a dinner attended by notables of all countries." Jackson treated him not as an enemy but as a head of state, even though Santa Anna had been succeeded in Mexico by Anastasio Bustamante.

The official greeting, reception, and dinner went extremely well, but the conversations involved nothing of substance. Not until the following day did the two men turn to the matter that had brought them together.

Santa Anna began by proposing the cession of Texas for a "fair consideration." The United States, responded Jackson, could do nothing about a cession until the "disposition of the Texians" was resolved. "Until Texas is acknowledged independent," said the President, this nation could make no official move. At some point in the conversation, Jackson outlined a proposal for the Mexican to take back to his

Texas rolls into the Union in one of the era's teeming political cartoons: as Houston waves the Lone Star flag, President Polk welcomes his new state from the federal shore.

country. Beginning with the supposition that Mexico would officially acknowledge the independence of Texas at some point early on, Jackson suggested that the boundary of the United States be extended to include Texas and northern California—in effect, this would run the "line of the U. States to the Rio grand—up that stream to latitude 38 north & then to the Pacific including north California." In return the United States would compensate Mexico with $3,500,000. "But before we promise anything," Jackson continued, "Genl Santana must say that he will use his influence to suspend hostilities." The President assured his visitor that the principal objective of the United States was not territorial acquisition or the further embarrassment of the Mexican Republic, but rather to "secure peace & tranquility on our respective borders & lay the foundation of a permanent tranquility between the U.S. and Mexico."

The interview ended on a polite but indefinite note. President Jackson provided Santa Anna with a warship to carry him to Veracruz, and the Mexican had nothing but gratitude for his treatment.

A little later Jackson mentioned his conversation with Santa Anna to William Wharton, recently arrived in Washington to represent Texas. Wharton protested: Texan independence was an accomplished fact achieved through her own military power, and Mexico had no right to make a treaty that in any way bound her. What the United States must do, insisted Wharton, was to recognize Texan independence; then the nation could move on to the question of possible annexation.

Jackson grimaced. Perhaps, suggested the President to Wharton, as a way of quieting the sectional rivalry that recognition was sure to provoke, Texas might claim California in order to "paralyze" Northern opposition to annexation. Acquisition of California along with Texas meant the continuation of representational balance in the Senate between free and slave states. The suggestion did not elicit much enthusiasm from Wharton. Texas could never legitimately claim California or undertake a war to assert its

claim. California was simply not on the negotiating table.

Congress, however, responded to the wishes of the "Texians" without grappling with the sectional consequences and, during the final days of Jackson's administration, recognized the independence of the Texas Republic. The President quickly appointed Alcée Louis La Branche of Louisiana as chargé d'affaires to Texas, and the Senate confirmed the nomination only hours before the final adjournment of Congress. Around midnight, when word came that La Branche had been confirmed, Jackson met with Wharton and a few others to celebrate. They lifted their glasses in a single toast: Texas!

But Jackson returned home defeated in his one great effort to reach the Rio Grande. He rightly feared his failure might jeopardize the integrity and tranquillity of the Union.

The more he thought about it, as he sat in his study at the Hermitage reading the reports that arrived from Washington, the more he convinced himself that the security of the United States demanded the acquisition of Texas. Never mind the machinations of abolitionists. They were nothing compared with the danger posed by foreign enemies: Great Britain, for example.

IF BRITAIN SHOULD DECIDE TO REENTER the continent through Texas and attempt a linkup with Canada, then war would be inevitable. "The safety of the republic being the supreme law, and Texas having offered us the key to the safety of our country from all foreign intrigues and diplomacy," Jackson wrote, "I say accept the key . . . and bolt the door at once." If England concluded an alliance with the "Texians"—which seemed under way at that very moment—then she would most likely move "an army from canady, along our western frontier," march through Arkansas and Louisiana, seize New Orleans, "excite the negroes to insurrection," "arouse the Indians on our west to war," and "throw our whole west into flames that would cost oceans of blood & hundreds of millions of money to quench, & reclaim. . . ." As

he wrote these words, Jackson worked himself into a passion. "Texas must be ours," he raged. "Our safety requires it." Later he repeated his demand with a little less passion but with the same determination. We must have Texas, "peaceably if we can, forcibly if we must."

Despite strong Northern pressure, the new President, John Tyler, obtained a treaty of annexation signed by representatives of Texas and the United States in April 1844 and submitted it to the Senate for ratification. It was accompanied by an extraordinary letter to the British minister to Washington, Richard Pakenham, written by the secretary of state, John C. Calhoun. In it Calhoun contended that the treaty had been signed for the express purpose of protecting American slavery from British attempts to bring about universal emancipation. The extension of the American slave interests into Texas, he said, would nullify that "reprehensible" goal.

Friends of annexation groaned when they read copies of Calhoun's provocative letter. The secretary had placed annexation "*exclusively* upon the ground of *protection* of *Slavery* in the *Southern States*!" and the senators from the nonslaveholding states who favored annexation were furious because "it would be death to them, politically, if they were to vote for the Treaty based on such principles."

Why had Calhoun done it? Why had he jeopardized the treaty by the gratuitous mention of slavery? Maj. William B. Lewis, one of Jackson's oldest friends, claimed to know. The secretary of state meant to kill the treaty, he wrote, in order to "drive off every Northern man from the reannexation" and thereby give him a "pretext to unite the whole South upon himself as the Champion of its cause." But simply, he meant to divide the Union, create a Southern confederacy, and make himself the "great man of this fragment which he expects to tear from the embrace of our glorious Govt." Like abolitionists, Lewis added, Southern hotheads were determined to disrupt the Union to achieve their own selfish objectives. Unfortunately, Texas had become a pawn in the fatal game of personal ambition. As far as Jackson was concerned, between "that arch fiend, J. Q. Adams" and that "*Cateline,* John C. Calhoun, they were tearing the Union apart.

So the treaty failed. And shortly thereafter the ostensible Whig and Democratic candidates for the Presidency in the next election, Henry Clay and Martin Van Buren, publicly announced their opposition to annexation. Clay (himself a slave owner) regarded annexation as dangerous to the country because it might provoke a war with Mexico, excite sectional passions over slavery, and prove financially disastrous, since the $10 million Texas debt would have to be assumed by the United States. Van Buren was especially concerned over the sectional rancor and possibility of war.

Jackson "shed tears of regret" when he read the letter of his old friend Martin Van Buren. "I would to god I had been at Mr. V. B. elbow when he closed his letter. I would have brought to his view *the proper conclusion.*" The only course of action left was to dump Van Buren as a presidential candidate and nominate someone else, someone who "is an annexation man," he wrote, "and from the Southwest." Other Democrats agreed, and at the national nominating convention in Baltimore, they "arranged" to replace Van Buren with James K. Polk.

Clay and Polk ran a close race. Among other things, Polk promised to "reannex" Texas, claiming like Jackson that it was part of the Louisiana Purchase and had been shamefully surrendered by that "crazy old man, John Quincy Adams." In the election, he won 170 electoral votes to Clay's 105. The popular vote was even closer: 1,337,243 to 1,299,062. Polk defeated Clay by a 1.4 percent margin. "A mere *Tom Tit,*" growled John Quincy Adams, had triumphed over the "old Eagle. The partial associations of Native Americans, Irish Catholics, abolition societies, liberty party, the Pope of Rome, the Democracy of the sword, and the dotage of a ruffian [Andrew Jackson] are sealing the fate of this nation, which nothing less than the interposition of Omnipotence can save."

Between the time of his election and inauguration, Polk met several times with Jackson at the Hermitage. Old Hickory instructed his friend on the necessity of annexing Texas in order to "put to rest the vexing question of abolitionism, the dangerous rock to our Union, and put at defiance all combined Europe, if combined to invade us." But Polk needed no instruction. Upon his arrival in Washington, he was queried by many members of Congress about his plans and goals. "He is for Texas, Texas, Texas," reported Sen. Willie P. Mangum of North Carolina, "& talks of but little else."

The outgoing President, John Tyler, saw his opportunity to capitalize on Polk's victory, and he helped arrange a joint resolution of annexation for both houses of Congress. After considerable politicking the House and Senate gave their approval, and Tyler signed the resolution on March 1, 1845, just three days before he was to leave office. A messenger was immediately dispatched to Texas with the "glorious" news.

"Texas is ours," trumpeted the newspapers. "The Union is safe." A feeble old man who had only a few months to live added his voice to the general acclaim. Andrew Jackson thanked God that he had lived to see this happy day. "I . . . congratulate my beloved country [that] Texas is reannexed," he wrote, "and the safety, prosperity, and the greatest interest of the whole Union is secured by this . . . great and important national act."

But others expressed more disturbing views. They feared that the admission of Texas would lead inevitably to war with Mexico and possibly civil war. And their direst predictions proved correct. Texas ratified annexation on July 4 and was admitted into the Union as a slave state on December 29, 1845. The following spring—on May 11, 1846—the United States declared war against Mexico. Later the North and South submitted their dispute over slavery to a frightful test of arms. Within twenty years the Union cracked apart, and to weld it back together did indeed take "oceans of blood & hundreds of millions of money."

Not Really Greek

Roger Kennedy's new book questions time-honored views of a favorite architectural style

With two sentences that could well change the way many of us look at architecture, Roger G. Kennedy begins his sixth book, *Greek Revival America:* "Architecture is always a public utterance. Willynilly, it conveys ideas." This book, "about the American Greek Revival, which flourished from 1825 to 1855," is generously illustrated with nearly two hundred splendid color photographs and thirty period illustrations (Stewart, Tabori and Chang, $85). In no sense, however, can it be considered a coffee-table or picture book. Kennedy's words—witty and urbane—are entirely too provocative to be overshadowed by mere photographs.

In the introduction, Kennedy, director of the Smithsonian's National Museum of American History, warns the reader that what he has to say is "not wholly conventional." After that he pulls no punches as he demolishes long-established notions about the style. "The American Greek Revival," he writes, "was not an expression of the founding fathers; it did not arise from any desire on their part to emulate the institutions of Greece or Rome. It was a statement on the part of their successors that was at once political and intimate, public and intensely private. It was often a party expression, and at the same time, it proceeded from the sexual anxieties of individuals."

Passages from Kennedy's introduction are reprinted in the pages that follow. Taken piecemeal, these quotations do not do justice to Kennedy's entire thesis, but from them the reader should be able to grasp at least one important point that the author emphasizes: "A few columns doth not a Greek Revival make." As this book well proves, architecture—and the ideas it conveys—does not lend itself to such easy categorization.

—*Michael S. Durham*

THE AMERICAN GREEK REVIVAL AROSE AS MANY AMERICAN MALES SENSED THE nation to be adrift after its heroic revolutionary accomplishments, and feared its centrifugal disorder. . . . The writings of the three decades before the Civil War are full of pride and—sometimes in the very same sentences—of remorse at disappointing the frugal expectations of the founders. Americans knew that they were engaged in a brash pursuit of riches, and they duly celebrated their successes. Yet they dutifully paid architectural tribute to two ideal societies, one ancient and distant, the other American and only a half century gone, both imagined as purer and worthier than their own, and left too quickly behind.

THE LARGEST, MOST AMBITIOUS, AND most sophisticated houses built during the Greek Revival, and the best of its cottages, are known to us by the names of their owners, not those of their architects. Though this does not mean their architects, or designers, were unimportant, it does indicate that the American Greek Revival was the social and political statement of a popular state of feeling as much as an aesthetic phenomenon.

PEOPLE WILLING TO EXTEND THEIR EXperience of New Jersey beyond the bogs, refuse barrens, and commuter suburbs that occupy its northeastern corner can discover that the Greek Revival flourished as far as its opposite, northwest corner. This remote region is still remarkably rural, portions of it as serene as Vermont or Wisconsin. Flemington, for example, was the home of a master carpenter named Mahlon Fisher, who lined Main Street with Grecian houses and grew prosperous enough to put up

one of the largest for himself. His counterpart in Princeton, Charles Steadman, built seventy or more houses, forty of which remain, most of them Grecian, providing America's most complete ensemble of small-town, middle-class housing during the reign of the Greek Revival. None of them, taken alone, is memorable, but as a group they are unsurpassed.

IT IS IN SMALL TOWNS IN THE AMERICAN countryside that one can sense what was best in the Greek Revival period. These accomplishments are felt most poignantly in the old Northwest Territory, the region south of the Great Lakes and north of the Ohio that was consciously and articulately shaped by the founding fathers. There, after 1788, they set out to build a new society. Their second chance might redeem the first, which, five years after independence, was already frustrating their hopes. In the West they might start anew; with fresh materials they might form a better reality than that possible within the refractory original thirteen states, cluttered and clogged by unexpungible bad habits such as human slavery and an unsuitable appetite for European luxuries.

LIKE ALL THINGS AMERICAN, THE GREEK Revival was never, anywhere, "pure." It had too much to do, too much symbolic freight to carry, too many cultural pressures to accommodate. Along the California coast and in the Southwest, it actually revived the real Greece, from life rather than from archaeology. Dwellings that might appear to an Englishman to be strange admixtures of the Greek and Hispanic were, in fact, adaptations to a climate and terrain similar to those

Reprinted from *Americana*, February 1990, pp. 43-49.

encountered by the ancient Greeks. These were courtyard buildings, turned inward around patios, with fountains and colonnaded passageways leading directly to the interior rooms. This is how the Greeks actually lived—not in temples presenting columns and porticos to the world.

FEW READERS WILL GO ABOUT AMERICA with measuring devices to see how many times the diameter of a column must be repeated to reach its height, though distinguishing a Roman from a Greek form often does require calipers and tape. . . . Even without calipers, one can observe that Greek columns were stubbier than their Roman counterparts, and that American designers, from the eighteenth century onward, showed a marked tendency to attenuate even Roman forms. Americans also tended toward Roman siting: They, like the Romans, more often than not placed columns and whole buildings upon artificial elevated platforms. The Greeks created a sacred precinct around their temples, and when an elevation like the Acropolis provided such a precinct naturally, they rejoiced in it, but their earliest columns, in the Doric mode, were not platformed; they were baseless.

BEFORE A YANKEE TINKERER NAMED ELI Whitney exploded the cotton belt outward by inventing his gin, the western claims of Georgia and South Carolina, reaching all the way to the Mississippi,

had little attraction to those cultivating crops for sale to world markets. Moreover, this relatively unappealing terrain was already occupied by intelligent native agriculturists with no interest in world markets, whose military prowess had held the Europeans within seventy miles of the shore for a century and a half. Something extraordinary was needed to draw Americans into a long campaign to conquer the region and to bring it within the international market system. Whitney provided that something, and the Greek Revival belt of Georgia, Alabama, and Mississippi resulted.

THOMAS JEFFERSON DEVELOPED HIS taste wholly in disregard of the rediscovery of Greece. So did his beloved Palladio. Consequently, those portions of the United States, especially in the Jacksonian South, that took architectural cues from Jefferson and Jefferson's un-Hellenic Virginia never had a *Greek* Revival. . . . On the contrary, it was the *northern* tradition in American architecture that showed the benefits of the direct observation of the work of the Greeks. For this we can be grateful to such men as George Hadfield, Benjamin Henry Latrobe, Nicholas Biddle, Ithiel Town, and to scores of carpenter-builders who worked from Maine to Wisconsin.

WHEN THE FLOWERING OF NEW ENgland occurred, its ingenuity did not rush into architecture; it gently flowed, instead, toward the introverted arts, liter-

ature and philosophy. Antebellum Massachusetts was not bold in architecture, nor was South Carolina, nor Virginia. For a Roman Revival of a swaggering sort, one must look to Greater Tennessee; for a more Grecian Greek—and in the United States one cannot be too strict about such matters—the traveler turns to the Finger Lake region, the western slopes of Vermont, the coastal villages of Maine and Ohio, the riverbanks of Indiana, Wisconsin, Michigan, Minnesota, Connecticut, and Massachusetts.

THE IMPRESSION THAT THE FOUNDERS commenced a Greek Revival requires the compression to the twinkling of an eye of a "classical lag" that actually lasted three decades, during which there was no Greek Revival. Nonetheless, some twentieth-century rewriters have depicted them as swept away by a "cult of Greek democracy, and housed accordingly."

CONTRARY TO A ONCE FASHIONABLE NOtion, the founding fathers were not eager to copy from the ancients either the government they founded or the buildings they erected. They had been *too* well trained in the classics to have emulated the practices of antiquity in any field. They knew too much. . . . As a result, they did not choose to emulate either Greek or Roman political institutions, for their thorough understanding of the experience of the ancients left them with few illusions. "Greek democracy" and the Roman "Republic" offered a catalog of experiences to avoid.

Legacy of Violence

Sociologists continue to be vexed by the pathology of urban violence: Why is it so random, so fierce, so easily triggered? One answer may be found in our Southern past.

Edward L. Ayers

Edward L. Ayers, an associate professor of history at the University of Virginia, is the author of Vengeance and Justice: Crime and Punishment in the 19th-Century American South *(Oxford, 1984) and is writing a history of the South in the three decades following Reconstruction.*

A jostle, a slightly derogatory remark, or a potential weapon in the hands of an adversary means something to many poor blacks and whites it does not mean to the middle and upper classes, some criminologists argue. "A male is usually expected to defend the name and honor of his mother, the virtue of womanhood . . . and to accept no derogation about his race (even from a member of his own race), his age, or his masculinity," write the sociologists Marvin Wolfgang and Franco Ferracuti. On the streets of our major cities, young men must guard against attacks on their status or demeaning words or glances. Fights over matters of pride seem to come easily and on occasion end in death.

This violence, while obviously fueled by the desperate poverty and bleak hopes of many young people, appears to have roots that stretch deep into America's past, into the world of the colonial era and the Old South and beyond there into the Britain of the seventeenth and eighteenth centuries. A culture of violence grew luxuriantly in the hothouse atmosphere of the slave South. Slave-owners cultivated the most self-conscious version of this culture, but the values flourished at all levels of white society and even took hold among blacks in slavery. After the Civil War and emancipation, this culture began to die from the top down, fading among the gentry even as it remained strong among poorer whites

and blacks. Fed by the weakness and perceived injustice of the law, the culture of violence grew in the cities and towns of the New South and followed Southerners of both races into their new homes in the twentieth-century North. Black and white Southerners from the 1830s or 1870s would understand the values of those who most often turn to violence today, North and South.

Southern violence became legendary early in the new nation's history. One visitor in the 1790s, appalled at the brutal fighting and eye gougings he found in Maryland and Virginia, was "credibly assured" that farther south, in the Carolinas and Georgia, "the people are still more depraved in this respect than in Virginia." An Englishman visiting those more southerly states several years later found the violence far bloodier and more widespread than he had expected: "The eye is not the only feature which suffers on these occasions. Like dogs and bears, they use their teeth and feet, with the most savage ferocity, upon each other."

Another traveler, Elkanah Watson, witnessed the affairs of honor within the lower class. At a Virginia courthouse on election day in 1778, Watson watched "a fight between two very unwieldy, fat men, foaming and puffing like two furies, until one succeeded in twisting his forefinger in a side-lock of the other's hair, and was in the act of thrusting, by this purchase, his thumb into his adversary's eye, when he bawled out 'King's cruse,' equivalent, in technical language, to 'enough.' " Watson himself came "near being involved in a boxing-match" when he rebuffed "with little respect" an Irishman who wanted to swap horses. The immigrant from Ireland, his pride wounded, swore belligerently that the Englishman did not "trate him like a jintleman."

While backwoodsmen were brawling and disfiguring one another, planters and politicians solemnly faced each other on the dueling grounds. In 1826 a victorious duelist rushed to his fallen foe. "White, my dear fellow," he said quietly, "I am sorry for you." His bleeding opponent answered, "I do not blame you," and the two duelists clasped hands. The wounded man recovered, and the other was elected governor of Tennessee a few months later. A student wrote home that college life in Virginia presented certain dangers: "Challenges are continually passing; fights are had almost every day." Another student assured concerned faculty members that the bowie knife he carried would be used only "against a person who should insult him and refuse to give him honorable satisfaction."

Every statistical index corroborates this eyewitness testimony. The South was far more violent than other parts of the United States from the earliest dates for which we have records. Even today a strong predictor of violence anywhere in the country is a heavy proportion of residents there who have a cultural tie to the South. Sociologists have long puzzled over the sources of the personal violence fistfights, shootings, stabbings—associated with the region. The complex answer has to begin with the Southern past.

Explanations for Southern violence have never been lacking. As early as the 1790s Thomas Jefferson observed that the unbridled authority wielded by slaveholders tended to breed impetuous behavior and shortness of temper, characteristics passed from one generation of masters to the next. Emily Burke, a New England schoolteacher who taught in Georgia in the 1840s, also located the origins of slaveholders' violence in the patterns of their upbringing: "At that tender age

From *American Heritage*, October 1991, pp. 102-109. Used with permission from *American Heritage*, a division of Forbes Inc.

when the earth is in its most plastic state, no attempts are made to subdue his (the Southerner's] will or control the passions, and the nurse, whether good or bad, often fosters in her bosom a little Nero, who is taught that it is manly to strike his nurse in the face in a fit of anger." The wife of a Georgia planter told C. G. Parsons that "slaveholders' children, instead of being taught to govern their tempers, are encouraged to indulge their passions; and, thus educated, they become the slaves of passion." But while slaveholders might act with impetuosity, they accounted for only one strand of Southern violence. Nonslaveholding whites were, if anything, more violent than their wealthier neighbors. There has to be more to the phenomenon.

The frontier's corrosive effect on the power of the law has often been offered as another explanation of Southern violence. The frontier, this argument runs, breeds lawlessness, and the frontier was, in effect, built into the South in the form of plantations. Our national mythology assumes violence to be a natural outgrowth of the frontier; the explanation seems almost commonsensical to most Americans. But in other British colonies, such as Canada and Australia, frontier challenges similar to those of the United States did not breed notoriously high levels of violence among the settlers. Moreover, recent studies of the American West and Midwest challenge the stereotypes of rampant violence on these frontiers as well. The violence that did erupt in Western cattle towns and on the open range in the post-Civil War years may well have been Southern violence transplanted, especially by way of Texas. If earlier Southern frontier areas did suffer from violence—and from all accounts, they did—then we need to look beyond the mere locale to explore the character of the people who lived and died there. Bloodshed was the product of a culture Southern frontiersmen brought with them, not something they found waiting in the wilderness. The frontier of the South did witness violence, but primarily because the frontier exaggerated cultural traits already in existence.

And those cultural traits bring us back to the explanations Southerners themselves gave. They said they fought for honor's sake. The word *honor*, though, now puts many of us on our guard. It is an anachronism and conjures up images as archaic as jousting knights or, in our own history, of aristocratic planters facing each other at dawn with leveled pistols. From the perspective of modern culture, honor that must continually be fought over has no resonance or meaning, when values antithetical to it rule. Middle-class children today are taught to shrug off insult, to avoid violence if at all possible. Yet, just as Southerners claimed, many of them recognized the dictates of honor, a system of values within which you have exactly as much worth as others confer upon you.

A society that is so concerned with the perceptions of others is also likely to be subject to extreme patterns of behavior. Contemporaries who described Southerners as gracious and hospitable described men who adhered to honorable conduct, but so did those who described Southerners as touchy and belligerent. Honor led people in the South to pay particular attention to manners, to ritualized evidence of respect. When that respect was not forthcoming between men, no matter how small or imagined the slight, satisfaction would be demanded by the offended party. The most common way of obtaining it was through fighting a duel, an "affair of honor."

But this most famous expression of Southern honor was merely the visible tip of the iceberg. In fact, the duel came to the South long after the code of honor; it was not until the 1770s, when English and French army officers made it the fashion within the American army, that duels appeared with any frequency in the New World. For a few decades Northerners as well as Southerners fought on the field of honor, but by 1830 dueling and the South had become virtually synonymous. By the last antebellum decade the South stood alone in the Anglo-American world in its toleration of dueling.

Because the lower boundary of the "aristocratic" class was poorly drawn in the early nineteenth century, especially on the cotton frontier of Alabama, Mississippi, Louisiana, Arkansas, and Texas, pretenders and outsiders sometimes persuaded themselves they could join the circle of the elect by fighting a duel. Timothy Flint, a Northerner who lived in the Mississippi Valley for many years, described how honor could become a commodity purchased with blood: "Many people without education and character, who were not gentlemen in the circles where they used to move, get accommodated here from the tailor with something of the externals of a gentleman, and at once set up in this newly assumed character. The shortest road to settle their pretensions is to fight a duel. Such are always ready for the combat." Fittingly enough, the published insult constituted the only American contribution to the ritual of the duel; the affronted party printed his "card" in a newspaper so that as many people as possible, including strangers, would know of his willingness to defend his honor—and know also that he possessed honor worthy of defense. An ambitious young man might make a name for himself just by challenging the right opponent in the fluid society of the Old Southwest.

Joseph G. Baldwin characterized with scorn and sarcasm the business of the courts of the cotton frontier of Alabama and Mississippi in the 1830s: "The major part of criminal cases, except misdemeanors, were for killing, or assaults with intent to kill. They were usually defended upon points of chivalry. The iron rules of British law were too tyrannical for free Americans, and too cold and unfeeling for the hot blood of the sunny south." A young lawyer from Alabama engaged in a revealing exchange with Alexis de Tocqueville, who asked: "Is it then true that the ways of the people of Alabama are as is said?"

"Yes. There is no one here but carries arms under his clothes. At the slightest quarrel, knife or pistol comes to hand. These things happen continually; it is a semi-barbarous state of society."

"But when a man is killed like that, is his assassin not punished?"

"He is always brought to trial, and always acquitted by the jury, unless there are greatly aggravating circumstances. . . . This violence has become accepted. Each juror feels that he might, on leaving the court, find himself in the same position as the accused, and he acquits."

The young lawyer then admitted that he too had fought, and exhibited four deep scars on his head. Tocqueville, incredulous, asked, " 'But you went to law?' . . . 'My God! No. I tried to give as good in return.' "

Honor did not reside only within the South's planter class. While some men faced each other under elaborate ritual on dueling grounds, many more combatants fought in obscure taverns and streets. The elite wrapped their violence in calm and detachment, directing one shot at their foes; the poor, on the other hand, gloried in boasting, improvisation, and inflicting as much damage as they could on their adversaries. Whatever the class of combatants, violence was not the product of mere impetuosity. It often began when men were stone sober, after a long period of frustration or series of conflicts. As one observer noted, "in by far the greater number of 'difficulties' it is known beforehand just what is about to happen, intimations of an impending struggle being whispered on the streets or in the country store, and everybody is listening for the reports of firearms that are to send one or more citizens into eternity." Southern violence possessed its own rules and unfolded on its own schedule.

White women played crucial roles in a society based on honor. A man who blustered his way into a duel might win honor among his male compatriots, but women would decide the full meaning of that honor. It was often women who defined the boundaries of who was and was not admitted to proper society, who determined whether a man's wife and family belonged. Many women refused to marry men who would not or could not defend their honor; no woman wanted to share in a dishonored name. And women's chastity and behavior played a crucial role in maintaining a family's honor, no matter how that honor had been won and no matter what class that family occupied.

Slavery constantly fed Southern honor among whites. It was slavery that systematically demeaned all black people, regardless of their character. It was slavery that inflated white people's sense of themselves, that allowed them to consider themselves benefactors, champions, and fathers to their slaves. It was slavery that allowed wealthy whites to consider themselves the heirs to the manners and pretensions of the English gentry. It was slavery that put violence and coercion behind moneymaking, that joined all white people in the domination of all black people. It was slavery that sealed off large parts of the South from the power of law, as slaveowners took the punishment of their slaves into their own hands.

Whites recognized no honor among slaves, but the slaves themselves refused to accept that. Without course to the power of the law, black men had no choice but to adjudicate conflicts among themselves. As a result, many of them, like many whites, turned to violence, display, boasting, and physical courage.

Some whites professed to be unable to understand the causes of violence among black men, but the descriptions of that violence bear a striking resemblance to descriptions of white-on-white bloodshed. One white wrote: "It is utterly confounding for what trivial causes they will take the life of a fellow-slave. Sometimes it is simply a dispute about a game of cards or marbles; sometimes the being supplanted by a rival in the confidence of the master or overseer is the exciting cause; but much more frequently jealousy leads to the fatal deeds."

Not infrequently, too, slaves of both sexes, pushed to the limit, assaulted white people, including their masters and mistresses. Violence might erupt when a young son of a master used his authority too arbitrarily, when a detested overseer pushed too violently against the wrong person, when a usually lenient owner asserted authority in an arbitrary or cruel way, when a widowed owner remarried and the new partner tried to wield authority unrecognized by the slaves. Honor, in other words, seems to have been working under the surface of slavery. Black Southerners turned to honor not out of imitation of their white owners but in enraged response to the capriciousness, inhumanity, and despair of the slavery in which they lived.

Things were increasingly different above the Mason-Dixon line. By the mid-nineteenth century the North had generated the core of a culture antagonistic to honor. Northerners could only shake their heads in disbelief at Southern violence. "About certain silly abstractions that no practical business man ever allows to occupy his time or attention, they are eternally wrangling," one observer wrote in the 1850s, "and thus it is that rencounters, duels, homicides, and other demonstrations of personal violence, have become so popular in all slaveholding communities." Northern culture, for its part, celebrated "dignity"—the conviction that at birth white males possessed an intrinsic value at least theoretically equal. In a culture of dignity men were expected to remain deaf to the same insults that Southern men were expected to resent. "Call a man a liar in Mississippi," an old saying went, "and he will knock you down; in Kentucky, he will shoot you; in Indiana, he will say 'You are another.' " Dignity might be likened to an internal skeleton, a hard structure at the center of the self; honor, on the other hand, resembles a cumbersome

and vulnerable suit of armor that, once pierced, leaves the self no protection and no alternative except to strike back in desperation.

The conflict between the rural cultures of North and South appeared in antebellum southern Illinois, where migrants from both regions settled. A Southerner who moved to Illinois recalled later that settlers from his native region scarcely saw notes, receipts, mortgages, or bonds until the Northerners arrived, and when the newcomers "sought to introduce their system of accounts, written notes, and obligations, they were looked upon with great suspicion and distrust, and their mode of doing business regarded as a great and unwarrantable innovation upon established usage." As one historian of the Midwest observes, "To the Southerner his own way of doing business affirmed confidence and personal honor. To the Yankee it was a lack of proper system, a sinful inefficiency." The Yankee settlers built schools and libraries and founded colleges and newspapers; the upland Southerners just got along. In fact, the Southerners were known among the Yankees primarily for "intemperance, profanity, and *fisticuffs* on all public days."

Both honor and dignity had roots in Old World cultures but developed new strains in the bracing environment of the New World. Almost from the very beginning a subtle and reinforcing sifting process created regional cultures in North America. Once British settlers arrived in America in the seventeenth and eighteenth centuries, they drew upon different elements of their diverse and changing culture as increasingly divergent economies led the Northern and Southern colonies farther and farther apart.

As they grew in power and wealth, the Southern gentry of the colonial era sustained the values of a proud and domineering English aristocracy, a class whose power and authority the Southerners planned to replicate in the New World. Honor and its violence were a part of the culture they regarded as their own, as the only culture worthy of emulation.

The violence of honor came to the South along other routes as well. Lower-class English and Scots-Irish emigrants carried to America expectations and tendencies of their own, and these soon combined with the aristocratic ideals of honor to spark violence on every level of colonial Southern society. Philip Vickers

Fithian, a tutor from New Jersey who kept a journal of his sojourn in Virginia in the 1770s, described the forms honor took among the common folk. One combatant might have offended another when he "has in a merry hour call'd him a *Lubber,* or a *thick-Skull,* or a *Buckskin,* or a *Scotchman,* or perhaps one has mislaid the other's hat, or knocked a peach out of his Hand, or offered him a dram without wiping the mouth of the Bottle; all these, and ten thousand more quite as trifling & ridiculous, are thought & accepted as just Causes of Immediate Quarrels, in which every diabolical Stratagem for Mastery is allowed and practised."

While Southern planters in the seventeenth and eighteenth centuries self-consciously modeled themselves on the English gentry, influential people in the North kept alive a sense of themselves directly and self-consciously opposed to worldly honor. Although the Puritans themselves faded away across the eighteenth century even in New England, aspects of their values endured to become known as the heart of the "Yankee" character. Where honor celebrated display, the ideal Puritan called for restraint. Where honor looked outward, the Puritans looked inward. Dignity also steadily gathered strength in the antebellum North because it was inextricably tied to the transformations of society and personality that accompanied the development and growth of a culture built around business. The ideal of the inherent value of the autonomous individual grew up simultaneously with the new ideals of character, of self-control, of discipline and delayed gratification that came to be the hallmark of the commercial middle class.

The North, however, was no more unanimous in its devotion to dignity than the South was in its devotion to honor. The various elements of dignity did not come together to form a coherent set of ideals until the 1830s, and even then dignity was constantly changing and growing. The spread of the gospel of dignity took on the dimensions of a crusade. Through educational and religious organizations, through publications and speaking tours, and through mass migration, New England colonized much of the North with the ideal.

Honor had its enemies in the South as well. From its earliest days evangelical Southern religion defined itself in opposition to the culture of honor. Not merely violence but the entire culture of display, ostentation, worldly hierarchy, sport, and amusement fell prey to its wrath.

Ministers urged women to help destroy the worldly and false system of values embodied in honor. "We would have every Christian young woman speak to these men of blood in the words of the patriarch, 'Instruments of cruelty are in their habitation. Oh! my soul come not thou into their secret,' " a Charleston pastor cried in the 1850s. "The mothers and daughters of Carolina are involved in a fearful responsibility on this subject. It is in their hands to stop this bloodshed, and in the name of God, I call upon them to do so."

Southern women embraced evangelicalism in ever-growing numbers and with ever-greater fervor throughout the nineteenth century. In a patriarchal society, piety gave women a system of belief that undermined the secular conception of females as mere bearers of children, household laborers, or mannequins of finery. Piety stressed woman's ability to discipline herself, to reject the world of fashion and prestige. The evangelical church gave women a new strength by offering them an autonomy found nowhere else, and in turn women constituted the church's greatest power. Honor increasingly became a male preserve.

Honor faced other enemies in the laws and courts. Honor and written laws against violence were incompatible, as the advice given to young Andrew Jackson by his mother reminded him: "The law affords no remedy that can satisfy the feelings of a true man." While honor reigned, a man who had taken the law into his own hands had little to fear from a jury. "Almost any thing made out a case of self-defense—a threat—a quarrel—an insult—going armed, as almost all the wild fellows did—shooting from behind a corner, or out of a store door, in front or from behind—it was all self-defense!" wrote Joseph G. Baldwin. And it usually really was self-defense, given the inexorable way insult bred violence. Even Sir William Blackstone, from whom Southern lawyers worshipfully learned their craft, admitted that honor was "a point of nature so nice and delicate that its wrongs and injuries escape the notice of the common law, and yet are fit to be redressed somewhere." That "somewhere" was the Southern dueling ground, tavern, and street.

In part it was the South's deep loyalty to honor that helped spawn secession and the Civil War. All the signals from the North—the abolitionists, John Brown's raid, the response to the Fugitive Slave Law, Lincoln's election—were read not merely for their overt political content but for their affront to Southern honor. White Southerners in 1860 did not feel they could in good conscience accept the North's apparent disregard for Southern rights and opinion. The states of the upper South refused to secede until they saw that Lincoln was calling up troops for South Carolina; considering themselves invaded, they joined the states of the Deep South that had seceded months earlier. Honor may even have shaped Southern strategy in the ensuing war, encouraging frontal assaults and other daring strategies instead of less glorious defensive maneuvers.

After the South's defeat, one thing remained constant. "Self-respect, as the Southerners understand it, has always demanded much fighting," a Connecticut native serving in the Freedmen's Bureau explained to fellow Northerners. "A pugnacity which is not merely war paint, but is, so to speak, tattooed into the character, has resulted from this high sentiment of personal value." As in the colonial and antebellum periods, all classes seemed touched with violence: "It permeates all society; it has infected all individualities. The meekest man by nature, the man who at the North would no more fight than he would jump out of a second story window, may at the South resent an insult by a blow, or perhaps a stab or pistol shot."

Nor was the pervasive violence confined to the turbulent years of Reconstruction. As late as the 1890s the bloodshed was still a sign of Southern distinctiveness. "People who have never visited the Southern States but only read of these deeds of violence, are not infrequently inclined to smile when the principals are referred to as 'members of prominent families' or 'leading citizens,' " a Southern writer admitted. But in fact, "farmers, merchants, bankers, physicians, lawyers, even ministers of the gospel, often slay their fellow-man in private warfare, and often after a mock trial are set at liberty, not only with no serious detriment to their reputation, but in many instances with increased popularity."

A few mannered duels still occurred in the South after Reconstruction, but dueling was increasingly eclipsed by less formalized and more deadly violence. Perhaps the mass slaughter of the Civil

War, the depersonalized and often senseless deaths in a losing cause, undermined Southerners' faith in ritualized violence. Perhaps, too, defeat forced members of the Southern elite to reconsider before ostentatiously engaging in a form of violence strictly reserved for an "aristocracy." Duelists who went upon the ground of battle "with all the hullaballoo and style imaginable," as one Georgia newspaper commented in 1889, "make themselves the laughing stock of the continent."

New avenues to respectability appeared in the South after the Civil War. Business now offered a legitimate and increasingly prestigious way to make a living, and there seemed little profit in a public ritual of bloodshed. One Southerner dreamed of a time when the values of business would purge the South of honor: in "the most highly civilized States . . . the foremost classes give little or no attention to enemies at all. . . . They do not care what any enemy says, and do not mind what he does, as long as he is not in debt to them. They keep up a disciplined police force to catch him and lock him up if he gets drunk, or threatens violence, or goes about calling names in the street." Another Southerner argued that "commerce has no social illusions" and that it would be commerce that would rid the region of "this historic, red-handed, deformed, and swaggering villain." As a Savannah newspaper put it, "In these modern times, character and honor depend upon a man's own life and conduct; not upon what another may say of him."

But even as business values, stronger churches, and a new mass culture worked in the New South to spread the values of dignity, Southern violence endured and escalated. Although dueling faded, a Southern professor warned, "the old spirit of so-called Chivalry has not declined with the 'Code': there is the same unwillingness—in a lessening degree—to go to the law; and in [the Southerner's] transition stage from the 'Code' to the courts we have fallen into the present lawless and cruel habit of street fighting." "The curse and shame of the South," lamented an 1882 article on the influence of homicide on Southern progress, "is the constant presence in the minds of all classes, from childhood up,

of homicide as one of the probable contingencies of ordinary social life." Robert Penn Warren remembered that in Kentucky in the early twentieth century "there was a world of violence that I grew up in. You accepted violence as a component of life."

The postwar South saw a widespread concern with black violence as well as with white. Whites charged that dangerous black men who had been controlled under slavery were now on the loose, most of their anger focused on other black men. Young blacks, one white newspaper claimed, carried knives and firearms as a habit, "most especially when a ball, frolic or entertainment is on hand. And being ready to fight it is not astonishing that they use the pistol on the slightest provocation." In language that sounded much like descriptions of colonial or antebellum white violence, Philip Bruce of Virginia held that arguments among black men could only be "settled by a resort to violence as desperate as it is impetuous; in the struggle no quarter is expected or allowed, and it is only terminated by the hasty retirement or the complete disablement of one of the parties."

Just as the antebellum Southern aristocracy believed itself to be above the law and thus adjudicated conflicts through honor, so did postwar black Southerners *know* themselves to be outside the law—whether they wanted to be or not. Blacks realized, after repeated painful experiences, that the law was what they called "white folks' law," its protections not extending to them. And black honor, which had grown in the vacuum of justice under slavery, acquired a force of its own that actively repelled the dictates of the written, abstract law. Manhood came to be equated with the extralegal defense of one's honor and unquestioning respect from peers. The contempt antebellum whites had felt for those who were so weak they had to go to the law for redress was amplified in the postbellum black community, for the law there represented not only an outside force but the force of the oppressor. Moreover, honor was often virtually all a poor black man owned, the only possession he could defend and identify with.

It might seem that the culture of honor and its violence should have soon with-

ered and died in the inhospitable atmosphere of Northern cities, where so many generations of Southern migrants have moved. Dignity, after all, had supposedly flourished since the mid-nineteenth century within the schools, factories, and active governments of the North.

Indeed, historians have discovered that Northern cities, like industrialized societies in general, did experience declining rates of violence from the mid-nineteenth century well into this century. The institutions of industry and state did apparently act to encourage self-control, deferred gratification, and fear of detection and arrest, to reduce violence. Many migrants from the South, however, especially blacks, have remained insulated from such forces, stranded in desperate Northern inner cities, where unemployment, ineffective schooling, and dangerous neighborhoods not only allow Southern-style honor to survive but actually generate an honor of their own. Honor has found new breeding grounds in cities, once the most advanced outposts of dignity. "Whenever the authority of the law is questioned or ignored, the code of honor re-emerges to allocate the right to precedence and dictate the principles of conduct," an anthropologist has observed. Honor springs up "among aristocracies and criminal underworlds, school-boy and street-corner societies, open frontier and those closed communities where reigns 'The Honorable Society,' as the Mafia calls itself."

Lower-class whites and lower-class blacks perpetuated honor after most educated middle-class Southerners had turned away from honor and violence as archaic relics of a glorious but impractical Southern past. An acute sensitivity to insult and a propensity for violence—the manifestations of honor—came with each passing decade of the twentieth century to be increasingly identified with poor rural whites and poor urban blacks. Honor is fed every day in places where courts are not trusted, where the American dream seems off limits, and where poverty and frustration reign. There values hundreds of years old get a new lease on life. Honor may eventually fade away, but it has proved remarkably durable and dangerous in its first three hundred years in America.

Eden Ravished

The Land, Pioneer Attitudes, and Conservation

Harlan Hague

Harlan Hague teaches history of the American West and American environmental history at San Joaquin Delta College, Stockton, California. He is the author of Road to California: The Search For a Southern Overland Route *and articles on western exploration and trails.*

In O. E. Rölvagg's *Giants in the Earth,* a small caravan of Norwegian immigrants stopped on the prairie, and the riders got down from their wagons. They scanned the landscape in all directions and liked what they saw. It was beautiful, all good plowland and clean of any sign of human habitation all the way to the horizon. After so much hoping and planning, they had finally found their place in the new land. One of the men, Per Hansa, still had difficulty comprehending what was happening:

"This vast stretch of beautiful land was to be his—yes, his. . . . His heart began to expand with a mighty exaltation. An emotion he had never felt before filled him and made him walk erect. . . . 'Good God!' he panted. 'This kingdom is going to be mine!' "

Countless others who went to the West reacted like Rölvaag's Per Hansa. They entered the Promised Land with high expectations, possessed the land and were possessed by it. They changed the land and in time were changed by it.

The influence of the West on the American mind has interested historians ever since Frederick Jackson Turner read his momentous essay in 1893 to a meeting of the American Historical Association. In the essay, Turner concluded: "The existence of an area of free land, its continuous recession, and the advance of American settlement westward, explain American development." Turner went on to describe in some detail the

various ways the western environment changed the frontiersman, molding him into the American. The processes and result of this evolution were in the end, by implication, favorable.

Writing in the early 1890s, Turner did not detect one of the most important themes, if not the most important, of the westward movement, a theme which would have immense impact on the shaping of the American character. This was the belief that the resources of the West were inexhaustible. Henry Nash Smith, in his influential *Virgin Land,* caught the point that Turner missed:

"The character of the American empire was defined not by streams of influence out of the past, not by a cultural tradition, nor by its place in a world community, but by a relation between man and nature—or rather, even more narrowly, between American man and the American West. This relation was thought of as unvaryingly fortunate."

This cornucopian view of the West was the basis of the frontiersman's attitude toward and his use of the land.

The typical trans-Mississippi emigrant in the last half of the nineteenth century accepted the assumption of inexhaustible resources. Yet the view of the West as an everlasting horn of plenty had been proven false long before the post-Civil War exodus. For example, commercial hunting of the sea otter along the California coast, which had begun in 1784, reached its peak around 1815; by the mid-1840s, the numbers of the animals had declined alarmingly, and the otter was soon hunted almost to extinction. The beaver's fate was similar. Soon after Lewis and Clark told about the teeming beaver populations in western streams, trappers moved westward to harvest the furs. They worked streams so relentlessly that the beaver began to disappear in areas where it had always been plentiful.

By 1840, the beaver had been trapped virtually to oblivion. No mountain man in the 1820s would have dreamed there could ever be an end to the hardy little animal. Yet unbridled exploitation had nearly condemned the beaver to extinction. The lesson was lost on Westerners.

Pioneers were not noticeably swayed by the arguments of the naturalists, who publicized the wonders of nature or went further and pled for its preservation. William Bartram, a contemporary of Jefferson, wrote eloquently about the beauty of American nature in his *Travels.* Originally published in 1791, his book was more popular in Europe than in the United States, which had yet to discover its aesthetic environment. John James Audubon had more influence in this country upon publication of his *Birds of America* series (1827–1844) and his subsequent call for protection of wildlife. Francis Parkman, while not famed as a naturalist, wrote firsthand accounts about the scenic West and the Indian inhabitants who lived in harmony with nature. It is no wonder that Parkman, who was enthralled with the outdoors, admired Indians and mountain men more than the settlers he encountered during his western travels.

There was indeed a whole body of romantic literature and art during the first half of the nineteenth century that might have persuaded Americans that environmental values could be measured in terms other than economic. William Cullen Bryant wrote-with such depth of feeling about the simple pleasures of the outdoors that he is still known as one of our foremost nature poets. The founding spirit of transcendentalism, Ralph Waldo Emerson, wrote in his first book, *Nature:*

"In the presence of nature, a wild delight runs through the man. . . . In the woods, is perpetual youth. . . . In the woods, we return to reason and faith. . . .

The currents of the Universal Being circulate through me; I am part or particle of God. . . . In the wilderness, I find something more dear and connate than in streets or villages."

Emerson's contemporary, Henry David Thoreau, was even less restrained in his adoration of untamed nature when he wrote: "In Wildness is the preservation of the World." At the same time, Thomas Cole and the Hudson River school of landscape painters captured on canvas the essence of nature that the romantic writers had recorded in prose and poetry. And farther west, beyond the Mississippi River, George Catlin, Karl Bodmer, and Alfred Jacob Miller were painting the exotic wilderness that increasingly drew the attention of Americans.

Unmoved by praise of the aesthetic quality of the environment, frontiersmen were even less impressed by warnings that its resources were not without end. Every American generation since the colonial period had been told of the virtue of using natural resources wisely. An ordinance of Plymouth Colony had regulated the cutting of timber. William Penn had decreed that one acre of trees be left undisturbed for every five acres cleared. In 1864, only a moment before the beginning of the migration that would cover the West within one generation, George Perkins Marsh published his book *Man and Nature,* the most eloquent statement up to that time of the disastrous result that must follow careless stewardship of the land. "Man has too long forgotten." he wrote, "that the earth was given to him for usufruct alone, not for consumption, still less for profligate waste." That is, man could and should both cherish and use the land, but he should not use it up. The significance in Marsh's warning was the recognition that the land could be used up.

While American ambassador to Italy, Marsh had theorized that ancient Rome's fall could be traced to the depletion of the empire's forests. He predicted a like fate for the United States if its resources were similarly squandered. Marsh's book appears to have been widely read by American intellectuals and probably favorably influenced the movements for national parks and forestry management. In it, indeed, were the seeds of the conservation movement of the early twentieth century. Yet it is unlikely that many frontiersmen read or were aware of—or at least they did not heed—Marsh's advice.

Pioneers heard a different drummer. They read descriptions about the West written by people who had been there. Lansford W. Hastings's glowing picture of California and Oregon thrilled thousands:

"In view of their increasing population, accumulating wealth, and growing prosperity, I can not but believe, that the time is not distant, when those wild forests, trackless plains, untrodden valleys, and the unbounded ocean, will present one grand scene, of continuous improvements, universal enterprise, and unparalleled commerce: when those vast forests, shall have disappeared, before the hardy pioneer; those extensive plains, shall abound with innumerable herds, of domestic animals; those fertile valleys, shall groan under the immense weight of their abundant products: when those numerous rivers shall team [sic] with countless steam-boats, steam-ships, ships, barques and brigs; when the entire country, will be everywhere intersected, with turnpike roads, rail-roads and canals; and when, all the vastly numerous, and rich resources, of that now, almost unknown region, will be fully and advantageously developed."

Once developed, hopeful emigrants learned, the area would become the garden of the world. In the widely-distributed *Our Western Empire: or the New West Beyond the Mississippi,* Linus P. Brockett wrote that "in no part of the vast domain of the United States, and certainly in no other country under the sun, is there a body of land of equal extent, in which there are so few acres unfit for cultivation, or so many which, with irrigation or without it, will yield such bountiful crops."

Other books described the routes to the Promised Land. The way west was almost without exception easy and well-watered, with plenty of wood, game, and grass.

There was not just opportunity on the frontier. Walt Whitman also saw romance in the westward migration:

Come my tan-faced children,
Follow well in order, get your weapons
ready,
Have you your pistols? have you your
sharp-edged axes?
Pioneers! O pioneers!
For we cannot tarry here,
We must march my darlings, we must bear
the brunt of danger,
We the youthful sinewy races, all the rest
on us depend,
Pioneers! O pioneers! . . .
We primeval forests felling,

We the rivers stemming, vexing we and
piercing deep the mines within,
We the surface broad surveying, we the
virgin soil upheaving
Pioneers! O pioneers! . . .
Swift! to the head of the army!-swift!
spring to your places, Pioneers! O
Pioneers!

The ingredients were all there: danger, youth, virgin soil. Well might frontiersmen agree with Mark Twain who wrote that the first question asked by the American, upon reaching heaven, was: "Which way West?" Thoreau also thought a westward course the natural one:

"When I go out of the house for a walk . . . my needle always settles between west and south-southwest. The future lies that way to me, and the earth seems more unexhausted and richer on that side. . . . westward I go free. I must walk toward Oregon."

Emigrants felt this same pull but for different reasons. Thoreau's West was a wild region to be enjoyed for itself and preserved untouched, while the West to the emigrants was a place for a new start. The pioneers would conquer the wilderness and gather its immeasurable bounty. This did not imply that Westerners were oblivious to the beauty of the land. Many were aware of the West's scenic attractions but felt, with the influential artist Thomas Cole, that the wilderness, however beautiful, inevitably must give way to progress. In his "Essay on American Scenery," Cole described the sweet joys of nature—the mountains, lakes, rivers, waterfalls, and sky. The essay, dated 1835, is nostalgic. Cole closed his paean with an expression of "sorrow that the beauty of such landscapes are quickly passing away . . . desecrated by what is called improvement." But, after all, he added, "such is the road society has to travel!" Clearly, Cole, like most of his nineteenth-century readers, did not question the propriety of "improvement" or the definition of "progress."

THE BELIEF IN THE INEXHAUSTIBILITY OF western resources was superimposed on an attitude toward the land that Americans had inherited from generations past. In the Judeo-Christian view, God created the world for man. Man was the master of nature rather than a part of it. The resources of the earth—soil, water, plants, animals, insects, rocks, fish, birds, air— were there for his use, and his proper role was to dominate. It was natural then for God's children to harvest the rich garden provided for them by their Creator. They went into the West to do God's bidding, to use the land as he willed, to fulfill a destiny.

This attitude of man-over-nature was not universal. Like most primitive cultures throughout history, it was not held by the American Indian. The Indian saw himself as a part of nature, not its master. He felt a close kinship with the earth and all living things. Black Elk, a holy man of the Oglala Sioux, for example, believed that all living things were the children of the sky, their father, and the earth, their mother. He had special reverence for "the earth, from whence we came and at whose breast we suck as babies all our lives, along with all the animals and birds and trees and grasses." Creation legends of many tribes illustrate the Indian's familial attachment to the earth and his symbiotic relationship with other forms of life.

The land to Indians was more than merely a means of livelihood for the current generation. It belonged not only to them, the living, but to all generations of their people, those who came before and those who would come after. They could not separate themselves from the land. Of course, there were exceptions. Some Indians fell under the spell of the white trader who offered them goods that would make their lives easier, not to say better. As they became dependent on white man's goods, the land and its fruits began to assume for them an economic value that might be bartered for the conveniences produced by the white man's technology. This is not to say that the Indian attitude toward the land changed. Rather it illustrates that some Indians adopted the white man's view.

To European-Americans, the western Indians' use of the land was just another proof of their savagery. The pioneers had listened to the preachers of Manifest Destiny, and they knew that the nomadic tribes must stand aside for God's Chosen People who would use the land as God intended.

And so they returned to Eden. While some went to California and some to Oregon, the most coherent migration before the rush for California gold began in 1849 was the Mormon exodus to Salt Lake Valley. The latter was not typical of the westward movement. The persecuted saints entered the West not so much for its lure as because of its inaccessibility. In 1830, the same year that the Mormon Church was founded, Joseph Smith announced a revelation which would lead eventually to—or at least foresaw—the great migration:

"And ye are called to bring to pass the gathering of mine elect . . . unto one place upon the face of this land [which] . . . shall be on the borders by the Lamanites [Indians]. . . . The glory of the Lord shall be there, and it shall be called Zion. . . . The righteous shall be gathered out from among all nations, and shall come to Zion, singing with songs of everlasting joy!"

Mormons who trekked to the Utah settlements in the late 1840s and 1850s knew they were doing God's bidding.

Other emigrants were just as sure that the Lord had prepared a place for them. "Truly the God in Heaven" wrote an Oregon-bound traveler in 1853, "has spread in rich profusion around us everything which could happily man and reveal the Wisdom and Benevolence of God to man." Oregon Trail travelers often noted in their journals that they were going to the "Promised Land." In A. B. Guthrie's *The Way West*, Fairman, who would be leaving Independence shortly for Oregon, proposed a toast "to a place where there's no fever." McBee, another emigrant, impatient to get started, responded:

" 'Y God, yes, . . . and to soil rich as anything. Plant a nail and it'll come up a spike. I heerd you don't never have to put up hay, the grass is that good, winter and all. And lambs come twice a year. Just set by and let the grass grow and the critters birth and get fat. That's my idee of farmin.' "

It seems that most emigants, in spite of the humor, did not expect their animals or themselves to wax fat in the new land without working. God would provide, but they must harvest.

Following close on the heels of the Oregon Trail farmers, and sometimes traveling in the same wagon trains, were the miners. This rough band of transients hardly thought of themselves as God's children, but they did nevertheless accept the horn-of-plenty image of the West. Granville Stuart wrote from the California mines that "no such enormous amounts of gold had been found anywhere before, and . . . they all believed that the supply was inexhaustible." Theirs was not an everflowing cornucopia, however, and each miner hoped to be in the right spot with an open sack when the horn tipped to release its wealth.

The typical miner wanted to get as rich as possible as quickly as possible so he could return home to family, friends, and a nabob's retirement. This condition is delightfully pictured in the frontispiece illustration in Mark Twain's *Roughing It*. A dozing miner is seated on a barrel in his cabin, his tools on the floor beside him. He is dreaming about the future: a country estate, yachting, carriage rides and walks in the park with a lady, an ocean voyage and a tour of Europe, viewing the pyramids. The dreams of other miners, while not so grand, still evoked pleasant images of home and an impatience to return there. This yearning is obvious in the lines of a miner's song of the 1850s:

Home's dearest joys Time soon destroys,
  Their loss we all deplore;
While they may last, we labor fast
  To dig the golden ore.

When the land has yielded its riches:

Then home again, home again,
  From a foreign shore,
We'll sing how sweet our heart's delight,
  With our dear friends once more.

Miners' diaries often reflected these same sentiments, perhaps with less honeyed phrases but with no less passion.

A practical-minded argonaut, writing in 1852 from California to his sister in Alabama, explained his reason for going to the mines: "I think in one year here I can make enough to clear me of debt and give me a pretty good start in the world. Then I will be a happy man." What then? He instructed his sister to tell all his friends that he would soon be "back whare (sic) I can enjoy there [sic] company." Other miners thought it would take a little longer, but the motives were the same. A California miner later reminisced:

"Five years was the longest period any one expected to stay. Five years at most was to be given to rifling California of her treasures, and then that country was to be thrown aside like a used-up newspaper and the rich adventurers would spend the remainder of their days in wealth, peace, and prosperity at their eastern homes. No one talked then of going out 'to build up the glorious State of California.' "

The fact that many belatedly found that California was more than worked-out diggings and stayed—pronouncing the state glorious and themselves founding fathers—does not change their motives for going there.

There was a substantial body of miners, perpetually on the move, rowdies usually, the frontier fraternity boys, whose home was the mining camp and whose friends were largely miners like themselves. They rushed around the West to every discovery of gold or silver in a vain attempt to get rich without working. Though they had no visions of returning east to family and fireside, they did believe that the West was plentifully supplied with riches. It was just their bad luck that they had not found their shares. Their original reason for going to the mining camps and, though they might enjoy the camaraderie of their fellows, their reason for staying, was the same as that of the more genteel sort of miner who had come to the western wilderness, fully expecting to return to the East. More than any other emigrant to the West, the miner's motive was unabashed exploitation. For the most part, he did not conserve, preserve, or enrich the land. His intention, far from honorable, was rape.

THE CATTLEMAN WAS A TRANSITION FIGure between the miner who stripped the land and the farmer who, while stripping the land, also cherished it. The West to the cattleman meant grass and water, free or cheap. The earliest ranchers on the plains raised beef for the eastern markets and for the government, which had decreed that the cow replace the buffalo in the Plains Indians' life-style. The Indians, except for a few "renegades," complied, though they were never quite able to work the steer into their religion.

It was not long before word filtered back to the East that fortunes could be made in western stock raising. James Brisbin's *Beef Bonanza; or, How to Get Rich on the Plains,* first published in 1881, was widely read. Readers were dazzled by the author's minutely documented "proof" that an industrious man could more than double his investment in less than five years. Furthermore, there was almost no risk involved:

"In a climate so mild that horses, cattle, and sheep and goats can live in the open air through all the winter months, and fatten on the dry and apparently withered grasses of the soil, there would appear to be scarcely a limit to the number that could be raised."

Experienced and inexperienced alike responded. Getting rich, they thought, was only a matter of time, not expertise.

Entrepreneurs and capital, American and foreign, poured into the West. Most of the rangeland was not in private ownership. Except for small tracts, generally homesteaded along water courses or as sites for home ranches, it was public property. Though a cattleman might claim rights to a certain range, and though an association of cattlemen might try to enforce the claims of its members, legally the land was open, free, and available.

By the mid-1880s, the range was grossly overstocked. The injury to the land was everywhere apparent. While some began to counsel restraint, most ranchers continued to ravish the country until the winter of 1886–1887 forced them to respect it. Following that most disastrous of winters, which in some areas killed as much as 85 percent of range stock, one chastened cattle king wrote that the cattle business "that had been fascinating to me before, suddenly became distasteful. . . . I never wanted to own again an animal that I could not feed and shelter." The industry gradually recovered, but it would never be the same. More land was fenced, wells dug, and windmills installed. Shelters for cattle were built, and hay was grown for winter feeding. Cattle raising became less an adventure and more a business.

In some cattlemen there grew an attachment, if not affection, for the land. Some, especially after the winter of 1886–1887, began to put down roots. Others who could afford it built luxurious homes in the towns to escape the deficiencies of the countryside, much as twentieth-century townsmen would build cabins in the country to escape the deficiencies of the cities. Probably most cattlemen after the winter of 1886–1887 still believed in the bounty of the West, but a bounty which they now recognized would be released to them only through husbandry.

Among all those who went into the West to seek their fortunes, the frontier farmers carried with them the highest hopes and greatest faith. Their forebears had been told for generations that they were the most valuable citizens, chosen of God, and that their destiny lay westward. John Filson, writing in 1784 about frontier Kentucky, described the mystique of the West that would be understood by post-Civil War emigrants:

"This fertile region, abounding with all the luxuries of nature, stored with all the principal materials for art and industry, inhabited by virtuous and ingenious citizens, must universally attract the attention of mankind." There, continued Filson, "like the land of promise, flowing with milk and honey, a land of brooks of water, . . . a land of wheat and barley, and all kinds of fruits, you shall eat bread without scarceness, and not lack any thing in it."

By 1865 the Civil War had settled the controversy between North and South that had hindered the westward movement, the Homestead Act had been passed, and the Myth of the Garden had replaced the Myth of the Desert. By the grace of God and with the blessing of Washington, the frontier farmer left the old land to claim his own in the new:

Born of a free, world-wandering race,
  Little we yearned o'er an oft-turned sod.
What did we care for the father's place,
  Having ours fresh from the hand of God?

Farmers were attracted to the plains by the glowing accounts distributed by railroads and western states. Newspapers in the frontier states added their accolades. The editor of the *Kansas Farmer* declared in 1867 that there were in his state "vast areas of unimproved land, rich as that on the banks of the far famed Nile, . . . acres, miles, leagues, townships, counties, oceans of land, all ready for the plough, good as the best in America, and yet lying without occupants." Would-be emigrants who believed this sort of propaganda could sing with conviction:

Oh! give me a home where the buffalo roam,
Where the deer and the antelope play;
Where never is heard a discouraging word,
And the sky is not clouded all day.

There was a reason for the sky's clarity, the emigrants learned when they arrived on the plains. It was not long before many had changed their song:

We've reached the land of desert sweet.
Where nothing grows for man to eat;
I look across the plains
And wonder why it never rains.

And, finally, sung to the cadence of a "slow, sad march":

We do not live, we only stay;
We are too poor to get away.

It is difficult to generalize about the experience of pioneer farmers. Those who continued their journeys to the Pacific Coast regions were usually satisfied with what they found. It was those who settled on the plains who were most likely to be disillusioned. Their experience was particularly shattering since they had gone to the West not just to reap in it but also to live in it. Most found not the land of milk and honey they expected, but, it seems, a life of drudgery and isolation.

The most persistent theme in the literature of the period is disenchantment. This mood is caught best by Hamlin Garland. In *Main-Travelled Roads,* Garland acknowledged two views of the plains experience when he wrote that the main-travelled road in the West, hot and dusty in summer, muddy and dreary in fall and spring, and snowy in winter, "does sometimes cross a rich meadow where the songs of the larks and bobolinks and blackbirds are tangled." But Garland's literary road is less cluttered: "Mainly it is long and wearyful, and has a dull little town at one end and a home of toil at the other. Like the main-travelled road of life it is traversed by many classes of people, but the poor and the weary predominate."

The opposite responses to the plains are more pronounced in O. E. Rölvaag's *Giants in the Earth,* one of the most enduring novels of the agricultural West. Per Hansa meets the challenge of the new land, overcomes obstacles and rejoices in each success, however small. He accepts the prairie for what it is and loves it. Meanwhile, his wife, Beret, is gradually driven insane by that same prairie. Where Per Hansa saw hope and excitement in the land, Beret saw only despair and loneliness. "Oh, how quickly it grows dark out here!" she cries, to which Per Hansa replies, "The sooner the day's over, the sooner the next day comes!" In spite of her husband's optimistic outlook, Beret's growing insanity dominates the story as it moves with gloomy intensity to its tragic end. It is significant that Per Hansa dies, a victim of the nature that he did not fear but could not subdue.

Willa Cather, the best-known novelist of nineteenth-century prairie farm life, treated relationships between people and their environment more sensitively than most. While her earlier short stories often dwell on themes of man against the harsh land, her works thereafter, without glossing over the severity of farm life, reveal a certain harmony between the land and those who live on it and love it.

Her characters work hard, and suffer; but they are not immune to the loveliness of the land.

The histories of plains farming dwell more on processes than suffering, but accounts that treat the responses of the settlers to their environment generally verify the novelists' interpretations. According to the histories, the picture of desperation painted by Garland and Rölvaag applies principally to the earliest years of any particular frontier region. By the time sod houses acquired board floors and women were able to visit with other women regularly, Cather's images are more accurate.

The fact that pioneer farmers were not completely satisfied with what they found in the Promised Land does not alter their reasons for going there. They had gone into the West for essentially the same reason as the trappers, miners, and cattlemen: economic exploitation. Unlike their predecessors, they also had been looking for homes. Yet, like them, they had believed fervently in the Myth of Superabundance.

THE IRRATIONAL BELIEF THAT THE WEST'S resources were so great that they could never be used up was questioned by some at the very time that others considered it an article of faith. George Perkins Marsh in 1864 warned of the consequences of a too rapid consumption of the land's resources. In 1878, John Wesley Powell attacked the Myth of the Garden when he pointed out that a substantial portion of western land, previously thought to be cultivable by eastern methods, could be farmed successfully only by irrigation. Overgrazing of grasslands resulted in the intrusion of weeds and the erosion of soil, prompting many ranchers, especially after the devastating winter of 1886–1887, to contract their operations and practice range management. Plowing land where rainfall was inadequate for traditional farming methods resulted in wind and water erosion of the soil. Before the introduction of irrigation or dry farming techniques, many plains farmers gave up and returned eastward. The buffalo, which might have numbered fifty million or more at mid-century, were hunted almost to extinction by 1883. Passenger pigeons were estimated to number in the billions in the first half of the nineteenth century: around 1810, Alexander Wilson, an ornithologist, guessed that a single flock, a mile wide

and 240 miles long, contained more than two billion birds. Yet before the end of the century, market hunting and the clearing of forest habitats had doomed the passenger pigeon to extinction. Examples of this sort led many people to the inescapable conclusion that the West's resources were not inexhaustible.

At the same time a growing number of people saw values other than economic in the West. Some plains farmers struggling with intermittent drought and mortgage could still see the beauty of the land. Alexandra in Cather's *O Pioneers!* could see it: "When the road began to climb the first long swells of the Divide, Alexandra hummed an old Swedish hymn. . . . Her face was so radiant" as she looked at the land "with love and yearning. It seemed beautiful to her, rich and strong and glorious. Her eyes drank in the breadth of it, until her tears blinded her."

Theodore Roosevelt wrote often of the "delicious" rides he took at his Badlands ranch during autumn and spring. He described the rolling, green grasslands; the prairie roses; the blacktail and whitetail deer; the songs of the sky-lark; the white-shouldered lark-bunting; and the sweet voice of the meadowlark, his favorite. Of a moonlight ride, he wrote that the "river gleams like running quicksilver, and the moonbeams play over the grassy stretches of the plateaus and glance off the wind-rippled blades as they would from water." Lincoln Lang, a neighbor of Roosevelt's, had the same feeling for the land. He called the Badlands "a landscape masterpiece of the wild, . . . verdant valleys, teeming with wild life, with wild fruits and flowers, . . . with the God-given atmosphere of truth itself, over which unshackled Nature, alone, reigned queen."

Even miners were not immune to the loveliness of the countryside. Granville Stuart, working in the California mines, was struck by the majestic forests of sugar pine, yellow pine, fir, oak, and dogwood. He described the songs and coloration of the birds and the woodpeckers' habit of storing acorns in holes that they meticulously pecked in tree limbs. He delighted in watching a covey of quail near his cabin each day. "Never was I guilty of killing one," he added. Bret Harte lived among the California miners, and his stories often turn to descriptions of the picturesque foothills of the Sierra Nevada. After the birth of "The Luck" in Roaring Camp, the proud, self-appointed godfathers decorated the baby's "bower with flowers and sweetsmelling shrubs, . . . wild honey-suckles, azaleas, or the painted blossoms of Las Mariposas. The men had suddenly awakened to the fact that there were beauty and significance in these trifles, which they had so long trodden carelessly beneath their feet."

Success of some sort often broadened the frontiersman's viewpoint. The miner, cattleman, or farmer who had succeeded in some way in his struggle with the land had more time and inclination to think about his relationship with it. Viewing his environment less as an adversary, the Westerner began to see what was happening to it.

At times, concern for the environment led to action. The mounting protests of Californians whose homes and farms had been damaged by the silt-laden runoff from hydraulic mining finally led to the outlawing of this mindless destruction of the land. Frederick Law Olmsted, who had designed New York's Central Park, initiated an era in 1864 when he and some friends persuaded Congress to grant to the state of California a piece of land in California's Sierra Nevada for the creation of a park, merely because the land, which included Yosemite Valley and the Mariposa Big Trees, was beautiful and the public would enjoy it. The idea took hold, and other parks soon followed, Yellowstone in 1872 being the first public "pleasuring ground" under federal management. The new art of landscape photography showed Easterners the wonders of the West, without the hardships of getting there, and revealed to many Westerners a land they inhabited but had never seen. With the improvement in transportation, principally railroads, more and more people ventured into the West to see these wonders firsthand.

A growing awareness that unrestrained exploitation was fast destroying the natural beauty of the West and that its resources, by the end of the nineteenth century widely acknowledged to be finite, were being consumed at an alarming pace led to considerable soul-searching. Frederick Jackson Turner, who had most eloquently described the influence that the great expanses of western land had on the shaping of American character, also hinted that the disappearance of available land was likely to cause some serious disruptions in American society. "The frontier has gone," he wrote, "and

with its going has closed the first period of American history."

If the first phase of American history, in which a dominant theme was the advance of the frontier, ran from 1607 to 1890, the second phase began with the emergence of the conservation movement which would lead to the alteration of fundamental attitudes toward the land nurtured during the first phase. While based generally on concern for the environment, the movement split in the early twentieth century into two factions. One faction argued for wise management of the country's resources to prevent their being wasted. This "utilitarian conservation" was not a break with the frontier view of exploitation. It was a refinement. While the frontier view was one of rapid exploitation of inexhaustible resources, the utilitarian conservationists rejected the myth of inexhaustibility and advocated the careful use of finite resources, without rejecting the basic assumption that the resources were there to be exploited. This view of conservation led to the setting aside and management of forest reserves, soil and water conservation projects, and irrigation and hydroelectric programs.

The other faction, whose ideology has been called "aesthetic conservation;' clearly broke with the frontier past when its members argued for the preservation of areas of natural beauty for public enjoyment. This group's efforts bore fruit in the establishment of national and state parks, monuments and wilderness areas. There are indications that the two factions are drawing closer together in the umbrella ecology movement of the 1970s, perhaps eventually to merge.

It is senseless to compare nineteenth-century frontier attitudes toward the land with today's more enlightened views. Faced seemingly with such plenty—billions of passenger pigeons, millions of buffalo, innumerable beaver, endless seas of grass, vast forests of giant trees, mines to shame King Solomon's—excess was understandable and probably inevitable. Excess in this case meant waste. Here the Turner thesis is most meaningful, for the belief in the inexhaustibility of resources in the West generated the unique American acceptance of waste as the fundamental tenet of a life-style. For this, the frontiersman is not entirely blameless. But certainly, he is less blameworthy than the neo-pioneer who continues, against reason and history, to cling hopefully to the myth of inexhaust-

ibility. Yet there were examples, however few, and voices, however dim, that the frontiersman might have heeded. It remains to be seen whether Americans today have learned the lesson their ancestors, four generations removed, failed to comprehend.

BIBLIOGRAPHIC NOTE

There are few comprehensive surveys of the evolution of American attitudes toward the environment. Three useful sources are Stewart L. Udall, *The Quiet Crisis* (New York: Holt, Rinehart, 1963); Hans Huth, *Nature and the American: Three Centuries of Changing Attitudes* (Berkeley: University of California, 1957); and Roderick Nash, *Wilderness and the American Mind*, rev. ed. (New Haven: Yale University, 1973), the last particularly concerned with the American response to wilderness. Frederick Jackson Turner's frontier thesis, which inevitably must be considered in any study of the reldtionship between Americans and their environment, is in his *The Frontier in American History* (New York: Henry Hoit, 1921). Invaluable to an understanding of what Americans thought the West was is Henry Nash Smith, *Virgin Land: The American West as Symbol and Myth* (New York: Vintage Books, 1950). The most influential book of the twentieth century in the development of a land ethic is Aldo Leopold, *A Sand County Almanac* (New York: Oxford University, 1949).

Selections from historical materials and literature were blended in this study to illustrate western emigrants' expectations for and responses to the new country. In addition to titles listed in the text, literary impressions of nature are in Wilson O. Clough, *The Necessary Earth: Nature and Solitude in American Literature* (Austin: University of Texas, 1964) and John Conron, *The American Landscape: A Critical Anthology of Prose and Poetry* (New York: Oxford University, 1974). Useful bibliographies of the literature of the westward movement are Lucy Lockwood Hazard, *The Frontier in American Literature* (New York: Thomas Y Crowell, 1927) and Richard W Etulain, *Western American Literature* (Vermillion, S.D.: University of South Dakota, 1972). Bibliographies of historical materials are in Ray Allen Billington, *Westward Expansion*, 4th ed. (New York: Macmillan, 1974), and Nelson Klose, *A Concise Study Guide to the American Frontier* (Lincoln: University of Nebraska, 1964).

Act One

Lois W. Banner

Lois W. Banner, 47, is professor of history and of the Program for the Study of Women and Men in Society at the University of Southern California. Born in Los Angeles, she received a B.A. from the University of California, Los Angeles (1960) and a Ph.D. from Columbia University (1970). She is the author of Elizabeth Cady Stanton: A Radical for Women's Rights (1980) and is co-editor of Clio's Consciousness Raised: New Perspectives on the History of Women (1976).

On July 19, 1848, in the village of Seneca Falls, New York, some 300 people crowded into a small Methodist chapel, drawn by an announcement in the daily *Seneca County Courier.* The notice proclaimed something unheard of—a two-day "Woman's Rights Convention." Despite a request that men stay away until the second day, about 40 curious males showed up at the start.

The organizers of the convention—Lucretia Mott, a 55-year-old Quaker activist from Philadelphia, and Elizabeth Cady Stanton, 32, the wife of a local lawyer—politician—would be remembered later as the founders of the American women's rights movement. But on that day in 1848, they lacked the temerity to preside over their own meeting and instead persuaded Mott's husband, James, a merchant, to serve as chairman. Not until Stanton rose to speak did anyone get a sense of what was to come.

"I should feel exceedingly diffident . . . having never before spoken in public," she told the audience," . . . did I not feel that the time had come for the question of woman's wrongs to be laid before the public, did I not believe that woman herself must do this work; for woman alone can understand the height, the depth, the length and the breadth of her degradation."

Stanton went on to read aloud the "Declaration of Rights and Sentiments" that she and several fellow organizers had drafted for the convention. A clever rewording of Thomas Jefferson's Declaration of Independence, its title borrowed from the 1833 covenant of William Lloyd Garrison's American Anti-Slavery Society, the broadside provoked 18 straight hours of debate among those present—farmers, local merchants, housewives, mill workers, abolitionists and sundry other reformers.

"We hold these truths to be self-evident," Stanton said, "that all men and women are created equal." Thus, Stanton positioned her declaration squarely withIn the American political tradition. But she underscored the radical roots of that tradition: "The history of mankind is a history of repeated injuries and usurpations on the part of man toward woman, having in direct object the establishment of an absolute tyranny over her. To prove this, let the facts be submitted to a candid world."

The facts Elizabeth Cady Stanton presented that day in Seneca Falls illustrated the social and legal liabilities attached to being a woman during the first 60 years of the republic.

As she pointed out, the status of the majority of American women at midcentury was vividly characterized by the common-law term "civil death." A throwback to British Colonial days (indeed to the Norman Conquest), civil death made married women, in effect, private property. Legally, they could not sign contracts, keep earnings, or control property.* Divorces were granted only in cases of nonsupport, desertion, or adultery; even then, fathers retained child custody. Single women had legal status, for they were expected to pay property taxes. But without the right to vote they incurred the very injury that provoked the American Revolution: taxation without representation.

---

*In 1848, New York had passed the Married Woman's Property Act, the nation's first reform of civil death. It gave certain real estate and personal property rights to wives.

Stanton's Declaration of Sentiments also deplored women's "social and religious degradation." Man, Stanton charged, had "deprived woman of a thorough education, all colleges being closed against her."† He "monopolized nearly all the profitable employments" and held women to a moral code by which *his* "delinquencies" were "deemed of little account." He "usurped the prerogative of Jehovah himself" and made women "willing to lead a dependent . . . life."

In its demand for suffrage—women's "inalienable right to the elective franchise"—the declaration must have appeared almost as revolutionary as another social tract of 1848, the *Communist Manifesto.* To the Seneca Falls group, this demand for the vote seemed so excessive that only the black abolitionist Frederick Douglass would take the floor in Stanton's support. Lucretia Mott warned her friend not to make their movement appear "ridiculous." Stanton's father, a New York State Supreme Court judge, was reportedly outraged. Her husband, Henry, ever the politician, quietly left town.

HOME RULE

After two days of impassioned rhetoric, only one-third of Seneca Falls' conferees were persuaded to sign the declaration. Some later retracted their signatures. An editorial in the *Philadelphia Public Ledger and Daily Transcript* plainly showed what fears Stanton had aroused: "A woman is nobody. A wife is everything. A pretty girl is equal to ten thousand men, and a mother is, next to God, all powerful. . . . The ladies of Philadelphia . . . are resolved to maintain their rights as Wives, Belles, Virgins, and Mothers, and not as Women." Was

---

†Oberlin College (Ohio), founded in 1833 to train missionaries, was coeducational; Mount Holyoke (Massachusetts), founded for women in 1837, received collegiate status in 1883.

not protection preferable to the risks inherent in equality? It was a question that would surface repeatedly for over a century.

Other American women had spoken out before Seneca Falls—the essays of Judith Sargent Murray, daughter of a Massachusetts sea captain, argued for equal rights 10 years before Mary Wollstonecraft's 1792 *A Vindication of the Rights of Women* appeared in England. By 1848, literate Americans of both sexes had pondered the "Woman Question," most of them apparently concluding, along with Thomas Jefferson, that "the tender breasts of ladies were not formed for political convulsion." But the Seneca Falls meeting became a mid-19th century media event; the nation's newspapers, newly linked by telegraph, gave it plenty of play. Stanton saw that bad publicity ("the most shocking and unnatural incident ever recorded in the history of womanity," pronounced a typical newspaper editorial) was better than no publicity. "There is no danger of the Woman Question dying for want of notice," she wrote.

It was an era of national expansion, radical hopes, and conservative fears. Sutter's Creek in California yielded gold, President James K. Polk's generals won the Mexican War, and a new antislavery political party was formed—the Free-Soilers—all in 1848. Midcentury America abounded with middle-class reformers, usually led by clergymen, variously upset by urban dislocation in the industrializing North, slavery in the South, and immorality out West.

In upstate New York, where Stanton was raised, the opening of the Erie Canal in 1825 brought thousands of settlers and entrepreneurs. After them came Evangelical Protestant revivalists, with so many hellfire sermons that the area became known as "the burned-over district." Preachers set up tents to warn against money-grubbing, declaring that "all men may be saved if they will" and taking public confessions from largely female audiences. While at Emma Willard's Troy Female Seminary, the young Stanton went to hear the Rev. Charles Grandison Finney, a tall, charismatic ex-lawyer who claimed to have seen Christ in Rochester, New York. She became ill from all the emotional intensity, and thereafter distrusted religion.

As Stanton learned early, American middle-class society was organized around the popular notion of "separate spheres"

for men and women. "Everything I liked and enjoyed," she wrote of her childhood, "was messy and injurious; . . . and . . . everything I disliked was just the thing." According to Sarah Hale—editor of the widely read *Godey's Lady's Book* and a kind of 19th-century Emily Post—"ladies" kept to "the chaste, disinterested circle of the fireside," where "purer, more excellent, more spiritual values" than "the contagion of moneymaking" prevailed. How much Stanton enjoyed such advice may be surmised by her depiction of home life in Seneca Falls: "How rebellious it makes me feel when I see Henry going about where and how he pleases," she wrote to a friend, while "I have been compelled . . . to be . . . a household drudge."

SEXUAL POLITICS

This was not quite the whole picture. Even household drudges could get out of the kitchen for a good cause—and there were plenty of those in the Northern states, from helping unwed mothers to hiding fugitive slaves. Indeed, social uplift became the main outlet for the talents of educated women such as Stanton. Inadvertently, reform organizations became a training ground for future women's rights leaders. Despite Stanton's contempt for the spheres ("A man has quite enough to do," she replied to one critic, "without being taxed to find out also where every woman belongs"), the custom of creating separate male and female groups within these organizations had a polarizing effect that led many women to seek greater equality.

The first social reform groups—"benevolence societies" such as the American Bible Society and the Home Missionary Society—bloomed in the early 1800s, and they tended to be highly conservative. Women raised money for missionaries laboring in the unruly West. They visited the poor, cared for orphans and widows, established schools, asylums, and workshops.

Over time, social reform took on a distinct coloration, the first sign of what Kate Millet would call "sexual politics." Uplift groups, such as the social purity and temperance movements, which campaigned against male carnality and drunkenness, signaled a widening rift between men and women over the state of the nation's manners and morals. By 1840, the American Female Moral Reform So-

ciety had over 500 auxiliaries and a weekly journal read by 20,000 subscribers. Its members battled prostitution by spying on prominent clients of brothels. In Utica, New York, "visiting committees" went into poor sections of town to solicit tales of men's sexual abuses at home. Meanwhile, temperance workers went on tour with stories of wife beating, child molesting, gambling, and other incarnations of "Demon Rum." Later in the century, it was common for temperance women to invade saloons in large "praying bands."

Most important to feminists were the antislavery organizations. In 1840, just before the convention at Seneca Falls, abolitionists split into factions, partly over whether women should speak out in "promiscuous" (mixed) company. The "political" wing, headed by several New Yorkers, among them Henry Stanton, favored gradual abolition and a no-talking policy for women. The radicals, led by William Lloyd Garrison, wanted an immediate end to slavery and had no qualms about letting women say so, giving many future feminists their first taste of political agitation.

It has been said that women abolitionists became feminists when they perceived the analogy between slavery and the plight of womankind. But Stanton and Mott became feminists when they saw how women were treated by certain male abolitionists. They met in 1840, at the first international antislavery convention in London. Mott had been dispatched by the Philadelphia Female Anti-Slavery Society; Stanton was simply accompanying her new husband. Forced, despite the objections of Garrison and Wendell Phillips, to keep silent in a curtained off section of the hall, the two women vowed to retaliate when they returned to the United States.

NATIONAL STRIDES

They envisioned the meeting at Seneca Falls as the first in a series of public forums on women's rights. Until the outbreak of the Civil War in 1861, conventions did take place almost every year. But the women's movement never attracted much of a popular following among women compared to temperance, abolition, and moral uplift. Its ideas were both too radical and too bourgeois, the product of upper-middle-class experience. Though they spoke of self-reliance, feminist leaders did not form their own independent organization for nearly two decades. And by relying on women in temperance and abolitionist groups to publicize their activities and provide a grassroots structure, the feminists antagonized conservative reformers and may have discouraged would-be supporters. Moreover, by focusing on property rights, marriage reform, and suffrage, they failed to arouse much support from one of their natural constituencies, a fast-growing group of women workers with grievances of their own.

By 1850, women—often unmarried, first generation teen-agers or farmers' daughters—constituted nearly 25 percent of the country's expanding manufacturing work force. Even in the textile mills around Lowell, Massachusetts (touted for model industrial conditions), women worked 13-hour shifts in overcrowded rooms. Many got sick from the fumes of kerosene lamps. They sometimes slept six to a room, two to a bed, in nearby boarding houses. Theirs was a separate sphere in one sense: women's pay, less than one-half that of male workers, ranged from $1 to $3 per week; much of it went for room and board.

Some of these women staged strikes and made sporadic attempts to form labor organizations during the 1830s and '40s. Sarah Bagley, one of the nation's first trade unionists, founded the Female Labor Reform Association in New England. But such efforts eventually foundered for lack of funds, time, and support from men's labor organizations. Only after the Civil War would women's rights leaders take up the factory workers' cause.

In 1850, feminists from seven states met in Worcester, Massachusetts. Some were already prominent among social reformers: Mott, Lucy Stone, and Angelina Grimké, who left her Southern plantation to work against slavery; Paulina Wright Davis, a wealthy one time moral reformer; Ernestine Rose, a Polish Jew active in the early temperance movement; Antoinette Brown, the first female Protestant minister. The leaders of this unusually large meeting—about 1,000 people came—set the agenda for subsequent conventions. They initiated petition campaigns in eight states for women's suffrage and established committees to report on women's educational, legal, and professional status.

Then as later, the press approached the Woman Question with hostility or scorn:

"What do women want?" ran an editorial in the *New York Herald*. "They want . . . to be lawyers, doctors . . . generals in the field. How funny it would sound . . . that Lucy Stone, pleading a cause . . . gave birth to a fine bouncing boy in court!" Other editors wrote of "petticoat rebellions" or "hen conventions" arranged by "love-starved spinsters."

Stanton stayed in Seneca Falls until the last of her seven children reached adolescence—surrounded, as she wrote to Wendell Phillips, "by small craft which I am struggling to tug up life's stream." Even so, her exceptional eloquence guaranteed her a central role during the early years of the movement; she wrote impassioned letters that were read aloud at each feminist convention. She was further encouraged when, through Amelia Bloomer, a neighbor who published *The Lily,* a monthly temperance newspaper, she met Susan B. Anthony, a Quaker temperance activist. In contrast to the high-spirited, talkative Stanton, Anthony was sober and introspective, yet the two became lifelong friends.

CHOOSING SIDES

This alliance proved essential to the women's movement. With Anthony's coaching, Stanton's ideas developed into powerful speeches and essays. Whereas all of the other feminist leaders had husbands and children to worry about, Anthony, unwed, could give all of her time to promoting the cause. Stanton fondly recalled how her friend would turn up with a briefcase full of slanderous diatribes by male politicians against women. "Whenever I saw that stately Quaker girl coming across my lawn," she wrote, "I knew that some happy convocation of the sons of Adam was to be set by the ears. She supplied the facts . . . I the philosophy."

In 1852, the New York State Men's Temperance Society invited women's groups to attend their annual meeting. However, they forbade the women to speak. Anthony, Mott, and other outraged delegates formed a rival New York State Women's Temperance Society, electing Stanton president. But Stanton's radical ideas—especially her insistence that women be permitted to divorce drunken husbands—dismayed conservatives. Even Bloomer took sides against Stanton. She was not reelected.

Anthony quit the temperance group out of loyalty to her friend. It was the beginning of both women's commitment to direct political agitation. Stanton outlined their goals: the full rewards of citizenship, including the right to vote; property and marriage reforms for wives—especially the right to dissolve unhappy marriages in divorce. (All were controversial, yet suffrage proved hardest to attain.)

Anthony organized a plan of action. She enlisted 60 women, one from every county in New York State, to be "captains" of a petition campaign. In six weeks she had signatures from over 10,000 women—5,931 for married women's rights; 4,164 for woman suffrage. But it was grueling work. Often women slammed their doors against the canvassers, Anthony reported, saying they had husbands, thank God, to look after their interests.

A SLAVE'S APPEAL

The petition campaign culminated in the Albany women's rights convention of 1854, timed by Anthony to take place while the New York legislature was in session. As she had hoped, the legislature allowed Stanton to present the petitions to the Joint Judiciary Committee. But the response to her plea came in a committee report asserting that since "the ladies always have the best place and choicest titbit at the table . . . the warmest place in the winter and the coolest place in the . . . if there is any inequity or oppression in the case, the gentlemen are the sufferers."

On Christmas Day 1854, Anthony set out alone to bring back more petition signatures, with $50 loaned by Wendell Phillips. During one of the coldest winters in New York's history, she traveled by train, sleigh, and often on foot, carrying a carpetbag full of tracts by Stanton. Often hungry and exhausted, she stayed in unheated hotels and passed the hat to cover her expenses. By May, she had canvassed 54 of New York's 60 counties.

This effort, and repeated efforts over the next five years, failed to stir Albany's male politicians. Not until 1860, when Stanton reappeared before the Judiciary Committee with a speech entitled "A Slave's Appeal," would legislators finally listen, though not to pleas for suffrage or changes in divorce law. They amended the existing Married Women's

Property Act to include child custody, control over earnings, and property rights for widows.*

However, marriage reform was not the most pressing issue in America by that time—not even to Stanton and Anthony. The country was on the verge of civil war over questions of slavery and states' rights, and these life-or-death issues consumed the attention of the reformers from whom feminists drew their support. Stanton and other leaders identified their aims with those of the abolitionists. At rallies sponsored by William Lloyd Garrison's American Anti-Slavery Society, women speakers argued that suffrage was a "natural right" both of white females and of the oppressed black race.

---

*Fourteen other states passed bills from 1848 to 1860 giving women limited property rights.

In 1857, the year the Supreme Court declared slavery permissible in the Dred Scott decision, Anthony started working as a paid organizer for Garrison. Stanton, whose husband allied himself with the conservative abolitionists, earlier had shared his fear that demanding an immediate end to slavery would provoke an unnecessary war. But by 1857 she had gone over to the radicals' cause, and in early 1861 she left home to join Anthony for a series of antislavery rallies in western New York. For suggesting that the newly elected president, Abraham Lincoln, commit himself to ending slavery, the two women often faced mobs throwing eggs and stones.

When the Civil War erupted in April 1861, all talk of women's rights abruptly stopped. Over Anthony's objections, Stanton and other feminists decided to devote themselves to supporting the war effort. They reasoned that a grateful government in Washington would reward their wartime loyalty with the right to vote. As Stanton later wrote, "It was a blunder." While she and others knitted socks and cared for the wounded, the New York legislature gutted its own 1860 marriage reform bill, banning joint child custody and revoking widows' property rights. Stanton and Anthony's wartime petition drive for universal enfranchisment would be seen by Congress as evidence of national support for black male suffrage only. The politics of postwar Reconstruction would divide the feminist movement over questions unrelated to women's rights. In the war's aftermath, feminists would have to start from scratch in many areas. But at least in a perverse way, the long, bloody conflict had advanced their cause: It showed how important civil rights could be.

Forgotten Forty-Niners

The common perception is that only "women of easy virtue" took part in the California Gold Rush. But a careful examination of the historical record shows that thousands of women engaged in virtually every occupation and inhabited every level of gold-rush society.

JoAnn Levy

Los Angeles author JoAnn Levy specializes in writing about California and Western history.

If Concord, Massachusetts is remembered for the "shot heard 'round the world," Sutter's Mill, in the foothills of California's Sierra Nevada, is remembered for the "shout heard 'round the world"—"Eureka!" As that cry reverberated across the globe in 1848 (and echoed into the 1850s), a flood of humanity converged on the land of golden opportunity. This human tide irrevocably changed the West, opening up the frontier as no other force in the nation's history has, before or since.

One of the most common assumptions about gold-rush-era California is that it was almost exclusively a male domain—and that such women as could be found there were prostitutes. As recently as 1983, a California historian asserted that "it was, literally, mankind which participated in the gold rush, for woman kind, at least of the 'proper' variety, was almost totally absent."

A careful study of surviving diaries, memoirs, newspapers, and census records from the period refutes this long-standing misperception, revealing that the vast wave of migration to California included thousands of "respectable" women—and numerous children, too.

Many of these adventurous women accompanied or followed their husbands, fathers, or brothers to the golden land; others arrived entirely on their own. Once in California, enterprising women engaged in almost every occupation and inhabited every level of society. They mined for gold, raised families, earned substantial sums by their domestic and entrepreneurial labors, and stayed on to help settle the land—contributing a facet of gold-rush history that until now has been largely overlooked or forgotten.

In actuality, so-called respectable women outnumbered prostitutes in California, even in 1850, by four to one. While 25 percent represents a large number, even if not in this instance a "respectable" one, it is far from a majority.

BEFORE THEY COULD AVAIL THEMSELVES of the opportunities afforded by the gold rush, woman argonauts, like their male counterparts, had to undertake and survive the arduous journey to California. Many travelers chose the Cape Horn route, braving gale, storm, and shipwreck on a voyage that consumed from five to seven months; others shortened the ocean journey by making the difficult crossing of the Isthmus of Panama via small boat and mule. In 1849, more than twenty thousand gold-seekers arrived at San Francisco by sea, and nearly twenty-five thousand more followed in 1850. Many journals and letters mention the presence of women on these routes, which travelers generally regarded as being safer for families than the even more daunting overland crossings.

Despite the hardships and dangers involved, thousands of other wealth-seekers trekked overland by wagon or on foot, crossing plains, deserts, and forbidding mountain ranges while carrying with them—and then often abandoning for survival's sake—their worldly possessions. Trail-journal entries suggest that of the twenty-five thousand people traveling overland in 1849, at least three thousand were women and fifteen hundred children. Forty-four thousand people crossed the plains the following year, and, given California's census of 1850, about ten percent of these may be assumed to have been female. News of hardship, starvation, and cholera stemmed the tide of overland emigrants in 1851 to little more than a thousand, but in 1852 an estimated fifty thousand again surged across the continent. By July 13, 1852 the Fort Kearny register had tallied for that year alone the passage of more than seven thousand women and eight thousand children.

"The country was so level that we could see long trains of white-topped wagons for many miles," recorded one woman of her experiences on the eastern segment of the overland trail. "And, when we drew nearer to the vast multitude and saw them in all manner of vehicles and conveyances, on horseback and on foot, all eagerly driving and hurrying forward, I thought, in my excitement, that if one-tenth of these teams and these people got [there] ahead of us, there would be nothing left for us in California worth picking up."

ON JUNE 28, 1849, THE "BUCKEYE ROVers," a company of young men heading from Ohio to California's gold fields, camped near Independence Rock on the overland trail. One of the group, John Banks, wrote in his diary that night of seeing "an Irish woman and daughter without any relatives on the way for gold. It is said she owns a fine farm in Missouri." Two weeks later, on the banks of the Green River, their paths converged again: "Last night the Irish woman and daughter were selling liquor near us. . . . Fifty cents a pint, quite moderate."

Some distance beyond the Green River, near the Humboldt River, a woman named Margaret Frink recorded in her journal for August 12, 1850: "Among the crowds on foot, a negro woman came tramping along through the heat and dust, carrying a cast-iron bake oven on her head, with her provisions and blanket piled on top—all she possessed in the world—bravely pushing on for California."

Frink and her husband had begun their westward trek in Indiana. Along the way they stopped at the home of a Mr. and Mrs. McKinney near St. Joseph, Missouri. "Mrs. McKinney," wrote Margaret in her diary, "told me of the wonderful tales of the abundance of gold that she had heard; "that they kept flour-scoops to scoop the gold out of the barrels that they kept it in, and that you could soon get all that you needed for the rest of your life. And as for a woman, if she could cook at all, she could get $16.00 per week for each man that she cooked for, and the only cooking required to be done was just to boil meat and potatoes and serve them on a big chip of wood, instead of a plate, and the boarder furnished the provisions.' I began at once to figure up in my mind how many men I could cook for, if there should be no better way of making money."

These vivid images of independent and determined women are strikingly at odds with the stereotypical picture of the long-suffering and sad-eyed pioneer wife peering wearily westward while a creaking covered wagon carries her ever farther from the comforts of home. Perhaps more startling is the departure from the perception of the gold rush as an exclusively male adventure.

ALL TRAVELERS ENDURED HARDSHIPS EN route to California, but the lure of gold enticed and beckoned like a rainbow's promise. Upon reaching the golden ground, numbers of women, as eager as any male red-shirted miner, grubbed in the dirt and creekbeds for the glittering ore. Gold fever raged in epidemic proportions, and women were not immune.

The journal of schoolteacher Lucena Parsons, married but a year, reveals her infection's daily progress. On May 30,

1851, Parsons confessed to "a great desire to see the gold diggings"; she accompanied the men and watched them mine for gold. On May 31, she wrote: "This morning the gold fever raged so high that I went again with the rest but got very little gold. . . ." On June 2, "again went to the canion [sic] to find that bewitching ore"; and June 3, "a general turn out to the mines . . . we made 10 dollars to day." On June 4, she went again "and did very well."

Elizabeth Gunn, who had sailed around the Horn with four young children to join her prospecting husband in Sonora, observed to her family back East that "a Frenchman and his wife live in the nearest tent, and they dig gold together. She dresses exactly like her husband—red shirt and pants and hat."

The editor of the *Alta California* reported a similar sighting: "We saw last April, a French woman, standing in Angel's Creek, dipping and pouring water into the washer, which her husband was rocking. She wore short boots, white duck pantaloons, a red flannel shirt, with a black leather belt and a Panama hat. Day after day she could be seen working quietly and steadily, performing her share of the gold digging labor. . . ."

Many of the women who tried mining, however, found the prize unworthy of the effort it required. Eliza Farnham, famed for attempting to deliver one hundred marriageable women to California, wrote that she "washed one panful of earth, under a burning noon-day sun . . . and must frankly confess, that the small particle of gold, which lies this day safely folded in a bit of tissue paper . . . did not in the least excite the desire to continue the search."

Louisa Clapp, wife of a doctor at Rich Bar, concurred, writing to her sister in the East: "I have become a *mineress;* that is, if the having washed a pan of dirt with my own hands, and procured therefrom three dollars and twenty-five cents in gold dust . . . will entitle me to the name. I can truly say, with the blacksmith's apprentice at the close of his first day's work at the anvil, that 'I am sorry I learned the trade'; for I wet my feet, tore my dress, spoilt a pair of new gloves, nearly froze my fingers, got an awful headache, took cold and lost a valuable breastpin, in this my labor of love."

Mary Ballou, at the mining camp of Negro Bar, wrote her son Selden, left behind in New Hampshire, that she "washed out about a Dollars worth of

"I like my Voyage very much so far and anticipate a great deal of pleasure yet to come[.] I have seen some things that I never could at home."

gold dust . . . so you see that I am doing a little mining in this gold region but I think it harder to rock the cradle to wash out gold than it is to rock the cradle for Babies in the States."

THE LABOR WAS INDEED DISCOURAGING, and most gold-rushing women found it easier—and more profitable—to market their domestic skills in exchange for the glittering metal. As Margaret Frink had heard, if "a woman could cook at all," she could earn her living. Boasted one fiercely independent woman: "I have made about $18,000 worth of pies—about one third of this has been clear profit. One year I dragged my own wood off the mountain and chopped it, and I have never had so much as a child to take a step for me in this country. $ 11,000 I baked in one little iron skillet, a considerable portion by a campfire, without the shelter of a tree from the broiling sun. . . ."

Forty-niner Sarah Royce, who journeyed overland to California with her husband and three-year-old daughter, met a woman at Weaverville who "evidently felt that her prospect of making money was very enviable." The woman received one hundred dollars a month to cook three meals a day, was provided an assistant, and did no dishwashing.

In San Francisco, Chastina Rix supplemented the family income by ironing. In one week she noted that she had ironed sixty shirts, thirty-five starched and twenty-five plain, plus "hosts of other clothes & I have made twelve dollars by my labor." Her husband Alfred wrote to friends in the East that Chastina "is making money faster than half the good farmers in Peacham. She has just bought her another silk dress & lots of toggery & cravats & gloves for me and all the nice things & has quite a fund at interest at 3 per cent a month."

Laundresses were in especially high demand in the gold fields: during the early days of the rush some desperate

In a rare 1852 daguerreotype of a California mining operation, a woman visits diggings near Auburn—perhaps to deliver a basket lunch to her husband and his partners. Other even more free-spirited women participated actively at the sluice box and cradle. Among the more fortunate of these was a Mrs. H. H. Smith who, while working with her husband in French Ravine, discovered a nugget weighing ninety-seven-and-a-half pounds, "estimated by Langton and Company, bankers, at Downieville . . . to be of nearly $13,000 in value."

miners shipped their laundry to the Sandwich [Hawaiian] Islands and even to China, waiting as long as six months for its return. Abby Mansur, at the Horseshoe Bar camp, wrote to her sister in New England about a neighbor who earned from fifteen to twenty dollars a month washing, "so you can see that women stand as good a chance as men[;] if it was not for my heart I could make a great deal but I am not stout enough to do it."

WHETHER WASHING OR COOKING, MINing or ironing, women at work in frontier California toiled arduously. No labor, however, seemed more intimidating than keeping a boarding house. In 1850, about one out of every hundred persons gainfully employed in California ran some sort of hotel. Many were women, and none attested more eloquently to the labor involved than forty-niner Mary Jane Megquier, who had crossed the Isthmus from Winthrop, Maine to run a San Francisco boarding house.

"I should like to give you an account

of my work if I could do it justice," Megquier wrote. "I get up and make the coffee, then I make the biscuit, then I fry the potatoes then broil three pounds of steak, and as much liver, while the [hired] woman is sweeping, and setting the table, at eight the bell rings and they are eating until nine. I do not sit until they are nearly all done . . . after breakfast I bake six loaves of bread (not very big) then four pies, or a pudding then we have lamb, for which we have paid nine dollars a quarter, beef, pork, baked, turnips, beets, potatoes, radishes, sallad [sic], and that everlasting soup, every day, dine at two, for tea we have hash, cold meat bread and butter sauce and some kind of cake and I have cooked every mouthful that has been eaten excepting one day and a half that we were on a steamboat excursion. I make six beds every day and do the washing and ironing[.] you must think that I am very busy and when I dance all night I am obliged to trot all day and if I had not the constitution of six horses I should [have] been dead long ago but I am going to

give up in the fall whether or no, as I am sick and tired of work. . . ."

Although Megquier fails to mention how much she earned from these herculean exertions, another female fortyniner formerly of Portland, Maine earned $189 a week from her ten boarders, clearing about $75 after expenses. The accommodations she shared with them were minimal, if not spartan:

"[We] have one small room about 14 feet square, and a little back room we use for a store room about as large as a piece of chalk. Then we have an open chamber over the whole, divided off by a cloth. The gentlemen occupy the one end, Mrs. H—and a daughter, your father and myself, the other. We have a curtain hung between our beds, but we do not take pains to draw it, as it is of no use to be particular here. . . . We sleep on a cot without any bedding or pillow except our extra clothing under our heads."

California's inflated economy required that everyone work who could, as fortyniner Luzena Wilson, an overlander with her husband Mason and two young sons,

vigorously affirmed: "Yes, we worked; we did things that our high-toned servants would now look at aghast, and say it was impossible for a woman to do. But the one who did not work in '49 went to the wall. It was a hand to hand fight with starvation at the first. . . ."

William Tecumseh Sherman, a goldrush banker before history called him to greater fame as a Union general in the Civil War, confessed to a friend that keeping his wife Ellen in California ruined him financially: "No man should have a wife in California. . . . Unless she be a working woman, no man can by his own labor support her."

Many women like Ellen Sherman, accustomed to servants and unaccustomed to labor, gave up and returned east. Those willing to work, however, received substantial rewards in an economy where a washer-woman earned more than a United States congressmen. Writing from San Francisco in 1850, one woman declared: "A smart woman can do very well in this country true there are not many comforts and one must

Instead of mining for gold, most women argonauts preferred to market their skills, cooking for the miners, doing their laundry, or running hotels. This 1850s view in Sonora includes several women and at least two children. Pioneering Californians found domestic work hardly less demanding than mining—and some found it discouraging. "Three times a day I set my Table which is about thirty feet in length," wrote boarding-house keeper Mary Ballou: "I would not advise any Lady to come out here and suffer the toil and fatigue that I have suffered for the sake of a little gold."

"THE WINTER OF 1849" BY FRANK MARRYAT (1855); COURTESY OF THE NEW-YORK HISTORICAL SOCIETY, NEW YORK CITY

Women arriving in gold-rush California discovered the region almost totally lacking in civilized amenities. One of the first nuisances they had to cope with was the abysmal state of San Francisco's streets—"one vast fathomless sea of mud . . . Its composition is heterogeneous, its character antipellucid, its adhesive qualities immense and antagonistic to a composed state of nerves." Commenting on appropriate female attire for such conditions, one newspaper editor observed that "in one or two cases we have detected bona fide pantaloons peeping out from beneath the 'flowing skirts' . . . If ladies go out . . . no objection ought certainly to be urged to their appearance in boots and whatdycallems to protect them from the mud."

work all the time and work hard but [there] is plenty to do and good pay[.] If I was in Boston now and know what I now know of California I could come out here[.] If I had to hire the money to bring me out. It is the only country I ever was in where a woman received anything like a just compensation for work."

MANY OTHER GOLD-RUSHING WOMEN both affirmed the necessity to work and observed that there were "not many comforts." Those who had arrived via the overland trail, for example, often continued to make their beds in tents and wagons, like Mrs. John Berry, who protested: "Oh! you who lounge on your divans & sofas, sleep on your fine, luxurious beds and partake of your rich viands at every meal know nothing of the life of a California emigrant. Here are we sitting, on a pine block, a log or a bunk; sleeping in beds with either a quilt or a blanket as substitute for sheets, (I can tell you it is very aristocratic to have a bed at all), & calico pillow-cases for our pillows."

Harriet Ward, already a fifty-year-old grandmother when she journeyed overland, wrote happy descriptions of her roomy cabin and pine-stump furniture in

"Everybody ought to go to the mines, just to see how little it takes to make people comfortable in the world."

remote Sierra County. But of the beds she penned only, "Oh, such beds! I will say nothing of them!"

One report of a comfortable California bed does survive in the reminiscence of a guest at a celebrated gold-rush hostelry. The St. Francis boasted that it was the first San Francisco hotel to offer sheets on its beds. The lady confirmed that her bed there was "delightful." Two "soft hair mattresses" and "a pile of snowy blankets" hastened her slumbers. On this occasion, however, the California deficiency was not the bed, but the *walls*:

"I was suddenly awakened by voices, as I thought, in my room; but which I soon discovered came from two gentlemen, one on each side of me, who were talking to each other from their own rooms *through* mine; which, as the walls were only of canvas and paper, they could easily do. This was rather a startling discovery, and I at once began to cough, to give them notice of my *interposition* lest I should become an unwilling auditor of matters not intended for my ear. The conversation ceased, but before I was able to compose myself to sleep again . . . a nasal serenade commenced, which, sometimes a duet and sometimes a solo, frightened sleep from my eyes. . . ."

The walls of most early California habitations consisted of bleached cotton cloth stretched tightly and fastened to the dwelling's frame, then papered over. "These partitions look as firm and solid as they do made the usual way," noted Mrs. D. B. Bates, wife of a ship's captain, "but they afford but a slight hindrance to the passage of sounds."

California construction astonished Sarah Walsworth, a missionary's wife, who watched a house being built in Oakland: "Only a slight underpinning is laid on the ground, upon which rest the joists of the floor which is carefully laid down *first thing.* This looked so odd to me at first, that I could but laugh[.] Give a carpenter a few feet of *lumber*, a few doors, & windows, a few pounds of nails & screws a few hinges; to a paperhanger, a few yards of cloth & a few rolls of paper—to them *both* a *good deal* of *gold* & you may have a house in 6 days—perhaps in less time. You will have no trouble with 'digging cellars,' laying wall, having a 'raising' nor with dirty 'masons'—but after it is all done it is but an improved speaking-trumpet[.]"

At Santa Cruz, forty-niner Eliza Farnham built her own house. "Let not ladies lift their hands in horror," she wrote, "[but] I designed supplying the place of journeyman carpenter with my own hands." She succeeded so well, she confessed, "that during its progress I laughed . . . at the idea of promising to pay a man $14 or $16 per day for doing what I found my hands so dexterous in."

WHILE MOST WOMEN MADE DO WITH tents, cabins, and flimsily constructed clapboard houses, a very few enjoyed luxurious surroundings. "See yonder house," wrote a San Francisco chronicler. "Its curtains are of the purest white lace embroidered, and crimson damask. . . . All the fixtures are of a keeping, most expensive, most voluptuous, most gorgeous. . . ." Upon the Brussels carpet "whirls the politician with some

sparkling beauty," he added, "as fair as frail. . . ."

The house described is thought to have been that of Belle Cora, a beauty from Baltimore by way of New Orleans, who crossed the Isthmus in 1849 with gambler Charles Cora. Belle and a handful of other successful parlorhouse madams lived extravagantly, but such magnificence was the exception among California's demimonde population.

The first prostitutes to gold-rush California sailed from Valparaiso, Chile, where news of the gold discovery arrived in August 1848 via the Chilean brig *J.R.S.* Many of these women not only married argonauts, but enjoyed the luxury of choosing among their suitors.

Other Latin women, however, fared poorly. Hundreds, through indenture arrangements, were destined for fandango houses, the poor man's brothels. José Fernandez, the first alcalde at San Jose under American rule, wrote: "They did not pay passage on the ships, but when they reached San Francisco the captains sold them to the highest bidder. There were men who, as soon as any ship arrived from Mexican ports with a load of women, took two or three small boats, or a launch, went on board the ship, paid to the captain the passage of ten or twelve unfortunates and took them immediately to their cantinas, where the newcomers were forced to prostitute themselves for half a year, during which the proprietors took the bulk of their earnings."

China, like Chile, received news of California's gold discovery in 1848. By 1854, San Francisco's burgeoning Chinatown included hundreds of Chinese girls imported for prostitution. Typically, agents took arriving Chinese girls to a basement in Chinatown where they were stripped for examination and purchase. Depending on age, beauty, and the prevailing market, they sold from $300 to $3,000.

American women were not exempt from similar exploitation, albeit more subtly executed. In late 1849 and early 1850, several prostitutes in the East received passage to California by signing contracts as domestics. Some unethical agencies subsequently adopted the ploy of advertising that "servants" were wanted in California and receiving exceptional wages. A number of girls innocently responded to these procurement fronts that masqueraded as employment offices.

France similarly pounced on the fortuitous discovery at Sutter's Mill. Recruiting agents, as well as the French government, assisted the emigration of French women, who arrived in California literally by the boatload. Testified one eyewitness: 'They have done the wildest kinds of business you can imagine in San Francisco, such as auctioning off women in the public square. I got there when matters had settled down somewhat: a ship arrived with sixty French women, none of them had paid her passage, so they offered a girl to anyone who would pay what she owed. Next day they did not have a single one left."

"[True] there are not many comforts, and one must work all the time and work hard. . . ."

A knowledgeable Frenchman noted that his countrywomen profitably hired themselves out to stand at gaming tables: "All in all, the women of easy virtue here earn a tremendous amount of money. This is approximately the tariff.

"To sit with you near the bar or at a card table, a girl charges one ounce ($16) an evening. She had to do nothing save honor the table with her presence. This holds true for the girls selling cigars. when they sit with you. Remember they only work in the gambling halls in the evening. They have their days to themselves and can then receive all the clients who had no chance during the night. . . . .

"Nearly all these women at home were streetwalkers of the cheapest sort. But out here, for only a few minutes, they ask a hundred times as much as they were used to getting in Paris. A whole night costs from $200 to $400."

PROVIDING THEATRICAL ENTERTAINMENT for lonesome miners offered a less notorious but equally profitable means of amassing California gold. Everywhere forty-niners could be found, from San Francisco's gilt-decorated theaters to the rough boards of a mining camp stage lit by candles stuck in whiskey bottles, actresses, dancers, singers, and musicians performed before appreciative audiences.

The pay varied as much as the venue. In Grass Valley, a black woman presented public piano concerts, charging fifty cents admission. The miners of

Downieville bestowed $500 in gold on a young female vocalist who made them homesick by sweetly singing old familiar ballads. A Swiss organ-girl, by playing in gambling halls, accumulated $4,000 in about six months. A Frenchwoman who played the violin at San Francisco's Alhambra gambling hall earned two ounces of gold daily, about $32.

In 1850, three French actresses opened at San Francisco's Adelphi Theatre. A critic observed that two of them "have been on the stage for a long time (I was about to write too long a time), and . . . have never definitely arrived." The women succeeded despite the quality of the performances, for the critic noted that they "have not done badly from a financial point of view, as they now own the building, the lot, and the scenery."

Renowned female performers willing to try their fortunes in far-off California achieved enormous success. Soprano Catherine Hayes, a tall blonde woman of imposing appearance, introduced costumed operatic presentations to the San Francisco stage and was rumored to have departed from the golden state with an estimated quarter-million dollars. Lola Montez cleared $16,000 a week for performing her titillating spider dance.

CALIFORNIA'S FREE AND OPEN SOCIETY also permitted women to pursue a variety of other employments nominally deemed unacceptable for their gender. The editor of the *Alta California* welcomed a female doctor with a cheerfully delivered jibe: "So few ladies in San Francisco that the new M.D. may attend them all. . . . No circumlocutions necessary. . . . Simply, as woman to woman: 'Saw my leg off!' "

The same newspaper advised "those wishing to have a good likeness are informed that they can have them taken in a very superior manner, by a real live lady, in Clay street, opposite the St. Francis Hotel, at a very moderate charge. Give her a call, gents."

The editor also boosted the business of a female barber with a shop on Commercial street by admitting that it was 'not an unpleasant operation . . . to take a clean shave at the hands of a lady fair."

Advertising her own skills in the San Francisco paper was "Madame St. Dennis—Late of Pennsylvania," who could be "consulted on matters of love, law and business, from 8 a.m. to 8 p.m. Office second brown cottage from Union

street, between Stockton and Dupont." Similarly self-promoting was the linguistically talented Madame de Cassins: 'The celebrated diviner, explains the past and predicts the future. Can be consulted in English, French, Italian, Greek, Arabic and Russian . . . No. 69 Dupont st." And, at the site of the future state capital, "Miss Chick begs to inform the inhabitants of Sacramento, that she has taken a suite of rooms . . . for the purpose of teaching all the new and fashionable dances."

CALIFORNIA'S EARLY NEWSPAPERS ARE a mother lode of rich and often surprising information about female gold-rushers; tidbits are as diverse as the experiences of these women.

Three women, for example, made one newspaper's December 14, 1850 listing of San Francisco millionaires: Mrs. Elizabeth Davis, Mrs. Fuller, and Mrs. Wm. M. Smith. And in September 1850, noted another article, a fire destroyed the capacious dwelling house of Mrs. Jane Smith, "erected a few months since at an expense of $10,000."

At the opposite end of the spectrum, on March 10, 1850, the *Alta* reported the particulars of a washerwomen's meeting at which laundry fees were discussed and jointly agreed.

Newspapers also reported what we would term gossip-column material today, such as an item appearing in the September 14, 1852 *Alta:* 'Forlorn: This was the charge written against Eliza Hardscrabble's name on the Recorder's docket. Unacquainted with the peculiar character of this offence, we referred to Webster, and found perhaps the proper definition, 'a lost forsaken, solitary person. Yes, Eliza is one of 'em. Whether blighted affection, harrowing care, or an erring be the cause, she is now an incurable rum-drinker, and is no longer fit to take care of herself."

Quite able to take care of herself was Dorothy Scraggs. Nonetheless, she advertised in a Marysville newspaper that she wanted a husband. She advised that she could "wash, cook, scour, sew, milk, spin, weave, hoe, (can't plow), cut wood, make fires, feed the pigs, raise chicks . . . saw a plank, drive nails, etc." She added that she was neither handsome nor a fright, yet an *old* man need *not* apply, nor any who have not a little more education than she has, and a great deal more gold, for there must be $20,000 settled on her before she will

"I get up and make the coffee, then I make the biscuit, then I fry the potatoes then broil three pounds of steak, and as much liver . . . after breakfast I bake six loaves of bread . . . then four pies, or a pudding . . . I make six beds every day and do the washing and ironing[.] you must think that I am very busy and when I dance all night I am obliged to trot all day and if I had not the constitution of six horses I should [have] been dead long ago . . ."

bind herself to perform all of the above."

Court records, too, provide intriguing glimpses into the lives of gold-rushing women. In July 1850 Mrs. Mary King testified in the Sacramento justice court that persons unknown had stolen from her two leather bags containing gold dust and California coin worth about $3,500.

According to the record of *People v. Seymour alias Smith,* Fanny Seymour was indicted on a charge of assault with intent to commit murder when she shot stage-driver Albert Putnam for refusing to pay for a bottle of wine.

In *People v. Potter,* Sarah Carroll's case against William Potter, whom she claimed stole $700 in gold coin from her trunk, was dismissed because she was black and Potter was white.

Equally interesting are the surviving letters, diaries, and reminiscences of men who encountered women during their California adventures. For instance, Enos Christman, a young miner, witnessed a bullfight in Sonora at which a "magnificently dressed" *matadora* entered the arena: "She plunged the sword to the hilt into the breast of the animal. She was sprinkled with crimson dye . . . and greeted with a shower of silver dollars."

In Weaverville, Franklin Buck, a trader, was smitten by a young woman who owned a train of mules by which she delivered flour to the distant mining community: "I had a strong idea of offering myself . . . but Angelita told me she had a husband somewhere in the mines . . . so I didn't ask."

Lawyer John McCrackan met a woman who, while en route to California, brought fresh produce from a Pacific island as a speculative venture: She sold some pieces of jewelry . . . which cost her about twenty dollars at home [and] purchased onions which she sold on arriving here for eighteen hundred dollars, quite a handsome sum, is it not?" . . . She also brought some quinces & made quite a nice little profit on them."

Most fascinating, however, are the women's own observations of life in the gold regions. Wrote Abby Mansur from Horseshoe Bar: "I tell you the women are in great demand in this country no matter whether they are married or not[.] You need not think [it] strange if you see me coming home with some good looking man some of these times with a pocket full of rocks . . . it is all the go here for Ladys to leave there [sic]

Husbands[.] two out of three do it."

In fact, the divorce rate in gold-rush California was startlingly high. One judge, growing impatient with incessant requests for divorces under California's permissive divorce law, sought to deter further applications to his court by publishing his negative decision in *Avery v. Avery* in *Sacramento Daily Union.*

BY THE END OF 1853, A CONTEMPORARY historian estimated California's female population at more than sixty thousand, plus about half that many children. In San Francisco alone, women numbered about eight thousand.

By that time, energy and gold had transformed San Francisco from a city of tents into a booming metropolis. No longer a hamlet, the city reflected the changes taking place throughout the newly admitted state. Its people were no longer simply transient miners. Men were bankers and businessmen, lawyers and doctors, farmers and manufacturers. They intended to stay.

So did the women, as California pioneer Mallie Stafford later recalled. "Very few, if any, in those [first] days

contemplated permanently settling in the country. . . . But as time wore on . . . they came to love the strange new country . . . and found that they were wedded to the new home, its very customs, the freedom of its lovely hills and valleys."

Thus tens of thousands of women, through choice, chance, or circumstance, found themselves in California during the "great adventure." And, after the gold fever eventually subsided, many of them remained to help settle the land. Although they are today a neglected part of gold-rush history, the "forgotten forty-niners" were there when history was being made and they helped to make it.

Reading Notes: Author Jo Ann Levy's *They Saw the Elephant: Women in the California Gold Rush* (Shoe String Press, 1990) is one of only a few volumes devoted exclusively to women in early California. Firsthand accounts of the gold rush by women include Louisa Clapps's *Shirley Letters from the California Mines, 1851–1852* (Peregrine Smith, 1983) and Sarah Royce's *A Frontier Lady: Recollections of the Gold Rush and Early California* (University of Nebraska Press, 1977). Also see *Covered Wagon Women: Diaries & Letters from the Western Trails, 1840–1890* (Arthur H. Clark, 1983).

The War Against Demon Rum

With alcohol consumption on the rise in 19th-century America, the temperance cause took root.

Robert Maddox

Robert Maddox, of Pennsylvania State University, is a distinguished historian whose article "War In Korea: The Desperate Times" appeared in the July 1978 issue of AHI. *For those interested in reading further on the subject of temperance he suggests* The Origins of Prohibition *(1925), by John Allen Krout and* Ardent Spirits *(1973), by John Kobler.*

"Good-bye, John Barleycorn," cried the Reverend Billy Sunday to an approving crowd, "You were God's worst enemy. You were Hell's best friend. I hate you with a perfect hatred. I love to hate you." The date was January 16, 1920, the day when the Eighteenth Amendment to the Constitution went into effect. Drys across the nation celebrated happily, while drinkers cursed and contemplated a future without alcohol. Both were premature. John Barleycorn was by no means dead, though he did go underground for more than a decade. But on that first day, those who had worked on behalf of prohibition could congratulate themselves on a victory over what at times had seemed insurmountable odds.

From the first settlements at Jamestown and Plymouth Rock, Americans have brewed, fermented, and distilled everything they could. Though their drinking customs were from Europe, the colonists displayed remarkable ingenuity in devising additional reasons for having a cup of this or a mug of that. Writers of early travel accounts express surprise as to the amount of alcohol the colonists consumed. Everything from the crudest beers and ciders to the most elegant wines ran down American throats in amazing quantities.

During the colonial period there were few attempts to restrict the availability of alcohol, much less to prohibit it entirely. Public houses and taverns abounded. Even in Puritan New England, contrary to popular legend, the people had virtually unrestricted access to spirits of all kinds. Indeed, alcohol was seen as one of God's blessings, to be enjoyed as He intended. When taken in moderation, it was believed to be beneficial for both the mind and the body.

Drunkenness was another matter. Defined in one colony as "drinking with excess to the notable perturbation of any organ of sense or motion," public inebriation was dealt with harshly. The penalties varied from place to place but ranged from fines for first offenders to hard labor or whippings for chronic indulgers. Still, drunkenness was seen as a personal weakness or sin, and the guilty party had no one save himself to blame. Alcohol bore the responsibility scarcely more than did the fire which burned down a careless person's home.

A number of people, principally clergymen, spoke out or wrote locally distributed tracts denouncing the intemperate use of intoxicants. This was particularly true after the middle of the 17th century when rum and whiskey replaced the milder ciders and wines. To some it appeared their communities were in danger of drowning in alcohol. It was not until 1784 that any single temperance tract received wide attention. In that year the eminent Philadelphia physician, Dr. Benjamin Rush, published his "An Inquiry into the Effects of Spiritous Liquors on the Human Body and Mind." This pamphlet went through many editions and portions of the work were widely reprinted in newspapers and almanacs across the entire country.

The reception accorded Rush's tract undoubtedly reflected a growing concern about the problems concerning alcoholic consumption. Aside from its popularity, the pamphlet differed from earlier ones in several ways. First of all, as a physician-general in the Continental Army during the Revolution, Rush had had ample opportunity to observe the effects of drinking on soldiers. Thus his words had the backing of what appeared to be scientific examination, rather than mere moral exhortation. Rush denied the popular notions that drinking helped prevent fatigue, protected one against cold, and many other popular myths of the day. Quite the contrary, he argued, in general the consumption of alcohol helped *bring on* diseases of both the mind and of the body. Second, his pamphlet differed from previous ones in that he not only warned against excessive amounts of drink, but claimed that even moderate use over an extended period of time would have harmful effects. It is interesting to note, however, that Rush's broadside was directed against distilled spirits only. Beers and light wines, he thought, *were* beneficial if taken in moderation.

How much effect, if any, Rush's pamphlet had on the consumption of alcohol at the time is uncertain. But it did inspire a number of reformers who took up the temperance cause in the years following. Perhaps the most important, and colorful, of these was the Reverend Lyman Beecher of East Hampton, Long Island. Father of thirteen children (including the famous Henry Ward Beecher and the even more famous Harriet Beecher Stowe), Beecher had been appalled by the drinking habits of his fellow students while at Yale and little he saw thereafter reassured him. Indeed, he came to believe, alcohol posed the greatest threat to the society's physical and spiritual well-being. Though males were the worst offenders, even women consumed im-

From *American History Illustrated*, May 1979. Reprinted through the courtesy of Cowles Magazines, publishers of *American History Illustrated.*

pressive amounts. Nor were the clergy immune.

Beecher spoke of attending one convocation where, after a time, the room came to look and smell "like a very active grog shop." Worse yet were the amounts of alcohol given to children of all ages. Fairfax Downey, in a recent article about Beecher, tells the story of a 7-year-old girl who visited her grandmother in Boston. When she learned she would be given no spirits, she angrily notified her parents. "Missy," the grandmother learned, "had been brought up as a lady and must have wine and beer with every meal." Beecher was so concerned about the situation that he claimed he never gave a child even the smallest amount of money without adding the warning "not to drink ardent spirits or any inebriating liquor."

Beecher frequently lectured his congregation on the dangers of drink, and became even more active in the cause after taking the pastorate at Litchfield, Connecticut, in 1811. He was instrumental in forming one of the first temperance groups, the Connecticut Society for the Reformation of Morals. Among other things, the Society printed and distributed large numbers of Dr. Rush's pamphlet. In 1825 Beecher delivered six sermons on the temperance issue which later were published in pamphlet form. Widely reprinted in the years following, the "Six Sermons" according to one scholar, "were as widely read and exerted as great an influence as any other contribution to the literature of the reform."

The Reverend Beecher went beyond earlier temperance leaders in several respects. Like Dr. Rush, he believed that the sustained use of liquor was harmful even if one never actually got drunk. "Let it therefore be engraven upon the heart of every man," he wrote, "that the daily use of ardent spirits, in any form, or in any degree, is intemperance." Beecher's prescription was radical; he called for nothing less than total abstinence from distilled beverages. He differed from Rush on the question of drinking wine as well. Rush had recommended it; Beecher thought it a treacherous way station on the road to stronger potions. Under the influence of Beecher, and others like him, the temperance movement had come a long way from mere denunciations of drunkenness.

The 1830's witnessed a remarkable growth of temperance societies. The United States Temperance Union (later renamed the American Temperance Union) was founded in 1833, though four years passed before it held its first national convention. Despite its increasing popularity, the cause suffered grievously from internal disunity. For some, temperance meant what the word itself meant: moderation. For others, such as Beecher, it had come to mean abstinence. And what was to be included in the list of harmful beverages: distilled spirits only, or wines and beers too? Finally, should temperance (however defined) be promoted exclusively by moral suasion, or should the societies enter the realm of politics? Members of the various groups wrangled over these questions in seemingly endless debates which did little to achieve effectiveness.

A new development took place after 1840. Until this time, the most visible leaders of the cause were opinion leaders such as clergymen, newspaper publishers, and college presidents. Beginning with a group which called itself the Washington Temperance Society, however, a new element came to the fore: reformed drinkers. These were men who, some way or another, had seen the light and who wanted to help save others. Who knew better the evils of drink than those who once had been in its clutches themselves? This "Washington revival," as it became known, spread throughout the country and produced a number of eloquent spokesmen for the temperance cause.

One of the most popular of the reformed drunkards was John H.W. Hawkins. Hawkins began drinking as a young lad while serving as an apprentice to a hatmaker. For more than twenty years he alternated between periods of excessive drinking and relative sobriety. Finally, as his bouts with alcohol became longer and more debilitating he was no longer able to provide for his family and became a public ward. According to his own account, Hawkins was redeemed when members of the Washington Temperance Society in Baltimore convinced him to sign a pledge of total abstinence. Possessing impressive oratorical talents, Hawkins went on to become one of the cause's most sought-after speakers. He later estimated that during his first ten years as a reformer he traveled more than 100,000 miles and delivered some 2,500 lectures.

John Bartholomew Gough was equally in demand. Gough too had begun drinking as a youngster, and his habit cost him job after job and several physical breakdowns. During one, when his seriously ill wife tried to nurse him through, the strain proved too much for her and she died. For some time after her death he rarely drew a sober breath. When finally converted by a friend, Gough pitched himself wholeheartedly into the cause. By several accounts he was a masterful speaker, able to manipulate the emotions of his audience as he wished. He boasted in his autobiography that singlehandedly he accounted for more than 15,000 converts to abstinence.

Things did not always go smoothly for Gough. Early in his career as a reformer he "fell off the wagon" and did so again at the height of his popularity in 1845. The latter occasion touched off quite a furor. While visiting New York City Gough disappeared for almost a week. After a desperate search, friends located him in a bawdy house in one of the seedier sections of the city. He was, it was obvious, recovering from a monumental drinking spree. The incident received wide publicity as the anti-temperance press had a field day at Gough's expense. He claimed innocence. An acquaintance, whose name he could not remember, had treated him to a glass supposedly containing only a soft drink. Having consumed the beverage, Gough claimed, he blanked out and did not know how he ended up where he did. How many people believed Gough's explanation—implying as it did that the liquor interests had conspired to do him in—is unknown, but he remained a popular speaker on the temperance circuit for another five years.

The temperance movement evolved one step more during the pre-Civil War years. It was becoming painfully evident to some that, despite the thousands of pamphlets issued, meetings held, and speeches delivered, the drinking habits of most Americans had not changed. Taverns and saloons prospered, men and women reeled about in the streets, and the gallons of drink consumed rose with each passing year. But what of all the converts? The usual evidence of success consisted of the number of signed pledges individuals or societies collected from "redeemed" individuals, who promised either moderation or total abstinence.

There were two problems with this approach. First, even in the most rewarding years no more than a tiny percentage of the adult population signed such promises. Second, how valid were they? To be sure, an effective speaker such as Hawkins or Gough could cause people to struggle in the aisles to sign up. But when emotions cooled, it was obvious, many resumed their old habits. Indeed, as one anti-temperance joke had it, some individuals became so elated by taking the pledge that they could scarcely wait to celebrate by having a few drinks. Increasingly, therefore, temperance advocates sought to strengthen moral persuasion with legal enforcement.

Some reformers had advocated legal controls in the 1830's and 1840's, but they were always in the minority. True conversion could only come through education, the majority had argued, and there was great fear that the purity of the cause would become sullied by entangling it in partisan politics. But this position became increasingly untenable as time wore on; unaided moral suasion simply had not achieved the desired effects. Nor was local-option legislation sufficient. This tactic had been tried in many communities, but serious drinkers could always lay in a supply from nearby towns or cities. Some reformers, therefore, came to believe that nothing less than statewide prohibition could get the job done. A formidable under-taking to be sure, but the prospects were dazzling.

Neal Dow was a successful businessman who looked the part. He wore expensive clothes, a lace-trimmed vest, and kept the time by a fat gold watch reportedly costing more than $200. He was dynamic, aggressive, and exuded vitality. Although slight of stature, Dow feared no man and used his fists effectively when the occasion demanded it. He was also a devout reformer. Dow devoted his life to the temperance cause and, as early as the 1830's, had become convinced that state prohibition was the only answer.

Born and raised in Portland, Maine, Dow practiced the teachings of his temperance-minded parents with a vengeance. At the age of 18 he joined the volunteer fire department of Portland and before very long somehow convinced the group to stop serving alcohol at its social get-togethers. Later, as captain, he enraged many drinkers by allowing a liquor store to burn to the ground

without turning a hose on it. Called before the city's board of alderman to account for his behavior, Dow claimed he had acted as he did to "save" adjacent buildings. On another occasion, when the casks of a wholesale dealer were erupting into fireballs, Dow remarked to an aide that it was a "magnificent sight." Small wonder that the liquor interests in Portland would have preferred another fire chief.

But Dow was after bigger game. Throughout the 1840's he worked tirelessly to bring the temperance issue into the political arena. At first he concentrated on turning Portland dry, but statewide legislation was his real goal. He was careful not to allow prohibition to become a partisan issue; he and his allies (he often used his own employees to do temperance work) supported all those who were "right" on the good cause. At last, in 1851, Dow won what had seemed an impossible victory. With many members of both houses indebted to him politically, he shepherded through the Maine legislature the first general prohibition law in American history. Dow, who was by this time mayor of Portland, prosecuted the new law to the best of his considerable abilities.

The Maine Law of 1851 served as rallying point for prohibitionists in other states. Dubbed "The Napoleon of Temperance," Dow became a hero to drys everywhere as the following song attests:

Come all ye friends of temperance, and listen to my strain,
I'll tell you how Old Alchy fares down in the State of Maine.
There's one Neal Dow, a Portland man, with great and noble soul,
He framed a law, without a flaw, to banish alcohol.

Unfortunately, as Dow himself admitted privately, alcohol was not "banished" from Maine, but flowed rather freely through illegal channels. Still, it was a step forward, and in the next four years two territories and eleven states enacted similar laws. Many people deserved the credit, if such it be, but no one more than Dow who advised and counseled his fellow reformers across the nation.

The hope that prohibition would become an irresistible tide proved illusory after the mid-1850's. The most important reason was the growing sectional struggle which culminated in thee Civil War. As compared to the great issues of slav-

ery and secession, prohibition seemed almost trivial except to the faithful. More than twenty-five years were to pass before another state would adopt prohibition. Equally ominous, though less obvious, was a simple statistic. During those years of temperance victories the per capita consumption of wine, whiskey, and beer *rose* from slightly over four gallons to almost six and one-half. Later prohibitionists ignored or downplayed the grim truth that laws in the books were ineffective so long as a sufficient number of people were willing to disobey them.

By the early 1870's, the temperance movement began stirring again. One of the most significant developments of this era was the role women played. Women always had constituted the backbone of the movement in terms of numbers, but men invariably held the positions of leadership. The first sign of change occurred in what became known as the "Women's Crusade." In communities across the nation groups of women assembled in front of saloons and taverns, vowing to remain until owners agreed to close. For hours, days, and even longer the women sang and prayed, and tried to discourage men from entering. Some places indeed did close, but usually only temporarily and the Crusade dwindled after a few years. Veterans of the Crusade were not about to quit, however, and in 1874 formed the Woman's Christian Temperance Union. This organization would play an important part in the drive for national prohibition.

The dominant force of the WCTU until her death in 1898 was Frances Willard. Born into a family dedicated to reform (her father was a member of the Washington Society), Willard was a

This temperance cartoon was captioned "Commit him for manslaughter in the greatest degree." ("Harper's Weekly," March 21, 1874)

zealous temperance advocate from youth. Endowed with a formidable intelligence and incredible energy, she received a good education and was a college faculty member at age 23. In 1871 Willard was named president of Northwestern Female College and, when that institution merged with Northwestern University, became dean of women. She subsequently resigned from this post, however, and thereafter dedicated herself to the temperance movement.

Under Willard the WCTU became the largest, best organized, and most powerful temperance organization in the country. It published tons of pamphlets, provided speakers, lobbied legislators. There were few aspects of society the organization failed to penetrate. Willard herself was a dynamo who, when not giving a speech or chairing a meeting, wrote letters and articles in behalf of the cause. Described by one individual as "organized mother love," the WCTU under Willard reached into every community.

Less important than Willard, though far more colorful, was Carry A. Nation ("carry a nation for temperance," she liked to say). A member of the WCTU, Nation circled in her own orbit and in fact was an embarrassment to some of the members. Having grown up in a family where eccentricity was the norm, Carry at age 19 married a man who drank himself to death very quickly. When the daughter of that union developed chronic illnesses of the cruelest sort, Carry concluded they were the results of her husband's addiction to alcohol and tobacco. These two substances became her lifelong enemies. Though she became involved in temperance work earlier, Carry made the full commitment after claiming to have received a direct communication from God during the summer of 1900.

Nation's methods were similar to the Women Crusaders—with a difference. She too prayed and sang that saloon keepers and their customers would repent. But in addition to her words she hurled bricks and bottles. Her favorite weapon came to be a hatchet which she wielded with remarkable verve for a middle-aged woman. "Smash! Smash! For Jesus' sake, Smash!" was her battle cry as she broke up saloons from Kansas to New York. Though she garnered a

great deal of publicity, and caused some other women to take up their own hatchets, Carry's impact was not lasting. Indeed, in later years she became a curiosity, touring county fairs and carnivals. At age 64 she collapsed after a lecture and died a few months later in the summer of 1911.

The temperance movement took on new life with the founding of the Anti-Saloon League of America in 1895. As was the WCTU, it was misnamed. Just as "temperance" really meant abstinence, the Anti-Saloon League was dedicated to banning all alcohol rather than just that dispensed by saloons. It was an effective ploy because the term "saloon" conjured up all sorts of negative images: drunken fistfights, scarlet women, and husbands drinking away their wages. The word "League" was accurate, however, because the organization was nonsectarian and accepted any individuals or groups dedicated to prohibition.

The League's dedication to a single goal made it more effective than its predecessors. It took on no other reforms, rarely got bogged down in internal disputes, and appealed to everyone interested in the cause. The organization was pragmatic to say the least, and subordinated everything to its goal. "Ethics be hanged," as one of the leaders put it, and they very often were. The League regularly supported politicians who were known drinkers, for instance, provided they could be depended upon to vote dry. In the South, League speakers and pamphlets often played upon racial prejudices by describing in lurid terms how alcohol heightened the lust black males had for white women. Dedicated, unscrupulous as to means, the League was able to bring great pressure to bear upon politicians across the country.

During the first decade of the 20th century, the League, the WCTU, and other organizations, succeeded in getting a number of state legislatures to pass prohibitory laws of various kinds. By 1913 the League went on record as favoring a constitutional amendment to make prohibition nationwide. Bills were introduced in Congress and the issue aroused considerable debate, which spurred the drys on to greater efforts. When the 1914 elections were over, men committed to voting dry had gained in both houses of Congress. During the next session a pro-

hibition bill introduced in the House won by a 197-190 majority. This was a good deal short of the two-thirds necessary to start the amendment process (three-fourths of the states have to concur), but still constituted a victory of which earlier temperance advocates could not have dreamed.

Would the prohibitionists ultimately have prevailed because of their own efforts? Or would the movement have peaked short of its goal, and then perhaps waned as had earlier temperance crusades? The answer is speculative. For it was the onset of World War I—and more particularly, American entry into the conflict—which assured a prohibitionist victory.

American participation in the war gave the drys two additional weapons which they employed with deadly effect. The first stemmed from the simple fact that various grains and sugar are the main ingredients of beer and liquor. At a time when Americans were being called upon to conserve food for the war effort, how could one defend the diversion of these materials into alcohol? Few politicians were prepared to defend themselves against charges that they were willing to see drunks get their liquor while boys in the trenches went hungry. That most breweries and many distilleries bore Germanic names provided a second boon to the drys. They were able to concoct all sorts of horror stories about German plots to undermine the war effort by encouraging soldiers and civilians to drink their vile products. Such allegations may seem absurd today, but they carried weight during a period when sauerkraut was renamed "victory cabbage."

Under these circumstances the prohibition movement was unstoppable. What was to become the Eighteenth Amendment was adopted by the Senate in August 1917 and by the House in December. The wets thought they had outmaneuvered their opponents when they worked in a seven-year time limit on the ratification process, but they were badly mistaken. The required number of states ratified within thirteen months of submission and the Eighteenth Amendment became law on January 16, 1919, (though it was not to take effect until one year from that date). The "Noble Experiment" would soon begin.

The Civil War and Reconstruction

Disputes over slavery had waxed and waned since the Constitutional Convention. Unlike matters such as the tariff question, slavery was a moral issue that made compromise difficult. Attempts were made in 1820 and 1850 to resolve the conflict, but these were accommodations that satisfied no one. Efforts to maintain "politics as usual" failed as the subject continued. Divisive quarrels destroyed the Whigs and led to the formation of the Republican Party, a sectional organization based entirely in the North. Southerners increasingly came to believe that Republican victory would mean the destruction of what they liked to call the "Southern way of life." Abraham Lincoln's election in 1860 was the Southerners' worst nightmare come true. One by one Southern states began seceding from the union. Lincoln hoped to avoid war, but refused to accept the legality of secession. When Southerners attempted to stop the reprovisioning of Fort Sumter, war began.

The Civil War was a watershed in American history with consequences that are still with us. This long, bloody conflict ushered in revolutionary political, social, and economic changes. That was not apparent at the outset. What many people believed would be a war of short duration lasted four years. President Lincoln at first tried to define the conflict as a war over union, but at last bowed to pressures to make it a crusade against slavery. Northern victory resulted in a new "critical period" of reconstruction in the South, a struggle to establish the rights and status of freedmen and women in the postwar society. Efforts to gain full citizenship for blacks failed, as the defeated Southerners ultimately gained the upper hand. This "aborted revolution" left Southern blacks at the mercy of their former masters.

"Dred Scott in History" describes how a Supreme Court decision about a former slave exacerbated sectional antagonisms and fears. When war came, the cry of "on to Richmond" reflected the optimism many Northerners felt about defeating the South within weeks. "First Blood to the South: Bull Run, 1861" shows how significant this battle was in revealing the false assumptions on both sides. Although slavery had long since been eliminated in the North, blacks were discriminated against in every way. Their efforts to participate in the war were met only with reluctance. "Black, Blue, and Gray: The Other Civil War" evaluates their contribution to the Northern war effort. Interpretations abound as to why the North won the war, and "Why The Confederacy Lost" argues that "Southern nationalism as a binding force in war was more apparent than real."

For a variety of reasons, among them fear of alienating the border states, Lincoln was reluctant to openly proclaim his intention to emancipate the slaves. "Lincoln and Douglass" tells the story of how, as a former bondsman, Frederick Douglass tried to persuade the president that nothing less than full equality for blacks was acceptable. The article "A Few Appropriate Remarks" discusses the origins of Lincoln's Gettysburg Address and how it was received.

The sectional struggle that led to the Civil War had lasting impact. "The War Inside the Church" discusses how the slavery dispute split most Protestant churches, and how it affected black religious life. James McPherson, in "A War That Never Goes Away," evaluates the struggle and argues that continuing interest in that monumental event is warranted. Two essays, "What Did Freedom Mean?" and "The New View of Reconstruction" analyze the conditions freedpeople had to cope with in the postwar era.

Looking Ahead: Challenge Questions

Why did the Dred Scott decision have such devastating implications for reaching compromise on the slavery question?

The North had superiority in population and industrial production, among other things. Was it therefore inevitable that the South should lose?

Those who imposed radical reconstruction on the South hoped to establish full political, economic, and social rights for freedpeople. Were they doomed to fail? Did anything good come out of reconstruction?

Dred Scott in History

Walter Ehrlich

Dr. Walter Ehrlich is Associate Professor of History and Education at the University of Missouri–St. Louis.

Dred Scott v. *John F.A. Sanford* stands as one of the most memorable and important cases in the history of the United States Supreme Court. Except for the celebrated *Marbury* v. *Madison,* which in 1803 established the Supreme Court's power to invalidate federal laws, perhaps more has been written about *Dred Scott* than about any other action of the American judiciary, either state or federal. Most of that literature deals with the controversial final decision, rendered on March 6, 1857, by Chief Justice Roger Brooke Taney. To comprehend the full significance and impact of that decision, it is imperative to understand clearly what the issues were; and to understand the issues necessitates an almost step-by-step unfolding of the litigation itself. It did indeed have a singular history.[1]

Born in Southampton County, Virginia, in the late 1790's or early 1800's, the property of Peter Blow, Dred Scott came with his master to Missouri, via Huntsville and Florence, Alabama, settling finally in St. Louis in 1830. Very little is known about the slave's early life. He was "raised" with the Blow children and apparently was close to them, performing menial labor one might associate with household slaves. Yet when Peter Blow found himself strapped financially, he sold Scott to Dr. John Emerson, a physician then residing in St. Louis. This was sometime before De-

Dred Scott, *by Louis Schultze, 1881. Courtesy of the Missouri Historical Society, St. Louis.*

cember 1, 1833, when Emerson embarked on a military career that took him, among other places, to Illinois and Wisconsin Territory (now Minnesota). Scott was with his master in both places until 1842, even though slavery was prohibited in Illinois by that state's constitution and in the northern Louisiana Purchase territory by the Missouri Compromise of 1820. Scott, however, made no effort to secure his freedom.

While Scott was in this service to Dr. Emerson, two weddings occurred which affected the slave's life. The first was Scott's, in 1836 or 1837, to Harriet Robinson, whose master, Major Lawrence Taliaferro, transferred her ownership to Emerson. This marriage was unique in American slave history, for it was a legal civil ceremony performed by a justice of

the peace. Dred and Harriet Scott had two daughters; Eliza was born in October, 1838, aboard the steamboat "Gipsey" while it was on the Mississippi River in "free," "northern" waters, and Lizzie was born about 1845 at Jefferson Barracks in Missouri. (Eliza never married. Lizzie married Wilson Madison of St. Louis, and through them exist the present descendants of Dred Scott.) The other wedding was Emerson's, on February 6, 1838, to Eliza Irene Sanford, whose brother later played a major role in Dred Scott's legal struggles for freedom.

In 1842 Dr. Emerson was posted to Florida where American military forces fought against the Seminole Indians. He left his wife and the slaves in St. Louis with Mrs. Emerson's father. The doctor

[1]For the best account of the case's chronology, especially in the Missouri courts, see Walter Ehrlich, *They Have No Rights: Dred Scott's Struggle for Freedom* (Greenwood Press, 1979). For further information, see Don E. Fehrenbacher's *The Dred Scott Case: Its Significance in American Law and Politics* (Oxford University Press, 1978) and David Potter's *The Impending Crisis, 1848–1861* (Harper and Row, 1976).

From *Westward,* Vol. 1, No. 1, Winter 1983, pp. 5-10. Published by The Jefferson National Expansion Memorial Historical Association. Reprinted by permission of the author.

returned from the wars in 1843, but died shortly thereafter at the age of forty, leaving a young widow with an infant daughter and the Dred Scott family.

The whereabouts of the slaves during these St. Louis years is unclear, except that they were hired out to various people, a frequent experience for city-dwelling slaves. Then on April 6, 1846, Dred and Harriet Scott sued their mistress Irene Emerson for freedom, initiating litigation in the local Missouri state circuit court that would take eleven years before culminating in the celebrated decision of the Supreme Court of the United States on March 6, 1857.

But what brought on that suit for freedom in 1846, when Scott had been "eligible" in free territory since 1833? The evidence is not exactly clear, but some facts are obvious. From 1833 to 1846 Scott was unaware of the law. (It should be noted that he was illiterate and had to mark an "X" for his signature, not uncommon for slaves.) Only after he returned to St. Louis was he apprised of the possibility of being free. But why, and by whom? Again all the details are not known, but it is now undeniable why the case was *not* brought. It was *not* instituted for political or financial reasons as many later imputed. The evidence is indisputable that Dred Scott filed suit for one reason and one reason only, to secure freedom for himself and his family, and nothing else.

But who told him now what he had been unaware of for thirteen years? Again the evidence could be stronger, but it points persuasively to several people. One was a white abolitionist lawyer, Francis Butter Murdoch, recently moved to St. Louis from Alton, Illinois, where as city attorney he had prosecuted criminal offenders on both sides in the infamous and bloody Elijah P. Lovejoy riots and murders. Another was Reverend John R. Anderson, himself a former slave and the black pastor of the Second African Baptist Church of St. Louis, in which Harriet Scott was a devout member. Like Murdoch, Anderson was an emigre from racial-torn Alton.

The exact sequence of events remains somewhat fuzzy; but it was Murdoch, on April 6, 1846, who posted the necessary bonds and filed the required legal papers which initiated the suit. Then, within a few months and before any further legal action occurred, Murdoch left for the west coast, where he lived the rest of his days in California. Having thus initiated the suit, he dropped out completely.

Now another group of Dred Scott's benefactors emerged: the sons and sons-in-law of Peter Blow, those "boys" with whom the slave had been "raised." Murdoch's departure left their ex-slave and childhood companion in limbo. Now the former owners stepped in, posted bonds, secured attorneys, and took over the process of seeking his freedom. They were to carry it through to the very end.

They anticipated no difficulty. According to the facts of the case and the legal precedents in Missouri, there is no question that Dred Scott was entitled to freedom; indeed, that it was such a patently open-and-shut case may even explain why the Blow family so readily came to their former slave's rescue. At any rate, two totally unexpected developments now changed the situation.

The first was the decision on June 30, 1847, in the trial court, denying Scott his freedom and ordering a new trial—not because of the law or the facts, but because of a legal technicality invalidating certain evidence introduced by Scott's attorney. The slave's freedom, which otherwise unquestionably would have been granted in 1847, now had to await a new trial. The second unexpected development was that it took three long years, until 1850, before that second trial finally occurred, a delay caused by events over which none of the litigants had any control. With that legal technicality of 1847 corrected, the court now, on January 12, 1850, unhesitatingly granted the slave his freedom. That should have ended the case.

But during that three-year delay more unexpected developments came into play. The first was Mrs. Emerson's departure from St. Louis and marriage to Dr. Calvin Clifford Chaffee, a Massachusetts abolitionist completely unaware of the litigation involving his new wife. When she left St. Louis, her local affairs were supervised for her by her businessman-brother, John F.A. Sanford. Among those affairs was the pending slave case.

A second development was monetary. Because Scott's eventual status was still undecided, the court had assigned the local sheriff as custodian of all wages the Scott family might earn, which would then accordingly be turned over to either a free Dred Scott or to his owner. The accrued wages, though by no means an inordinate amount, nevertheless made ownership of the slaves in 1850 much more worthwhile than it had been in 1846 or 1847. The result was, therefore, that Mrs. Emerson (actually her attorney hired for her by her brother Sanford) immediately appealed to the Missouri Supreme Court to reverse the freedom decision of the lower court.

This set the stage for the most consequential development yet, the injection of slavery as a political issue. Up to this point the legality or morality of slavery had never entered into the case to any degree. But by the early 1850's, stimulated by national discord over the seemingly uncompromisable slavery issues, and exacerbated by local Missouri factionalism centering on Senator Thomas Hart Benton, some judges of the Missouri Supreme Court took it upon themselves to reinterpret and reverse Missouri's longstanding legal principle of "once free always free," that a slave once emancipated in free territory would remain free even after returning voluntarily to the slave state of Missouri. By sheer coincidence, the case just appealed to the Missouri high court contained the necessary circumstances for such a ruling. This singularly irregular political partisanship on the part of the judges was abetted by an equally dissolute legal brief introduced at the last moment by Mrs. Emerson's attorney, Lyman D. Norris, a document characterized more by its vituperative pro-slavery tirades than by its legal reasoning.

The result was that on March 22, 1852, the Missouri Supreme Court reversed the lower court's decision and remanded Dred Scott to slavery. What the court now said in effect was, even though the law of a free state and a free United States territory may have emancipated a slave, the slave state of Missouri no longer would accept that status within its own borders. In other words, "once free always free" became "maybe once free, but now back to slavery." It was a radical change in Missouri law, overturning precedent and clearly endorsing the extreme pro-slavery point of view. What had been a simple and genuine emancipation case seeking only freedom for a slave under longstanding law and principle had been transformed into a matter focusing on the most divisive issue the nation had ever experienced.

This was precisely why the case appealed to the Supreme Court of the United States: to clarify "once free always free" and to determine to what degree, if at all, a state could reverse

Since it was rendered, the Dred Scott case has been one of the most discussed and written about court cases in American history. This booklet, containing the Supreme Court decision in the Dred Scott case, was published in 1857. It is preserved in the Jefferson National Expansion Memorial archives, located in St. Louis' Old Courthouse.

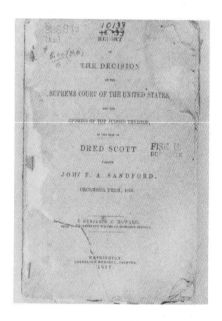

freedom once granted through the implementation of the Northwest Ordinance of 1787, prohibiting slavery in the Northwest Territory, and the Missouri Compromise of 1820. Note that this did not question the validity of granting freedom in a free state or territory; the power to prohibit slavery or to manumit slaves taken into free territory was universally recognized. In question was whether that freedom *once granted* could be lost by returning to a slave state. It was a highly controversial and delicate political and moral issue which the United States Supreme Court had deliberately sidestepped even when the opportunity to decide had been present. The Court had shown that judicial restraint as recently as 1850, in *Strader* v. *Graham*. Instead of deciding on the merits in that particular case, the Court took a procedural approach: it fell back on a long-standing and safe (albeit unpopular to some) prin-

ciple that the Court simply would abide by the decision of a state's supreme court as the definitive arbiter of that state's law, in this instance Kentucky.

Some time before the Missouri high court rendered its drastic decision, Dred Scott's situation came to the attention of Roswell M. Field, one of St. Louis' leading lawyers. A native of Vermont and an abolitionist, Field for some time had articulated the need for clarification of "once free always free." He realized *Dred Scott* v. *Irene Emerson* could be the vehicle through which to appeal to the Supreme Court for that, clarification. But he also was aware of the *Strader* case. *Strader* v. *Graham* had gone to the Supreme Court of the United States on direct appeal from the high court of Kentucky. If Dred Scott's case were appealed the same way, directly, the Court could easily evade the controversial and delicate merits by using *Strader* as a precedent and then simply fall back on the Missouri decision, foredooming Scott to slavery. The only way Scott might attain his freedom was to get the Supreme Court to examine the case's merits; and the only way to do that was to institute a case in a lower *federal* court and appeal from it to Washington. In that way *Strader* might not be a precedent and it could open the door for an examination of the substantive issues.

Thus was born *Dred Scott* v. *John F.A. Sanford* in the federal Circuit Court of the United States, docketed in St. Louis in 1853 and tried on May 15, 1854.[2] Sanford was named defendant for two reasons. The first was to make the case eligible for the federal court system. A long-time resident of St. Louis, Sanford had moved to New York, though he still maintained business and social ties in St. Louis. Scott as a citizen of Missouri

---

[2]Contrary to widespread St. Louis tradition that all the local Dred Scott trials occurred in the historic Old Courthouse, this trial was conducted elsewhere, in an inauspicious upstairs room in what was then the Pap in Building on First Street between Chestnut and Pine Streets. Normally the federal courts sat free of charge in the Old Courthouse. But since that structure was state-owned, state courts had priority on use of the courtrooms, and if there was no room available then the United States marshall simply had to make other arrangements. This was the situation in May, 1854. And so the private room in the Papin Building was rented.

suing Sanford as a citizen of New York created a federal case on the grounds of diversity of citizenship. The second reason for naming Sanford as defendant was as executor of his brother-in-law's estate and thus the virtual, if not real, owner who was "holding" Scott in slavery.

As an interesting and fascinating side issue, the presumption of Sanford as executor was in fact not true. Sanford had been named in Dr. Emerson's will as executor, but by a unique set of circumstances he never legally qualified. For some curious and unknown reasons, though, neither he nor, apparently, his attorneys realized this, and he accordingly managed the estate as though he was indeed the executor. When Dred Scott sued Sanford, therefore, the latter could not and did not deny that he was at least "holding" Scott as a slave, and so whether he was the executor or the actual owner made no difference. What counted legally was that he was "holding" Scott as a slave.

And so *Dred Scott* v. *John F.A. Sanford* was instituted to clarify "once free always free." But again a new issue unexpectedly appeared. Sanford's attorney Hugh A. Garland (his partner Lyman D. Norris had died) now claimed that Scott was not a citizen of Missouri and therefore could not sue in a federal court. The reason, argued Garland, a native of Virginia with pro-slavery proclivities, was that Scott was "a negro of African descent." Now injected into the case was the right of a black man to be a citizen of the United States. As if "once free always free" was not delicate enough!

More was to come. It was a foregone conclusion that the lower federal court decision would be appealed to the Supreme Court, as of course it was. Moving to the highest court in the land brought more changes. One was that both sides acquired outstanding and nationally-reputed attorneys and spokesmen for their political and legal points of view. Another was that the case was now publicized throughout the country as one involving important and highly controversial issues.

Yet another change transformed this case from the obscure freedom suit it had been in 1846 to the *cause celebre* which it now became. It will be recalled that *Scott* v. *Sanford* came into the federal courts to seek clarification of "once free always free," and that the original right and power to emancipate a slave in a free

*A*lthough her
name does not enjoy the widespread
recognition of her husband's,
Harriet Scott's (above) freedom was tied
to the fate of her husband's court cases.
The Scott's two daughters
(right) Eliza, left, and Lizzie,
were also affected by the litigation
involving their parents.

state or territory was universally accepted. Now that too was changed, when Sanford's attorneys, Senators Henry S. Geyer of Missouri and Reverdy Johnson of Maryland, introduced the extreme pro-slave doctrine that slaves were private property protected by the Constitution and therefore Congress did not have the power to abolish or forbid slavery in the first place. In other words, the Missouri Compromise, and presumably any similar slavery prohibition, was unconstitutional. Applied specifically to this case, the issue was no longer whether Missouri could remand Dred Scott to slavery; the issue was whether he had ever been free in the first place.

This, then, was the case and these the issues thrust before the Supreme Court of the United States. At any other time these matters would have been difficult enough to deal with, for they could not be divorced from their political and sociological implications. In the tense and discordant national atmosphere of the 1850's, those political and sociological implications made an acceptable solution virtually impossible. In addition, the pressures on the Court were appalling. It was precisely because the issues were so delicate that many looked to the Supreme Court as the only institution which could

solve them, indicative of the esteem in which the Court was held.

Nevertheless, it appeared that judicial restraint would prevail, as the Court found a way to skirt the divisive substantive questions. Even though *Dred Scott* had come up from a lower federal rather than a state supreme court, *Strader* v. *Graham* still would be used as a precedent, and how the state (Missouri) supreme court had ruled on its own state law would be acceptable to the United States Supreme Court. This was a safe and long-accepted principle, and most important it would avoid dealing with the volatile substantive slavery questions. Justice Samuel Nelson of New York was assigned the task, and he began to write what apparently would be a very bland Court's Opinion.

Then all the unbridled forces of the time came to a head. The exact sequence of events is not absolutely clear, but the key event was the proposal by Justice James M. Wayne of Georgia that the decision be changed to include the two controversial issues Nelson was deliberately omitting, the citizenship of blacks and the constitutionality of the Missouri Compromise. Though Wayne made the specific proposal, responsibility for precipitating the drastic step falls on at least

four of his colleagues, Chief Justice Taney and Associate Justices John McLean, Benjamin R. Curtis and Peter V. Daniel. At any rate, a bare majority, all from slave states, concurred with Wayne. Chief Justice Taney would write the new Court Opinion. As delivered on March 6, 1857, it is the famous—or infamous—"Dred Scott Decision."

Dred Scott was declared to be still a slave, for several reasons. (1) Although blacks could be citizens of a given state, they could not be and were not citizens of the United States with the concomitant right to sue in the federal courts. Dred Scott's suit therefore was dismissed because the Court lacked jurisdiction. (2) Aside from not having the right to sue in the first place, Scott was still a slave because he never had been free to begin with. Slaves were property protected by the Constitution, and Congress exceeded its authority when it passed legislation forbidding or abolishing, slavery in the territories. The Missouri Compromise was such an exercise of unconstitutional authority and was accordingly declared invalid. (3) Whatever the status of an erstwhile slave may have been while he was in a free state or territory, if he voluntarily returned to a slave state, his status there depended upon the law of that slave state as interpreted by its own courts. In Scott's case, since the Missouri high court had declared him to be still a slave, that was the status and law which the Supreme Court of the United States would accept and recognize. "Once free always free" went by the wayside.

In the tense sectional-ridden atmosphere of the time, it is no wonder that the decision triggered a violent reaction. The Court had sought to solve the volatile slavery issue; instead, what it did has been recorded as the most ill-advised and unfortunate moment in its history. It unleashed irreconcilable passions, both North and South, that merged with those already building toward civil war. The press, the pulpit, the political stump and the halls of Congress now reverberated with scathing condemnations as well as vigorous defenses of the Court's action.

The intrusion of the Court into the slavery issue created an unprecedented political dilemma. *Dred Scott* appeared to give constitutional sanction to slavery. If so, that compromised the new anti-slave Republican party, whose very *raison d'etre* now seemed undermined. Existence as a national political party demanded respect for the law; but that existence also demanded the overturn of *Dred Scott* law. The political realities of the time offered little likelihood of either. Undoing *Dred Scott,* therefore, involved a hard new look at existing American institutions. To many in both North and South, any compromise over slavery now was impossible. The attack on slavery consequently was bound to involve action and measures more radical and drastic than anything the American democratic process had ever before experienced, and in like manner, the defense of slavery was destined to become equally inflexible. Once the Court had spoken, the two sections, irrevocably moved down a road that could lead only to disaster. *Dred Scott* might well have been the point of no return.

Anti-slavery forces now rose in righteous anger, determined to prevent the next fearful step, the legalizing of slavery everywhere. For that was the frightful specter which *Dred Scott* foreshadowed. If slaves were property protected in the territories, which was the consequence of the Missouri Compromise being declared unconstitutional, then they were also property which could be protected in the states. One more decision like *Dred Scott* and slavery would be a na-

tional institution. "Slavery national" rather than "freedom national" loomed on the horizon.

Forces intent on ridding the nation of slavery now mounted an unprecedented assault. Ironically, *Dred Scott* and Chief Justice Taney showed the way. Pro-slave states' rights Jeffersonian agrarians, for all their political philosophy, had utilized *national* institutional machinery to strengthen slavery. If that machinery was strong enough to *legalize* slavery throughout the nation (as some feared it now would), was it not also strong enough to *destroy* slavery throughout the nation? If Repub-

D*red Scott's final resting place is in St. Louis' Calvary Cemetery. The descendents of Scott's last owner, Taylor Blow, paid to have this monument erected in 1957.*

licans could just hold the line on slavery and prevent any further expansion, all they had to do was gain control of the national machinery *without weakening it institutionally.* They could then use it to reverse whatever gains agrarianism and slavery had made. (After all, slavery was not the only concern of the new Republican party.) Gaining control of the executive and legislative branches had to come first; "proper" appointments to the federal judiciary would eventually follow.

In the meantime, the Court had to be prevented from legalizing slavery nationally, not by subverting its institutional

decision-making power, but by diminishing its influence and prestige *temporarily.* This was done by a vicious assault upon the *Dred Scott* decision. The charge of *obiter dictum* rang throughout the country, meaning once the Court had decided Dred Scott could not sue for lack of jurisdiction, then any incidental opinion on issues having no bearing upon the case was uncalled for. Legal scholars today overwhelmingly agree that Taney's rulings were not *obiter dicta,* but many contemporaries were convinced otherwise.

Taney and his concurring colleagues were derided and ridiculed to such a degree, not only for their legal abilities but also for personal matters, that confidence gradually eroded in their ability to render unbiased judgments. At the same time, Republicans and abolitionists heightened the fear of a "slave-power conspiracy" that purportedly included even members of the Supreme Court. This vicious attack on the Court was the spearhead of an unprecedented furious campaign to gain control over the national government, and then to run it under a centralized-power philosophy. It succeeded; in 1860, Abraham Lincoln was elected President of the United States.

The *Dred Scott* decision played a most significant role in those troubled days in still another way. As noted, individual judges were singled out for abuse and vilification because of their legal opinions. Inevitably, the assault on these individuals affected the institution itself, degrading it as a partisan body no longer capable of rendering justice without bias. Prior to *Dred Scott* there was a willingness—even an eagerness—to look to the Court to solve difficult constitutional problems, including slavery; after *Dred Scott,* confidence in the Court on such issues evaporated. Perhaps never before in the history of the United States was there so much need for the stabilizing influence, the sobriety, and the sound guidance that a respected Court might have provided. But it was no longer there. True, it would return later, but too late. Instead, bloodshed and violence prevailed.

The Dred Scott case, then, was of momentous consequence. Originating as an obscure open-and-shut freedom litigation, it literally was dragged by circumstances into prominence and notoriety. Little could that slave anticipate, when his benevolent friends went into St.

Louis' Old Courthouse to seek his freedom, that they were unleashing one of the most exciting and traumatic episodes in American constitutional history.

POSTSCRIPT: With the Taney pronouncement caught up in the dramatic events that exploded into bloody civil war, historians have largely overlooked what happened to Dred Scott the person. According to the Court, of course, he remained a slave. But whose? A careful examination of the record revealed that he still belonged to Mrs. Emerson, now Mrs. Chaffee, whose husband was a prominent Massachusetts abolitionist. Incredulously, though, Chaffee did not learn of his wife's association with the now-famous slave until only a few weeks before the Court rendered its final deci-

sion. His embarrassment was compounded because Massachusetts law considered his wife's property as his. The law also prevented him from freeing the slave until the pending legal action had been concluded. Once the Court announced its decision, however, Chaffee issued a quitclaim transferring ownership to Taylor Blow in St. Louis. (Dred Scott and his family had remained in St. Louis throughout the entire litigation.) Then, on May 26, 1857, in accordance with Missouri law, Taylor Blow formally freed Dred Scott, his wife Harriet, and their two daughters. That action occurred in the same courtroom in St. Louis where the case had started eleven years earlier in 1846. And so, despite the Supreme Court decision, Dred Scott and his family now were free.

Dred Scott worked as a porter in a St. Louis hotel for more than a year. But his popularity and new-found fame were short-lived. On September 17, 1858, he died of tuberculosis (some called it consumption). He was buried in the Wesleyan Cemetery just outside the St. Louis city limits. In 1867, as the city expanded westward, the cemetery was abandoned. Through the efforts again of Taylor Blow, Dred Scott's remains were reinterred in Calvary Cemetery in what is now northern St. Louis. For a long time the grave remained unmarked. In 1957, through the generosity of Taylor Blow's granddaughter, a stone marker was installed. It stands there today as a historical monument, a reminder of one of the most famous episodes in America's legal and constitutional history.

First Blood to the South: Bull Run, 1861

The rebel yell that dispelled hopes of a quick Union victory—Brian Holden Reid looks at the battle that set the scene for the American Civil War's protracted and bloody conflict.

Brian Holden Reid

Brian Holden Reid is Lecturer in War Studies at King's College, London and co-editor of American Studies: Essays in Honour of Marcus Cunliffe *(Macmillan, 1991).*

The First Battle of Bull Run, fought around a stream of that name on a boiling hot day on July 21st, 1861, in northern Virginia, was a salutary and traumatic experience for its participants. It was to date the greatest battle fought on North American soil. It has been the subject of two fine books, R.M. Johnston's *Bull Run: Its Strategy and Tactics* (1913), and more recently, William C. Davis' *Battle at Bull Run* (1977). Both works are examples of traditional campaign studies. The former was influential in examining the art of war within a narrative framework and expounding those elements upon which that art rested; the latter relies comfortably on archival research and is less didactic. But both books share a common characteristic which is the besetting sin of Civil War historiography, namely, that the military operations are studied in a vacuum. From the moment the campaign begins it is studied in isolation from those political and social issues that not only surrounded it, but governed it.

This campaign cannot be understood adequately unless it is connected with the social and political sources of warmaking in North America. It serves as a representative symbol, a culmination of the illusions and miscalculations, as well as the wisdom enshrined in the American military tradition. In the words of the late Marcus Cunliffe, the First Battle of Bull Run 'epitomised the variegated confusion of a century and more of American warfare'.

The campaign itself formed the climax of a dramatic series of events that began with the bombardment of Fort Sumter on April 12th 1861. Three days later Abraham Lincoln issued 'By the President of the United States, A Proclamation'. In this document Lincoln stressed his determination 'to suppress said combinations [of rebels] and to cause the laws to be duly executed'. In so doing he promised that 'the utmost care will be observed . . . to avoid any devastation; any destruction of, or interference with, property, or any disturbance of peaceful citizens in any part of the country'. He called for 75,000 volunteers for three months. On May 3rd, he issued another call for a further 42,000 volunteers for three years.

This political imperative governed the workings of the campaign—the need for a short, sharp victory over traitorous combinations of troublesome politicians. This political factor was accentuated by a decision of the Confederate government to give up its quarters at Montgomery, Alabama, to move to the more cosmopolitan surroundings of Richmond, Virginia, about fifty miles south of Washington. This decision, which brought the capitals so close together, led to an obsessive focus on the war in Virginia. Politicians are invariably of the opinion that the world revolves around their sayings and doings, and American politicians are more voluble than most. It was a desire to occupy Richmond before the Confederate Congress reconvened there on July 20th that provoked the somewhat hysterical cry of 'On to Richmond'.

Most professional soldiers complain at some stage that their operations are hamstrung by politicians. But the position of Washington in 1861–62 was a special case. It is rare that a war of such scale and intensity was fought so close to the political heart of a country in which political decisions had such important strategic implications. Military action had been resorted to because American political mechanisms had broken down. From the outset, therefore, soldiers were exposed, not only to the political aspects of the war, but to the cut and thrust of political life. This was especially true of the opening months of war because the secession crisis had been such a painful experience that many politicians were infected by hysteria. The chairman of the Joint Committee on the Conduct of the War, Senator Benjamin F. Wade, was to write of this period that:

There was treason in the Executive mansion, treason in the Cabinet, treason in the Senate, treason in the House of Representatives, treason in the Army and Navy, treason in every department, bureau and office connected with the government.

This statement was a trifle exaggerated, but is a striking indicator of the sense of outrage and betrayal that secession had kindled into flame.

In May 1861 Brigadier-General Irvin B. McDowell was appointed to command the newly formed Army of the Potomac. He was a solemn and humourless man prone to over-eating, but a competent commander. McDowell laboured under the intense strain of political pressure for an immediate triumph over the rebels. This emanated from members of Congress, the administration and perhaps most important of all, the newspapers. Hugh Brogan has written that Americans are not schooled to the long haul; they expect everything to happen quickly. In 1861 both War Democrats, whose views on slavery were cautious (believing that Congress had no right to interfere with property rights in the states), and the more radical Republicans (who demanded its abolition), were impatient to see an early and decisive victory. The conservatives were anxious for an immediate end to the rebellion as a signal that there would be no change either to property rights or race relations in the Southern states. Before 1860 the South had been a fastness of the Democratic Party; its dominance of the presidency could not be restored until Southern electoral votes could be counted in its column. The Radical Republicans demanded an immediate overthrow of secession as a prelude to the destruction of the Southern plantocracy—the infernal 'Slave Power' that threatened to subvert democracy with its brutal, aristocratic mores. But whatever the aspirations of various party factions and their vociferous spokesmen in the newspapers, all assumed as a matter of course that the war would be short and that the Confederacy would be overthrown in one great, decisive, pitched battle. Congressman George Washington Julian, a Radical Republican, 'found everybody taking it for granted [that] when the first fight began our forces would prove triumphantly victorious'.

The expectations loaded on to McDowell's ample shoulders were therefore not light. He drew up a respectable plan to advance overland towards Richmond, outflanking the left of any Confederate forces he might meet, and advance on the city, whose fortifications were then infinitely weaker than they would soon become. Central to his plan was the need to pin down the Confederate forces commanded by General Joseph E. Johnston in the Shenandoah Valley. He could not risk any Confederate concentration against his forces north of Richmond.

McDowell was able but inexperienced. He was overworked and lacked a group of able staff officers to help him. The *Times* war correspondent, William Howard Russell, met McDowell harassed and care-worn, as he arrived in Washington on July 16th. 'He asked where I came from and when he heard from Annapolis, inquired eagerly if I had seen two batteries of artillery . . . which he had ordered up and was waiting for, but which had "gone astray". Russell continued:

I was surprised to find the General engaged in such duty, and took leave to say so. 'Well it is quite true, Mr Russell; but I am obliged to look after them myself, as I have so small a staff, and they are all engaged out with my headquarters. You are aware I have advanced? No! Well, you have just come in time, and I shall be happy, indeed, to take you with me. I have made arrangements for the correspondents of our papers to take the field under certain regulations, and I have suggested to them they should wear a white uniform, to indicate the purity of their character'.

A sense of humour was not one of McDowell's strong points, and the irony of this last remark passed him by. But it is clear from Russell's account that the command system was chaotic, geared at the wrong level, and the commanding general was wasting his energies on trivia.

The same was true of the Confederate command system. General P.G.T. Beauregard commanding the Confederate forces north of Richmond (also confusingly called the Army of the Potomac) and General Johnston were hardly the two most modest men in the Confederate army. And much as Beauregard welcomed the arrival of Johnston's troops by rail the day before the battle, he did not welcome the arrival of their commander. He was jealous and suspicious of Johnston as a rival. Both men were under considerable pressure to justify the reputations they had either cultivated or built up on the basis of very slender experience. As Governor Pickens of South Carolina wrote of Beauregard, he was:

too cautious, and his very science makes him hesitate to make a dash. His knowledge of Batteries and cannon and engineering is great, but he relies nothing upon the spirit and the energy of troops, and has not experience in the management of Infantry. His Reputation is so high that he fears to risk it, and yet he wants the confidence of perfect genius.

Pickens expressed a widely felt view that war would be determined by moral, and not material, factors. William Howard

'Reading the War News in Broadway, New York' – an 1861 *Illustrated London News* sketch. Facile optimism (on both sides) about a speedy war began to recede in the aftermath of Bull Run.

Russell, became very irritated by the blithe Southern assumption of moral superiority. He asked, 'Suppose the Yankees . . . come with such preponderance of men and *matériel,* that they are three to your one, will you not be forced to submit?' 'Never [was the reply]. The Yankees are cowardly rascals'.

From the northern point of view the battle went well, at first. Beauregard had concentrated his forces in the centre and on the right along the Bull Run and neglected his left. But as the day wore on, mainly under Johnston's influence, Beauregard was persuaded to move more of his forces to the left so that he could counter McDowell's out-flanking move. This switch was greatly aided by the futile attrition of Federal strength on the right and centre. For example, within hours Colonel Ambrose E. Burnside's brigade had been reduced to one regiment, the 2nd New Hampshire, which Burnside personally commanded. All commanders, no matter how senior, felt happiest at this level of command. It was in this sector that General Bernard Bee's immortal remark concerning Jackson's 'stone wall' was coined—which had much more significance in Confederate folklore than as a turning point in this battle.

Even by the late afternoon, the battle had not gone badly for McDowell. But his plan was simply too complex for his untrained and raw army to implement. Because he lacked a good staff, McDowell was frequently absent from the main point of decision attending to other people's work, and co-ordination was lacking. Discipline broke down. 'No curse could be greater', concluded Colonel William T. Sherman, 'than invasion by a volunteer army . . . Our men are not good soldiers. They brag, but don't perform, complain sadly if they don't get everything they want, and a march of a few miles uses them up'. The crisis of the battle was reached shortly after 3pm. The Confederate army had virtually turned 90 degrees to face McDowell's outflanking force. Colonel Oliver O. Howard's brigade was severely mauled in an attack on Henry Hill and was driven back in confusion. It was symptomatic of the amateurish deployment on both sides that the success of McDowell's assault rested on one brigade, and that the arrival of three Confederate regiments, two from South Carolina and the 28th Virginia, was sufficient to steady the Confederate line. It was this movement, the repulse of one brigade and the arrival

Feeble Yankees – the Southern sense of moral (and physical) superiority over their Northern counterparts is reflected in this cartoon comment on the 1856 caning of Charles Sumner by Brooks in the senate, after the former's attack on South Carolina's policies.

of three regiments that triggered off the Federal retreat. Some parts of this turned into a rout which swept up a number of important political personages who had come out to watch the crushing of the impertinent rebels. Thus ended, with such ignominy, the campaign of Bull Run, in which so much hope had been invested. What were the main factors that had led to this unexpected (but for the South welcome) Union defeat?

The main feature of this campaign was the complete lack of preparation on both sides for sustained military operations. During the secession crisis very little had been done to organise the United States Army for a punitive expedition against the rebels. Seven warships had been ordered by Congress to help the revenue service collect the duties and enforce the blockade of Southern ports. Some money had been voted by Northern legislators to improve the militia— but this did not amount to very much. After Sumter there was a burst of martial enthusiasm. The decision was taken to raise volunteers rather than to expand the regular army. In the South a plan was mooted to raise a regular army but here, too, the volunteer system was preferred. McDowell found the three month volunteers an embarrassment. If he had insisted on waiting until he was properly prepared and trained before attacking the

Confederates, then he would have lost 10,000 of his best men once their terms of enlistment had expired. In July 1861 President Lincoln called for a further 400,000 volunteers, again for three years.

These troops were undisciplined and poorly trained. As McDowell wrote in his report, Union troops were 'unaccustomed to marching . . . and not used to carrying even the load of "light marching order" '. The opinionated and obstreperous behaviour of American soldiers so struck observers that one recorded after Bull Run that 'I doubt if our democratic form of government admits of that organisation and discipline without which an army is a mob'. And it must be stressed that such was the novelty of seeing large bodies of uniformed troops drilling, that many of the favourable impressions recorded by politicians were exaggerated. Lincoln's friend, Orville Hickman Browning, described a regiment of Rhode Island volunteers in the following glowing terms: 'I have never seen troops to surpass [them] in appearance or perfection of discipline, or accuracy of drill'—but he had seen so few others to compare them with. On the Southern side, the secessionist fire-eater, Edmund Ruffin, was disgusted to find that there were as many men retiring from the victorious field of Bull Run as advancing. 'But I was struck with the strange fact, that of all these men reported as either wounded or worn down by exertion, not one was sitting or lying as if to rest'. They were, of course, making a rapid withdrawal from the scene of maximum danger.

Ruffin's comments are interesting because they contradicted a widely held view that the South was better equipped in every way to wage war than the North; indeed that the South had its own military tradition. This overlooked rather conveniently the fact that the Confederacy won a defensive victory and that it was much more difficult for the Union Army to organise offensive movement. But it was assumed that such a military tradition did exist; that Southerners were inherently superior at the profession of arms. It was also believed that the secession conspiracy had been years in the making—and not just an impulsive reaction to the election of a Republican president in 1860. This, too, was an assumption that was based on fragmentary evidence. The only evidence that secession had been carefully nursed was found in a novel published in 1836 by Nathaniel Beverley Tucker, *The Partisan Leader,* which predicted the coming of civil war as the result of the courageous Southern efforts to resist Northern tyranny. 70,000 copies of this work were circulated during May 1861. Conspiracy theories tend to proliferate when the evidence is fragmentary or non-existent. The commandant of cadets at West Point, Colonel (later Major General) John F. Reynolds, believed that when the Confederate President, Jefferson Davis, was Secretary of War in the Pierce Administration (1853–57) he had seduced Southern officers from their true allegiance and planted instead 'the poisonous weed of secession, . . . the depth of his treachery has not been plumbed yet', he predicted. But because public opinion in the South was convinced that the South had been well prepared for the battle, the meaning of Bull Run was misinterpreted. Far from seeing that chance had proved to be the decisive factor in a battle between two unprepared armies, many concluded that Southern martial prowess was the key.

These elements fitted into a vision of war that assumed it would be short. Consequently, there would be no need to train or prepare in the North because the South would be crushed quickly; and in the Confederate States faith in Southern martial prowess would suffice to bring a

rapid victory over the Northern masses. The model that fitted these preconceptions of what a future war would be like was George B. McClellan's advance in May and June 1861 into the Unionist counties of West Virginia who stubbornly refused to be coerced by the Confederacy. Lightning advances, striking gains, little fighting but pleasing victories advertised by bombastic Napoleonic pronouncements, were its prominent, comforting features, at least for the North. The occupation of these counties came as a shock to the South and threw a (temporary) cloud over the career of Robert E. Lee. Southerners were convinced, as Russell noted in a visit to the deep South, 'that the white men in the slave States are physically superior to the men in the free States'; their moral superiority had been proven by confrontations between politicians in Congress—especially the caning of Senator Charles Sumner in 1856. According to Louis T. Wigfall, this was an example 'of the manner in which the Southerners would deal with Northerners generally . . . [and] in which they would bear their "whipping" '.

Even taking into account that Wigfall was drunk during this conversation, it is a somewhat hazy description of the shape a future war would take. In the West Virginia instance, it had been the South that had been 'whipped'—though this verdict was reversed by Bull Run. Nevertheless, the view that the war would remain short persisted long after the battle. In January 1862, a wealthy Georgia planter, Edgeworth Bird, wrote to his wife, Sallie, 'I believe the war will not last long . . . England's interest unerringly points to an issue with them [the Federal Government], and it will surely come [and lead to British intervention on behalf of the South]. Let us keep our cotton and let not a single bag go, except in exchange for necessary articles'. Thus the illusion of a short war was buttressed by another illusion—that Great Britain would rescue the Confederacy because of her desperate need for cotton.

That the war did not take the expected form led to some confusion and a severe oscillation in morale on both sides. Before Bull Run, Congressman Joseph Medell was of the opinion that 'The idea of waiting until frost set in, and merely defending our capitol was a preposterous one in a political point of view, and our struggle is not a purely military one'. The main spokesman for this view was

Horace Greeley of the New York *Tribune* whose opinions were as impulsive as its chimerical editor. Before 1861 Greeley had seen no need for an army. After Fort Sumter Greeley urged 'condign punishment' on the South. The leader-writer, Charles A. Dana, sketched the headline 'Forward to Richmond'. This was just one more influential voice that swelled a chorus demanding swift and decisive action. It underestimated both the enthusiasm and determination of Southern soldiers. Commentators were too easily persuaded that the war would resemble an affray like Shay's Rebellion in Massachusetts in 1786, in which a body of discontented farmers were dispersed without effort. Consequently, the North was over-confident before Bull Run and the South over-confident after it. Russell was convinced that both sides in 1861 were too prone to boast about their martial prowess without experiencing the realities of war. Here Bull Run was a salutary shock.

The expected short war would be brought to an end by a great and decisive battle. This was a naive and romantic vision, that would rise again before 1914. In so far as it envisaged fighting at all (as opposed to picturesque movement and heroics), this involved hand-to-hand fighting. John S. Mosby convinced himself of Southern martial superiority when he noticed that the Federals 'never once stood to a clash of the bayonet—always broke and ran'. But bayonet fights were rare. Another Southern observer remarked that 'We were taken out into an open field and formed in line of battle where we made excellent marks for the enemy who commenced firing at us'. Other observers expressed frustration at not being able to see the enemy: 'The enemy can't see us and we cannot see them being covered by trees . . . Nothing but trees to fire at'. The concern with dash expressed in all of these comments—an obsession with reckless movement, led by officers of a feckless and histrionic mien, buttressed the supposition that the whole war would be over in one great battle—an illusion that would prevail for at least another nine months. It was revealed as foolish by the First Battle of Bull Run.

As Northern confidence was uneven, and oscillated between boastfulness and despair, so the defeat at Bull Run was followed by a search for scapegoats. McDowell was sacked and replaced by the hero of West Virginia, George

B. McClellan—prematurely dubbed the 'Young Napoleon'. After three months of hostilities the Federal Government was still on the strategic defensive. It would remain so—even after the Battle of Shiloh—until General McClellan set out on his ill-fated Peninsular Campaign in the spring of 1862. Thus the campaign ended with politicians blaming one another for urging McDowell on to his premature advance—even though he had no choice but to move when he did. The true significance of this somewhat unedifying controversy lay in its convenience as a pretext for discrediting the President and his cabinet. Attempts were made to reconstruct it in favour of one pressure group or another. Earlier efforts had failed before the firing on Fort Sumter, and they would be repeated during the Cabinet Crisis in December 1862 following the Union defeat at the Battle of Fredericksburg. Lincoln's dominance of his administration depended crucially on the progress of military events, mainly in the Virginian theatre.

Certainly, the Lincoln administration wanted the battle. There were some dissident voices, such as the general-in-chief, Winfield Scott, who always thought that untrained volunteers could not be trusted. But the campaign went ahead on the Northern side because of the overwhelming faith that the war would soon be over. Hardly anyone challenged this belief. The South similarly was inspired by the expectation that the war would be short. Success at Bull Run, despite the lack of a pursuit, fortified Southern confidence that their martial skills, now abundantly vindicated, would bring an early triumph. The First Battle of Bull Run had revealed starkly the illusions and false expectations cherished about the character of warfare in the mid-nineteenth century. This is a task often discharged by early battles. Yet these illusions persisted. So strong was the yearning for a dramatic, decisive victory that would bring the fratricidal conflict to an end, that in February 1862 William H. Seward, the Secretary of State, informed Senator Charles Sumner that he had 'authentic information from Virginia that the Rebellion would be over there in four weeks'. The source of this startling intelligence was not divulged. Four more years might have been a more accurate prediction.

FOR FURTHER READING:

Marcus Cunliffe, *Soldiers and Civilians: The Martial Spirit in America, 1775-1865* (Eyre and Spotiswoode, 1969); William C. Davis, *Battle at Bull Run* (Louisiana State U.P., 1977); William Howard Russell, *My Diary North and South* (ed.) Eugene H. Berwanger (Alfred A. Knopf, 1988); Kenneth M. Stampp, *And the War Came: The North and the Secession Crisis* (Louisiana State U.P., 1950); Michael C.C. Adams, *Our Masters the Rebels* (Harvard U.P., 1978); Brian Holden Reid, 'General McClellan and the Politicians,' *Parameters*, XVII (September 1987).

Black, Blue and Gray: The Other Civil War

African-American soldiers, sailors and spies were the unsung heroes

Ride in, kind Saviour!
No man can hinder me.
O, Jesus is a mighty man!
No man can hinder me.
We're marchin' through Virginny fields.
No man can hinder me.

—Spiritual

Far off to the east, far out over the Atlantic Ocean, the first faint glow of the sun tinged the blue-black sky*. In a ravine near Richmond, Va., Black men in blue hugged the ground and watched the blotch of red widen and glow. Shells howled and burst over their heads, bullets whined and whacked into the trees.

The men waited, watched, listened.

A general came and said it was necessary to capture the Confederate redoubt over the hill and that they—the Third Division of the Eighteenth Corps of the Army of the James—had to do it. The men fixed their bayonets and listened to the words and the heavy beating of their hearts.

The land before the troops sloped down to a swamp and a shallow brook, then rose sharply to the crest of a hill commanded by a Confederate redoubt and some 1,000 troops. The Confederates, noticing the Black troops on the opposite hill, gave a wild whoop and urged the soldiers on. On they came, getting mired in the muck of the swamp, splashing across the brook with their guns held over their heads, faltering, reforming and moving up the hill, one man falling and another man replacing him in line, the whole column swept by grape shot and canister, the ground wet

*Excerpted from *Before The Mayflower*, by Lerone Bennett Jr., revised 1987 edition, copyright © 1987, Johnson Publishing Co.

with the blood, the entrails and the brains of the dead.

After what seemed like an eternity of minute-hours, the troops reached the first barricade. By now most of the White officers were wounded or dead, and Black sergeants and corporals were commanding companies and platoons. Cursing, pleading, threatening, they drove the men on. On they went, stepping over the wounded, to the Confederate redoubt. A rebel officer jumped on the parapet, waved his sword and shouted, "Hurrah, my brave men." Pvt. James Gardiner rushed forward, shot the officer and ran him through with his bayonet. The Confederate soldiers then abandoned their posts and ran up the road to Richmond. With a resounding cheer, the Black men in blue clambered over the parapet of the dearly purchased real estate on New Market Heights. Behind them on the hill running down to the swamp lay 543 of their comrades.

It had been a bloody 30 minutes' work. But on this day and largely in these 30 minutes, 12 Blacks, including Pvt. Gardiner, won Congressional Medals of Honor.

With the New Market Road secured, the Union troops pressed on toward Richmond, but the advance ground to a halt outside Richmond. The next day Robert E. Lee sent 10 of the South's finest brigades against the Union soldiers. The first charge and the second charge were neatly repulsed. And then someone—was it Lee?—had a bright idea. The rebel soldiers came back again, but this time the charge was against the Black New Market veterans. The long gray lines swept forward, came to the very edge of the earthwork, and Black and rebel soldiers fought hand to hand.

For an agonizing moment the issue hung in dispute. Then the Confederates

broke in disorder, a witness said, "while the Union troops shouted themselves hoarse with delight."

It was a bitter moment for the South. Robert E. Lee had failed to retake an important position within sight of the steeples of the Confederate capital. Lt. R. B. Prescott, a White Union soldier, stood cheering on the parapet of Fort Harrison and he believed he could see "the beginning of the end."

THAT BLACK SOLDIERS SHOULD PLAY AN important role in this action seems somehow poetic. For in the beginning, in the middle and in the ending of the Civil War, the Black American—as soldier and civilian—was central.

In the beginning, people tried hard to get around this fact. In the first blast of emotion that followed the fall of Fort Sumter, even Abraham Lincoln tried to get around it. For when Black volunteers thronged the recruiting stations, eager for a chance to fight for Black freedom, the Lincoln administration sent them home with an understanding that the war was a "White man's war."

That Lincoln's policy was changed at all is due not to humanitarianism but to rebel battlefield brilliance—the South knew what it was fighting for—and the daring and hope of fugitive slaves. By digging in and fighting, the South brought the North to a realization that it was in a real brawl and that it needed all the weapons it could lay hands on.

And so, while Lincoln temporized, three generals stretched out their hands to Ethiopia. Without waiting for official approval, David ("Black David") Hunter organized the First South Carolina Volunteers, the first Black regiment, and Jim Lane organized the First Kansas "Colored" Volunteers. In New Orleans, Gen.

From *Ebony*, February 1991, pp. 96, 98, 100, 103, 105. Excerpt from *Before the Mayflower*, revised 1987 edition. Copyright © 1987 by Johnson Publishing Co.

Benjamin Butler issued the necessary papers and the First Louisiana Native Guards became the first Black regiment to receive official recognition.

When Lincoln issued the Emancipation Proclamation—which didn't apply to slaves in loyal Border States or slaves in Southern sections controlled by the Union Army—the Black South exploded in a mass movement that was, John Eaton said, like "the oncoming of cities."

No more driver's lash for me,
No more, no more.
No more driver's lash for me,
Many thousand gone.

Many thousands found employment in the Union Army. By the end of 1863 there were some 50,000 Black soldiers in Union ranks. Although Black soldiers were promised $13 a month (the pay of White privates), they were insulted with an offer of $7 a month.

Black soldiers were paid less money, but they faced grimmer hazards. Some Black POWs were murdered or sold into slavery. In the ugliest incident of the war, a rebel force, commanded by Maj. Gen. Nathan Bedford Forrest—a Confederate hero who is still honored in Memphis—massacred a predominantly Black group at Fort Pillow, Tennessee.

LONG BEFORE FORT PILLOW, AND LONG before Sherman's dagger thrusts in Georgia, Black soldiers and sailors became indispensable elements in a war that could not have been won without their help. In the fall of 1862, they participated in minor actions at Island Mounds, Mo., and in skirmishes in Georgia and Florida. But their first major battles came in the summer of 1863 at Port Hudson, the last Confederate obstacle to the capture of Vicksburg, and in the famous "Glory" charge of the Fifty-fourth Massachusetts Volunteers at Fort Wagner in the Charleston, S.C., harbor.

In 1864 Black soldiers entered the big tent. When Ulysses S. Grant settled down for the 10-month siege that ended in April 1865, with the fall of Petersburg and Richmond, 34 Black Union regiments were with him. Black troops were especially prominent in the disastrous Battle of the Crater and engagements at Darbytown Road, Fair Oaks, Deep Bottom, Hatcher's Run, New Market Heights and Fort Gilner.

Black soldiers were in on the kill. The Second Division of the all-Black Twenty-fifth Corps was one of the Union divisions that chased Lee's tattered army from Petersburg to Appomattox Courthouse. When the end came, the Black and White troops were moving forward at the double and Lee's men were retreating in confusion.

The triumph of Union forces was due to a number of factors, including Northern technology and the spirit of the age. But a central, perhaps preeminent, factor was the contribution of Black Americans—slaves and freedmen—who provided the margin of difference that turned the tide against the Confederate forces in 1864 and 1865. There were, according to official records, 185,000 Black soldiers in the Union Army. These soldiers, generally identified as United States Colored Troops, were organized into 166 regiments (145 infantry, 12 heavy artillery, 7 cavalry, 1 light artillery, and 1 engineer).

Most of these soldiers—93,000—came from the South. Northern states contributed 52,000 Black soldiers, and 40,000 soldiers came from the Border States. The largest number of Black soldiers came from Louisiana (24,052), followed by Kentucky (23,703), and Tennessee (20,133). Since the War Department discouraged Black applicants, there were few Black officers. The highest-ranking of the 70 to 100 Black officers was Lt. Col. Alexander T. Augustana, a surgeon.

For various reasons, almost all of them linked to racism, the Black mortality rate was disproportionately high. Union records list 37,638 Black casualties, roughly 21 percent of the total number of Black soldiers.

Black soldiers participated in 410 military engagements and 39 major battles, including Port Hudson, Fort Wagner, Olustee, Petersburg Mine Assault, Chaffin's Farm, Nashville, Overton Hill, Honey Hill, Yazoo City, Poison Springs, Tupelo, Bermuda Hundred, Dutch Gap, Hatcher's Run, Fort Fisher, the fall of Richmond, Deep Bottom and Appomattox. Sixteen Black soldiers received Congressional Medals of Honor for gallantry in action.

Equally visible—and heroic—were the sailors in the Union Navy, which accepted Blacks from the beginning of the conflict. Twenty-nine thousand Blacks—one out of every four Union sailors—served on Union ships as coal heavers, stewards, boatswains, firemen and gunners. These sailors were quartered and messed with Whites and shared equally in the danger and glory. Four Black sailors received Medals of Honor.

In addition to these forces, the Union effort was forwarded by the more than 200,000 civilians, mostly freed slaves, who worked in Union camps as mechanics, cooks, barbers, teamsters, nurses and common laborers. Particularly important to the war effort were the Black laborers who built fortifications and groundworks, freeing soldiers, Black and White, for combat duty.

Black civilians, in and out of the army, served as spies and scouts. Of these spies, none was more successful than John Scobell, a former slave of a Scotsman who could sing Scottish ballads with impeccable diction and imitate Southern field hands. Disguising himself as a laborer and as a cook and peddler, Scobell infiltrated Southern lines at Fredericksburg, Leesburg and Manassas.

The most remarkable of all Union spies was a woman—the celebrated abolitionist Harriet Tubman. Working in South Carolina and other states, she organized slave intelligence networks behind enemy lines and led scouting raids. She also became the first woman to lead U.S. Army troops in battle. A graphic account of one of these battles appeared in the Boston *Commonwealth* on July 10, 1863:

HARRIET TUBMAN

Col. Montgomery and his gallant band of 300 Black soldiers, *under the guidance of a Black woman*, dashed into the enemy's country, struck a bold and effective blow, destroying millions of dollars worth of commissary stores, cotton and lordly dwellings, and striking terror into the heart of rebeldom, brought off near 800 slaves and thousands of dollars worth of property, without losing a man or receiving a scratch. It was a glorious consummation.

After they were all fairly well disposed of in the Beaufort charge, they were addressed in strains of thrilling eloquence by their gallant deliverer . . .

The Colonel was followed by a speech from the Black woman who led the raid, and under whose inspiration it was organized and conducted [Emphasis supplied].

By these different methods, by fighting and spying and weakening the Confederate war effort, Black Americans did as much as any other group to free themselves and American freedom. There is no better authority on this point than Abraham Lincoln, who initially opposed use of Black troops. But when it became apparent that "no human power" could subdue the rebellion "without the use of the emancipation policy," Lincoln changed his mind and told critics: "ABANDON ALL THE POSTS NOW GARRISONED BY BLACK MEN: TAKE TWO HUNDRED THOUSAND MEN FROM OUR SIDE AND PUT THEM IN THE BATTLEFIELD OR CORNFIELD AGAINST US, AND WE WOULD BE COMPELLED TO ABANDON THE WAR IN THREE WEEKS."

With the defeat of Confederate forces, the Black South exploded in a series of Jubilees that continued until the winter of 1865.

Free at last!
Free at last!
Thank God Almighty,
We're free at last!

The basic demand of the freedmen was land. They had lived for centuries in a primary relationship with the land, and it was inconceivable to them that the U.S. government would turn them loose without providing the economic wherewithal that would make freedom meaningful. And so it was believed in the summer of 1865 that each adult freedman would receive 40 acres of land on January 1, 1866. But there was no land on January 1, 1866, or on January 1, 1867. Without the means to realize their freedom, most freedmen were driven back to the plantations by hunger and violence.

It was in this setting, with booby traps all around them and all the high ground in the hands of their adversaries that the freedmen and freedwomen of America began their long march down a road some called freedom.

Family and Freedom:

BLACK FAMILIES IN THE AMERICAN CIVIL WAR

Ira Berlin, Francine C. Cary, Steven F. Miller, Leslie S. Rowland

No event in American history matches the drama of emancipation. More than a century later, it continues to stir the deepest emotions, and properly so. Emancipation accompanied the military defeat of the world's most powerful slaveholding class. It freed some four million slaves, a larger number than were emancipated in all other New World slave societies combined.

Born of a bloody civil war that raged for four long years (1861–65), emancipation accomplished a profound social revolution. It destroyed forever a way of life

based upon the ownership of human beings, restoring to the former slaves proprietorship of their own persons, liquidating without compensation private property valued at billions of dollars, and forcibly substituting the relations of free labour for those of slavery. In designating the former slaves as citizens, emancipation placed citizenship upon new ground, defined it in the national Constitution and thenceforth removed it beyond the jurisdiction of the states. By obliterating the sovereignty of master over slave, emancipation handed a monopoly of sovereignty to the newly consolidated nation-state. The freeing of the slaves simultaneously overturned the old regime of the South and set the entire American nation upon a new course.

With emancipation in the South, the United States enacted its part in a worldwide drama. Throughout the western world and beyond, the forces unleashed by the American and French revolutions and by the industrial revolution worked to undermine political regimes based upon hereditary privilege and economic systems based upon bound labour. Slavery had already succumbed in the Northern states and in the French and British Caribbean before the Civil War, and it would shortly do so in its remaining strongholds in Spanish and Portuguese America. Almost simultaneously with the great struggle in the United States, the vestiges of serfdom in central and eastern Europe yielded to the pressure of the age. Only small pockets in Africa

From *History Today*, January 1987, pp. 8-15. Reproduced by kind permission of History Today, Ltd., 83-84 Berwick Street, London W1V 3PJ England.

and Asia remained immune, and their immunity was temporary. The fateful lightning announced by the victorious Union army was soon to strike (if it had not already struck) wherever men and women remained in bonds of personal servitude.

For all systems of bondage, emancipation represented the moment of truth. The upheaval stripped away the patina of routine, exposing the conflicts that had smouldered beneath the surface of the old order. Throwing off habitual restraints, freed men and women reconstituted their lives in ways that spoke eloquently of their hidden life in bondage, revealing clandestine institutions and long cherished values. In confronting new restraints, they abandoned their customary caution in favour of direct speech and action, alive to the realisation that they were setting radically new precedents for themselves and for future generations.

Because they thrust common people into prominence, moments of revolutionary transformation have long occupied historians. While those who enjoy political power and social authority speak their minds and indulge their inclinations freely and often, their subordinates generally cannot. Only in the upheaval of accustomed routine can ordinary men and women give voice to the assumptions that guide their world as it is and as they wish it to be.

Encompassing in full measure the revolutionary implications of all transitions from bondage to freedom, emancipation in the American South has left behind an unparalleled wealth of documentation permitting direct access to the thoughts and actions of the freed men and women themselves. As the Civil War became a war for liberty, the lives of slaves and ex-slaves became increasingly intertwined with the activities of both the Union and Confederate governments. Following the war, agencies of the federal government, especially the army and the Freedmen's Bureau, figured prominently in the reconstruction of Southern economy and society. The records created and collected by these governmental agencies and now housed in the National Archives of the United States provide an unrivalled manuscript source for understanding the passage of black people from slavery to freedom.

In these archival files, alongside official reports, hundreds of letters and statements by former slaves give voice to people whose aspirations, beliefs, and behaviour have gone largely unrecorded. Not only did extraordinary numbers of ex-slaves, many of them newly literate, put pen to paper in the early years of freedom, but hundreds of others, entirely illiterate, gave depositions to government officials, placed their marks on resolutions passed at mass meetings, testified before courts-martial and Freed-

The newly-found voices of the slaves caught up in the American Civil War, and heard through letters to their families, are a testimony to their tenacity and unity in the struggle for emancipation.

men's Bureau courts, and dictated letters to more literate blacks and to white officials and teachers. The written record thus created constitutes an unparalleled outpouring from people caught up in the emancipation process.

The Freedmen and Southern Society Project (University of Maryland) is a collaborative effort to draw upon these remarkable records to write a documentary history of emancipation in the American South. During three years of systematic research in the National Archives, the project editors made an initial selection of more than 40,000 documents (about 2 per cent of the items they examined). These documents serve as the basis for *Freedom: A Documentary History of Emancipation, 1861–1867*, a multi-volume history combining interpretative essays with documents. Two volumes have reached print thus far, both published by Cambridge University Press: *The Destruction of Slavery* (1985) and *The Black Military Experience* (1982). Subsequent volumes will be concerned with the wartime genesis of free labour; land, labour, and capital in the postwar South; race relations, law, and justice; and black community life, including family, religion, education, and politics.

What follows is a sample of documents regarding one aspect of the story of emancipation—slave families in the wartime struggle for freedom. As slaves, black people had worked hard to maintain the sanctity of their family life. Despite enormous difficulties, they managed to create a dense network of kinship which stood at the centre of black society, not only performing the tasks of reproduction and socialisation that commonly fall to familial institutions but also giving meaning and direction to the lives of people who had no legal right to their own person or their progeny. The Civil War opened the way for slaves to put their family life on a firmer footing. When the opportunity arose, they hastily gathered their children, their parents, and other kin and fled toward safe—and, they hoped, free—ground. But the war created difficulties as well as opportunities for black families. Slaves had to balance the possibility of escape against the harsh retribution that would surely face family members left behind. Often they concluded that the only way to achieve their family's freedom was to strike out alone, with the hope of returning later as liberators. In short, wartime emancipation put black families to the test. The documents presented below reflect the dimensions of the ordeal.

The documents are transcribed exactly as written, with no correction of spelling, punctuation, capitalisation, or syntax. Extra space marks the end of unpunctuated sentences. Italicised words which are enclosed in brackets have been added by the editors; letters or words in ordinary roman type and enclosed in brackets indicate conjectural readings of illegible passages.

The free-born can perhaps never know the triumph and pain felt by the slave who gained liberty. John Boston, a Maryland slave, seized freedom early in the war by escaping to a Union army regiment, where he obtained employment as the servant of a Northern officer. This route out of slavery held less promise for women, children, and old people, who were regarded as encumbrances by an army on the march. John Boston therefore fled alone, to share with the family

This day i can adress you thank god as a free man...

RATHER DIE FREEMAN THAN LIVE TO BE SLAVES

3RD UNITED STATES COLORED TROOPS

Shield and motto of a Black regiment. Liberty, with the fasces — symbol of authority — hands the Union Flag to the regimental sergeant.

Upton Hill [*Virginia*] January the 12 1862
My Dear Wife   it is with grate joy I take this time to let you know Whare I am   i am now in Safety in the 14th Regiment of Brooklyn   this Day i can Adress you thank god as a free man   I had a little truble in giting away But as the lord led the Children of Isrel to the land of Canon So he led me to a land Whare fredom Will rain in spite Of earth and hell Dear you must make your Self content i am free from al the Slavers Lash   and as you have chose the Wise plan Of Serving the lord i hope you Will pray Much and i Will try by the help of god To Serv him With all my hart   I am With a very nice man and have All that hart Can Wish But My Dear I Cant express my grate desire that i Have to See you   i trust the time Will Come When We Shal meet again   And if We dont met on earth We Will Meet in heven Whare Jesas ranes   Dear Elizabeth tell Mrs Own[ees] That i trust that She Will Continue Her kindness to you and that god Will Bless her on earth and Save her In grate eternity My Acomplements To Mrs Owens and her Children may They Prosper through life   I never Shall forgit her kindness to me   Dear Wife i must Close   rest your-self Contented i am free   i Want you to rite To me Soon as you Can Without Delay   Direct your letter to the 14th Reigment New york State malitia Uptons Hill Virginea In Care of Mr Cranford Comary   Write my Dear Soon As you C   Your Affectionate Husban Kiss Daniel For me

John Boston
Give my love to Father and Mother

---

he left behind not only the triumph of his new freedom, but also its pain.

When circumstances permitted, slave families attempted to escape bondage together. The risks were enormous because slaveowners mobilised to prevent flight and recapture runaways, but proximity to Union army lines or to federally controlled territory like the District of Columbia could improve the chances. From the first days of the war, the District served as a haven for fugitive slaves from adjacent portions of Maryland and

Virginia. However, freedom remained insecure even for those who successfully reached its borders. A military labourer who had fled slavery with his family described the re-enslavement and punishment of his mother, wife, and infant child.

Black men and women who reached freedom behind Union lines did not rest satisfied with their own liberty. Like former slaves in other parts of the Union-occupied Confederacy, black military labourers in eastern Virginia organised an

expedition to liberate families and friends left behind. Union General Edward A. Wild, whose brigade of black troops comprised ex-slaves from Virginia and North Carolina, assigned several of his soldiers to accompany the dangerous raid and reported its outcome to his superior officer. Slaves who gained freedom under the auspices of the Union army were not thereby assured of maintaining either their families or their liberty. The members of an Alabama slave family found themselves re-enslaved, separated, and sold to new masters in

[*Washington, DC*] 6th day of Feb. 1864 Grandison Briskoe being duly sworn says he is about 25 years of age was born in Maryland & has been married to his wife since 1861   Came to reside with his wife in this City in April—4th day of April 1862 & has resided in said City Since that period of time except a part of the time   he has been in the Service of the United States all the time & is now in Said Service in Virginia—That his wife & his mother were taken away from Washington in April (on the 7th day) 1862 & as fugitive Slaves & taken to Piscatawa to Broad Creek to their master's [farm?] whose name is John Hunter & My mothers masters name was & is Robert Hunter—They were both taken to the barn & severely whipped Their clothes were raised & tied over their heads to keep their screams from disturbing the neighborhood & then were tied up & whipped very severely whipped and then taken to Upper Marlborough to jail My wife had a Child about nine month's old which was taken from her & died soon after. Some six or eight months after my wife was imprisoned she had a

Child but the inhuman master & mistress though the[y] knew she was soon to be Confined or give birth to a Child made no arrangements provided no Clothing nor anything for the Child or mother   I have sent them Clothing & other articles frequently until the first or near the first of January 1864 Since which the new jailor has refused to allow them to receive any thing from me

They have been in prison for the Crime of Coming to Washington to reside, ever since about the fourth of April 1862 now a year & ten months. They are confined in Jail at Upper Marlborough Prince George's County Maryland

Grandison Briscoe

Kentucky, a Union state where slavery remained untouched by the Emancipation Proclamation or other war-time emancipation measures.

The recruitment of black soldiers into the Union army beginning late in 1862 helped speed both emancipation and Union victory. In the Union's own slave states (Delaware, Maryland, Missouri,

Newport-News, [Va.]. Sept. 1st, 1864. Sir, I have the honor to report that some Government employees (colored) came up here from Fort Monroe and Hampton hospitals, having been allowed a short leave of absence for the purpose of getting their families if possible. I told them I had no boats, but would help them with men. They reappeared the next day with sailboats. I sent with them a Captain and 15 men (dismounted Cavalry). The families were in and about Smithfield. I gave them strict instructions to abstain from plundering—to injure no one if possible—to get the women and children merely, and come away as promptly as possible. They were to land in the night. They followed these directions closely: but became delayed by the numbers of women and children anxious to follow, whom they packed in extra boats, picked up there, and towed along. They also had to contend against a head tide, and wind calm. So that their progress down Smithfield Creek in the early morn was exceedingly slow. The inhabitants evidently gathered in from some concerted plan of alarm or signals.

'Reading the Proclamation', J.W. Watts' emotive engraving of 1864.

4. THE CIVIL WAR AND RECONSTRUCTION

Slave into Soldier: two photographs of Hubbard Pryor during the Civil War.

For, 3 miles below, the party were intercepted by a force of irregular appearance, numbering about 100—having horses and dogs with them;—armed variously with shot guns, rifles, &c, and posted behind old breastworks with some hurried additions. They attacked the leading boats, killed a man and woman, and wounded another woman therein. The contrabands then rowed over to the opposite bank and scattered over the marshes. How many more have been slaughtered we know not. Two (2) men have since escaped to us singly.—When the rear boats, containing the soldiers, came up, the Captain landed, with the design of attacking the rebels. But then the firing revealed their full numbers. He found they outnumbered him, more than 6 to 1, and that the *revolvers* of our Cavalry, in open boats or on the open beach, would stand no chance against their rifles behind breastworks. He embarked again, and they made their way past the danger, by wading his men behind the boats, having the baggage and bedding piled up like a barricade. They then had a race with 3 boats, which put out from side creeks to cut them off. But for the coolness and ingenuity of Capt. Whiteman, none would have escaped.

None of the soldiers are known to have been severely wounded; but 3 are missing in the marshes and woods. We have since learned that there are signal Stations in that neighborhood—which ought to be brooken up. I would also earnestly recommend the burning of a dozen or 20 houses in accordance with your General Order No. 23. Very respectfully Your obt. Servant

Edwd A. Wild

and Kentucky), where the Emancipation Proclamation bad no force, recruitment itself constituted the chief route to freedom. But it also created numerous difficulties for black soldiers' families, who remained legally slaves. Masters manipulated their slaves' family ties to try to deter the men from enlisting, and then turned their wrath upon the relatives of slave men who joined the Union army despite threats. When Martha Glover, a Missouri slave, wrote the following letter to her husband soon after he enlisted, her troubles had in fact only begun. Six weeks later, her master was apprehended while transporting her and her three youngest children to Kentucky for sale.

Mexico Mo. Dec 30th 1863
My Dear Husband   I have received your last kind letter a few days ago and was much pleased to hear from you once more. It seems like a long time since you left me. I have had nothing but trouble since you left. You recollect what I told you how they would do after you was gone. they abuse me because you went & say they will not take care of our children & do nothing but quarrel with me all the time and beat me scandalously the day before yesterday—Oh I never thought you would give me so much trouble as I have got to bear now. You ought not to left me in the fix I am in & all these little helpless children to take care of. I was invited to a party to night but I could not go I am in too much trouble to want to go to parties. the children talk about all you the time. I wish you could get a furlough & come to see us once more. We want to see you worse than we ever did before. Remember all I told you about how they would do me after you left—for they do worse than they ever did & I do not know what will become of me & my poor little children. Oh I wish you had staid with me & not gone till I could go with you for I do nothing but grieve all the time about you. write & tell me when you are coming.

Tell Isaac that his mother come & got his clothes she was so sorry he went. You need not tell me to beg any more married men to go. I see too much trouble to try to get any more into trouble too—Write to me & do not foget me & my children—farewell my dear husband from your wife
Martha

Slave men who enlisted in the Union army assumed that their military service should assure their families' freedom as well as their own. When Joseph Harris, a sergeant in the 82nd US Colored Infantry, found himself stationed in Florida, far from his Louisiana home and unable to accomplish his family's liberation, he

Barrancas Fa. Dec 27. 1864
Sir I beg you the granterfurction of a Small favor will you ples to Cross the Mississippia River at Bayou Sar La. with your Command & jest on the hill one mile from the little town you will finde A plantation called Mrs Marther. H. Turnbull & take a way my Farther & mother & my brothers wife with all their Childern & U take them up at your Hed Quarters. & write to me Sir the[y] ar ther & I will amejeately Send after them. I wishes the Childern all in School. it is

beter for them then to be their Surveing a mistes. Sir it isent mor then three or four Hours trubel   I have bain trying evry sence I have bin in the servis it is goin on ner 3. years & Could never get no one to so do for me   now I thinks it will be don for you is my Gen. I wishes evry day you would send after us. our Regt. ar doing all the hard fightin her   we have disapointe the Rebes & surprizeed theme in all. importan pointes   they says they wishes to Captuer the 82nd Regt that they woul murdar them all   they Calls our Regt the Bluebellied Eagles   Sir my Farthers Name Adam Harris   he will Call them all to gether. & tel him to take Cousan Janes Childarn with hime

     Joseph. J. Harris

Sir I will remain Ob your Soldiar in the U.S.A.

[*Louisville, Ky. August 14?, 1865*]

Amy Moore Colored, being duly Sworn deposeth and Says, that in the Summer of 1863 [*1862*] the United States Soldiers under command of Major McMillen came to her masters house in Huntsville Alabama, (her master and his family having left them) and carried away deponent together with her mother and three Sisters, that they brought us all to Nashville Tenn where we were put on board of a transport and Started for Cincinnati Ohio   that when we arrived at Louisville Ky we were arrested by a man who Said he was a watchman and taken to the Slave pen on Second Street Louisville Ky and kept there two or three days when we were taken to the Depot of the Louisville and Nashville Rail Road and there another watchman took charge of us and took us to Shepherdsville Ky and kept us confined several weeks when we were sold at auction by the Sherriff of Bullett County Ky. Dr. McKay bought deponent and paid for her the sum of Five Hundred (500) dollars   *Jam(es) Funk* bought deponents mother and youngest Sister paying Six Hundred (600) dollars for the two, and Soon after Sold her mother to *Judge Hoegner* who now holds her as a Slave   *James Shepherd* bought my Sister Nora and *Richard Deets* bought my sister Ann, and further deponent saith that she and her mother and Sisters have been held as Slaves Since the above Sale and Still continue to be so held.

     her
    Amy X Moore
     mark

---

sought the assistance of General Daniel Ullmann, who had supervised the recruitment of several black regiments in Louisiana.

The transformation of slaves into soldiers altered the expectations of both former slaves and slaveowners. Once black men donned the Union uniform, nothing was the same. When Private Spotswood Rice, a Missouri ex-slave, learned that the woman who owned his daughter Mary refused to permit the child to visit him and charged that he had tried to 'steal' her, he exploded in anger.

Chaplain Warren of the Freedman's bureau officiating at a military wedding, Vicksburg.

His letters, the first to his enslaved daughters and the second to Mary's mistress, suggest how military service made loving fathers into fierce liberators.

[*St. Louis, Missouri, September 3, 1864*]

My Children   I take my pen in hand to rite you A few lines to let you know that I have not forgot you and that I want to see you as bad as ever   now my Dear Children I want you to be contented with whatever may be your lots   be assured that I will have you if it cost me my life   on the 28th of the mounth. 8 hundred White and 8 hundred blacke solders expects to start up the rivore to Glasgow and above there thats to be jeneraled by a jeneral that will give me both of you   when they Come I expect to be with, them and expect to get you both in return. Dont be uneasy my children   I expect to have you. If Diggs dont give you up this Government will and I feel confident that I will get you   Your Miss Kaitty said that I tried to steal you   But I'll let her know that god never intended for man to steal his own flesh and blood. If I had no cofidence in God I could have confidence in her   But as it is if I ever had any Confidence in her I have none now and never expect to have   And I want her to remember if she meets me with ten thousand soldiers she [will?] meet her enemy   I once [*thought*] that I had some respect for them but now my respects is worn out and have no sympathy for Slaveholders. And as for her cristianantty I expect the Devil has Such in hell   You tell her from me that She is the frist Christian that I ever hard say that aman could Steal his own child especially out of human bondage

You can tell her that She can hold to you as long as she can   I never would expect to ask her again to let you come to me because I know that the devil has got her hot set against that that is write-now my Dear children I am a going to close my letter to you   Give my love to all enquiring friends   tell them all that we are well and want to see them very much and Corra and Mary receive the greater part of it you sefves   and dont think hard of us not sending you any thing   I you father have a plenty for you when I see you   Spott & Noah sends their love to both of you   Oh! My Dear children how I do want to see you

[*St. Louis, Missouri, September 3, 1864*]

I received a leteter from Cariline telling me that you say I tried to steal to plunder my child away from you   now I want you to understand that mary is my Child and she is a God given rite of my own and you may hold on to hear as long as you can but I want you to remembor this one thing that the longor you keep my Child from me the longor you will have to burn in hell and the qwicer youll get their   for we are now makeing up a bout one thoughsand blacke troops to Come up tharough and wont to come through Glasgow and when we come wo be to Copperhood rabbels and to the Slaveholding rebbels for we dont expect to leave them there root neor branch   but we thinke how ever that we that have Children in the hands of you devels we will trie your [vertues?] the day that we enter Glasgow   I want you to understand kittey diggs that where ever you and I meets we are enmays to each orthere   I offered once to pay you forty dollers for my own Child but I am glad now that you did not accept it   Just hold on now as long as you can and the worse it will be for you   you never in you life befor I came down hear did you give Children any thing not eny thing whatever not even a dollers worth of expencs   now you call my children your property   not so with me   my Children is my own and I expect to get them and when I get ready to come after mary I will have bout a powrer and autherity to bring hear away and to exacute vengencens on them that holds my Child you will then know how to talke to me   I will assure that and you will know how to talk rite too   I want you now to just hold on to hear if you want to   iff your conchosense tells thats the road go that road and what it will brig you to kittey diggs   have no fears about geting mary out of your hands   this whole Government gives chear to me and you cannot help yourself

Spotswood Rice

Fearing that their families would be abused by angry masters, slave volunteers brought their wives, children, and other relatives with them to the Union recruitment centres. In the Union-occupied Confederacy, many of the black soldiers' families joined earlier fugitive slaves in 'contraband camps' established by the army for ex-slaves not suited to military labour or armed service. Others were employed on plantations supervised by Union authorities, or took up residence in the shantytowns that proliferated near military posts. Some Union army officers, however, had little regard for the family ties of black soldiers and

express permission of the aforementioned Officer and never received any notice to leave until Tuesday November 22" when a mounted guard gave my wife notice that she and her children must leave Camp before early morning. This was about six o'clock at night. My little boy about seven years of age had been very sick and was slowly recovering   My wife had no place to go and so remained until morning. About eight Oclock Wednesday morning November 23" a mounted guard came to my tent and ordered my wife and children out of Camp   The morning was bitter cold. It was freezing hard. I was certain that it would kill my sick child to take him out in the cold. I told the man in charge of the guard that it would be the death of my boy   I told him that my wife and children had no place to go and I told him I was a soldier of the United States. He told me that it did not make any difference. He had orders to take all out of Camp. He told my wife and family that if they did not get up into the wagon which he had he would shoot the last one of them. On being thus threatened my wife and children went into the wagon   My wife carried her sick child in her arms. When they left the tent the wind was blowing hard and cold and having had to leave much of our clothing when we left our master, my wife with her little one was poorly clad. I followed them as far as the lines. I had no Knowledge where they were taking them. At night I went in search of my family. I found them at Nicholasville about six miles from Camp. They were in an old meeting

house belonging to the colored people. The building was very cold having only one fire. My wife and children could not get near the fire, because of the number of colored people huddled together by the soldiers. I found my wife and children shivering with cold and famished with hunger   They had not recieved a morsel of food during the whole day. My boy was dead. He died directly after getting down from the wagon. I know he was Killed by exposure to the inclement weather   I had to return to camp that night so I left my family in the meeting house and walked back. I had walked there. I travelled in all twelve miles   Next morning I walked to Nicholasville. I dug a grave myself and buried my own child. I left my family in the Meeting house—where they still remain   And further this deponent saith not

his
(Signed) Joseph Miller
mark

labourers and—deeming the women, children, and old people a nuisance—periodically evicted them from military camps. Private Joseph Miller, who had recently enlisted in the 124th US Colored Infantry, testified to the cruel fate of his family when they were forced out of Camp Nelson, Kentucky.

The war ended when the Confederacy surrendered in April 1865, but many black soldiers were not mustered out of

'Contrabands' coming into a Union Camp, by A.R. Ward, 1862.

Camp Nelson Ky, November 26, 1864   Personally appered before me E. B W Restieaux Capt. and Asst. Quartermaster Joseph Miller a man of color who being duly sworn upon oath says   I was a slave of George Miller of Lincoln County Ky. I have always resided in Kentucky and am now a Soldier in the service of the United States. I belong to Company I 124 U.S.C. Inft now Stationed at Camp Nelson Ky. When I came to Camp for the purpose of enlisting about the middle of October 1864 my wife and children came with me because my master said that if I enlisted he would not maintain them and I knew they would be abused by him when I left. I had then four children ages respectively ten nine seven and four years. On my presenting myself as a recruit I was told by the Lieut. in command to take my family into a tent within the limits of the Camp. My wife and family occupied this tent by the

Flight to Freedom: Fugitive slaves with a Black military escort in Virginia.

service for months or even years. As former masters returned home and reasserted their authority, black soldiers' families became special objects of abuse.

One Louisiana black soldier received the following letter from his wife about the difficulties forced upon his family in his absence. A sympathetic officer granted the soldier a furlough to attend to his family and then, in the second letter, warned the newly organised Freedmen's Bureau that Union military authorities were unwittingly assisting erstwhile slaveowners in their persecution of black soldiers' families.

General Wild and his brigade of Black troops liberating slaves in North Carolina.

4. THE CIVIL WAR AND RECONSTRUCTION

Roseland Plantation [St. Charles Parish, La.] July 16th 1865 My Dear Husband I received a letter from you week before last and was glad to hear that you were well and happy.

This is the fifth letter I have written you and I have received only one—Please write as often as you can as I am always anxious to hear from you. I and the children are all well—but I am in a great deal of trouble as Master John Humphries has come home from the Rebel army and taken charge of the place and says he is going to turn us all out on the Levee unless we pay him (8.00) Eight Dollars a month for house rent—Now I have no money of any account and I am not able to get enough to pay so much rent, and I want you to get a furlough as soon as you can and come home and find a place for us to live in. and besides Amelia is very sick and wants you to come home and see her if possible she has been sick with the fever now over two weeks and is getting very low—Your mother and all the rest of your folks are well and all send their regards & want to see you as soon as you can manage to come—My mother sends her compliments & hopes to see you soon

My children are going to school, but I find it very hard to feed them all, and if you can not come I hope you will send me something to help me get along

I get all the work I can and am doing the best I can to get along, but if they turn me out I dont know what I shall do— However I will try & keep the children along until you come or send me some assistance

Thank God we are all well, and I hope we may always be so Give my regards to all the boys. Come home as soon as you can, and cherish me as ever Your Aff wife

Emily Waters

Fort St. Philip. La. Aug. lst, 1865 Sir. I am an officer in a co. of 140 men.— have been with them continually Since their organization as a Co., and most of the time the Sole officer with them. Feeling an interest in the advancement and prosperity of the colored race and always sympathizing with them in their trials and Sufferings, which are now very great, owing to the peculiar condition of the country, and their people, those under my immediate charge have learned to look to me for consolation in regard to many matters not Strictly military. I always do what I can but frequently that is nothing at all. One of the most frequent complaints brought to me is the mistreatment of Soldiers wives, and in Some cases their ejectment for non-payment of rent by *returned rebels* who seem to be resuming their old positions all over the country. This of course is inhuman as well as contrary to Genl. Orders. No. 99. Hd Qrs. Dept. of the Gulf. June 30th, 1865, which declares that the families of Soldiers in the Service of the Gov't. either on land or water, Shall not be ejected for rent past due, and no collections of rent forced until further orders. . . .

My object in writing you this letter is to call your attention to a Mr. John Humphrey, who I am told is a returned rebel officer, now living on Roseland Plantation, St. Charles Parish, who is Said to have made innumerable threats and at least one attempt to put out the family of one of my Soldiers.—*for non-payment of rent.*—I gave the man a furlough and he got home just in time to find a *Provost Guard* at his house for the purpose of ousting his wife and children. These look like Strange proceedings viewed at this distance with my understanding of the law. The fact is, persecution is the order of the day amongst these

returned rebels, against the colored race in general, and Soldiers families *in particular.* And I am grieved to Say that many wearing the U.S. uniform are too easily bought body and Soul over to the evil designs and purposes of these same individuals. It seems to me that your Bureau and its agents are the "forlorn hope" of the colored people.—These rebels Strongly object to these agents, and declare that they will only keep up a confusion and disturbance, continually. That means that they do not intend to manifest the "good faith" for which Genl. Howard hopes, but intend to take Such a course with the colored people as will *oblige* the interference of the agents of your Bureau.

These are my views, although I owe you an apology for expressing them at Such length. If it pleases you I shall be glad to lay the frequent cases which arise in my Co. before you, as I know your voice is very potent With respect I am Your Most Obt. Servt.

Hugh P. Beach.

FOR FURTHER READING:

Freedom: A Documentary History of Emancipation, 1861–1867, Series 1, vol. I, *The Destruction of Slavery,* eds. Ira Berlin, Barbara J. Fields, Thavolia Glymph, Joseph P. Reidy and Leslie Rowland; Series 2, *The Black Military Experience,* eds. Ira Berlin, Joseph P. Reidy and Leslie S. Rowland (Cambridge University Press, 1985 and 1982); W. E. B. DuBois, *Black Reconstruction in America 1860–1880* (1935, reprinted Atheneum, 1969); Herbert G. Gutman, *The Black Family in Slavery and Freedom, 1750–1925* Pantheon, 1976); Leon F. Litwack, *Been in the Storm So Long: The Aftermath of Slavery* (Knopf, 1979); Willie Lee Rose, *Rehearsal for Reconstruction: The Port Royal Experiment* (Oxford University Press, 1976).

Lincoln and Douglass

Dismantling the
Peculiar Institution

A bestselling author of the 1990s is, surprisingly, Abraham Lincoln. The Library of America has reissued his speeches and writings; in Eastern Europe, translations of Lincoln now serve as classroom texts on democracy. But few know about the evolution of Lincoln's thinking on the race question, or how he was influenced by the ex-slave and brilliant orator Frederick Douglass. Dorothy Wickenden describes the relationship between the two men—a relationship that would alter the history of race in America.

Dorothy Wickenden

Dorothy Wickenden is the managing editor of The New Republic. *Born in Norwalk, Connecticut, she received her B.A. from William Smith College (1976).*

In late July, 1863, in the middle of the Civil War, an imposing man with stern features arrived at the White House hoping to meet Abraham Lincoln. Describing their interview later, he declared that, though he was the "only dark spot" in the throng of supplicants lining the stairway, he was received a few minutes after presenting his card. Elbowing his way to the front, he heard another visitor grousing, "Yes, damn it, I knew they would let the n——r through." Lincoln, surrounded by documents and hovering secretaries, sat in a low armchair, with his feet "in different parts of the room." The president's guest observed that "long lines of care were already deeply written on Mr. Lincoln's brow; and his strong face, full of earnestness, lighted up as soon as my name was mentioned." He approached Lincoln, who "began to rise, and he continued rising until he stood over me; and, reaching out his hand, he said, 'Mr. Douglass, I know you; I have read about you, and Mr. Seward has told me about you.' "

The president's visitor was, of course, Frederick Douglass, the editor of a respected abolitionist newspaper, a man internationally famous for his oratorical powers and anti-slavery activities. A self-taught former slave who had fled to

freedom 25 years before, Douglass was the first black man in America to receive a private audience with the president. There was every reason to expect, however, that the meeting would not go well. Douglass was a pitiless critic of Lincoln's harebrained "colonization" schemes, which would have dispatched freed slaves to Africa or Central America to establish their own republic. What's more, Lincoln could hardly have relished Douglass's reason for coming to the White House—to press him to pay black and white soldiers equally, a highly sensitive political issue. The two men had very different goals: The president's mission in the war was to save the Union; Douglass's was to free the slaves and transform them into citizens. Douglass's demands were not met that day, but he was evidently delighted by his reception. ("I tell you I felt big there!" he boasted.) And the meeting launched an exchange between Lincoln and Douglass that eventually did more than alter each of their views about the proper conduct of the war. It helped to rewrite the history of race in America.

If Frederick Douglass had the courage of Abraham Lincoln's convictions on racial equality, Lincoln perhaps more accurately gauged both the depth of prejudice permeating American society and the staggering complexity of replacing the institution of slavery with all of the safeguards of true democracy. Douglass's dream of a color-blind, integrated society in which blacks would share the privileges of education, voting, public

accommodations, and political office seemed on the point of being realized a century later, in the Supreme Court's *Brown* v. *Board of Education* decision (1954) and the 1964 Civil Rights Act. Today, Lincoln's tortured views about equal rights seem sadly prescient. Segregation can still be seen in schools, neighborhoods, and workplaces; and the separatist creeds of extremist politicians—white and black—are again making themselves heard. With current schisms confirming some of Lincoln's worst fears, it is worth reconsidering how he and Douglass came to terms over the future of blacks in America.

DURING THE 1950S AND '60S, REVISION-ist historians went back to reexamine Lincoln's views on racial equality and emerged with disturbing news. Kenneth M. Stampp asserted, " . . . if it was Lincoln's destiny to go down in history as the Great Emancipator, rarely has a man embraced his destiny with greater reluctance than he." A black journalist, Lerone Bennett, Jr., wrote a provocative article for the February 1968 issue of *Ebony* magazine entitled, "Was Abe Lincoln a White Supremacist?" The very question, asked in a black magazine during the racial strife of the 1960s, hinted at its answer.

Both those who defend Lincoln's racial politics and those who deplore them prop up their arguments with the speeches and writings of Frederick Douglass. Douglass's commitment to emancipa-

From *The Wilson Quarterly*, Autumn 1990, pp. 102-112. Copyright © 1990 by Dorothy Wickenden. Reprinted by permission.

tion, black enlistment in the army, and universal suffrage was as clear and consistent as Lincoln's was equivocal and changing. Douglass found himself maddened by Lincoln's faltering progress toward emancipation and by his seemingly inexhaustible solicitude toward the border states and northern conservatives. Yet by the end of the war, Douglass had come to admire Lincoln's tactical genius, and with considerable pride he also saw him as an ally and a friend. Douglass's changing opinions about the president reveal as much about his own political evolution as they do about Lincoln's.

Race was the issue that launched Lincoln's career in national politics. In the famous debates of 1858, the other Douglas—Stephen A. Douglas, Lincoln's opponent for the U.S. Senate in Illinois that year and again for the presidency in 1860—dwelled incessantly on the theme of racial inferiority. Douglas charged that the Negro race was inferior and thus not entitled to the inalienable rights accorded to whites. Conservative voters responded enthusiastically when Douglas referred to Lincoln as a "black Republican" and an extreme abolitionist (like "Fred. Douglass, the Negro") who was advocating intermarriage and Negro suffrage and officeholding. Lincoln tried to rise above Douglas's distortions and racial slurs, insisting that he was fighting for the nation's moral foundations. The crucial issue, Lincoln said, was that of human rights, not race. And he warned—as the abolitionists did—that the nation could not survive "permanently half slave and half free."

Yet Lincoln's liberal philosophy was countered by his pragmatism and his strong political conservatism. He realized that any attempt to secure all rights for blacks at once would scare the skittish white community and thus defeat the precarious enterprise of building a more equitable society. His goal during the 1850s was to stop the spread of slavery, not to liberate the slaves—hence the seeming contradictions in his views on race. He deplored the extension of slavery but defended southern states' rights to their slaves as "property." He also supported the southern demand for a tough fugitive slave law and opposed Negro voting and officeholding. During the ruthless political campaign of 1858, Lincoln sounded deeply pessimistic about the prospects for racial equality. In the now infamous Charleston speech he baldly declared that

there is a physical difference between the white and the black races which I believe will for ever forbid the two races living together on terms of social and political equality. And inasmuch as they cannot so live, while they do remain together there must be the position of superior and inferior, and I as much as any other man am in favor of having the superior position assigned to the white race.

The best he could do was to invoke the views of two slaveholders—Thomas Jefferson and Henry Clay—advocating gradual emancipation and voluntary emigration of freed slaves as the only viable solutions to slavery and racism.

Frederick Douglass, who was not running for office in 1858, had a different agenda. While Lincoln was trying to win over antislavery voters without unduly alarming conservatives in the state, Douglass was speaking out for abolition and dismissing colonization as a delusion that "serves to deaden the national conscience when it needs quickening to the great and dreadful sin of slavery."

Yet Douglass campaigned hard for Lincoln both in his Senate race in 1858 and in his 1860 run for the presidency. He, too, was a political pragmatist. He was saddened, he wrote in the June 1860 issue of *Frederick Douglass's Paper,* that the Republicans would not "inscribe upon their banners, 'Death to Slavery,' instead of 'No More Slave States,' " but he was willing to "work and wait for a brighter day, when the masses shall be educated up to a higher standard of human rights and political morality." He described Lincoln approvingly as a "radical Republican," calling him "a man of will and nerve. . . . He is not a compromise candidate by any means." Douglass was willing to overlook Lincoln's statements about racial superiority and his schemes for colonization. After all, Lincoln had pledged to stop the spread of slavery and to work toward "its ultimate extinction," and he had a good chance to win the presidential election.

But disillusionment quickly followed his endorsement. By December 1860 Douglass was describing Lincoln not as an abolitionist (which Lincoln had never remotely professed to be), but as a protector of slavery. "Mr. Lincoln proposes no measure which can bring him into antagonistic collision with the traffickers in human flesh," he declared. Douglass's worries were exacerbated by the country's unstable political condition. In the wake of the election, southern states

were threatening to secede. Northerners were urging compromise, not confrontation, and Douglass and other abolitionists expected the Republican Party to back down on slavery. "The feeling everywhere," he wrote later, "seemed to be that something must be done to convince the South that the election of Mr. Lincoln meant no harm to slavery or the slave power." Douglass no longer advised against disunion. He sought "any upheaval that would bring about an end to the existing condition of things." As Lincoln desperately sought ways to restore national harmony, Douglass looked forward to war as the beginning of the end of slavery.

THE NEW PRESIDENT DID NOT INTEND TO turn the war into an abolitionist crusade. He said in his first Inaugural Address in March 1861, "I have no purpose, directly or indirectly, to interfere with the institution of slavery in the States where it exists. I believe I have no lawful right to do so, and I have no inclination to do so. . . ." Douglass described the address as "double-tongued"—a shrewd description of Lincoln at the time. Caught between abolitionists and their Republican sympathizers on one side and Northern Democrats and the volatile border states on the other, Lincoln struggled to arrange a compromise. He hoped that he could move the remaining slave states still in the Union slowly toward emancipation by offering financial compensation for freed slaves. At the same time, he sought to soothe racial fears, in the North and the South, by advocating the colonization of freedmen.

For months after the Civil War broke out, public opinion in the North tended to endorse Lincoln's view of his mission. In November 1861, the three major New York papers, the *Tribune,* the *Times,* and the *World,* all denied that the war's purpose was to abolish slavery. Even Senator Charles Sumner, a friend of Douglass and a longtime supporter of the abolitionists, wrote: "You will observe that I propose no crusade . . . making it a war of abolition instead of a war for preservation of the union." Emancipation was "to be presented strictly as a measure of military necessity, and the argument is to be thus supported rather than on grounds of philanthropy." Though the abolitionists found this a cold-blooded approach, they too argued that the war could be won only if the slaves were freed. "The

Frederick Douglass: His Bondage and His Freedom

The life of Frederick Douglass (1817–1895) has the shape of an American myth—even more, perhaps, than that of Honest Abe, rail-splitter. Douglass's autobiographies (he wrote three) show a man who not only demanded that the nation accept the black dream of freedom and equality, but who embodied the dream in his own life.

Born to a black slave and a white father he never knew, Douglass's early childhood on a Maryland plantation was marked by paralyzing hunger and cold. He recalled his feet being "so cracked with the frost, that the pen with which I am writing might be laid in the gashes." At age six or seven, he was sent to a family in Baltimore, where the mistress of the house broke state laws by teaching him the rudiments of reading. This interlude came to an end when the master found out, admonishing his wife that if she taught "that nigger . . . how to read, there would be no keeping him. He would at once become unmanageable, and of no value to his master." Few warnings have proved so prophetic.

With the help of local schoolboys, Douglass taught himself to read and write. Now literate, he became even more eager for release from the "peculiar institution." In September 1838, at the age of 21, he escaped from slavery by fleeing to New York City, there marrying a freed woman, Anna Murray, whom he had known in Baltimore. They then moved to New Bedford, Massachusetts, where he changed his name from Bailey to Douglass to elude slaveholders. For three years he supported himself by shoveling coal, sawing wood, and sweeping chimneys, until, as he put it, "I became known to the anti-slavery world."

Soon after his arrival in New Bedford, Douglass became a subscriber to the abolitionist paper *The Liberator* and a protégé of its founder, William Lloyd Garrison. His first opportunity to speak before a white audience came in August 1841, when he addressed an anti-slavery convention in Nantucket. His gift for oratory was immediately apparent, and

the Massachusetts Anti-Slavery Society hired him as a lecturer. Using no notes, Douglass could speak for hours at a time, possessing, as one observer said, "wit, argument, sarcasm, pathos" and a voice "highly melodious and rich." Hecklers and skeptics claimed that so articulate a man could never have been a slave. To refute them, Douglass wrote an autobiography in 1845, which he rewrote 10 years later as *My Bondage and My Freedom.* Fearing recapture because of what he revealed in the autobiography, Douglass went on a two-year lecture tour in the British Isles, promoting his book and raising funds for the Massachusetts reformers. Douglass was soon an international celebrity.

In December 1846 friends purchased his freedom, and he returned home with a new ambition: to start his own abolitionist newspaper. After moving to Rochester, he began publishing the *North Star* (later renamed *Frederick Douglass's Paper),* which he described as "a terror to evil-doers."

In 1851, Douglass made a crucial decision. At the convention of the American Anti-Slavery Society he opposed Garrison's assertion that the Constitution was a pro-slavery document, citing the "noble purposes avowed in its preamble." He made it clear that he no longer supported Garrison's call for the dissolution of the republic.

Soon Douglass's work as an agitator and Lincoln's as a campaigner intersected. The passage of the Kansas-Nebraska Act in 1854, sponsored by Stephen A. Douglas, marked a turning point for the two men, as it did for the country. The opening of the territories to slavery unleashed Northern sentiment against the South, sending many voters to the new Republican Party. Impressed by Lincoln's eloquent attacks on slavery and by the promise of the new party, Douglass joined, too, in August 1856.

The victories of emancipation and black enlistment that Douglass helped to achieve during the Civil War never seemed to him sufficient. During the 1860s and '70s, when racial animosity appeared more pervasive than ever, he pushed for black suffrage and integrated schools. (He was also one of the few influential men of his time, black or white, to agitate for women's rights.) Douglass's work on behalf of the Republicans was rewarded with government posts: In 1877 he was appointed Marshal of the District of Columbia, in 1881 Recorder of Deeds for the District, and in 1889 he became American ambassador to Haiti.

During the 1880s and '90s, while many of his disillusioned contemporaries were preaching self-help and racial solidarity, Douglass became stubbornly more assimilationist. In 1884 he remarried, this time a white woman, Helen Pitts. Many blacks were appalled, but Douglass denounced their reaction as a dangerous eruption of "race pride." In a message that sounds particularly pointed today, he insisted that "a nation within a nation is an anomaly. There can be but one, American nation . . . and we are Americans."

very stomach of this rebellion is the Negro in the condition of a slave," Douglass wrote. "Arrest that hoe in the hands of the Negro, and you smite the rebellion in the very seat of its life."

Lincoln was an astute politician who moved only when the time seemed right. He was as concerned about the limits of federal power as he was about the evils of slavery. As president he did not express his abhorrence of slavery with the passion he had in the debates with Stephen Douglas. Frederick Douglass was astonished when Lincoln revoked General John C. Frémont's order freeing Missouri's slaves in August 1861. He could not understand Lincoln's refusal to make use of Negro soldiers:

The national edifice is on fire. Every man who can carry a bucket of water or remove a brick, is wanted; but those who have the care of the building, having a profound respect for the feeling of the national burglars who set the building on fire, are determined that the flames shall only be extinguished by Indo-Caucasian hands. . . .

After a series of devastating Union defeats in 1861, however, the public moved closer to the abolitionist view that the war could be won only by destroying slavery. So did the president. Although he still declared that the purpose of the war was to restore the Union and urged the border states to accept gradual, compensated emancipation, he simultaneously initiated a number of tactical changes. In August, the month he revoked Frémont's order, he also signed the first Confiscation Act, which freed all slaves who had participated against the Confederate war effort. In April 1862 he signed a bill abolishing slavery in the District of Columbia, and in May he acceded to General Benjamin Butler's "contraband" policy toward fugitive slaves, virtually granting them freedom. In July he signed the Second Confiscation Act. And, despite Lincoln's worries that arming the Negro would turn the border states against him, in August Secretary of War Stanton authorized Brigadier General Rufus Saxton at Beaufort, South Carolina, to recruit black volunteers. Most telling of all, that summer Lincoln privately discussed emancipation with his cabinet.

Lincoln had made each of these decisions reluctantly. That is unsurprising, given his cautious political disposition. More troubling to some historians is that Lincoln continued his tenacious support

for the voluntary emigration of freed slaves, an idea Douglass described, accurately enough, as "an old Whig and border state prepossession."

On August 14, 1862, Lincoln received at the White House a small group of free black men who had been carefully selected by the Commissioner of Emigration, the Rev. James Mitchell, an avid proponent of colonization. Lincoln thought he could convince them that racial prejudice was immutable and emigration inevitable, and he asked them to lead a movement for voluntary colonization. "You and we are different races," he said. "[T]his physical difference is a great disadvantage to us both. . . ." Furthermore, he told them, the Negro was the source of the current troubles: "But for your race among us there could not be war." Incensed at what he perceived as a case of blaming the victim, Douglass wrote a withering account of the inconsistencies in Lincoln's argument, concluding that he was "a genuine representative of American prejudice and Negro hatred and far more concerned for the preservation of slavery, and the favor of the Border Slave States, than for any sentiment of magnanimity or principle of justice and humanity."

FEW REALIZED THAT AS LINCOLN WAS making one final push for his tired old Whig solutions to slavery, he was also laying the groundwork for a social revolution. One month before receiving the black delegation, Lincoln had privately presented the "preliminary" Emancipation Proclamation to his cabinet, and one month later he released it. In December 1862, he proposed amendments to the Constitution that would provide for gradual, compensated emancipation and colonization. But by January 1, 1863, when the final proclamation took effect, Lincoln no longer considered colonization an active political option. Many scholars have claimed that Lincoln supported colonization mainly as a political tool to chip away at conservative worries about black freedom. Certainly, once the slaves were freed and allowed to fight in the war, Lincoln recognized that the obvious next step was citizenship, not banishment.

Douglass wished that the proclamation had gone further. It was, after all, only a war measure that excluded the loyal border states and those areas of the South under occupation by Union troops. It

justified emancipation as a "military necessity" and did not condemn slavery. Nevertheless, as he later wrote, he "saw in its spirit a life and power far beyond its letter." The final document made no mention of colonization (as the preliminary one had) or compensation, and it had a provision for incorporating blacks into the Union army. On New Year's Eve in 1862, Douglass waited with crowds of expectant blacks at Boston's Tremont Temple for the momentous announcement from Washington and joined in hours of rejoicing when it came. He set off on an extended lecture tour to explain the proclamation's significance to the public and to press for Negro enlistment. He agreed immediately to Major George L. Stearns's request to help recruit Negro troops. Douglass had begun to work within the political establishment.

FOR DECADES, HISTORIANS HAVE ARgued about whether Lincoln ever foresaw genuine civil rights for liberated blacks. Frederick Douglass, of course, had much to say on the subject. Although he continued his attacks on the administration after the Emancipation Proclamation, the tone of his remarks changed. Both men faced two pressing questions during the last years of the war—the role of blacks in the army and the future of blacks in America—which they discussed with mutual respect at the White House. The three conversations between the "ex-slave, identified with a despised race" and "the most exalted person in this great Republic," as Douglass put it in his 1892 autobiography, vividly capture how the two leaders practiced the arts of politics and persuasion. The talks also reveal how far each had gone toward accepting the other's views on how best to achieve a more just society.

Douglass intended to demand nothing less than "the most perfect civil and political equality." That included, of course, Negro suffrage. He was convinced that enlistment of blacks in the Union army was the first step toward citizenship, and on February 26, 1863, he published a widely distributed broadside, "Men of Color, to Arms!" urging blacks to fight for their own freedom. Undeterred by complaints of pay inequity, he told an audience of young black men in Philadelphia: "Once let the black man get upon his person the brass letters U.S. . . . and there is no power on the earth . . . which can deny that he has earned the right to citizenship in the United States.'' He even defended the administration: ''I hold that the Federal Government was never, in its essence, anything but an anti-slavery government.''

Six months later, after the bloody defeat of the Massachusetts 54th regiment at Fort Wagner, South Carolina (a battle in which his two sons fought), Douglass grew disheartened. Faced with growing evidence of the Confederates' brutal mistreatment of captured black soldiers, he wrote to Major Stearns that he intended to stop recruiting. ''How many 54ths must be cut to pieces, its mutilated prisoners killed and its living sold into Slavery, to be tortured to death by inches before Mr. Lincoln shall say: 'Hold, Enough!' ''

At Stearns's suggestion, Douglass went to the president himself with his complaints. In late July, 1863, accompanied by Senator Samuel C. Pomeroy of Kansas, Douglass entered the White House. During that first meeting, the president recalled Douglass's criticism of his ''tardy, hesitating, vacillating policy'' toward the war (''I think he did me more honor than I deserve,'' Douglass said somewhat disingenuously), and Lincoln told him that this charge of vacillating was unfair. ''I think it cannot be shown that when I have once taken a position, I have ever retreated from it.'' Douglass was more impressed with this statement than with anything else Lincoln said during the interview.

Douglass proceeded bluntly to make his demands: equal pay for black soldiers, equal protection for black prisoners of war, retaliation for Confederate killings, and promotions of blacks for distinguished service in battle. Lincoln replied that eventually black soldiers would receive the same pay as whites, but that the current inequity ''seemed a necessary concession to smooth the way to their employment at all as soldiers.'' Lincoln resisted the suggestion of retaliation, arguing that it would encourage further Confederate atrocities, but he said he would ''sign any commission to colored soldiers'' recommended by Secretary of War Stanton. Douglass left the interview finally convinced of the president's concern for blacks as a people, not just as a military tool.

At the War Department, Douglass said, Stanton not only ''assured me that justice would ultimately be done my

race''; he promised Douglass a commission as assistant adjutant. The pledge prompted Douglass to cease publishing his paper, and in his valedictory he proudly told his readers, ''I am going south to assist Adjutant General Thomas in the organization of colored troops, who shall win the millions in bondage the inestimable blessings of liberty and country.'' Although he was informed of his salary, the order for a commission never came. Douglass was displeased, but he later wrote with resignation, rather than resentment, that Stanton must have decided ''the time had not then come for a step so radical and aggressive.''

Lincoln called Douglass back to Washington the following August. The Rev. John Eaton, who helped run the government's program for freedmen in the Mississippi Valley, had reported to the president Douglass's continuing dissatisfaction with the treatment of black soldiers. Lincoln asked Eaton to set up another interview, telling him that, ''considering the conditions from which Douglass rose, and the position to which he had attained, he was, in his judgment, one of the most meritorious men in America.''

This encounter was even more revealing than the first. On August 19, 1864, while waiting in the reception room, Douglass was mistaken for the president. Joseph T. Mills, another visitor that day, told Lincoln:

It was dark. I supposed that clouds & darkness necessarily surround the secrets of state. There in a corner I saw a man quietly reading who possessed a remarkable physiognomy. I was rivetted to the spot. I stood & stared at him. He raised his flashing eyes & caught me in the act. I was compelled to speak. Said I, Are you the President? No replied the stranger, I am Frederick Douglass.

The meeting itself perpetuated this eerie confusion of identities, with Douglass assuming the role of wise statesman and Lincoln proposing a radical scheme to ensure black freedom.

The Union troops were foundering, and Lincoln (in the midst of his reelection campaign) was afraid he would be forced into a premature peace agreement. He told Douglass he would like his advice on two matters, doubtless fully calculating the disarming effect the request would have. Horace Greeley, the editor of the *New York Tribune,* and others had been pressing for peace. In his

reply to Greeley, Lincoln had made the abolition of slavery an explicit condition for the restoration of the Union. This ''To whom it may concern'' letter inflamed moderate Republicans and Copperheads (Democrats who pressed for reunion through negotiations), and Lincoln showed Douglass a response he had drafted, in which he said, in his usual circumspect manner, that even if he wanted to wage the war for the abolition of slavery, the country would not go along. Douglass emphatically urged the President not to send the letter, warning that it would be interpreted as a ''complete surrender of your anti-slavery policy.'' In the end, Lincoln did not send it.

Lincoln told Douglass that, if peace were forced upon them now, he must find a way to get as many blacks as possible behind Union lines. He proposed a kind of underground railroad that curiously resembled John Brown's early plan of attack on slavery: a small band of black scouts would infiltrate rebel states and accompany their charges to the North. Douglass worried that Lincoln was implicitly conceding that the Emancipation Proclamation could be suspended after the war, but he agreed to cooperate. He wrote the president a letter several weeks later suggesting the number of agents to be assigned, their salaries, and how to assure their safety. He also proposed some temporary government support for the freed slaves.

In his autobiography, Douglass recorded his impressions of the meeting: ''What he said on this day showed a deeper moral conviction against slavery than I have ever seen before in anything spoken or written by him. . . . I think that, on Mr. Lincoln's part, it is evidence conclusive that the proclamation, so far at least as he was concerned, was not effected merely as a 'necessity.' '' Moreover, Douglass added, ''In his company, I was never in any way reminded of my humble origin, or of my unpopular color.''

At the time Douglass had only a partial picture of the president's intentions. He did not know that Lincoln was deliberately making his way from the Emancipation Proclamation toward the 13th Amendment, which the President would describe as ''the King's cure for all the evils.'' He had already moved from an acceptance of black soldiers to enthusiasm for their performance. In August 1863 he had written a letter to his old friend James C. Conkling, stating:

The largely black Massachusetts 55th Regiment marches into Charleston on February 21, 1865. Douglass had championed the idea of blacks serving as soldiers as a step toward citizenship.

I know, as fully as one can know the opinions of others, that some of the commanders of our armies in the field who have given us our most important successes believe the emancipation policy, and the use of colored troops, constitute the heaviest blow yet dealt to the rebellion; and that, at least one of those important successes, could not have been achieved when it was, but for the aid of black soldiers.

Furthermore, Lincoln had made the crucial connection between arming the Negro and allowing him the privilege of voting. Louisiana, where Reconstruction had begun before the end of the war, was a test case. In March 1864, Lincoln wrote a letter to the newly elected Union governor, Michael Hahn, saying that the elective franchise might be offered to some blacks, "as, for instance, the very intelligent, and especially those who have fought gallantly in our ranks." He closed on a timid note: "But this is only a suggestion, not to the public, but to you alone." Nevertheless, on April 11, 1865, in his last public address a few days before his assassination, he returned to the idea, advocating limited suffrage and public education for blacks in reconstructed Louisiana.

Douglass disliked Lincoln's approach to Reconstruction, which allowed each state to decide for itself whether to confer the vote upon blacks. Like Senator Sumner, Douglass argued that Congress should demand universal suffrage as a condition for a state's readmission into the Union. Still, he did finally support Lincoln's reelection effort, agreeing with him "that it was not wise to 'swap horses while crossing a stream,' " and he attended the inauguration.

LINCOLN'S TRANSCENDENT SECOND Inaugural Address thrilled Douglass as much as the first had disappointed him. He was particularly struck by the president's conviction that slavery was "one of the offenses which . . . [God] now wills to remove," and that "this terrible war" was the "woe due to those by whom the offenses came." In Lincoln's words about the bond-man's 250 years of unrequited toil and suffering under the lash, Douglass could not have asked for a more stirring tribute to his people and the righteousness of the war against slavery.

The evening of the Inauguration Douglass went to the White House for the third time, to pay tribute to the president. He was turned away at the door, an affront that was quickly atoned for when an acquaintance of Douglass's let the president know he was there. Douglass entered the elegant East Room, and there, as he remarked in his autobiography, "Like a mountain pine high above all others, Mr. Lincoln stood, in his grand simplicity and homely beauty. Recognizing me, even before I reached him, he exclaimed, so that all around could hear him, 'Here comes my friend Douglass.' "

Lincoln, ever the politician, took Douglass's hand and said: " 'I am glad to see you. I saw you in the crowd today, listening to my inaugural address; how did you like it?' " Douglass demurred, afraid of detaining the president. " 'No, no,' he said. 'You must stop a little, Douglass; there is no man in the county whose opinion I value more than yours.' " Douglass, an equally adept flatterer, told him that the speech was "a sacred effort," and Lincoln replied, "I am glad you liked it!" His black friend "moved on, feeling that any man, however distinguished, might well regard himself honored by such expressions, from such a man."

On April 14, 1876, the eleventh anniversary of Lincoln's assassination, Frederick Douglass gave a speech at the unveiling of the Freedmen's Monument in Washington. It was a ceremonious occasion attended by senators, Supreme Court justices, and President Ulysses S. Grant and his cabinet. The oration is a favorite both with historians who cast Lincoln as a white supremacist and with those who see him as the Great Emancipator. In it, Douglass began with what sounded like sharp criticism: "Abraham Lincoln was not, in the fullest sense of the word, either our man or our model. In his interests, in his associations, in his habits of thought, and in his prejudices, he was a white man. He was preeminently the white man's president, entirely devoted to the welfare of white men.'' Black Americans, continued Douglass, ''are only his step-children . . . children by force of circumstances and necessity.'' Yet later in the speech, Douglass's praise for the President was unstinting:

His great mission was to accomplish two things, first to save his country from dismemberment and ruin; and second, to free his country from the great crime of slavery. To do one or the other, or both, he needed the earnest sympathy and the powerful cooperation of his loyal fellow countrymen. . . . Had he put the abolition of slavery before the salvation of the union, he would have inevitably driven from him a powerful class of the American people and rendered resistance to rebellion impossible. From the genuine abolition view, Mr. Lincoln seemed tardy, cold, dull, and indifferent, but measuring him by the sentiment of his country—a sentiment he was bound as a statesman to consult—he was swift, zealous, radical, and determined.

Douglass was far from immune to the sentimental view of Lincoln that so many Americans acquired after his death. And the president's apparent fondness for him was reciprocated. He was deeply touched that Lincoln had left his walking stick to him. According to his biographer Benjamin Quarles, Douglass cherished this more than any other gift he received—including those from Charles Sumner and Queen Victoria.

Nevertheless, Douglass was not one to let sentiment override truth, and in his oration he was groping toward a painful recognition that the president's ultimate triumph was due in part to those distasteful concessions he made to white prejudice. As Richard Hofstadter acknowledged in *The American Political Tradition* (1948), Lincoln ''knew that formal freedom for the Negro, coming suddenly and without preparation, would not be real freedom, and in this respect he understood the slavery question better than most of the Radicals, just as they had understood better than he the revolutionary dynamics of the war.'' The abolitionists and the radical Republicans could not have won their war against slavery. Nor would Lincoln's early support for black rights have prevailed without the determination of extreme idealists like Douglass.

At the time of his death Lincoln had not yet made a clear commitment to full citizenship for blacks. But in the Gettysburg Address in November 1863, he described a nation that, ''conceived in liberty and dedicated to the proposition that all men are created equal,'' would be given ''a new birth of freedom.'' This was not the old Jeffersonian social order he had set out to defend. It was, in fact, very close to the ''new Union'' Douglass talked about the next month: ''We are fighting for something incomparably better than the old Union.'' In the new union there would be ''no black, no white, but a solidarity of the nation, making every slave free, and every free man a voter.'' In strikingly similar terms, Abraham Lincoln and Frederick Douglass thus described a more perfect union, one they together helped to construct.

TODAY, AMID THE POLITICS OF SELF-interest and racial resentment, this sense of shared purpose is ever more fragile. Douglass saw that the country would be susceptible to such fragmentation, and he fought against it throughout his political life. "Nothing seems more evident," he repeatedly insisted to blacks who despaired of finding common ground with whites, "than that our destiny is sealed up with that of the white people of this country, and we believe that we must fall or flourish with them."

"A Few Appropriate Remarks"

President Lincoln had been invited to speak at the new national cemetery almost as an afterthought. His speech lasted barely two minutes. But those few well-chosen words—uttered 125 years ago this month—endure as the best-remembered oration in American history.

Harold Holzer

Harold Holzer, co-author of The Lincoln Image *(1984), was awarded this year's Lincoln Diploma of Honor by Lincoln Memorial University in Harrogate, Tennessee.*

By noon the procession had made its way up Gettysburg's Baltimore Street, along Emmitsburg and Taneytown roads, and across the hillside to the ceremony area. Bands played as the dignitaries, President Abraham Lincoln among them, dismounted from their horses and walked between rows of soldiers to the speakers' stand. The crowd pressed so tightly about that the marshals' horses were completely encircled.

As Lincoln ascended the three-foot-high platform, he could see thousands of spectators spread out across the grounds before him, all the way to the distant trees where a few onlookers perched in the branches. A photographer to the rear of the throng exposed a single plate as Lincoln took his seat.

America's sixteenth president was in town on this nineteenth day of November 1863 to make "a few appropriate remarks." The occasion: the dedication of a national cemetery for Union soldiers killed in the Battle of Gettysburg in July 1863, less than five months before.

THE THREE-DAY BATTLE AT GETTYS-burg had irrevocably changed the course of the Civil War, all but guaranteeing the eventual suppression of the rebellion and the restoration of the Union. But the cost had been staggering: over 3,000 Federal dead, 14,500 wounded, and another 5,000 missing. More than 24,000 Confederate soldiers were also missing or wounded.

"For seven days it literally ran blood," a nurse had recalled of the harrowing scenes in makeshift hospitals that filled to overflowing after the battle. The surgeons who staffed the Union medical corps were too few to tend to all the wounded, and many of those who received the scarce medical attention died anyway.

The less fortunate wounded had remained on the field for up to a week, filling the hot summer days and nights with moans of suffering and pitiful cries for help. All around them, bodies of men and horses swelled and decomposed in the fearsome heat. Torrential rains just after the fight washed the topsoil off the few mass graves that had been hastily dug.

During the days and weeks that followed the battle, as the rest of the North celebrated victory, grieving relatives descended on the once-obscure Pennsylvania village to search for their loved ones. What they saw was the horrible aftermath of man's inhumanity and Nature's downpour: stiffened arms and legs jutting akimbo from half-exposed burial sites, accompanied by a stench so overpowering that visitors and townspeople alike held sachets to their noses.

When Pennsylvania Governor Andrew Curtin arrived, he was understandably appalled. He quickly asked a thirty-two-year-old Gettysburg attorney, David Wills, to organize a mass cleanup. Wills accepted the challenge and went to work.

At first he suggested the impossible: place each body in its own coffin, label it, and ship it home. But the foul odor, the fear of pestilence, and the oppressive July heat all combined to make the job hopeless. After only a few hundred bodies had been processed, the task was abandoned. Wills sent new instructions: bury the dead where they had fallen, one hundred at a time if necessary.

VISITORS FROM MASSACHUSETTS, searching for casualties from their home state, were the first to suggest setting aside ground in Gettysburg for a national cemetery. It would be a grateful nation's gift to "those who here gave their lives that that nation might live," as Lincoln poignantly described the site in his brief address when, exactly 125 years ago this month, he visited the battle-scarred village.

"It is altogether fitting and proper that we should do this," Lincoln declared at the cemetery's dedication, using words that even the southern *Atlanta Constitution* conceded in retrospect were "abundantly justified by the march of time." The mesmerizingly simple words of his Gettysburg Address, woven into poetic phrases and beautiful sentences, were destined to become even more famous than the battle itself.

But for all the misty legends that have come to enshroud Lincoln's speech—his

From *American History Illustrated*, November 1988, pp. 37-46. Reprinted through the courtesy of Cowles Magazines, publishers of *American History Illustrated*.

supposedly careless preparation and off-hand delivery, to name but two—he almost didn't make the trip to Gettysburg.

For one thing, he was only halfheartedly invited to attend the ceremony. Even then, he wasn't immediately asked to speak. And he almost cancelled his trip at the last minute to nurse his gravely ill son Tad. Had the event been scheduled only a few days later, Lincoln himself might have been incapacitated by illness.

Actually, for all his fame as an orator, the President did not ordinarily agree to make public speeches. Compared to modern presidents, Lincoln was practically a White House recluse. Following his publicly delivered 1861 inaugural address, he virtually retired from the presidential rostrum. Only an occasional White House serenade could elicit a brief thank-you or a clumsy, extemporaneous apology for having failed to prepare formal remarks.

"This is . . . the occasion for a speech," he admitted to such an impromptu gathering at a July 7 serenade to celebrate the Gettysburg victory. "But I am not prepared to make one worthy of the occasion. . . . Having said this much, I will now take the music."

Lincoln's reputation as debater and raconteur notwithstanding, the carefully recorded transcripts of such bumbling meanderings reveal him as an astonishingly awkward public speaker—that is, when he was not meticulously prepared. This makes the most stubborn and widely known of the Lincoln Gettysburg legends—that he scribbled his speech on the back of an envelope during the train ride to the event—highly improbable.

Lincoln had almost immediately sensed Gettysburg's historical watershed importance. And when he was finally asked there to make an address on the battle and its meaning, he readily agreed to do so.

The Gettysburg triumph was "a glorious theme" and "the occasion for a speech," the President had acknowledged to the White House serenaders. The battle could become a symbolic rallying cry—of sacrifice, honor, freedom, equality, and hope for the future. Lincoln could use the occasion to remind his fellow citizens that their struggle was not being waged solely to restore national authority, but to rescue and sustain the pure, original dream of American democracy, through a bitter and painful "new birth of freedom."

BY AUGUST 1863, WILLS HAD SUCCESSfully negotiated with seventeen Northern states for approval of the cemetery plan and for sharing the costs of creating it. For $2,475 his group purchased seventeen boomerang-shaped acres alongside the town graveyard, and planned a series of graceful, semicircular grave areas identifiable by state—with several sections set aside for the unknown dead. By November 1863 some twelve hundred bodies would be reinterred there.

The cemetery dedication might have taken place two months earlier than it did, had it not been for sixty-nine-year-old Edward Everett of Massachusetts—ordained minister, professor of Greek, congressman, governor, ambassador, college president, secretary of state, U.S. senator, candidate for vice president (against Lincoln's ticket in 1860), and the best-known American public speaker of his time. On August 28, the Gettysburg committee surprised no one by asking him to give the keynote oration one month later.

In the second-floor guest bedroom of the Wills home, Lincoln labored on his address for the next day. As always, even with a looming deadline, he worked slowly.

Everett was eager to participate—but not so soon. He was recovering from a stroke, and he needed more time to prepare. Would it not be possible, he asked, to postpone the dedication to a later date—November 19 at the earliest? Wills desperately wanted Everett to be the main speaker, so November 19 it would be.

Printed invitations were soon sent to assorted Union dignitaries, and when Curtin next visited Washington, D.C., in late October, he personally presented one to the President. To everyone's surprise, Lincoln accepted.

A presidential "no" had been all but assumed—and probably with a sense of relief. The organizers may have remembered that, soon after the Battle of Antietam the year before, scandal-mongers had asserted that Lincoln had wandered

through a field littered with corpses, heartlessly asking a companion to sing a comical song. Although the vicious claim was false, the prospect of an awkward, wisecracking Lincoln at Gettysburg likely concerned Wills and his committee.

As an astute Illinoisian on Wills's committee pointed out, propriety dictated that the President of the United States be invited to speak, even though the principal oration was to be delivered by someone else, and, even though, as one organizer remembered, "it did not seem to occur to anyone that he could speak on such an occasion." And so Lincoln was invited as "an afterthought."

On November 2—just seventeen days before the great day—Wills sent a perfunctory, almost rude notice to Lincoln. "These Grounds will be Consecrated . . . on Thursday the 19th," he wrote, adding that "Hon Edward Everett will deliver the Oration. I am authorized by the Governors of the different States to invite you to . . . participate in these ceremonies."

Lincoln's role was carefully described. "After the Oration, you as Chief Executive of the Nation" will "formally set apart these grounds to their Sacred use by a few appropriate remarks." And just to make sure that Lincoln's remarks would not be *in*appropriate, Wills presumptuously reminded him that the "ceremonies . . . will doubtless be very imposing and solemnly impressive."

Later Wills sent the President a warmer and more personal note. "As the hotels in our town will be crowded and in confusion . . . Governor Curtin and Honorable Edward Everett will be my guests at the time and if you will come you will please join them at my house."

LINCOLN WAS NOT ABOUT TO ALLOW THE reluctant summons to deter him. He likely began giving thought almost immediately to the occasion before him—such was his style—and to slowly formulate ideas and thoughts until they took shape in his mind and, eventually, on paper.

For the inspiration of his immortal opening lines, Lincoln needed to look back only twelve weeks, for the idea had apparently come to him even as the dead were lying exposed in the hot fields of Gettysburg. He had expressed it on the evening of July 7, as the crowd of serenaders gathered outside the White House in celebration of the Gettysburg victory.

"I am very glad indeed to see you tonight," Lincoln had welcomed them from an open window. "How long ago was it?—eighty odd years—since on the Fourth of July for the first time in the history of the world a nation by its representatives, assembled and declared as a self-evident truth that 'all men are created equal.' [Cheers] That was the birthday of the United States of America."

Four months later, those stumbling references would be refined into a pristine salutation: "Four score and seven years ago, our fathers brought forth upon this continent a new nation, conceived in liberty and dedicated to the proposition that all men are created equal."

Minute guns sounded as the parade moved up Baltimore Street, accompanied by military bands playing dirges. Lincoln rode "easily, bowing occasionally to left and right."

How much time Lincoln took to nurture his idea, no one can be sure, but its July 7 expression, albeit in rough form, suggests that Lincoln did *not* wait until the last minute to create the Gettysburg Address either because of carelessness *or* divine inspiration.

Lincoln had been developing many of the themes in the speech throughout his political career. In a eulogy to Henry Clay, written twenty-three years before Gettysburg, he spoke of "men who . . . are beginning to assail and ridicule . . . the declaration that 'all men are created equal' "—the sacred "proposition" of his 1863 masterpiece spoken at Gettysburg.

Speaking in Peoria, Illinois, nine years earlier, he had told an audience: "Near eighty years ago we began by declaring that all men are created equal. . . . Let us re-adopt the Declaration of Independence, and with it, the practices and policy, which harmonize with it. . . . If we do this, we shall not only have saved the Union, but we shall have so saved it, as to make, and to keep it, forever, worthy of the saving." A Union, in other words, that "shall not perish from the earth."

He had spoken of the "great task which events have devolved upon us" in

his 1861 Message to Congress; in the Gettysburg Address it became "the great task remaining before us."

And in a special message to Congress that year he had asked whether "a government of the people, by the same people—can, or cannot, maintain its territorial integrity . . . against its own domestic foes."

An eyewitness to Lincoln's Gettysburg Address said of the speech, "it seems as though he must have been preparing it all his life." In a way, he had been.

ON NOVEMBER 8, TWO WEEKS BEFORE the Gettysburg dedication, Lincoln visited Alexander Gardner's Washington photography gallery, where he sat for a series of portraits. Asked there whether he had yet written his speech, Lincoln admitted: "Not yet . . . not finished anyway." But, he said, he had decided it would be "short, short, short."

As Lincoln posed, an envelope could be seen beside his elbow on the studio table. Some have claimed that inside was an advance copy of Everett's oration, which the President read between exposures.

The next day, Lincoln wrote his first known words *about* Gettysburg. The President's old friend and self-appointed bodyguard, Ward Hill Lamon, had been named marshall for the ceremony, an appointment that apparently precluded a planned reunion with his wife and her father Stephen Logan, Lincoln's former Illinois law partner. Trying to placate Logan, Lincoln wrote: "Now, why would it not be pleasant for you to come" to Gettysburg instead? "It will be an interesting ceremony," the President promised, "and I shall be very glad to see you." (To Lincoln's pleasure, Judge Logan came; to Lamon's delight, the judge brought Mrs. Lamon.)

That night, Lincoln encountered John Wilkes Booth at Ford's Theatre. Their final, fatal encounter was still nearly two years away. But this evening, President and Mrs. Lincoln looked on happily as the athletic young actor entertained them in *The Marble Heart.* "Rather tame than otherwise," Lincoln's young assistant private secretary, John Hay, wrote of the performance in his diary.

Tension in the family grew just days before the dedication ceremony when the Lincolns' youngest son, Tad, contracted a serious illness—probably smallpox. Only a year-and-a-half earlier, the couple's

third—and favorite—child, Willie, had died in the White House. As Tad's condition worsened, Mary, her longstanding emotional fragility already strained by Willie's death, was reported near hysteria. Lincoln may seriously have considered cancelling his appearance at Gettysburg. But, as with most conflicts between the public and private Lincoln, the public won out. Despite his wife's protests, Lincoln affirmed his decision to go.

With only a few days left, Lincoln began focusing in earnest on his "short, short, short" speech. On November 17, he admitted to Attorney General James Speed that he had only written half of it. Speed's Cabinet colleague, Secretary of War Edwin M. Stanton, apparently saw a rough copy—"written with a lead pencil on commercial notepaper," he recalled later. Only half of such a penciled copy has survived, suggesting that Lincoln soon rewrote the first half in ink, discarding his draft in the process.

To Lamon, Lincoln confessed he was struggling. Only hours before their departure, he slowly took some sheets from his hat and said, "Hill, here is what I have written for Gettysburg tomorrow. It does not suit me, but I have not time for any more." He then read it aloud as Lamon listened intently. Lincoln's friend offered no response. Possibly he did not like what he heard. Surely he knew there was no time to make major revisions. So he said nothing at all.

Other intimates may have seen the work-in-progress, too. Not surprisingly, their numbers swelled when the speech became famous. In any case, enough eyewitnesses claimed to have seen at least a draft of the address to disprove the legend that Lincoln began composing it while en route to Gettysburg.

That scenario would have been even more unlikely had Secretary of War Stanton had his way. Stanton had proposed that Lincoln leave on the morning of November 19, a plan that certainly appealed to Mrs. Lincoln, who was still nursing both an ailing son and a lingering hope that she could keep her husband home. One newspaper even reported that Mary had developed "an opportune chill" in an attempt to win her husband's sympathy.

But Lincoln rejected Stanton's itinerary. Rail travel in 1863 was anything but dependable—in fact, Pennsylvania Governor Curtin's train would later run into difficulty on its short trip from Harrisburg to Gettysburg. "I do not like this arrangement," Lincoln complained. "I do not want to go that by the slightest accident we fail entirely, and, at the best, the whole to be a mere breathless running of the gauntlet." So the departure was moved ahead one day.

LATE ON THE MORNING OF NOVEMBER 18, Lincoln bade his family farewell, urging his wife to keep him posted about their son's condition, and stepped into a carriage bound for the depot.

Many friends and acquaintances were on board the special train—cabinet ministers such as Secretary of State William H. Seward and Postmaster General Montgomery Blair; ambassadors from France and Italy; Lincoln's secretaries, John Hay and John G. Nicolay; Edward Everett's daughter-in-law; a Marine band; and an honor guard. The four-car train pulled out of Washington nearly on schedule, bunting and steamers flapping in the wind.

On the tedious journey that followed—a trip that would take no more than two hours today by automobile—Lincoln stayed for the most part in a partitioned-off section of the rear car, listening as the band up ahead practiced its music, inviting people back to talk to him, telling a few lighthearted stories, and sharing a lunch in a converted baggage car furnished with a long table. No one could later recall what was served.

One "detail" nearly everyone recalled differently was whether or not Lincoln took out his speech during the trip; whether, as legend persistently claimed, he wrote all of it on an envelope while he rode. "I have no recollection of seeing him writing or even reading his speech during the journey," insisted one of Lincoln's military escorts, General James B. Fry. Another eyewitness reported "hardly any opportunity to read, much less to write."

But newspaperman Ben Perley Poore insisted that the address was "written in the car on the way from Washington to the battlefield, upon a piece of pasteboard held on his knee." And years later Andrew Carnegie said that it was he, then an aide to the head of the B&O Railroad, who had personally handed Lincoln the pencil he used on board to write his speech. A fellow passenger went so far as to say that Lincoln had completed the speech by the time the train reached Baltimore.

But even if Lincoln seriously thought of writing a draft on the train, he may

well have remembered the cold February morning in 1861 when he had delivered a beautiful farewell speech to his Springfield neighbors from the back of a railroad car like this one, just before departing for his inauguration. Once inside the car and underway, reporters and admirers had urged the president-elect to write down his remarks, and Lincoln had tried to do so. But midway through the effort he gave up. The jostling of the primitive cars had rendered his usually precise penmanship an indecipherable scrawl. A secretary took over the task. The surviving copy of that speech bears little resemblance to the neat drafts of the Gettysburg Address. If Lincoln did write anything en route to Gettysburg, it has not survived. Chances are he recalled the Springfield experience and did not even try.

The slow journey home was far from pleasant. Lincoln was depressed, certain his speech had been a failure. And he was ill with symptoms of varioloid, a mild form of smallpox.

Along the way the President did get to see some of his constituents. At one stop he kissed a "little rosebud" of a child, as he called her, and later gave a brief talk in Hanover, Pennsylvania, when a man called out from a crowd of admirers, "Father Abraham, your children want to see you!" Stepping onto the platform, Lincoln told them: "Well, you had the Rebels here last summer . . . did you fight them any?" The crowd seem perplexed.

FINALLY, AT 5 P.M., THE PRESIDENTIAL special chugged into Gettysburg. After exchanging greetings with Everett and other dignitaries at the station, Lincoln got his first look at the village that had become famous throughout America. There is no record of what he said as he walked slowly to the town square and the Wills home. But as the crowd neared the mansion, the large presidential party "broke like a drop of quicksilver split."

In the Wills residence, Lincoln was shown to a beautifully furnished second-

floor bedroom dominated by a four-poster bed. Later that evening, the Gettysburg lawyer hosted a lavish dinner for twenty-four people. Observing Lincoln there, Everett thought him "the peer of every man at the table."

Before the President excused himself to return to his room, he was handed a telegram that undoubtedly relieved him tremendously. It was from Stanton: "By inquiry, Mrs. Lincoln informed me that your son is better this evening."

Lincoln now needed time to work, but as the Wills house grew quieter, the noise from the streets below grew louder. The town was choked with visitors, many of whom had found no lodging and were now roaming around aimlessly, drinking and singing. By 9 P.M. a large and noisy crowd had gathered outside the Wills home, and the din was further magnified when the New York Fifth Artillery Band struck up a serenade. Well-wishers called for "Old Abe" until he appeared outside Wills's front door.

Lincoln was "loudly cheered," according to a New York reporter, and proceeded to offer "half a dozen words meaning nothing," as Hay remembered. "I appear before you, fellow-citizens, merely to thank you for this compliment," Lincoln told them. "The inference is a very fair one that you would hear me for a little while at least, were I to commence to make a speech."

The audience perked up, but quickly Lincoln added: "I do not appear before you for the purpose of doing so, and for several substantial reasons. The most substantial of these is that I have no speech to make." The audience laughed heartily, and Lincoln went on: "In my position it is somewhat important that I should not say any foolish things."

A voice from the crowd shot back *"If you can help it!"* and there was more laughter.

Lincoln quickly replied: "It very often happens that the only way to help it is to say nothing at all." That got more laughs, Lincoln added a few pleasantries, and he begged to be excused.

Not yet satisfied, the crowd slowly moved on to the house next door, where Seward had been installed, and called for a speech from him. The crowd had better luck with the secretary of state, who offered a longer address to this curious mixture of mourners and celebrants.

AS SEWARD INTONED NEXT DOOR, LINcoln went back to work on his address.

As always, even with a looming deadline, he worked slowly. At one point he asked his valet to summon Wills, whom the President questioned closely about the arrangements for the ceremony. Later, Curtin made his belated entrance, and was ushered into Lincoln's room to proffer apologies and greetings. Then, at around 11 P.M., Wills was summoned again, and this time Lincoln asked for Seward. His host offered to go next door and fetch him, but Lincoln replied, "No, I'll go and see him."

Gathering up the sheets of paper (the President "would read from the same paper" the next day, Wills later insisted, although others disagreed), Lincoln followed his host into the "Diamond" (as the town square was called), through still-thick crowds, to the home where Seward was lodged. There the President read his speech to his chief minister and asked for comments—just as he had done with his first inaugural address and his Emancipation Proclamation. If Seward made any suggestions this night, they were not recorded. All we know is that Lincoln later stepped back into the street to return to the Wills house by 11:30, pushing his way past well-wishers with a pleasant, "I will see you all tomorrow."

Minutes later, Lincoln received another heartening bulletin about Tad, this time from Mary. "The doctor has just left. We hope dear Taddie is slightly better. Will send you a telegram in the morning." Curtin thought he saw Lincoln holding a "long yellow envelope"—presumably containing his speech. "Now, gentlemen, if you will excuse me," Lincoln told his fellow guests, "I will copy this off." It was midnight. Alone, he returned to his writing.

SOME, SEWARD AMONG THEM, LATER claimed that Lincoln roused himself early the next morning and secretly drove off in a carriage for a firsthand look at the battlefield. Surely Lincoln would have liked to view the site of the war's greatest conflict, but it is doubtful he could have made such a tour, even around dawn, without being observed by the hundreds of shelterless visitors in the vicinity. The "preaddress battlefield tour" is probably another of the many stubborn Lincoln-at-Gettysburg legends.

Lincoln certainly awoke by 7 A.M., when "salvos of artillery rolled through the air," signaling the start of this solemn day of tribute. "November 19th dawned

bright and clear—a perfect day for the ceremonial," a local minister recalled. But the *Washington Chronicle* reported early morning rain showers.

In either case, by sunrise the little town of 1,300 was filled with thousands more (some estimate 100,000 visitors, but the number was probably closer to a still-impressive 15,000). Over the next two hours, the Diamond began to swell to overflowing with smartly dressed officers, military bands, assorted dignitaries, and impatient horses, and, by 9 A.M., an honor guard. At that hour, Nicolay arrived at the Wills house to help the President make final preparations. He found Lincoln in his room busily copying his speech onto clean sheets of paper.

At 10 A.M. precisely, a resplendent Lincoln, wearing a black frock coat and white gloves—the official garb for the day—and a mourning band around his familiar stovepipe hat, stepped out into the Gettysburg town square. As the crowd quickly pressed around him, Lincoln was shown to the horse chosen for him for the processional.

According to yet another Gettysburg legend, the steed was too small for the President, whose legs dangled practically to the ground. Other witnesses remembered that the diminutive mount had been brought out as a joke on the well-known jester, one local man howling as Lincoln sat awkwardly on the pony: "Say Father Abraham, if she goes to run away with yer, you just stand up and let her go!"

Such irreverence seems inappropriate for so solemn an occasion, but how else to explain the conflicting recollections of those who subsequently observed the President as he rode along the parade route, looking tall and dignified, towering over all others "like Saul of old?" People who saw him that day would go to their graves insisting that Lincoln had been astride a "white horse," "a light bay," "a brown charger," a "black steed," or even "the largest . . . Chestnut horse . . . in Cumberland County."

All that is known for certain is that Lincoln had requisitioned his horse himself. A presidential message scribbled that morning read: "Capt. Blood furnish one horse for bearer. A. Lincoln."

The actual procession did not commence for a full hour, during which time Lincoln remained in his saddle, greeting well-wishers, reading military reports, and happily devouring the promised tele-

gram from Washington, which brought word that his son's health was "a great deal better." Tad "will be out to-day," it promised.

With that encouraging news no doubt buoying his spirits, Lincoln heard the drums start to roll, signaling, at last, the start of the procession to the cemetery. With a military escort in the lead—color guard, staff officers, detachments of artillery and cavalry, and ranks of infantrymen with shouldered rifles and bayonets—the parade lurched forward "in an orphanly sort of way." Minute guns sounded as the procession slowly moved up Baltimore Street, accompanied by military bands playing dirges, past small townhouses decorated with mourning crepe and flags, their residents gazing out of the open windows.

The three-quarters-of-a-mile trek was traversed in fifteen minutes. At first Lincoln sat erect on his horse, riding "easily, bowing occasionally to left and right." At one point he gave a pretty little girl a brief ride with him, so apparently the mood was not altogether forbidding. But well before he reached the cemetery, Lincoln fell into deep thought, slouching in his saddle, his head hanging and bobbing to the horse's pace, lost in a reverie of melancholy and contemplation.

LATER, OBSERVING THE "ENSEMBLE" AS it gathered on the platform, the correspondent of the *Cincinnati Daily Commercial* described "the central figure" to be that of Everett, "his head white with the snows of seventy winters, but his form erect. . . ." Nearby, "in a strange contrast," was "a thoughtful, kindly, care-worn face, impassive in repose, the eyes cast down, the lids thin and firmly set, the cheeks sunken, and the whole indicating weariness, and anything but good health. This is the President."

Attention now focused on the opening of the formal program. The crowd was given another dirge, and then an invocation so long and fiery that Hay remembered it as "a prayer which thought it was an oration." Then the Lord's Prayer was recited, and some eyewitnesses noted men and women alike dabbing at their eyes with handkerchiefs. Letters were read from dignitaries who could not attend, including General George Meade, who had excused himself with the observation that "this army has duties to perform."

At last Lamon was ready to introduce the main speaker—not Lincoln, of course, but the "central figure" from Massachusetts. Everett stood up, and, bowing to Lincoln, began, "Mr. President." "Mr. Everett," Lincoln replied aloud, bowing from his chair. And then, in a booming, rich voice, Everett launched into his oration.

"Standing beneath this serene sky," he proclaimed, "overlooking these broad fields now reposing from the labors of the waning year . . ." And so the speech went on—skillfully punctuated by oratorical gestures—for the next hour and fifty-seven minutes.

Not once did Everett refer to his thick manuscript. Although many would praise his effort, others would call the oration "utterly inadequate," even if "smooth as satin." *Harper's Weekly* called it "smooth and cold." And even Lincoln could offer no more in the way of congratulations than a tactful, "perfectly satisfactory."

As Everett reached his oratorical climax, bidding "farewell to the dust of these martyr-heroes," many in the crowd could be seen wandering about the battlefield. "Seldom has a man talked so long and said so little," concluded the *Philadelphia Daily Age*. A rival Philadelphia paper disagreed, exulting: "What a wonderful man is Edward Everett."

Then amateur poet Benjamin B. French, who was working as Lamon's chief aide for the cemetery dedication, stepped forward and recited an amateurish poem. (Henry Wadsworth Longfellow, John Greenleaf Whittier, and William Cullen Bryant had each refused to compose an ode for the occasion.)

BY TWO O'CLOCK THAT AFTERNOON THE weather had turned warm—Indian summer, people would recall.

Lamon returned to the center of the platform and shouted, as loud as he could, to an audience still murmuring about the Everett marathon they had just endured: "The President of the United States." As Lincoln stepped forward, he was greeted with "repeated cheers of enthusiasm."

"The President rises slowly," a reporter wrote, "draws from his pocket a paper, and when commotion subsides," begins his "brief and pithy remarks." Lincoln's "care-worn face" was "now lighted and glowing with intense feeling."

"Four score and seven years ago," Lincoln began. Barely two minutes later

he concluded with the words, "that government of the people, by the people, for the people, shall not perish from the earth."

The President had spoken approximately 271 words—"a few appropriate remarks."

Hay remembered Lincoln speaking "in a firm, free way, and with more grace than is his wont." But the Cincinnati correspondent described a "sharp, unmusical treble voice."

There have been countless descriptions of Lincoln's outdoor speaking style—few of them alike. Surely his was a good, clear, audible voice—after all, he had spoken at mammoth rallies during his debates with Stephen A. Douglas. If he couldn't claim the baritone bombast of a Douglas or an Everett, Lincoln possessed something just as useful: a bell-like tone that reportedly could be heard to the farthest reaches of any crowd.

The trouble on this occasion, as his contemporaries later recalled, was that Lincoln, who needed a full ten minutes to get his "outdoor voice," spoke only a fraction of that time. His voice, as a consequence, seemed "raspy but penetrating" to one eyewitness, but "loud, and far-reaching" to another. One sympathetic onlooker claimed that "more of that immense crowd heard him than heard Everett."

How many actually heard Lincoln is impossible to determine; on this aspect of his Gettysburg appearance, as on so many others, there is no consensus. Many witnesses reported that there was much noise and shuffling about from the fringes of the crowd throughout the talk. But from the platform, former Ohio governor William Dennison felt "a thrill of feeling" as Lincoln spoke, that, "like an electric shock" had "pervaded the crowd."

Nor is it certain whether Lincoln *read* the Gettysburg Address or recited it from memory. Lincoln's secretary, Nicolay, insisted the President "did not read from a manuscript." A college student in the audience recalled that Lincoln kept a "hand on each side of the manuscript" throughout the speech, though "he looked at it seldom." Yet another eyewitness insisted that Lincoln "barely took his eyes" off the speech as he read it. Some thought they saw him gesture as he spoke. Others saw him holding his hands behind his back. And there were those who insisted he had kept his thumbs locked into the inside of his lapels.

There is also wide disagreement on how the crowd reacted. An Associated Press reporter was so transfixed by Lincoln's "intense earnestness and depth of feeling" that he "unconsciously stopped taking notes and looked up at him." Yet he still had to file a transcript, and when he later filled in the gaps in his text by borrowing Lincoln's manuscript, he charitably added several interruptions for "applause," plus "long continued applause" at the conclusion.

A number of spectators were sure they did hear applause. French, the would-be laureate who had read the day's memorial ode, remembered a "hurricane of applause." The *Illinois State Journal* reported that its favorite son had been rewarded with "immense applause and three cheers." And an eyewitness insisted he heard not only "roars of applause" but "sobs and cheers," exclaiming: "My God! It was so impressive!" But another onlooker, W. H. Cunningham, reported "not a word, not a cheer, not a shout," and a man nearby agreed there had been "no applause of any kind."

Some in the audience may have reacted as if to a solemn prayer—in response to which applause was simply unthinkable. An Ohio journalist on the scene did report "sobs of smothered emotion," after Lincoln concluded, adding, "scarcely could an untearful eye be seen." A one-armed Gettysburg veteran in the crowd "sobbed aloud while his manly frame shook with no unmanly emotion" when Lincoln proclaimed, "The world will little note nor long remember what we say here, but it can never forget what they did here."

But perhaps the best explanation for the possible silence that greeted the Gettysburg Address was that the crowd simply wasn't sure Lincoln had finished—not after only two minutes. Even the poem had been longer. In fact, as the President resumed his seat, a perplexed journalist boldly leaned toward him and asked, "Is that all?" Undoubtedly embarrassed, Lincoln responded: "Yes . . . for the present."

EVEN THE OTHER DIGNITARIES ON THE platform seemed convinced at first that Lincoln's address had fallen flat. "It is not what I expected of him," Everett confessed to Seward. "I am disappointed." To which Seward admitted: "He has made a failure and I am sorry of it." Lamon

What Did Lincoln Actually Say?

Abraham Lincoln may or may not have read from his manuscript when he delivered his Gettysburg Address.

Some eyewitnesses insisted that he "read from a sheet of paper . . . held in his hand," as the *New York Times* stated. But others were just as certain that he had spoken without consulting his text. Either way, and surviving drafts notwithstanding, what, precisely, did Lincoln say?

The Associated Press reporter at the dedication stopped taking notes midway through Lincoln's brief address, later borrowing the President's own manuscript to complete his copy, and adding six interruptions for "applause." His copy, therefore, is an inaccurate record.

Other correspondents did no better. According to the *Philadelphia Inquirer,* Lincoln said: "We *imbibe* increased devotion." And the *Chicago Times*—perhaps maliciously—began its transcript: "Four score and *ten* years ago. . . ."

Fortunately, joining the Associated Press on the scene was correspondent Charles Hale, nephew of principal orator Edward Everett. Hale not only carefully transcribed a shorthand copy but added punctuation and underlining to indicate where Lincoln had paused and added emphasis. His copy is considered by scholars to be the most reliable record of what the President actually said.

But Hale made no note of whether, in his famous conclusion, Lincoln emphasized the prepositions *of* the people, *by* the people, *for* the people—or the critical word itself: "people." Again, other eyewitnesses remembered different versions. We will probably never know for sure.

The following is the so-called "Hale Copy" of Lincoln's Gettysburg Address:

"Four score and seven years ago, our fathers brought forth upon this continent a new nation, conceived in liberty and dedicated to the proposition that all men are created equal.

Now we are engaged in a great civil war, testing whether that nation—or any nation, so conceived and so dedicated—can long endure.

We are met on a great battle-field of that war. We are met to dedicate a portion of it as the final resting-place of those who have given their lives that that nation might live.

It is altogether fitting and proper that we should do this.

But, in a larger sense, we cannot dedicate, we cannot consecrate, we cannot hallow, this ground. The brave men, living and dead, who struggled here, have consecrated it, far above our power to add or to detract.

The world will very little note nor long remember what we say here; but it can never forget what they did here.

It is for us, the living, rather, to be dedicated, here, to the unfinished work that they have thus far so nobly carried on. It is rather for us to be here dedicated to the great task remaining before us; that from these honored dead we take increased devotion to that cause for which they here gave the last full measure of devotion; that we here highly resolve that these dead shall not have died in vain; that the nation shall, under God, have a new birth of freedom, and that government of the people, by the people, for the people, shall not perish from the earth."

"Of the People, by the People, for the People"

Lincoln's closing thoughts at Gettysburg may well be the most famous words ever spoken by an American: " . . . that government of the people, by the people, for the people shall not perish from the earth."

But whose thoughts are they? No one ever expressed the idea as simply and beautifully as Lincoln did. But others *did* express similar thoughts before the President said them, and he could have read these at any point in his long political career. The following are some of the known antecedents, as first collected by Lincoln scholar William E. Barton in his 1930 volume, *Lincoln at Gettysburg.*

" . . . a government of all the people, by all the people, for all the people."—Theodore Parker, at an antislavery convention in Boston, May 29, 1850

" . . . the people's government, made for the people, made by the people, and answerable to the people."—Daniel Webster, January 26, 1830

" . . . a government made by ourselves, for themselves, and conducted by themselves."—John Adams, 1798

"I am in favor of the democracy . . . that shall be of the people, by the people, for the people."—attributed to Cleon, 420 B.C.

Similar thoughts are also attributed to John Marshall, James Monroe, and others.

concurred: "I am sorry to say it does not affect me as one of his great speeches."

And Lincoln could not have agreed more. "That speech won't scour," he confessed to Lamon. "It is a flat failure." And even when Everett tried to offer some consoling words, Lincoln stopped him in mid-flattery. "We shall try not to talk about my address. I failed, I failed, and that is about all that can be said about it." But, as Hay remembered the aftermath, "music wailed as we went home through crowded and cheering streets."

The long day was not yet over. Lincoln attended a midafternoon luncheon at the Wills home, where "thousands shook him by the hand." He met John Burns, an old man who had joined the battle the previous summer with a squirrel gun and a grim determination to chase out the Rebels. And the President briefly visited a local church event.

Not until 6:30 P.M. was Lincoln back on the train to Washington. "All is now quiet on the streets of Gettysburg," the *Boston Journal* reported, "the imposing ceremonies of the day having been completed in admirable order and without being marred in any respect." As the *New York Herald* put it, "the air, the trees, the graves" were now silent. "Even the relic hunters are gone now."

THE SLOW JOURNEY HOME WAS FAR from pleasant. Lincoln was depressed, certain that his speech had been a failure. And to make matters worse, he was feeling ill with the first symptoms of varioloid, a mild form of the dreaded smallpox. He lay down with a wet cloth over his throbbing forehead as the train lurched along. It would not reach the capital until 1:10 the next morning.

Just before their arrival, Wayne Mac-Veagh, a member of the presidential party, walked back to tell Lincoln he had reconsidered the impact of the Gettysburg speech. Apparently he had criticized it earlier, but now MacVeagh declared: "I can only say that the words you spoke will live in the world's language." A weary, bilious Lincoln waved him away: "You are the only person who has such a misconception of what I said."

But later the same day Lincoln received a compliment from another person—none other than Edward Everett. "Permit me . . . to express my great admiration of the thoughts expressed by you, with such eloquent simplicity & appropriateness," the nation's most famous orator wrote, adding, "I should be glad, if I could flatter myself that I came as near to the central idea of the occasion, in two hours, as you did in two minutes."

Lincoln replied: "In our respective parts yesterday, you could not have been excused to make a short address, nor I a long one. I am pleased to know that, in your judgment, the little I did say was not entirely a failure."

Indeed, he would soon know otherwise. Admirers, among them the respected historian George Bancroft, would besiege the President with flattering requests for copies of the address—some to be sold to raise funds for the war wounded.

Newspaper approval followed quickly (along with typical partisan criticism). In the opinion of the *Philadelphia Evening Bulletin:* "Thousands who would not read the long, elaborate oration of Mr. Everett will read the President's few words, and many will not do it without a moistening of the eye and a swelling of the heart." As *Harper's Weekly* put it, Lincoln's Gettysburg Address was nothing less than "the most perfect piece of American eloquence." "A perfect thing in every respect," echoed the *Cincinnati Gazette.*

Reading such tributes, Lincoln may have recalled one of the many brief stops his train had made en route to Gettysburg. The father of a soldier killed at the battle had come aboard to shake the President's hand, and Lincoln had confessed to him: "When I think of the sacrifices yet to be offered . . . my heart is like lead within me, and I feel at times like hiding in deep darkness." Hours later, speaking at the soldiers' cemetery, Lincoln had opened his heart to call for "increased devotion," and had illuminated "a new birth of freedom" for his unhappy, divided country.

"The world will little note, nor long remember what we say here," he had predicted.

Those may have been the only false words he spoke.

The world *has* long remembered.

Recommended additional reading: A New Birth of Freedom *by Philip Kunhardt (Little, Brown, & Company, 1983).*

Why the Confederacy Lost

Brian Holden Reid *opens our two-headed debate on the American Civil War by Arguing that the South failed to use revolutionary methods to full advantage.*

Mao Tse-Tung once remarked that a revolutionary war is not a dinner party. A revolutionary war may be defined as the seizure of political power by armed force. The American Civil War was a good example of a revolutionary war—but one in which the side seeking to seize political power—the Southern Confederacy—failed to use revolutionary methods to its full advantage. What was the reason for this failure, and why did the Confederacy allow itself to be ground down in a war of attrition in a conflict in which the war aim on the Union side was nothing less than the unconditional surrender of the Confederate armies and the destruction of their warmaking potential? As nation states existed, according to Hobbes, either to maintain internal order or protect themselves from external aggression, this is the criterion by which to assess the strength of Southern society to resist invasion and the imposition on it of political measures, including ultimately the emancipation of slavery, which it had gone to war to resist. Indeed it could be suggested that by 1864-65 the Confederacy had no other justification for its existence other than to maintain armed forces in the field.

It was Napoleon, who was in a position to know, who said that in war moral factors are to the physical as three is to one. The study of social factors in the American Civil War presents a curious paradox. It is undoubtedly true that the Confederacy secured from its soldiers

The will to win; a Confederate print of Robert E. Lee and his colleagues stressing pride in the Southern military tradition.

extraordinary courage, dedication and endurance, and the *élan* of Southern soldiers, their dash in the attack, the rebel 'yell', were legendary. But there is another side to the coin: defeatism, desertion, war weariness, doubts about the validity of the Southern cause and guilt over slavery. These factors need to be taken into account and given their due weight beside the more glorious elements in histories of the Confederacy's gallant struggle against great odds. They cer-

From *History Today,* November 1988, pp. 32-41. Reproduced by kind permission of History Today, Ltd., 83-84 Berwick Street, London W1V 3PJ, England.

tainly need to be related to a fundamental problem which emerges from a study of the South's participation in the Civil War. In the Confederate states the war opened decisively and abruptly in April and July 1861 with the bombardment of Fort Sumter and the victory at the First Battle of Bull Run. These events were celebrated with great popular enthusiasm. The war ended just as abruptly with the surrender of General Robert E. Lee at Appomattox in April 1865, but without a glimmer of enthusiasm—a gritty determination to fight on irrespective of the odds. Why was this? Why did the war not continue, perhaps in some irregular form? Popular support for opening a war is usually a gauge for some measure of support for continuing it after defeat appears inevitable. Why did the South fail to field guerrilla columns like the resolute Boer commandos of 1899-1902? It may be that Southern nationalism as a socially binding force in war was more apparent than it was real.

There are two ways in which one state can exert power over another using military force. They have been well codified by the German military writer, Hans Delbruck, and developed as a tool to analyse the American Civil War by Major General J.F.C. Fuller. The first is the strategy of annihilation. In accordance with the strategy, the enemy's armies are destroyed by rapid manoeuvre and battle. This strategic form conforms to a more limited type of war and may be equated with the modern generic term, *blitzkrieg*. The second category is the strategy of exhaustion or attrition: belligerents attempt to wear one another down in a long drawn out struggle. It was in the South's interests, if its independence could not be secured quickly, to persuade the North that it could not win because of the unacceptable human and material cost. Or alternatively, the North could destroy the South because Confederate resources were insufficient to prevent Union armies occupying large areas of territory and their war-making potential; the South would also find it difficult to prevent the creeping disintegration of its armed forces through war weariness and despondency. The strategy of exhaustion adheres more to an unlimited kind of war—'total war'. In both forms of strategy, geographical, economic and moral factors are crucially important. 'Whereas in the first', commented General Fuller, 'the aim is the decisive battle, in the second battle is but one of several means,

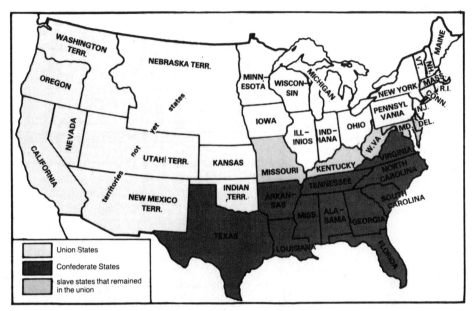

such as manoeuvre, economic attack, political persuasion and propaganda, whereby the political end is attained.'

There is a long tradition in American writing which contends that the South had a distinct military tradition, that the South was a singularly militaristic region of the United States. Marcus Cunliffe, in his influential and penetrating study, *Soldiers and Civilians: The Martial Spirit in America, 1775–1865* (1968), has shown convincingly that this view has been greatly exaggerated and that elements of a supposed Southern military tradition were shared by the North. Nonetheless, these martial attitudes are important because they assist in delineating the Southern reaction to strategic reverses irrespective of whether they were unique to this region or not. They can be distinguished with reference to three main themes.

Firstly, optimism mixed with fatal dread. As General J.E.B. Stuart told George C. Eggleston in 1861:

In regard it as a foregone conclusion . . . that we shall ultimately whip the Yankees. We are bound to believe that anyhow; but the war is going to be a long and terrible one, first we've only just begun it, and very few of us will see the end.

There is a contradiction in Stuart's view: war consists in 'whipping' the enemy. But this does not appear to be sufficient. Faith in an eventual Confederate victory rested on the moral strength of the Southern cause—not on the political and economic strength of the Confederacy. Yet the view propounded by Stuart did not

take into account the effects on morale of a strategy of attrition. As he observed in 1864, 'I would rather die than be whipped', a wish that was, alas, fulfilled at the Battle of Yellow Tavern later that year.

Secondly, a romantic nineteenth-century heritage. This attitude dominated the Southern outlook and was personified by Stuart again, although many others saw themselves as dashing cavaliers—gentlemen at war. As gentlemen they were chivalrous, like knights of the Middle Ages, a spirit that was captured by groups such as the 'Knights of the Golden Spurs'. This romantic spirit fed on the novels of Sir Walter Scott, which were immensely popular in the South. It persuaded many that war could be viewed in a distinctly glamorous, even sentimental light, so that campaigns took on the character of a 'quest', indeed a light-hearted 'lark'. Thus warfare came to be regarded as a game on an extended scale, such as Stuart's 'Ride Around McClellan's Army', which captured the South's imagination in June 1862.

Thirdly, these attitudes engendered an enigmatic sense of triumph. The enemy would be 'whipped', but his forces remained in the field despite the demonstrable superiority of Southern arms. The victories of Robert E. Lee reminded some Southern observers of the pyrrhic triumphs of Hannibal. Thus the final test would depend on the will of God.

These factors operated to sustain Southern morale while military operations appeared to favour the Confederacy. None of them, however, served to stiffen morale in a war of exhaustion. Despite their enigmatic asides to the contrary, most Southerners had expected a short war, or at least a longer war which conformed to the strategy of annihilation. This view contrasts clearly with the Boers of South Africa, for instance, who did not think in such European-orientated and romantic terms and were innured to the hardihood of the veldt.

Nevertheless a number of factors did operate in the South's favour. The Confederacy occupied a vast geographical area—certainly twice the size of South Africa which the British army had occupied with such difficulty in 1900-02. Clearly an army of occupation would have problems in holding down such an enormous area. Indeed it should be recalled that Sherman's 'March to the Sea' did not constitute an occupation of territory, only a raid in which his forces traversed three Southern states, destroying warmaking potential *en route,* but making no effort to hold them down. Secondly, the Confederate armies, despite setbacks, were still in being in 1864-65. Their organisation, equipment and performance in set-piece battles were a considerable advance over comparable efforts in the American Revolution. Here was a considerable source of experienced manpower if Confederate commanders had chosen to disperse their forces in guerrilla groups throughout the countryside and in the back-country. Such a move would have been aided by the diffusion of the population over a great area and low wooded terrain, highly suitable for guerrilla warfare.

Finally, the importance of military time can hardly be underestimated in calculating the Confederacy's chances of survival. Time was on the side of the Confederacy, not in the sense that it required time to organise its resources (indeed time would dissipate these), but rather in that the South had to defer a military decision in the North's favour and assert its independence in the eyes of foreign powers. In other words, show to the world, and not least the federal government, that it could not be extinguished. Guerrilla action in the Carolinas against Lord Cornwallis in 1780-81 had achieved precisely this in the Revolution. But by 1865 a consensus had developed that the war should be ended. There had been a number of voices calling for the Confederacy to adopt a guerrilla strategy, the most famous being John Hunt Morgan,

but these were a minority. How had this consensus taken such a firm hold? During the Boer War a mere 60,000 Boers had held at bay the might of the British Empire for two years, despite a much greater disparity of resources and the disadvantage of operating in a smaller theatre of operations.

In considering why the South collapsed so decisively, it should be recalled that loyalty in wartime is usually shaped and inspired by a state's war aims. But it was not altogether clear *what* the South was fighting for. Was it defence of property rights as exemplified by the defence of slavery? Or was it the independence of the Southern states? In pursuit of independence and as a vital aid to the maintenance of its armed forces by saving manpower, the Davis Administration began to emancipate slaves in 1865 in return for their joining the Confederate army. Considering the gigantic gamble represented by secession and the impassioned rhetoric that had marked the Confederate states' ordinances of secession from the Union, and the fatal (and greatly exaggerated) threat that Southerners perceived faced the South's 'peculiar institution' after the election of the Lincoln Administration in 1860, this desperate action five years later surely forms a *reductio ad absurdum* of the Confederate position and strengthened the voices of those who had claimed in 1861 that slavery was better protected *within* the Union than without.

In addition, there can be no doubt that Southern morale was volatile. It oscillated between extremes of depression and exultation. By 1864, after extensive territory—especially in the west—had been given up, a widespread feeling developed that so much had been sacrificed for nothing. As Mary Chestnut wrote in her diary:

Think of all those young lives sacrificed! If three for one be killed, what comfort is that? What good will that do? '. . . The best and bravest of one generation swept away!' . . . literally in the tide of blood.

Many Southerners could not understand that the South could afford to trade space for time, so long as her armed forces retained their fighting power. Southern morale had not the sophistication or endurance to sustain the blows inflicted by a strategy of exhaustion. Every withdrawal, even if it made military sense, depressed and caused consternation. One newspaper editor commented:

Courts of Heaven resound with one great prayer; the supplications of a sorrowing people for the return of *peace* . . . appalled at the dire calamities which war has inaugurated, the heart of a nation pants for relief.

Many Southerners were prone to think that withdrawals or defeats in battle were a heavenly sign of the Lord's displeasure with the sins of the South. This only served to weaken morale. Typical comments in the newspapers and the pulpits include, 'Without special interposition we are a ruined people', and 'God will avenge himself on this American people, if this unnatural fratricidal butchery continues much longer'.

Confederate nationalism was a fragile reed. In a war against fellow Americans very few negative reference points existed for it to feed upon. Americans were not divided by any linguistic differences or fundamental cultural divergences of the type which so clearly differentiated the Boers from the British during the Boer War. The appeal of the Southern military tradition can be explained as an attempt to mark Southerners out as different from other Americans, inaccurately as it turns out. The only fundamental divergence that can be found concerns views about Negro slavery. But even here the Confederate Constitution imitated the Federal Constitution faithfully, save for additional clauses enshrining the protection of slavery. Yet by 1865, because of the pressure of Federal advances, the Confederate Government was beginning to emancipate slaves.

Finally, there was a widespread fear of what recourse to an uncontrolled revolutionary war would do to Southern Society. This was especially strong among Confederate generals such as Robert E. Lee and Joseph E. Johnston, who were very keen to negotiate acceptable terms of surrender before guerrilla action developed on any sizeable scale. Irregular war might lead to the arming of blacks, and confirm the very worst Southern fears of race wars which had haunted whites before 1861. In the end, Southern leaders were not prepared to inflict guerrilla warfare on their people, who were in any case not prepared to carry its burdens.

In 1863 President Jefferson Davis claimed that Confederates:

. . . Have added another to the lessons taught by history for the instruction of man; . . . they have afforded another example of the impossibility of subjugating a people determined to be free.

Actually, the opposite was the case: the Confederacy showed that whatever advantages had accrued to it, a rebellion may be crushed if the rebels show insufficient *will* to seek and secure their independence. Southerners simply lacked a sense of national identity during the war years. They staked a claim for independence which mortgaged too heavily their moral and psychological resources.

Bruce Collins *looks at the factors that made guerrilla warfare, Boer-style, an unlikely option for the South.*

Why the Southern Confederacy collapsed in April 1865 is naturally a question long debated by historians. Recent work on the subject has emphasised the lack of internal cohesion and sustained political will. It does not wholly concur in W.E. Gladstone's celebrated judgment of October 1862:

Jefferson Davis and other leaders of the South have made an army; they are making, it appears, a navy; and they have made what is more than either, they have made a nation.

Instead, it sees feebleness of national spirit and fragmentation of political power as key contributors to Confederate defeat. In assessing this weakening of morale, Dr Holden Reid has particularly focused on comparisons with the Boers' struggle against the British in 1899-1902 and on asking why the Confederates, unlike the Boers, failed to continue their fight for independence by guerrilla action once regular warfare had failed. The comparison of Confederates and Boers is most instructive, for the Boers resembled Southerners in conducting a farming people's war against fellow whites. The South African struggle may have been an imperial conflict but it was not a 'colonial war' in the classic nineteenth-century sense, where British regulars and allied levies overwhelmed non-European forces, often defective in training and/or weaponry. Boers and Southerners saw themselves as gallant individualists

trying to preserve a traditional agrarian order against spreading industrialism and 'cosmopolitan' ideas. In many ways African subordination was less an issue for the Boers than slavery was for the Southerners, but Boers distrusted British policymakers' attitudes towards Africans. More generally, Boers and Confederates typically appear as opponents to national consolidation, advocates of localism, and upholders of increasingly anachronistic values. If one is thinking of nation-building and the role of war in it, and of morale, the comparison of Boers and Confederates is far from being strained.

Yet comparison in detail reveals important contrasts which in turn help explain Confederate collapse. The Boers undertook extensive, prolonged guerrilla campaigns against the British from late 1900 to May 1902 partly because that style of warfare matched their conceptions of armed struggle. The Boers had no experience of formal warfare worth the name; small-scale frontier policing operations were all they had engaged in. No West Point of the high veldt turned out regular officers. Although very well equipped in 1899-1900, they saw no virtue in giving battle in classic style. Their preferred dispositions against British regulars in the field took the form of large-scale ambushes, with the aim of doing damage from a distance rather than rushing enemy lines and seizing enemy positions. Even at the height of their success, their military organisation creaked. At councils of war, at least in theory, corporals and cornets could outvote commandants. More important, the Boers lacked the manpower to sustain big battles once the British reinforced in strength. Their male population of arms-bearing age totalled only about 55,000. Their manpower losses in fighting *throughout* the war (about 7,000 killed) probably failed to match Confederate losses at Antietam. In terms of their training, past experience, and numbers, guerrilla warfare offered their *only* viable means of resistance once the British—to the surprise of some leading Boers—assembled an overwhelmingly superior army in South Africa during the winter of 1899-1900. From that point the Boers had little choice but to act, as was said at the time, as 'the gadfly of regular armies'. This was especially the case after no fewer than 13,900 men (of 35,000 initially raised) accepted Lord Roberts' terms for laying down their

arms during March-July 1900. But when the Boers switched to guerrilla action they did so under existing leaders and with existing forces. The total number of *bittereinders* who did not surrender until the war's end in 1902 (17,000) represented about half the strength of the initial Boer mobilisation in 1899. They formed not so much a stubborn rump, as a principal campaign force.

The Confederates possessed a very different military background and very different military aspirations. Nothing in their past prepared them for Antietam, Gettysburg or the Virginia campaign from May 1864. Formal warfare American-style was, like General Zachary Taylor's nickname, rough and ready. The greatest battle fought on Southern soil before 1861 was New Orleans in 1815, a bizarre and triumphant affair of assorted American contingents against British regulars. Indian warfare required planning, manpower, and commitment to more than just brief forays, but, again, it scarcely imbued officers or men with European military codes of behaviour. Yet Southerners entertained more formal ideas of warfare than the Boers. The crucial difference lay in the Mexican war of 1846-48 and in military education. The Southern states had provided a disproportionate contribution in manpower to the Mexican campaign, which required fairly elaborate planning and logistical organisation. And Confederate generals were mostly West Point graduates. They believed in decisive battle. They boasted that Southerners enjoyed superior classic military skills to Northerners. Guerrilla warfare was neither desirable nor necessary; and it was scarcely honourable. To the Boers, it was formal warfare that seemed alien or aberrant.

Confederates' distrust of guerrilla warfare stemmed also from the nature of the war they waged. While secession was a revolutionary act, in overthrowing the constitutional Union established in 1787-89, politicians, not generals, created the Confederacy and they extended its area in the spring of 1861 because the North challenged its legitimacy, not because they conquered any territory. In that sense, the Civil War did not fit a major pattern of twentieth-century revolutionary wars in which armed struggle carries a political movement to power and then helps consolidate that movement's dominant position. The Confederates achieved their initial objectives by

4. THE CIVIL WAR AND RECONSTRUCTION

political means; they fought the war defensively to secure Northern recognition of their independence. This fact partly explains also why the Confederate government lacked sweeping domestic powers. Accustomed to controlling their individual states' affairs, presiding over properly administered state governments, and imbued with highly articulated ideas of state rights, Confederate leaders distrusted central authority. They also distrusted unstructured power. Ultimately they would rather work within a political structure dominated by their enemies than take their chance with informal government appended to and supported by guerrilla movements.

But did such reluctance to resort to informal means after 1865 suggest a lack of will? Like all armies, including the Northern, the Confederate forces suffered from periodic losses of confidence, desertions, and soldiers' resentment against their officers. These characteristics have to be seen against the nature of the war, one not lightly called the first modern war for its heavy casualties sustained in frontal infantry assaults upon well-secured positions strengthened by artillery, and for its mass mobilisation of manpower. Desertions did not soar until autumn 1864, and did not reach epidemic proportions until early 1865, just before the surrender in April. The last returns of the Confederate armies gave 160,200 officers and men present, and no fewer than 198,500 absent from the flag. But by October 1864, the Confederate military cause was hopeless. The trans-Mississippi states of Arkansas, Louisiana and Texas had been virtually cut off from the rest of the Confederacy by the end of 1862. Those states in 1860 contained 1³/₄ million of the 9 million people of the Confederacy. Their isolation was no mean loss. The Confederacy was further fragmented when Sherman's army invaded Georgia and, on September 2nd, 1864, entered Atlanta. No Confederate army stood between Sherman and Lee's forces in Virginia. Sherman began marching northwards into South Carolina and subsequently into North Carolina in January 1865. The Confederate government controlled very little territory by then. No wonder men slipped away to rejoin and perhaps rescue their families and homesteads.

This final collapse must be seen against the preceding years of armed resistance. It was remarkable that the South fought for so long. By the end of

1862 the Confederate position was already grim. The border South had not seceded. Much of Tennessee had been lost. The Federals had captured the Confederacy's principal city and port, New Orleans. They also seized Norfolk, Virginia's main port, and blockaded the key remaining Confederate ports of Charleston, Mobile and Savannah. The international front offered no comfort, since no country recognised the Confederacy as a belligerent. One wonders if Northern refusal to recognise Confederate independence would have survived equivalent pressure; an effective Confederate blockade of the Atlantic seaboard ports, Confederate capture of New York City and Chicago, Confederate control of a belt of land cutting off everything west of Indiana from the rest of the North, and the establishment of pro-Confederate governments in southern Pennsylvania, southern Ohio, and southern Indiana. Given the panic and dismay Northerners evinced when faced with far more limited Confederate advances, it seems improbable.

The collapse of morale during the winter of 1864-65 must be seen against several facts. First, during the war about one in every three Confederate males of military age died in, or as a result of, war service. Many more received injury. That amounted to an unprecedented level of bloodletting in a major modern war. When one adds that by early 1865 very large tracts of the Confederacy had been invaded, it is little wonder that morale sank. Those still in arms had every reason to feel hopeless. For their part, the Boers did not sustain a level of casualties anywhere approaching that withstood by the Confederates. And their guerrilla campaign petered out when the British army devastated their farms and livestock and removed civilians into concentration camps. If, as in so many historical instances, we are to judge whether the jug was half full or half empty, it is surely right to conclude that, by any standard of comparison, the Confederate measure of resistance looks more full than empty. Bell Wiley, the pre-eminent historian of Johnny Reb, warts and all, concluded:

Few if any soldiers have had more than he of *élan,* of determination, of perseverance, and of the sheer courage which it takes to stand in the face of withering fire.

This certainly was a view shared by the Confederates' opponents. Grant in his memoirs recorded:

Up to the battle of Shiloh, I, as well as thousands of other citizens, believed that the rebellion against the government would collapse suddenly and soon, if a decisive victory could be gained over any of its armies.

Sherman justified the scorched earth campaigns of 1864–65 on the grounds that:

We are not only fighting hostile armies, but a hostile people and must make old and young, rich and poor, feel the hard hand of war, as well as organized armies.

It was this combination of civilian depredations, loss of military manpower, and loss of territory that wrecked the Confederate, just as it wrecked the Boer, war effort.

But the loss of an attainable political objective was also vital. When the Boers' Assembly of the People debated submission to the British in May 1902, one of their generals, Jan Smuts, took as his theme the keynote of Lincoln's Second Inaugural: 'to bind up the nation's wounds'. From a military point of view, he told the Assembly, the contest could continue, for 'We have still 18,000 men in the field, veterans, with whom you can do almost any work'. But the Assembly had to consider not merely this army, but the Afrikaner people, those in concentration camps as well as the free, those who had already given their lives, and 'those who will live after we are gone'. Independence was an honourable objective; 'But we may not sacrifice the Afrikaner people for that independence'. The Boers' prolongation of the war after 1900 had been aimed at sapping British morale. Their dramatic raid into Cape Colony failed, however, to stir the 'Dutch' population there to revolt. And, in Britain, although strong Liberal attacks on General Kitchener's concentration camps—'methods of barbarism' according to Campbell-Bannerman—surfaced in 1901, they failed to dent the Conservative Government's commitment to the war. By 1865, the Confederates faced a similar prospect of sacrificing the white South for an independence which could clearly not be attained. Invading the North had been tried and had failed to produce significant results. Confederate recourse to guerrilla fighting in 1865 would probably have stiffened Northern opinion even further politically against the Confederates and it is unlikely that the North would have refused the expenditure necessary to suppress guerrilla bands; the war, after all, had already cost enormous sums. Moreover, the last obvious chance for the Confederates to score a political settlement had already passed, just as the Boers' political strategy crumbled in 1902. For the Confederacy the last, best hope was the presidential election of 1864. If Lincoln had lost (and as late as August, before Atlanta fell on September 2nd, his prospects appeared by no means certain), some form of negotiated settlement might have been secured. Once Lincoln won re-election, then the Confederates had virtually no realistic political objective for which to fight. It was by no means illogical that Southern morale slumped after Atlanta's fall (the occasion of much public relief among Northerners) and after Lincoln's electoral victory in early November. Sherman set off from Atlanta on his march to the sea, and then inland, a few days after the Republicans' victory.

Behind these military and political events was a further cause of Confederate distress. However staunchly Confederate soldiers continued to fight the Yankees, their self-sacrifice could not stem the erosion of slavery at home. A recent study of wartime Georgia (by Clarence Mohr) shows how slavery became increasingly undermined, despite state politicians' efforts to maintain it in full force. Raids by the Federal navy drove coastal slave owners with their valuable chattels inland. Inflation drove up land prices and made it difficult for these migrants to purchase fresh lands. Inflation also cut back on paternalism as clothing and other items became 'luxuries' for slave owners to bestow upon their work forces. The absence of white males on military service weakened racial control of the slaves. Rising demand for manufactured goods and urban services encouraged the hiring-out of slaves in towns, where, again, racial control became increasingly difficult. Slaves themselves exploited these openings to weaken the oppressive institution. Some ministers of religion began even to urge reform in the laws governing slavery. Finally, acute manpower shortages fostered proposals that slaves be armed and

sent to war. As Howell Cobb, a former governor of Georgia and the United States Secretary of the Treasury, remarked in January 1865, 'If slaves will make good soldiers, our whole theory of slavery is wrong'. Georgia's experience was repeated throughout the South. If the very institution which Southerners left the Union to preserve against ultimate extinction was crumbling around them, it surely made more sense to uphold some vestige of white supremacy at home than to struggle for political objectives that, with Lincoln's re-election, were palpably unattainable. More generally, when the war ended, this collapse of traditional racial order was matched by the decline of settled relations between whites. Returning ex-soldiers indulged in a good deal of looting and lawlessness. Many Southerners saw any form of government as preferable to threatened anarchy.

Unfolding political circumstances also reduced possible pressures to continue resistance. Almost immediately after the Confederate surrender, Lincoln's assassination placed the vice-president, Andrew Johnson, in the White House. Johnson, a Tennessee Democrat before 1861, had been a wartime Unionist. While he often opposed the slave-holding planters as a social and political caste, his position towards the ex-Confederate leaders during 1865 shifted from hostility towards accommodation. So, too, Southern Unionists appointed to office within the shattered Confederacy lacked the numerical support and the ideological venom to press radical reform. Thus the political prospects in the former confederacy in the eight months following surrender resembled somewhat those obtaining in 1907-08 in South Africa. The ex-Confederates faced a leader who was no longer their wartime adversary, but a politician more amenable to their arguments. And many former secessionists accepted the need for cautious, conciliatory Southern leadership to restore the Southern economy and to safeguard social stability. Former Confederate leaders were soon winning elections to Congress. Interestingly enough, when

Radical Republicans found this sort of reconstruction unacceptable and changed the very lenient rules of Andrew Johnson's political game, Southerners did indeed resort to armed resistance in 1868-71. But this took the form of widespread terrorism, directed by the Ku Klux Klan against black voting and office-holding.

Some efforts to continue the contest were made after Lee's surrender to Grant on April 9th. Jefferson Davis sought to fight on, possibly from across the Mississippi, but made it only to Georgia before being captured by Federal soldiers on May 10th. By then, it should have been clear that the Confederacy had fought itself to a standstill. Even the pugnacious Nathan Bedford Forrest refused to go on. 'To make men fight under such circumstances', he said in early May from southwest Alabama, 'would be nothing but murder'. His force was massively outnumbered, even for informal conflict. 'Any man who is in favor of a further prosecution of this war is a fit subject for a lunatic asylum'. Given the whole range of social, political and military events in the previous six months, that was surely an apposite judgement.

FOR FURTHER READING:

Marcus Cunliffe, *Soldiers and Civilians: The Martial Spirit in America, 1775-1865* (Little, Brown, 1968); George M. Frederickson, 'Blue Over Gray : Sources of Success or Failure in the Civil War', in G.M. Frederickson (ed), *A Nation Divided* (Minneapolis, 1975); Richard Beringer et al, *Why the South Lost the Civil War* (University of Georgia Press, 1986); Clarence L. Mohr, *On the Threshold of Freedom* (University of Georgia Press, 1986); James M. McPherson, *Battle Cry of Freedom* (Oxford University Press, 1988); Brian Holden Reid and John White, "'A Mob of Stragglers and Cowards": Desertion from the Union and Confederate Armies', *The Journal of Strategic Studies,* VIII (March, 1985); Michael C. C. Adams, *Our Masters the Rebels* (Harvard University Press, 1978); Bruce Collins, *White Society in the Antebellum South* (Longman, 1985); Thomas Pakenham, *The Boer War* (Weidenfeld & Nicolson, 1979); W. K. Hancock, *Smuts,* Vol. I *The Sanguine Years 1870-1919* (Cambridge University Press, 1962).

The War Inside the Church

Which Side Are You On, God?

Analysis By Herman Hattaway And Lloyd A. Hunter

Decades before the first shots of the Civil War thundered over Fort Sumter, South Carolina, an equally ominous sound echoed through America. In churches across the land, hands hammered on pulpits, and impassioned preachers roared for the purification of God's favored nation. In the North, this fiery call seared the South for its sinful ways. In the South, it scathed the wayward North. And eventually, the call helped crack America's delicate Union in two.

This crack, this great schism between Christians of North and South, began during the 1830s and 1840s. So bitter was the division that the Methodist, Baptist and Presbyterian churches split into separate northern and southern denominations. And still other churches, most notably the Episcopal community, were on the verge of tearing apart at the Mason-Dixon Line, lingering just short of official division. Only recently have scholars probed deeply into the origins of these schisms. Their investigations show that religious belief and influences dramatically affected the South's decision to secede. And religion influenced the way Northerners and Southerners conducted the Civil War, and it affected the way people adjusted to life in the postwar South.

The breach in American Christendom came at a time when the issue of slavery was one of the foremost national issues. For reasons ranging from moral concerns to political pragmatism, there were attempts to regulate slavery by refusing to admit slave states to the Union, or by admitting such states only when a free state could be admitted simultaneously. Against such attempts, and against the endless stream of abolition petitions

from the Northern public, legislators from slave states fought bitterly. Slavery was the most volatile topic of debate in Congress, and there was talk of Southern secession in the 1830s.

At the state level, several Southern slaveholding states passed laws in the 1830s, forbidding the dissemination of abolitionist propaganda. Grave penalties—in some cases, death—were prescribed for violators of these codes. There was a fear in the South that abolitionists, who sought the end of slavery and sometimes worked for their goal by helping slaves escape, would bring on violent slave revolts.

For the churches, too, slavery was a heated issue. Northern Christians tended to view bondage as immoral, and struggled over whether they could tolerate the "peculiar institution" with a clear conscience. Ultimately, the general consensus was a firm no. Slavery had to be eradicated.

In the South, the churches responded to the North's condemnation of slavery by returning the anathema—the Northern interpretation of Christianity was incorrect, they charged. What resulted was a great schism, with Northern believers crying "Unclean!" at the South, and Southern faithful returning the accusation in kind. The controversy that began as a moral, theological debate, quickly deteriorated into a battle of sectional politics; the true faith was defined by geography, and entire regions were suddenly on the side of right or wrong.

The chasm between the churches of North and South had a profound destructive impact on America's already turbulent political life. By severing the religious ties between North and South, the schism bolstered the South's strong inclination toward secession from the Union. It helped bring about a breakup in the national political parties, which splintered into factions rooted in sec-

tional concerns. And the shattering of the parties led to the breakup of the Union itself.

That religious disputes could lead citizens to take up arms and fight a civil war is not surprising when seen in the context of the 19th-century vision of the United States. American nationalism had a religious base. Much of the populace believed theirs was a nation blessed by God, endowed with a divine mission to be an example of right living to the rest of the world. This perception was largely the result of evangelical Christianity, an interdenominational Protestant movement ablaze with militant, crusading zeal. Evangelicalism, which emphasized good, lengthy sermons rather than ceremony and ritual, spread its message rapidly through ardent preachers. The movement suffused its religious nationalism throughout both North and South during the early antebellum period.

At first, the notion that America was God's chosen country helped nurture national unity. And spectacular numbers of conversions gave mainline denominations—especially the Baptists, Methodists and Presbyterians, and to a lesser extent the Congregationalists and Episcopalians—a strong voice in the nation's social and political spheres. But with the idea of a "chosen" America came a deep sense of national responsibility to God. When Americans failed to do their duty by following the will and laws of the Almighty, it was a serious matter, a mark on the soul of the Republic. And so, to many Northerners, the Southerners' justification or tolerance of slavery was more than an ethical problem requiring change—it was a violation of America's sacred mission, and had to be stopped at once, even if by radical means.

In the sectional dispute that grew out of this urgent matter of conscience, Northern and Southern Christians turned on each other with the same zeal that had

From *Civil War Times Illustrated*, January 1988, pp. 29-33. Reprinted through the courtesy of Cowles Magazines, publishers of *Civil War Times Illustrated*.

won so many souls. Each side viewed the other as transgressor, as the sinner sullying God's Republic with moral abominations. So intense were these convictions that both sides perceived and portrayed the controversy in cosmic terms. They would come to regard the Civil War as "Armageddon," the ultimate struggle of eternal right against eternal wrong prophesied in the Bible's New Testament Book of Revelation (16:16).

If the church leaders of North and South, laymen and clerics alike, had molded different solutions to the moral problems they believed were besmirching America, the war itself might have been avoided. Instead, they watched the breakup of the nation, seeing in it the vindication of their schisms. The secession of the South had confirmed their beliefs that one region was morally right, the other morally wrong. And with their dramatic interpretation of events, the churches not only became catalysts in breaking the nation, they became intimately involved with the war effort, because they saw it as a holy crusade.

Thanks to the fresh scholarship of recent years, we have a new picture of how religion affected the thinking and fighting spirit of the Civil War's combatants. The churches, more than any other institution, seem to have been the underpinning of Civil War morale, at times buoying it, at times eroding it. One of the most inspiring religious concepts in the mind of Civil War-era Northerners seems to have been the doctrine of millenarianism—the belief that the Devil would be restrained and Jesus Christ would come again, possibly quite soon, to establish his kingdom on earth for 1,000 years. This belief in the "millenium" was based on a passage in the Book of Revelations (20:1-4): "And I saw an angel come down from heaven. . . . And he laid hold on the dragon . . . which is the Devil . . . and bound him a thousand years . . . and I saw the souls of them that were beheaded for the witness of Jesus . . .; and they lived and reigned with Christ a thousand years."

Church historian James Moorhead found a striking degree of "post-millenialist" thought in "the four mainline manifestations of Protestantism in the North": the Congregational Church, the Presbyterian Church (both Old Light and New Light), the Northern Baptist Church (later renamed American Baptist), and the Methodist-Episcopal Church, North. Post-millenarianism fed the no-

tion that the Civil War was Armageddon. Those who held the doctrine believed that by their actions they could fulfill necessary conditions for the coming of God's kingdom on earth—that they could hasten the second coming of Christ through their deeds.

SOUTHERNERS HAD A DIFFERENT RELI-gious mind-set. Leery of post-millenarianism, they were instead somewhat fatalistic. The typical Southern Christian believed there was nothing he could do to influence the flow of final events. But this idea in no way implied lack of religious fervor. Southerners believed God had a plan, a divine will to which it was crucial to adhere. If people followed God's will, he would bless them and things would go well. If they did not, things would go badly. The problem of course, was trying to discern the divine plan.

These particular aspects of Southern Protestant thought had no denominational boundaries. Indeed, there was a great blurring of denominational differences in the region. Southerners were religious in a cultural way more than in a theological or liturgical way. When a person changed denomination, it was usually for social, cultural or class reasons rather than as a matter of faith.

Northern Christians could not understand this sort of religious attitude. They took denominational differences more seriously, and were very much more evangelical. As time passed, Northern churchmen increasingly came to view the South not as differently "churched," but quite simply "unchurched." After the war, typical Northerners perceived the South as a great, fertile field for proselytization and reform, and Northern missionaries traveled south to spread Christianity among the heathen. One Northern Methodist minister chortled during the Civil War that events were crushing the "Dagon god of the South" (Dagon was an idol worshipped in Old Testament times by the Philistines).

Based on this understanding of what American Christians of the Civil War era believed, religious historians have added a new answer to the weighty question. "Why did the South lose the war?" Religion's impact on the outcome of the conflict was dramatic. As the war progressed, Northerners were impelled more and more to push on to victory, because they believed that by doing so they were hastening the coming of the

Lord's kingdom. But Southerners, as they looked at the ongoing tragedies and mounting casualty lists, with no future victory apparent, came to feel they had veered away from the will of God. Slowly, and despite their indisputable and awesome sacrifices in the war effort, they began to feel their best recourse was to give up. Other factors contributed to the erosion and ultimate collapse of Southern will, but religion played a vital role.

The South's spirits had fallen far since the war's outset. In 1861, both sides were confident God was on their side. If they made the proper sacrifices, they believed, victory would be theirs. As a Confederate soldier wrote his wife in early 1862, "when we lay *all* upon the altar of our country, the God of Nations will give us a permanent happy existence. How near akin is patriotism to religion."

Though this unknown soldier could not have known it, his words underscored a religious element in the American experience that was altered and intensified by the Civil War. Known as "civil religion," something not taken seriously by most scholars until recently, this dimension of America's faith centered upon the nation itself. Much like the religious nationalism of the evangelicals, with which it was clearly infused, it viewed the United States as a redeemer nation, its citizens as a chosen people. It interpreted America's meaning and destiny in light of God's activity among the nations.

Though remarkably similar to evangelical beliefs, civil religion had its differences. As its foremost student, Robert N. Bellah, explains, civil religion "actually exists alongside of and rather clearly differentiated from the churches," but it uses Biblical symbols and themes as vehicles for the nation's self-understanding. Like all religions, says Bellah, it "has its own prophets and its own martyrs, its own social events and sacred places, its own solemn spirituals," such as presidential inaugurations, and the recent rededication of the Statue of Liberty.

Though it blossomed during the War Between the States. American civil religion existed much earlier. In 1630, Puritan John Winthrop told his fellow English colonists aboard the *Arbella* that their new "plantation" at Massachusetts Bay must be God's "City Upon a Hill," to which all humankind would look for guidance. From then on, Americans—

4. THE CIVIL WAR AND RECONSTRUCTION

Northerners and Southerners alike—infused their history with religious meaning. An example is Julia Ward Howe, author of the most famous war poem set to music, who saw "the glory of the coming of the Lord" in the marching ranks of the Union Army of the Potomac. But the same trumpet call easily could have been sounded in Dixie. The renowned "fire-eater" or radical secessionist Benjamin Morgan Palmer, a Presbyterian preacher in New Orleans, proposed the Confederacy was "the cause of God Himself." With this firm conviction, Palmer echoed Howe's "Battle Hymn Of The Republic," vowing he would "never call retreat." Civil religion became a way to make sense of the Civil War, of its triumphs and tragedies, and of its outcome.

The Christian theme of sacrifice, death and rebirth became a permanent ingredient of American civil religion, receiving ritual expression in another outgrowth of the Civil War: Memorial Day. But the theme of sacrifice was most tragically symbolized in the assassination of President Abraham Lincoln on Good Friday, 1865. On the Easter Sunday that followed, Americans immediately proclaimed the fallen president a Christ-symbol in the national religion. Lincoln became the perfect human who had willingly sacrificed himself for the ultimate good, the Union's preservation.

It was perceived that Lincoln's was the final blood offering to purify America, and to purchase its resurrection to holiness. Yet, for many, he was more than a martyr. Most of all, he had become a much-needed prophet of the civic faith. Indeed, he had been that throughout his presidency, and that was a significant factor in the North's achievement of victory. Interestingly, Lincoln struggled continually to understand the meaning of the war in light of God's purpose. Ever cognizant of divine judgment, Lincoln labeled his countrymen God's *almost chosen people."* And in his marvelous second inaugural address, he touched at some length on the topic of God's will, and the strong tendency of Americans to identify national goals with that divine will, even when the identification is false.

While Lincoln and others added new dimensions to the old civil religion, Southerners created an entirely new one. Speaking to Confederate veterans in Joplin, Missouri, in Autumn 1906, Lawrence M. Griffith, a state official of the

Sons of Confederate Veterans, commented that when Dixie's soldiers returned "to find their homes despoiled, their families hungry, and their estates dissipated, there was born in the South a new religion." This regional faith focused, as religious historian Charles Reagan Wilson phrased it, on "a Redeemer Nation that Died." An amalgam of the South's fervent Protestantism and the powerful myth of the Lost Cause, Southern postwar civil religion elevated the old Confederacy, with its symbols and story, to sacred significance, and commemorated it in periodic rituals.

This "religion of the Lost Cause" took institutional form in a host of memorial and veterans groups, notably the United Confederate Veterans and the United Daughters of the Confederacy. Southern clergy, many of whom were themselves Civil War veterans, lent zealous support. Like its Northern counterpart, Southern civil religion stressed the sacrifices made by the warriors in gray that the Confederate nation might be cleansed through "the baptism of blood." Wherever Southern veterans and their ladies gathered to share in a reunion, decorate graves, or dedicate a monument—all of which they did countless numbers of times—they recalled their heroes and the sacred ideals for which they had offered their lives. Before them were the symbols of the cause: the gray jacket, the melodic and stirring "Dixie," and the battle flag, itself immortalized in the poetry of Father Abram Ryan, "poet priest of the Confederacy":

Furl that banner! softly, slowly,
Treat it gently—it is holy . . .

Father Ryan himself, incidentally, became one of the "saints" in this civil religion: he is memorialized in a stained glass window at the Confederate Memorial Hall in New Orleans, Louisiana.

There were other saints in Southern civil religion, the spiritual giants of the Confederacy. There was General Robert E. Lee who, like Christ in Gethsemane, grappled with an agonizing dilemma when he chose to fight for his beloved Virginia. There was President Jefferson Davis, who suffered symbolic crucifixion in his postwar imprisonment without trial. And there was the Moses-like Lieutenant General Thomas J. "Stonewall" Jackson—whose piety was perhaps the most notorious among all Civil War soldiers—who never reached the "Promised Land" of a victorious Confederacy.

Surely, declared the devotees of the Lost Cause, a nation with such holy symbols could never know final defeat.

THE SOUTH HAD BEEN BROUGHT LOW BY "overwhelming numbers and resources," as Lee conceded in his farewell to the defeated Army of Northern Virginia. But, taught Southern civil religion, in God's own time, the Confederacy, like Israel of old, would be vindicated, and in a transcendent sense, ultimately victorious. And so the South, like the North, was cast as an instrument of God. As such, it too contributed to the civil religion of a people "on the road," not only the road to reunification of the United States, but to the pervasive belief articulated by historian and U.S. Senator Albert J. Beveridge, that God "has marked the American people as His chosen nation to finally lead in the redemption of the world."

The religion of Northern and Southern Protestant Christians had urged America into war, carried it through the struggle, and helped it deal with the end, whether bitter or joyous. And through its contributions to the nation's civil religion, Civil War spirituality left its legacy, a lasting mark on the way America viewed itself. But there was yet another great spiritual legacy that came from the Civil War: the modern American black churches, which continue even today as essentially racially-defined Christian institutions.

Union forces had occupied Richmond only four days when more than 1,000 blacks, some sporting the blue jackets they had worn as Federal soldiers, packed into the First African Church to celebrate their new day of freedom. As they had in the days of slavery, they vented their heartfelt sentiments in exuberant and deeply emotional song. As their voices grew louder and their joy peaked, they reached the lines that best expressed their keenest feeling at that moment:

I'm going to join in this army;
I'm going to join in this army of the Lord.

In every state of the former Confederacy, newly freed Negroes echoed these sentiments. In the language of these former bondsmen, the fall of Richmond had been "de Lawd's work." God had acted through "Massa Linkum's army" to bring about the deliverance he had promised for so long. This was the only way some blacks could understand the recent dramatic events, for they, like almost all Americans, were deeply religious. The freed men believed in a God who, like the Old Testament Yahweh, intervened in the affairs of the world, and on the side of the oppressed. Ironically, they had learned this message from the very people who had used it to sustain enslavement: the white preachers who had endlessly invoked the apostle Paul's injunction, "Servants, obey your masters."

Blacks rejected the slaveholders' interpretation of this scripture, but clung passionately to Christianity's gospel of liberation, mixing it with remnants of African beliefs. Even in the days of slavery, blacks would sometimes "steal away" to a hollow or some other secluded spot, and indulge in their own churching—their "invisible institution." There they would "shout" and sing of freedom:

O my Lord delivered Daniel
O why not deliver me too?

In this way, Negroes established their own brand of Christianity even before the Civil War. But in the war's aftermath, the religious culture of the slaves changed dramatically. It came into the open, and soon became the very foundation for the black community in freedom. The informal congregations of slaves, now free, joined themselves to the already extant black churches, and together became, according to famed church historian Martin Marty, "the most powerful and durable of black institutions in the century."

But despite the emergence of their powerful religious tradition and their newfound freedom, blacks in the postwar years faced a new day that was not always hallmarked by the joy felt at the war's end. The Civil War, besides ensuring freedom for former slaves, also demolished whatever orders and stability had existed in the Old South. The old, paternalistic ecclesiastical system, in which blacks worshipped under the eyes of white preachers and in white congregations, had broken down. Its demise was traumatic, for both whites and blacks.

One educated mulatto cleric observed in Charleston, South Carolina, "There was no one to baptize their children, to perform marriages, or to bury the dead. A ministry had to be created at once—created out of the material at hand." And so, being free, and preferring Negro leadership in their spiritual life, the former bondsmen not only launched a gigantic "black exodus" from the white congregations, they also began rapidly spawning their own clergy. Assisted by Northern missionaries, the black churches molded themselves after the antebellum Protestant denominations of the North, but added their own cultural leaven to become unique.

So, the Civil War's chief legacy to slavery's children, the black church, made the "invisible institution" visible. And as this new church took on structure, it became the social center of the Negro experience. Whether Baptist, Methodist, or Presbyterian, the Afro-American denominations provided their people not only with spiritual interaction and fellowship, but with economic and educational development. It was through the exemplary work of numerous black preachers and Northern supporters from the American Missionary Association and other benevolent groups that blacks were helped to adjust to life as free men.

The black churches' social mission was not limited to the period immediately after the war, though. In years to come, these spiritual communities would serve as platforms for political life. This function proved particularly crucial when, as Reconstruction failed to fulfill the federal government's goal of equality, white supremacy eventually prevailed again. Then, only the black church gave Southern Negroes the faith and strength to persevere, never despairing that their people might "overcome someday." It is surely no coincidence that the Reverend Dr. Martin Luther King, Jr.'s dream of a Dixie that would "be transformed into an oasis of freedom and justice" emerged from institutions founded by those blacks who rejoiced that April day in 1865 when Richmond collapsed.

A War That Never Goes Away

More than the Revolution, more than the Constitutional Convention, it was the crucial test of the American nation. The author of **Battle Cry of Freedom,** *a most successful book on the subject, explains why the issues that fired the Civil War are as urgent in 1990 as they were in 1861.*

James M. McPherson

James M. McPherson is the Edwards Professor of American History at Princeton University. His most recent book is Battle Cry of Freedom *(Oxford University Press).*

"Americans just can't get enough of the Civil War." So says a man who should know, Terry Winschel, historian of the Vicksburg National Military Park. Millions of visitors come to Vicksburg and to more than a dozen other Civil War national battlefield and military parks every year. More than forty thousand Civil War reenactors spend hundreds of dollars each on replica weapons, uniforms, and equipment; many of them travel thousands of miles to help restage Civil War battles. Another two hundred and fifty thousand Americans describe themselves as Civil War buffs or "hobbyists" and belong to one of the hundreds of Civil War round tables or societies, subscribe to at least one of the half-dozen magazines devoted to Civil War history, or buy and sell Civil War memorabilia.

Above all, Americans buy books on the Civil War. This has always been true. More than fifty thousand separate books or pamphlets on the war have been published since the guns ceased firing 125 years ago. In recent years some eight hundred titles, many of them reprints of out-of-print works, have come off the presses annually. Nearly every month a new Civil War book is offered by the History Book Club or the Book-of-the-Month Club, often as the main selection. Many bookstore owners echo the words of Jim Lawson, general manager of the Book 'N Card shop in Falls Church,

Virginia. "For the last two years," he said in 1988, "Civil War books have been flying out of here. It's not [just] the buffs who buy; it's the general public, from high school kids to retired people."

Although we are approaching the end of the 125th-anniversary commemorations of Civil War events, the boom shows no signs of fading. As a beneficiary of this popular interest in the Civil War, I am often asked to explain what accounts for it—in particular, to explain why my own recent contribution to the literature on the war and its causes, *Battle Cry of Freedom,* was on national best-seller lists for several months as a hardcover book in 1988 and again as a paperback in 1989. I have a few answers.

The war did in fact pit brother against brother, cousin against cousin, even father against son.

First, for Americans, the human cost of the Civil War was by far the most devastating in our history. The 620,000 Union and Confederate soldiers who lost their lives almost equaled the 680,000 American soldiers who died in all the other wars this country has fought combined. When we add the unknown but probably substantial number of civilian deaths—from disease, malnutrition, exposure, or injury—among the hundreds of thousands of refugees in the Confederacy, the toll of Civil War dead may exceed war deaths in all the rest of American history. Consider two sobering facts about the Battle of Antietam, Amer-

ica's single bloodiest day. The 25,000 casualties there were nearly four times the number of American casualties on D-day, June 6, 1944. The 6,500 men killed and mortally wounded in one day near Sharpsburg were nearly double the number of Americans killed and mortally wounded in combat in all the rest of the country's nineteenth-century wars combined—the War of 1812, the Mexican War, and the Spanish-American War.

This ghastly toll gives the Civil War a kind of horrifying but hypnotic fascination. As Thomas Hardy once put it, "War makes rattling good history; but Peace is poor reading." The sound of drum and trumpet, the call to arms, the clashing of armies have stirred the blood of nations throughout history. As the horrors and the seamy side of a war recede into the misty past, the romance and honor and glory forge into the foreground. Of no war has this been more true than of the Civil War, with its dashing cavaliers, its generals leading infantry charges, its diamond-stacked locomotives and paddle-wheeled steamboats, its larger-than-life figures like Lincoln, Lee, Jackson, Grant, and Sherman, its heroic and romantic women like Clara Barton and "Mother" Bickerdyke and Rose O'Neal Greenhow, its countless real-life heroines and knaves and heroes capable of transmutation into a Scarlett O'Hara, Rhett Butler, or Ashley Wilkes. If romance is the other face of horror in our perception of the Civil War, the poignancy of a brothers' war is the other face of the tragedy of a civil war. In hundreds of individual cases the war did pit brother against brother, cousin against cousin, even father against son. This was especially true in border states like Kentucky, where the war divided

From *American Heritage,* March 1990, pp. 41-44, 46-47, 49. Used with permission from *American Heritage,* a division of Forbes Inc.

such famous families as the Clays, Crittendens, and Breckinridges and where seven brothers and brothers-in-law of the wife of the United States President fought for the Confederate States. But it was also true of states like Virginia, where Jeb Stuart's father-in-law commanded Union cavalry, and even of South Carolina, where Thomas F. Drayton became a brigadier general in the Confederate army and fought against his brother Percival, a captain in the Union navy, at the Battle of Port Royal. Who can resist the painful human interest of stories like these—particularly when they are recounted in the letters and diaries of Civil War protagonists, preserved through generations and published for all to read as a part of the unending stream of Civil War books?

Indeed, the uncensored contemporary descriptions of that war by participants help explain its appeal to modern readers. There is nothing else in history to equal it. Civil War armies were the most literate that ever fought a war up to that time, and twentieth-century armies censored soldiers' mail and discouraged diary keeping. Thus we have an unparalleled view of the Civil War by the people who experienced it. This has kept the image of the war alive in the families of millions of Americans whose ancestors fought in it. When speaking to audiences as diverse as Civil War buffs, Princeton students and alumni, and local literary clubs, I have sometimes asked how many of them are aware of forebears who fought in the Civil War. I have been surprised by the large response, which demonstrates not only a great number of such people but also their consciousness of events that happened so long ago yet seem part of their family lore today.

THIS CONSCIOUSNESS OF THE WAR, of the past as part of the present, continues to be more intense in the South than elsewhere. William Faulkner said of his native section that the past isn't dead; it isn't even past. As any reader of Faulkner's novels knows, the Civil War is central to that past that is present; it is the great watershed of Southern history; it is, as Mark Twain put it a century ago after a tour through the South, "what A.D. is elsewhere; they date from it." The symbols of that past-in-present surround Southerners as they grow up, from the Robert E. Lee Elementary School or

Jefferson Davis High School they attend and the Confederate battle flag that flies over their statehouse to the Confederate soldier enshrined in bronze or granite on the town square and the family folklore about victimization by Sherman's bummers. Some of those symbols remain highly controversial and provoke as much passion today as in 1863: the song "Dixie," for example, and the Confederate flag, which for many Southern whites continue to represent courage, honor, or defiance while to blacks they represent racism and oppression.

This suggests the most important reason for the enduring fascination with the Civil War among professional historians as well as the general public: Great issues were at stake, issues about which Americans were willing to fight and die, issues whose resolution profoundly transformed and redefined the United States. The Civil War was a total war in three senses: It mobilized the total human and material resources of both sides; it ended not in a negotiated peace but in total victory by one side and unconditional surrender by the other; it destroyed the economy and social system of the loser and established those of the winner as the norm for the future.

Civil War soldiers were the most literate up to that time. Their diaries and letters have had a lasting appeal.

The Civil War was fought mainly by volunteer soldiers who joined the colors before conscription went into effect. In fact, the Union and Confederate armies mobilized as volunteers a larger percentage of their societies' manpower than any other war in American history—probably in world history, with the possible exception of the French Revolution. And Civil War armies, like those of the French Revolution, were highly ideological in motivation. Most of the volunteers knew what they were fighting for, and why. What were they fighting for? If asked to define it in a single word, many soldiers on both sides would have answered: liberty. They fought for the heritage of freedom bequeathed to them by the Founding Fathers. North and South alike wrapped themselves in the mantle of 1776. But the two sides interpreted

that heritage in opposite ways, and at first neither side included the slaves in the vision of liberty for which it fought. The slaves did, however, and by the time of Lincoln's Gettysburg Address in 1863, the North also fought for "a new birth of freedom. . . ." These multiple meanings of freedom, and how they dissolved and reformed in kaleidoscopic patterns during the war, provide the central meaning of the war for the American experience.

When the "Black Republican" Abraham Lincoln won the Presidency in 1860 on a platform of excluding slavery from the territories, Southerners compared him to George III and declared their independence from "oppressive Yankee rule." "The same spirit of freedom and independence that impelled our Fathers to the separation from the British Government," proclaimed secessionists, would impel the "liberty loving people of the South" to separation from the United States government. A Georgia secessionist declared that Southerners would be "either *slaves in the Union or freemen out of it.*" Young men from Texas to Virginia rushed to enlist in this "Holy Cause of Liberty and Independence" and to raise "the standard of Liberty and Equality for white men" against "our Abolition enemies who are pledged to prostrate the white freemen of the South down to equality with negroes." From "the high and solemn motive of defending and protecting the rights which our fathers bequeathed to us," declared Jefferson Davis at the outset of war, let us "renew such sacrifices as our fathers made to the holy cause of constitutional liberty."

BUT MOST NORTHERNERS RIDICULED these Southern professions to be fighting for the ideals of 1776. That was "a libel upon the whole character and conduct of the men of '76," said the antislavery poet and journalist William Cullen Bryant. The Founding Fathers had fought "to establish the rights of man . . . and principles of universal liberty." The South, insisted Bryant, had seceded "not in the interest of general humanity, but of a domestic despotism. . . . Their motto is not liberty, but slavery." Northerners did not deny the right of revolution in principle; after all, the United States was founded on that right. But "the right of revolution," wrote Lincoln in 1861, "is never a legal right. . . . At most, it is but a moral right, when exercised for a morally justifiable cause. When exercised without such a cause revolution is no right, but simply a wicked exercise of physical power." In Lincoln's judgment secession was just such a wicked exercise. The event that precipitated it was Lincoln's election by a constitutional majority. As Northerners saw it, the Southern states, having controlled the national government for most of the previous two generations through their domination of the Democratic party, now decided to leave the Union just because they had lost an election.

For Lincoln and the Northern people, it was the Union that represented the ideals of 1776. The republic established by the Founding Fathers as a bulwark of liberty was a fragile experiment in a nineteenth-century world bestridden by kings, emperors, czars, and dictators. Most republics through history had eventually been overthrown. Some Americans still alive in 1861 had seen French republics succumb twice to emperors and once to the restoration of the Bourbon monarchy. Republics in Latin America came and went with bewildering rapidity. The United States in 1861 represented, in Lincoln's words, "the last, best hope" for the survival of republican liberties in the world. Would that hope also collapse? "Our popular government has often been called an experiment," Lincoln told Congress on July 4,1861. But if the Confederacy succeeded in splitting the country in two, it would set a fatal precedent that would destroy the experiment. By invoking this precedent, a minority in the future might secede from the Union whenever it did not like what the majority stood for, until the United States fragmented into a multitude of petty, squabbling autocracies. "The central idea pervading this struggle," said Lincoln, "is the necessity . . . of proving that popular government is not an absurdity. We must settle this question now, whether, in a free government, the minority have the right to break up the government whenever they choose."

Many soldiers who enlisted in the Union army felt the same way. A Missourian joined up as "a duty I owe my country and to my children to do what I can to preserve this government as I shudder to think what is ahead of them if this government should be overthrown." A New England soldier wrote to his wife on the eve of the First Battle of Bull Run: "I know . . . how great a debt we owe to those who went before us through the blood and sufferings of the Revolution. And I am willing—perfectly willing—to lay down all my joys in this life, to help maintain this government, and to pay that debt."

Freedom for the slaves was not part of the liberty for which the North fought in 1861. That was not because the Lincoln administration supported slavery; quite the contrary. Slavery was "an unqualified evil to the negro, to the white man . . . and to the State," said Lincoln on many occasions in words that expressed the sentiments of a Northern majority. "The monstrous injustice of slavery . . . deprives our republican example of its just influence in the world— enables the enemies of free institutions, with plausibility, to taunt us as hypocrites. . . . "Yet in his first inaugural address, Lincoln declared that he had "no purpose, directly or indirectly, to interfere with . . . slavery in the States where it exists." He reiterated this pledge in his first message to Congress, on July 4, 1861, when the Civil War was nearly three months old.

Civil War armies mobilized a larger percentage of volunteer manpower than any other war in our history.

What explains this apparent inconsistency? The answer lies in the Constitution and in the Northern polity of 1861. Lincoln was bound by a constitution that protected slavery in any state where citizens wanted it. The republic of liberty for whose preservation the North was fighting had been a republic in which slavery was legal everywhere in 1776. That was the great American paradox—a land of freedom based on slavery. Even in 1861 four states that remained loyal to the Union were slave states, and the Democratic minority in free states opposed any move to make the war for the Union a war against slavery.

BUT AS THE WAR WENT ON, THE SLAVES themselves took the first step toward making it a war against slavery. Coming into Union lines by the thousands, they voted with their feet for freedom. As enemy property they could be confiscated by Union forces as "contraband of war." This was the thin edge of the wedge that finally broke apart the American paradox. By 1863 a series of congressional acts plus Lincoln's Emancipation Proclamation had radically enlarged Union war aims. The North henceforth fought not just to restore the old Union, not just to ensure that the nation born in 1776 "shall not perish from the earth," but to give that nation "a new birth of freedom."

Northern victory in the Civil War resolved two fundamental, festering issues left unresolved by the Revolution of 1776: whether this fragile republican experiment called the United States would survive and whether the house divided would continue to endure half slave and half free. Both these issues remained open questions until 1865. Many Americans doubted the Republic's survival; many European conservatives predicted its demise; some Americans advocated the right of secession and periodically threatened to invoke it; eleven states did invoke it in 1860 and 1861. But since 1865 no state or region has seriously threatened secession, not even during the "massive resistance" to desegregation from 1954 to 1964. Before 1865 the United States, land of liberty, was the largest slaveholding country in the world. Since 1865 that particular "monstrous injustice" and "hypocrisy" has existed no more.

In the process of preserving the Union of 1776 while purging it of slavery, the Civil War also transformed it. Before 1861 the words *United States* were a plural noun: "The United States *are* a large country." Since 1865 *United States* has been a singular noun. The North went to war to preserve the *Union;* it ended by creating a *nation.* This transformation can be traced in Lincoln's most important wartime addresses. The first inaugural address contained the word *Union* twenty times and the word *nation* not once. In Lincoln's first message to Congress, on July 4, 1861, he used *Union* forty-nine times and *nation* only three times. In his famous public letter to Horace Greeley of August 22, 1862, concerning slavery and the war, Lincoln spoke of the Union nine times and the nation not at all. But in the Gettysburg Address fifteen months later, he did not refer to the Union at all but used the word *nation* five times. And in the second inaugural address, looking back over the past four years, Lincoln

McPherson's Basic Reading List

Allan Nevins. **Ordeal of the Union,** 2 vols. (New York: Charles Scribner's Sons, 1947). **The Emergence of Lincoln,** 2 vols. (New York: Charles Scribner's Sons, 1950). **The War for the Union,** 4 vols. (New York: Charles Scribner's Sons, 1959–71). These eight volumes are a magisterial account of the crisis-laden years from the Mexican War to Appomattox, covering social, economic, political, and military events in compelling prose.

David M. Potter. **The Impending Crisis, 1848–1861** (New York: Harper & Row, 1976). The best single-volume survey of the political events that led to secession and war.

Shelby Foote. **The Civil War: A Narrative,** 3 vols. (New York: Random House, 1958–74). A superbly readable military history by a novelist who did a massive amount of historical research.

Bruce Catton. **The Centennial History of the Civil War,** 3 vols. (Garden City, N.Y: Doubleday and Co., 1961–65). Fast-paced chronicle of the fighting on the battlefield and the infighting in the political capitals of Washington and Richmond. **Mr. Lincoln's Army** (Garden City, N.Y: Doubleday and Co., 1951). **Glory Road** (Garden City, N.Y: Doubleday and Co., 1952). **A Stillness at Appomattox** (Garden City, N.Y: Doubleday and Co., 1953). Catton's superb trilogy on the Army of the Potomac emphasizes the gritty determination of private soldiers despite the incompetent commanders who led them so often to defeat until Grant finally took charge.

Douglas Southall Freeman. **R. E. Lee: A Biography,** 4 vols. (New York: Charles Scribner's Sons, 1934–35). A classic study in leadership and command. **Lee's Lieutenants,** 3 vols. (New York: Charles Scribner's Sons, 1942–44). The story of the Army of Northern Virginia seen through the eyes of its principal officers.

Bell Irvin Wiley. **The Life of Johnny Reb** (Indianapolis: Bobbs-Merrill Co., 1943). **The Life of Billy Yank** (Indianapolis: Bobbs-Merrill Co., 1952). Thoroughly researched and superbly written studies of the common soldiers in both armies.

---

spoke of one side's seeking to dissolve the Union in 1861 and the other side's accepting the challenge of war to preserve the nation. The old decentralized Republic, in which the post office was the only agency of national government that touched the average citizen, was transformed by the crucible of war into a centralized polity that taxed people directly and created an internal revenue bureau to collect the taxes, expanded the jurisdiction of federal courts, created a national currency and a federally chartered banking system, drafted men into the Army, and created the Freedman's Bureau as the first national agency for social welfare. Eleven of the first twelve amendments to the Constitution had limited the powers of the national government; six of the next seven, starting with the Thirteenth Amendment in 1865, radically expanded those powers at the expense of the states. The first three of these amendments converted four million slaves into citizens and voters within five years, the most rapid and fundamental social transformation in American history—even if the nation did back-slide on part of this commitment for three generations after 1877.

From 1789 to 1861 a Southern slaveholder was President of the United States two-thirds of the time, and two-thirds of the Speakers of the House and presidents pro tem of the Senate had also been Southerners. Twenty of the thirty-five Supreme Court justices during that period were from the South, which always had a majority on the Court before 1861. After the Civil War a century passed before another resident of a Southern state was elected President. For half a century after the war hardly any Southerners served as Speaker of the House or president pro tem of the Senate, and only nine of the thirty Supreme Court justices appointed during that half-century were Southerners. The institutions and ideology of a plantation society and a caste system that had dominated half of the country before 1861 and sought to dominate more went down with a great crash in 1865 and were replaced by the institutions and ideology of free-labor entrepreneurial capitalism. For better or for worse, the flames of Civil War forged the framework of modern America.

So even if the veneer of romance and myth that has attracted so many of the current Civil War camp followers were stripped away, leaving only the trauma of violence and suffering, the Civil War would remain the most dramatic and crucial experience in American history. That fact will ensure the persistence of its popularity and its importance as a historical subject so long as there is a United States.

What Did Freedom Mean?

The Aftermath of Slavery as Seen by Former Slaves and Former Masters in Three Societies

Dean C. Brink

Dean Brink is chairman of the history department at Roosevelt High School in Seattle, Washington.

"Most anyone ought to know that a man is better off free than as a slave, even if he did not have anything," said the Reverend E. P. Holmes, a black Georgia clergyman and former house servant, to a Congressional committee in 1883. "I would rather be free and have my liberty. I fared just as well as any white child could have fared when I was a slave, and yet I would not give up my freedom."(1) Holmes was just one of over six million individuals held in bondage in the Western Hemisphere who were freed either by force and violence (as in Haiti between 1793–1803 and the United States between 1861–1865) or by government decree (as in Jamaica in 1838, Cuba in 1886, and Brazil in 1888). Four million of these slaves lived in the Southern United States. In Russia, two years before Lincoln issued the Emancipation Proclamation, Czar Alexander II freed fifty million serfs. Certainly the abolition of slavery was one of the most revolutionary and far-reaching developments of the nineteenth century.

Undoubtedly most of these former slaves would echo the Reverend Holmes statement that "I would not give up my freedom." But what did freedom mean? One way for the student of history to begin to answer this question is to analyze the accounts of former slaves and former masters on the ending of slavery in several societies. The accounts presented here illustrate some of the difficulties of adjusting to freedom. The first set of readings consists of the observations of former masters—two from the Southern United States, where the masters were white and the slaves were black, and one from Zaria, a region in northern Nigeria, where both slaves and masters were black. The second set of readings is a collection of letters written by former slaves to their former masters during the first years of Reconstruction in the South. A final set of readings contains the recollections of former slaves in Cuba and the Southern United States many years after abolition.

ACCOUNTS OF FORMER MASTERS

Frances B. Leigh was the daughter of the acclaimed British actress Frances (Fanny) Kemble and Peter Butler, a Georgia planter. At the beginning of the Civil War, Butler had nearly one thousand slaves on two plantations. In 1866, Frances Leigh returned to Georgia with her father to manage the plantations. She described her experiences in *Ten Years on a Georgia Plantation Since the War* (1883).

The year after the war between the North and South, I went with my father to look after our property in Georgia and see what could be done with it.

A Freedmen's Bureau station issuing rations to the old and sick. Although the Bureau, with the help of Union troops, tried to protect the civil rights of Southern blacks, brutal riots against blacks occurred in Memphis and New Orleans in 1866.

Reprinted from *OAH Magazine of History*, Vol. 4, No. 1., Winter 1989, pp. 35-46. Copyright © 1989 by the Organization of American Historians.

41. What Did Freedom Mean?

A Currier and Ives print, "Freedom to the Slaves," depicts Lincoln breaking the chains of bondage for a slave family.

we wanted and nothing could induce our people to go anywhere else. My father . . . could attend to nothing but the planting, and we agreed that he should devote himself to that, while I looked after some furniture. . . .

The prospect of getting in the crop did not grow more promising as time went on. The negros talked a great deal about their desire and intention to work for us, but their idea of work is very vague, some of them working only half a day and some even less. I don't think one does a full day's work, and so of course not half of the necessary amount is done and I am afraid never will be again, and so our properties will soon be utterly worthless, for no crop can be raised by such labor as this, and no negro will work if he can help it, and is quite satisfied to scrape along doing an odd job here and there to earn money enough to buy a little food. . . .

My father was quite encouraged at first, the people seemed so willing to work and said so much about their intentions of doing so; but not so many days after they started, he came in quite disheartened, saying that half of the hands had left the fields at one o'clock and the rest by three o'clock, and this just at our busiest time. Half a day's work will keep them from starving, but won't raise a crop. Our contract with them is for half the crop; that is, one half to be divided among them, according to each man's rate of work, we letting them have in the meantime necessary food, clothing, and money for their present wants (as they have not a penny) which is to be deducted from whatever is due to them at the end of the year.

This we found the best arrangement to make with them, for if we paid them wages, the first five dollars they made would have seemed like so large a sum to them, that they would have imagined their fortunes made and refused to work any more. But even this arrangement had its objections, for they told us, when they missed working two or three days a week, that they were losers by it as well as ourselves, half the crop being theirs. But they could not see that this sort of work would not raise any crop at all. . . . They were quite convinced that if six days' work would raise a whole crop, three days work would raise half a one, with which they as partners were satisfied, and so it seemed as if we should have to be too. . . .

In May 1867, Leigh and her father moved to their second plantation on a sea

The whole country had of course undergone a complete revolution. The changes that a four years' war must bring about in any country would alone have been enough to give a different aspect to everything; but at the South, besides the changes brought by the war, our slaves had been freed. . . . The South was still treated as a conquered country. The white people were disfranchised, the local government in the hands of either military men or Northern adventurers, the latter of whom, with no desire to promote either the good of the country or the people . . . encouraged the negroes in all of their foolish and extravagant ideas of freedom, set them against their masters, . . . in order to secure for themselves some political office which they hoped to obtain through the negro vote. . . .

We had, before the North, received two letters from Georgia, one from an agent of the Freedmen's Bureau, and the other from one of our neighbors both stating very much the same thing, which was that our former slaves had all returned to the

island and were willing and ready to work for us, but refused to engage themselves to anyone else, even to their liberators, the Yankees; but they were very badly off, short of provisions, and would starve if something were not done for them at once. . . .

On Wednesday, when my father returned, he reported that he had found the negroes all on the place, not only those who were there five years ago, but many who were sold three years before that. . . . They received him very affectionately, and made an agreement with him to work for one half the crop. . . . Owing to our coming so late, only a small crop could be planted, enough to make seed for another year and clear expenses. . . . Most of the plantations were lying idle for want of hands to work them, so many of the negroes had died; . . . Many had taken to the Southwest, and other[s] preferred hanging about the towns, to working regularly on the plantations; so most people found it impossible to get any laborers, but we had as many as

The Lilly Library

island off the coast of Georgia. Her account continues.

The rice plantation becoming unhealthy early in May, we removed to St. Simon's, a sea island on the coast, about fifteen miles from Butler's Island where the famous Sea Island cotton had formerly been raised. This place had been twice in the possession of the Northern troops during the war, and the negroes had consequently been brought under the influence of Northerners, some of whom had filled the poor people's minds with all sorts of vain hopes and ideas, among others that their former masters would not be allowed to return, and the land was theirs, a thing many of them believed, and they had planted both corn and cotton to a considerable extent. To disabuse their minds of this notion my father determined to put in a few acres of cotton. . . .

My father spent . . . time in talking to the negroes, of whom there were about fifty on the place, making arrangements with them for work, more to establish his right to the place than from any good work we expected to do this year. We found them in a very different frame of mind from the negroes on Butler's Island. . . . They were perfectly respectful, but quiet, and evidently disappointed to find they were not the masters of the soil and that their friends the Yankees had deceived them. . . .

In all other ways the work went on just as it did in the old times. The force, of about three hundred, was divided into gangs, each working under a head man— the old negro drivers. . . . To make them do odd jobs was hopeless, as I found when I . . . tried to make them clear up the grounds about the house, cut the undergrowth and make a garden. . . . Unless I stayed on the spot all the time, the instant I disappeared they disappeared as well. . . . And I generally found that if I wanted a thing done I first had to tell the negroes to do it, then show them how, and finally do it myself. Their way of managing not to do it was very ingenious, for they were always perfectly good tempered, and received my orders . . . and then always somehow or other left the thing undone.

In August of 1867 my father died, and . . . I went down to the South to carry on his work, . . . but before anything else could be done the negroes had to be settled with for the past two years, and their share of the crops divided according to the amount due each man. . . .

Notwithstanding their dissatisfaction with the settlement, six thousand dollars was paid out among them, many getting as much as two or three hundred a piece. The result was that a number of them left me and bought land of their own, and at one time it seemed doubtful that I should have hands at all left to work. The land they bought, and paid forty, fifty dollars and even more for an acre, was either within the town limits, for which they got no title, and from which they were soon turned off, or out in the pine woods, where the land was so poor they could not raise a peck of corn to the acre. . . .

Most frightfully cheated the poor people were. But they had got their land, and were building their little log cabins on it, fully believing that they were to live on their property and incomes the rest of their lives, like gentlemen. (2)

Mary Boykin Chestnut was a woman of wit and intelligence who kept an intimate diary of life in the Confederacy during the Civil War. The daughter of one of South Carolina's finest families, she was married to James Chestnut, an aide to Jefferson Davis and a Brigadier General of the Confederacy. These two entrees are from *Mary Chestnut's Civil War,* the most recent edition of her diary.

May 2, 1865

Old Mr. Chestnut had a summer resort for his invalid negroes and especially for women with ailing babies. Myrtilla, an African, was head nurse then. She was very good, very sensible, very efficient, and her language a puzzle to me always. She went off with the Yankees. "Old Aunt Myrtilla run away," said Smith with a guffaw. Ellen (said)

"She was a black angel—she was so good."

"Yes," said Smith, "her arms hung back of her jis' like wings. She was always more like flying than walking—the way she got over ground."

"And Marster did treat her like a lady. She had a woman to wash and cook for her. You think the Yankees gwine do that for her? And then, she is that old—she is so old—I thought she only wanted in this world a little good religion to die with."

And now from Orangeburg comes the most pathetic letters. Old Myrtilla begs to be sent for. She wants to come home. Miss C, who feels terribly any charitable distress which can be relieved by other people, urges us to send for "poor old Myrtilla."

"Very well," says her brother. "You pay for the horses and the wagon and the driver, and I will send."

And that ended the Myrtilla tragedy as far as we were concerned, but poor old Myrtilla, after the first natural frenzy of freedom subsided, knew all too well on which side her bread was buttered—and knew too, or found out, where her real friends were. So in a short time old Myrtilla was on our hands to support once more. How she got back we did not inquire. (3)

June 12, 1865

Captain Barn well came to see us. . . . He gave us an account of his father's plantation from which he had just returned.

"Our negroes are living in great comfort. They were delighted to see me with overflowing affection. They waited on me as before, gave me breakfast, splendid dinners, etc. But they firmly and respectfully informed me: 'We own this land now. Put it out of your head that it will ever be yours again.' " (4)

Baba was a Hausa woman who lived

President Abraham Lincoln entering the city of Richmond, Virginia, former capital of the Southern States, April 4, 1865. He is said to have told the masses of freed slaves, "You must kneel to God only, and thank Him for the liberty you will hereafter enjoy. I am but God's humble instrument."

in the Nigerian states of Kano and Zaria between 1890 and 1951. The Hausa are a group of west African peoples who speak a similar language. They are traditionally village farmers who adhere to the Islamic faith. When the British abolished slavery in Zaria in 1901, Baba was a young girl. Her father owned about 200 slaves. She described her experiences in an autobiography, *Baba of Karo: A Woman of the Moslem Hausa.* (1964).

When I was a maiden the Europeans first arrived. Ever since we were quite small the malams (scholars of the Koran) had been saying that the Europeans would come with a thing called a train, they would come with a thing called a motor-car, . . . They would stop wars, they would repair the world, they would stop oppression and lawlessness, we should live at peace with them. We used to go and sit quietly and listen to the prophecies. . . .

I remember when a European came to Karo on a horse, and some of his foot soldiers went into the town. Everyone came to look at them, but . . . everyone at Karo ran away—"There's a European, there's a European!" He came from Zaria with a few black men, two on horses and four on foot. . . . Later we heard that they were in Zaria in crowds, clearing spaces and building houses. . . .

The Europeans said that there were to be no more slaves; if someone said 'Slave!' you could complain to the alkali (a judge) who would punish the master who said it, the judge said "That is what the Europeans have decreed!" The first order said that any slave, if he was younger than you, was your younger brother, if he was older than you he was your elder brother—they were all brothers of their master's family. No one could use the word 'slave' anymore. When slavery was stopped, nothing much happened at our rinji (a slave village) except that some slaves whom we had bought in the market ran away. Our father went to his farm and worked, he and his son took up large hoes; they loaned out their small farms. Tsoho our father and Kadiri my brother . . . and Babambo worked, they farmed guinea-corn and millet and groundnuts and everything; before this they had supervised the slaves' work—now they did their own. When the midday food was ready, the women of the compound would give us children the food, one of us drew water, and off we went to the farm to take the men their food at the foot of the tree; I was about eight or nine at the time, I think. (5)

LETTERS OF FORMER SLAVES TO FORMER MASTERS

Because they were kept illiterate while in bondage, few former slaves were able to record their thoughts about the meaning of freedom or their hopes and aspirations for life in a society without slavery. Still, some letters from former slaves to former masters exist, and they reflect the memories and emotions that they had about slavery, freedom, and the ties that bound master and slave together. These three letters express some of the feelings and attitudes that millions of other illiterate former slaves may have held.(6)

Montgomery, February 10, 1867

My Dear Old Master,—I am anxious to see you and my young masters and mistresses. I often think of you, and remember with pleasure how kind you all were to me. Though freedom has been given to the colored race, I often sigh for the good old days of slave-times, when we were all so happy and contented. . . . I am tolerably pleasantly situated. I hired to a Mr. Sanderson , who treats me very well. I am very well and hope I may have an opportunity of coming to see you all next Christmas. I am still single and don't think very much about a beaux. I don't think the men in these days of freedom are of much account. If I could find one whom I think a real good man, and who would take good care of me, I would get married. Please, dear old master, ask some of my young mistresses to write me.

My kind and respectful remembrances to all.

Your former servant and friend,

Alice Dabney

February 5,1867

Mas William,

I guess you will be somewhat surprised to receive a letter from me. I am well & doing just as well as I could expect under the circumstances, one blessing is that I have plenty to eat & have plenty of work to do, & get tolerable fair prices for my work. I have but two small children, they are good size boys, able to plow & help me out a great deal. I still work at my trade. I once thought I wanted to come back to that old country, but I believe I have given up that notion. Give my respects to old Mas Henry & his family Miss Jane & all the family.

Tell Austin howdy for me & tell him I want him to write me & give me all the news of that old country who has married who had died give me all the news I am anxious to hear from them all tell Austin to give them all my love to all I havent time to mention all ther names, but I wish to hear from all remember me to Coleman especially. As I am in a great hurry I will close please send me word, direct your letters to Camden in the Case or in the name of S. B. Griffin, Camden, Washita County, Arksas.

*I remains as ever Respt
Your humble Servent
Jake*

Dayton, Ohio, August 7,1865

*To My Old Master, Colonel P. H. Anderson
Big Spring, Tennessee*

Sir: I got your letter and was glad to find you had not forgotten Jourdon, and that you wanted me to come back and live with you again, promising to do better for me than anyone else can. I have often felt uneasy about you. I thought the Yankees would have hung you long before this for harboring Rebs they found at your house. . . . Although you shot at me twice before I left you, I did not want to hear of your being hurt, and am glad you are still living. . . .

I am doing tolerably well here; I get $25 a month, with victuals and clothing; have a comfortable home here for Mandy (the folks here call her Mrs. Anderson), and the children, Milly, Jane and Grundy, go to school and are learning well. . . . Now if you will write and say what wages you will give me, I will be better able to decide whether it would be to my advantage to move back again.

As to my freedom, which you say I can have, there is nothing to be gained on that score, as I got my free papers in 1864. . . . Mandy says she would be afraid to go back without some proof that you are sincerely disposed to treat us justly and kindly—and we have concluded to test your sincerity by asking you to send us our wages for the time we served you. This will make us forget and forgive old scores, and rely on your justice and friendship in the future. At $25 a month for me, and $2 a week for Mandy, our earnings would amount to $11,680. Add to this the interest for the time our wages have been kept back and deduct what you paid for our clothing and three doctor's visits for me, and pulling a tooth for Mandy, and the balance will show that we are in justice entitled to. Please send the money by Adams Express. . . . We trust the good Maker has opened your eyes to the wrongs which you and your fathers have done to me and my fathers, in making us toil for you for generations without recompense. . . . Surely there will be a day of reckoning for those who defraud the laborer of his hire.

In answering this letter please state if there would be any safety for my Milly and

Jane, who are now grown up and both good-looking girls. . . . You will also please state if there are any schools opened for colored children in your neighborhood, the great desire of my life now is to give my children an education, and have them form virtuous habits.

P.S.—Say howdy to George Carter, and thank him for taking the pistol from you when you were shooting at me.

From your old servant,

Jourdan Anderson

RECOLLECTIONS OF FORMER SLAVES

Esteban Montejo was a runaway slave who spent ten years hiding in the forests of central Cuba before slavery was abolished. He described his experiences after slavery had ended in *The Autobiography of a Runaway Slave* (1973). He was over one hundred years old at the time.

All my life I have liked the forest, but when slavery ended I stopped being a runaway. I realized from the way people were cheering and shouting that slavery had ended, an so I came out of the forest. They were shouting, 'we are free now.' But I didn't join in, I thought it might be a lie. I don't know . . . anyway, I went up to a plantation and let my head appear little by little till I was out in the open. . . . When I left the forest and began walking, I met an old woman carrying two children in her arms. I called to her, and when she came up I asked her, 'Tell me, is it true we are no longer slaves?' She replied, 'No, son, we are now free.' I went walking the way I was going and began looking for work. . . .

After this time in the forest I had become half savage. I didn't want to work anywhere, and I was afraid they would shut me up again. I knew quite well that slavery had not ended completely. A lot of people asked me what I was doing and where I came from. Sometimes I told them, 'My name is Stephen and I was a runaway slave.' Other times I said I had been working on a certain plantation and could not find my relations. I must have been about twenty at the time.

Since I didn't know anyone I walked from village to village for several months. I did not suffer from hunger because people gave me food. You only had to say you were out of work and someone would always help you out. But you can't carry on like that forever. I began to realize that

work had to be done in order to eat and sleep in a barracoon (barracks for housing slaves) at least. By the time I decided to cut cane, I had already covered quite a bit of ground. . . .

The first plantation I worked on was called Purio. I turned up there one day in the rags I stood in and a hat I had collected along the way. I went in and asked the overseer if there was work for me. He said yes. I remember he was Spanish, with moustaches, and his name was Pepe. There were overseers in these parts until quite recently, the difference being that they didn't lay about them as they used to do under slavery. But they were men of the same breed, harsh, overbearing. There were still barracoons after Abolition, the same as before. Many of them were newly built of masonry, the old ones having collapsed under the rain and storms. The barracoon at Purio was strong and looked as if it had been recently completed. They told me to go and live there. I soon made myself at home for it wasn't too bad. They had taken the bolts off the doors and the workers themselves had cut holes in the walls for ventilation. They had no longer to worry about escapes or anything like that, for the Negroes were free now, or so they said. But I could not help noticing that bad things still went on. There were bosses who still believed that the blacks were created for locks and bolts and whips, and treated

them as before. It struck me that many Negroes did not know that things had changed, because they kept saying, 'Give me your blessing, my master.'

Those ones never left the plantation at all. I was different in that I disliked having anything to do with the whites. They believed they were the lords of creation. . . .

The work was exhausting. You spent hours in the fields and it seemed as if the work would never end. It went on and on until you were worn out. The overseers were always bothering you. Any worker who knocked off for long was taken off the job. I worked from six in the morning. The early hour didn't bother me since in the forest it had been impossible to sleep late because of the cocks crowing. There was a break at eleven for lunch, which had to be eaten in the workers' canteen, usually standing because of the crowd of people squashed in. This was the worst and hottest time. Work ended at six in the afternoon. Then I would take myself off to the river, bathe for a while, and go back to get something to eat. . . .

The Negroes who worked at Purio had almost all been slaves; they were so used to life in the barracoon they did not even go out to eat. When lunch-time came they shut themselves up in their rooms to eat, and the same with dinner. They did not go out at night. They were afraid of people, and they said they would get lost if they

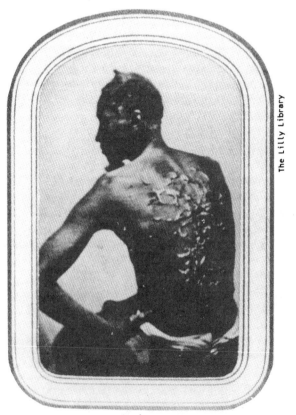

A slave.

did, they were convinced of this. I wasn't like that—if I got lost I always found myself again. . . .

On Sundays all the workers who wanted to could work overtime. This meant that instead of resting you went to the fields and cleared, cleaned or cut cane. Or if not that, you stayed in, cleaning out the troughs or scraping the boilers. . . . As there was nothing special to do that day, all the workers used to go and earn themselves extra money. . . .

In those days you could get either permanent or temporary work on the plantations. Those employed on a permanent basis had to keep a time-table. This way they could live in the barracoons and did not need to leave the plantations for anything. I preferred being a permanent worker myself.

The barracoons were a bit damp, but all the same they were safer than in the forest. There were no snakes, and all us workers slept in hammocks which were very comfortable. Many of the barracoons were made of sacking. The one tiresome thing about them was the fleas; they didn't hurt, but you had to be up all night scaring them off with the Spanish broom, which gets rid of fleas and ticks. . . .

After months of work on the plantation of Purio, Montejo left to go work at a sugar mill on a plantation at Ariosa.

But life grew wearisome on the plantations. It was boring to see the same people and fields day after day. The hardest thing was to get used to one place for a long time. I had to leave Purio because life seemed to have stopped still there. I started walking South, and I got to San Agustin Ariosa sugar-mill, near the villiage of Zulueta. At first I did not intend to stop there because I preferred walking . . . but as luck would have it I found myself a mistress there and so I stayed. . . .

I stayed a long time at Ariosa. . . . The plantation was of medium-size, owned by a man called Ariosa, a pure-blooded Spaniard. It was one of the first plantations to become a mill, and a large-gauge line ran through it, bring the cane direct from the fields into the boiler-house. It was much the same as everywhere else. There were the usual yes-men and toadies to masters and overseers alike. This was on account of the hatred which has always existed between the groups of slaves, because of ignorance. This is the only reason for it. The freed slaves were generally very ignorant and would lend themselves to anything. It happened that if some fellow became a nuisance, his own brothers would undertake to kill him for a few centenes. . . .

They didn't give work to just anyone . . . and at Ariosa you had to work hard. (The overseers) watched you the whole time, and they would book you for nothing at all. I remember a criminal by the name of Camilo Polavieja, who became Governor of Cuba in the Nineties. No one liked him. He said the workers were cattle and he kept the same views he had during slavery. Once he ordered all the workers (to have cards). . . . The cards were slips of paper . . . with the worker's address on. Anyone caught without his card got a good belting across the shoulders. . . . It was always given in a gaol, because that's where they took you if you were caught without your card. The card cost twenty-five cents . . . and it had to be renewed every year. . . .

There were lots of workers at Ariosa, I think it must have been one of the biggest plantations . . . The owner was an innovator and made many changes in the mills. Some plantations gave very bad food because the cooks didn't care, but Ariosa wasn't like that, you ate well there. . . .

When the dead season came everything stopped. . . . There was less work and fewer duties at this time, and naturally this led to boredom. . . .

The women carried on as usual, there was no such thing as dead time for them. They washed the men's clothes, mended and sewed. . . . They had plenty of other things to do, like raising pigs and chickens. . . . There was no freedom. (7)

In the 1930s the Federal Writers' Project of the Works Progress Administration (WPA) sent teams of interviewers into the South to interview surviving former slaves. The results of the interviews of over two thousand ex-slaves were compiled in the Slave Narrative Collection. Two-thirds of those interviewed were over eighty years of age and the interviews gave them an unparalleled opportunity to describe their lives both under slavery and after emancipation. These four narratives are taken from *Life Under the "Peculiar Institution": Selections from the Slave Narrative Collection* (1970) by Norman P. Yetman.(8)

1. Mary Anderson, age 86
Interviewed near Raleigh, North Carolina

I was born on a plantation near Franklinton, Wake County, North Carolina, May 10, 1851. I was a slave belonging to Sam Brodie, who owned the plantation at this place. . . .

We had good food, plenty of warm clothes, and comfortable houses. . . . The plantation was very large and there was about two hundred acres of cleared land that was farmed each year. . . . There were about one hundred and sixty-two slaves on the plantation. . . .

The War was begun and there were stories of fights and freedom. The news went from plantation to plantation and while the slaves acted natural and some even more polite than usual, they prayed for freedom.

Then one day I heared something that sounded like thunder and Marster and Missus began to walk around and act queer. The grown slaves were whispering to each other. Sometimes they gathered in little gangs in the grove. . . .

In a day or two everybody on the plantation seemed disturbed and Marster and Missus were crying. Marster ordered all of the slaves to come to the Great House at nine o'clock. . . . Then Marster said, "Good morning," and Missus said, "Good morning, children." They were both crying. Then Marster said, "Men, women, and children, you are free. You are no longer my slaves. The Yankees will soon be here. . . ."

The slaves were awfully excited. The Yankees stayed there, cooked, ate, drank, and played music until about night. . . .

When they left the country, lots of the slaves went with them and soon there were none of Marster's slaves left. They wandered around from place to place, fed and working most of the time at some other slave owner's plantation and getting more homesick every day.

The second year after the surrender our Marster and Missus got on their carriage and went and looked up all the Negroes they heard of who belonged to them. Some who went off with the Yankees were never heard from again. . . . Some were so glad to get back they cried, 'cause fare had been mighty bad part of the time they were rambling around and they were hungry.

2. Frank Bell, age 86
Interviewed at St. Louis, Missouri

I was owned by Johnson Bell and born in New Orleans . . . and my master . . . was real mean to me. . . . When war come, Master swear he not gwine to fight, but the Yankees they capture New Orleans and throws Marster in a pen and guards him. He gets a chance and escapes.

When war am over he won't free me, says I'm valuable to him in his trade. He say, "Nigger, you's supposed to be free but I'll pay you a dollar a week and if you run off I'll kill you." So he makes me do like before the War, but gives me a dollar a month, 'stead week. He says I cost more'n I'm worth, but he won't let me go. Times I don't know why I didn't die before I'm growed, sleepin' on the ground, winter and summer, rain and snow.

Master helt me long after the War. If anybody get after him, he told them I stay 'cause I wants to stay, but told me if I left he'd kill him another nigger. I stayed till he gits in a drunk brawl one night . . . and . . . got killed.

Then I am left to live or die, so I wanders from place to place. I nearly starved to death before I'd leave New Orleans, 'cause I couldn't think Master am dead and I afraid. Finally I gets up nerve to leave town. . . .

Then I gets locked up in jail. I didn't know what for, never did know. One of the men says to me to come with him and takes me to the woods and give me an ax. I cuts rails till I nearly falls, all with chain locked round feet, so I couldn't run off. He turns me loose and I wanders again. Never had a home. Works for me long 'nough to get fifty, sixty cents, then starts roamin' again, like a stray dog.

After a long time I marries Feline Graham. . . . We has one boy and he farms and I lives with him. I worked at a sawmill and farms all my life, but never could make much money.

3. Elidge Davison, age 86
Interviewed at Madisonville, Texas

My birth was in Richmond . . . in Old Virginy. . . . Massa and Missus were very good white folks and was good to the black folks. . . . Us work all day till just before dark. Some times us got a whipping. . . . Massa learn us to read and us read the Bible. He learn us to write too.

I 'member plenty about the War, 'cause the Yankees they march on to Richmond. . . . When the War over Massa call me and tells me I'se free as he was. 'Cause them Yankees win the War. He gives me five dollars and say he'll give me that much a month iffen I stays with him, but I starts to Texas. I heared I wouldn't have to work in Texas, 'cause everything growed on trees and the Texans wore animal hides for clothes. I didn't get no land or mule or cow. There warn't no plantations divided that I knowed about.

It about a year before I gets to Texas. I walks nearly all the way. . . . Sometimes I work for folks along the way and gets fifty cents and start again. I get to Texas and try to work for white folks and try to farm. I couldn't make anything at any work. I made five dollars a month for I don't know how long after the War. Iffen the woods wasn't full of game us . . . all starve to death them days.

4. Henri Necaise, age 105
Interviewed in Mississippi

I was thirty-one years old when I was set free. My Marster din't tell us about bein' free. De way I found out about it, he started to whip me once and de young marster up and says, "You ain't got no right to whip him now; he's free." Den Marster turn me loose.

Dey went out and turned us loose, just like a passel of cattle, and didn't show us nothin' or give us nothin'. Dey was acres and acres of land not in use, and lots of

timber in dis country. Dey should-a give each one of us a little farm and let us get out timber and build houses.

I never did look for to get nothin' after I was free. I had dat in my head to get me eighty acres of land and homestead it. As for the government making me a present of anything, I never thought about it.

I did get me this little farm, but I bought it and paid for it myself. I got de money by workin' for it. . . .

Many of the major developments or experiences in American history are local topics for comparative study and analysis—the Revolution, the frontier experience, slavery and race relations, to name just a few. The growing body of research by scholars into the aftermath of emancipation in different societies now offers teachers and students an opportunity to study Reconstruction from a comparative perspective. The following suggestions from a lesson in comparative history are based on the assumption that students will have a good knowledge of American slavery and race relations including events during the Civil War leading to emancipation. The lesson can be used to introduce a unit on Reconstruction.

To begin, tell your students that you are going to have them assume the role of a slave who has been freed as a result of the Civil War. "It is 1866 and you have been free for nearly a year. What is freedom like? How is it different from slavery? You have the opportunity to write your former master a letter. What would you tell him or her about being free?" Spend a day having students read their letters in class, giving them the opportunity to draw comparisons about their descriptions of freedom. Have them speculate whether their letters would reflect the feelings of slaves who were freed at the time of the Civil War.

Next, tell your students that they will read "eyewitness accounts" about the aftermath of slavery by former masters and former slaves in three different societies—the United States, Cuba, and Zaria. Divide the class into small groups of equal size and give each group a different set of accounts—accounts by former masters, letters of former slaves, and recollections of former slaves. Appoint a discussion leader and tell each group to read and analyze the accounts and agree on three generalizations about what freedom meant to either former masters or former slaves. Students should consider such matters as attitudes toward

work, changing roles of masters and slaves, how and when slaves learned about freedom, attitudes toward land ownership, and so on. Allow several days for this activity, and when each group has reported and defended its generalizations, lead a class discussion about the difficulties of adjusting to freedom and whether the attitudes about freedom stated by students in their letters were shared by the writers of the accounts they have just analyzed.

Finally, present to your students some of the insights about the aftermath of slavery in several societies from Thomas J. Pressly's article, "Reconstruction in the Southern United States: A Comparative Perspective." This might include a discussion of the common desire for land ownership by former slaves and the extent to which it was obtained, the reasons why former masters were able to retain their control after abolition, and the degree of political power, health care, and education gained by former slaves. Encourage the students to use the eyewitness accounts they have analyzed to support some of the ideas you have presented to them.

At this point you might turn to a more detailed study of the Reconstruction Era. By reading, analyzing, and discussing accounts about the aftermath of emancipation in different settings, students will be able to develop a better understanding about the problems associated with the ending of slavery in the nineteenth century United States.

NOTES

1. Foner, Eric. *Nothing But Freedom: Emancipation and Its Legacy,* 7. Baton Rouge: LSU Press, 1983.

2. Leigh, Frances B. *Ten Years on a Georgia Plantation Since the War,* 1–3, 13–16, 24–28, 32–33, 56–57, 73–74, 78–79. London: Richard Bentley & Son, 1883.

3. Vann Woodward, C., ed. *Mary Chestnut's Civil War,* 805–806. New Haven: Yale University Press, 1981.

4. Ibid., 827.

5. Smith, Mary B. *Baba of Karo: A Woman of the Moslem Hausa,* 66–68. New York: Praeger, 1964.

6. These letters are reprinted in Litwack, Leon F. *Been In The Storm So Long: The Aftermath of Slavery,* 333–335. New York: Vintage Books, 1979.

7. Montejo, Esteban. *The Autobiography of a Runaway Slave,* 59–60, 63–69, 83–85, 91–92, 171. New York: Vintage Press, 1973.

8. Yetman, Norman R. *Life Under the "Peculiar Institution": Selections From The Slave Narrative Collection,* 15, 17–18, 21–23, 91–93, 237–239. New York: Holt, Rinehart and Winston, Inc., 1970.

The New View of Reconstruction

Whatever you were taught or thought you knew about the post–Civil War era is probably wrong in the light of recent study

Eric Foner

Eric Foner is Professor of History at Columbia University and author of Nothing but Freedom: Emancipation and Its Legacy.

In the past twenty years, no period of American history has been the subject of a more thoroughgoing reevaluation than Reconstruction—the violent, dramatic, and still controversial era following the Civil War. Race relations, politics, social life, and economic change during Reconstruction have all been reinterpreted in the light of changed attitudes toward the place of blacks within American society. If historians have not yet forged a fully satisfying portrait of Reconstruction as a whole, the traditional interpretation that dominated historical writing for much of this century has irrevocably been laid to rest.

Anyone who attended high school before 1960 learned that Reconstruction was an era of unrelieved sordidness in American political and social life. The martyred Lincoln, according to this view, had planned a quick and painless readmission of the Southern states as equal members of the national family. President Andrew Johnson, his successor, attempted to carry out Lincoln's policies but was foiled by the Radical Republicans (also known as Vindictives or Jacobins). Motivated by an irrational hatred of Rebels or by ties with Northern capitalists out to plunder the South, the Radicals swept aside Johnson's lenient program and fastened black supremacy upon the defeated Confederacy. An orgy of corruption followed, presided over by unscrupulous carpetbaggers (Northerners who ventured south to reap the spoils of

office), traitorous scalawags (Southern whites who cooperated with the new governments for personal gain), and the ignorant and childlike freedmen, who were incapable of properly exercising the political power that had been thrust upon them. After much needless suffering, the white community of the South banded together to overthrow these "black" governments and restore home rule (their euphemism for white supremacy). All told, Reconstruction was just about the darkest page in the American saga.

Originating in anti-Reconstruction propaganda of Southern Democrats during the 1870s, this traditional interpretation achieved scholarly legitimacy around the turn of the century through the work of William Dunning and his students at Columbia University. It reached the larger public through films like *Birth of a Nation* and *Gone With the Wind* and that best-selling work of myth-making masquerading as history, *The Tragic Era* by Claude G. Bowers. In language as exaggerated as it was colorful, Bowers told how Andrew Johnson "fought the bravest battle for constitutional liberty and for the preservation of our institutions ever waged by an Executive" but was overwhelmed by the "poisonous propaganda" of the Radicals. Southern whites, as a result, "literally were put to the torture" by "emissaries of hate" who manipulated the "simple-minded" freedmen, inflaming the negroes' egotism" and even inspiring "lustful assaults" by blacks upon white womanhood.

In a discipline that sometimes seems to pride itself on the rapid rise and fall of historical interpretations, this traditional portrait of Reconstruction enjoyed remarkable staying power. The long reign of the old interpretation is not difficult to

explain. It presented a set of easily identifiable heroes and villains. It enjoyed the imprimatur of the nation's leading scholars. And it accorded with the political and social realities of the first half of this century. This image of Reconstruction helped freeze the mind of the white South in unalterable opposition to any movement for breaching the ascendancy of the Democratic party, eliminating segregation, or readmitting disfranchised blacks to the vote.

NEVERTHELESS, THE DEMISE OF THE traditional interpretation was inevitable, for it ignored the testimony of the central participant in the drama of Reconstruction—the black freedman. Furthermore, it was grounded in the conviction that blacks were unfit to share in political power. As Dunning's Columbia colleague John W. Burgess put it, "A black skin means membership in a race of men which has never of itself succeeded in subjecting passion to reason, has never, therefore, created any civilization of any kind." Once objective scholarship and modern experience rendered that assumption untenable, the entire edifice was bound to fall.

The work of "revising" the history of Reconstruction began with the writings of a handful of survivors of the era, such as John R. Lynch, who had served as a black congressman from Mississippi after the Civil War. In the 1930s white scholars like Francis Simkins and Robert Woody carried the task forward. Then, in 1935, the black historian and activist W.E.B. Du Bois produced *Black Reconstruction in America*, a monumental reevaluation that closed with an irrefutable indictment of a historical profession that had sacrificed scholarly objectivity on the altar of racial bias. "One fact and one alone," he wrote, "explains the attitude of most recent writers toward Reconstruction; they cannot conceive of Negroes as men." Du Bois's work, however, was ignored by most historians.

It was not until the 1960s that the full force of the revisionist wave broke over the field. Then, in rapid succession, virtually every assumption of the traditional viewpoint was systematically dismantled. A drastically different portrait emerged to take its place. President Lincoln did not have a coherent "plan" for Reconstruction, but at the time of his assassination he had been cautiously contemplating black suffrage. Andrew Johnson was a stubborn, racist politician who lacked the ability to compromise. By isolating himself from the broad currents of public opinion that had nourished Lincoln's career, Johnson created an impasse with Congress that Lincoln would certainly have avoided, thus throwing away his political power and destroying his own plans for reconstructing the South.

The Radicals in Congress were acquitted of both vindictive motives and the charge of serving as the stalking-horses of Northern capitalism. They emerged instead as idealists in the best nineteenth-century reform tradition. Radical leaders like Charles Sumner and Thaddeus Stevens had worked for the rights of blacks long before any conceivable political advantage flowed from such a commitment. Stevens refused to sign the Pennsylvania Constitution of 1838 because it disfranchised the state's black citizens; Sumner led a fight in the 1850s to integrate Boston's public schools. Their Reconstruction policies were based on principle, not petty political advantage, for the central issue dividing Johnson and these Radical Republicans was the civil rights of freedmen. Studies of congressional policy-making, such as Eric L. McKitrick's *Andrew Johnson and Reconstruction,* also revealed that Reconstruction legislation, ranging from the Civil Rights Act of 1866 to the Fourteenth and Fifteenth Amendments, enjoyed broad support from moderate and conservative Republicans. It was not simply the work of a narrow radical faction.

EVEN MORE STARTLING WAS THE REVISED portrait of Reconstruction in the South itself. Imbued with the spirit of the civil rights movement and rejecting entirely the racial assumptions that had underpinned the traditional interpretation, these historians evaluated Reconstruction from the black point of view. Works like Joel Williamson's *After Slavery* portrayed the period as a time of extraordinary political, social, and economic progress for blacks. The establishment of public school systems, the granting of equal citizenship to blacks, the effort to restore the devastated Southern economy, the attempt to construct an interracial political democracy from the ashes of slavery, all these were commendable achievements, not the elements of Bowers's "tragic era."

Unlike earlier writers, the revisionists stressed the active role of the freedmen in shaping Reconstruction. Black initiative established as many schools as did Northern religious societies and the Freedmen's Bureau. The right to vote was not simply thrust upon them by meddling outsiders, since blacks began agitating for the suffrage as soon as they were freed. In 1865 black conventions throughout the South issued eloquent, though unheeded, appeals for equal civil and political rights.

With the advent of Radical Reconstruction in 1867, the freedmen did enjoy a real measure of political power. But black supremacy never existed. In most states blacks held only a small fraction of political offices, and even in South Carolina, where they comprised a majority of the state legislature's lower house, effective power remained in white hands. As for corruption, moral standards in both government and private enterprise were at low ebb throughout the nation in the postwar years—the era of Boss Tweed, the Credit Mobilier scandal, and the Whiskey Ring. Southern corruption could hardly be blamed on former slaves.

Other actors in the Reconstruction drama also came in for reevaluation. Most carpetbaggers were former Union soldiers seeking economic opportunity in the postwar South, not unscrupulous adventurers. Their motives, a typically American amalgam of humanitarianism and the pursuit of profit, were no more insidious than those of Western pioneers. Scalawags, previously seen as traitors to the white race, now emerged as "Old Line" Whig Unionists who had opposed secession in the first place or as poor whites who had long resented planters' domination of Southern life and who saw in Reconstruction a chance to recast Southern society along more democratic lines. Strongholds of Southern white Republicanism like east Tennessee and western North Carolina had been the scene of resistance to Confederate rule throughout the Civil War; now, as one scalawag newspaper put it, the choice was "between salvation at the hand of the Negro or destruction at the hand of the rebels."

At the same time, the Ku Klux Klan and kindred groups, whose campaign of violence against black and white Republicans had been minimized or excused in older writings, were portrayed as they really were. Earlier scholars had con-

Until recently, Thaddeus Stevens had been viewed as motivated by irrational hatred of the Rebels (left). Now he has emerged as an idealist in the best reform tradition.

NEW YORK PUBLIC LIBRARY, PRINT ROOM

EDWARDS ELLIS, *The History of Our Country*, VOL. 5, 1900

Reconstruction governments were portrayed as disastrous failures (left) because elected blacks were ignorant or corrupt. In fact, postwar corruption cannot be blamed on former slaves.

SCHOMBERG CENTER, NEW YORK PUBLIC LIBRARY

veyed the impression that the Klan intimidated blacks mainly by dressing as ghosts and playing on the freedmen's superstitions. In fact, black fears were all too real: the Klan was a terrorist organization that beat and killed its political opponents to deprive blacks of their newly won rights. The complicity of the Democratic party and the silence of prominent whites in the face of such outrages stood as an indictment of the moral code the South had inherited from the days of slavery.

By the end of the 1960s, then, the old interpretation had been completely reversed. Southern freedmen were the heroes, the "Redeemers" who overthrew Reconstruction were the villains, and if the era was "tragic," it was because change did not go far enough. Reconstruction had been a time of real progress and its failure a lost opportunity for the South and the nation. But the legacy of Reconstruction—the Fourteenth and Fifteenth Amendments—endured to inspire future efforts for civil rights. As Kenneth Stampp wrote in *The Era of Reconstruction,* a superb summary of revisionist findings published in 1965, "If it was worth four years of civil war to save the Union, it was worth a few years of radical reconstruction to give the American Negro the ultimate promise of equal civil and political rights."

As Stampp's statement suggests, the reevaluation of the first Reconstruction was inspired in large measure by the impact of the second—the modern civil rights movement. And with the waning of that movement in recent years, writing on Reconstruction has undergone still another transformation. Instead of seeing the Civil War and its aftermath as a second American Revolution (as Charles Beard had), a regression into barbarism

(as Bowers argued), or a golden opportunity squandered (as the revisionists saw it), recent writers argue that Radical Reconstruction was not really very radical. Since land was not distributed to the former slaves, they remained economically dependent upon their former owners. The planter class survived both the war and Reconstruction with its property (apart from slaves) and prestige more or less intact.

Not only changing times but also the changing concerns of historians have contributed to this latest reassessment of Reconstruction. The hallmark of the past decade's historical writing has been an emphasis upon "social history"—the evocation of the past lives of ordinary Americans—and the downplaying of strictly political events. When applied to Reconstruction, this concern with the "social" suggested that black suffrage and officeholding, once seen as the most radical departures of the Reconstruction era, were relatively insignificant.

RECENT HISTORIANS HAVE FOCUSED THEIR investigations not upon the politics of Reconstruction but upon the social and economic aspects of the transition from slavery to freedom. Herbert Gutman's influential study of the black family during and after slavery found little change in family structure or relations between men and women resulting from emancipation. Under slavery most blacks had lived in nuclear family units, although they faced the constant threat of separation from loved ones by sale. Reconstruction provided the opportunity for blacks to solidify their preexisting family ties. Conflicts over whether black women should work in the cotton fields (planters said yes, many black families said no)

and over white attempts to "apprentice" black children revealed that the autonomy of family life was a major preoccupation of the freedmen. Indeed, whether manifested in their withdrawal from churches controlled by whites, in the blossoming of black fraternal, benevolent, and self-improvement organizations, or in the demise of the slave quarters and their replacement by small tenant farms occupied by individual families, the quest for independence from white authority and control over their own day-to-day lives shaped the black response to emancipation.

In the post–Civil War South the surest guarantee of economic autonomy, blacks believed, was land. To the freedmen the justice of a claim to land based on their years of unrequited labor appeared self-evident. As an Alabama black convention put it, "The property which they [the planters] hold was nearly all earned by the sweat of *our* brows." As Leon Litwack showed in *Been in the Storm So Long,* a Pulitzer Prize–winning account of the black response to emancipation, many freedmen in 1865 and 1866 refused to sign labor contracts, expecting the federal government to give them land. In some localities, as one Alabama overseer reported, they "set up claims to the plantation and all on it."

In the end, of course, the vast majority of Southern blacks remained propertyless and poor. But exactly why the South, and especially its black population, suffered from dire poverty and economic retardation in the decades following the Civil War is a matter of much dispute. In *One Kind of Freedom,* economists Roger Ransom and Richard Sutch indicted country merchants for monopolizing credit and charging usurious interest rates, forcing black tenants into debt and lock-

4. THE CIVIL WAR AND RECONSTRUCTION

ing the South into a dependence on cotton production that impoverished the entire region. But Jonathan Wiener, in his study of postwar Alabama, argued that planters used their political power to compel blacks to remain on the plantations. Planters succeeded in stabilizing the plantation system, but only by blocking the growth of alternative enterprises, like factories, that might draw off black laborers, thus locking the region into a pattern of economic backwardness.

IF THE THRUST OF RECENT WRITING HAS emphasized the social and economic aspects of Reconstruction, politics has not been entirely neglected. But political studies have also reflected the postrevisionist mood summarized by C. Vann Woodward when he observed "how essentially nonrevolutionary and conservative Reconstruction really was." Recent writers, unlike their revisionist predecessors, have found little to praise in federal policy toward the emancipated blacks.

A new sensitivity to the strength of prejudice and laissez-faire ideas in the nineteenth-century North has led many historians to doubt whether the Republican party ever made a genuine commitment to racial justice in the South. The granting of black suffrage was an alternative to a long-term federal responsibility for protecting the rights of the former slaves. Once enfranchised, blacks could be left to fend for themselves. With the exception of a few Radicals like Thaddeus Stevens, nearly all Northern policy-makers and educators are criticized today for assuming that, so long as the unfettered operations of the marketplace afforded blacks the opportunity to advance through diligent labor, federal efforts to assist them in acquiring land were unnecessary.

Probably the most innovative recent writing on Reconstruction politics has centered on a broad reassessment of black Republicanism, largely undertaken by a new generation of black historians. Scholars like Thomas Holt and Nell Painter insist that Reconstruction was not simply a matter of black and white. Conflicts within the black community, no less than divisions among whites, shaped Reconstruction politics. Where revisionist scholars, both black and white, had celebrated the accomplishments of black political leaders, Holt, Painter, and others charge that they failed to address the economic plight of the black masses.

Painter criticized "representative colored men," as national black leaders were called, for failing to provide ordinary freedmen with effective political leadership. Holt found that black officeholders in South Carolina mostly emerged from the old free mulatto class of Charleston, which shared many assumptions with prominent whites. "Basically bourgeois in their origins and orientation," he wrote, they "failed to act in the interest of black peasants."

In emphasizing the persistence from slavery of divisions between free blacks and slaves, these writers reflect the increasing concern with continuity and conservatism in Reconstruction. Their work reflects a startling extension of revisionist premises. If, as has been argued for the past twenty years, blacks were active agents rather than mere victims of manipulation, then they could not be absolved of blame for the ultimate failure of Reconstruction.

Despite the excellence of recent writing and the continual expansion of our knowledge of the period, historians of Reconstruction today face a unique dilemma. An old interpretation has been overthrown, but a coherent new synthesis has yet to take its place. The revisionists of the 1960s effectively established a series of negative points: the Reconstruction governments were not as bad as had been portrayed, black supremacy was a myth, the Radicals were not cynical manipulators of the freedmen. Yet no convincing overall portrait of the quality of political and social life emerged from their writings. More recent historians have rightly pointed to elements of continuity that spanned the nineteenth-century Southern experience, especially the survival, in modified form, of the plantation system. Nevertheless, by denying the real changes that did occur, they have failed to provide a convincing portrait of an era characterized above all by drama, turmoil, and social change.

Building upon the findings of the past twenty years of scholarship, a new portrait of Reconstruction ought to begin by viewing it not as a specific time period, bounded by the years 1865 and 1877, but as an episode in a prolonged historical process—American society's adjustment to the consequences of the Civil War and emancipation. The Civil War, of course, raised the decisive questions of America's national existence: the relations between local and national authority, the

definition of citizenship, the balance between force and consent in generating obedience to authority. The war and Reconstruction, as Allan Nevins observed over fifty years ago, marked the "emergence of modern America." This was the era of the completion of the national railroad network, the creation of the modern steel industry, the conquest of the West and final subduing of the Indians, and the expansion of the mining frontier. Lincoln's America—the world of the small farm and artisan shop—gave way to a rapidly industrializing economy. The issues that galvanized postwar Northern politics—from the question of the greenback currency to the mode of paying holders of the national debt—arose from the economic changes unleashed by the Civil War.

Above all, the war irrevocably abolished slavery. Since 1619, when "twenty negars" disembarked from a Dutch ship in Virginia, racial injustice had haunted American life, mocking its professed ideals even as tobacco and cotton, the products of slave labor, helped finance the nation's economic development. Now the implications of the black presence could no longer be ignored. The Civil War resolved the problem of slavery but, as the Philadelphia diarist Sydney George Fisher observed in June 1865, it opened an even more intractable problem: "What shall we do with the Negro?" Indeed, he went on, this was a problem *incapable* of any solution that will satisfy both North and South."

As Fisher realized, the focal point of Reconstruction was the social revolution known as emancipation. Plantation slavery was simultaneously a system of labor, a form of racial domination, and the foundation upon which arose a distinctive ruling class within the South. Its demise threw open the most fundamental questions of economy, society, and politics. A new system of labor, social, racial, and political relations had to be created to replace slavery.

The United States was not the only nation to experience emancipation in the nineteenth century. Neither plantation slavery nor abolition were unique to the United States. But Reconstruction was. In a comparative perspective Radical Reconstruction stands as a remarkable experiment, the only effort of a society experiencing abolition to bring the former slaves within the umbrella of equal citizenship. Because the Radicals did not achieve everything they wanted, histo-

Some scholars exalted the motives of the Ku Klux Klan (left). Actually, its members were part of a terrorist organization that beat and killed its political opponents to deprive blacks of their rights.

rians have lately tended to play down the stunning departure represented by black suffrage and officeholding. Former slaves, most fewer than two years removed from bondage, debated the fundamental questions of the polity: What is a republican form of government? Should the state provide equal education for all? How could political equality be reconciled with a society in which property was so unequally distributed? There was something inspiring in the way such men met the challenge of Reconstruction. "I knew nothing more than to obey my master," James K. Greene, an Alabama black politician later recalled. "But the tocsin of freedom sounded and knocked at the door and we walked out like free men and we met the exigencies as they grew up, and shouldered the responsibilities."

"YOU NEVER SAW A PEOPLE MORE EXcited on the subject of politics than are the negroes of the south," one planter observed in 1867. And there were more than a few Southern whites as well who in these years shook off the prejudices of the past to embrace the vision of a new South dedicated to the principles of equal citizenship and social justice. One ordinary South Carolinian expressed the new sense of possibility in 1868 to the Republican governor of the state: "I am sorry that I cannot write an elegant stiled letter to your excellency. But I rejoice to think that God almighty has given to the poor of S. C. a Gov. to hear to feel to protect the humble poor without distinction to race or color. . . . I am a native borned S. C. a poor man never owned a Negro in

my life nor my father before me. . . . Remember the true and loyal are the poor of the whites and blacks, outside of these you can find none loyal."

Few modern scholars believe the Reconstruction governments established in the South in 1867 and 1868 fulfilled the aspirations of their humble constituents. While their achievements in such realms as education, civil rights, and the economic rebuilding of the South are now widely appreciated, historians today believe they failed to affect either the economic plight of the emancipated slave or the ongoing transformation of independent white farmers into cotton tenants. Yet their opponents did perceive the Reconstruction governments in precisely this way—as representatives of a revolution that had put the bottom rail, both racial and economic, on top. This perception helps explain the ferocity of the attacks leveled against them and the pervasiveness of violence in the postemancipation South.

The spectacle of black men voting and holding office was anathema to large numbers of Southern whites. Even more disturbing, at least in the view of those who still controlled the plantation regions of the South, was the emergence of local officials, black and white, who sympathized with the plight of the black laborer. Alabama's vagrancy law was a "dead letter" in 1870, "because those who are charged with its enforcement are indebted to the vagrant vote for their offices and emoluments." Political debates over the level and incidence of taxation, the control of crops, and the resolution of contract disputes revealed

that a primary issue of Reconstruction was the role of government in a plantation society. During presidential Reconstruction, and after "Redemption," with planters and their allies in control of politics, the law emerged as a means of stabilizing and promoting the plantation system. If Radical Reconstruction failed to redistribute the land of the South, the ouster of the planter class from control of politics at least ensured that the sanctions of the criminal law would not be employed to discipline the black labor force.

AN UNDERSTANDING OF THIS FUNDAmental conflict over the relation between government and society helps explain the pervasive complaints concerning corruption and "extravagance" during Radical Reconstruction. Corruption there was aplenty; tax rates did rise sharply. More significant than the rate of taxation, however, was the change in its incidence. For the first time, planters and white farmers had to pay a significant portion of their income to the government, while propertyless blacks often escaped scot-free. Several states, moreover, enacted heavy taxes on uncultivated land to discourage land speculation and force land onto the market, benefiting, it was hoped, the freedmen.

As time passed, complaints about the "extravagance" and corruption of Southern governments found a sympathetic audience among influential Northerners. The Democratic charge that universal suffrage in the South was responsible for high taxes and governmental extravagance coincided with a rising conviction among the urban middle classes of the

4. THE CIVIL WAR AND RECONSTRUCTION

North that city government had to be taken out of the hands of the immigrant poor and returned to the "best men"—the educated, professional, financially independent citizens unable to exert much political influence at a time of mass parties and machine politics. Increasingly the "respectable" middle classes began to retreat from the very notion of universal suffrage. The poor were no longer perceived as honest producers, the backbone of the social order; now they became the "dangerous classes," the "mob." As the historian Francis Parkman put it, too much power rested with "masses of imported ignorance and hereditary ineptitude." To Parkman the Irish of the Northern cities and the blacks of the South were equally incapable of utilizing the ballot: "Witness the municipal corruptions of New York, and the monstrosities of negro rule in South Carolina." Such attitudes helped to justify Northern inaction as, one by one, the Reconstruction regimes of the South were overthrown by political violence.

IN THE END, THEN, NEITHER THE ABOLItion of slavery nor Reconstruction succeeded in resolving the debate over the meaning of freedom in American life. Twenty years before the American Civil War, writing about the prospect of abolition in France's colonies, Alexis de Tocqueville had written, "If the Negroes have the right to become free, the [planters] have the incontestable right not to be ruined by the Negroes' freedom." And in the United States, as in nearly every plantation society that experienced the end of slavery, a rigid social and political dichotomy between former master and former slave, an ideology of racism, and a dependent labor force with limited economic opportunities all survived abolition. Unless one means by freedom the simple fact of not being a slave, emancipation thrust blacks into a kind of no-man's land, a partial freedom that made a mockery of the American ideal of equal citizenship.

Yet by the same token the ultimate outcome underscores the uniqueness of Reconstruction itself. Alone among the societies that abolished slavery in the nineteenth century, the United States, for a moment, offered the freedmen a measure of political control over their own destinies. However brief its sway, Reconstruction allowed scope for a remarkable political and social mobilization of the black community. It opened doors of opportunity that could never be completely closed. Reconstruction transformed the lives of Southern blacks in ways unmeasurable by statistics and unreachable by law. It raised their expectations and aspirations, redefined their status in relation to the larger society, and allowed space for the creation of institutions that enabled them to survive the repression that followed. And it established constitutional principles of civil and political equality that, while flagrantly violated after Redemption, planted the seeds of future struggle.

Certainly, in terms of the sense of possibility with which it opened, Reconstruction failed. But as Du Bois observed, it was a "splendid failure." For its animating vision—a society in which social advancement would be open to all on the basis of individual merit, not inherited caste distinctions—is as old as America itself and remains relevant to a nation still grappling with the unresolved legacy of emancipation.

Index

Credits/ Acknowledgments

Cover design by Charles Vitelli

1. The New Lamp
Facing overview—Courtesy of The Library of Congress.

2. Revolutionary America
Facing overview—National Archives.

3. National Consolidation and Expansion
Facing overview—Courtesy of The Library of Congress. 120—(left) Anderson Collection, Print Room, New York Public Library; (middle) Sears Roebuck Catalog; (right) The Bettmann Archive. 121, 122—American Antiquarian Society. 123—*Legion of Liberty,* (Albany, 1845), New York Public Library. 124—Anderson Collection, Print Room, New York Public Library. 125—American Antiquarian Society. 130—Free Library of Philadelphia.

4. The Civil War and Reconstruction
Facing overview—Courtesy of The Library of Congress. 183—Mansell Collection. 184—HT Archives. 192, 194—Courtesy of The Freedom & Southern Society Project Collection. 193, 195, 196, 197—Courtesy of The Library of Congress. 201, 204—Courtesy of The Library of Congress. 214—Library of Congress/Weidenfeld Archives. 215—HT map by Ken Wass. 228, 230—The Bettmann Archive.

ANNUAL EDITIONS ARTICLE REVIEW FORM

■ NAME: _____ DATE: _____

■ TITLE AND NUMBER OF ARTICLE: _____

■ BRIEFLY STATE THE MAIN IDEA OF THIS ARTICLE: _____

_____

_____

_____

_____

_____

■ LIST THREE IMPORTANT FACTS THAT THE AUTHOR USES TO SUPPORT THE MAIN IDEA:

_____

_____

_____

_____

_____

_____

■ WHAT INFORMATION OR IDEAS DISCUSSED IN THIS ARTICLE ARE ALSO DISCUSSED IN YOUR TEXTBOOK OR OTHER READING YOU HAVE DONE? LIST THE TEXTBOOK CHAPTERS AND PAGE NUMBERS:

_____

_____

_____

_____

_____

_____

_____

■ LIST ANY EXAMPLES OF BIAS OR FAULTY REASONING THAT YOU FOUND IN THE ARTICLE:

_____

_____

_____

_____

_____

■ LIST ANY NEW TERMS/CONCEPTS THAT WERE DISCUSSED IN THE ARTICLE AND WRITE A SHORT DEFINITION:

_____

_____

_____

_____

_____

*Your instructor may require you to use this Annual Editions Article Review Form in any number of ways: for articles that are assigned, for extra credit, as a tool to assist in developing assigned papers, or simply for your own reference. Even if it is not required, we encourage you to photocopy and use this page; you'll find that reflecting on the articles will greatly enhance the information from your text.

ANNUAL EDITIONS:
AMERICAN HISTORY, Vol. I
Pre-Colonial Through Reconstruction
Article Rating Form

Here is an opportunity for you to have direct input into the next revision of this volume. We would like you to rate each of the 42 articles listed below, using the following scale:

1. **Excellent: should definitely be retained**
2. **Above average: should probably be retained**
3. **Below average: should probably be deleted**
4. **Poor: should definitely be deleted**

Your ratings will play a vital part in the next revision. So please mail this prepaid form to us just as soon as you complete it.
Thanks for your help!

Annual Editions revisions depend on two major opinion sources: one is our Advisory Board, listed in the front of this volume, which works with us in scanning the thousands of articles published in the public press each year; the other is you—the person actually using the book. Please help us and the users of the next edition by completing the prepaid article rating form on this page and returning it to us. Thank you.

Rating	Article	Rating	Article
	1. America Before Columbus		22. From Utopia to Mill Town
	2. Was America a Mistake?		23. The Secret Life of a Developing Country (Ours)
	3. California's Spanish Missions		24. The Jacksonian Revolution
	4. Colonists in Bondage: Indentured Servants in America		25. "Texas Must Be Ours"
	5. Anne Hutchinson: "A Verye Dangerous Woman"		26. Not Really Greek
	6. "Under an Evil Hand"		27. Legacy of Violence
	7. Remapping American Culture		28. Eden Ravished
	8. The Shot Heard Round the World		29. Act One
	9. Declaration of Independence		30. Forgotten Forty-Niners
	10. Winter at Valley Forge		31. The War Against Demon Rum
	11. A Troubled League		32. Dred Scott in History
	12. The American Revolution: A War of Religion?		33. First Blood to the South: Bull Run, 1861
	13. Philadelphia Story		34. Black, Blue, and Gray: The Other Civil War
	14. Philadelphia 1787		35. Family and Freedom: Black Families in the American Civil War
	15. The Founding Fathers and Slavery		36. Lincoln and Douglass: Dismantling the Peculiar Institution
	16. 'A Nauseous Project'		37. "A Few Appropriate Remarks"
	17. River of the West		38. Why the Confederacy Lost
	18. The Lives of Slave Women		39. The War Inside the Church
	19. The Great Chief Justice		40. A War that Never Goes Away
	20. Indians in the Land		41. What Did Freedom Mean?
	21. The Odd Couple Who Won Florida and Half the West		42. The New View of Reconstruction

(Continued on next page)

ABOUT YOU

Name_____ Date_____

Are you a teacher? ☐   Or student? ☐

Your School Name _____

Department _____

Address _____

City _____ State _____ Zip _____

School Telephone # _____

YOUR COMMENTS ARE IMPORTANT TO US!

Please fill in the following information:

For which course did you use this book? _____

Did you use a text with this Annual Edition?   ☐ yes   ☐ no

The title of the text? _____

What are your general reactions to the Annual Editions concept?

Have you read any particular articles recently that you think should be included in the next edition?

Are there any articles you feel should be replaced in the next edition? Why?

Are there other areas that you feel would utilize an Annual Edition?

May we contact you for editorial input?

May we quote you from above?

AMERICAN HISTORY, Vol. I, Twelfth Edition
Pre-Colonial Through Reconstruction

BUSINESS REPLY MAIL

First Class   Permit No. 84   Guilford, CT

Postage will be paid by addressee

The Dushkin Publishing Group, Inc.
Sluice Dock
DPG **Guilford, Connecticut 06437**